Grant Seekers Guide

Grant Seekers Guide

Third Edition

National Network of Grantmakers

Jill R. Shellow and Nancy C. Stella,
Editors

Moyer Bell Limited

Published by Moyer Bell Limited
Colonial Hill/RFD 1
Mt. Kisco, New York 10549
(914) 666–0084

Copyright © 1989 **National Network of Grantmakers**
% Partnership for Democracy
2335 18th Street NW
Washington, D.C. 20009
(202) 483–0030

Although some of the material in the source listings of foundations and corporate-giving programs and the appendixes thereto may be available elsewhere in one form or another, it is primarily the organization and presentation of these data in a format designed to offer speed of reference that is original in this publication. The collections, computation, and verification of information has been done carefully and represents a significant employment of staff, time, and resources of the National Network of Grantmakers.

Second Printing, August, 1990

Library of Congress Cataloging-in-Publication Data
Grant seekers guide : funding sourcebook / National Network of Grantmakers ; Jill R. Shellow and Nancy C. Stella, editors.—Rev. and expanded.
    p.   cm.
  Includes bibliographies and indexes.
  ISBN 0-918825-83-0 : ISBN 0-918825-84-9 (pbk.)
  1. Endowments—United States—Directories. I. Shellow, Jill R.
HV97.A3G73 1989
361.7′632′02573—dc19   8812052
ISBN: 0-918825-83-0(CL)   CIP
      0-918825-84-9(PB)

Printed in the United States of America
Distributed by Rizzoli

Contents

Contents

The National Network of Grantmakers

The National Network of Grantmakers is an association of individuals involved in grantmaking who are committed to social and economic justice. Its members represent a broad spectrum of grantmaking interests, from individual philanthropists and representatives of religious grantmaking programs to staff and trustees of large and small private, public, corporate, and community foundations. While many Network members have the opportunity to work directly on social and economic justice issues through their work, others have joined because of their personal beliefs and commitments.

The goals of the Network are: (1) to share information and provide support across grantmaking sectors; (2) to develop strategies for social and economic justice and for using existing resources to that end; (3) to be a voice for issues of social and economic justice within the philanthropic community and to educate others in government, business, labor, education, and political parties; and (4) to promote affirmative action and open democratic processes within the Network and the larger grantmaking community.

The National Network of Grantmakers is not a staffed organization. The development and activities of the organization are the result of efforts by individual Network members who volunteer their time.

National Network of Grantmakers

Management Committee 1986–87*

Sasha Hohri, Co-convenor, Ms. Foundation for Women, Inc.
Susan K. Kinoy, Co-convenor, The Villers Foundation
Kathy Acey, Astraea Fund
Dave Bockmann, A Territory Resource
Prentice Bowsher, Bowsher-Booher Foundation
Jean Entine, Boston Foundation
Erica Hunt, The New World Foundation
Mindy Lewis, Cummins Engine Foundation
Lois Roisman, Jewish Fund for Justice

*Affiliation provided for identification only

Tricia Rubacky, The Youth Project
Cinthia Schuman, Rockefeller Family Fund
Betsy Taylor, Ottinger Foundation
Dagmar Thorpe, Seventh Generation Fund for Indian Development

Grantseekers Guide Advisory Committee 1987–88
Judy Austermiller, The Boehm Foundation
Adisa Douglas, Campaign for Human Development
Susan K. Kinoy, The Villers Foundation

Foreword

The Grantseekers Guide is designed to meet the specific fundraising needs of those organizations that address issues, proffer solutions, and advocate for social and economic justice. While its contents may prove useful to larger, established institutions, it is structured for the smaller organization, often grassroots or community-based, whose fundraising potential is often unfairly limited.

These grantseekers have unique fundraising needs which are not fulfilled by the standard tools of the fundraiser's trade. It was with these needs in mind that a process was developed for determining which grantmaking programs to include. Many funders were closely scrutinized. The result is a select group of grantmaking organizations whose members share an interest in, an understanding of, and a commitment to the kinds of projects for which *The Grantseekers Guide* is intended.

As a general rule only grantmaking programs with assets in excess of $1 million or grantmaking budgets of $100,000 or more per year were considered. Of course, there were several exceptions. By its very nature, this publication is exclusionary. Although some grantmakers specifically requested either to be included or excluded, the substantive decisions on content were made by the Book Committee in consultation with the editors. The bottom line is that only those grantmakers that have demonstrated a receptivity to proposals and past financial support of social and economic justice projects are included.

Decisions were based on a thorough analysis of current and past annual reports, grants lists, other publications and written statements, and input from grantmakers and grantseekers alike who had personal experience with funders under consideration. Where the assembled data clearly indicated strong support for social and economic justice from a grantmaker across several program areas, the funder was included and its program described in the entirety. In other instances, where funding patterns demonstrated traditional giving, but a particular programmatic interest appeared compatible with the objectives of this book, the grantmaker was included and that specific program highlighted. Every effort was made to portray accurately the grantmaker's program interests, financial data, and application procedures, and each grantmaker was afforded the opportunity to review its entry before publication and make corrections as appropriate.

In sum, *The Grantseekers Guide* is designed to help social and economic justice groups overcome the myriad social, political, and economic factors that have combined over the last decade to heighten the competition among all nonprofits and put social and economic justice groups on an even plane with their traditional charitable counterparts. It achieves this objective by providing an in-depth analysis of those grantmaking programs that display commitment to citizen participation in the institutions and decision-making processes that affect both the individual citizen and the society as a whole.

Editors' Acknowledgments

It seems hard to believe that almost ten years have passed since work was started on the first edition of *The Grantseekers Guide.* And it's grown so much thicker. Part of its heft this time around is attributable to the thoroughness of the individual authors of the first nine chapters, to whom we are deeply grateful. At the same time, the number of funders described in its pages has more than doubled. While perhaps we as a collective society are no closer to achieving the equity, freedom, and justice underlying the reasons this book was written in the first place, in countless individual settings progress has been made which is no doubt attributable to the people who helped us put this book together.

A person who comes immediately to mind is Terri Shuck. When Jill was first approached about doing a third edition, she hesitated. Then Terri—an experienced hand from the Youth Project—agreed to help, and the book seemed not just possible, but worth doing. Terri gave tremendously of her time and energy during research and thinking stages when hard decisions needed to be made about which funders to include. She was no more sorry to have to set it aside when she became executive director of the Forum Institute than we were to see her go. Finding her replacement was not easy; there were few volunteers. Indeed, the only volunteer was Phil Lerman, an organizer whom activist Jill has known since childhood. He knew Jill needed help and was willing to abandon his recent retirement. With the help of his wife, Sara Dean, Phil edited several of the entries before Nancy was recruited.

The Book Committee—comprised of longtime colleagues who know how valuable a shield can be and were there when we needed them— was indispensable, and the Network Management Committee—grant-makers on the front lines—provided more than mere encouragement. Tricia Rubacky acted as liaison between Moyer Bell Limited and the Management Committee, dotting every *i* and crossing every *t.* Susan Kinoy devoted careful attention to both Jill and to the product. Early one Sunday morning, on her way out of town, she came over to Jill's house with an orchid in one hand and her proofreader's glasses in the other to help get out the first draft mailing. Three months later—this time on a Saturday— she was back with a red-penciled copy of the manuscript.

Editors' Acknowledgments

Important in another respect are those funders whose contributions to the Network made this edition possible: the Boehm Foundation, the Joyce Foundation, the Edna McConnell Clark Foundation, the Sophia Fund, the Chicago Resource Center, the Benton Foundation, and the Funding Exchange.

From the point of view of substance, a number of people—far too many to do justice in this space—served as sounding boards, some admittedly louder than others. Among those to whose expertise and guidance the pages of this book are witness are Karl Stauber (whose idea it was to replace his chapter on economic development with something more practical, namely, Jon Pratt's work on earned income); Michael Seltzer (whose deep involvement with the leading funders of projects addressing the civil rights/social justice/public health aspects of the AIDS epidemic enabled us to stay current on the latest developments down to the very minute before press time); Frank Chapper (a lawyer at Caplin & Drysdale, who used his many years of accumulated wisdom about the way the IRS really operates to point Jill, in a friendly sort of way, in the right direction as she labored with the tax chapter); and Barrie Pribyl (whose invaluable insights on community foundations sent us scurrying to do more research and resulted in important additions to the book).

Barbara Parker, Sue Vogelsinger, and Jennifer Sarmiento, collectively known as the communications consulting firm of Parker/Vogelsinger & Associates, agreed initially to be a convenient mail drop/center of operations. Little could they have known it would turn out to be more than that, a lot more. Their help and good humor (a much-needed commodity) in the face of mountains of extra mail and an extra person in rotation on their computer was invaluable. Our last-minute addition to the team was Audrey Stone. On less than a day's notice, Audrey—who acknowledged she has a well-worn copy of edition number two on her desk at the National Women's Law Center—appeared at the door eager to help and found typos our glazed eyes couldn't see.

Our publishers, Britt Bell and Jennifer Moyer, bring to this endeavor perhaps a critical service above and beyond mere production. Moyer Bell Limited has the distribution channels that enable the book to travel from the South Pacific to the inner cities. Their efforts fill us with confidence that the audience for whom it was written will easily be able to put it to use.

Finally, there are friends and family. Timmy Napolitano and Jill go back a long time as colleagues and trusted friends. When Jill would trust no one else to look over the final pages, Timmy put aside her own schedule and came to our rescue. Adam and Sarah Stella were model children—

at home with Mommy always at work on the computer, and at Jill's (where Mommy was still working on the computer), and Frank Stella bore the brunt of the inconvenience with grace, humor, and the moral equivalent of a chef's hat. To all, we say thank you.

J.R.S.
N.C.S.

User's Guide

Before you head straight to the descriptions of the funders in Chapters 10 and 11 and the indexes, the editors offer the following advice. There are nine excellent chapters on various aspects of raising money that come first. Read them. You do yourself a disservice by getting ahead of yourself.

These chapters—all by experienced fundraisers and grantmakers—put grantsmanship in its proper perspective by explaining its limitations and presenting alternatives that should be given serious consideration. They range from the history of foundation support for social justice movements to the importance of making certain you do not jeopardize your tax-exempt status by engaging in excessive grassroots lobbying (which would without a doubt cramp your ability to raise money), raising money from individuals, and earned income. They also explain corporate and religious contributions as distinguished from foundation grants. Finally, there is the all-important chapter on planning, which is the key to fundraising success. The more you know when you finally turn to read the descriptions, the more helpful they will be.

You should also keep in mind that this book has several significant limitations:

- Like all compilations of reference material, it is quickly dated. Addresses and telephone numbers change, as do grantmaker's priorities and procedures.

  Get the most current information from a grantmaker before planning to submit a proposal.

  Do not count on *The Grantseekers Guide* as the ultimate authority on critical parts of the application process such as deadlines or page and format requirements. You may be very disappointed!
- Use the book as a Rolodex of funders; that's one of its great features. They are all in one place.

  But don't use it to create fundraising mailing lists. You'll only be wasting postage.

These grantmakers are too involved with the very issues you work on to pay attention to mass-mailed proposals and fundraising solicitations.

- Use the book to develop your own ideas; don't let something as inconsequential as the index by subject areas stifle your creativity.
- Look behind the descriptions of the funders.

  Request lists of past grantees; talk to them.

  Look at annual reports (new and old), study application forms and guidelines, and read between the lines.

  Only after you have educated yourself about a funder's agenda and priorities, and are convinced a proposal would have merit, should you sit down and write.
- Pay attention to the grant limitations and requirements, but don't accept them unquestioningly. The rules are often defined by their exceptions.
- Finally, don't ignore the numbers. A lot of time and energy has gone into providing meaningful figures to convey to you the realistic level of resources from which these funders make grants. Note:

  When assets are listed, they are at market value as of a fixed date.

  Where support and revenue figures are provided, this strongly suggests the funder is not endowed and depends on a major donor or the public to secure its grantmaking budget.

  Where neither assets nor support or revenue are included in the description, the grantmaker is probably dependent on some individual's income or some corporation's profits for its grantmaking budget. The only measure of that grantmaker's potential future activity is the grants budget information.

  For the most part, the grants information presented is based on grants paid not grants approved. While limiting in the sense that multiyear commitments are excluded, it realistically reflects the size grant an organization might expect in any one year.

  Look carefully at the median grant size and use it to judge the size of any contemplated request.

  A median is not an average. It is a measure of distribution, i.e., in a grants list organized by size from largest to smallest, it is the middle grant.

One-half of all grants made during the period were larger than the median; one-half were smaller.

Use this figure in planning how much you might ask for and realistically expect to receive.

1

Chapter One
Foundation Funding of Progressive
Social Movements (Revisited)
By J. Craig Jenkins*

Foundations that fund progressive social change have frequently been targets of political controversy. In the early 1950s, the Cox and Reese Committees in the House of Representatives held hearings on charges that the foundations were financing subversion, atheism, and "behavioral science." In the early 1960s, Congressman Wright Patman of Texas launched an investigation into the tax privileges of foundations. Spurred by publicity about the Ford Foundation involvement in the school decentralization controversy in New York and support of voter registration campaigns, Patman ultimately pressed through the Tax Reform Act of 1969. In the early 1980s, several foundations supporting the nuclear freeze campaign were criticized for their political associations. Invariably, the critics questioned the tax exemption of foundations making these grants, arguing their funding constitutes a subsidy of political expression and promotes elite meddling in the affairs of private citizens. In response, the foundations have argued that they are funding significant social innovations, especially expanding access to the political system for disadvantaged and unrepresented groups. Yet, despite considerable debate about the propriety of social-movement funding, there has been little empirical study of the issue.[1]

This chapter summarizes my research on the sources, scope, and impact of private foundation support for progressive social movements. This support is the most controversial and yet often the most effective approach available to foundations attempting to bring about social change. While there are many other approaches to social change, foundations seriously concerned with altering social institutions will almost invariably

*J. Craig Jenkins, Ph.D., is a professor of sociology at the Ohio State University, Columbus, Ohio. Research for this chapter was conducted in cooperation with the Program on Nonprofit Organizations at Yale University and the Center for Policy Research, New York. It was supported in part by a grant from the Russell Sage Foundation, New York, New York, and the National Endowment for the Humanities.
[1]For normative discussions, see Simon (1973 and 1987), Nielsen (1979), Metzger (1979), Arnove (1980), and Asher (1983). For the few empirical studies, see Nielsen (1972), Carey (1977), and Roelofs (1983).

consider at some point the possibility of funding social-movement advocates.

Defining "Social Movements"

By a "social movement" I mean any collective effort to bring about progressive social change on behalf of some marginal or excluded interest through innovative or rebellious means. The recipient of the grant must have been a group or organization with a collective focus and emphasis on the alteration of institutional patterns.[2] Organizing campaigns and legal advocacy of group interests are classic examples. Individual service projects were included only if their underlying purpose was collective advocacy. For example, the Earl Warren Project, a service project of the NAACP Legal Defense and Education Fund, was included because its purpose was on-the-job training of civil rights lawyers.

For purposes of this study, the primary constituency also had to be a marginal or excluded group whose interests were not routinely taken into account in elite decisions. Minority groups are, of course, the archetypical case, but even the general public are often ignored in their role as consumers or users of the environment. The actions must also have been innovative, either using existing advocacy methods in novel ways or shaking up social routines. Ralph Nader's advocacy projects, for example, have made innovative use of research and publicity to get their message across. The NAACP and the Gray Panthers have used demonstrations and protests alongside more staid policy advocacy.

Finally, a social movement is also a politically marginal actor. At least at the outset, social movements will not enjoy clear and firm recognition by centers of political authority. This does not imply, however, that social-movement grants will always go to politically marginal organizations. As we will see, many movement grants have actually been channeled through established nonprofit organizations such as churches and universities that assumed administrative responsibility for a movement project. A critical question, then, will be the extent to which movement funding is channeled through established rather than social-movement organizations.

Methodology

The list of social change foundations was compiled from the first edition of this book, studies such as Carey's (1977), and "snowball" interviews in which movement funders were asked to identify other funders.

My list was then passed to several social-movement fundraisers who

---

[2] For a fuller discussion, see Jenkins (1983, 1987, and forthcoming).

nominated additions. The annual reports and IRS 990 forms for the resulting list of 131 grant-giving foundations were then content-coded for those grants going to social-movement efforts during the period 1953 to 1980. Of these, 103 were private foundations, fifteen public charities, five community foundations, seven corporate foundations, and one was an operating foundation. Each movement grant item was coded in terms of the major beneficiary group, the primary issue which the grant addressed, the political status and action style of the recipient organization, and the amount of the grant. The year of the grant was treated as that in which funds were reportedly paid out. In other words, foundation decisions were frequently made prior to the actual payment of grant dollars, possibly as much as a year in advance.

Profile: Foundations that Fund Social Movements

Foundations funding progressive social movements have been extremely innovative and unconventional actors within their own world. Foundation support goes overwhelmingly to conventional charitable activities and established institutions.[3] Social-movement grants have always constituted less than one percent of total foundation giving, averaging about one-half of a percent during this study period. Moreover, the 131 foundations in this study represent only a minute fraction of the more than 22,000 active grantmaking foundations in American society.

What distinguishes movement funders from other foundations? Although many of the newer, smaller foundations are more aggressive and willing to take risks, the big funders (in terms of total dollars and grant items) have been the larger, more established foundations with professional staff and more sophisticated evaluation procedures. The typical movement funder was founded in the late 1940s or early 1950s, with about a quarter dating back to the first decades of the twentieth century. Forty-three percent reported assets of less than $5 million with another 48.8 percent reporting between $5 and $100 million and 8.3 percent holding over $100 million.[4] Reflecting their large size, the movement funders, overwhelmingly, were staffed foundations. The average such funder had two to six staff members, at least one a program or grants officer specializing in grants evaluation and monitoring. Only 30 percent

---

[3]For classic evidence on this contention, see the Peterson Commission Report (1971), Cunninggim (1972), and Nielsen (1972).

[4]By comparison, the general survey of foundations conducted by Odendahl, Boris, Nelson, and Rudney found a much smaller average foundation, 91.89 percent with less than $5 million in assets and only .53 percent with $100 million or more (Boris, p. 68).

of these social-change funders lacked staff while, among foundations in general, one-half operated without staff, typically out of a family business office or a bank trust department.

As among foundations in general, the programs of these change funders closely reflects the views of donors and their family members. Only 16.4 percent did not have either a donor or at least two family members as trustees, about one-half having donors and two-thirds with family members of their boards, figures that compare with those found by Boris, et al. (1987). In general the nonfamily foundations were the largest, having gradually drifted away from family control. Like philan-thropic assets generally, these foundations are concentrated in the north-eastern region of the country, with 51.5 percent in New York State alone and another 12 percent in California.

The most distinctive feature that sets off these social-change funders is the religious background of their donors. By checking biographical backgrounds, I managed to identify the religious background of 85 per-cent of the original donors. Of these, 27.7 percent were Jewish and 42.3 white Protestant, with 3.1 percent Catholic, and 1.5 percent Black. By contrast, the general survey by Odendahl and Boris found only 13.4 percent of the major donors to be Jewish and 65.7 Protestant. The public-spirited political outlook of the Jewish community, coupled with the heritage of religious discrimination, has created a group of philanthropists who are highly sensitive to social-change issues. I also inquired into the industrial origins of the family assets that were used to endow the foun-dations and, aside from a slight over-representation from the retail/whole-sale trade and banking/finance industries and an under-representation from the mining and manufacturing industries, found these movement funders quite comparable to foundations in general.

Profile: Organizations that Receive Funding

In many ways these pathbreaking foundations have been rather conven-tional in their approach to social-movement giving. Many of the grants have gone to established organizations like the National Council of Churches or Georgetown University rather than to politically marginal movement organizations like the Teamsters for Union Democracy or Massachusetts Fair Share. Although these grants have still been designated for social-movement activities, it is significant that 7.5 percent of grant dollars and 4.7 percent of the grant items have been channeled this way. This, of course, only skims the full range of foundation support for these more established organizations, since most have supporters outside this small universe of movement funders. There have been several reasons for channeling movement funding in this way. Some movement groups have lacked a 501(c)(3) nonprofit tax exemption and, hence, have been ineligible for foundation grants. In these instances, movement activists used their contacts with established nonprofits like universities and church agencies to sponsor their bids for support. Channeling movement funding through established organizations has also reflected reluctance on the part of the foundations to support new, less established organizations without a track record where there was less assurance that the projects would be seriously pursued. This intermediary relation has also buffered the foundations from the movements, protecting them against potential controversy and charges of fiscal improprieties. The foundations have also looked at this use of intermediaries as a matter of efficiency. Supporting a large number of small movement groups, such as neighborhood groups and tenant unions, through a single technical support entity like The Youth Project or the Center for Community Change, has seemed more efficient than dealing with all the groups directly.

Even more dramatic has been the preference of these social change foundations for professional advocacy projects such as research organizations, legal defense funds, and technical support groups over grassroots membership organizations. Organizations like the Natural Resources Defense Council and the NAACP Legal Defense and Education Fund have received priority over membership organizations like the Friends of the Earth and the National Organization for Women. Of social movement grants, 75.5 percent of the dollars and 74.7 percent of the grant items have gone to professional projects while only 16.6 percent of the dollars and 13.7 percent of the grants have gone to grassroots organizations. In part this is because professional projects have been relatively expensive and enjoyed few other sources of support. Foundations have also assumed that grassroots organizations can generate resources from their membership base and therefore have less need for foundation support. Many membership organizations have also been ineligible because of their 501(c)(4) nonprofit status from the IRS, although several have created 501(c)(3) affiliates to secure foundation grants for their tax-exempt activities.

Political caution has been another major factor leading foundations to give preference to the social-movement work of established institutions. Grassroots movement organizations tend to be more informal and decentralized, lacking the fiscal and management devices that foundations have often expected from their recipients. Professionalized organizations are typically centralized, controlled by a single executive or a professional staff. Top-down structure has been more intelligible to foundation trustees who have been drawn overwhelmingly from the world of business and universities. Centralization has also afforded greater assurance that the money would be prudently used as specified in a grant proposal. Grassroots organizations have also been more likely to become involved in controversial actions with the potential for embarrassment to their sponsors.

How have these foundations become involved in the support of movements? Although critics [5] have frequently charged foundations with meddling and stirring up movement activities, the evidence shows quite clearly that they have overwhelmingly been reactive. Foundations have responded to an issue or concern already raised by some movement or citizens' group. They have rarely played the role of an instigator, creating concern about an issue or proposing social changes in the absence of a prior grassroots demand for change. Although the overlap between specific movement demands and particular supported projects has never been complete, the general concerns have been generated by the movements. This reflects the traditionalism of the foundations as well as the prevalent philosophy that the role of foundations is to facilitate, not initiate, social change. This reactiveness shows up dramatically in the timing of social movement grants. Figure 1 charts the growth of movement funding in both nominal and real (i.e., adjusted for inflation) dollars. Figure 2 traces these grants in terms of their proportion of total foundation giving.[6]

The Growth of Social-Movement Funding

Social-movement funding was negligible until the mid-1960s, taking off in 1965 and rising rapidly to $18.6 million in 1971, stabilizing through the peak of $25.2 million in 1977, and then falling slightly through the end of the decade. Two processes were probably important in accounting for this pattern. The total level of both foundation giving and private social welfare giving rose steadily throughout the 1960s, reaching a peak in the very years that movement funding rose sharply. During the 1960s, American society experienced a general liberalization trend, both politically and in terms of private efforts to deal with social problems. Economic affluence and the concomitant growth in foundation assets and giving facilitated this marked rise in movement funding, providing "slack"

---

[5]For quite different versions of this critique, see Moynihan (1972) and McLlhnay (1979).

[6]The earlier version of this article contained an erroneous time-trend that created the appearance of a peak in 1971 and a sharper decline after 1977. This error was apparently created by a flaw in the program used for computation. The corrected figures here were created with the help of the Statistical Analysis System.

6

Figure 1. Philanthropy and Social Movement Giving

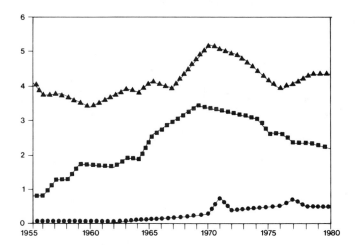

● Percent of foundation grants going to social movements
■ Total private foundation grants
▲ Total social welfare philanthropy, all sources

resources that could be invested in discretionary endeavors like social causes. Affluence bred a general optimism about the possibility of solving social problems. Increased professionalism in the larger foundations also encouraged a shift from traditional "Band-Aid" charity to social change as a basis for long-term solutions.

In contrast, the decline in movement funding during the late 1970s reflected, among other things, less promising economic times, a general squeeze on foundation assets and giving, and pessimism about the possibility of solving social problems. It also reflected an emergent division of labor between the larger and smaller foundations. The total number of foundation grants continued to rise through 1979 before falling off, while the average size of the grants fell much earlier. The larger foundations were withdrawing, while smaller, sometimes more radical public charities and private foundations with smaller grants were becoming more central to the support of social movements.

The second and more immediately relevant trend was the general explosion of grassroots social-movement activity during the 1960s. Between 1963 and 1971 American society witnessed a steady and accelerating proliferation of new causes. The civil rights movement started it all, rapidly followed by a student movement, opposition to the war in

7

Figure 2. Movement Grants as a Percent of
Total Foundation Giving

Vietnam, women's rights advocates, environmentalism, consumer advocates, community organizing, prisoners' rights efforts, Native American
movements, homosexual rights, antinuclear campaigns, and so on. It was
as if virtually every conceivable social cause became the center of intense
political concern. This tumultuous period served as a critical stimulus
for foundations by identifying new social problems, creating an impending
sense of crisis, and generating a host of new political-advocacy organizations—all bidding for foundation support. The turbulence of the period
was remarkable. In the decade from 1960 to 1971 there was an average
of 225 mass demonstrations per year as compared to five per year in the
1950s and forty to fifty in the late 1970s. In 1967 alone there were more
than 200 major riots, and virtually every city in the country experienced
a major disorder.[7]

The new movements and political turbulence generated a profound
sense of crisis among national elites. They came to see the "system" as
challenged, perhaps even as breaking down, adopting grandiose diagnoses
such as the "urban crisis," the "race relations crisis," and the "eco-disaster"

---

[7]Charles Lewis Taylor and David A. Jodice, *World Handbook of Social and Political
Indicators,* (New Haven: Yale University Press, 1983), pp. 92–93; 110–11.

as images of reality. According to Senator Daniel Patrick Moynihan,[8] at that time chief domestic policy adviser to President Nixon, the domestic turbulence was seen at the elite level as "cataclysmic." Because of their close links to holders of large personal wealth and elite policy centers, many private foundations shared these perceptions. The period also witnessed a boom in new political organizations, especially those advocating social change. Beginning in 1969, the annual number of new political associations registered in the *Encyclopedia of Associations* rose from about twenty to eighty per year and stayed at that level through 1978. Many of these new organizations were eligible for foundation grants and, by bidding for support, reinforced the general expansion of social-movement funding.

The Foundation as "Gatekeeper": Change with Order

The ideology guiding most social-movement philanthropy has been what Theodore Lowi (1979) has called "interest group liberalism," namely, the belief that the public interest is best served by a political order that is accessible to all social groups. Since some groups lack the resources, organization, or leadership to make political claims, or like racial minorities have been deliberately excluded from political representation, the American political order is imperfect. By sponsoring organizations that claim to represent the interests of these groups, these foundations see themselves as correcting a major flaw in the American political system. Of these social movement grants, 40.5 percent have gone to racial minorities, another 22.5 percent to public interest organizations advancing consumer rights, protecting the environment and the like, and another 15.5 percent went to groups such as women, children, the aged, and the handicapped, who could either draw on the analogy with racial discrimination or obviously lacked political capacities. In general, these foundations were not particularly interested in issues such as peace, union organizing, or workplace reform, where the claims of political authorities to expertise was seen as dominant, or existing interest groups were seen as already representing these interests.[9] In short, a proposal to protect the constitutional rights of some minority group was far more likely to

---

[8]Daniel P. Moynihan, *The Politics of a Guaranteed Income,* (New York: Free Press, 1971), p. 120.

[9]Recent foundation interest in the peace movement and the nuclear freeze developed only after the freeze movement had been launched in the late 1970s. Peace has, of course, been a longstanding concern, but funding has gone almost exclusively to nonmovement organizations.

win foundation support than one to organize Black slum dwellers into tenant unions or to challenge the national foreign policy establishment. Figure 3 shows the distribution of social movement grants by main beneficiary groups.

The overwhelming concentration of these grants on professionalized advocacy organizations also reflects this interest-group liberalism. As mentioned earlier, 42.6 percent of these grant dollars went to professional advocacy projects such as law firms and research centers and another 32.9 percent to technical support centers, while only 16.6 percent went

Figure 3. Distribution of Grants (dollars)

Millions of dollars

| | 0 | 10 | 20 | 30 | 40 | 50 | 60 |

Racial Minorities
Black Americans
Mexican Americans
Native Americans
Puerto Ricans
Asian Americans
Minorities in General

Ethnic Groups
Appalachians
White Ethnics

Economic Justice
Poor People's Advocacy
Working Class Advocacy

Other Groups
Womens Rights
Childrens Advocacy
Prisoners Rights
Handicapped Rights
Aged Advocacy
Homosexual Rights

Peace & World Order
Student Movement
Peace Movement
Third World Advocacy
Veterans Rights

Public Interest Movement
Environmentalism
Anti-Nuke Movement
Consumer Rights
Other Public Interests

10

to grassroots organizations. Foundations have favored professional advocates as representatives of the unrepresented, balancing their commitment to a more responsive and accessible political order against their concern for orderly social change. This caution also shows in the foundation preference for movement organizations that abstain from unruly actions. Two-thirds of the grant dollars went to organizations that had never been involved in protests, while on the order of one-third went to organizations with some history of scrappiness. As one foundation officer explained to me: "We fund *responsible militancy*."

Yet foundation grants have frequently been extremely significant in the process of social reform. In general, foundation support for movements has helped institutionalize reforms that have been pushed onto the political agenda by the grassroots movements. The foundations have been political "gatekeepers," funding the movement initiatives that were successfully translated into public policy and institutional reforms. In the process, they have also selected the new organizations that became permanent features of the political landscape. For example, the idea of voter registration originated from civil rights activists in the Student Non-Violent Coordinating Committee and the Southern Christian Leadership Conference, but did not become a major area of activity until foundations supported the Voter Education Project in 1963. This in turn contributed to the passage of the Voting Rights Act of 1964 and the institutionalization of voter education and registration work that has followed. This "gatekeeper" role is also visible in the types of projects and organizations that have received support. Grassroots movement organizations, which played major initiatory roles in pressing for social changes, received less support, while professional advocacy projects emphasizing the formulation of specific policy alternatives, the monitoring of governmental programs, and legal efforts to insure the implementation of new laws were major beneficiaries. These professional advocacy organizations have typically been more critical in the policy formulation and implementation stages of social reform than the gestation of new ideas and the mobilization of mass support for social change. At the very point that the mass movements began to secure a serious hearing, the foundations stepped in with support for professional advocacy and technical support that addressed these concerns and consolidated social reforms.

If this is the case, then there are several interesting paradoxes underlying the role of foundations and movements in the process of social reform. Social movements themselves frequently fail to bring about the social changes they intend, but the political pressures they set off may

11

well force through reforms anyway. The foundations do not initiate the reforms, but their funding determines which movement concerns and actors become permanent fixtures. The civil rights experience offers an instructive model. The civil rights movement began as an effort to challenge Jim Crow racism and remedy the economic plight of Blacks. Its greatest success lay in uprooting Jim Crow, but the pressures let loose by the movement also crystallized the War on Poverty and several decades of federal efforts to alleviate poverty for the white as well as Black poor. The foundations funded an array of professional advocacy projects like the Southern Poverty Law Center and the Children's Defense Fund, which have played a key role in monitoring and implementing federal policies to alleviate poverty. While the movement *initiated*, the foundations and their professional projects *controlled* the design of the actual reforms that were eventually put into place.

Foundations that fund social movements have played a critical role, not as initiators, but as gatekeepers to the political system. The mass movements, which were never the major beneficiaries of foundation grants, were the initiators of social reform. But foundation support for professionalized advocacy was instrumental in designing the actual policy reforms that were eventually implemented. Foundation support also insured that new political advocates were brought into centers of political decision-making as the representatives of previously marginal or excluded groups.

REFERENCES

Asher, Thomas R. "Why Foundations Should Support Advocacy Groups." *Foundation News*. 23 (1983):56–58.

Arnove, Robert, ed. *Philanthropy and Cultural Imperialism*. Boston: G. K. Hall, 1980.

Boris, Elizabeth. "Creation and Growth: A Survey of Private Foundations." In *America's Wealthy and the Future of Foundations*, edited by Teresa Odendahl. New York: Foundation Center, 1986.

Carey, Sarah C. "Philanthropy and the Powerless." In *Research Papers II*. Commission on Private Philanthropy and Public Needs (Filer Commission). II (1977):1109–1164.

Cunninggim, Merrimon. *Private Money and Public Service*. New York: McGraw-Hill, 1972.

Hart, Jeffrey. "Foundations and Public Controversy: A Negative View." In *The Future of Foundations* edited by Fritz Heimann. Englewood Cliffs, N.J.: Prentice-Hall, 1973.

Jenkins, J. Craig. "Resource Mobilization Theory and the Study of Social Movements." *Annual Review of Sociology,* 9 (1983):527–53.

———. "Nonprofit Organizations and Policy Advocacy." In *The Nonprofit Sector* edited by Walter W. Powell. New Haven: Yale University Press, 1987.

———. "Channeling Black Insurgency: Elite Patronage and the Professional Social Movement Organizations and the Development of the Black Movement." *American Sociological Review.* (1986):812–29.

———. "Social Movement Philanthropy and American Democracy." *Philanthropic Giving* edited by Richard Magat. New York: Oxford University Press, forthcoming.

Lowi, Theodore. *The End of Liberalism*, 2d ed. New York: Norton, 1979.

McLlhany, William H. *The Tax-Exempt Foundations*. Westport: Arlington House, 1980.

Metzger, Peter. *The Coercive Utopians: Their Hidden Agenda*. Denver: Public Service Company of Colorado, 1979.

Moynihan, Daniel P. *The Politics of a Guaranteed Income*. New York: Free Press, 1971.

———. "Social Welfare: Government vs. Private Efforts." *Foundation News*, 12 (1972):5–8.

Nielsen, Waldemar. *The Big Foundations*. New York: Columbia University Press, 1972.

———. *The Endangered Sector*. New York: Columbia University Press, 1979.

Peterson Commission. *Foundations, Private Giving and Public Policy*. Chicago: University of Chicago Press, 1971.

Roelofs, Joan. "Foundation Influence on Supreme Court Decision-Making." *Telos*, 13 (1983): 1–24.

Simon, John. "Foundations and Public Controversy: An Affirmative View." *The Future of Foundations,* edited by Fritz Heimann. Englewood Cliffs, N.J.: Prentice-Hall, 1973.

———. "Tax Treatment of Nonprofit Organizations: A Review of Federal and State Policies." In *The Nonprofit Sector,* edited by Walter W. Powell. New Haven: Yale University Press, 1987.

Taylor, Charles Lewis and David A. Jodice. *World Handbook of Social and Political Indicators*. New Haven: Yale University Press, 1978.

2

Chapter Two
Tax-Exempt Status for
Your Organization
By David B. Hopkins and Jill R. Shellow*

The primary focus of this chapter is the importance of acquiring and maintaining federal tax-exempt status. As will be discussed, there are several advantages that flow from establishing your own tax-exempt organization. However, you can also obtain the most important of these advantages—the ability of a donor to take certain deductions from his or her income for charitable contributions—by operating under the auspices of a tax-exempt "sponsoring" organization, but at the cost of fiscal, and thus operational, independence.

For example, in order for donors to your program to take advantage of the tax benefits of making charitable contributions, all their contributions will be paid not to you, but to your sponsoring organization. That extra detail alone may discourage some donors. The sponsor must retain full discretion and control over the funds received, and will apply those donations to your "account" only once its internal recordkeeping and management procedures have been satisfied. For this service the sponsor will generally take a percentage of your funding to cover its administrative costs.

Nevertheless, many programs operate under sponsoring organizations to avoid the organizational and operational responsibilities of acquiring and maintaining their own IRS tax-exempt status. This chapter sets out an overview of those requirements to help you decide which route is right for you.

First, a note of caution. This chapter contains only a broad-brush outline of the topics covered. It is neither sufficiently detailed nor tailored to the activities of any particular organization to serve as a practical guide for obtaining and maintaining tax-exempt status.

This brief chapter cannot address all the exceptions or qualifications contained in this area of tax law. At the risk of being criticized for adding to the overlegalization of America, see a lawyer, preferably a lawyer who has experience in servicing tax-exempt organizations. The requirements

---

*David Hopkins is a lawyer with Hillyer & Erwin in San Diego, California. Jill R. Shellow is a graduate of Georgetown University Law Center.

for getting and keeping your tax-exempt status are highly technical. If they are not met precisely, your status may be denied or revoked despite your best intentions. The Internal Revenue Service (IRS) generally is not impressed by meeting the "spirit" of the Code or Regulations; usually it requires compliance with "the letter of the law." Obtaining experienced legal counsel may save you substantial time and money in the long run.

To obtain tax-exempt status for your organization, you must apply for it with the Internal Revenue Service under one of the subsections of Section 501(c) of the Internal Revenue Code (IRC). There are twenty-five subsections of Section 501(c) each describing a different type of tax-exempt organization. This chapter concentrates specifically on Section 501(c)(3), since these organizations are the ones eligible to receive contributions that are tax deductible to the donor.

The application for tax-exempt status also serves as the application for classification as a public charity or an operating foundation. Absent a specific request for classification, once your application is approved, your organization will automatically be considered a private (nonoperating) foundation. Additional requirements are imposed on organizations that want to upgrade their tax-exempt status to the even more favorable status of either a private operating foundation or a public charity. But more on this later.

The Advantages of Tax Exemption

Why bother to obtain tax-exempt status? The most important advantage is that it greatly enhances your ability to attract funding. But several other tax and tax-related advantages flow directly from tax-exempt status.

Having applied for and obtained tax exemption from the IRS, your organization will enjoy significant—but not total—exemption from tax liability. Any income earned in furtherance of your exempt purpose—that is, your charitable, educational, or civic activities—as well as investment income is exempt from federal income taxation. On the other hand, your organization must pay tax like any other entity on all income it earns from "unrelated business activities" (except for the first $1,000 of such income). Keep in mind that if your exempt organization does earn unrelated business income, your tax liability will be based on your net income, that is, income after deducting all of the expenses directly connected with that activity, the same as any other business.

Generally speaking, unrelated business income that is subject to tax is revenue derived from any significant income-producing activity that is regularly carried on by the organization (like a commercial enterprise) that is not substantially related to the organization's exempt purpose. To satisfy the "substantially related" test, there must be a substantial, direct cause-and-effect relationship between the activity itself and the organization's exempt purposes. The mere fact that an income-producing activity generates revenue which is used to subsidize exempt program costs, or that the income-producing activity uses the same facilities and personnel as the exempt programs, does not make the income-producing activity related. Income from games of chance operated by your organization (i.e., lotteries, raffles, etc.) is tax exempt provided there is a state law that permits organizations such as yours to conduct such activities.

The statute contains specific exemptions from the definition of unrelated business income including: activities carried on primarily for the convenience of the organization's members; activities conducted primarily by volunteers; selling donated merchandise; rent from real property; and interest, dividends, and royalty income.

As this chapter is going to press, the Congress—perceiving substantial abuses of the laws related to unrelated business income—is currently reexamining tax-exempt organizations and specifically the relationship between their exempt-function income and unrelated business income. New legislation is being considered which could, perhaps, impose additional restrictive definitions, reporting requirements, tax liabilities, and penalties for failure to report unrelated business income.

Another benefit of obtaining tax-exempt status is that most tax-exempt organizations are eligible to acquire surplus real and personal property from the federal government by applying to the appropriate state agency for surplus property and/or the regional property coordinator for the Department of Health and Human Services. Further, many federal agencies maintain programs to assist qualified organizations in obtaining leases, loans, or insured mortgages for the construction or remodeling of facilities.

Finally, one of the most valuable benefits is reduced postage rates. All tax-exempt organizations can apply for a nonprofit mailing permit that enables them to send large bulk mailings at reduced prices; public charities receive even more favorable postage rates. Application forms may be obtained at the post office your organization utilizes.

Having obtained federal tax exemption, it is generally a simple matter, in most states, to obtain state tax exemption as well, relieving your organization from state (and usually local) income, sales, and property taxes. In most states it is necessary to apply separately for state tax-exempt status, although acquiring it is often virtually automatic after obtaining federal tax exemption. Proof of state tax exemption is what is referred to when someone—usually a vendor—asks for your "tax-exempt identification number." While several states assign identification numbers to their tax-exempt organizations, the IRS does not assign numbers to organizations exempt from federal income tax.

In addition to all of these tax benefits, 501(c)(3) organizations are eligible to receive tax-deductible charitable contributions by virtue of parallel descriptive language in IRC Section 170(c)(2) which defines such contributions. Obviously, this greatly enhances your ability to obtain funding from individuals and businesses since the availability of the tax deduction seems to increase the generosity and social awareness of donors. Acquiring 501(c)(3) status will also enhance your ability to obtain funding from major foundations, since it constitutes adequate verification that their funds are being used for purposes that are consistent with keeping their own tax-exempt status.

Classification as a Private Foundation or a Public Charity

All Section 501(c)(3) organizations are classified either (in reverse order of desirability) as private nonoperating foundations, private operating foundations, or public charities. An organization receiving Section 501(c)(3) status is automatically considered to be a private nonoperating foundation. The more advantageous status of private operating foundation or of public charity must be specifically requested on the application forms.

To qualify as an operating foundation, your organization must spend at least eighty-five percent of its yearly income on its own exempt-program activities. Operating foundations have fewer government reporting obligations. More important, a donor may generally obtain greater tax advantages from contributions to operating foundations than to nonoperating foundations. Thus, operating foundations may attract funds more easily than nonoperating foundations.

Public charities are allowed to engage in lobbying; private nonoperating or operating foundations cannot. Further, public charities are exempt from the two percent excise tax on investment income to which all private foundations are subject. Public charities status is generally limited to religious, educational, or governmental organizations, hospitals and schools, or to organizations that are publicly funded. The specific requirements are set forth in IRC Section 170(b)(1)(A). In all probability, you will seek public charity status because of your public support, specifically under Section 170(b)(1)(A)(vi).

The Treasury Department has developed two alternative tests for determining whether an organization meets the public support criteria appearing in the statute, a "mechanical test" and a "facts and circumstances test." If you meet either of these tests, your organization will receive the coveted classification of "not a private foundation."

Generally speaking, when you first apply for public charity classification as a publicly supported organization, you tell the IRS you expect that over the first four years of your existence you will satisfy the requirements. Thereafter, every year you must provide documentation that your organization continues to satisfy the requirements.

Under the "mechanical test" the organization must receive at least one-third of its total support from contributions by the general public or from government sources. If this one-third test is not met, the organization can still qualify as "publicly supported" under the "facts and circumstances" test, provided that (1) at least ten percent of its total support is derived from the general public or from governmental sources (again using the four-year time period for computation); (2) it carries on an active program of soliciting public support; and (3) it possesses a combination of certain other factors indicative of public support, the most significant of which are the public composition of the organization's governing board and the extent to which the organization's facilities or programs are available to the public.

The one-third and ten-percent thresholds for public support are determined by a "support fraction" which measures the percentage of the organization's "total support" that comes from public sources. What is included in the numerator and denominator of the "support fraction" is precise, but in typical IRS fashion not necessarily intuitive or logical.[1]

---

[1] The denominator of the fraction, "total support," includes the gross amounts of (1) gifts, grants, and contributions; (2) net income from any unrelated trade or business; plus (3) gross investment income, such as interest, dividends, and rents (but not capital gains).

The numerator of the fraction includes the full amount of grants, gifts, and contributions received from governmental units and publicly supported charities (i.e., tax-exempt organizations not classified as private foundations). Contributions from individuals, trusts, and corporations and grants from private foundations are also included in the numerator, but only to the extent that the contributions or grants from any one individual or entity do not exceed two percent of the organization's total support over the four-year computation period.

For the purposes of calculating the "support fraction" the IRS ignores completely and excludes from both the denominator and the numerator (1) amounts received by the organization from the performance of its exempt functions; (2) capital gains; (3) loan repayments; and (4) "unusual grants," i.e., grants that are unusually large, unexpected, and which if taken into account would adversely affect the organization's status as publicly supported.

An alternative mechanical test is available to organizations with substantial exempt function income and investment income. It is functionally quite similar, except that the "support fraction" is calculated slightly differently to account for the different revenue mix. If you want the specifics, check Section 509(a)(2) of the IRC.

Read the requirements carefully, plan ahead, and periodically check your progress during the four-year period and thereafter.

A third means of avoiding private foundation status is to qualify as a "support organization," that is, one formed and operated for the benefit of a specific public charity (or group of educational institutions) and which is operated, supervised, and controlled by or in connection with the supported public charity.

Statutory Definition of a Tax-Exempt Organization

The statute describes Section 501(c)(3) organizations as:

> Corporations and any community chest, fund or foundation organized and operated exclusively for religious, charitable, scientific . . . library or educational purposes, or for the prevention of cruelty to animals, no part of the net earnings of which inures to the benefits of any private shareholder or individual, no substantial part of the activities of which is carrying on propaganda, or otherwise attempting to influence legislation, and which does not participate in (including the publishing or distributing of statements) any political campaign on behalf of any candidate for public office.

Several points should be made about this language. In order to qualify as a tax exempt, you must: have an organization; be organized exclusively for exempt purposes; operate exclusively as an exempt organization; insure that no benefits inure to any private individuals; refrain from any involvement in political campaigns; and engage in no more than the statutorily limited amounts of direct and grassroots lobbying. Each of these requirements is addressed in turn below.

A Recognized Legal Entity

First, in order to qualify under Section 501(c)(3), there must exist an organization. Section 501(c)(3) is not available for individuals or for groups not cognizable as legal entities. The most common type of organization is the nonprofit (as opposed to business) corporation, although other forms, such as a trust or association, may also be used. The requirements for establishing these types of legal entities are governed by state law. However, be sure to consult your tax counsel at the time your organization drafts its articles or bylaws, since many provisions normally utilized for other types of organizations may run afoul of the technical requirements of Section 501(c)(3).

The Organization's Legal Structure

Second, the entity must be organized exclusively for one or more of the exempt purposes identified in the statute. This means that the organizational documents, i.e., the articles of incorporation or association and bylaws or trust instruments, must expressly limit the purpose of the entity to those specified in Section 501(c)(3). These documents should not expressly empower the organization to engage in activities not in furtherance of its exempt purpose, except to an insubstantial extent. If your applicable state laws do not require a more specific listing of your organization's powers to qualify as a legal entity, it is advisable to list your powers as "all those permitted by applicable state law which are also consistent with Section 501(c)(3)." Often, qualification depends upon including "magic words" such as these in your organizational documents and avoiding "buzz words" such as business or profit.

Operating Exclusively for Exempt Purposes

Third, the organization must be operated exclusively for exempt purposes. However, in typical IRS fashion, exclusively does not really mean exclusively. The regulations promulgated under Section 501(c)(3) establish that this test will be met if the organization "engages primarily" in activities that accomplish its exempt purpose. An organization will not meet this test if "more than an insubstantial part of its activities" is not in furtherance of its exempt purpose. There is, unfortunately, no bright-line test for distinguishing insubstantial from substantial. For example, the IRS has ruled that an organization that conducts religious retreats and that also includes recreational activities qualifies under Section 501(c)(3), while an organization that conducts a cruise that includes four hours per day of organized religious activity did not qualify. Although the two rulings may satisfy one's sense of justice, it is difficult to determine how much nonexempt activity is so substantial that exempt status will be denied.

Prohibition on Private Benefit

Fourth, your organization must be both organized and operated so that no part of its net earnings benefits any private shareholder or individual. From an organizational standpoint, this means, in part, that your charter or deed of trust should provide that upon dissolution, your assets will be distributed for Section 501(c)(3) purposes or to a federal, state, or local government for a public purpose. From an operational standpoint, financial transactions between the organization and its principals other than fair payment for services should be avoided, as should other private benefits such as permitting individuals to use your facilities, mailing per-

21

mits, etc., for activities that do not further the exempt purpose of the organization.

This also means that you cannot pay unreasonably high salaries which can easily be interpreted as benefiting a private individual. Running afoul of this prohibition was considered by many in the know to be part of the reason such highly visible television ministers as Jim and Tammy Bakker and their tax-exempt organizations were the subject of substantial scrutiny by the IRS and Congress in late 1987 and early 1988.

Prohibition on Political Activities

Fifth, the law clearly prohibits organizations exempt under Section 501(c)(3) from intervening in political election campaigns. All intervention—whether in favor of or opposed to any particular candidate for public office—is barred. This includes not only endorsing candidates, distributing campaign literature, holding campaign rallies on the premises of a tax-exempt organization, and making political campaign contributions (which might also violate federal and state election campaign finance laws), but any form of activity.

Certain types of nonpartisan voter education, voter registration, and get-out-the-vote activities are permitted. However, before venturing into these activities, consult a lawyer who can advise you about the strict rules that must be followed. Failure to heed this admonition carries stiff penalties and can cost an otherwise charitable organization its tax-exempt status.[2]

Restrictions on Lobbying

And sixth, no substantial part of your operating activities can be for purposes of disseminating propaganda or influencing legislation. This is the so-called "lobbying restriction."

Lobbying is prohibited for private foundations. For public charities, lobbying is allowable within permissible—but vaguely defined—limits. Lobby expenditures greatly in excess of these limits may result in loss of tax-exempt status. Obviously, understanding these limitations and exactly what constitutes lobbying activities is vital. Unfortunately, the definitions are not clear.

A safe harbor defining the amount of permissible lobbying is available for public charities filing a specific election to engage in lobbying activities. Activities exceeding the levels permitted by the election are subject

---

[2]Although political campaign activities are prohibited to Section 501(c)(3) organizations, organizations described in other subsections of Section 501 may engage in such activities, subject however to the strict requirements of IRC Section 527.

to a twenty-five percent excise tax. In 1987, the IRS issued proposed regulations implementing the election, but they have been withdrawn. In early 1988, the IRS announced plans to issue new, different proposed regulations by midyear. The Independent Sector in Washington, D.C., as well as other organizations, is monitoring these developments. Stay tuned.

Different permissible limits are applicable to the two types of lobbying recognized by the IRC: direct lobbying and grassroots lobbying. Direct lobbying relates to legislative activities such as encouraging or discouraging actions by Congress, state legislatures, local councils, or public referenda and initiatives. Grassroots lobbying refers to exhortations to an organization's members or the general public to support or oppose legislation being considered, or soon to be considered, by a legislative body. An organization will be disqualified if its main or primary purpose or objective may be obtained only by achieving the passage of legislation, or the defeat of proposed legislation, and it advocates or campaigns for or against such legislation. However, self-defense lobbying, i.e., "appearances before or communications by any legislative body with respect to a possible decision of such body which might affect the existence of the organization, its powers and duties, its tax-exempt status or the deduction of contributions to the organization" is also permitted. In addition, an organization may engage in and publicize nonpartisan analysis, study, or research of issues that are the subject of legislation. The key word is nonpartisan. Section 501(c)(3) organizations may also provide technical advice or opinions to legislatures, committees, or subcommittees in response to a written request.

The lobbying restrictions on tax-exempt organizations have been the subject of heated controversy. The proposed regulations issued by the IRS in 1987 (and since withdrawn) implemented Sections 501(h) and 4911 of the IRC which were enacted by Congress in the mid-1970s to provide tax-exempt organizations with some guidance about the extent to which lobbying would be permitted. The new law permits public charities to elect to have their lobbying expenditures quantified against specific· dollar expenditures limits. The proposed regulations tried to define the types of activities encompassed in the vague and amorphous language of the statutes. Although technically the proposed regulations pertained only to those organizations making the specific election, they were widely perceived to be applicable to defining when a nonelecting organization crossed the line between a permitted insubstantial amount of lobbying and impermissible substantial lobbying.

The new regulations anticipated in mid-1988 may shed additional light on these issues. Three critical issues remain: what is meant by "substantial," what kinds of activities constitute lobbying, and how should an organization go about allocating lobbying costs.

Two approaches can be taken to defining "substantial." The first looks to an organization's specific expenditures on lobbying activities. The second is a subjective analysis by the IRS of how much of the organization's total activities is—in reality or merely perceived to be—direct or grass-roots lobbying.

The easiest way to define "substantial" is to look to Sections 501(h) and 4911 of the IRC, which allow public charities the option of electing to have their lobbying activities measured against specific dollar expenditure limits. The electing public charity may spend twenty percent of its first $500,000 of exempt-purpose expenditures (and a lesser percentage of further exempt-purpose expenditures) for lobbying, up to a total of $1.0 million. Up to one-fourth of that total may be spent for grassroots lobbying, i.e., attempting to influence the public on legislation matters. Lobbying expenditures in excess of the limits are subject to a twenty-five percent excise tax. An electing organization that either normally, or for a period of four years, exceeds an average of 150 percent of its limit for either grassroots or total lobbying expenditures will lose its tax-exempt status. The election must be made annually; it may be made anytime during the year and, once made, applies retroactively to all lobbying during the year.

Organizations that do not elect pursuant to Section 501(h) are highly vulnerable. The lobbying activities of these organizations are evaluated using subjective criteria such as the amount of attention their activities receive in the media, the controversy the activities generate, and public perception of the organization's goals in carrying out their lobbying. In practice it works like this:

> Assume your organization has been granted tax-exempt status to operate a women's health program. Your annual budget is $500,000, and all of your activities during a given year are related to the operation of your program. However, in the political climate prevailing in 1988, you decide to run a series of television advertisements during prime time in your community, urging the public to contact their elected representatives and oppose pending legislation which would require parental consent before young women would be allowed to receive family planning counseling and services. The advertisements cost a total of $10,000.
>
> 1. If your organization has elected under Section 501(h),

24

you have not engaged in excessive lobbying. Section 4911 permits you to spend twenty percent of your total expenditures for exempt purposes (i.e., all of your program costs plus the $10,000 for the ad) on direct lobbying, i.e., twenty percent of $500,000 = $100,000; of which twenty-five percent may be for grassroots lobbying, or twenty-five percent of $100,000 = $25,000.

2. If your organization has not made the election, however, the IRS may look at the high visibility of the advertisements and the controversy they generated, and find you have engaged in "substantial lobbying" in violation of the statute.

The second problem goes to exactly what is meant by lobbying. The 1987 proposed regulations suggested that grassroots lobbying activities would be identified as: statements "pertaining to" pending or imminent legislation, statements which "imply" a view on the desirability of certain legislation, and statements that reach policy conclusions requiring legislative solutions or legislative action. Accordingly, organizations are well advised to avoid explicitly calling for specific legislative action, advocating one side of specific legislation, and using such well-worn phrases as "contact your local representatives in Congress." Another problem is dissemination of an organization's positions on legislative issues.

In January 1988 the IRS took the position that opposing the nomination of Judge Robert Bork to the United States Supreme Court, although not a prohibited political campaign activity, did constitute lobbying activity even though technically the congressional issue was confirmation not legislation.[3] This example illustrates that organizations must be sensitive to the lobbying regulations when making statements on public policy issues.

Objective analysis of a public policy issue should be permissible, but it could become grassroots lobbying if distributed in a manner that favors one side of an issue, i.e., in the words of the proposed regulations, if it is targeted to individuals "reasonably expected to share a common view." While it would appear that communications with an organization's own membership on legislation of direct self-interest to the organization may not be lobbying, the proposed regulations suggested it could be quickly transformed into a lobbying activity if it directly encourages the

---

[3]In addition, the IRS identified such expenditures as falling within the definition of "political activity" appearing in IRC Section 527, discussed in note 2, above.

25

membership to engage in their own direct or indirect grassroots lobbying activities.

The last problem raised by the proposed lobbying regulations relates to allocating lobbying costs. Once a communication is deemed to be lobbying, an organization must determine how much of its cost constitutes direct lobbying, indirect grassroots lobbying, or educational communications. The proposed regulations suggested that with three exceptions, there should be a "reasonable allocation, based on all of the facts and circumstances." The three exceptions relate to advertising, fundraising, and mixed lobbying (direct and grassroots). The regulations said that "if any part of" an advertisement "constitutes grassroots lobbying, the entire amount expended for, or in connection with the advertisement, constitutes a grassroots (lobbying) expenditure." Expenditures made for both grassroots lobbying and fundraising combined were also to be treated, *in toto*, as grassroots lobbying expenditures. Expenditures made for "both direct lobbying and grassroots lobbying purposes" were to be treated, the IRS suggested, as grassroots lobbying expenditures except to the extent that the organization could prove that the expenditure was "incurred solely for direct lobbying purposes."

As the foregoing discussion should make clear, the proposed regulations—promulgated with a view toward drawing some bright lines— do exactly the opposite. For example, what is meant by dissemination; does this include media coverage? What constitutes an expenditure "in connection with" a lobbying activity? What if the problem addressed by an organization is susceptible not only to legislative solutions but to other nonlegislative solutions as well? What about newsletters; are they fundraising pieces or grassroots lobbying statements? The 1987 proposed regulations were withdrawn after an outcry by certain public interest groups and exempt organizations. But it is uncertain what the new proposed regulations, anticipated in mid-1988, will provide.

In addition to the statutory lobbying restrictions of the Tax Code, on April 25, 1984, the Office of Management and Budget (OMB) adopted a regulation prohibiting any organization from using federal funds for lobbying purposes. The OMB regulation applies to all organizations, including public charities, that either receive federal grants or have cost-plus contracts with federal agencies. However, the OMB regulation restricts only the federal funds themselves; it does not affect other funds or activities of the organization that are not federally funded. Any organization receiving federal funds and involved in any way in legislation-oriented activities should review the OMB regulation carefully since it differs from the IRC requirements in several important respects.

One thing to keep in mind is that if your organization cannot take advantage of the election and plans to be involved in substantial lobbying, it should consider qualification under Section 501(c)(4) as an "organization ... not organized for profit but operated exclusively for the promotion of social welfare." However, 501(c)(4) organizations may not receive tax-deductible charitable contributions.

Purposes Deemed to be Exempt

The specific types of exempt purposes for which a 501(c)(3) organization must be exclusively organized and operated are construed very broadly. According to applicable treasury regulations, a charitable purpose would include (among other things): relief of the poor; erection or maintenance of public buildings; lessening of the burdens of government; and the promotion of social welfare through lessening neighborhood tensions, eliminating prejudice and discrimination, defending human and civil rights secured by law, or combatting community deterioration and juvenile delinquency. However, this last category of organization may be determined to constitute a Section 501(c)(4) civic organization if its membership and its activities are too restricted. Examples of 501(c)(3) charities have included such diverse activities as the building and operating of a drag strip for the purpose of reducing drag racing on public streets. It is even possible for a public interest law firm to receive 501(c)(3) status provided that it is operated by an independent board that is representative of the public interest and is not identified with a private firm.

Educational purposes are also broadly defined as including the instruction or training of the individual for the purpose of improving or developing his capabilities. Educational organizations accorded 501(c)(3) status have had as their subject matter: a particular method of painless childbirth, marital adjustment, gardening instruction, and sailboat racing (to improve the quality of the U.S. Olympic sailing team).

For tax years beginning after July 18, 1984, there is a new Section 501(k) that expands the definition of "educational" purposes to include child care centers that are available to the public (i.e., not limited to children of parents who work for particular employers) if substantially all of the care provided is to permit individuals (presumably the children's parents or custodians) to be gainfully employed. By a corresponding amendment to IRC Section 170, contributions to qualifying child care centers are tax deductible.

Applying for Tax-Exempt Status

An organization applies for Section 501(c)(3) status by filing with the IRS Form 1023 (Form 1024 in the case of a Section 501(c)(4) organization).[4] The application must include copies of the applicant's organizational documents. The IRS forms ask the organization to provide details about its proposed activities, the background and experience of its principals, its relationship to other organizations, its anticipated sources of funding, and its projected use of funds. This information must be provided in much greater detail than is required by state law in the organization's charter or other organizing document. It is best to be as specific as possible in delineating particular projects and activities that will be undertaken. In most cases the IRS office in the district in which the organization is formed will issue a determination letter. However, in some cases the application will be referred to the national office of the IRS in Washington, D.C. As a result of the Tax Reform Act of 1986, all organizations that receive their tax-exempt status after July 15, 1987, are required to make their exemption applications available for public inspection at their own offices. All other organizations are required to make provision for public disclosure only if, on July 15, 1987, they had in their files a copy of the application. (Under the old law, public access was available only through the IRS.)

An organization that applies for and is granted tax-exempt status within fifteen months of the date on which it was formed will be considered by the IRS to have been tax exempt retroactively to the date of its incorporation. By waiting longer than fifteen months to apply, the tax-exempt status, when it is granted, will be deemed to have been in effect only from the date on which the application was filed. If your organization is new but you expect it will qualify as a public charity (as discussed above), the IRS will provide, upon request, an advance ruling for five years treating you as a public charity. However, within ninety days after the advance ruling period ends, the organization must provide documentation that the public support tests have been satisfied. If the IRS determines that your organization did not satisfy the requirements, the organization will be liable for all the taxes levied on private nonoperating foundations.

When your organization receives its determination letter from the IRS identifying it as tax exempt, be sure to keep the letter in a safe place. If at some point you lose it, consult the IRS Cumulative List of Section 501(c)(3) organizations, IRS Publication 78. If the name of your organization is included—and it should be—you may obtain a duplicate copy

---

[4]The IRS publishes a relatively easy to understand booklet entitled "How to Obtain Tax-Exempt Status," Publication No. 557. It is well worth reading before completing an application, and available free of charge by telephoning your local IRS district office.

of your IRS exemption letter by contacting your local IRS district director. If your name does not appear, it is probably time to consult a lawyer well versed in the problems of exempt organizations, to clarify your organization's tax status.

Tax-Exempt Status Does Not End All Contact with the Federal Government

It is vital to remember that while approval of your application for tax-exempt status relieves your organization of most of its liability for income taxes (as well as those other benefits described earlier in this chapter), qualification as an exempt organization does not relieve you of filing tax returns. In fact, such qualification carries with it an obligation to file certain specific returns.

Public charities qualified under Section 501(c)(3) must file annually IRS Form 990, the "Return of Organization Exempt from Income Tax." Private foundations qualified under Section 501(c)(3) are required to file a longer return, IRS Form 990-PF, "Return of Private Foundation Exempt from Income Tax." These forms must be filed on or before the fifteenth day of the fifth month following the close of the organization's annual accounting period, at the IRS service center noted in the instructions. Further, any of these organizations having more than $1,000 in unrelated trade or business income must file a Form 990-T. This form must be filed on or before the fifteenth day of the fourth month following the close of the annual accounting period. All these forms, just like your original application, must be made available to the public.

Furthermore, exemption from income taxes does not exempt an organization from filing withholding, social security, and unemployment tax returns, as well as other documents and reports too numerous and detailed to mention in this space. Moreover, as a result of the Tax Reform Act of 1986, tax-exempt organizations with unrelated business income tax liabilities are now required to estimate this income and make quarterly payments of estimated taxes. In addition, most states have laws regulating activities of exempt organizations, including fundraising activities, and may require additional filings.

The message should be clear. Exemption from income tax is not the same as exemption from government regulation.

3

Chapter Three
Planning for Fundraising
By Tricia Rubacky*

Successful fundraising begins with a clear organizational mission and people committed to achieving it. These ingredients are critical; without them, your attempts to raise money will surely suffer. Assuming your organization satisfies these basic conditions, my advice is to follow these three commandments of fundraising:

I. Thou shalt always plan, plan, and plan some more;
II. Thou shalt always strive for a diversified fundraising plan;
III. Thou shalt tie thy program and budget planning to thy fundraising planning.

The information on funding sources in this book can prove lucrative for your organization. However, without careful planning, your investment in grantseeking can have disappointing—even disastrous—results.

A frequent complaint from grantseekers is: "I sent in all these proposals and I haven't heard anything from the foundations. We're headed for a financial crisis if we don't hear something soon!" This is the classic "blame the funder" approach, which you should decide right now to abandon. It assumes it is up to the foundations to prevent your funding problems.

A plan alone cannot solve a financial crisis. However, it can help prevent one, because it incorporates the steps you must take over a prescribed period of time, the strategies you can employ to make your program attractive to a variety of funding sources, and the internal back-up systems for times when your strategies and plans fall short.

A fundraising plan is much more than a list of funders and amounts requested. A real plan reflects an income goal that is tied to your organization's program goals and incorporates the following components:

1. A list of all sources from whom you are seeking funds (both grant and nongrant fundraising) organized by likelihood of

---

*Tricia Rubacky, a consultant and trainer in fundraising and development, was formerly director of development at the Youth Project.

      support and priority of effort,
2. A calendar including all deadlines and a follow-up schedule,
3. An income projection based on likely funding, and
4. A cash flow projection.

The most successful fundraising plans also demonstrate a commitment to diversified fundraising. Diversity in fundraising prevents organizational overdependence on one source of funding (e.g., foundation grants or direct mail), and provides a greater margin of safety for those inevitable times when circumstances prevent one source from continuing its support. In addition, dependence on a single type of fundraising limits your group's exposure in other arenas—exposure which is necessary to achieving familiarity needed for attracting new support. It is true that considerable organizational resources must be used to achieve funding diversity; however, it is also true that your organization's future could be in serious jeopardy without the stability provided by diverse income streams.

A good fundraising plan also produces important management benefits. It can forestall the need for crisis-mode fundraising and keep you informed of where you stand at all times. A plan helps you identify progress and anticipate problems, and it forms the basis for informed decisions and budget adjustments as new developments occur or new information is received. A plan also helps you set and balance priorities and avoid the pitfalls of competing goals and timetables. Finally, a plan helps build the organization's confidence in its fundraising capacity.

Step One: Goals and Timelines

Before making a plan, considerable preparation work is needed. First, you must have a ballpark idea of how much money you need to raise and when it is needed. This ballpark figure will help you build the plan, but it is important that the program and budget goals are informed by the fundraising plan and vice versa. The most logical place to start is with the amount you raised during the previous year. Later, armed with a realistic estimate of what can be raised and from what sources, you may decide that no increases for new programs are feasible. Or you may determine that adding to your program and budget is feasible in light of your fundraising potential and the time and resources you have available for raising the funds. Before committing to a budget and a fundraising plan, all the people involved in your program, finance, and fundraising, operations, including members of your governing board, should review the plan and agree on goals that are both realistic and achievable.

Step Two: Identify Potential Funding Sources

The next step is to create a list of all the potential sources of income for your organization. Here are some possibilities to consider:

Grant Fundraising. Sources of grants include corporations, foundations, government programs, religious organizations, and individuals who make grants through philanthropic institutions, labor unions, or professional associations.

Nongrant Fundraising. This fundraising can be grouped in two categories, as follows: (1) Individual solicitation, including personal requests, phonathons, telemarketing, mail appeals via the media (radio or telethons), workplace and payroll deduction, special events, canvassing, and membership drives; and (2) Earned income, including sales of products, fees for services, and interest income.

While you may already be raising funds through a variety of means, as part of the planning process you must determine whether to try to raise more from current sources or to explore new avenues. Some combination of tested and untested sources is a positive goal for any organization if the resources are available to undertake new ventures. Before deciding, you need to do some research and learn as much as you can about both grant and nongrant fundraising. Armed with this information, you are in a position to determine what the potential is for your group.[1]

Step Three: Record Keeping

Once you have decided which avenues of support you will pursue, you need a system for managing the information you compile about these sources. Essential facts (such as contact person, address, phone number, deadlines, and board meeting dates) and strategy should be organized for every source you are planning to approach. This information should be kept within easy reach at all times, either in a notebook or on a computer. (See Sample 1 for a Fundraising Strategy Sheet format.)

Basic information on individual contributors, whether major donors

---

[1]There are many excellent reference works available to help you formulate and diversify your fundraising program. Among the best are the books by Klein, Flanagan, and Seltzer, which are listed in the bibliography.

Sample 1. Fundraising Strategy Sheet

Name of funding source:

Address:

Telephone:

Contact person:

Other known staff/board members:

Known interest areas:

History of support:

Total annual grants: Average grant size:
Who knows or has connections?

Step 1:
    Results:

Step 2:
    Results:

Step 3:
    Results:

Notes from meetings, telephone calls, etc.:

or members, should also be well organized in a profile book, a card file, or a computer data base. (See Sample 2 for a model Donor Profile Sheet.)

The information system you devise should be easy to update regularly, since grantseeking requires you to handle many important details at once, and you cannot afford to allow any to fall through the cracks. Indeed, the system itself is critical to developing and refining your strategy in approaching funders and should be considered among the most priceless tools of your plan. In addition, you need to establish a filing system

Sample 2. Individual Donor Profile Sheet

Name:

Home address: Telephone:

Business address: Telephone:

Title/Occupation:

Preferred place for being contacted:

Personal/financial background information:

General philanthropic interests:

Any foundation connections:

Who knows/has connections?

Donor history:

Date   Amount   Restricted/Unrestricted

on funders to provide new staff and board members with a sense of the organization's history with its funders, and with those from whom it has tried unsuccessfully to raise funds. This information is critical to the future relationship of organizations to their grantmakers, and holds many clues to understanding problems a group may be having raising funds from particular sources.

Step Four: The Calendar

The next component in organizing your fundraising is a calendar, preferably a fifteen-month calendar to plan fundraising for the year—since much of fundraising requires advance planning that you normally need to begin at least three months before your fiscal year even starts.

As you lay out your plan, keep the calendar nearby and fill in as many deadlines or dates for your fundraising activities as possible. You will add to the calendar and change it frequently throughout the year. The calendar will also help you decide whether new program activities can be added or must be deferred because they compete with each other or with other organizational activities. You may want to set aside a copy of your original calendar and go back to it at the end of the year to see how realistic it was as a planning tool.

Deadlines mean nothing unless they are accompanied by a work plan. Your next step, therefore, is to take the deadlines calendar and create another calendar for all the activities listed. Every aspect of your fundraising, including preparation of proposals, letters, printing newsletters, travel, board and committee meetings, individual meetings, events, and all follow-up should be built into the work plan calendar. If the work plan is mapped out using the same fifteen-month format, then, when you are ready, the fundraising and work plan calendars can be integrated and converted to whatever calendar system works best for you—six-month, three-month, one-month, or weekly.

Keep in mind, in order to be effective planning tools, the calendars must be developed in conjunction with your overall program and fundraising plans, incorporating enough of your organization's activity to know what will affect or drive your fundraising.

Step Five: Income Projections

A significant part of the fundraising plan is an income projection. Because budget and program decisions will be based upon the fundraising plan, extra caution must be taken not to overestimate the potential for funding from any source, whether a traditional one or an entirely new one. All funding sources should be organized in order of probability, according to a likelihood rating based on your most informed judgment. For example, all things being equal, your potential for raising $5,000 from an annual mail appeal should be very likely in the second or third year. However, before counting on that income, you must ask yourself if all factors that produced that level of response last year are unchanged. Maybe you have more names to approach than last year, which could enable you to raise more money. Perhaps staff turnover during the year kept the organization from communicating with donors since their last contribution, which could cause you to lose support. Use this kind of information to estimate your proceeds, and when in doubt, err on the conservative side.

Similarly, if last year the XYZ Foundation made a $10,000 grant, and the year before a $7,500 grant, would it be safe to assume the foundation would renew again? What about planning for a similar increase? The answers must be based on your most recent information about the funder. Have you stayed in touch with them to know their impressions of your work? Does the foundation still fund groups working on the same issues? Has there been staff turnover at the foundation? Has anything happened that would affect their level of grants, or the timing of their grant cycles?

The point is that in order to anticipate income realistically you must have current information upon which to base your probability estimates.

Figures 1 and 2 show what a hypothetical completed annual plan looks like, and should provide you with an idea of what is meant by probability-based planning. This hypothetical organization had a fund-raising goal of $110,000, but the conservative projection was $105,000, so the budget was based on the latter figure.

At the close of the year, this group raised more than their conservative projection of $105,975. Perhaps when they did not receive the $20,000 grant from the Jones Foundation, they put more effort into the phonathon and product sales to make up the difference. The important thing to see is that this kind of plan enables an organization to evaluate its progress continuously, to monitor its fundraising successes and evaluate its program accordingly, and to correct for disappointments in a timely manner.

A few rules in the preparation of income projections should be followed to increase their reliability.

1. Base percentages on an informed sense of what is likely, even if the sources in a category are only twenty-five to fifty percent likely. This sample plan was based primarily on renewals, and this organization had a considerable amount of com-

Figure 1. Sample Plan 1987

Adopted 12/15/86   **GOAL:** $110,000
Current as of 12/31/87

Source	Projection	Committed to Date
Secure (at beginning of year)		
New World Fdn.	$10,000	$10,000
Norman Fnd.	10,000	10,000
CHD	22,000	22,000
Ms. Smith	2,500	2,500
Carryover from 1985	1,800	1,800
subtotal	**$46,300**	**$46,300**
Very Likely Renewals		
Mr. Heir	$20,000	$20,000
March Mail Appeal	8,000	8,425
Jones Fnd.	20,000	-0-
Payroll Deduction gifts	6,500	7,850
subtotal	**$54,500**	**$36,275**
Running Total	**$100,800**	**$82,575**
Possible Renewals		
J.C. Penney Fnd.	$10,000	$ 5,000
Joint Fdn. Support	10,000	10,000
Topsfield Fdn.	5,000	5,000
Mr. Anonymous	5,000	10,000
General Mills Co.	5,000	-0-
October phonathon	5,000	6,350
subtotal	**$40,000**	**$36,350**
Running Total	**$140,800**	**$118,925**

Sample Plan continued on next page

mitted income when it started the year. Many plans will not allow for such high probability of success.

2. Do not include "prospects" in the income projection. (A prospect is a source that is untried as well as one for which you have no reliable experience or information upon which

Figure 1. Sample Plan 1987 (*continued*)

Earned Income

Book sales	$ 2,500	$ 2,200
T-shirt sales	3,500	1,500
Calendars/cards sales	1,500	2,400
subtotal	**$ 7,500**	**$ 6,100**
Running Total	**$ 48,300**	**$125,025**

Prospects

Mr. Stockbroker	$ 2,500	$ 1,000
Ms. Investor	1,500	1,500
Ms. Banker	1,000	1,000
Spring party	5,000	5,750
subtotal	**$ 10,000**	**$ 9,250**
Running Total	**$158,300**	**$134,275**
TOTAL	**$158,300**	**$134,275**

Figure 2. Income Projection 1987 Compared to Actual Income

Source	Original Projection				Conservative Projection	Actual Income
Secure	46,300	@	100%	=	$ 46,300	$46,300
Very Likely	54,500	@	90%	=	49,050	36,275
Possible	40,000	@	50%	=	20,000	36,350
Earned Income	7,500	@	75%	=	5,625	6,100
Prospects	10,000	@	0%	=	-0-	9,250
	$158,300				**$120,975**	**$134,275**

to evaluate the probability of support.) Groups often become so caught up with efforts to raise funds from other categories of support that they never get around to the prospects list. Therefore, it is better to treat income from these sources as the funds to expand your program if they are raised. If prospects do not yield success, your existing program will not suffer if they were not included in your original income projection.

3. Once the plan is approved, do not change the placement of sources or the likelihood rating you assigned to each category. If you change the plan midyear, you will not be able to evaluate your original projections, nor will you be able to make informed judgments about expenditures during interim budget review periods.
4. Remember that you are developing a plan, and like any plan, it needs constant monitoring to determine progress. It is not a foolproof calculation and should not be considered immune to failure. Your projections may be wrong, but if they are, you will know what the impact will be relative to your other fundraising activity.

Step Six: The Income Cash Flow Projection

The last piece of the fundraising plan is the income cash flow projection. This is a necessary complement to the expense cash flow projection which your organization needs in order to meet monthly bills. To prepare your income cash flow projection, begin with an accounting sheet with twelve columns. List all the sources of income on your fundraising plan down the left side, and label the top of each column with the names of the months. (See Figure 3.)

Then, go over your potential sources and make a realistic and conservative projection of when grants might be expected, when income from individual contributions is likely to be received, when the proceeds from sales and events are possible. Put the conservative projected amount in the column under the month the income is anticipated.

It will soon be obvious which months will be your high income months and which will be low. This will help you plan your expenses, especially those which can be deferred or spread over time.

As you can see from the sample, none of the prospect income is included in the cash flow plan. Because you have not made an income projection for the sources in that category, you should not include those sources in the cash flow plan. You should also exercise caution with some of sources you have categorized as "possible." It may be advisable to project less income or to put the projection later in the year when it is not as vital. While this conservative approach means that your cash flow projection will not equal your income projection, this is a precautionary measure to prevent over-extending your organization's cash flow.

You should regularly adjust the cash flow plan based on new information about your funding sources and the projected outcomes of fund-

Figure 3. Sample Income Cash Flow Projection 1987

	Jan.	Feb.	Mar.	April	May	June	July	Aug.	Sept.	Oct.	Nov.	Dec.
Foundations												
New World			$10,000									
Norman	$10,000											
CHD	$7,500			$7,500			$7,000					
Jones					$10,000							
J.C. Penney				$5,000								
JFS						$10,000						
Topsfield							$5,000					
General Mills					$2,500							
Major Donors												
Ms. Smith	$2,500											
Mr. Heir				$20,000								
Mr. Anonymous												$5,000
Individuals/Events												
March mail appeal				$4,000	$3,000	$1,000						
Fall payroll Deduction campaign										$1,500	$2,000	$3,000
October phonathon										$1,000	$2,000	$2,000
Product Sales												
Books	$100	$200	$200	$250	$150	$150	$250	$100	$200	$200	$300	$300
T-shirts				$750	$250	$500				$250	$250	$500
Calendars/ Cards									$300	$300	$400	$500
Total	$20,100	$200	$10,200	$37,500	$15,900	$11,650	$12,250	$100	$500	$3,250	$4,950	$11,300

raising events. Constant oversight of income and expenses is one way of preventing a cash flow crisis, provided that the other facets of the fundraising plan are being followed carefully throughout the year.

Planning an organization's fundraising does not require sophisticated systems. All the suggestions offered here are, rather, means to help keep fundraising efforts organized. They are simple to use, and can be modified to meet an individual organization's particular needs. While planning alone cannot guarantee fundraising success, it can do the next best thing: It can enhance the organization's capacity and bring order to what is too often an overwhelming process.

4

Chapter Four
Approaching the Grantmaker
and Preparing a Proposal
By Jill R. Shellow

Writing a proposal seems to be the part of the grant-seeking process that always gets the most attention. Numerous articles and whole volumes have been published on how to write a good proposal. All this attention, however, is not in direct proportion to the relative importance of the proposal in the process.

The proposal is only one part. It must be preceded by an ongoing project with a proven track record, or good, articulated plans for implementing a new idea. The proposal must also be preceded by thorough planning and research on the universe of potential funding sources. As Tricia Rubacky points out in Chapter 3, fundraising proposals should be consistent with both your programmatic and financial plans. Before you submit a proposal you should also make certain that your board or other governing body knows about it and approves of both the proposed activities and the proposal itself. It is also a good idea to inform senior staff. Foundations are not reticent about checking with board members and staff other than those specifically mentioned in a proposal, and you do not want your allies to be taken by surprise.

For each source that you contemplate approaching, you should read the annual report, review the list of grantees, know the program priorities, and familiarize yourself with the decision-making process. For example, most foundations that you will approach have at least two steps in the decision-making process. There is a staff that screens proposals, conducts interviews, and makes field visits. There is a board of directors or trustees that makes the final decisions, usually based on staff recommendations. In some cases, only proposals that receive a favorable review from the staff ever get to the board of directors. The decision makers rarely get to see proposals rejected at the staff level. What this means is that you should develop a good working relationship with the staff early on. It is important to honor any explicit preferences for time and method of contact expressed by the foundation. If, in its literature, the foundation recommends a telephone call for the initial approach, then by all means call. On the other hand, if the grantmaker prefers that you make the initial contact by letter, it is unwise to telephone.

Grantseekers always seem to prefer a meeting or interview before submitting anything in writing. When the foundation is amenable, this can certainly work to your advantage. Usually, though, foundations and corporate grantmakers prefer to see what your program looks like on paper before they invest time preparing for, conducting, and evaluating a meeting. It is in this pre-meeting stage that the first of what may be many proposals is prepared.

The experts all generally agree that a proposal, at minimum, must include:

1. The organization contact person, his or her title, the organization's address and telephone number;
2. A brief summary of the proposed project;
3. The goals and specific objectives of the organization and/or project;
4. A statement of how your organization will go about conducting the proposed project;
5. Plans for evaluating both the project and the grant;
6. An annual budget for the organization and, if appropriate, for the project;
7. An indication of other sources of support that you are currently receiving, have applied for, or expect to apply for.

In addition, if you have received a "Letter of Determination" from the Internal Revenue Service stating that you are a tax-exempt organization, attach this to the proposal. If you are not tax exempt but have made arrangements with another organization that will act as your fiscal agent, attach a copy of the agreement and a copy of your sponsor's tax-exempt determination letter. Also include some background on the key personnel involved in your organization and their experience as well as a list of the members of your board of directors or other governing body with their professional and voluntary affiliations identified. If possible, you should also include the organization's most recent audited financial statements.

The components of a proposal are just that: pieces. In order to convey your message, they must be formed into a cohesive document. Whether you are writing a letter of introduction or an elaborate funding proposal, generally the same rules apply. Keep it short. Say only what you need to say in order to get your point across. Then stop. It is better to have the grantmaker respond to you with questions about specific details of your program. If it is too long, your proposal may never be read. Wherever possible, avoid jargon. What is commonplace language for you may mean something else entirely to someone not familiar with your community. Write clearly, and do not let your philosophical rhetoric get the best of you. Remember, there are grammatical rules that in the end work to your advantage. (If you need a reference, try *The Elements of Style* by William Strunk, Jr., and E. B. White, published by Macmillan, an 85-page paperback that is well worth the investment.)

After you have written a draft, show it to other people and ask for their comments. Sometimes it is helpful to review your proposal with someone with experience getting grants, and sometimes it is better to go to a disinterested person. While the experienced proposal writer may be able to spot something you have left out, be careful not to adopt any bad habits. The person who reads your proposal who has no experience with grants may be very helpful with the organization and style, but keep in mind that if you have inadvertently left out something critical, it may be forgotten entirely. The best approach is to review your proposal with both types of people. Then, after you have had a few days (or a few hours) to think about their comments, synthesize them into a second or even third draft.

Sometimes one proposal is sufficient to meet the requirements of several funding sources. In that case, by all means prepare a standardized proposal and leave your adaptations for the cover letter. If, on the other hand, you have to adapt the proposal to meet special application procedures, do so with caution. Be consistent. You may rearrange the format, even change some of the language, but do not say one thing in the first proposal and then say something quite different in another. It is not unusual for grantmakers to consult one another about projects and proposals. This is especially true at the community level, when many grantmakers may get together on a regular basis to share information. Inconsistencies can come back to haunt you. It is acceptable, however, to submit different types of proposals for the same project. Indeed, at times this strategy can work to your advantage. It is called "leveraging the funding," and it has two forms:

1. The matching grant. Let us assume that you need $12,000. You can propose to a grantmaker that he fund $6,000 and that as a condition of that grant, you will raise the other $6,000. This would be a one-to-one match, i.e., for every dollar you raise, the foundation will match it.

Some foundations want as much as a five-to-one match, i.e., you must raise five dollars in order to receive one dollar from the funding source.

In some circumstances you can negotiate with the grantmaker so that the matching requirement you need to supply is not all cash. Using donated services, supplies, or space—"in-kind contributions"—is a generally accepted practice, up to a certain point. It is best to calculate low, a twenty-five or thirty-five percent in-kind match is common. When using in-kind contributions, be careful to keep good records. You will have to show that the value you have assigned is consistent with the market value in your community.

The cash match can be raised from a variety of sources, usually without limitation. It can consist of individual contributions, membership dues, subscription sales, or other grants from government agencies, churches, or foundations. This leads to the second type of leveraging.

2. Splitting the budget. One proposal technique is to request only a portion of your budget and state that you have or are in the process of seeking co-funders. Grantmakers like to fund projects together when their interests are compatible. Each feels that his or her funder is getting a little more from the grant because the costs are being shared. If you are going to try this approach, do your homework and talk to the grantmakers before you submit a final proposal. If you are unprepared, you may find yourself having funded only two-thirds of your program. This might mean either cutting back on the project's scope or returning the grant money. Before you have a crisis, it is always a good idea to discuss with funders how they will respond, and by all means, do not proceed on a project that you have promised will be completed if you know in advance you will not be able to raise the rest of the needed funds without checking with those funders who have already made grants to the project.

This chapter is not intended as a thorough treatment of the grantmaking process. The only purpose is to provide an introduction. Check the bibliography and select one or two of the publications specifically devoted to proposals. Read through them, paying particular attention to some of the sample proposals that are often included. Another helpful source of information about proposal writing is often the grantmaker's own annual report or brochure. Many of them specify a proposal format, the types of information required, and the supplementary materials that you should attach. Keep in mind, too, that an initial proposal can be revised and resubmitted if necessary. Sometimes new ideas may come to mind when you are meeting with potential funding sources. After digesting these ideas, you can revise the proposal and perhaps make the project easier to fund the next time around.

A few general words of caution. Remember, the first impression you make to the grantmaker may be the most important. Type your proposal or proposal letter, preferably on your organization's letterhead. Read it through carefully, and do not send it out with typographical errors. A correction or two neatly written with a pen is always preferable to a misspelled word or a word left out.

If you have written one general proposal for your program and want to send it to several funding sources, write individual cover letters. No one likes getting form letters. Tailor each letter to reflect the grantmaker's program priorities. Show that you have done your homework and that you believe your project deserves careful consideration in light of its interests and concerns.

Finally, do not let your grantseeking frustrations dampen the enthusiasm with which you started. Raising money from foundations and corporations is difficult, and it consumes time and energy. Most grantmakers try to acknowledge receipt of all proposals promptly. Sometimes this notification takes weeks. Then a few more weeks (or months) may elapse before you hear whether they will even consider your application. If you have not heard anything about the status of your proposal after a reasonable length of time, a follow-up letter or telephone call is in order. Be understanding—your proposal may simply have been misplaced or lost. If this is the case, send a second copy and keep on working with whatever other fundraising projects are on your agenda. Eventually, you will hear whether or not your proposal has been accepted for funding.

5

Chapter Five
Corporate Support for Social Justice
By David Dodson*

Over the last decade there has been a lot said and written about the emergence of corporate giving as a major force in American philanthropy—and for good reason. Open almost any magazine or newspaper and you are likely to see stories about corporate generosity—scholarship grants made to the local college, funds for computers given to the neighborhood school. Visit a museum and more often than not a major exhibition has been funded in part or entirely with corporate funds.

Corporate dollars seem to be doing good works everywhere. In fact, since 1975 there has been an explosion in charitable giving by corporations. In less than fifteen years, total gifts from business have more than tripled, from $1.2 billion in 1975 to approximately $4.5 billion in 1986. Corporate philanthropy has become a full partner along with private and community foundations in the business of giving.

But what about corporate giving to progressive causes? How much has the social and economic justice agenda benefited from the flood of new business dollars? Unfortunately, no reliable statistics exist, but it is not hard to guess the answer. Community organizing, civil rights, and environmental action groups have fared less well at getting a share of the growing corporate pie compared to such established institutions as colleges and universities, museums and symphony orchestras.

According to the annual surveys of corporate contributions conducted by the Conference Board and the Council for Financial Aid to Education, over the last three years, for which information is available, education has consistently taken the largest slice of corporate philanthropy, followed by health and human services, civil and community activities, culture and art, and miscellaneous (see Table 1). While it is not really known what is meant by either contributions for "civic/community activities" and "other contributions," taken as a whole, these

---

*David Dodson is executive vice-president of MDC, Inc., a nonprofit public policy research firm in Chapel Hill, North Carolina, that is concerned with economic development, employment, and education issues facing the South. From 1983 to 1987 he was executive director of Cummins Engine Foundation in Columbus, Indiana.

figures really should not surprise us. Progressive causes have never figured prominently on the agenda of organized philanthropy in general.

Stories still circulate in corporations and foundations about grants to advocacy organizations and community groups that have come back to haunt their donors. There is the celebrated case of a corporate executive whose firm made a grant to the National Black United Fund to support its campaign against the United Way's monopoly of the federal employee payroll deduction program. No sooner had the grant been announced than a flood of protest calls began rolling in from the executive's peers, all of them ardent supporters of the United Way: to their eyes, the executive was breaking ranks, showing disloyalty. The corporation made good its commitment for the grant, but the emotional reaction of his peers made the executive think hard before making another grant to an unpopular cause. Trivial as this example may seem today, it underscores a basic truth: corporations and foundations still find it hard, and their leaders sometimes find it personally painful, to buck the status quo and address unpopular causes. The pressure to play it safe is strong.

The truth remains, however, that progressive organizations can improve their track record with corporate donors by learning how corporate donors think and what they value, recognizing where the interests of the grantseeking organization intersect with the corporation's interests, and by tailoring requests for support so that it is easier for a corporation to

Recipients of Corporate Contributions, 1983-85
(in millions of dollars)

	1983*		1984*		1985*	
Education	$ 498.8	39.0%	$ 561.7	38.9%	$ 650.0	38.3%
Health & Human Services	367.6	28.7	399.9	27.7	494.1	29.2
Civic/Community Activities	188.8	14.8	271.6	18.6	279.5	16.5
Arts and Culture	145.2	11.4	154.7	10.7	187.4	11.1
Other	78.0	6.1	56.4	3.9	83.5	4.9
TOTAL	$1,278.4	100.0%	$1,444.3	99.8%	$1,694.5	100.0%

*Data based on 471 companies responding to survey in 1983; 415 companies in 1984; and 436 companies in 1985.

SOURCES: American Association of Fund Raising Counsel, *Giving USA*, 1986; The Conference Board, Council for Financial Aid to Education, *Annual Survey of Corporate Contributions*, 1985.

respond favorably. This chapter will help you see how to apply these principles to your organization.

How Did We Get Where We Are Today?: A Short History of Corporate Giving

The best way to understand how corporate donors think and work is to understand how corporate philanthropy has developed and how it is changing. Organized corporate giving is a recent development; most corporate foundations and giving programs are less than twenty-five years old. Until the early 1970s, when the leadership of a handful of prominent corporate executives began to stress its importance as a means of responding to social ills, corporate giving was often viewed as indefensible. The business of business was making money, not giving it away. Few corporate-giving programs had trained staff or even well-defined program goals. Much of the giving corporations did was random, and little of it ever trickled down to civil rights, organizing, or other social and economic justice causes.

Major changes followed the urban riots of the 1960s. Led by the insurance industry and other businesses with substantial investments in troubled center cities, corporations began to define their public missions differently. Business leaders began to talk of their companies' "social responsibility." Corporations became junior partners with government in trying to address the problems of the cities—poverty, poor schools, inadequate housing—and corporate philanthropy emerged as a tool in the battle for improving society.

At the heart of the social-responsibility movement was the principle of "enlightened self-interest." Corporations could now defend the giving away of profits because they were buying something of value, namely, a more stable and secure environment in which to operate. Suddenly, philanthropy became a wise and prudent business strategy.

Much of the money that was given to fight social problems in the 1970s went to mainline organizations (notably community chests) that funded services rather than advocacy for change. Still, overall corporate giving had started to grow, and a few companies —Cummins Engine, Levi Strauss, Aetna—began small but aggressive programs of support for legal services, civil rights organizing, community-based economic development organizations, voter registration, and other progressive causes.

Throughout the 1970s a number of factors kept corporate support for progressive causes fragile at best. First, corporations often found themselves the targets of the consumer, environmentalist, civil rights, or other public interest advocacy groups that formed the core of the progressive movement. Many advocacy groups would have found it unthinkable to seek funding from private business, just as many corporations would have found it equally out of the question to grant them support. Second, business, being conservative by nature, generally chose to define "corporate social responsibility" conservatively as well. Gifts to museums, colleges, or hospitals carried little risk and were often a safer and easier means to exhibit concern for the community than support for an untested or upstart community group. Finally, and perhaps most important, business knew that ultimately it had to defend its philanthropy to its owners—the stockholders.

Since corporate giving was itself a new thing, it was easier to justify support for the Boy Scouts than to defend support for voting rights litigation. When business did embrace the progressive agenda, it was either because of extraordinarily committed and visionary leadership—as at Cummins, Levi Strauss, and Aetna—or, in the case of certain consumer-oriented businesses, out of fear of losing its Black, Hispanic, or women customers.

The election of Ronald Reagan in 1980 changed the face of corporate philanthropy just as it changed the face of American politics. Having sounded the retreat of government from social and welfare concerns, President Reagan called immediately for business to assume a leading role in meeting community needs. Business responded by major increases in charitable giving, but the public soon realized that $4 billion in annual corporate giving could hardly soothe the pain of $50 billion in reduced government funding for social programs. So just as the supply of corporate dollars began to expand, the competition for those dollars grew more intense. In some communities, the withdrawal of government support produced new coalitions of business and community groups and use of creative new funding mechanisms, such as the Local Initiatives Support Corporation, that blended private capital, philanthropic dollars, and public funds to support community-based development. But for progressive groups, who had never been on the inside track for corporate support, the net result was a standstill.

By the mid-1980s, things were worse. A recession and growing foreign competition began to erode business profits, and many of the most progressive corporate grantmakers were forced to cut back their giving, often dramatically. Some, like Cummins Engine, tightened their scope geographically, limiting grants to areas in which the company had employees or did significant business. Other corporations restricted their philanthropy by focusing on specific issues—education, economic development, hunger. In some cases, such as the absorption of Gulf Oil into Chevron, corporate mergers eliminated generous donors entirely.

Above all, in nearly every corporate-giving program the corporate pressure to reduce operating costs spilled over into attitudes toward grantees. It was no longer enough that a program was well intentioned; it had to produce results and operate efficiently. The result of these changes? Nonprofit organizations saw and felt that they were just as vulnerable as corporations to the ups and downs of the business cycle: when corporate profits sank, philanthropy frequently vanished. Suddenly events as foreign and mysterious as the devaluation of the Mexican peso took on new meaning to nonprofits, especially when the result was depressed exports—and therefore lower profits—for a loyal corporate donor. Unlucky organizations in communities without a corporate benefactor or with a cause that didn't fit on the narrowed corporate agenda saw the flow of dollars tighten and, often, disappear.

The Implications of This History
for Support of Progressive Causes

So, what do these trends mean for you and your organization? What are your chances for winning and keeping corporate support for your program? If the odds of success are getting worse with time, is it even worth trying to tap the corporate coffer?

Let's first face the hard truth: corporate grantseekers are competing in a very tough market today, with more institutions and groups chasing fewer dollars. Young and inexperienced community-based and progressive organizations face a particularly hard struggle for the corporate dollar, in part because the historical focus of corporate giving is on more traditional activities and in part because limited resources now make it hard for corporations to begin relationships with new grantees. Recent trends make location and program focus more important factors than ever in securing corporate support, and not all organizations are equally well situated to meet these new, stricter standards. Add to these developments an uncertain economy—a factor that always makes corporations reluctant to expand their charitable giving—and the picture is far from bright.

Yet, it is important to recognize a number of promising trends that offset, at least in part, the depressing picture just painted. Despite economic uncertainty and demands that exceed their resources, there is still a strong corps of corporations firmly committed to advancing social justice concerns through their philanthropy. The growth in corporate listings in *The Grantseekers Guide* underscores this point. The first edition

53

(1981) listed fifteen corporate foundations and giving programs; the current edition lists twenty-six. This growth is an encouraging sign.

Furthermore, there is mounting evidence of new coalitions between corporations and organizations whose agendas include social justice concerns. These relationships may be the seeds of new and expanded business support for community-based and advocacy organizations in several areas of common concern. For instance, major corporations, child and welfare advocates, and civil rights groups have recently begun to unite around the problems facing poor and minority children. Business has realized that today's youth will be the foundation of tomorrow's competitive workforce, and that each child who is deprived of a sound start in life represents a lost future resource. The labor force of the future will be proportionately more Black and Hispanic than it is today. Business now understands that it must begin to invest in improving the quality of life for minority youth as much for its own future as for that of the children themselves. The result: the opportunity for an unprecedented partnership between corporations and youth and minority advocacy groups.

There are bright signs, too, in the area of community economic development. Programs such as the Local Initiatives Support Corporation (LISC) and the Enterprise Foundation have given a new generation of corporate executives their first exposure to community groups as partners in addressing urban decay and neighborhood revitalization. This contact has given community organizations new credibility with corporations and may make it easier for other community groups to approach the business community in the future.

Finally, in certain sectors, notably the financial services community, business has discovered that support for the activities of community-based organizations can be an ideal means for discharging obligations placed on them by government regulation. It is common now for banks to work with community development corporations to meet the reinvestment requirements of the Community Reinvestment Act (CRA), and while much of the visible CRA activity has occurred in urban areas, the growing trend toward statewide banking has brought CRA investment capital within the reach of rural community groups who previously would not have benefited from corporate support.

So the opportunities are out there, despite many discouraging trends. Yet the would-be corporate grantseeker needs to remember that the rules of the game have changed. The scarcity of dollars and an emerging sophistication about philanthropy within business mean that nonprofit organizations need to think carefully about their needs and relate them convincingly to the interests of the corporation.

The Basic Rules About Raising Money from Corporations

I suggest six rules to remember as you go through the grantseeking process.

1. Never forget that corporations justify their philanthropy out of enlightened self-interest—"ESI".

This is what motivates their giving. Businesses may vary in the way they define and conceive the term, but in the end, all share the belief that philanthropy makes sense only if it produces some tangible benefit in the corporation's eye. At Cummins Engine, our definition of "ESI" embraced a wide universe. The company believed that its existence depended on a free and open society with no obstacles to opportunity and justice; this led us to support legal services and voter education efforts that most other corporations would have rejected. But our motivation for funding advocacy and justice programs always tied back to our definition of ESI. It was good for society, and therefore good for Cummins, to make sure the society was free of barriers based on race and sex.

Many businesses take a more restricted view of ESI. Some choose to relate it to the quality of life in the communities where they operate. Others see it in their interest to address issues related to the purpose of their business—Pillsbury and hunger issues or B. Dalton books and the Gannett newspaper chain and illiteracy. Consumer products companies— food, beverage, retailing—are particularly concerned about their public image and have strong business incentives to support projects that will appeal to the groups that make up their market. Thus, Philip Morris and Anheuser Busch contribute heavily to Black and Hispanic organizations. Because concepts of self-interest can vary dramatically, it's wise to begin your fundraising by getting inside the mind of the corporation to understand how it defines "ESI." Once you do this, the task becomes "how can we show that it's in the corporation's interest to give our program support?"

How do you begin? If the corporation has a formal giving program or a corporate foundation, your task is relatively easy. Most formal giving programs have operating statements and program guidelines that indicate both why they give and what their priorities are. Increasingly, corporate foundations and giving programs publish their own annual reports that list both their giving priorities and their recent grants. If your target corporation has no organized giving program, call the public relations or community affairs office and ask for corporate annual reports or statements by corporate executives on community involvement or corporate responsibility. These are often useful tools in figuring out the public issues a corporation thinks are important. Look closely, too, at the business the corporation is in. Does your organization work on an issue that is important to the corporation's customer base? Will a grant to you enable the corporation to show the people who buy its products that it is a good and responsible corporate citizen?

Most corporations prefer to contribute to programs in the communities where they do business, so you should begin your fundraising research by exploring the interests of companies that have headquarters or major operations in your area. Be particularly alert to subsidiaries of major corporations that operate under different names from their parent company—a common occurrence given the recent wave of corporate mergers. Most likely the subsidiary will have the same philosophy of philanthropy as its better-known parent (this is the case at Cummins Engine and Dayton Hudson, for instance). Corporate annual reports will often list the communities where a business and its subsidiary companies operate, so it's worth doing research on the best-known corporate givers to determine all the locations where they have a presence. You may have an active corporate donor in your community and not even know it. Newspaper and retailing chains such as Gannett, Federated Stores, Dayton Hudson, and *The New York Times* are examples of active corporate givers with a broad national reach.

When you finally get to the point of making a formal request, relate your organization's program to the corporation's interests and philosophy. Show how you are responding to an issue or problem that the corporation believes is important, how an investment in you will advance their philanthropic goals.

Note: While increasing numbers of corporate giving programs have full- or part-time staff, often the grants function is handled by a public affairs or community affairs department. Since employees in these areas perform a variety of jobs in the company, they may not have a deep understanding of the issue or problem your organization is facing. Don't assume your audience understands the fine point of an issue as well as you do. Take time in your proposal or letter of inquiry to explain why your project matters and why it should be important to the corporation.

2. Keep your proposal focused on results. Be clear about what you will accomplish and how you will measure your success.

Businesses are increasingly results-oriented. They want to know what they are buying with their dollars, what the return will be on their investment. This attitude spills over into the way business makes philanthropic decisions. You'll do well to remember that the people who will review and rate your request inside the corporation, often corporate executives or division managers, will be looking for measurable outcomes. Think hard about the tangible results your program will deliver and be clear about them in your request.

Two good questions to ask yourself are: "What will be different as a result of this project?" and "What will be the consequences if we don't get the corporation's support?" If you can answer these honestly and convincingly for yourselves, you'll have helped your chances within the corporation.

3. Look for ways to build relationships with the corporation that can strengthen your case for funding.

Many corporations give special consideration to projects and organizations in which their employees are involved either as volunteers or as board members. Some, such as Levi Strauss and Fel-Pro/Mecklenburger, have special giving programs that make employee involvement a requirement for receiving a grant. Others have matching gift programs that enable employees to augment their personal gifts to nonprofit organizations. As part of your strategy for attracting corporate support, consider recruiting volunteers from businesses that are active in your community. Not only will corporate volunteers bring skills to your organization and be a formal link between you and the corporation, they can also be an invaluable source of inside information on the best way to approach their employer for financial support—information that will not be available to you in any of the corporation's formal statements about community involvement or philanthropy. And if you are successful in attracting corporate volunteers, be sure to ask if their company has a matching gift or special grants program for which you might be eligible.

4. Be creative about your request. Look at the full range of your needs and don't ask just for dollars.

Unlike other sources of charitable support, businesses have resources other than cash. We have talked about employee volunteers; corporations also can lend services such as printing; consulting in management, finance, and planning; new and used equipment; facilities for meetings and retreats. Certified public accounting firms have been known to perform financial audits for community organizations at reduced cost as a charitable gesture. Larger businesses frequently have the capacity to place employees "on loan" to community organizations for extended periods of time, sometimes as long as a year. As the pressure on the dollar resources of corporations intensifies, community organizations may find it easier to get nonmonetary, in-kind support for projects. In fact, requesting in-kind donations of services and equipment is often a good means of beginning a relationship with a corporation that may be reluctant to make a dollar contribution to an unfamiliar organization.

5. Break projects into segments that may make it more attractive to a corporate donor if necessary.

As you examine a corporation's funding interests and priorities, you may also find it useful and necessary to identify sections or segments of your project that the corporation can find it easiest to support. Most corporations like to see tangible results for their money. Visible projects have better public relations value. A business may refuse you outright if you ask for a grant for research, but if you ask for a grant to hold a community meeting on the same topic—an event that will get the business public recognition as a good citizen—you may have a winning proposal. Similarly, if a business finds aspects of your organization's program too experimental or controversial to support but is in sympathy with your overall goals, give them the option of underwriting something they are comfortable with—perhaps the cost of an annual report or volunteer recognition dinner. Make it easy for the corporation to say yes.

6. Be persistent. Keep trying until you succeed.

It isn't easy to break into world of corporate support. As we've seen, there's more demand than there is money; competition is tough. Many companies are new to the business of giving away money—especially for unfamiliar and potentially controversial causes—and may shun nontraditional groups. You're just as likely to be disappointed in your first attempt to get corporate funding as you are to strike pay dirt. But don't give up. Businesses sell for a living, and business people appreciate someone who believes enough in what they are doing to keep selling even when the first answer is no. If you're turned down for dollars, ask for a noncash contribution—equipment or printing. If you fail there, recruit a corporate employee to your board. When your persistence pays off, you will find that the range of resources that a willing corporation can make available to you will have been worth the hard work.

6

Chapter Six
An Overview of Church Resources for
Social and Economic Justice
By Douglas M. Lawson*

Throughout history, organized religions have actively supported social justice and self-development. While the Catholic bishops' pastoral letters of recent years on nuclear war and the United States' economic policy have made this participation perhaps more evident to the general public, seldom do people realize that organized religious entities of all denominations play an unparalleled role in supporting nonprofit organizations, including projects seeking to correct social injustices throughout the world. Indeed, such support is viewed by many in religious communities as an integral part of fulfilling biblical and theological missions.

This chapter will help prospective grantees understand the historic and contemporary role of organized religious institutions as resource providers for social justice. Initially, the magnitude of these resources is set forth in a few statistics on church giving. The chapter then discusses the biblical motivation for religious support, the structure of religious organizations, and the kinds of activities they support. Also included are some of the unusual benefits of receiving religious support and a few of the ways grantseekers may improve their chances of gaining support from church-related programs. It concludes with a partial list of religious resources.

Little is really known about the full extent of church giving. While some religious funding sources go out of their way to publicize their grantmaking programs, others keep very much to themselves, citing inappropriate mechanisms to determine the precise level of financial resources available, fear of unwanted government reporting requirements, fear of government intrusion or public reprisal, and a desire to use the networks within their own religious communities for determining recipients. Grantseekers might prefer this situation to be different, but religious grantmakers themselves have to become convinced that additional information will leverage additional resources.

---

*Douglas M. Lawson is the deputy director, foundations and grants at the Campaign for Human Development, the grantmaking action/education program of the United States Catholic Conference, Washington, D.C.

Thus, a strong word of caution is in order. There currently exist no national directories of church funding sources that completely and accurately tell the story. The list of denominations and grantmaking programs that appears in Appendix III should be used with the utmost discretion. Read this chapter through from start to finish and do your research carefully. **Do not use this information as the basis for mass mailing proposals.** Some church grantmakers work hard to develop and maintain contacts and cooperative programs with foundations and corporations. Nobody benefits, least of all grantees, if, as a result of mass-mailed proposals, cooperation that has been increasing in recent years ceases.

Quantifying Church-Related Grantmaking

For all the reasons given above, it is difficult to estimate church giving for social justice activities. We must rely instead on a few other general figures to provide a sense of the magnitude of church resources. For example, in 1983, Constant H. Jacquet, who compiles financial data on forty of the United States' religious bodies in *The Yearbook of American and Canadian Churches*, reported that together these organizations had income of slightly more than $11.6 billion.[1] Using this data, the American Association of Fundraising Counsel, Inc., projected that in 1983 the American people gave approximately $31.03 billion to religious groups.[2] A rule of thumb used by some knowledgeable people about the financial workings of the religious sector suggests that approximately twenty percent of these receipts is allocated annually to charitable, research, medical, educational, relief, advocacy, and development efforts in the United States and abroad. Indeed, this $6.0 billion is probably on the conservative side.

In 1984 the Council on Foundations conducted a survey of 2,700 religious groups in an effort to discover the extent of religious funding (exclusive of funding solely to promote specific religious purposes). Based on the responses of 485 organizations and programs and other collected data, Jean A. McDonald estimated that giving by religious organizations in 1983 was about $7.5 billion and even as high as $8.5 billion if the giving of individual congregations had been included.[3] This means,

---

[1] Constant H. Jacquet, Jr., ed., *Yearbook of American and Canadian Churches, 1984* (Nashville: Abingdon Press, 1984).

[2] American Association of Fundraising Counsel, Inc., *Giving USA 1984 Annual Report*. (New York, 1984).

[3] Jean A. McDonald, "Survey Finds Religious Groups Strongly Favor More Collaboration," *Foundation News*, 25 (1984).

as shown in Figure 1, that church-related giving in 1983 exceeded the total of all foundation and corporate contributions combined.

Figure 1. Religious Giving Compared to Foundation and Corporate Giving, 1983

All Religious organizations	$7.5 billion
Corporations	$3.1 billion
Foundations	$3.5 billion

SOURCE: Council on Foundations, 1984

This should not be taken to mean that $7.5 billion was allocated for social justice activities. This figure includes not only budgets for social justice grantmaking, but also budgets for religious service agencies supporting their own institutions such as schools, hospitals, homes for seniors, and so forth. Furthermore, while about two-thirds of these resources supported domestic programs, the remainder went for international activities.

The Biblical and Theological Traditions of Giving

While it may not be possible to know how many dollars are used by religious institutions to support nonprofit programs and social justice activities, the rationale for religious charity is clearly articulated in biblical and theological traditions. Concern for the welfare of the people was a part of Middle Eastern law and thinking before the Old Testament, evidenced for example in the Code of Hammurabi, but the writings of the Old and New Testaments strengthened the concepts about justice and mercy toward the poor and oppressed and together contain the ethical foundations of contemporary religious charity.

The Old Testament contains scriptures common and sacred to Jews, Catholics, and Protestants, and rabbis, priests, and ministers have commented with eloquence on the social responsibility and charity implied and explicitly mandated. Consider, for example, the following passage: "I command thee, saying thou shall open thine hand wide unto thy brother, to thy poor, and to thy needy, in thy land" (Deut. 15:11); Cain's question, "Am I my brother's keeper?" (Gen. 4:9); or the instruction to Joshua to designate certain cities as places of safe haven for persons seeking refuge from political and social injustice (Josh. 20:1-9). The

Israelites were taught that what remained in the fields after harvest and the gathering of olives and grapes should not be collected; it was for the alien, the orphan, and the widow. Even more, the fields were not to be harvested to the very edge so that food would remain to be eaten by the poor and the refugees. (Lev. 19:9).

The biblical concept of the jubilee year was radical. Every seven years all refugees, aliens, and slaves had to be freed and land redistributed or returned to its original owners if it had once been taken from them (Lev. 25:9,10,31). The Old Testament prophets were even stronger defenders of the poor and critics of the injustices of the powerful. They did not stop at calling for charity; they pointed to social injustice as the root cause of poverty (Amos 5:7; Jer. 5:28). For them poverty resulted not from fate; it was caused by injustices condemned by God (Isa. 10:1–2).

In the following statement from the New Testament, Jesus is talking to a young man of inherited wealth. "If thou wilt be perfect, go and sell that thou hast, and give to the poor, and thou shalt have treasure in heaven: and come and follow me." The sense of this passage conveys a broad meaning of poor; it can be translated weak, needy, refugee, deprived, helpless, i.e., all kinds of poor. Its challenge is to the ultimate spirit of charity: selling that which has been acquired and giving to the poor. Other parts of the New Testament make even more clear that worldly goods are not a sign of God's favor and that there is incompatibility between the accumulation of things and love of neighbor (Matt. 19:22–24; I John 3:17). The book of James teaches that the appropriation of wealth implies that injustice has been done somewhere. James chides his readers for showing favoritism toward the rich, reminding them that God prefers the poor (James 2:2–7).

In the Judaic tradition, the principles of charity are set forth in the traditions of *tzedakah,* which literally means "righteousness," or in a more contemporary interpretation has come to mean "charity" or "justice" interchangeably. The foremost authority on *tzedakah* was Moses Maimonides, a medieval scholar who in *The Book of Seeds* ("Agriculture") of the Mishnah Torah, the code of Jewish laws based on the Talmud and other authoritative legal writings, summarizes rules relating to the conduct of charity in the context of economic activity. Maimonides identified eight degrees of *tzedakah,* each one more important or significant than the next. The essence is stated in the first three: (1) the encouragement of self-sufficiency and self-determination, helping those who are without help themselves; (2) the preservation of dignity, giving anonymously so that those who are without know not from where the charity comes and those that give know not who is receiving; and (3) the sense of spirit, giving in a friendly manner that which is needed without having to be asked. The bottom line is that the manner of giving in the name of charity and justice is equally as important as what is given.

Understanding the Hierarchies of Religious Institutions

Religious grantmaking programs made up of contributions from hundreds of millions of congregants are the contemporary means—vehicles of convenience—for carrying out the biblical and theological imperatives of charity and justice. They are administrative units of the churches that created them. Therefore, it is important for grantseekers to have a working knowledge of the church structures of which these agencies are a part. Failure to understand how churches are organized to carry out their work may result in limited access to church funds.

Before stating specifics, however, a few parameters need to be established. There are too many established religious traditions in our society to describe each one in a chapter this length. Therefore, the following discussion of church structure focuses on those that have known national grantmaking capabilities and a history of supporting progressive social change, specifically the Roman Catholic Church and seven Protestant churches: American Baptist Churches in the U.S.A., Christian Church (Disciples of Christ), the Episcopal Church, Evangelical Lutheran Church in America, Presbyterian Church U.S.A., United Church of Christ, and the United Methodist Church. Also included are two branches of the Religious Society of Friends (Quakers): the Friends United Meeting and the Friends General Conference.

Noticeably absent are descriptions of the Jewish and Unitarian structures. Although Jewish philanthropy has long been identified with the causes of social justice, this is primarily a function of philanthropy by individuals and family-affiliated foundations. Jewish federations, sometimes perceived as grantmaking organizations, raise money from the Jewish community that is almost always allocated to their local member agencies. Unlike the Catholic and Protestant denominations, historically there has been no national administrative structure for channeling Jewish support into social justice activities. However, since 1984, the Jewish Fund for Justice, an independent public charity, has been a vehicle for American Jews to both articulate and financially support the Jewish commitment to justice for all citizens. The Fund is a national grantmaking organization that channels support from the American Jewish community into efforts to combat the root causes of poverty in the United States. Likewise, while there are at least two grantmaking organizations associated with the Unitarian tradition of supporting social justice in the United States—The Veatch Program, on Long Island, New York, and the Social Concerns Panel Fund of the First Unitarian Society in Minneapolis, Minnesota—both are congregationally based. Neither is linked directly into the religious administrative hierarchy.

A common characteristic of all national church bodies is that they are structured along geographical lines. The three primary geographical levels of structure are local churches or congregations, middle judicatories, and national or headquarters' offices.

Local churches are found in every community in the United States and are composed of individual members who give their time, energy, and money to support the work of the local church and in some cases the work of the larger structures of their religious communions. The local membership is the true basis on which the superstructure of religious bodies stand. In a limited number of cases, local churches have sufficient income and social consciousness to establish and operate their own grantmaking programs. The Riverside Church and the Parish of Trinity Church (both located in New York City) are perhaps best known among local congregations that have grants programs.

A middle judicatory is simply the descriptive reference for regional subunits of Protestant and Roman Catholic churches. Middle judicatories do not follow a uniform pattern from denomination to denomination. Each religious body chooses its own name for its middle judicatories. Names most commonly used are diocese, synod, district, association, conference, regional office, and convention. Boundaries also differ greatly. One religious body may have four or five middle judicatories in a state while another may have one middle judicatory for the whole of that state and yet another may include that same state plus two or three other states in one middle judicatory. Roles played by middle judicatories may also differ.

Some judicatories operate programs while others do not; some manage grants programs while others do not. Most provide a wide range of services to the member churches within their jurisdiction, including training, program coordination, technical assistance, and interpretation of national church policy. In those instances where a middle judicatory manages a grants program which is a subunit of a national program, as some do, the middle judicatory may have independent discretion and its own board to decide which grants will be made. Its guidelines will probably be essentially the same as the national program except that it will be limited to funding projects within its geographical jurisdiction. It may also be possible for qualified projects to receive a grant from both the national grantmaking program and from the regional component. Understanding how judicatories in your area operate and getting to know their staff may result in new avenues to resources—both financial and in-kind.

The national church or the headquarters is where general administrative, policy-making, program, personnel, and financial affairs for the church are coordinated. While many people mistakenly assume that New York is the location of most national church offices, national religious bodies are headquartered in various cities. If a denomination operates a funding program for social and economic justice projects, the office that administers that program will be based in the national headquarters.

Many religious bodies are of the persuasion that social action is not a proper activity for them to support. This view may be held because the group is basically conservative politically and theologically. Nevertheless, the astute grantseeker will be on the lookout for exceptions to this rule. Even within denominations where no formal channel exists for support of social action projects, there may be individual staff or local pastors personally committed to social justice who can prove to be strong allies.

In those religious bodies that do have a stated commitment to work for social and economic justice, prospects for help may be good. First, that commitment is likely to be reflected at all levels of the church structure. They are more likely to have established and staffed grant-making programs that operate at both the national and the regional levels. Written guidelines for these grantmaking programs may be available upon request. Second, even where grantmaking programs do not exist, the staff of these religious bodies are likely to be receptive to requests for technical assistance and in-kind contributions to social and economic justice activities.

The following religious bodies are among those most likely to have organized channels for support of projects that work for social and economic justice in the society.

American Baptist Churches in the U.S.A.
Valley Forge, Pennsylvania 19481
(215) 768-2000
The American Baptist Churches (ABC) have staffed administrative and program units in a range of social concerns paralleling the issues and social policy questions being addressed by community-based projects. These ABC programs are not grantmaking programs, but local projects may find the ABC national staff to be knowledgeable and resourceful. American Baptist middle judicatories are known as either associations or conventions. There are approximately thirty-seven American Baptist judicatories; some cover only a major city, others are statewide or include several states.

The Christian Church (Disciples of Christ)
222 South Downey Street
Post Office Box 1986
Indianapolis, Indiana 46206
(317) 353-1491
The national office of The Christian Church (Disciples of Christ) houses several program units with social and economic justice as their primary mandate. These include the Division of Homeland Ministries and the Reconciliation Program of the Christian Church. The Christian church has approximately thiry-two middle judicatories, which are known as regional offices.

The Episcopal Church
815 Second Avenue
New York, New York 10017
(212) 867-8400
The Episcopal Church is divided into dioceses of which there are one hundred in the United States. The national headquarters houses the office of the presiding bishop and several program units, including the National Mission in Church and Society and the World Mission in Church and Society.

Evangelical Lutheran Church in America
8765 West Higgins Road
Chicago, Illinois 60631
(312) 380-2700
The Evangelical Lutheran Church in America (ELCA) is the successor church following the merger of the American Lutheran Church and the Lutheran Church in America in 1987. The major program units of the ELCA include the divisions for ministry, education, outreach, global missions, congregational life, and social ministry organizations. The middle judicatories of the ELCA are known as synods. There are sixty-five synods in the country.

Presbyterian Church (U.S.A.)
100 Witherspoon Street[4]
Louisville, Kentucky 40202
(502) 580-1900
The Presbyterian Church (U.S.A.) was created in 1983 when the Pres-

---

[4]The Presbyterian Church (U.S.A.) is combining its New York City and Atlanta offices in Louisville in summer 1988. At the time this book went to press, this was their expected address and telephone number.

byterian Church in the U.S., headquartered in Atlanta, merged with the United Presbyterian Church in the USA, based in New York City. Specific grantmaking programs include the Self-Development of People Fund and the Presbyterian Hunger Program.

The Religious Society of Friends (Quakers)

The Religious Society of Friends (Quakers) has four branches: the Friends General Conference, the Friends United Meeting, the Evangelical Friends Alliance, and the Conservative Friends. Two branches, historically linked with supporting progressive social change, are described below.

THE FRIENDS UNITED MEETING[5]
101 Quaker Hill Drive
Richmond, Indiana 47374
(317) 962-7573
The Friends United Meeting is an international body that represents about half the Friends in the world. The functional equivalent of a middle judicatory is called a yearly meeting, and there are approximately twenty-five yearly meetings in the United States. Yearly meetings are made up of monthly meetings, which in common usage would be called congregations. Many of the yearly meetings of the Friends United Meeting are affiliated with the Friends General Conference (See below).

FRIENDS GENERAL CONFERENCE
1529-B Race Street
Philadelphia, Pennsylvania 19102
(215) 241-7270
There are about 121 yearly meetings of the Friends General Conference, many of which are affiliated with the Friends United Meeting (See above).

The Roman Catholic Church

The United States Catholic Conference
1312 Massachusetts Avenue, N.W.
Washington, D.C. 20005
(202) 659-6600
The United States Catholic Conference (USCC) is a civil entity of the America Catholic bishops that provides an organization and structure for

---

[5]The Political and social action arms of the Religious Society of Friends are the Friends Committee on National Legislation (FCNL) and the American Friends Service Committee (AFSC) respectively. The FCNL is a lobbying organization in Washington, D.C. The AFSC is a service organization headquartered in Philadelphia with ten regional offices (whose boundaries differ from the yearly meetings). The AFSC has three divisions, all concerned with social justice: the International Division, the Peace Education Division, and the Community Relations Division.

service, coordination, and studies on educational and social concerns. The education-action unit of the USCC that makes grants is the Campaign for Human Development. Middle judicatories are called dioceses, and there are approximately 175 in the United States There are also about twenty-four archdioceses, many of which have offices of social justice, urban affairs, justice and peace, or other similar names with small funds available to support social and economic justice activities.

The United Church of Christ
105 Madison Avenue
New York, New York 10016
(212) 683-5656
Among the several program units of the United Church of Christ, the United Church Board for Homeland Ministries, the Office of Church in Society, and the Commission for Racial Justice are involved in social and economic justice ministries. United Church of Christ middle judicatories are known as conferences and total thirty-eight in number.

United Methodist Church
475 Riverside Drive
New York, New York 10115
(212) 870-3800
Several national boards and agencies of this church have responsibilities to address social and economic justice needs in society. Key boards working on justice concerns are the Board of Church and Society (Washington, D.C.), the Commission on Church and Race (Washington, D.C.), and the Board of Global Ministries (New York). There are approximately seventy-three middle judicatories of the United Methodist Church, which are called conferences. Each conference has a superintendent and a council of ministries concerned with social justice, among other issues.

Ecumenical Organizations
In addition to the structures described above, it is common practice for national church agencies (and occasionally regional agencies) to join together to create and support ecumenical agencies. These bodies enable national church agencies to cooperate on special problems, conduct research, address public policy issues, supply technical assistance to local churches and community-based projects, and in some instances provide financial support. Among the ecumenical agencies working on social and economic issues are:

The Ecumenical Minority Bail Bond Fund
475 Riverside Drive
New York, New York 10115
(212) 870-2298
A limited number of denominations have organized and jointly support this fund which is used to provide bail bond money for persons they judge to be victims of racial or social injustice. A thorough screening process is used to determine if their criteria for funds have been met before support is provided.

The Ecumenical Review Board
475 Riverside Drive, Room 572
New York, New York 10115
(212) 870-2307
The Ecumenical Review Board is a process through which several member Protestant denominations and the Campaign for Human Development share information about domestic hunger projects, evaluate them, and cooperatively determine if assistance should be provided.

The Interfaith Center on Corporate Responsibility
475 Riverside Drive
New York, New York 10115
(212) 870-2936
The Interfaith Center on Corporate Responsibility (ICCR) is an organization through which several Protestant and Catholic bodies cooperate to insure that investment resources of religious agencies maximize corporate responsibility. Its members conduct research and education programs in areas such as transnational corporations, equal employment opportunity, nuclear weapons production, plant closings, and environmental hazards. From time to time ICCR focuses on other selected economic justice issues.

The Interreligious Foundation for Community Organization
420 West 145 Street
New York, New York 10031
(212) 926-5757
The Interreligious Foundation for Community Organization (IFCO) is committed to providing technical assistance and fundraising counsel for community-based and social justice action organizations. Occasionally, IFCO conducts educational campaigns to inform chosen publics on social or economic justice needs and issues.

The National Farm Workers Ministry
Post Office Box 302
Delano, California 93216
(805) 725-7445
The National Farm Workers Ministry brings together people and resources to support efforts seeking improved working conditions among farm workers and farm worker organizing activities. Its primary efforts are through support of workers on subsistence stipends.

An Overview of Religious Giving
With a sense of the structures of organized religious organizations and ecumenical bodies, we can now look at ways in which church-based agencies support social justice. Of immediate interest, of course, are cash grants. The Council on Foundations, based on responses to its survey and other information it collected, reported that there are at least 231 church-related grantmaking programs operating in many ways like foundations and corporations, i.e., they receive proposals and make grants and/or loans. In the following table, this data is broken down by religious affiliation. Their grantmaking during 1983 totaled $1.03 billion.

Figure 2. Grantmaking Religious Organizations by Religious Tradition, 1983

Religious Tradition	Organizations	Grantmaking Dollars
Baptist	14	$ 26,202,000
Catholic	62	117,232,667
Episcopal	36	12,523,263
Jewish	24	554,514,000
Lutheran	8	16,467,253
Methodist	7	124,460,000
Presbyterian	45	18,677,063
Other	22	7,736,000
Interreligious	3	405,600
Nondenominational religious	10	153,500,000
TOTAL	**231**	**$1,031,717,846**

SOURCE: Council on Foundations, 1984

The survey tabulations also show that most religious grantmakers have committees to review proposals, and many have boardlike entities that make the final decisions. Almost ninety percent of religious grantmakers do some sort of postgrant evaluation to measure how effectively their funds have been spent. Grant decisions may take from as little as one week to as long as one year from the time a proposal is submitted, but most are acted upon within three months. Grant sizes run the entire range from $10 to $17 million, with small grants typically in the range of $500 to $10,000 and large grants ranging from $10,000 to $50,000. The average number of grants made by religious organizations included in the council's data ranged from six to ten, with the average number of loans from one to three. The two most common types of grants were seed money and project funding. The most exciting part of all, however, comes to light in the ten most frequently mentioned domestic funding interests of church-related grantmaking programs. As shown in Figure 3, education and justice activities ranked fourth and fifth respectively.

What does not show up in this table, however, is that when asked whether their funding patterns had changed in recent years, 150 religious organizations replied they had—with most of these moving toward in-

Figure 3. Most Frequently Mentioned Domestic Activities, All Religious Groups

(Top Ten)

Activity	Percent of Respondents
1. Food, nutrition	55.7
2. Refugee aid, resettlement	48.7
3. Day care, camps, recreation for youth	47.4
4. Issue education, advocacy	47.0
5. Justice, human rights, for particular groups	46.8
6. Emergency assistance, disaster relief	46.2
7. Clothing	43.3
8. Temporary shelter	41.2
9. Schools (preschool through high school)	40.8
10. Adult education, tutoring	40.0

SOURCE: Council on Foundations, 1984

cluding more self-help, economic justice, and social-change activities and more support for new, grassroots, and neighborhood groups without proven track records.

While there maybe no substitute for the exhilaration of receiving a grant, there are other benefits that working with churches can bestow. Church agencies are more likely than other funding sources to share in-kind resources such as space for meetings, temporary office space, assistance with bookkeeping and accounting, staff training, printing, and the use of audio and visual equipment. Remember that the limit on ways to be helped is proscribed only by the creativity of the parties involved. Another unusual benefit of religious funding is the credibility it can provide. This may be especially crucial in the start-up stages of a community-based organization caught in the usual catch-22 of needing to show it can successfully raise money in order to raise money. This is the time when who funds a project in its initial stages may determine who else will later provide support. Church support can be an early seal of approval in the eyes of both the funding and service communities.

Approaching Religious Institutions for Support

The dos and don'ts of approaching religious grantmakers are not very different from the rules for approaching foundations and corporations. Doing the basic research required to know how a funding source operates is essential. If you know they are available, write for guidelines and descriptive materials. Find out what they are interested in, their geographic limitations, and the things they will not fund. Determine the types of projects they have supported in the past, and if it is appropriate and necessary (and the staff seems amenable), ask for an appointment to increase your understanding of how the funding source works. Remember, however, that most religious funding sources do not have the staff resources and printed materials of foundations and corporations. Furthermore, many church agencies consider their funding programs part of their church mission to be interpreted to the membership of the church but not in reports for a more general public.

Admittedly, this makes the research more difficult. Start by talking to people active in your own organization who may also be active in their own churches. Religious organizations at the congregational level tend to be a natural network for support of social and economic justice groups. Indeed, while some religious grantmakers have no requirements that your work or project involve members of their faith, others—especially those that do not have published guidelines—make it a requirement.

While there are many reasons to seek church funding, it is important to be aware that churches, unlike most foundations, have a constituency and that frequently a certain quid pro quo is helpful in your approach to church funding sources. At the least, your program goals should be in line with the social teachings of the church to which you are applying. A brief review of Figure 3 can give you a general idea of the most frequently mentioned activities funded by church groups. The strongest case you can make for your program is the involvement of the particular religious organizations' constituency. In fact, some religious groups (particularly religious organizations of women) will entertain only proposals that have members involved or that have been submitted by their members.

The requirement that you have church members involved in your program is not as onerous as it may initially seem. Most Americans have at least a nominal affiliation with a church. No doubt you already have churchgoers among your staff, board, and constituency. At any rate, seeking relationships with churches can help to broaden your constituency. Try to decide why church-related organizations would be interested in working with your group. It may be that they are interested in the same issues, or you may be helping to educate their constituents about social justice. You might have volunteers that could work to strengthen their activities, or you might be providing services to their members.

National church funding sources frequently have a review process that involves people at the local or midjudicatory level. For example, the Campaign for Human Development normally has a "diocesan director" who, in conjunction with a local committee, reviews and makes funding recommendations to the national office on the proposals submitted from within the geographic boundaries of the diocese. Establishing a relationship at this level before you submit a proposal to the national office can be helpful. You may receive technical assistance in developing your proposal, and probably will have a better recommendation than if your proposal came in "cold" to the judicatory.

REFERENCES

American Association of Fundraising Counsel, Inc. *Giving USA 1984 Annual Report*. New York: 1984.

Council on Foundations. *The Philanthropy of Organized Religion: A Nationwide Survey by the Council of Foundations*. Washington, D.C.: 1985.

Greater Minneapolis Council of Churches. *Church Funding for Social Justice*. Minneapolis: 1984.

Jacquet, Jr., Constant H., (ed.). *Yearbook of American and Canadian Churches, 1984*. Nashville: Abingdon Press, 1984.

Kelley, Dean M. *Why Conservative Churches are Growing*. New York: Harper & Row, 1972.

Maimonides, Moses. *The Book of Seeds*. Chapter 10.

McDonald, Jean A. "Survey Finds Religious Groups Strongly Favor More Collaboration." *Foundation News*. 25 (1984).

Mead, Frank S. (ed.). *Handbook of Denominations in the United States*. Seventh Edition. Nashville: Abingdon Press, 1980.

Netting, F. Ellen. "Secular and Religious Funding of Church-Related Agencies." *Social Sciences Review,* December, 1982.

Pryde, Paul and Louis Knowles. *Church Investment in Community Development: Past, Present and Future*. Washington, D.C.: American Enterprise Institute, 1983.

Robinson, Peter S., ed. *Foundation Guide for Religious Grant Seekers*. Missoula, Montana: Scholars Press, 1979.

Seltzer, Michael S. "Approaching Religious Institutions." *Securing Your Organization's Future: A Complete Guide to Fundraising Strategies*, New York: The Foundation Center, 1987.

National Catholic Conference of Bishops. "The Challenge of Peace: God's Promise and Our Response." *Origins, National Catholic Documentary Service* National Catholic News Service. 13 (1983).

National Catholic Conference of Bishops. *Economic Justice for All: Pastoral Letter on Catholic Social Teaching*. Washington, D.C.: National Catholic Conference, 1986.

Women's Technical Assistance Project. *Resource Guide: Church Funding Sources*. Washington, D.C.: Center for Community Change, 1984.

7

Chapter Seven
Fundraising from Individuals
By Kim Klein*

There are two broad sources of funds for America's nonprofit organizations: the public sector, which is all types of government funding, and the private sector, which is made up of foundations, corporations, and individuals. Surprisingly, ninety percent of the money donated by the private sector is given by individuals.

Every year, the American Association of Fund Raising Counsel (AAFRC) compiles and analyzes philanthropic giving by the private sector from the previous year. For the past thirty-five years that AAFRC has compiled these figures, the percentages have varied by only one or two points, and have consistently shown that ninety percent of the money given away by the private sector took the form of donations and bequests from individuals. Figure 1 illustrates private sector giving for 1986, the latest year for which figures are available.

Who are these individuals?
Many studies have profiled the people who tend to be donors. Some surprising facts have emerged. One of the most recent studies, conducted

Figure 1.

Contributions (in billions)		Contributions as Percent of total	
Individuals	$71.72	Individuals	82.2%
Bequests	5.83	Bequests	6.7
Foundations	5.17	Foundations	5.9
Corporations	4.50	Corporations	5.2
TOTAL	**$87.22**		

SOURCE: American Association of Fund Raising Counsel, *Giving USA*, 1987

---

*Kim Klein conducts training programs on various techniques for raising funds from individuals, she is also the executive director of Appalachian Community Fund in Knoxville, Tennessee.

for the Rockefeller Brothers Fund by Yankelovich, Skelly and White, showed that households with incomes of $50,000 and over (13 percent of all households) gave 37 percent of the total given, while 63 percent came from households with incomes of $50,000 and under.[1] A 1985 United Way study showed that 85 percent of all money contributed by individuals came from households with incomes of $50,000 and under.[2] An Independent Sector study in 1982 of giving by income bracket showed, among other findings, that families with incomes of $5,000 gave away an average of $238.[3] Organizers and service providers who work with low income people bear out the fact that generosity increases with lack of resources. Measured as a percentage of income, poorer people give away much more income than wealthy people do. Although the precise figures vary from study to study, the conclusion is the same: It is the middle class and below that give away the most money in America.

Studies consistently show that even among the very wealthy, tax advantages for giving are the least important factor in deciding whether or not to be a donor. In her book, *America's Wealthy and the Future of Foundations,* Teresa Odendahl describes a study done by Eugene Steuerle. Steuerle showed that wealthy people tended to retain their assets during their lifetimes, making their largest contributions as bequests. Odendahl remarks: "This pattern of wealth retention is remarkable in light of the fact that lifetime giving offers more tax advantages than do bequests. In effect, the rich hold on to wealth that they will most likely never consume, and they pay a greater price for it. ... The wealthy tend to show a preference for wealth-holding itself, regardless of the tax consequences."

Other studies show that people who attend religious services tend to give more to all charities than people who do not. In 1984, according to Yankelovich, Skelly and White, 86 percent of people attending religious services made 94 percent of the total contributions to all charities.[4]

Finally, the prime giving ages are 35 to 64. As more and more Americans enter that population, we can expect giving by individuals to increase accordingly.

---

[1]Yankelovich, Skelly and White, Inc. In *Giving USA.* (New York: American Association of Fund Raising Counsel, 1987).

[2]*Grassroots Fundraising Journal.* (Knoxville, August, 1987).

[3]*Patterns of Charitable Giving by Individuals II, A Research Report.* (Washington, D.C.: Independent Sector, 1982).

[4]Yankelovich, Skelly and White, Inc.

Where did this money go?

AAFRC divides nonprofits into eight broad categories and analyzes amount and percent of giving to each. These categories and the 1986 figures for each appear in Figure 2.

The vast majority of private sector funding goes to religion. Religious institutions—primarily churches—raise money through a combination of three basic techniques:

1. Churches ask for money constantly.
2. Churches encourage everyone to give. If you have $1.00 to give, they encourage you to give it. If you have $1 million, you are equally encouraged. No gift is too small or too ostentatious.
3. Churches provide a variety of places to give. You are expected to give not only to the general collection but also to overseas missions, the building fund, flowers for the sanctuary in memory of someone, the soup kitchen or homeless shelter run out of the church basement, and the local shelter for battered women as a domestic mission of the Women's Group.

None of the above techniques are restricted to religious institutions. Any organization can request funds, encourage donors to give as much as they possibly can, and ask for additional gifts for special programs all year long.

Basic Principles

Four basic principles govern all fundraising, and can be extrapolated from organizations with successful fundraising records. These principles are as follows:

Figure 2.

Distribution (in billions)		Distribution as Percent of total	
Religion	$40.90	Religion	46.9%
Education	12.73	Education	14.6
Health	12.26	Health	14.0
Human Services	9.13	Human Services	10.5
Arts, Culture	5.83	Arts, Culture	6.7
Public/Society Benefit	2.38	Public/Society Benefit	2.7
Other	3.99	Other	4.6

SOURCE: American Association of Fund Raising Counsel, *Giving USA*, 1986.

1. People give out of self-interest.

Your organization is a business. Perhaps it is incorporated and has tax-exempt status from the federal government as a Section 501(c)(3) or Section 501(c)(4) organization. Certainly, someone must keep track of money coming in and going out, and provide budgets, financial reports, and so on. From a fundraising standpoint, the fact that your organization is a business means that your donors are customers who "buy" your "products", which are your services, your organizing, your advocacy, or whatever it is you do.

People will give their money to your organization when it serves their self-interest to do so. Some rewards of giving to support social change are that a donor helps to move the world a little closer to his or her vision of what it should be. Maybe a local situation is changed and the "little guys" win. Or maybe the donor is recognized by friends as a generous or caring individual. Sometimes self-interest is more direct: the donor's water is cleaned up, the donor's candidate wins, the donor is no longer discriminated against because of sex, race, or sexual orientation.

The first task in effective fundraising is to figure out the different rewards donors will have if they give to your group. Each donor will have multiple motives, and donors will have different motives from each other. However, if you do not touch on one of their motives, you will not get your gift.

2. Fundraising is a long-term process.

It is not enough to get a donor to give; we must always be thinking about how to get that person to give again, to give more, to encourage friends to give, and to become involved. The first gift is just that. As you develop strategies to raise money, you need to balance your fundraising plans by including some strategies whose main purpose is to bring in new donors (i.e. direct mail, special events, canvassing) as well as strategies to encourage donors to give bigger gifts (i.e. personal solicitation, pledge programs) and strategies to encourage donors to give several times a year (i.e. special mail appeals, phonathons, house parties).

3. Personal contact is most effective.

In general, the most effective strategies for raising money involve personal contact with the donor. The most effective specific strategy is for one person to ask someone he or she knows in the context of a personal visit. As a rule, the closer you get to the donor, the more likely you are to get the gift.

4. Diversify funding sources.

To implement principles 1, 2, and 3, you need two things: diversified sources of funding and an active volunteer force involved in fundraising. (An active volunteer force means five or more people committing eight to ten unpaid hours a month to your organization. For service organizations, this group of people would be in addition to hotline volunteers, crisis counselors, and so forth.) This volunteer force should be generally led by the main decision-making body of the organization. An organization cannot maintain successful diversity without also having a large number of people working on fundraising. Further, an organization that relies on one or two people, whether paid or volunteer, to do all the fundraising is no more secure than an organization with only one or two funding sources. The same things happen to people that happen to funding sources: they die, they move, they move on, they get mad, they run out of energy, or they change their priorities.

Summary of Basic Principles

Successful fundraising is built on marketing and sales principles, a fact of life that sometimes makes progressive people and organizations queasy.

It is important to understand that like money itself, marketing and sales are neutral. Positive values and behavior can be marketed, such as wearing seat belts, or practicing safe sex. Important "products" can be "sold" such as a bilateral, verifiable nuclear arms freeze, or pay equity. "Abolish Apartheid" is as much a sales slogan as "Coke is it."

There are now 1.2 million registered 501(c)(3) and (c)(4) nonprofit tax-exempt corporations in America,[5] and up to eight million organizations that may not have any kind of tax exemption.[6] With all these groups raising money, there is a great deal of competition for the billions of dollars available. As more and more organizations are forced to raise private sector dollars to replace previous federal funding, the competition increases every day. The organizations that will survive and grow in the next few years will be those who apply the adage "Work smarter, not harder" to their fundraising by implementing effective fundraising techniques.

Fundraising Strategies

The rest of this chapter will describe briefly the most common fundraising strategies. All these strategies involve, to varying degrees, identifying

---

[5] *Non-Profit Times*. Vol.1. Princeton: 1987.
[6] Carl Bakal, *Charity USA*.

prospects and asking for money. There is really no such thing as fundraising if it does not involve these two points. Therefore, we begin the strategy discussion with them.

Identifying Prospects

A prospect is someone who is likely to give. A prospect is different from a stranger, and is not just a name. For someone to be a prospect, three things must be true of the person:

1. He or she must have the *ability* to make a gift. Part of prospect identification is to determine what size gift is possible and what strategy should be used in getting the gift.
2. He or she must believe in your cause or in something similar to your cause.
3. He or she must be known to the group in some way. The organization must have a way to contact the person.

When you have positive verifiable evidence of these three factors, you have a prospect. Depending on your strategy, your prospect may be an individual (for a major gift solicitation) or may be a part of a group that exhibits the above characteristics (all the donors to one group may be approached by mail for another group).

Asking for Money

Asking for money seems to be the great stumbling block to raising money, which is unfortunate since there is really no other way to raise money effectively. The reason why people find it difficult to ask for money is simple: we find it difficult to talk about money. If we can't talk about it, clearly we can't ask for it.

Most people in the United States are raised to think that it is rude to ask someone what her salary is or what he paid for his house. At the same time, most people are curious about other people's salaries or purchases, and will use alternative methods to find out.

Our attitudes are full of contradictions on the subject. On the one hand, we believe, "If you are a good person and work hard, you will get what you deserve." At the same time, we assert that you cannot measure a person's character by how much money he or she has. We fiercely maintain that money can't buy happiness while thinking that we would be happier if only we had more money. We claim: "Time is money," yet ask each other for time much more easily than for money, and do not value large gifts of time from our volunteers nearly as much as large gifts of money.

The inability to get money we need for social justice work comes, in great part, from the inability to ask for money. This is learned behavior. Children have no trouble asking for money, or anything else. We learn it, and we can retrain our thinking in order to raise the money we need for our work.

There are two things to remember in asking for money:

1. Success is *asking*. Whether you get the money or you don't is up to the prospect, not up to you. The only thing you can do is *ask*—ask straightforwardly and clearly, but *ask*. Failure in fundraising is a failure to ask.
2. Most people will say no. If you ask through a direct mail appeal, up to ninety-nine percent of the people will not respond; in a phonathon, up to eighty-five percent of the people will turn you down; and even in the most successful strategy, the personal visit, up to fifty percent of the people will say no.

Fundraising is a numbers game. If you ask enough people, you will get your money. Once you know that your task is simply to ask and that you will get turned down some of the time, there is no longer anything to fear—and no longer any reason not to do it.

The Strategies

Personal Solicitation

First, identify your prospect. The prospect usually should have a giving ability of $50 or more because of the time involved in getting each gift, and should also be personally known to someone in the organization. He or she does not have to be known to the solicitor, but the solicitor will need to use someone's name to gain access to the prospect, i.e. "Fred Murphy gave me your name. . . ."

In the most formal approach, the solicitor writes the prospect a letter which says, in effect: "I am raising money for Good Organization. I would like to talk with you about being a major donor. I'll call you in a few days to see when we can meet." The letter is then followed by a phone call to set up the meeting, and the meeting to get the answer to the request. In each step, keep in mind the purpose of the step.

Step One: The letter is to tantalize the prospect. Don't say much about your organization. Simply tell the person you want

81

to talk to him or her about making a gift, but ask the prospect, in effect, not to decide until you have had a chance to visit personally.

Step Two: The phone call is to set up the meeting. Sometimes the prospect will wish to make a decision on the phone, and you should accept graciously. However, you should offer to meet with all your prospects even if some of them give the money with just a phone call.

Step Three: The meeting's purpose is to ask for the money. The meeting, however, has been preceded by at least one, and perhaps two, indications that you are going to talk about money (the letter and the phone call). In the meeting, then, you don't focus on the prospect's money but on your organization, and why it is important. Remembering the basic marketing principle of the first part of this chapter, you should prepare for the meeting by thinking through why it is in this prospect's self-interest to support your group. What does he or she support now? Believe in? Whom does he or she want to look good in front of? What kind of self-image does he or she have? By thinking through these things, you can focus the conversation on the prospect's interests and concerns.

The most important aspect of each step is what is called "the close"— where you name what it is you want. In the case of the letter, it is simple. The close is "I'll call you to set up a meeting." Don't say "Call me if you want to meet" or "I'm hoping we can run into each other sometime."

The "close" of the phone call is "When can we meet?" Or "Tuesday is better than Wednesday for me. How is it for you?" Not "Shall we meet?" or "I was hoping that sometime we could see each other."

Clearly, the most difficult and critical close takes place in the meeting. At this close, the prospect will either become a donor or will reject your offer. You must decide if the prospect is ready to tell you a decision, and then you should look straight at him or her say clearly and distinctly, "Will you help us with $" and name an amount. After you say exactly what you want, you have nothing else to say, so be quiet.

The close must be specific and clear. Sometimes solicitors will claim that they asked someone for money but that they don't know what the person's response was. This is impossible unless the solicitor has amnesia or the prospect lapsed into a foreign language at the end. If you ask clearly and unambiguously, the prospect can only say "yes" or "no" or "I'll think about it." In the case of the latter, respect the person's need to think.

Many people cannot make decisions in a hurry. However, set a time by which the thinking will be done. Say, "May I call you Wednesday?" Or "I'll call you next week if that will be enough time?"

The final point to clarify in individual solicitation is how the money will be paid. Let's assume you have asked for $1,000. The prospect says she would be delighted to give. After thanking her, you say, "How would you like to pay that?" The donor says, "I'll give you a check" or "I'll send stock or a check" or whatever.

The end of the whole interaction is a thank-you note.

Direct Mail

The purpose of direct mail, which means simply two hundred or more identical letters sent by bulk mail rates, is to acquire donors. Here the prospects are all of one group, and the group meets the three criteria, although each individual within the group may not. Also, the level of personal contact is greatly reduced. Your contact with these people is an address list.

Mass direct mail (sending ten thousand to one million letters) is generally not a strategy small social change organizations can or even should undertake. However, even the smallest group can compile a list of all the people they know, send that group a mail appeal, and ask the respondents for names of people they know.

There are three parts to a mail appeal: the "carrier envelope" (the outside envelope), the letter, and the enclosures (which are the return envelope and the reply device). Direct mail must be easy to understand and should carry an emotional message rather than relying on an intellectual grasp of the subject.

For organizations seriously considering direct mail, there are many good books available.

Special Events

Special events are the most common grassroots fundraising strategy and probably the most misunderstood. Special events such as dances, auctions, luncheons, walkathons, and so forth, should be used first to promote the organization, second to increase the overall visibility of the organization, and only third to raise money. For the amount of time they take, special events are an inefficient way to raise money, but they are the most efficient way (short of a media campaign) to get attention.

The variety of special events is almost limitless. Organizations contemplating or planning a special event should consult some of the many excellent books and articles on the subject.

Fundraising by Telephone

Telephone solicitation is rapidly becoming as common as direct mail appeals, but unfortunately is much more disliked by the public. Many people feel that phone solicitation is an invasion of privacy, and many people distrust phone solicitors, and thus the organization doing the phoning. Still, it is an effective way both to raise money and to teach volunteers how to ask for money directly in a less charged setting than a major gift solicitation.

Names of prospects are critical. To get names, send an appeal to your current donors and ask them for names, addresses, and phone numbers of people they think would be interested in your organization. Ask volunteers to bring the names of five people who they think would be interested but whom they are uncomfortable about asking for a large gift face-to-face. Those volunteers will trade names. Call all the people who gave you money last year but have failed to respond to renewal letters this year. Or call to follow up on a mail appeal.

Set aside a three-hour block of time, ideally six to nine on any evening from Monday to Thursday. Ask volunteers to come thirty minutes before the phoning for orientation and to stay thirty minutes afterward to finish up and clean up. Have in place: phones, lists of names, and instructions for handling gifts. Each volunteer should be able to call twenty people per hour, so you can figure out how many volunteers you will need for your prospects.

Provide volunteers with a script which they are free to adapt, a list of common and hard questions about your organization, and make them practice with each other. Let them know that most people will say no, and some will say it rudely. Success in a phonathon is a donation from about fifteen percent of the people reached.

Workplace Fundraising

Once the sole domain of the United Way, federated fundraising, or raising money through payroll deduction, is now being used by many alternative funds around the United States. The most well known of these are the Black United Funds, Womens Way in Philadelphia, and Community Shares in Knoxville, Tennessee.

The first step in workplace fundraising is to see if the United Way will accept your organization as an agency. If you are in social change or social justice work, the answer is almost certain to be no. However, if you are a service provider, you may have a chance. United Ways vary from community to community and are worth looking into. If the United

Way says no, check to see if there are alternative funds in your community that you could join. If there are none, or you do not qualify, you can create your own federation. For an excellent introduction to workplace fundraising, see Chapter 9, "Workplace Giving: United Way or Alternative Ways?" by Robert O. Bothwell.

Canvassing

Canvassing involves a team of people going door to door to request contributions for your work. Canvassing is used extensively by local groups and by local chapters of state or national organizations.

While part-time or temporary canvasses can be run with volunteers, most canvassing is a full-time operation involving salaried or commissioned employees who work forty hours a week and solicit in neighborhoods on a regular and revolving basis. Well-run canvasses can bring in $50,000 to $500,000 or more in gross income. Because they are labor intensive, however, the high cost of most canvasses absorbs at least sixty percent of their gross earnings.

Canvassing works best when the organization has an issue that affects the people being canvassed, when that issue is easy to explain, and when the canvass is run in a metropolitan area. Although there have been rural canvasses, they have not lasted because of the distance between homes or towns, and the labor required to reach a small population.

Summary

There are dozens of other fundraising strategies, and within each of the strategies described here there are hundreds of variations and applications. Many people wonder how to choose a fundraising strategy. The first part of picking strategies is fairly simple: every organization, regardless of size, location, or age, should raise some money from personal solicitation, some from mail appeals, and some from special events. Every organization should use a variety of strategies, so it is not a question of picking one strategy, but picking several. In choosing which variation or application of a strategy, groups need to look at considerations such as volunteers available, amount of money needed and when, front money available, and other goals of the strategy (such as recruiting new donors or getting publicity).

The basics of individual donor fundraising are the same throughout all the strategies, and are simple and straightforward. To summarize, to raise money from individuals, you must:

1. Ask for it by name, clearly and boldly.
2. Know what the money will be used for, and make it clear that the donor is important to the success of the organization.
3. Ask for additional gifts during the year.
4. Use a broad base of volunteers led by the board of directors to do fundraising. It should not be a staff-dominated activity.
5. Use a wide variety of strategies to maximize visibility, the number of donors, and sources of income.
6. Remember that people give money when it serves their self-interest, and that fundraising is built on principles of marketing and sales.
7. Success in fundraising is asking for the money; failure is a failure to ask.
8. If you are having trouble talking about money, remember this old fund-raisers' saying: "If you are afraid to ask for money, kick yourself out of the way and let the cause talk."

REFERENCES

Andres, Susan. "A Primer on Mailing Lists." *The Grantsmanship Center* NEWS. September/October 1982.

"Asking for Money: Getting Over the Fear of Asking." *Grassroots Fundraising Journal*. April 1983.

Ballenger, Bruce. "Direct Mail on a Shoestring." *NRAG Paper*. Helena: Northern Rockies Action Group, Spring 1984.

Bergen, Helen. *Where the Money Is: A Fundraiser's Guide to the Rich*. Alexandria: BioGuide Press, 1985.

Direct Mail Fundraiser's Association. *A Guide to Direct Mail Fundraising*. New York: Direct Mail Fundraiser's Association.

Independent Sector. *The Charitable Behavior of Americans: Findings from a National Survey*. Washington, D.C.: 1986.

8

Chapter Eight
Workplace Giving: United Way
or Alternative Ways?
By Robert O. Bothwell*

Which would be easier? Asking someone to give you $50? Or asking them to give you $1.00 a week. Clearly the latter, and that is a key reason that workplace fundraising is being seen by more and more organizations today as a new source of private contributions.

Traditionally the preserve of United Ways (united funds and community chests as they were known in previous incarnations), workers in the United States contribute $1.6 billion a year at their workplaces, mainly through payroll deductions.[1] Now more than $100 million a year is raised by non–United Way charities: health agencies, social action organizations, arts groups, international agencies, minority organizations, women's groups, environmental organizations, and others. While United Way payroll deduction revenues continue to grow ten percent annually, non–United Way employee contributions grew an average of thirty-seven percent annually during the first half of the 1980s.

Large corporations, small and medium-sized businesses, the government at all levels, public school systems, public and private universities—basically all types of today's workplaces, blue collar and white collar—are sites for fundraising. These worksites provide several advantages: all the workers are employed and earning regular incomes; they often are concentrated geographically; and they provide a cadre of supervisors and regular workers to perform the actual solicitation on time paid for by the employer. It is no wonder that donating by payroll deduction, a post–World War II phenomenon, has expanded to nearly one-third of the size of all foundation grantmaking.

Who Is Doing Payroll Deduction Fundraising?
Can any organization benefit from this fundraising phenomenon? Which groups today are most successful at workplace fundraising? Where? How?

*Robert O. Bothwell is the executive director of the National Committee for Responsive Philanthropy (NCRP) in Washington, D.C. NCRP is a watchdog organization monitoring foundation and corporate philanthropy and United Ways and providing organizing and technical support for new forms of collective fundraising.
[1]The figures used throughout this chapter come from a wide variety of sources, all of which are identified at the end of this chapter in the reference section.

First and foremost, United Ways dominate the scene, raising 93.5 percent of all employee contributions (excluding corporate employee-matching gift programs). United Ways exist in 2,300 locations, providing funds to 37,000 agencies large and small. For every two dollars of corporate employee donations, United Ways also secure one dollar in corporate grants—thereby substantially expanding their grantmaking base. Adding in other revenues, United Ways' total projections for 1987 amount to $2.6 billion.

Health agencies such as the Muscular Dystrophy Association conduct workplace fundraising in the federal government, in many state and local governments, and in more than 2,500 private workplaces. There are forty-one federations of health agencies now operative.[2] They are mostly made up of national health agencies or their local affiliates. Rarely are local clinics or hospitals involved. At the federal level, health agencies raise $27 million a year; at state and local levels, their federations raise anywhere from $5,000 to $3.8 million annually.

International agencies such as CARE and Save the Children raise payroll deduction gifts in the federal government and many state governments, and are now beginning to solicit local governments and corporations. Combined they raise $11 million each year.

There are more than sixty united arts funds across the country; eleven conduct payroll deduction solicitation, mostly from corporations, raising $2 million annually.

The first Black United Fund (BUF) was organized in 1968. BUFs are not organized as federations of agencies in the same way as the organizations mentioned previously. (BUFs are described in greater detail below.) There are ten BUFs operating today, mostly soliciting governmental workplaces but starting to make serious inroads into corporate worksites. They raise approximately $3.5 million a year.

Social action agencies—ranging from neighborhood organizations to consumer activist groups to day care associations— have organized in twenty-one federations across America. While also soliciting mainly in government worksites, they are gearing up to seek access to corporations. All together, they raise $2.2 million a year, of which fifty-two percent is from payroll gifts and forty-eight percent is from other sources.

Women's and environmental groups complete the list of those currently undertaking workplace fundraising. Three women's federations are

---

[2]Basically, a federation is an organization of member charities where the umbrella helps its members raise money and distributes it to members and sometimes nonmembers, according to a predetermined formula.

active, and three additional women's funds are organizing to solicit payroll dollars. Womens Way in Philadelphia raises $230,000 through payroll deduction plans (plus $570,000 from nonpayroll sources). One environmental federation is well under way in California (raising more than $200,000); another is in formation in Washington.

Individual Charities Successful in the Workplace

Thousands of individual charities not a part of United Way (or any other grouping) collect substantial payroll deduction monies—more than $37 million in 1985–86. They do it through United Way donor option programs, which allow employees to "write-in" their favorite charities which are not included in official brochures. (Donor option programs are discussed below.) Individual charities also raise money in the workplace through the federal government's Combined Federal Campaign, either as write-ins or by passing an eligibility test. Some state and local governments (such as California and Massachusetts) also allow individual charities to participate in their annual employee charity campaigns.

Back to "Go": Consider the United Way

Let's return to the United Ways. As the dominant organizations in the field, they are the appropriate starting point. They have lots of money to give away, for example, $78 million in Los Angeles and $14 million in Providence, Rhode Island. Some of their members receive several hundred thousand dollars annually; others receive only a few thousand. According to United Way, any human care service nonprofit organization can join or receive special funding. So what's the first step?

The initial approach should be through the local membership application office. Find out what the local United Way is looking for other than just what is requested on the application form. For example, is it looking to fund only successful agencies, or will it support those just getting started? (More on the unwritten criteria later).

The boards of directors of United Ways—comprised of the most well known and respected civic and business leaders in each community—have committees assigned to check out membership applications. Applicants should find out who these committee people are and look for connections to their own board and staff members. Meetings should then be arranged. Applicants stand a better chance for membership if respected civic or business leaders provide support at these meetings.

There is no substitute for this person-to-person contact. The formal application should be completed and submitted only after sifting through all that has been learned. After submitting an application, be prepared to wait. It may not be acted upon for several months, or in some cases several years (yes, years). But one should not sit on one's heels. Call, write, follow up, seek new meetings with additional United Way staff and board. Be persistent. Applications should be supplemented as more is learned about United Way's expectations.

United Way Membership: The Realities

When all is said and done, however, it is very difficult, regardless of the type of program being operated, to become a new member of a United Way; although in some localities it is somewhat easier to receive special nonmember funding. According to data from United Way of America (a separate national organization providing research and public policy support to local United Ways), only one or two new members are admitted annually to large city United Ways; in smaller city United Ways the numbers are probably less encouraging.

Organizations engaged in advocacy, litigation, lobbying, or citizen organizing usually have a tougher time gaining membership than purely service organizations. Those that deal with economic issues (such as consumer interests, the environment, or pay equity) can face an almost impossible barrier, since two-thirds of most United Way boards are usually made up of businessmen who may see their own business interests threatened by such groups. Frequently such organizations have gone through elaborate procedures to gain membership only ultimately to be turned down. Such is the recent experience of the AIDS Foundation of Houston, a public health project in Anchorage, and a nutritional food service in Baltimore.

Denominators common to most rejected groups are that they were formed only in recent years; they serve previously neglected sectors of society; they offer innovative approaches and/or advocate citizen empowerment as ways to solve problems.

United Way Membership: The Realpolitik Approach

United Ways should not be written off by progressive organizations; their membership policies and procedures vary substantially from community to community. If one's research suggests membership is possible—even if it's a long shot—the possible monetary results should be carefully weighed against the costs of seeking admission before making the decision whether or not to apply.

However, it is often necessary to discern the reality between the official United Way line that all human care service organizations have an opportunity to join and the preceding examples of groups that did not make it. J. Dawn Hodson, former United Way associate director in Ventura, California, offers some clarity.

"Being a United Way agency is not for everyone. If you do join, you will have to adhere to some rules regarding the timing and nature of your other fundraising activities, and you will also have to submit to program evaluations and to loan staff to United Way, among other things. . . . And there are, of course, subtle but important issues of political perspective, values, style, and priorities."

Hodson likens admission to United Way to joining an exclusive club: You have to meet the entrance requirements and you also need a sponsor. She outlines three ground rules:

1. The Golden Mean. "No matter how United Way bills itself, it is a middle class organization with middle-class values. In trying to reach a consensus among its constituencies, it usually plays it safe.by taking in only those organizations which offend no one. Your chances of being admitted depend to a considerable extent on how well you fit into mainstream America."

2. The Banker's Law. "Always remember that United Way is a business, even if it is raising money for charities. It is like a bank in that it does not want your business unless you are so successful that you can do without its support."

3. Running the Gauntlet. "The less power you have in the community, the more closely you will be scrutinized when you apply. United Way will evaluate you not only for the usual entrance requirements, but also for . . . your other sources of support and the attitudes, personalities, and skills of the people who run your agency. . . . You must be perceived either as part of [a community's] power base, or develop a power base of your own."[4]

If Not United Way, Then How?
Groups that fail to obtain United Way membership or special funding, or decide not to undertake the effort, can select other ways of obtaining

---

[3] J. Dawn Hodson, "United Ways: Have You Considered Joining?" *The Grantsmanship Center News,* 1982.
[4] *Id.*

payroll deduction contributions. But be warned: There is no easy street to securing workplace contributions. If non–United Way charities so far have been able to capture only 6.5 percent of the market for payroll deduction contributions, there must be a reason. The reason is it takes lots of effort.

The flip side to this coin is that if a group actually gains access to workplace donations, it is not nearly as tough to keep them rolling in. Once employers decide to allow access, they rarely change their minds. Moreover, when workers get over the shock of being allowed to give to non–United Way charities, they generally expand their gifts to these groups over time. Workplace donations, thus, become one of the more predictable sources of funds. Equally important, they are unrestricted general-support funds, the gold-coin funds that are rarely available from government agencies, foundations, or corporations, which prefer to make "special project" grants.

United Way Donor Option Programs

One of the easiest routes to payroll donations is through United Way "donor option" programs. Even though an individual organization is not a United Way member or a recipient of United Way special funding (and thus is not listed in official United Way brochures), workers may still donate by specially requesting a donor option card from the employer during the annual United Way fundraising drive (generally one month or more during the fall). Each card features spaces for writing in the organization's name and indicating how much money per pay period is to be contributed through deduction.

In 1982, a United Way study showed that fifty-three United Ways were offering donor option programs. Based on figures in this study and a 1986 study by the National Committee for Responsive Philanthropy, it is estimated that $18 million was contributed to individual, non–United Way charities in 1985–86 through donor option programs. Amounts varied from $4.5 million in Philadelphia to less than $100,000 in two-thirds of the other locations (e.g., Augusta, Georgia; Springfield, Illinois; St. Cloud, Minnesota).

Total contributions to organizations receiving donor option gifts varied just as much. A few got over $20,000; some received $5,000 or more; most ended up with under $100. However, organizations that made special efforts to obtain these dollars—by using brochures, handouts, and advertising—often got back $10 for every $1 they spent on brochures and other advertising.

The best way to begin securing donor option dollars is to contact the local United Way to see if it runs a donor option program, and remember, it may operate under another name. If so, ask United Way staff for the names of the charities receiving donor option funds. (You may have to ask several times.) The largest recipients should be approached for advice; find out how much they receive and how they seek these moneys.

Many United Ways have a rule forbidding distribution of brochures or other advertising for donor option contributions. Some United Ways rigidly enforce this rule and refuse to give pledged contributions to groups that advertised; other United Ways don't enforce the rule. Check with local charities receiving donor option money to learn the prevailing practice. If advertising is strictly forbidden, this source of payroll deduction contributions is not likely to yield very much.

What if a United Way has no donor option program? Can one be established? In Baltimore and Pittsburgh, local charities organized and prompted their establishment. These programs now flourish. In most communities with donor option, however, it arrived for other reasons— usually pressure from the business community. Some business leaders wanted to respond to employee desires for more choice in their payroll deduction charity drives (San Francisco); others wanted to accommodate local non–United Way charities which had been confronting United Way with substantial adverse publicity for refusing to let them participate (Los Angeles, Philadelphia). In still other communities, United Ways instituted donor option programs as a means to undercut competition from new alternative federations (Providence, Rhode Island).

Participation in Government Charity Drives

What additional avenues are open to charities not affiliated with any federation (United Way or otherwise) that want payroll deduction contributions? While very few business charity drives are open to nonaffiliated charities; many government employee charity drives are open.

The Combined Federal Campaign

First and foremost is the Combined Federal Campaign (CFC)— the federal government's $140-million-a-year operation—which is the largest workplace campaign in the country, involving four million workers. Open to United Ways, United Way agencies, and large, long-established national health agencies and international service agencies since its inception in the early 1960s, the CFC has become increasingly open to newer, nontraditional, and even advocacy charities during the past eight years. Court decisions, congressional intervention, White House executive orders and (in December 1987) permanent new legislation have changed the face of the CFC in major ways. Local nonaffiliated charities have been able to participate in the CFC since 1980 by meeting the eligibility requirements in the local communities where they operate. This qualifies them to receive payroll deductions from federal government workers employed in the local community.

The CFC operates in 523 locations across the country under rules drafted and administered by the Office of Personnel Management (OPM) in Washington, D.C. As this chapter is being written, these rules are being revised to bring the CFC into compliance with the new legislation. However, even once the new rules are in place, local federal officials will continue to play a role in their interpretation, deciding on local agency eligibility, choosing who runs the local campaign on behalf of all participating charities (usually the United Way), and generally overseeing the planning and operation of the campaign. National charities may now participate legally by securing a determination of national eligibility from OPM in Washington, D.C. Once a national organization is included, it functionally has access to payroll deduction contributions from all federal government workers regardless of where they work. Thus, local affiliates of these national charities may not participate in a local CFC if their national parent has already secured eligibility. However, local affiliates may join the drive in their own communities when their national group has not been approved for national eligibility.

Non–United Way federations of charities can gain local or national eligibility. The new legislation provides for more than mere participation. For example, all approved federations will now share in twenty-five percent of all CFC contributions which are not designated to any specific charity.

Eligibility rules, published annually in the Federal Register, can be obtained for free or nominal cost from local and regional OPM offices, from OPM in Washington, D.C., or in some communities from the local federal executive board. A technical assistance packet, including the rules, is available for $20.00 from the National Committee for Responsive Philanthropy.

The rules permit any charity with Section 501(c)(3) tax-exempt status serving human health and welfare needs to participate, if it meets rigorous public accountability criteria (such as publishing an annual report of its program and finances, having an annual audit by an independent CPA, keeping combined fundraising and administrative costs to twenty-five percent or less of their total support and revenue, although exceptions are allowed for these latter two). Under new rules, charities must apply very early in the calendar year to be considered for the fall campaigns.

About one-half of the annual $140 million CFC contributions goes to United Ways and their member agencies, while the other one-half goes to non–United Way charities, including approximately $8 million to nontraditional social justice and environmental organizations.

State and Local Government Charity Drives

Nineteen state government charity drives are open to single nonaffiliated charities. Many more local government charity campaigns are similarly open. Other state and local government charity drives are open only to United Way or to United Way and other federations.

To find out how to gain access, telephone the office of the secretary of state, board of administrative control, or office of administration. Ask for the top person and talk to whomever you get, asking for their boss if you do not get satisfactory answers to your questions. If all else fails, call the governor. Another route is to start with the office that actually handles all payroll deductions (such as withholding taxes and savings bond deductions), and then work your way back to the person responsible for the state's employee charity drive.

Many states have executive orders and formal regulations; some have mere "guidelines"; only a few have laws behind their charity drives (for example, California, Illinois, and South Carolina). In any event, seek out the written authority and rules. If none exist, this strongly suggests a United Way–only state, which means applying for United Way membership, or starting a political drive to open up the state to non–United Way charities. (More on this later.)

The employee charity drives of dozens of local governmental units— cities, counties, public school districts, or sanitation districts—also are open to single nonaffiliated charities. Again seek out the written authority or guidelines. Start with the head of administration. Go to the mayor, a county commissioner or school board president if necessary. If you get nowhere, try the payroll office. Be persistent. If nothing exists, again, it is probably a United Way–only campaign.

For all state and local governmental drives, find out if any groups participate in addition to United Way. Maybe health agencies do, or international agencies, or one of the other previously mentioned federations or funds. Talk with them about how the charity drive works. Somebody may fill you in on the unwritten rules that govern eligibility and conduct of the campaign. These often are as important as the written rules.

Charities Working Together to Expand Payroll Donations to Non–United Way Nonprofits

Unfortunately, because single nonaffiliated charities rarely cooperate in organized fashion to help shape government employee charity drives, United Ways usually organize charity drives in ways that cause far more money to flow in their direction than to all other participating charities. The CFC is the most visible exception, but this occurred only after eleven years of battle by individual charities and non–United Way federations.

Across America, other charities have been organizing to open up state and local government and business charity drives by forming "alternative funds." There were ninety-one such funds operating in fall 1988. They included Combined Health Appeals and National Voluntary Health Agencies (41); united arts funds (11), international service agencies (three national federations); national service agencies (one national federation); Black United Funds (10); social action funds (21); women's funds (3); and one environmental fund.

Of these, six are national; eighty-five are statewide or local. Some were just getting started with their first solicitation in fall 1987; others have been around for five to ten years or longer. Some raised as little as a few thousand dollars in fall 1987, but forty-five raised more than $100,000 in 1986–87; ten raised between $500,000 and $1 million; and eight raised more than $1 million.

Some have yet to distribute any funds to their members; others have distributed only a few hundred dollars; still others, generally those that have been around five years or more, are distributing $10,000 to $100,000 per year to their members. Health funds are the largest; social action funds the smallest distributors. But those funds distributing $10,000 annually to each of their members fully expect to double this amount over the next three to five years.

If United Way is not for you, and your state and local governments do not allow their employees to give to nonaffiliated charities (or they do but the returns appear meager), then investigate joining an alternative fund. A list of these funds appears at the back of this book, in Appendix III. National organizations should approach only those identified as national federations. Local groups should telephone the director of any potentially compatible fund in its area to find out more about it. If the discussion seems promising, make an appointment for a meeting. Follow up with a meeting with the fund's board chair.

Funds are organized somewhat differently, and membership committees, board chairs, and fund directors have varying degrees of influence within a particular fund. Nevertheless, these funds do periodically accept new members and one must approach the process of seeking membership in the same political way as was discussed in the context of seeking membership in a United Way.

One of the most important things to learn from a fund is its expectations of its member organizations. Some Combined Health Appeals (CHAs) work in partnership with United Ways and thus generally their member agencies are not expected to be involved in the actual workplace solicitation campaigns. Their members simply must participate in the usual board of directors and committee meetings. Members of other CHAs, social action funds, women's funds, and environmental funds not only have the normal board and committee meeting obligations, they also have the full burden of seeking access to new employers and orchestrating the actual solicitations.

Black United Funds are not federations; they have no member agencies. They act like foundations, raising money and distributing it in the form of grants to charities serving Blacks and the poor. Their boards of directors involve prominent leadership from the Black community, and welcome community volunteers, whether or not from nonprofit organizations.

The critical difference between a United Way and an alternative fund is that while United Way does it for you, alternative funds do it for themselves. As a result, those who are part of alternative funds generally feel as if they are more in control of their futures and the futures of their constituents.

When None of the Above Options Are for You, Then What?

When none of the prior options are suitable, a group can still obtain payroll deduction contributions by organizing its own alternative fund. Those who have ever organized anything know already that this option isn't easy. Nevertheless, those who have done it now look back with great pride on their role in creating new community institutions that are raising previously untapped private monies for their favorite causes.

Moreover, they see a bright future for alternative funds. Remember, employee contributions to non–United Way charities grew by 184 percent from 1980 to 1985—whereas those to United Ways grew by only fifty-four percent. Payroll contributions from all sources to social action funds grew forty percent from 1985 to 1986, the last year for which figures are available. International Service Agencies' payroll gifts from local and state government and business charity drives grew by forty-six percent.

What are the top considerations before undertaking the organization of a new alternative fund? The first is determining whether there is an adequate employee base to support an alternative fund. If there already is a United Way in a local community, that's a positive sign. But most United Ways have succeeded by gaining access to the larger local employers, both business and government.

Most alternative funds first gain access to government employees before they turn to workers in private corporations. So, a fundamental consideration is the size of the government workforce—at all levels. A minimum base of 25,000 government workers is essential for the success of a new alternative fund so that it may secure a respected spot in the community before seeking access to business charity drives. However, arts funds and some CHAs, because of the high-powered business people they attract to their boards, can start accessing corporate charity drives immediately. Therefore, one could organize an arts fund or CHA in communities with as few as 25,000 total employees, regardless of the number of government workers.

In smaller communities, rather than attempting to launch a federation that will solicit contributions only in the workplace, payroll deductions should be considered in conjunction with other fundraising activities such as canvassing or special events using a federation approach. Yes, usually individual charities feel competitive when doing these kinds of fundraising. But since federated workplace fundraising is usually most successful when organizations cooperate closely, this tends to encourage additional kinds of collective fundraising.

Once groups decide to form an alternative fund, they must identify a solid core of seven or more individuals to function as a sponsoring committee, representing up to fifteen organizations. Each of these people would have to routinely spend ten hours per month in organizing the new fund. Seed money has to be found to hire part-time staff. Free office space, a telephone, and postage have to be secured. A minimum of $4,000 to $30,000 will be required for the first year, depending on the extent of in-kind resources, staff salary requirements, and the local standard of living. Also essential is a spiritual leader—someone who has the vision, who will attend every meeting, rally the troops, and coordinate with outside groups.

These challenges are formidable enough. Yet the one factor that makes organizing an alternative fund even tougher than organizing any new organization is that most funds are federations of charities. Therefore, rather than simply raising money and hiring staff as one would do to put together a normal nonprofit organization, one has to do all that while also persuading already existing organizations to define a common goal and to work together to achieve it. This is like organizing a campaign to change public policy, or sometimes like organizing an election campaign for public office.

Of course, for some organizations this coalition building is a routine fact of life. For them organizing a new alternative fund would be simply another variation of what they have already done. But for others, coalition building—getting people with diverse skills and diverse-size egos working in harness—is a genuine challenge.

If this challenge is appealing, refer to Appendix III, where you will find a list of resource persons who can give you some good ideas on how to get started.

REFERENCES

U.S. Office of Personnel Management. *Combined Federal Campaign: Historical Statistics.* Washington, D.C.: U.S. Government Printing Office, 1988.

Cook, Richard V.; Steketee, Nancy L.; and Wenocur, Stanley. *United Way Donor Option Programs: Opportunity or Diversion for Non-Member Organizations?* Washington, D.C.: National Committee for Responsive Philanthropy, 1981.

Cook, Richard V. *Study of United Way Donor Option Programs.* Washington, D.C.: National Committee for Responsive Philanthropy, 1986.

Fulham, Erin. *State Employee Charitable Campaigns: Who Participates and How?* 2d ed., rev. Washington, D.C.: National Committee for Responsive Philanthropy, 1986.

Hodson, J. Dawn. "United Ways: Have You Considered Joining?" *The Grantsmanship Center News.* Los Angeles: 1982.

National Committee for Responsive Philanthropy. *Charity Begins at Work.* Washington, D.C.: 1986.

———. *An Inside Look at United Ways and Foundations.* Washington, D.C.: 1986.

———. *The Workplace Giving Revolution.* Washington, D.C.: 1987.

———. *Alternative Fund Statistics 1986.* Washington, D.C.: 1988.

Sumariwalla, Russy D. "Donor Option: Some Thoughts on Future Modeling." Alexandria: United Way of America, March 14, 1983. Unpublished.
United Way of America Public Information Office, 701 North Fairfax Street, Alexandria, Virginia 22314-2045.

9

Chapter Nine
Manna from Earth?
Earned Income for Nonprofits
By Jon Pratt*

In the wake of the 1981 budget cuts, two pieces of dubious wisdom entered the nonprofit world. The first was that nonprofits, churches, and volunteers could take on the social needs of the poor abandoned by the Reagan administration. When nonprofits pointed out that the cuts affected them, too, and that $2 billion in foundation grantmaking couldn't make up for $200 billion in federal cutbacks, they went searching for their own cash cows. Hey, this is the decade of the entrepreneur. Why not just go out and start a business enterprise and use the profits to support your charitable work?

The Search for Cash Cows
Enough foundation program officers and consultants dropped broad hints like "Have you ever thought of starting a business?" that the nonprofit watchwords of the early 1980s became regenerative funding, self-sufficiency, for-profit subsidiaries, and entrepreneurship. Grants and financing became available for new enterprises, and at conferences and in the media, earned income was held up to all as the wave of the future.

As it turns out, the idea of nonprofits starting businesses irks some people. The White House Conference on Small Business in 1985 cited unfair competition from nonprofits as the number three problem facing business—just ahead of the $2 trillion federal deficit. Nonprofits, they complained, could afford to undercut their prices for comparable goods and services because these groups receive tax deductible contributions and are exempt from paying taxes on income substantially related to their charitable programs. Congressional hearings on the extent of income earned by nonprofits and specifically unrelated business income in June 1987 prodded the IRS to schedule 3000 tax compliance audits of nonprofits to evaluate enforcement of the federal Unrelated Business Income Tax (UBIT). The House of Representatives' Ways and Means Committee

---

*Jon Pratt is an attorney and executive director of the Minnesota Council on Nonprofits in St. Paul, Minnesota.

is expected to issue its report in spring 1988, and legislation will probably be introduced shortly thereafter.[1]

Despite the attention and small business fears, nonprofit ownership of fast food franchises, dry cleaning establishments and the like—providing big monthly income with little time investment by the nonprofit— is a myth. The reality is that nonprofits are most frequently, and most successfully, selling what they already have and know well to the people they already serve.

What Is Earned Income? Pitfalls and Payoffs

Earned income includes fees, charges, and dues paid directly by clients, members, or others in exchange for some kind of product or service. In its most familiar forms, it is fees charged for services provided by a counseling agency, tuition required by a private school, tickets sold to those who attend performances by nonprofit dance and theater companies. Less obvious, however, is the university that licenses for commercial use a new laser technology developed in its teaching laboratories, the think tank that sells what would otherwise be downtime on its main frame computer, or the advocacy organization that licenses the use of its logo for umbrellas, tote bags, playing cards, or calendars. Earned income in this sense does not comprise fundraising methods that include purchases, such as raffles, auctions, or dinners, though many of the same considerations apply. It is a long-term resource—not a quick fix for the $15,000 cash flow crisis—which if successful enables nonprofit organizations to gain a measure of independence from their other major sources of income, namely private giving (from individuals, corporations, foundations, churches, or federated fund drives), government, and interest.

Earned income is desirable because it gives the organization a great deal of latitude in how the funds are spent. It builds skills, can get clients involved in the "marketplace," and offers a long-term supply of income limited only by the market size not by funder cash or time constraints. Earned income activities under community control are an exercise in self-determination, and can more effectively promote initiative and creativity than traditional services. They also place greater control and responsibility in the organization, and can be approached and designed to

---

[1]In March 1988, a wide range of proposals were being discussed from revising IRS Form 990 to make it more clear to nonprofits under what circumstances they are required to complete IRS Form 990-T reporting their unrelated business income, to new penalties on nonprofits and their managers for failing to report completely such income and pay the taxes due, to a wholesale restructuring of the definition of unrelated business income.

achieve the collateral benefits of strengthening resolve and increasing community autonomy.

Research conducted by the Urban Institute's Nonprofit Sector Project in twelve American cities found that sixty-nine percent of nonprofits receive at least some earned income, amounting to thirty percent of nonprofit income overall. The remainder of nonprofit revenue is from government (38 percent), private giving (21 percent), interest (five percent), and other (six percent).[2]

This research also showed low reliance on service fees among organizations that primarily serve the poor (eight percent) or Blacks (five percent).[3] This is explained by the fact that unless these organizations go outside the income group they were formed to serve, affordability places a limit on what they can charge. Nonetheless, nonprofits would be making a mistake to rule out charging appropriate service fees, scaled to income level. At times a well-meant flexibility on fee collection intended to communicate concern for clients translates into a weak, unenforced policy that in the long run harms the organization. A better route would be to establish clearly from the beginning what is to be charged, and then follow through.

The crucial issue about earned income from the perspective of guarding one's tax-exempt status with the IRS is whether or not the income-generating activity is "substantially related" to the exempt purpose of the

Figure 1. Income from Service Fees by Type of Organization (in percent)

Type of Organization	Percent
Employment/housing/legal services/advocacy	9
Social services	12
Multiservice	27
Culture/arts/recreation	34
Health/mental health/institutional care	44
Education/schools/colleges/research	45

SOURCE: The Urban Institute, 1987

[2]Barbara Lukerman, Lester M. Salamon, eds., *The Twin Cities Nonprofit Sector in a Time of Government Retrenchment* (Washington, D.C.: Urban Institute Press, 1984).
[3]Lester M. Salamon, *Twin Cities Nonprofit Organizations: The Challenge of Retrenchment* (Washington, D.C.: Urban Institute Press, 1987).

nonprofit organization. It does not matter how the money would be spent—the question is how the money was made.

A nonprofit corporation is obligated to pay UBIT if the trade or business is regularly carried on and not substantially related to its exempt purpose. If an organization has gross income of $1,000 or more from an unrelated trade or business, the income is required to be reported to the IRS on Form 990-T. The UBIT tax rate for nonprofit taxable income (gross income less allowable deductions) is the same as the rate levied on for-profit business corporations: 15 percent of the first $50,000; 25 percent on the next $25,000; and 34 percent on any amount over $75,000. Similarly, as a result of the Tax Reform Act of 1986, tax-exempt organizations—just like their for-profit counterparts—are required to estimate their corporate profits and make quarterly estimated tax payments.

An added danger for nonprofits is that excessive unrelated business income (no fixed ration but variously cited as more than 20 percent or 33 percent of gross revenue) could result in loss of the organization's overall tax-exempt status. Although 501(c)(3) tax-exempt status is granted to groups "operated exclusively" for exempt purposes, the test applied to earned income activities obviously is not one of strict exclusivity. Rather, a tax-exempt organization risks losing its status when the IRS considers its unrelated business activities substantial enough to overshadow its charitable activities.

The test of the "relatedness" of the income-producing activity, is whether it "contributes importantly" to the accomplishment of the organization's exempt purpose. Among the factors the IRS will consider are: (1) whether the articles and bylaws contain clear references demonstrating how the income-earning activity in question is related to the organization's charitable mission, and (2) whether the organization is operating its business in a manner that is substantially related to its exempt purposes.[4] Accordingly, the activity that earns the income (the sale of goods or services) should be mentioned in an organization's governing documents as part of the way it will achieve its charitable goals (improving health care, creating jobs, etc.)

In addition, to be considered related, the manner of operation should achieve an exempt purpose, such as by including free or reduced-cost service to low income persons, or providing employment for people with limited skills, or providing leadership development along with recreation.

---

[4]Edward Skloot, "Enterprise and Commerce in Nonprofit Organizations," in *The Nonprofit Sector,* ed. Walter W. Powell, (New Haven: Yale University Press, 1987), p. 390.

(For more information about the relationship between the legal require-ments for maintaining tax-exempt status and earned income, *see* Chapter 2, "Tax-Exempt Status for Your Organization" by David B. Hopkins and Jill R. Shellow.)

Most nonprofit earned income passes the relatedness test, including nonprofit hospital charges, advocacy group research report sales, Sesame Street product licensing, art museum sales of reproductions, thrift shop sales of donated merchandise, Planned Parenthood condom sales, and Girl Scout cookie sales (young people learn responsibility and spread the Scout mission). Since the conduct of the activity determines whether it is related, an imprecise definition, organizations with substantial earned income should consult an attorney or an accountant familiar with this area.

One strategy for avoiding UBIT is to form a for-profit subsidiary to run an unrelated business activity. This has the added benefits of achieving a separation of disparate activities, sheltering the parent organization's assets against the liabilities of the business, and easing the transfer of ownership.

Although the for-profit subsidiary would be subject to the corporate income taxes, like any other business it can use operating loss carryovers to offset taxable profits, thereby reducing the amount of profit otherwise subject to taxation. Net operating losses of the for-profit subsidiary can be carried back three years and forward five years. As a result, many subsidiaries of this kind have little or no tax liabilities yet are still able to make substantial contributions to the parent organization. The dis-advantages of subsidiaries include the nature and extent of control the nonprofit parent may be able to exercise over a formally separate or-ganization, extra personnel and overhead costs, increased difficulty in achieving community participation, and the administrative burdens of creating and liquidating subsidiaries.[5] Again, legal and tax advice is a must.

In addition to the tax advantage of substantially related activities, they are also the most practical. Experience has shown that earned income activities are most likely to succeed when they are based on the expe-rience base and market of the organization—what the organization is already doing.

Getting into the market does have its hazards. The high rate of failure of small businesses managed by people with business backgrounds is often cited as a reason for nonprofits not to venture into business. En-

---

[5]*A Lawyers Manual on Community Based Economic Development,* (Berkeley: National Economic Development and Law Center, 1978), pp. 589–601.

terprise development also requires investments of time, talent, and money that nonprofits may not have to spare. If the business activity is unrelated, board and staff time may be diverted from the core of the organization. On the other hand, when an organization building on its capabilities starts with a properly defined and executed business strategy, the results may not only bring earned income but can enhance service related to the nonprofit's mission. Since a third of nonprofit income is earned, those organizations must be doing something right.

The goal of nonprofit enterprise should be service maximization and community empowerment as opposed to the maximization of private profit in business. The question is how to structure the enterprise to maximize service in support of its mission and make it accountable to the community. If money is going to be lost, it should not exceed what was planned for and thus expected.

Considerations in Developing Earned Income Opportunities

Developing earned income plans calls for a methodical approach to information gathering, evaluation, and decision-making. The task lends itself to making lists and step-by-step planning.

Several excellent resources offer in-depth treatment of this process, including Peter C. Brown's book noted at the end of this chapter. The following is a basic set of considerations involved in developing an earned income project.

Internal Organizational Assessment

What resources does the organization have to apply to an enterprise (staff time and expertise, board time and contacts, organizational reputation, membership, volunteers, cash, credit, information unique to the organization, flexibility, community contact, market research ability, etc.)? What goods or services the organization now produces could be sold in the market? What activities would be appropriate for the organization? What impact would the enterprise have on the rest of the organization?

Market Assessment

Is there a market similar to the organization's clientele that would pay for the organization's goods or services? What opportunities exist for goods or services similar to those produced by the organization? What other goods or services are needed by the current clientele of the organization? Who else provides the same or similar goods or services? How good are they? Are they making money? Is there room in the market for a new entrant? Is assistance available to help the organization? Is the proposed product or service feasible? What is the future of the market? What are the negative repercussions of going ahead with the enterprise? What are the benefits to the community?

Establish Criteria for Possible Earned Income Ventures

Among the goods and services within the capability and expertise of the organization, is there anything the organization would not do for money? Is there a limit to how much staff time or money would be invested? What are the dollar goals for income? What type of impact on the organization would be unacceptable?

A serious risk is that the pursuit of earned income can divert an organization's time, energy, and attention to paying clients, thereby deflecting it from its original mission. Ideally, clients who can afford a service should pay for it; clients who can pay part should pay part; and clients who cannot pay should still be served. The danger is that nonprofits will become resource-directed, oriented to the source of their income rather than to their mission. It is the difference between asking "What can we get money to do?" and "What is it we want to do?" This pitfall can be avoided by maintaining an ongoing planning process, regularly asking how programs relate to the mission.

Develop the Business Plan

Most decisions about earned income, like instituting service fees or charging for a publication, are fairly simple and do not require a full-blown business plan. In these cases a brief written review of the financial and programmatic implications is usually sufficient for decision-making and evaluation by staff and board members. However, if more complex ventures are contemplated, the formulation of a business plan is a must. A formal business plan is intended as both an internal document that serves as guide and timeline for future actions and as an external document to convince others to invest the resources necessary to launch the enterprise.

That should sound familiar to anyone who has ever written a foundation proposal, and the similarities don't end there. A business concept is like a program description; market analysis is analogous to a need or problem statement; ownership and management equals staff and board description; and finances always come at the end. There are many ways to organize a business plan; the following is typical:

a.   **Business Concept**
     Define product or service
     Describe process of development

Determine materials/personnel needed
Determine availability of materials/personnel
Describe benefit to the community

b. **Market Analysis**
Cite evidence of need or demand
Describe structure of industry
Describe competition
Determine estimated sales potential
Determine the impact of price on demand
Determine unique features
Describe marketing strategy
Outline pricing and promotional approach
Give status of commitments or contracts to purchase

c. **Ownership and Management**
Describe form of organization
Give status of organization
List names of owners
Describe impact on parent organization
List names of investors (if not active in management)
Describe tax and legal consequences
Describe background and experience of principals
Describe other earned income activities of organization
Describe management structure
Give job descriptions and describe hiring plan
Outline training plan

d. **Financing**
Describe current financial status
Outline capital budget, including equipment
Outline operating costs, including labor, materials,
    administration, sales, space, utilities.
Give projections of revenues, costs, and income
Describe sources and uses of funds
Determine capital structure (investor payouts, loan
    schedules)

e. **Implementation**
List activities needed
Give schedule, tasks, and responsibilities
Contingency plans

One caveat is that the value a nonprofit attributes to providing quality services may not be recognized in the marketplace. On the other hand, some nonprofits underprice their services out of misplaced modesty or a willingness to unnecessarily subsidize services offered to the public. A well-conceived pricing strategy is required for any business venture.

Obtain or Allocate Sufficient Resources for Enterprise Financing

Sufficient is the key word here—undercapitalization is a notorious cause of business failure. Assuming that income will be less than expected, and expenses more, how much will it take to launch and sustain the venture through the start-up period? Provisions should be made to retain earnings for long-term stability of an enterprise—don't assume that the flow of money will always be from the enterprise to the checking account.

While some investors in business enterprises may be traditional types (e.g., lending institutions), most are more likely to be nontraditional—alternative loan funds, foundations, members, and clients. Foundations displayed much of the early enthusiasm about money-making ventures for nonprofits both through grants and program-related investments (PRIs) in nonprofits and continue to be a valuable resource.[6] In some cases low-interest loans are available from nontraditional investors whose investment goals include paybacks of nonmonetary dividends, i.e., social benefit to a particular community.

Get Help

Nonprofits, with a tradition of autonomy and self-reliance, are often hesitant to get outside assistance and learn from the experience of others. Like many things, good information often comes with a bill. Reluctance to pay for intangible services can be a strategic error in an information economy.

Venturing into a new area can also create the opposite problem: the inability to perceive when sufficient information is at hand and a decision

---

[6]PRIs are a form of investment for foundations, but they count toward the foundation's five percent payout requirement. They are called "program-related" because generally they relate directly to the same charitable purposes for which the foundation awards grants from its interest and investment income.

Several of the foundations described in Chapters 10 and 11 make PRIs and have developed specific guidelines for such investments which they will make available upon request. Often the first place a nonprofit approaches for financing an earned income plan is the same foundation with which it has developed a solid grantor-grantee relationship over the years, regardless of whether that foundation has ever before made a program-related investment.

ready to be made. Here again outside advice can help. It is worth the time and money to invest in information-gathering and consultation.

Sources of help include forming a board of advisers for the enterprise, meeting businesses engaged in similar ventures, and retaining professionals in the field—an attorney, an accountant, and a market consultant with sensitivity to nonprofit organizations.[7] Perhaps most useful is talking with other nonprofits that have been down the same road. There is a valuable body of knowledge based on the expansion of nonprofit earned income and the school of failed enterprises waiting to be tapped.

Conclusion

The long-term trend for nonprofit income has been increased reliance on earned income and decreased reliance on charitable contributions. The result has been more money for programs, but the resulting visibility has made nonprofits the nail that sticks up. Attacks on nonprofit tax exemptions will likely increase, and greater effort will be made to tax income from fees and services. In the long run it is in the nonprofit sector's interest to relate clearly earned income to charitable purposes, and to communicate to the public and public officials the role of earned income in serving the public mission.

REFERENCES

Brown, Peter C. *The Complete Guide to Money-Making Ventures for Nonprofit Organizations.* Washington, D.C.: The Taft Group, 1986. (Available from The Taft Group, 5130 MacArthur Boulevard, N.W., Washington, D.C. 20016.)

IRS Publication 598 (revised), *Tax on Unrelated Business Income of Exempt Organizations,* updated to include an explanation of changes in the law as a result of the Tax Reform Act of 1986. (Available free by telephoning 1-800-424-FORM.)

[7]One resource for nonprofit enterprise and business incubation consulting with extensive experience in low-income communities is Pryde, Roberts and Company, 1275 K Street N.W., Suite 501, Washington, D.C. 20005, (202) 371-6688; regional offices in California and Minnesota.

10
Chapter Ten
National Grantmakers

Overview

This chapter contains descriptions of 102 grantmaking organizations, 26 of which were not included in the last edition of *The Grant Seekers Guide* published in 1985. While they differ from one another in significant respects, the common denominator is that over the last several years all have made grants to support national or community-based efforts to promote social and economic justice. The similarities, however, stop here.

This chapter describes: 65 private foundations, 17 public charities (which raise money and in turn use those funds to make grants to other organizations), 16 corporate giving programs, three religious grantmakers, and the philanthropic interests of one individual. Their priorities range from preventing nuclear war to promoting economic development and new jobs and protecting civil rights and civil liberties. For some, grants to support social and economic justice activities are their exclusive focus. For others, such grants are a small part of a grantmaking program directed primarily toward traditional charitable institutions. Descriptions of the latter emphasize the program priorities, budget allocations, and application procedures that pertain most applicable to proposals for social and economic justice projects. It is not uncommon for what might be characterized as a "traditional funder," with a national focus, to support social and economic justice work in the local community in which it is located, or in which (for corporate grantmakers) it has substantial business interests.

The tables that follow list the grantmakers described in this chapter by their assets,[1] the amount of support and revenue received (for those that are not endowed)[2], and total grantmaking activity[3]. Statisticians would

---

[1] The assets are stated at fair market value and are the most recent data available. Consult the individual entries for footnotes which may contain additional explanatory information.

[2] Support and revenue includes contributions and other revenue, such as interest, received by the funder during the period of time indicated. Consult the individual entries for footnotes which may provide additional information.

[3] Several adjustments have been made to the figures provided by the funders indicating their total grantmaking activity, in an effort to arrive at the most realistic indicator of the funders' annual grants budget. For example, employee matching gifts and money earmarked for specific organizations by the donor or trustees, and thus not available to other organizations, are routinely excluded. While most figures are based on grants paid, some are based on grants approved or authorized. Please consult the individual description of the grantmakers, especially the footnotes, for specific exclusions and other information more fully explaining these figures.

point out that because these data cover different years (most are from 1987, but several are based on 1986 and a few are based on 1985) and sometimes, in the case of grantmaking activity, cover some period greater or less than one year, strictly speaking they are not comparable. Nonetheless, they illustrate the relative financial resources each one brings to the support of charitable activities, including social and economic justice projects.

Grantmakers Arranged by Assets

NAME	LOCATION	ASSETS	YEAR
Ford Foundation	New York, NY	$5,500,000,000	1987
MacArthur Foundation, The	Chicago, IL	2,271,057,000	1986
Kresge Foundation, The	Troy, MI	1,047,073,511	1986
Carnegie Corporation of New York	New York, NY	807,142,249	1987
Johnson Foundation, The	Princeton, NJ	804,599,529	1986
Mott Foundation, The	Flint, MI	736,873,249	1986
Gannett Foundation	Rochester, NY	577,757,400	1986
Hewlett Foundation, The	Menlo Park, CA	565,201,000	1987
Clark Foundation, The	New York, NY	384,509,000	1987
Kaiser Family Foundation, The	Menlo Park, CA	359,265,215	1986
Rockefeller Brothers Fund, Inc.	New York, NY	220,733,767	1986
Public Welfare Foundation	Washington, DC	198,808,000	1986
AT&T Foundation	New York, NY	165,300,000	1987
Jones Foundation, Inc., The	Charlottesville, VA	159,232,806	1987
Prudential Foundation, The	Newark, NJ	117,410,000	1986
Revson Foundation	New York, NY	78,501,928	1985
Markle Foundation, The	New York, NY	72,548,034	1986
Noyes Foundation, Inc.	New York, NY	60,963,723	1986
Kendall Foundation, The	Boston, MA	53,994,039	1985
Schumann Foundation, The	Montclair, NJ	51,652,873	1986
Donner Foundation, Inc., The	New York, NY	42,337,185	1985
Scherman Foundation, The	New York, NY	36,391,869	1986
Compton Foundation, Inc.	New York, NY	33,815,812	1985
HKH Foundation	New York, NY	28,458,581	1986
Mertz-Gilmore Foundation	New York, NY	28,410,268	1986
Rockefeller Family Fund	New York, NY	27,749,266	1986
New World Foundation, The	New York, NY	26,246,075	1986
MacArthur Foundation	Niles Chicago, IL	26,000,000	1988
McIntosh Foundation, The	West Palm Beach, FL	21,024,662	1986
Norman Foundation, Inc.	New York, NY	20,733,984	1987
Bingham Foundation, The	Cleveland, OH	20,355,000	1986
Arca Foundation, The	Washington, DC	19,912,864	1986
Levi Strauss Foundation	San Francisco, CA	19,834,894	1987
New-Land Foundation, The	New York, Ny	17,717,464	1986

Grantmakers Arranged by Assets *(cont.)*

NAME	LOCATION	ASSETS	YEAR
Villers Foundation, The	Washington, DC	16,807,708	1987
Town Creek Foundation	Oxford, MD	16,710,000	1986
General Mills Foundation	Minneapolis, MN	16,530,422	1986
General Service Foundation	Boulder, CO	15,824,387	1986
Ittleson Foundation, Inc.	New York, NY	15,668,006	1986
Huber Foundation, The	Rumson, NJ	15,270,178	1986
Hitachi Foundation	Washington, DC	14,958,518	1987
Skaggs Foundation, The	Oakland, CA	14,247,504	1986
Mailman Family Foundation	White Plains, NY	14,097,547	1986
Sunnen Foundation	St. Louis, MO	13,941,313	1987
Sunflower Foundation	New York, NY	13,000,000	1984
Burden Foundation	New York, NY	12,474,470	1986
Rubin Foundation	New York, NY	11,640,900	1987
Reed Foundation, The	New York, NY	11,620,332	1985
Benton Foundation, The	Washington, DC	11,279,000	1987
Aetna Life and Casualty Foundation, Inc.	Hartford, CT	10,448,029	1986
Harder Foundation	East Detroit, MI	8,974,026	1987
Cummins Engine Foundation	Columbus, IN	8,904,603	1986
Hazen Foundation, The	New York, NY	8,783,770	1986
Bydale Foundation, The	New York, NY	8,526,257	1985
South Branch Foundation, The	Somerville, NJ	8,045,058	1986
American Foundation for AIDS Research	New York, NY	6,112,267	1987
Needmor Fund, The	Boulder, CO	5,400,000	1986
Levinson Foundation, The	Sante Fe, NM	4,946,000	1986
Deer Creek Foundation	St. Louis, MO	4,904,037	1986
Penney Foundation	New York, NY	4,341,963	1987
ARCO Foundation	Los Angeles, CA	3,233,232	1987
Ottinger Foundation	Washington, DC	3,057,670	1986
Best Products Foundation	Washington, DC	3,000,000	1986
Edwards Foundation, The	South Londonderry, VT	2,694,113	1987
Winston Foundation for World Peace, The	Boston, MA	2,683,278	1987
Boehm Foundation, The	New York, NY	2,476,510	1986
CarEth Foundation, The	Cambridge, MA	1,853,575	1986
Ploughshares Fund	San Francisco, CA	1,803,183	1986
New York Times Company Foundation, Inc., The	New York, NY	1,696,762	1986
Crowe Foundation	Washington, DC	1,677,597	1986
Eastman Fund, Inc.	Los Gatos, CA	1,050,000	1987
Muste Memorial Institute	New York, NY	213,313	1986
Chicago Resource Center	Chicago, IL	141,383	1986

Grantmakers Arranged by Support and Revenue

NAME	LOCATION	SUPPORT AND REVENUE	YEAR
Campaign for Human Development	Washington, DC	$9,175,000	1987
Tides Foundation, The	San Francisco, CA	8,708,400	1987
Funding Exchange/National Community Funds, The	New York, NY	5,423,029	1987
Youth Project, The	Washington, DC	4,748,997	1987
Mott Fund	Flint, MI	2,840,130	1985
Ms. Foundation for Women, Inc.	New York, NY	1,947,458	1986
Forum Institute, The	Washington, DC	1,827,593	1987
C.S. Fund	Freestone, CA	1,229,221	1986
Threshold Foundation	San Francisco, CA	1,168,239	1986
Peace Development Fund	Amherst, MA	1,162,605	1987
Design Industries Foundation for AIDS	New York, NY	1,149,722	1987
Seventh Generation Fund for Indian Development	Lee, NV	837,296	1987
Jewish Fund for Justice	Washington, DC	497,281	1987
Windom Fund, The	Washington, DC	340,000	1987
Ark Foundation, The	Lafayette, CA	255,429	1986
Topsfield Foundation, Inc.	Pomfret, CT	211,991	1986

Grantseekers Arranged by Grants Paid or Grants Approved

NAME	LOCATION	GRANTS PAID OR APPROVED	YEAR
Ford Foundation	New York, NY	$204,300,000	1987
MacArthur Foundation, The	Chicago, IL	120,931,635	1986
Johnson Foundation, The	Princeton, NJ	94,605,533	1986
Kresge Foundation, The	Troy, MI	42,480,000	1986
Carnegie Corporation of New York	New York, NY	32,815,589	1987
AT&T Foundation	New York, NY	25,910,276	1987
Mott Foundation, The	Flint, MI	21,663,260	1986
Gannett Foundation	Rochester, NY	19,051,296	1986
Clark Foundation, The	New York, NY	16,096,302	1987
Revson Foundation	New York, NY	13,549,000	1986
Jones Foundation, Inc., The	Charlottesville, VA	11,272,738	1987
ARCO Foundation	Los Angeles, CA	10,322,525	1986
Dayton Hudson Foundation	Minneapolis, MN	10,132,325	1986
Aetna Life and Casualty Foundation, Inc.	Hartford, CT	10,000,000	1986
Hewlett Foundation, The	Menlo Park, CA	9,230,658	1987
Kaiser Family Foundation, The	Menlo Park, CA	8,440,345	1986
Public Welfare Foundation	Washington, DC	7,427,500	1986
Pillsbury Company Foundation, The	Minneapolis, MN	6,906,164	1987
Rockefeller Brothers Fund, Inc.	New York, NY	6,820,024	1986

Grantseekers Arranged by Grants Paid or Grants Approved *(cont.)*

NAME	LOCATION	GRANTS PAID OR APPROVED	YEAR
Campaign for Human Development	Washington, DC	6,494,000	1987
General Mills Foundation	Minneapolis, MN	5,584,212	1986
Prudential Foundation, The	Newark, NJ	5,125,830	1986
Apple Computer, Inc.	Cupertino, CA	4,700,000	1987
Markle Foundation, The	New York, NY	4,536,137	1986
Veatch Program	Plandome, NY	4,517,014	1987
American Foundation for AIDS Research	New York, NY	4,508,379	1987
New York Times Company Foundation, Inc., The	New York, NY	4,300,494	1986
Youth Project, The	Washington, DC	3,973,028	1987
Noyes Foundation, Inc.	New York, NY	3,773,946	1986
Cummins Engine Foundation	Columbus, IN	3,365,626	1986
Schumann Foundation, The	Montclair, NJ	3,157,685	1986
Mertz-Gilmore Foundation	New York, NY	3,130,341	1987
Funding Exchange/National Community Funds, The	New York, NY	2,822,307	1987
Skaggs Foundation, The	Oakland, CA	2,504,600	1987
Scherman Foundation, The	New York, NY	2,497,200	1986
Villers Foundation, The	Washington, DC	2,422,888	1987
Levi Strauss Foundation	San Francisco, CA	2,248,463	1987
Kendall Foundation, The	Boston, MA	2,207,110	1985
Tides Foundation, The	San Francisco, CA	2,175,200	1987
Compton Foundation, Inc.	New York, NY	2,165,756	1986
Reed Foundation, The	New York, NY	2,107,400	1985
Joint Foundation Support, Inc.	New York, NY	2,010,777	1986
MacArthur Foundation	Niles Chicago, IL	2,000,000	1988
Donner Foundation, Inc., The	New York, NY	1,771,907	1985
Rockefeller Family Fund	New York, NY	1,623,000	1986
New World Foundation, The	New York, NY	1,575,000	1986
New-Land Foundation, The	New York, NY	1,502,062	1986
Mott Fund	Flint, MI	1,446,278	1987
Avon Products Foundation, Inc.	New York, NY	1,312,145	1985
Hitachi Foundation	Washington, DC	1,288,628	1987
Sunnen Foundation	St. Louis, MO	1,276,000	1987
Chicago Resource Center	Chicago, IL	1,246,580	1987
Beldon Fund, The	Washington, DC	1,231,773	1987
HKH Foundation	New York, NY	1,196,500	1986
Town Creek Foundation	Oxford, MD	1,165,500	1986
General Services Foundation	Boulder, CO	1,161,500	1986
Needmor Fund, The	Boulder, CO	1,082,474	1986
Ploughshares Fund	San Francisco, CA	996,793	1987
Best Products Foundation	Washington, DC	939,760	1986
C.S. Fund	Freestone, CA	939,500	1987
Forum Institute, The	Washington, DC	935,217	1987

Grantseekers Arranged by Grants Paid or Grants Approved *(cont.)*

NAME	LOCATION	GRANTS PAID OR APPROVED	YEAR
Huber Foundation, The	Rumson, NJ	920,800	1986
Ittleson Foundation, Inc.	New York, NY	917,784	1987
Rubin Foundation	New York, NY	854,541	1987
Bingham Foundation, The	Cleveland, OH	816,127	1986
Bydale Foundation, The	New York, NY	755,164	1985
Winston Foundation for World Peace, The	Boston, MA	745,636	1987
Threshold Foundation	San Francisco, CA	720,329	1986
Norman Foundation, Inc.	New York, NY	663,450	1987
McIntosh Foundation, The	West Palm Beach, FL	634,800	1986
Stern Family Fund, The	Washington, DC	623,715	1987
Arca Foundation, The	Washington, DC	618,333	1986
Burden Foundation	New York, NY	602,895	1986
Mailman Family Foundation	White Plains, NY	556,096	1986
South Branch Foundation, The	Somerville, NJ	548,000	1987
Harder Foundation	East Detroit, MI	528,788	1987
Benton Foundation, The	Washington, DC	526,857	1987
Sunflower Foundation	New York, NY	500,000	1987
Streisand Foundation, The	Washington, DC	465,000	1987
Hazen Foundation, The	New York, NY	451,374	1986
Boehm Foundation, The	New York, NY	403,165	1986
Penney Foundation	New York, NY	385,991	1987
Ms. Foundation for Women, Inc.	New York, NY	345,400	1986
Levinson Foundation, The	Santa Fe, NM	333,672	1987
Mott Charitable Trust	Washington, DC	330,575	1986
Windom Fund, The	Washington, DC	260,500	1987
Peace Development Fund	Amherst, MA	239,570	1987
Deer Creek Foundation	St. Louis, MO	234,260	1986
Design Industries Foundation for AIDS	New York, NY	226,582	1987
Ottinger Foundation	Washington, DC	221,000	1986
Ark Foundation, The	Lafayette, CA	216,549	1986
Topsfield Foundation, Inc.	Pomfret, CT	159,850	1986
Pacific Peace Fund	Seattle, WA	149,472	1987
Edwards Foundation, The	South Londonderry, VT	134,837	1987
Jewish Fund for Justice	Washington, DC	123,374	1987
Seventh Generation Fund for Indian Development	Lee, NV	109,590	1987
CarEth Foundation, The	Cambridge, MA	100,750	1986
Playboy Foundation	Chicago, IL	100,000	1988
Crowe Foundation	Washington, DC	89,000	1986
Eastman Fund, Inc.	Los Gatos, CA	55,650	1987
Muste Memorial Institute	New York, NY	41,800	1987

ARCO Foundation
515 South Flower Street, Room 40107
Los Angeles, California 90071
(213) 486-3342

Contact Person
Eugene R. Wilson, President

Purpose
The ARCO Foundation concentrates its grantmaking in selected geographic areas where its sponsor, ARCO, has major operations. The foundation gives preference to organizations that deliver programs or services of regional or national impact. For organizations providing more localized services, preference is given to programs serving Dallas, Denver, Los Angeles, and Anchorage, and their immediate metropolitan areas.

Areas of Interest
Generally, the foundation's grantmaking can be divided into the following categories: (1) institutions of higher education, precollegiate programs aimed at improving the quality of urban public education (but not specific schools or school districts), and a few education-related organizations; (2) programs in the humanities and arts; (3) nonprofit community service organizations; (4) environmental programs; (5) programs in elementary and secondary education that focus on high-risk youth; and (6) United Funds. For purposes of this publication, the foundation's support for community programs, environmental programs, and public policy are highlighted.

Support for community programs is directed toward organizations whose activities and programs improve the economic and social well-being of people and communities. Grants are awarded primarily to social welfare organizations whose focus includes community economic development, ethnic minorities, women, youth, and older Americans. In particular, the foundation helps organizations that emphasize job creation, training, and placement and leadership development as well as those that provide managerial and technical assistance to other local groups.

The foundation supports selected environmental research organizations as well as national land preservation, wildlife conservation, and environmental protection programs that strike a balance between the nation's needs and its diminishing natural resources. The foundation has

ARCO Foundation

made grants to a few organizations and institutions for objective research on environmental matters. Support is also provided to national educational programs aimed at informing the public about environmental and natural resource issues.

In the public policy program, a few national and regional organizations studying and conducting action programs on issues raised by demographic, social, and economic shifts in the U.S. also receive support from the foundation. Grants support dissemination and implementation of new approaches to existing problems. The foundation is especially interested in organizations whose concerns include strengthening the private nonprofit sector; jobs and employment; self-fulfillment for older Americans through volunteer work and second careers; and improved participation by the underrepresented. Grants awarded in the public policy program may also include support for innovative or experimental programs that do not fall within other specific foundation categories.

Financial Data (year ended 12/31/86)
The foundation's assets on December 31, 1986, were valued at $52,261,523. However by December 31, 1987, they had fallen to $3,233,232. While a 1987 grants list was not available for analysis in time to be included, the following table reviews the foundation's 1986 national and regional grants. The data are broken down specifically to illustrate regional and programmatic funding patterns. For completeness, note grants of $1,000 and less are not itemized in the foundation's annual report and hence are not included. Moreover, approximately $1.0 million in grants made in the Philadelphia area is excluded because this region is no longer a priority of the foundation.

Application Procedures
The foundation operates on a calendar year. Requests for support may be submitted at any time. Proposals are accumulated by category and judged with similar requests on a periodic basis.

National organizations should write directly to the foundation's president. Local and regional organizations should contact the appropriate

ARCO Foundation
Analysis of 1986 Grantmaking Activity

	All Grants	Community Programs	Public Information	Environmental
NATIONAL PROGRAMS[1]				
Total Grants Paid	$4,296,748	$653,900	$291,000	$800,000
Number of Grants	212	47	36	17
Highest Grant	$52,500	$50,000	$50,000	$30,000
Lowest Grant	$1,500	$1,500	$1,500	$5,000
Median Grant Size	$10,000	$10,000	$5,000	$10,000
WESTERN GRANTMAKING PROGRAM[2]				
Total Grants Paid	$2,658,722	$974,322	$120,000	$236,500
Number of Grants	265	110	15	24
Highest Grant	$85,000	$65,000	$25,000	$35,000
Lowest Grant	$1,500	$1,500	$1,500	$2,000
Median Grant Size	$5,000	$5,000	$5,000	$5,000
SOUTHWESTERN GRANTMAKING PROGRAM[3]				
Total Grants Paid	$1,514,300	$689,300	$17,000	$73,000
Number of Grants	127	55	4	5
Highest Grant	$50,000	$45,000	$6,000	$25,000
Lowest Grant	$1,500	$1,500	$3,000	$3,000
Median Grant Size	$10,000	$5,000	$4,000	$15,000
ALASKA GRANTMAKING PROGRAM[4]				
Total Grants Paid	$513,775	$189,925	$6,000	$53,500
Number of Grants	55	31	1	2
Highest Grant	$40,000	$11,347	$5,000	$40,000
Lowest Grant	$1,500	$1,500	$5,000	$12,500
Median Grant Size	$5,000	$5,000	$5,000	$26,250
ROCKY MOUNTAIN GRANTMAKING PROGRAM				
Total Grants Paid	$298,500	$138,500	$19,000	$20,000
Number of Grants	35	19	3	1
Highest Grant	$20,000	$15,000	$10,000	$20,000
Lowest Grant	$2,000	$2,000	$4,000	$20,000
Median Grant Size	$5,000	$5,000	$5,000	$20,000

[1]In National Programs, the figure supplied for highest grant paid (all grants) excludes six unusually large grants of $100,000 and more totaling $1,259,098. The highest environmental grant in this program excludes one unusually large grant of $600,000.
[2]The highest grant in this program area excludes two unusually large grants of $100,000 and more totaling $250,000. Further, the highest environmental grant in this program excludes one unusually large grant of $54,750.
[3]The figure supplied for highest community program grant in the Southwestern Grantmaking Program excludes one unusually large grant of $45,000.
[4]In the Alaska Grantmaking Program, the figure supplied for highest community grant excludes one unusually large grant of $36,000.

ARCO Foundation

subsidiary for their area. The list of subsidiaries appears at the end of this entry.

Requests should be concise and in letter form, not more than two pages long. Elaborate and lengthy proposals will not be considered. The letter should describe the applicant organization and its purpose and explain how it meets the foundation's stated guidelines and priorities. It should also include a statement of need for the proposed project, a description of the methods chosen to meet the project goals, the amount of time needed to complete the project and milestones that will be used to measure its progress, the total cost of the project, other sources and levels of funding, the amount requested from the ARCO Foundation, and community support for and involvement in the project and organization.

In addition, a current budget showing income and expenses, the most recent audited financial statement, an annual report (if available), and a copy of the IRS letter designating the applicant as tax exempt should be included, along with the organization's most recently filed IRS Form 990 and a list of the organization's board of directors, including their organizational affiliations or occupations.

Grant Limitations

As stated above, preference is given to programs serving the cities of Dallas, Denver, Los Angeles, and Anchorage, and their immediate metropolitan areas. Local organizations located outside these regions are discouraged from making application. In addition, to qualify for a grant from the foundation, organizations must be designated by the Internal Revenue Service as nonprofit tax-exempt public charities.

The foundation does not consider grants to the following: programs with direct benefit to ARCO; individual applicants for support of their personal needs; religious activities or organizations; private grantmaking or operating foundations; specialized single-issue health organizations; fraternal organizations, including veteran and military organizations, or professional associations; political organizations or campaigns; endowments; benefit dinners, advertisements, and tables at fund-raising events; annual or automatic renewal grants; and multiyear pledges for any program.

ARCO Foundation

Meeting Times
The board of directors of the ARCO Foundation meets semiannually to review major funding requests. All other grant requests are reviewed monthly by the foundation officers.

Publications
The foundation publishes an annual report which is available on request.

Company Subsidiaries
Local and regional organizations must initiate their requests through representatives of the ARCO corporate office listed below:

Western Region and Los Angeles
Manager, Public Affairs
ARCO Western Region
515 South Flower Street
Los Angeles, CA 90071
(213) 486-8176

Rocky Mountain Region and Denver
Manager, Public Affairs
ARCO Coal Company
555 17th Street
Denver, CO 80202
(303) 293-4670

Central Region and Dallas
Manager, Public Affairs
ARCO Oil and Gas Company
1601 Bryan Street
Dallas, TX 75201
(214) 880-4945

ARCO Foundation

Alaska Region and Anchorage
Manager, Public Affairs
ARCO Alaska
Post Office Box 100360
Anchorage, AL 99510
(907) 265-6133

AT&T Foundation
550 Madison Avenue, Room 2700
New York, New York 10022
(212) 605-6734

Contact Persons
Reynold Levy, President
Edward Bligh, Executive Director
Sheila A. Connolly, Secretary

Purpose
The AT&T Foundation was created in 1984 as the principal instrument of corporate philanthropy of AT&T and its subsidiaries after the breakup of the Bell System. The foundation's staff and trustees look both within the company and outward at the nonprofit sector with the objective of identifying critical crossroads where business perspectives and philanthropic needs converge.

Two components of the company's philanthropy are highlighted in this summary: foundation grants for organizations of national and regional significance, and corporate contributions to local groups in communities where the company has a substantial business presence. Other company-sponsored activities include the provision of pro bono management assistance and loaned executives; in-kind contributions such as equipment and facilities space; and an employee matching-gift program.

In all areas, the foundation stresses its consistent commitment to the following goals: advancing the prospects of women and minorities more fully to realize their personal and professional potential; strengthening the capacity of public and nonprofit institutions to deliver high-quality services to citizens in need; helping to redress inequities rooted in socioeconomic, historic, geographic, racial, and sexual difference; supporting public and nonprofit leadership at the community, regional, and national levels; encouraging and reinforcing excellence where it is found and cultivating the promise of excellence where it is not; and assisting efforts to keep the U.S. competitive in a service and industrial economy increasingly characterized by foreign challenge and global interdependence.

Areas of Interest
Grants and contributions are made in the areas of higher education, health, social action, and arts and culture. Of particular note is the foundation's

AT&T Foundation

support for social action projects with national application and national institutions addressing socioeconomic problems.

In the social action area, projects of special interest are those that advance one or more of the following objectives: fostering the progress of equal opportunity throughout society for minorities and women, the physically and mentally disabled, and young people and the elderly; improving the quality of life in the U.S. by undertaking initiatives in community development, job training and employment, and conservation of energy and the environment; and enhancing the effectiveness of the not-for-profit and the public sectors. The foundation advises that projects should serve as models for other organizations and lend themselves to evaluation of results that can be disseminated to a wide audience. In addition, the foundation guidelines note that organizations engaged in the study of international trade, tax, and industrial competitiveness within and without the field of telecommunications may apply for project support.

Financial Data (year ended 12/31/87)

As of December 31, 1987, the assets of the foundation were approximately $165.3 million. National grants and local contributions highlighting support for social action organizations are presented below.

AT&T Foundation Grants and Contributions
Analysis of 1987 Payments

	AT&T Foundation	AT&T Local Contributions	Foundation Grants for Social Action
Total Grants Paid	$25,910,276[1]	$6,293,495	$2,385,000
Number of Grants	1,058	1,598	123
Highest Grant	$400,000	$50,000	$200,000
Lowest Grant	$1,000	$50	$1,000
Median Grant Size	$25,000	$4,000	$15,000

[1]This analysis excludes employee matching gifts to educational and cultural institutions totaling $4,397,974.

AT&T Foundation

Application Procedures

The foundation urges that applicants not telephone either the headquarters office in New York or the company's regional contributions coordinators with questions or to determine the foundation's interest in receiving a proposal.

Rather, applicants should address a brief letter of inquiry to the foundation. Nonprofit organizations in New York City, national organizations, and universities should address their inquiries to the foundation secretary at the address listed above. All other organizations should consult the list of regional contributions coordinators at the end of this entry, and direct their inquiries accordingly.

Letters of inquiry about potential support should be no longer than three pages but should include the following: a description of the organization and a statement relating its purpose to the general interests and specific priorities of the foundation, a summary of the purpose for which the grant is being sought and evidence of need for the activity, and an overall operating budget for the current fiscal year showing anticipated sources of revenue and expenses and (if project support is being sought) a detailed budget for the project.

The foundation encourages the participation of its employees in foundation decisions and often consults experts within the company about the state of a given cause or particular institution. Decisions on local contributions are made at the local community level, and proposals for projects of national and regional significance initiated at the local level are forwarded to the foundation after approval at the local level. Foundation grants in excess of $25,000 must be approved by the foundation's board of trustees.

Grant Limitations

The foundation does not award grants to individuals, buy advertisements, or donate equipment. Except in rare instances, it does not fund conferences or contribute to the creation of new organizations. Other excluded organizations and purposes are: organizations not classified as tax exempt under Section 501(c)(3) of the Internal Revenue Code; organizations that discriminate by race, color, creed, gender, or national origin; organ-

AT&T Foundation

izations whose chief purpose is to influence legislation; political organizations or campaigns; religious organizations that are denominational or sectarian in purpose; operating expenses or capital campaigns of local health and human service agencies other than hospitals; local chapters of national organizations; sports teams or athletic competitions; and banquets or other fundraising events.

It should be noted that within each of the foundation's specific areas of interest there are additional limitations. For more information consult the foundation's application guidelines.

Meeting Times
The board of trustees of the AT&T Foundation meets quarterly.

Publications
The foundation publishes an biennial report and a brochure describing its guidelines and application procedures.

Regional Contributions Coordinators
As indicated below, local organizations should initiate contact with the foundation by writing to the address indicated.

Organization Location	Foundation Contact
Alabama, Florida, Georgia, Kentucky, Louisiana, Mississipi, North Carolina, South Carolina, Tennessee	AT&T Contributions Coordinator Room 4036 1200 Peachtree Street, N.E. Atlanta, GA 30309
New England, New York, Pennsylvania, Delaware	AT&T Contributions Coordinator Room 2427 550 Madison Avenue New York, NY 10022
New Jersey	AT&T Contributions Coordinator Second Floor 188 Mount Airy Road Basking Ridge, NJ 07920

AT&T Foundation

Maryland, Virginia, Washington, D.C., West Virginia	AT&T Contributions Coordinator 2000 L Street, N.W., Suite 815 Washington, D.C. 20036
Illinois, Indiana, Iowa, Michigan, Minnesota, Nebraska, North Dakota, Ohio, South Dakota, Wisconsin	AT&T Contributions Coordinator Fourth Floor One North Wacker Drive Chicago, IL 60606
Arkansas, Kansas, Missouri, Oklahoma, Texas	AT&T Contributions Coordinator Suite 7100 5501 LBJ Freeway Dallas, TX 75240
Arizona, Colorado, Idaho, Montana, New Mexico, Utah, Wyoming	AT&T Contributions Coordinator Ninth Floor 7979 East Tufts Avenue Denver, CO 80237
Alaska, Northern California, Northern Nevada, Oregon, Washington	AT&T Contributions Coordinator Room 920 201 Third Street San Francisco, CA 94103
Southern California, Southern Nevada, Hawaii	AT&T Contributions Coordinator Suite 1250 611 West Sixth Street Los Angeles, CA 90017

Aetna Life and Casualty Foundation, Inc.
Aetna Life and Casualty Company
151 Farmington Avenue, A105
Hartford, Connecticut 06156
(203) 273-3340

Contact Persons
Sanford Cloud, Jr., Vice-President and Executive Director, Foundation
Glenda C. Reed, Assistant Vice-President, Corporate Public
   Involvement
Gail Promboin, Director, Corporate Public Involvement

Purpose
The public involvement programs of Aetna Life and Casualty Company
include grantmaking, employee involvement in public service organizations, contributions of in-kind services, and corporate investment in
community-based enterprises.

   The interests of the foundation and the corporation are parallel. With
a particular focus on Hartford, the purpose of Aetna's philanthropic programs is to help preserve a viable society in which to live, work, and do
business; to support those programs and organizations that will have a
real impact on solving social problems by advocating innovative solutions;
and to provide this support in a manner that will stimulate other donors.

Areas of Interest
The foundation's priorities are: (1) education and youth employment
with particular emphasis on the needs of minority and disadvantaged
youth; (2) urban revitalization, including programs that will improve
neighborhood residents' opportunities in the areas of housing, commercial enterprises, and jobs; (3) reform of the civil justice system through
support of programs that result in effective changes in the cost, efficiency,
and predictability of the system; and (4) leadership development, particularly programs that emphasize leadership to work effectively on the
foundation's priority issues in collaborative efforts among the public,
private, and nonprofit sectors. Of particular interest are programs that
enable women and minorities to develop the skills needed to assume
leadership roles in their communities.

   In addition to the national grants program, the foundation operates
an extensive local grants program through selected Aetna field offices.

Aetna Life and Casualty Foundation, Inc.

The FOCUS program, administered by field office general managers, makes grants in the interest areas listed above and in human services and the arts. In 1988 the FOCUS program operated in forty-two cities across the country. A complete list is available from the foundation.

Wholly separate and apart from the foundation, there is also the Corporate Responsibility Investment Committee (CRIC) comprising vice-presidents from Bond Investment, Common Stock, Real Estate Investment, Treasurers, Corporate Public Involvement, Law, Employee Benefits, and International divisions. Its purpose is to oversee corporate investments that strengthen community-based enterprises, increase economic development opportunities, leverage Aetna dollars, and provide leadership for new program development. Through CRIC Aetna made loans of over $80.2 million in 1987. These loans have placed particular emphasis upon urban revitalization projects and minority- and female-owned businesses.

Financial Data (year ended 12/31/86)
Assets of the Aetna Foundation total $10,448,029. The grand total of all contributions for the year is $6.9 million for the foundation and $3.1 million for the corporation (see the table on the next page).

Application Procedures
The first step in applying for a grant is for an applicant to submit a preliminary proposal that should include: (1) a description of the organization, its history, and purposes; (2) evidence of the organization's tax-exempt status; (3) an overview and budget of the proposed project; (4) a description of the expected results; and (5) a description of the total plan for funding. If it is determined that the project falls within the scope of funding interests, Aetna will invite submission of a formal proposal.

Organizations seeking a loan from Aetna's Corporate Responsibility Investment Committee should write a letter of no more than three pages addressed to Glenda C. Reed. The letter should include the following information: (1) the applicant's name and address; (2) the amount being requested and an explanation of how the money will be used; (3) project name and location; (4) a description of the type of project involved,

129

Aetna Life and Casualty Foundation, Inc.

including those facts that are particularly relevant to CRIC's interests; (5) a description of the applicant's development history, including previous Aetna-supported projects, if applicable; and (6) other sources of support for the project, both private and public. There are no geographic restrictions on this program. CRIC invests on a nationwide basis, and applications are accepted throughout the year.

Grant Limitations

Grants are restricted to tax-exempt organizations located in the United States and to programs taking place in the United States, with the exception of a small international program starting in 1988. About one-third of the grants are concentrated in the Hartford, Connecticut, area. No grants are made: (1) for medical research; (2) in support of religious organizations to fulfill their sacramental or theological functions; (3) to individuals; (4) for construction of buildings, or for endowments outside the Greater Hartford area; (5) for consolidated fundraising drives in cities outside of Hartford other than United Way and Selected Combined Health

Aetna Life and Casualty Foundation, Inc.
Aetna Life and Casualty Company
Analysis of 1986 Grantmaking Activity[1]

	General Grants (Foundation)	FOCUS Grants (Foundation)	Corporate Grants
Total Grants Paid	$2,019,282	$2,125,553	$2,986,543
Number of Grants Paid	73	197	95
Highest Grant	$250,000	$200,000	$106,000
Lowest Grant	$500	$1,000	$300
Median Grant Size	$15,000	$5,000	$5,000

[1]The grants and contributions tabulated here do not include employee-driven contributions totaling over $1.3 million. Nor do they include United Way contributions ($1 million), the Aetna Life and Casualty Foundation scholarship program ($405,000), the Greater Hartford Chamber of Commerce ($324,000), Neighborhood Housing Services Insurance Partnerships ($125,500), the Neighborhood Reinvestment Program ($110,752), Pro Bono Programs ($322,728), or various miscellaneous, unitemized donations and small grants. Also excluded is a one-time donation of property valued at $794,187 to the Greater Hartford Arts Council.

Aetna Life and Casualty Foundation, Inc.

Appeal campaigns; (6) for unrestricted operating funds for colleges, universities, social service agencies, secondary schools, museums, hospitals, or other such institutions located outside of the Greater Hartford area.

Meeting Times

The board of directors of the Aetna Life and Casualty Foundation, Inc., meets quarterly, in February, May, July, and November. The Corporate Responsibility Investment Committee meets monthly.

Publications

Annual reports are available which describe the activities of the foundation and the company. Separate materials describe the foundation's grant application procedure and the guidelines for CRIC.

American Foundation for AIDS Research
1515 Broadway, Suite 3601
New York, New York 10036
(212) 719–0033

5900 Wilshire Boulevard
Second Floor, East Satellite
Los Angeles, California 90036
(213) 857–5900

Contact Persons
J. Theodore, Grants Officer
Trish Halleron, Director of Education (New York)

Purpose
The mission of the American Foundation for AIDS Research (AmFAR) is to help prevent and find a cure or improve treatment for acquired immunodeficiency syndrome (AIDS) and related disorders. In addition to its grantmaking activities, AmFAR serves as a resource for responsible information on the clinical, psychological, public health, and public policy aspects of AIDS.

Areas of Interest
The bulk of AmFAR's grantmaking is directed toward basic biomedical research; however, AmFAR also awards grants for clinical, behavioral, legal, ethical, and humanistic research and has made a significant commitment of resources to public education and community outreach activities. In addition to traditional written materials, radio, and film aimed at young people and minorities, AmFAR has supported leadership training for corporate executives and educators, efforts to educate employees in the workplace, and community-based networking and organizing.

Financial Data (year ended 6/30/87)
On June 30, 1987, AmFAR's assets were $6,112,267. Following is an analysis of grant awards made in July and December 1987 that distinguishes basic research from education-related grants.

American Foundation for AIDS Research

Research Grants

Total grants awarded:	$	4,014,193
Number of grants awarded:		74
Highest grant:	$	60,000
Lowest grant:	$	4,432
Median grant size:	$	59,996

Education-related Grants

Total grants awarded:	$	494,186
Number of grants awarded:		9
Highest grant:	$	60,000
Lowest grant:	$	21,389
Median grant size:	$	59,996

Application Procedures

AmFAR conducts two grant cycles annually. The deadlines are usually in February and August; however, potential applicants are urged to contact AmFAR to ascertain the specific dates. Grant awards are announced approximately two months later.

Proposals for education-related activities should be directed to the foundation's New York office and should include: the project title; the name of the person responsible for the project; a description of the target audience, project goals, methodology, and evaluation plans; a full budget, including amount of funding requested; organization information including staff résumés; a list of other sources of support; and appropriate letters of support. Proposals are reviewed by a committee of educators and social science professionals and referred to AmFAR's board of directors.

There are highly specific application guidelines for basic research grants, and before submitting a grant application, the principal investigator must receive approval of a letter of intent submitted in response to a request for proposals. For complete information, contact the grants officer in AmFAR's Los Angeles office.

American Foundation for AIDS Research

Meeting Times
The board of directors of the American Foundation for AIDS Research meets twice a year to award grants.

Publications
AmFAR publishes an annual report, and grant application guidelines are available upon request.

Apple Computer, Inc.
Community Affairs Program
20525 Mariani Avenue M/S 38J
Cupertino, California 95014
(408) 974–2974

Contact Person
Community Affairs Office

Purpose

The Community Affairs Program of Apple Computer, Inc., makes computer donations to nonprofit organizations, schools (kindergarten through grade 12), and in partnership with large umbrella groups. This entry focuses primarily on Apple's grants to nonprofit organizations.

The Community Affairs Program makes grants of Apple personal computer systems with software, training, and follow-up support to organizations that want to work with other groups with values and activities similar to their own and that want to establish micronetworks. Under exceptional circumstances, grants will be made to one organization not working in a network, but only if its work is truly unique and groundbreaking.

Areas of Interest

Grants to nonprofit groups are awarded for three categories of organizations: (1) citizen action, offering services or advocacy in areas such as job development, housing improvement, environmental protection, substance abuse, and equal rights; (2) the arts, using computers for administrative or artistic applications in either the performing or visual arts; and (3) support for the disabled, developing computer information systems or researching and developing computer applications for the disabled.

Grants to nonprofits are also awarded within two special categories: research and development, including medical, scientific, and social science investigations; and skills development, for innovative community-based training programs that enhance educational and vocational opportunities for disabled, disadvantaged, or at-risk individuals. In order to qualify, groups must be innovative, useful, and able to serve as positive models for others.

Grants are also made to educational institutions for kindergarten through grade 12. The focus of this grantmaking program changes each

Apple Computer, Inc.

year, and applicants should call or write to the Community Affairs Department to ascertain deadlines and current program focus, and to request guidelines and application forms.

Grants from Apple consist of equipment and software selected by the company, with portions contributed by other manufacturers and service providers. The package consists of a computer, printer, modem, and disk drive; basic software; initial training; technical support from grants staff; access to on-line systems; publications produced by Apple Community Affairs; and the opportunity to network with fellow service providers and arts groups. The application forms contain a specific list of hardware and software currently being offered. Substitutions and/or additions cannot be made.

In addition to its grantmaking, Apple, along with other hardware and software manufacturers, supports a number of computer learning labs. These labs, managed by nonprofit organizations with the financial support of local foundations, enable nonprofits to obtain ongoing technical assistance, including an assessment of their computer needs, hands-on computer training, and access to computer equipment.

Financial Data (year ended 9/30/87)

In the fiscal year ending September 30, 1987, Apple donated approximately 900 computer systems, with a total fair market value of $4.7 million.

Application Procedures

The first step in contemplating a grant application to Apple, Inc., is to contact a group of two to four other organizations besides your own to ascertain your common needs and determine how a microcomputer network can enhance your collective goals. All members of the proposed network must meet the following criteria: (1) an annual budget of no more than $1 million for each organization; and (2) nonprofit, with each organization holding its own Section 501(c)(3) tax-exempt status, or nonprofit and operating under an umbrella 501(c)(3) as an autonomous group with its own board of directors or advisory panel. Furthermore, all organizations must have paid staff and operate during normal business

Apple Computer, Inc.

hours. Networks must consist of three to five separate organizations. Multiple departments or offices within one organization are not eligible to be members of the same network. Grants are not made for personal residence placement.

If your network meets the above criteria, you should request an application form. The application package lays out precisely what information must be developed as part of your proposal. It also describes the current computer packages that are being offered and lists application deadlines. Apple requests that information about every organization in the network be submitted simultaneously. Apple acknowledges receipt of all proposals within three weeks of the application deadlines. Grant decisions usually take place eight to ten weeks after the deadlines.

Grant Limitations

Grants will be made only to organizations meeting the criteria described under Application Procedures, above. Grants will not be awarded to individuals, to organizations using a classroom situation, government agencies (unless they serve a vital link in a network of private nonprofit groups), and groups seeking grants for political or religious uses. Grants are awarded to educational institutions only under the separate guidelines of that program; the program for nonprofit organizations does not make grants to educational institutions.

Meeting Times

The committee that reviews grant applications for Apple's Community Affairs Program consists of company management and employees. It awards grants to nonprofit groups twice a year, and to schools once a year.

Publications

The Community Affairs Program of Apple Computer, Inc., distributes program guidelines and application forms, and a variety of publications for grantees.

The Arca Foundtion
1425 21st Street, N.W.
Washington, D.C. 20036
(202) 822-9193

Contact Persons
Janet Schenk, Executive Director
Cooki Collinet, Grants Administrator

Purpose
The Arca Foundation supports a wide variety of organizations struggling for social and economic justice. It is committed to sustaining these organizations in their different missions of analysis and outreach to a wider public.

From time to time the priority issues of the Arca Foundation have changed in response to newly perceived needs. In general the foundation will support organizations with strategies that: provide direct accounts of the impact of U.S. policy in given regions of the third world; analyze human rights, democracy, economic, and social justice issues in the third world in depth and provide that information to the American public; advocate for policies based on these values; provide opportunities for U.S. citizens to visit third world countries and understand issues from new perspectives; and promote active citizen participation in foreign policy development.

Areas of Interest
Over the past four years, fully eighty percent of the foundation's resources have been devoted to changing U.S. attitudes and policies toward the third world in order to bring about U.S. foreign, military and economic policies that meet both domestic and international needs and which make economic growth and development the center of U.S. policy toward the third world. The foundation has sponsored many fact-finding missions to Central America as well as to South Korea, Chile, and Paraguay, and has supported a broad array of research, advocacy, and human rights organizations concerned with conditions in these countries and in South Africa. In 1987 the board of directors voted to spend a portion of the foundation's grantmaking budget to conduct studies of public policy concerning U.S.-Cuban relations and to educate the American public.

The remainder of the foundation's grantmaking, fifteen to twenty

The Arca Foundation

percent, is reserved for domestic projects that empower people to take charge of their own communities. Generally, these grants support: projects that address problems of powerlessness in America with emphasis on the constituencies most affected, such as the poor; work that takes on abuses of power; program activities that embody risk-taking and innovation around social issues; organization-building that empowers those left out and left behind; work that advances civil rights and civil liberties; and projects that encourage and develop citizen participation.

Financial Data (year ended 12/31/86)

Assets:	$ 19,912,864
Total grants awarded:	$ 618,333
Number of grants awarded:	46
Highest grant:	$ 25,000
Lowest grant:	$ 5,000
Median grant size:	$ 11,000

Application Procedures

Applicants should submit a brief two- or three-page summary of the project with budget figures and proof of tax-exempt status (if the organization has such status). There should be a clear identification of the problem, the proposed solution, and the value of the project. If the program or idea falls within the areas of interest of the foundation, applicants may be asked to submit a formal proposal, guidelines for which appear in the foundation's annual report. All letters are promptly acknowledged.

Once a formal proposal has been requested by the foundation, the application deadlines are March 15 and September 15. Grants are awarded six to eight weeks after these dates, and applicants are notified promptly once a grant has been awarded. The foundation states that it will not accept responsibility for keeping a grant application confidential and that proposals to the foundation may be discussed with outside consultants.

The Arca Foundation

Meeting Times

The board of directors of the Arca Foundation meets semi-annually in late spring and fall.

Publications

The foundation publishes an annual report.

The Ark Foundation
250 Lafayette Circle, Suite 301
Lafayette, California 94549
(415) 283-7920

Contact Persons
Don W. Carlson, President
Craig Comstock, Senior Associate
Linda Lazare, Senior Associate

Purpose
The Ark Foundation was established in 1984 to provide support for organizations seeking to bring about global security and real peace.

Areas of Interest
The foundation's primary focus is on organizations that can help improve America's competence to resolve conflict and promote constructive changes in international politics. It favors efforts to design and promote alternative security strategies based on nonviolent methods of channeling conflict and creating stronger international institutions and peacemaking mechanisms over traditional projects focused on military issues and weapons systems. Furthermore, it supports efforts that empower the individual to take an active role in the global community via citizen diplomacy and grass roots activity.

The foundation stresses that its interests are in practical projects, not academic or theoretical research. It is particularly interested in the public policy implications of proposed projects, including constructive criticisms of current policy and especially the development of practical alternatives.

Financial Data (year ended 10/31/87)

Support and revenue:	$	255,429
Total grants approved:	$	216,549
Number of grants approved:		39
Highest grant:	$	25,000
Lowest grant:	$	100
Median grant size:	$	5,000

The Ark Foundation

Application Procedures

Organizations interested in applying to the foundation for support should write a preliminary letter (no more than two pages long) describing the organization and the project for which funds are sought. This letter should describe the organization's mission and goals; the objectives of the proposed project, why the organization thinks they can be realistically attained, and the criteria against which the project will be evaluated; the capability of the organization to carry out the proposed project; the relationship of the organization and the project to others working in the same field; the public policy implications or the potential for the project to be used as a model; and a statement describing what, if the project is successful, would be the follow-up.

The letter should also include information on the budget of the proposed project, the amount to be requested from the foundation, and the amount that can be expected from other sources of funding. The enclosures should be the organization's annual report or other program description, the most recent financial statements, and proof of tax-exempt status under Section 501(c)(3) of the Internal Revenue Code.

If the foundation is interested in the proposed project, a more formal proposal may be requested and a site visit or other meeting may be arranged.

Grant Limitations

The foundation provides support only to organizations with tax-exempt status or projects working through a tax-exempt fiscal sponsor. The foundation does not support individuals, endowment campaigns, building funds, and projects that are primarily international, that is, projects where most of the work and the impact will take place outside of the United States.

Meeting Times

The board of directors of the Ark Foundation meets monthly.

The Ark Foundation

Publications
The foundation has no publications. A sister organization, the Ark Communications Institute, publishes books on peace issues (including *Citizen Summitry, Securing Our Planet,* and *Global Partners,* and a series of monographs that can be purchased directly from the foundation at the address above.)

Avon Products Foundation, Inc.
9 West 57 Street
New York, New York 10019
(212) 546-6729

Contact Persons
Glenn S. Clarke, President
Mary P. Quinn, Manager

Purpose
The Avon Products Foundation is a company-sponsored foundation of Avon Products, Inc., the manufacturer of cosmetics, toiletries, and costume jewelry. The foundation's activities focus primarily on supporting organizations whose programs improve, enhance, and serve the needs and interests of Blacks, Hispanics, women, and the elderly and programs to prevent alcohol and substance abuse.

Areas of Interest
The foundation's interests can be divided into four categories: health, education, humanities, and community service. The foundation makes grants for operating budgets and special projects.

Health care grants include support for hospitals, clinics, and hospices that provide direct services, preventive care, and treatment. Of particular interest are programs that recruit, train, and educate volunteers and administrators to help families provide home care for patients. In education, the foundation supports institutions and organizations that emphasize business, employment, and leadership development programs for youth and the disadvantaged. The foundation also supports scholarship programs for women and minorities. In the third area, humanities, the main emphasis is on performing arts groups, particularly on minority programs. Finally, in the area of community and social services, the foundation supports United Ways, programs for the elderly, children, and youth who are socially and economically deprived, and programs to prevent alcohol and substance abuse. Grants in this area are also made to organizations providing technical assistance to minority businesses.

Financial Data (year ended 12/31/85)
In fiscal 1985 the foundation made grants totaling over $1.4 million, both at the national level through home office grants and regionally or locally

Avon Products Foundation, Inc.

through its location grants. The analysis below presents a breakdown of grants in each category.

Home Office Grants

Total grants paid:[1]	$	942,150
Number of grants paid:[2]		126
Highest grant:	$	50,000
Lowest grant:	$	500
Median grant size:	$	2,000

Location Grants

Total grants paid:	$	369,995
Number of grants paid:		180
Highest grant:	$	10,000
Lowest grant:	$	200
Median grant size:	$	1,000

Application Procedures

There are no application deadlines. Applicants should submit a two-page letter addressing the following: the goals and objectives of the organization, the need or the problem and the manner in which a grant would be used, the number of persons who would be served by the program and the geographic area to be covered, and the cost of the program and the amount being requested. This letter should be accompanied by an annual report, a program budget, a list of the board of directors, a copy of the tax-exemption letter from the IRS, an audited report, and a list of other corporate contributors. Site visits and/or meetings will be scheduled, if appropriate, based on a review of the materials submitted.

Applications from programs that operate nationally should be sent to the New York City address. Regional and local organizations should

---

[1] These tabulations do not include $91,316 in matching gifts.
[2] This figure and those below exclude three unusually large grants of $100,000 each.

Avon Products Foundation, Inc.

send their applications to the local Avon facility (see list at end of this entry).

Grant Limitations
Eligibility is limited to national programs and to local and regional programs operating near an Avon location. The foundation does not make grants for building or endowment funds, for study and research programs, or to member agencies of the United Way and United Fund, or individuals.

Meeting Times
The board of directors of the Avon Products Foundation, comprising officers of the company, meets quarterly.

Publications
The foundation does not publish an annual report, but information and application guidelines are available upon request.

Avon Locations
Organizations operating nationally should forward their requests to the foundation's office in New York City. Regional and local organizations should contact their local Avon facility, as follows:

California
Retirement Inns of America
10960 Wilshire Boulevard, Suite 2440
Los Angeles, California 90024

Avon Products, Inc.
2940 East Foothill Boulevard
Pasadena, California 91121

Delaware
Avon Products, Inc.
2100 Ogletown Road
Newark, Delaware 19711

Avon Products Foundation, Inc.

Georgia
Avon Products, Inc.
Post Office Box 105541
Atlanta, Georgia 30303

Illinois
Avon Products, Inc.
6901 Golf Road
Morton Grove, Illinois 60053

Massachusetts
The Mediplex Group, Inc.
15 Walnut Street
Wellesley, Massachusetts 02181

New York
Avon Products, Inc.
Division Street
Suffern, New York 10901

Ohio
Avon Products, Inc.
175 Progress Place
Springdale, Ohio 45246

Pennsylvania
Foster Medical Corporation
1000 Conshohocken Road
Conshohocken, Pennsylvania 19428

Virginia
Avon Direct Response
Avon Lane
Newport News, Virginia 23606

Bauman Foundation
1731 Connecticut Avenue, 4th Floor
Washington, D.C. 20009–1146
(202) 234–8547

Contact Persons
Patricia Bauman, Co-Director
John L. Bryant, Jr., Co-Director

Purpose

The principal focus of the Bauman Family Foundation is prevention of occupational and environmental health problems. In particular, through grants and operating its own programs, the foundation is interested in devising policy changes, developing new approaches, and strengthening existing programs and strategies for reducing toxic substances in the workplace and general environment.

Areas of Interest

The foundation will support whatever activities are needed to achieve results, including advocacy, public education, litigation, and policy research. However, the foundation board believes it can best help to achieve strategic social goals by supporting organizations that have the capacity and willingness to work with state and local grassroots groups. Therefore, it prefers not to support state or local programs unless there is a clear plan for their dissemination and use as models. Similarly, policy analysis and other theoretical and planning work should be demonstrably capable of reaching relevant target audiences.

While the foundation recognizes that collaboration is not always possible, favorable consideration will be given to joint applications such as consortia of public interest, community and environmental groups, and labor organizations that have subcontract arrangements with university scientists or other technical experts.

Financial Data

The foundation's first grantmaking year was not complete when this book went to press. It is expected that from 1988–90 the total grants budget will be approximately $250,000 annually, with most grants in the $10–15,000 range. Small emergency grants are available.

Bauman Family Foundation

Application Procedures

There are no application deadlines, and grant requests may be acted upon by the foundation at any time during the year. Before submitting a complete application, interested organizations should send a brief letter to the foundation describing the proposed project. The foundation will attempt to respond with an indication of its interest within a few weeks.

If the foundation requests a complete application, organizations should be prepared to provide a statement of the project's objectives and the need and rationale for the project; a plan describing how the objectives will be achieved; a description of how the project relates to other activities of the applicant organization; information about the relationship between the proposed activity and other groups in the same field; anticipated outcomes and their evaluation criteria; and background information on the project staff. Applicants must also submit proof of tax-exempt status from the IRS; financial statements (a balance sheet and income statement, preferably audited); a description of other sources of funding, both long- and short-term; and a list of the members of the organization's governing body. A brief narrative about the organization, or its annual report should also be submitted.

After preliminary screening, applications may be submitted to peer reviewers appropriate to the subject of the proposed project.

Grant Limitations

The foundation prefers to make grants for specific projects, and shies away from general support. It will not cover overhead expenses for established institutions such as universities or large public interest organizations. Grants are not made for medical, epidemiologic, or laboratory research, and grants are not made to individuals. The foundation stresses that it supports organizations that do the empowering, not local initiatives.

Meeting Times

The board of directors of the Bauman Family Foundation meets quarterly in January, March, June, and September.

Bauman Family Foundation

Publications
The foundation expected to publish its first annual report in 1988.

The Beldon Fund
2000 P Street, N.W., Suite 410
Washington, D.C. 20036
(202) 293-1928

Contact Persons
John R. Hunting, President
Judy Donald, Executive Director

Areas of Interest
The Beldon Fund's primary interest is in strengthening national, regional, and statewide environmental organizations that educate and train their members or the general public about significant environmental issues.

The fund is also interested in a few specific issue areas. In 1987 these issues on a national level were: deep well injection, solid waste disposal, and large ecosystem coalitions. Internationally, the fund has two project areas: development of Antarctica as a world park and prevention of tropical deforestation.

The Beldon Fund occasionally supports national gatherings concerned with the spiritual aspects of the environmental movement and also contributes to environmental films through an underwritten screening process.

Financial Data (year ended 4/30/87)
Total grants paid:	$	1,231,773
Number of grants paid:		118
Highest grant:	$	30,000
Lowest grant:	$	500
Average grant size:	$	10,000

Application Procedures
The fund has no standard application form or procedures. Applicants are encouraged to telephone or to submit a letter of inquiry outlining the proposed program prior to submission of a formal proposal.

Grant Limitations
The fund makes grants only to tax-exempt organizations. The fund does not make grants to individuals, for capital or endowment campaigns, or for research projects.

The Beldon Fund

Meeting Times

Grant decisions are made by the Beldon Fund at least once a month throughout the year.

Publications

The fund does not publish an annual report.

The Benton Foundation
1776 K Street, N.W., Suite 605
Washington, D.C. 20006
(202) 429-7350

Contact Persons
Larry Kirkman, Executive Director
Karen Menichelli, Associate Director

Purpose
The Benton Foundation is committed to enhancing public understanding and use of the traditional and emerging media of communications. The foundation seeks to examine the major issues raised by the rapid growth of communications technologies, and to encourage the development of communications policies and systems consistent with the democratic principles on which this nation is based.

Areas of Interest
The foundation both initiates projects and provides grant support to other organizations for work in three broad program areas: (1) research on the societal impact of communications technologies, systems, and services, and on the resulting implications for public policy; (2) innovative applications of communications media to improve public debate and understanding of national and international issues; and (3) efforts to increase public awareness of the role of communications and information systems in society and to promote the informed use of those systems.

Financial Data (year ended 12/31/87)
Assets:	$ 11,279,000
Total grants paid:	$ 526,857
Number of grants paid:	56
Highest grant:	$ 50,000
Lowest grant:	$ 75
Median grant size:	$ 5,000

Application Procedures
Organizations interested in applying for a grant should contact the foundation to ascertain proposal deadlines. Applicants are asked to submit a brief description of the proposed project, including a statement of goals,

The Benton Foundation

the personnel involved, and the funds requested. A complete budget should also be submitted. The foundation does not have a standard application form. If necessary, the staff will request additional information.

Grant Limitations

Grants are made primarily to educational and charitable institutions rather than to individuals. Projects of national or regional significance are given priority. The foundation does not ordinarily support book writing or the preparation of newsletters or other periodicals. Nor will requests for contributions to capital fund campaigns for equipment or for general operating support normally be considered.

Meeting Times

The board of directors of the Benton Foundation generally meets three times a year.

Publications

The foundation publishes a biennial report and a brochure that provide an overview of the foundation's history and interests and outlines application procedures.

Best Productions Foundation
1616 P Street, N.W., Suite 100
Washington, D.C. 20036
(202) 328-5188

Contact Person
Susan L. Butler, Executive Director

Purpose
In general terms, the purpose of the Best Products Foundation is to enhance the quality of life in those communities in which Best Products Co., Inc., has facilities. The corporation is headquartered in Richmond, Virginia. Much of the foundation's grantmaking activity is concentrated in Virginia. The foundation also supports projects in those localities where there are Best Products showrooms. As of 1988, there were 197 Best stores across the country.

The foundation prefers to fund creative and model projects at the grassroots level, and is prone to make "seed money grants." In addition, the foundation provides scholarship funds for students at several private universities in Virginia and at the University of Michigan.

Areas of Interest
Program priorities of the foundation include: the prevention of teenage pregnancy; reproductive rights and other special problems of women; community-based programs for educationally at risk youth; local programming on public television stations; special civil liberties litigation (no general support for legal defense funds); neighborhood revitalization; and established (not community) cultural arts institutions.

Financial Data (year ended 9/30/86)[1]

Assets:	$	3,000,000
Total grants paid:[2]	$	939,760
Number of grants paid:		61
Highest grant:[3]	$	30,000
Lowest grant:	$	50
Median grant size:	$	5,000

---

[1] This analysis reflects a grants list for 1986 supplied by the foundation. As this book went to press, such a list was not available for 1987. However, the foundation reported that it had made grants totaling $807,000 in 1987, and that, in addition, showroom contributions and matching gifts for the year totaled $81,210 and $23,886 respectively.
[2] These figures do not include small grants made by individual Best stores, in amounts from $100 to $500.
[3] Not reflected in this figure are several grants to set up scholarship funds for women and minorities, and United Way contributions.

Best Products Foundation

Application Procedures
The foundation has no application forms but does require the grantseeker to prepare a proposal consistent with a specified format. The requirements are fully set forth in a policies/application brochure available upon request. Application deadlines vary with each board meeting.

Requests to a Local Showroom
In addition to its regular grantmaking and scholarship programs, each Best Products showroom manager is given a very small budget for supporting local projects. These grants range from $100 to $500. All requests for merchandise are handled by the local showroom manager.

Grant Limitations
The foundation makes grants only to tax-exempt organizations and is not disposed to supporting: building funds, annual operating funds, organizations deriving major support from any governmental unit, "goodwill" or journal advertisements, religious institutions, elementary or secondary educational institutions, national organizations, publications, conferences, seminars, and research. Because the foundation makes contributions to the United Funds in those cities where it has facilities, contributions are not made directly to member agencies of the United Fund.

Meeting Times
The board of directors of the Best Products Foundation meets four times per year.

Publications
The foundation will provide a brochure titled *Foundation Policies and Grant Application Procedure* and showroom addresses upon request.

The William Bingham Foundation
1250 Leader Building
Cleveland, Ohio 44114
(216) 781–3275

Contact Person
Laura Hitchcox, Director

Areas of Interest
The William Bingham Foundation contributes to a wide variety of organizations in the areas of education, the arts, health, and welfare, primarily in the eastern United States. The foundation also gives special attention to programs that educate the public about nuclear issues. As part of this effort, several of the foundation's grants in education and the arts are awarded to support films, conferences, research, and publications that illustrate the consequences of nuclear war.

Financial Data (year ended 12/31/86)
Assets:	$ 20,355,000
Total grants paid:	$ 816,127
Number of grants paid:	39
Highest grant:	$ 100,000
Lowest grant:	$ 550
Median grant size:	$ 15,000

Application Procedures
To initiate a request to the foundation, applicants should submit a letter no longer than two pages outlining the nature of the project, budget requirements and the amount requested. Telephone inquiries are discouraged. If the project coincides with the foundation's interests, a trustee or the executive director will contact the applicant and request a detailed grant proposal which must be completed at least two months before the semiannual meetings of the trustees. At that time applicants will be asked to provide financial statements and documentation of tax-exempt status. The foundation may request to meet with an applicant in order to evaluate a request. The foundation encourages applicants to seek additional funding from other sources and asks to be informed promptly of other grants received.

The William Bingham Foundation

Grant Limitations
The foundation prefers to support organizations in the eastern United States and makes awards only to qualified applicants that are tax exempt under Section 501(c)(3) of the Internal Revenue Code. Grants are not awarded to individuals.

Meeting Times
The board of trustees of The William Bingham Foundation meets twice a year in the spring and fall, usually in May and October.

Publications
The foundation publishes an annual report.

The Boehm Foundation
500 Fifth Avenue
New York, New York 10110-0296
(212) 354-9292

Contact Person
Judy Austermiller, Executive Director

Purpose
The purpose of The Boehm Foundation is to assist the development of human democratic rights at home and abroad and to assist in promoting and maintaining world peace. These aims are premised on the belief that unless the full range of democratic rights are protected and respected and unless nations and peoples are able to live together peacefully, none of the educational and creative aspects of the human spirit can be developed.

Areas of Interest
The primary interests of the foundation are promoting human rights (through the elimination of racism and sexism, protection of domestic political rights, promotion of international human rights, and recognition of economic rights as human rights) and promoting peace (through projects seeking nuclear disarmament; peace and human rights in Central America, South Africa, and the Middle East; and cooperation and friendship with the peoples of the Soviet Union).

Secondarily, the foundation is interested in encouraging young people to work for human rights and peace (through projects offering scholarships and internships in these fields) and insuring public awareness of human rights and peace issues (through investigative journalism and other media projects). It should be noted that grants for film and video projects are made only upon the recommendation of the Paul Robeson Fund for Film and Video at The Funding Exchange, and applications must be made through The Funding Exchange.[1]

---

[1]For more information about the Paul Robeson Fund for Film and Video, see the entry for The Funding Exchange that appears in this chapter.

159

The Boehm Foundation

Financial Data (year ended 12/31/86)

Assets:	$	2,476,510
Total grants paid:[2]	$	403,165
Number of grants paid:		94
Highest grant:[3]	$	12,000
Lowest grant:	$	500
Median grant size:	$	2,000

Application Procedures

There are no application deadlines. Applications are accepted throughout the year, and applicants can expect to receive a decision on their request within two months.

Applicants should submit a brief proposal or two-to three-page letter describing the goals and objectives of the organization or project and the work that will be carried out to realize these objectives. Appended financial information should include the organization's annual budget and a project budget if applicable; an up-to-date accounting of funds raised toward the budget, including sources; and a copy of the organization's tax-exemption ruling from the IRS.

Grant Limitations

The foundation does not make grants to individuals, nor does it generally make grants for capital expenditures, endowment funds, or individual research and writing projects.

Meeting Times

The board of directors of The Boehm Foundation generally meets once every two months.

Publications

The foundation distributes application guidelines and a list of past grantees.

---

[2] This excludes eight grants totaling $78,300 which were made at the request of a family member and which do not represent actions taken by the foundation board as a whole.
[3] This excludes three unusually large grants totaling $145,500 to organizations with which the foundation has historic relationships.

**Florence V. Burden Foundation
630 Fifth Avenue, Suite 2900
New York, New York 10111
(212) 489-1063**

Contact Person
Barbara Greenberg, Executive Director

Purpose
The Florence V. Burden Foundation has two specific programmatic interests: (1) the problems of the elderly; and (2) crime and justice. Generally the foundation supports projects that are, in the foundation's words, "at the cutting edge of social innovation"—genuinely innovative solutions to problems not effectively dealt with in the past. This includes pilot programs that, if successful, can be more widely adopted.

The foundation prefers that its initial grants be of a research character that promise to shed light on fundamental issues within its areas of interest, including both applied research and demonstration programs that are designed to provide specific information to decision-makers. The foundation prefers that research grants cover adequate initial exploration of the idea, i.e., grants of $5,000 or more. If a research grant shows the idea holds real promise, the foundation is prepared to follow up with a demonstration grant to fund pilot projects that will demonstrate feasibility and effectiveness.

Areas of Interest
In its focus on the elderly, the foundation concentrates on projects that encourage the continued independence of seniors and that enable them to remain productive members of society. Programs falling within this category include practical assistance in the provision of employment, preventive health care, housing alternatives, retirement planning projects, and other similar approaches. It is particularly interested in projects that use older people to help solve social problems. The foundation specifically wants to explore nongovernmental solutions to the problems faced by older persons. This means that it looks for projects that do not require large additional commitments of public funds in order to succeed.

In its crime and justice program, the foundation considers projects that prevent or control crime, help offenders outgrow criminality, enhance productivity of the system, and aid victims of crime. The foundation

Florence V. Burden Foundation

is also interested in raising the level of public debate on justice and providing new insights into policy issues. The foundation takes special interest in juvenile justice and youthful offenders.

Financial Data (year ended 12/31/86)

Assets:	$ 12,474,470
Total grants authorized:	$ 602,895
Number of grants authorized:	45
Highest grant:	$ 55,000
Lowest grant:	$ 500
Median grant size:	$ 10,000

Application Procedures

Before a formal proposal is made, a preliminary letter of intent is required. This letter should briefly describe the capabilities of the sponsoring organization and explain why funds are needed, what will be accomplished, and indicate the amount requested. A complete application form and other material may be subsequently requested and meetings arranged if the foundation decides to consider a formal request. Letters of intent must be submitted by the first of April, August, or December in order to receive prompt attention. Complete grant applications, provided by the foundation, must be returned by May 1, September 1, or January 1 for consideration at the board meeting in the following month.

Grant Limitations

In its elderly program, the foundation is not likely to make grants to programs that serve the elderly within institutional settings, such as hospitals or nursing homes. Usually, the foundation does not make general support grants to existing programs, nor does it provide funds for individuals, building construction, purchase of equipment, endowments, or general operating expenses.

Meeting Times

The board of directors of the Florence V. Burden Foundation meets three times a year, in June, October, and February.

Florence V. Burden Foundation

Publications
The foundation publishes an annual report.

The Bydale Foundation
299 Park Avenue
New York, New York 10171
(212) 207–1800

Contact Person[1]
Milton D. Solomon, Vice-President

Areas of Interest

The Bydale Foundation is a family foundation with diverse grantmaking practices. Its grantmaking can generally be divided into the following priority areas: (1) national energy and environmental policy, specifically progressive environmental strategies; (2) domestic economic policy; (3) foreign policy, specifically peace issues, disarmament, and world order; and (4) the arts, primarily traditional programs in New York City, but also an expressed interest in community arts programs.

On occasion, the foundation has supported publications and other media projects related to its priority interests. Seed moneys and general support are available.

Financial Data (year ended 12/31/85)

Assets:	$ 8,526,257
Total grants paid:	$ 755,164
Number of grants paid:	107
Highest grant:	$ 50,000
Lowest grant:	$ 250
Median grant size:	$ 5,000

Application Procedures

The deadline for proposals is November 1. The foundation specifically requests that all inquiries and applications be made in writing. Proposals should be brief and should include a statement of purpose and strategies, staffing capabilities, and detailed budget materials on both the organization and the proposed project. Supporting materials should be included.

---

[1]If, having complied fully with its guidelines, you need additional assistance, it is suggested that you contact Jill Niemond, Administrative Assistant, 16 West 61 Street, Tenth Floor, New York, New York 10023, (212) 603-7700.

The Bydale Foundation

Grant Limitations

The foundation makes grants only to tax-exempt organizations. No grants are made to individuals.

Meeting Times

The board of directors of the Bydale Foundation meets three or four times a year.

Publications

The foundation does not publish an annual report.

C.S. Fund
Warsh-Mott Legacy
469 Bohemian Highway
Freestone, California 95472
(707) 874–2942

Contact Persons
Martin Teitel, Executive Director
Roxanne Turnage, Assistant to the Executive Director

Purpose
The goals of the C.S. Fund and the Warsh-Mott Legacy are to support organizations and projects that work to challenge and change individual and institutional habits, behavior, attitudes, and beliefs that endanger humanity. These include the ways in which different people think of their rights of ownership, security, and freedom; the ways in which they form political, religious, and social values; the stated and assumed rights and responsibilities among individuals and between citizens and their institutions and the ways they have learned to solve problems. The funds seek to expand the collective thinking beyond habitual limits in order to discover and create imaginative and effective strategies for planetary survival.

Areas of Interest
The funds concentrate on four program areas: (1) dissent, including protecting the right to dissent and hold divergent opinions, preserving society's right to hold accountable all of its institutions and officials (both public and private), and preventing human rights violations and civil rights limitations; (2) genetics, including conserving and fostering the rich iversity of the earth's genetic pool and preventing the gross reduction and irreversible alteration of that genetic legacy; (3) peace, including pursuing effective paths to peace, particularly through alternative models of security; and (4) toxics, including reducing or eliminating the use of toxic materials through development of alternative policies, processes, and products and fostering comprehensive evaluation of the total burden of toxics on the biosphere.

The funds make grants to projects that demonstrate national or international impact and which will lead directly to changes in policy or practice. Grants are available for both organizational support and specific

C.S. Fund
Warsh-Mott Legacy

project support. The majority of grants are made for one year, however there is no limit to the number of years a program can receive support.

Financial Data (year ended 12/31/87)

C.S. Fund

Support and revenue:[1]	$	1,229,221
Total grants paid:[2]	$	939,500
Number of grants paid:		50
Highest grant:	$	50,000
Lowest grant:	$	1,500
Median grant size:	$	15,000

Warsh-Mott Legacy

Total grants paid:[2]	$	75,000
Number of grants paid:		7
Highest grant:	$	15,000
Lowest grant:	$	5,000
Median grant size:	$	10,000

Application Procedures

Application deadlines are January 15, May 15, and September 15. When the deadline falls on a weekend, proposals will be accepted the following Monday. Proposals must be in the C.S. Fund office by 5:00 P.M., Pacific time, on the day of the deadline. Late proposals are automatically included in the next funding cycle. All proposals received are acknowledged by mail.

Requests for support should be made in writing and submitted on letter-size paper. The funds provide the following proposal checklist:

---

[1] For the year ended December 31, 1986.

[2] These grants analyses are based on awards made separately by the C.S. Fund and the Warsh-Mott Legacy. They do not include grants made from the Legacy Fund, a donor-advised fund of the Institute for Regional Education, or from the C.R. Fund, a donor-advised fund of The Youth Project.

C.S. Fund
Warsh-Mott Legacy

Preliminarily, applicants should (1) identify the organization, the contact person and the contact person's address, and telephone number; (2) specify whether general support or project support is sought and, if appropriate, give the title of the project; and (3) prepare a summary of the proposal in 500 words or less (in addition to the full proposal). The full proposal should: (1) define the issue and explain the proposed approach (including what will be done by whom and differences the project will make in the issue area); (2) detail a brief history of the organization, including information about members of the governing body and staff and the overall vision of the organization; (3) include an accurate, itemized budget for the organization and the specific project (if appropriate); (4) report the source and amount of income received in the most recent fiscal year; (5) itemize existing and anticipated support for the current fiscal year; and (6) include evidence of federal tax-exempt status.

Grant Limitations
The funds do not support endowments, capital ventures, emergency requests, or film and video production. Failure to honor the conditions of a past grant, particularly timely reporting, will adversely affect an organization's chances of receiving future support.

Meeting Times
The boards of directors of the C.S. Fund and the Warsh-Mott Legacy meet three times a year to review grant requests.

Publications
The funds publish an annual report that includes funding goals, application guidelines, and a list of grantees.

Campaign for Human Development
United States Catholic Conference
3211 4th Street, N.E.
Washington, D.C. 20017
(202) 541–3210

Contact Persons
Rev. Alfred LoPinto, Executive Director
Douglas M. Lawson, Allocation Specialist

Purpose
The Campaign for Human Development (CHD) is an action-education program sponsored by the Catholic Bishops of the United States. It funds projects throughout the country that aim to attack the basic causes of poverty and to empower low income persons. CHD specifically encourages applications from poverty organizations working to bring about institutional change.

CHD makes grant awards on a nondenominational basis. However, all activities for which support is sought must conform to the moral teachings of the Catholic Church.

Areas of Interest
Grants are made in seven general areas of interest: communications, economic development, education, health, housing, legal aid, and social development. Each is briefly described below.

Communications. These are projects that give a voice to groups traditionally denied a voice in the media so that they can bring about changes in attitudes, organize listeners, and thus effect institutional change. Existing television, radio and print media may be changed, or alternative media established.

Economic Development. Economic development projects are businesses or projects set up by low-income groups to provide goods and services and generate profits. They may be worker or consumer cooperatives, community-owned, or tribally-owned.

Education. In this area, projects assist low-income groups to participate more fully in society and to influence its institutions. These projects work toward reform of educational sys-

Campaign for Human Development

tems or involve the education of special groups in advocacy skills required to bring about institutional change.

Health. Health projects advocate for the reform or establishment of health care delivery systems where present health care services are inadequate. Such projects focus on increasing the involvement of poverty groups in the planning and implementation of comprehensive health programs for an area.

Housing. These projects aim to develop decent, affordable housing, including both rehabilitation and new-construction programs. Projects can range from multiunit buildings to a complex of single-family detached homes. Many of the projects are housing cooperatives, but low-income rental and non-cooperative ownership structures are also funded.

Legal Aid. Legal aid projects emphasize using the legal system to redress injustices and to bring about needed institutional change. Projects may counter the exclusion of, or discrimination against, a particular group through class action lawsuits, administrative reform or other legal measures.

Social Development. These are projects that organize community groups around issues that affect their lives. Most are community organizing projects that enable people in a geographic area to work on a variety of issues. Others focus on organizing workers—such as farmworkers, factory workers, office workers—or other special groups—tenants, elderly, the handicapped. Some target a single complex issue like hunger or welfare or transportation. The common theme is building an effective organization so that people working together can bring about change.

CHD has specific grantmaking criteria. Briefly, all organizations receiving CHD support must benefit a poverty group, i.e., at least fifty percent of those benefitting from the project must be from the low-income community. Members of the poverty group must have the dominant voice in the project, i.e., at least fifty percent of those who plan, implement, and make policy, such as the board of directors, should be

Campaign for Human Development

persons who are involuntarily poor. Projects not meeting this criterion must document why and what steps will be taken for the poverty group to assume leadership and control.

Priority is given to projects that are innovative and demonstrate a change from traditional approaches to poverty by attacking the basic causes of poverty and by effecting institutional change which directly benefit a relatively large number of people, which generate cooperation among and within diverse groups, and which document that as a result of CHD funding there is the possibility of generating funds from other sources or of becoming self-sufficient. Grant awards range from a minimum of $10,000 to a maximum of $100,000.

Financial Data (year ended 12/31/87)

Projected income:[1]	$ 9,175,000
Total grants paid:	$ 6,494,000
Number of grants paid:	215
Highest grant:	$ 67,000
Lowest grant:	$ 10,000
Median grant size:	$ 30,000

Application Procedures

The deadline for submitting completed application materials to CHD is January 31. However, CHD starts distributing materials in September, and organizations that want to apply must complete a preapplication. The preapplication is mandatory and the deadline for submitting it is November 1.

Specific forms are required for both the preapplication and the final application; these, along with instructions, will be provided upon request. The forms are available in English and Spanish, and interested applicants are urged to contact their local CHD diocesan office or the national office staff if they want assistance in completing the process. Applicants are

---

[1]CHD receives 75 percent of the funds collected by each diocese on one day specially set aside for a social-justice collection. This figure is a projection that includes CHD's 1986 share, direct contributions, and investment income.

Campaign for Human Development

urged to follow the instructions carefully. Failure to provide the information requested, in the form requested will result in a negative evaluation of the request. Ten copies of the application and attachments must be submitted.

Grant Limitations
CHD makes grants only to organizations that are tax-exempt under Section 501(c)(3) of the Internal Revenue Code or that are working with a tax-exempt fiscal agent. The following general classifications do not meet CHD's funding criteria and guidelines: direct service projects; projects controlled by government, educational or ecclesiastical bodies; research projects, surveys, planning and feasibility studies; projects that have been operating for several years on funds from other funding agencies; projects sponsored by organizations which, at the time of application, receive substantial sums from other funding sources (unless the applicant documents that the proposed project cannot be funded by these agencies); and individually owned, for-profit businesses.

Funding will not be considered for projects that can be funded by money available from the private or public sector unless applicants document that they are unable to obtain funds from these sources. However, proposals that request seed money or matching funds will be considered. No CHD funds will be granted to organizations that would utilize the money to support other organizations.

Meeting Times
The CHD National Committee reviews proposals in June, and nonfunded projects are notified. Also in June, the Ad Hoc Committee of Bishops reviews the National Committee recommendations. Funding decisions are announced in July.

Publications
CHD publishes an annual report, a description of funded projects, application guidelines and instructions (in English and Spanish), and various other educational materials.

The CarEth Foundation
3 Church Street
Cambridge, Massachusetts 02138
(617) 354-8343

Contact Person
Carol Gruman, Vice-President

Purpose
The principal purpose of the CarEth Foundation is to stimulate the application of Judeo-Christian ethics to current U.S. foreign policy by supporting projects explicitly promoting world peace without directly seeking to influence legislation or partisan elections.

Areas of Interest
The foundation supports: (1) wide-scale educational efforts presented to well-defined, unpersuaded populations; (2) efforts that have a nonpartisan educational impact on the political process in Washington, D.C.; (3) church, ecumenical, or interfaith social action efforts; and (4) professional, practical, and efficient administration in the peace movement and cooperation and networking among social action groups avoiding unnecessary duplication of efforts; and (5) research programs that show pragmatic application of results.

Financial Data (year ended 12/31/86)

Assets:	$	1,853,575
Total grants paid:	$	100,750
Number of grants paid:		38
Highest grant:	$	4,000
Lowest grant:	$	500
Median grant size:	$	3,000

Application Procedures
The foundation's application deadlines change every year, and applicants should contact the foundation and request application forms and deadline information. The foundation requires both a proposal and a completed application form before a request can be considered.

The CarEth Foundation

Grant Limitations

The foundation makes grants only in the area of peace and does not support organizations seeking to influence legislation or partisan elections. Grants are made only to tax-exempt organizations or the projects of tax-exempt organizations, and no grants are made to individuals.

The foundation states that conferences, speakers bureaus, and special events are low priorities for support. Further, the foundation does not support projects that will have ended before foundation review of the proposal; coordinating or networking activities; fundraising and capital improvements; human rights projects (unless clearly connected with U.S. foreign or domestic policy); organizations primarily based outside the U.S.; relief efforts; and proposals from schools, colleges or universities intended for workshops and courses primarily for their own constituencies.

Meeting Times

The board of directors of The CarEth Foundation meets once each spring and fall to consider proposals.

Publications

The foundation distributes a description of its program interests along with application forms.

Carnegie Corporation of New York
437 Madison Avenue
New York, New York 10022
(212) 371-3200

Contact Persons
David Hamburg, President
E. Alden Dunham, Education: Science, Technology, and the Economy
Vivien Stewart, Toward Healthy Child Development: The Prevention of
   Damage   to Children
Adetokunbo O. Lucas, Strengthening Human Resources in Developing
   Countries
Frederic A. Mosher, Avoiding Nuclear War
Avery Russell, Director of Publications
Barbara D. Finberg, Executive Vice President and Special Projects

Purpose
The Carnegie Corporation of New York is a philanthropic foundation created "for the advancement and diffusion of knowledge and under-standing." The corporation has long been primarily concerned with ed-ucation, young children, and certain aspects of public policy with respect to strengthening human resources in developing countries and avoiding nuclear war.

Areas of Interest
The foundation focuses its efforts on the following four program areas:

> *Education: Science, Technology, and the Economy.* This first program area emphasizes grants with wide applicability and leverage in three areas of concentration: (1) improving edu-cation in science, mathematics, and technology; (2) encouraging minorities and women in science; (3) examination of the impact of science and technology on the economy and of ways in which the society can prepare for change, especially through educa-tional reform.

> *Toward Healthy Development: The Prevention of Damage to Children.* This program seeks ways to prevent failure in

175

Carnegie Corporation of New York

school, school-age pregnancy, childhood injury, and substance abuse. In two areas—school failure and school-age pregnancy—grant applications will be accepted; in the other two areas—childhood injury and substance abuse—the corporation initiates projects.

Strengthening Human Resources in Developing Countries. This program aims to engage the scientific and scholarly communities in the U.S. and developing countries in this effort and to heighten understanding in the U.S. of the role America can play. The program focuses on the health of children and mothers and on basic education, nutrition, family planning, and the status of women, with particular emphasis on English-speaking Africa, the Caribbean, and the U.S.-Mexican boarder. Grants are made to foster dialogue between experts and leaders from developing countries and the U.S., to provide support for technical and scientific cooperation, to evaluate past lessons in development and assess their applicability in other settings, and to communicate the lessons learned to American audiences including the general public.

Avoiding Nuclear War. This program has four areas of particular interest: (1) the development of new ideas and understanding and relating this development closely to the policy-making, policy-advising community; (2) using public education to build a broad base of nonpartisan interest in these ideas; (3) explorations of what the behavioral sciences have to offer in the way of advice about negotiations, decision-making, and conflict resolution in the near term and about human conflict and its resolution over the longer term; and (4) the possibilities for fundamentally changing the long-term relationship between the U.S. and the Soviet Union.

Carnegie Corporation of New York

Financial Data (year ended 9/30/87)

Assets:[1]	$ 806,295,988
Total grants paid:[2]	$ 32,815,589
Number of grants paid:	341
Highest payment:	$ 750,000
Lowest payment:	$ 975
Median payment size:	$ 60,000

Application Procedures

There is no application deadline; proposals are reviewed throughout the year. There is no formal procedure for submitting a proposal to the corporation. Applicants should first submit a statement describing the aims and methods of the project, the personnel involved, and the amount of financial support required. The program officers review all proposals in light of their knowledge of the field and in relation to the corporation's current program priorities. Requests for supplementary information or for meetings are made when either would be helpful in making a judgment on the grant request.

It should be noted that grant requests of $25,000 or less can be approved at the staff level.

Meeting Times

The board of directors of the Carnegie Corporation of New York meets in October, December, February, April, and June.

Publications

The corporation publishes annual and quarterly reports, as well as a general information brochure and list of grantees.

---

[1] As of November 30, 1987, the corporation reported the market value of its assets at approximately $730,000,000.

[2] This excludes studies and projects administered by officers of the corporation, totaling $1,627,442, and program-related investments totaling $384,411.

Chicago Resource Center
53 West Jackson Boulevard, Suite 315
Chicago, Illinois 60604
(312) 461-9333

Contact Person
Mary Ann Snyder, Director

Purpose
The Chicago Resource Center is a private foundation that supports organizations throughout the country addressing issues of domestic violence, gay and lesbian rights, and AIDS. It also makes a few miscellaneous out-of-program grant awards primarily related to women's issues.

Areas of Interest
Requests for start-up monies, operating expenses, and special project funding will be considered in all three programs, however, each program area has its own specific guidelines. Of special interest to the center in the area of domestic violence are coalition building, community education, volunteer programs, model programs, and shelter operating expenses. The center will consider a wide range of programs in the area of gay and lesbian issues, including direct services, civil and legal rights, coalition building, and outreach to educational and community institutions. Further, as a separate program interest, the Center will consider funding programs in the area of AIDS services and education.

Financial Data (year ended 12/31/87)
At December 31, 1986, the assets of Chicago Resource Center were $141,383. During 1987, however, it approved 188 grants totaling $1,525,218. Following is an analysis by program area. It excludes 10 miscellaneous grants totaling $278,638 (see table on the next page).

Application Procedures
The center annually issues requests for proposals in each program area, and copies may be obtained by telephoning the office. Essentially, the proposal guidelines are identical for each area, and proposals prepared for other funders will be accepted only if they contain all the information required by the center.

Proposals prepared expressly for the center should not exceed 10

Chicago Resource Center

pages, including budget information. Other materials may be attached, but will not be considered a part of the proposal. Proposals prepared for other funders that exceed the page limit must be accompanied by a one-to-two page description of the organization and project for which funds are requested. All proposals must be accompanied by the summary sheet form contained in the RFP package and by proof of Section 501(c)(3) tax-exempt status. Organizations that have applied but have not yet received tax-exempt status may submit proposals, however, funded monies will not be available until the IRS has made its determination.

Briefly, all proposals (except those submitted by organizations affiliated with universities) must describe the purpose, goals, history, activities, and achievements of the organization. Also included should be a list of other organizations familiar but not affiliated with the applicant's program. (Letters of support may be submitted, but the maximum is three.) The proposals should also describe the project for which funds are requested, including purpose, need, how the project differs from other work in the field, impacts, staffing, and criteria that will be used to measure success. Grant applications must also include a current annual operating budget, income statement, and a proposed project budget. Specific items to be included are detailed in the guidelines. Overhead charges should be listed as a separate item, and in-kind commitments should not be included in the total budget.

The deadlines for submitting proposals are as follows: March 31 for

Chicago Resource Center
Analysis of 1987 Grantmaking Activity

	AIDS Services and Education	Gay and Lesbian	Domestic Violence
Total Grants Authorized	$164,446	$316,409	$765,725
Number of Grants Authorized	21	43	114
Highest Grant	$15,000	$15,000	$13,550
Lowest Grant	$1,396	$800	$3,000
Median Grant Size	$7,500	$75,000	$6,000

Chicago Resource Center

consideration by the board at its May meeting; June 30 for consideration in August; September 30 for consideration in November; and December 21 for consideration in February. Applications received after the deadlines will be considered in the following grant cycle. Applicants can expect to be notified of a decision during the month following the board meeting. Telephone calls should not be placed to the center to find out about funding decisions. This information is not released by telephone.

Grant Limitations
In the domestic violence program the center will not consider batterers' programs or programs for children. Grants are made only to organizations with proof of tax-exempt status from the IRS.

Meeting Times
The board of directors of the Chicago Resource Center meets quarterly to review grant applications.

Publications
The center does not have an annual report. Program guidelines are distributed.

The Edna McConnell Clark Foundation
250 Park Avenue
New York, New York 10017
(212) 986-7050

Contact Persons
Peter D. Bell, President
Peter W. Forsythe, Vice President and Program Director, Children
M. Hayes Mizell, Program Director, Disadvantaged Youth
Kenneth F. Schoen, Program Director, Justice
Joseph A. Cook, Program Director, Tropical Disease Research
Susan Notkin, Program Director, Special Grants

Purpose
The goals of the Edna McConnell Clark Foundation are to improve conditions for persons who are poorly or unfairly served by the established institutions of society. To do this it seeks basic adjustments in the way institutions and agencies work to meet social needs and seeks opportunities to make a difference where other funding is not available.

Areas of Interest
The foundation has four specific programs: children, disadvantaged youth, justice, and tropical disease research. While many grants are made to well-established organizations, a number of community-based advocacy groups received support (especially in the first three program areas).

Children. This program seeks to assure that dependent, neglected, and troubled children have permanent families. It supports efforts to: (1) develop policies and programs that will avert the unnecessary removal of children from their families; (2) aid courts, advocates, and public agencies to implement the Adoption Assistance and Child Welfare Reform Act of 1980; and (3) protect reforms that have successfully reunited children with their biological parents or provided for the adoption of hard-to-place children.

Disadvantaged Youth. The Program for Disadvantaged Youth works to improve the education of disadvantaged youth by supporting: (1) projects aimed at the reform of school sys-

181

The Edna McConnell Clark Foundation

tems; (2) responses to the needs of disadvantaged youth in the middle grades; and (3) programs involving the business community as an advocate for improvements in the education of middle school students. The foundation is phasing out its support of school-to-work transition projects formerly carried out by the Program for Jobs for the Disadvantaged.

Justice. The Program for Justice seeks a more humane, rational, and effective criminal justice system by encouraging the use of alternatives to unnecessary incarceration and by supporting litigation and related work, both to correct specific abuses in prisons and jails and to enforce constitutional standards for the care of offenders.

Tropical Disease Research. This program seeks to prevent the two major causes of infectious blindness, onchocerciasis and trachoma, by supporting research to help develop better diagnostic methods, a vaccine, and effective control strategies. The program also continues to support well-targeted projects to develop means to control schistosomiasis, a parasitic disease which infects over 200 million people in the developing world.

Most grants are restricted to the programs listed above, and virtually all grants reflect the foundation's commitment to serve the disadvantaged. The foundation has traditionally maintained a special grants category in order to respond to a few important or interesting projects that may not fall into one of its four major program areas. It has recently sought to bring more programmatic coherence to special projects. Currently, for example, approximately half of the grants in this area are for projects to prevent or to end homelessness among families in New York City. Special grants, however, continue to enable the foundation to meet some of its responsibilities to the poor and disadvantaged in New York City, to support the advancement of national social policy issues on behalf of the disadvantaged, and to keep a margin of flexibility.

The Edna McConnell Clark Foundation

Financial Data (year ended 9/30/87)

As of September 30, 1987, the foundation reported assets totaling $384,509,000. Grants in all categories totaled $16,096,302. The following table analyzes grants for the year, according to the categories listed by the foundation in its annual report. This analysis does not include medical research grants totaling $4,130,997 paid during 1987.

Application Procedures

Initially, the foundation requests only a brief letter describing the program. If the staff determines that the request falls within the scope of the foundation's priorities, more detailed information and a formal proposal will be requested. Within each application, the staff looks for the strategy, skills, and commitment to accomplish the proposed project as well as the potential of the project to make substantial impact on specific program objectives.

Grant Limitations

The foundation welcomes the opportunity to cooperate with other funders with relevant interests. The foundation will not consider requests for capital purposes, scholarships, endowment or deficit operations, and does not make grants to individuals.

The Edna McConnell Clark Foundation*
Analysis of 1986-87 Grantmaking Activity

	National Social Policy	Ensuring Constitutional Conditions	National Job-Readiness Strategies	Family Preservation
Total Grants Paid	$1,398,026	$4,152,068	$2,183,956	$4,232,181
Number of Grants Paid	42	55	34	71
Highest Grant	$125,000	$485,000	$230,000	$266,000
Lowest Grant	$6,900	$5,853	$703	$5,000
Median Grant Size	$25,000	$50,000	$46,895	$47,500

*This table includes medical research grants totaling $4,130,997 paid during 1986–87.

The Edna McConnell Clark Foundation

Meeting Times

The board of trustees of the Edna McConnell Clark Foundation meets five times per year, in February, April, June, September, and December.

Publications

The foundation publishes a brochure titled *Current Goals & Programs,* an annual report, and a quarterly listing of grants awarded.

Compton Foundation, Inc.
10 Hanover Square
New York, New York 10005
(212) 510-5039

Contact Person
James R. Compton, President

Areas of Interest
The Compton Foundation's program priorities are (1) global and human survival, including arms control, international relations, population growth, environmental quality, preservation of natural resources, and protection of individual rights and human dignity; (2) education with a special emphasis on equal educational opportunity; (3) social justice, including the provision of adequate social services at the local level wtih a particular interest in programs directed at youth; and (4) culture and the arts, with an emphasis on regional programs.

The foundation has two programs. One is national and often addresses concerns that are global in scope. The other is regional, focused on the East and West Coasts, with a particular interest in local communities.

Financial Data (year ended 12/31/86)

Assets:[1]	$ 33,815,812
Total grants paid:	$ 2,165,756
Number of grants paid:	408
Highest grant:[2]	$ 60,000
Lowest grant:	$ 30
Median grant size:	$ 750

Application Procedures
A letter of inquiry is the preferred method of initial contact with the foundation. It should clearly and concisely set out the objectives of the project, the means by which the objectives are to be accomplished, the qualifications of the personnel involved, and an estimated budget. Evidence of the organization's tax-exempt status should be included. If further information is needed or a site visit is determined by the foundation to be warranted, the applicant will be notified. The foundation does not

[1] As of December 31, 1985.
[2] This excludes three unusually large grants totaling $325,000.

185

Compton Foundation, Inc.

acknowledge receipt of proposals, nor does it grant interviews with applicants.

Grant Limitations
No support is provided by the foundation for building funds or for individuals, and the foundation does not make loans.

Meeting Times
The board of directors of the Compton Foundation, Inc., meets semiannually, in May and November.

Publications
The foundation publishes a biennial report.

Pettus Crowe Foundation
1616 P Street, N.W., Suite 100
Washington, D.C. 20036
(202) 328-5186

Contact Person
Irene Crowe, President

Purpose
The Pettus Crowe Foundation is a small, family foundation organized for general charitable purposes and staffed part-time. Its grantmaking is directed primarily toward small, innovative, and risk-taking projects that promote justice and equality in society and that lack access to traditional funding sources.

Areas of Interest
The foundation is particularly interested in progressive women's issues including reproductive rights and how AIDS affects women of color; promoting and protecting civil rights and civil liberties; and exploring ethical issues. It will consider requests for support from service organizations as well as those conducting research and advocacy.

Financial Data (year ended 12/31/86)

Assets:	$	1,677,597
Total grants paid:	$	89,000
Number of grants paid:		32
Highest grant:	$	6,000
Lowest grant:	$	250
Median grant size:	$	2,500

Application Procedures
The foundation specifically requests that applicants not telephone, as the foundation is not staffed to handle telephone inquiries about potential support. Thus, the first step in initiating contact with the foundation is a brief letter of inquiry outlining the background of the organization, the proposed project and what it hopes to accomplish, and the amount of the grant request. Initially, full proposals should not be submitted. If the foundation is interested in the project, it will acknowledge the request and ask for a more complete proposal.

Pettus Crowe Foundation

Grant Limitations
The foundation will support only organizations with evidence of tax-exempt status or projects working with a tax-exempt fiscal sponsor.

Meeting Times
The board of directors of the Pettus Crowe Foundation meets twice a year to consider grant applications.

Publications
None.

Cummins Engine Foundation
500 Jackson Street
Mail Code 60814, Box Number 3005
Columbus, Indiana 47202-3005
(812) 377-3114

Contact Person
Adele J. Vincent, Associate Director

Purpose
The grantmaking activities of the Cummins Engine Foundation represent one portion of the corporate responsibility program of Cummins Engine Company, Inc., the manufacturer of high-speed diesel engines and component parts. The foundation supports local programs in communities in which the company has facilities or subsidiaries.

Areas of Interest
The activities of the Cummins Engine Foundation support three general principles: empowerment (to develop independence and equip people to help themselves and to serve others); inclusiveness (to expand opportunity for those who lack it); and community (to build and sustain quality in our common life).

The foundation has four funding priorities: youth and education, equity and justice, community development/arts, and public policy. Within each priority, the foundation has identified several areas for concentration.

In the youth and education program, the foundation looks for ways to eliminate barriers to the healthy development of young people, encourages organizations serving youth in creative ways, and supports efforts to improve elementary and secondary schools, including key institutions with which Cummins has historic relationships.

In equity and justice, Cummins focuses on those who face discrimination, are dispossessed, or are poorly served by society. It looks for organizations that are responding creatively and vigorously to meet their needs, engaging in constructive public advocacy and working to ensure protection of civil rights for women and racial and ethnic minorities. It also encourages opportunities for leadership development among women and minorities and supports efforts to increase minority economic participation.

The community development/arts program looks for programs that

Cummins Engine Foundation

enhance the general environment of Cummins plant communities. In community development, the foundation supports projects that encourage a high quality of life for the entire community. In the arts area, support is aimed primarily at developing opportunities for young or emerging artists in local Cummins communities and encouraging involvement in the arts, especially by youth.

The public policy program provides a vehicle for the foundation to make general support grants to national organizations working to strengthen the debate on key issues facing society. For the most part, impetus for these grants comes from the board of the foundation and not as a response to unsolicited proposals.

Financial Data (year ended 12/31/86)

Assets:	$ 8,904,603
Total grants paid:[1]	$ 3,365,626
Number of grants paid:	154
Highest grant:[2]	$ 50,000
Lowest grant:	$ 300
Median grant size:	$ 2,500

Application Procedures

There are no application deadlines. The foundation prefers that initial inquiries be made in writing and that interested applicants prepare a preliminary proposal for the foundation's review. This preliminary application should include a brief description of the problem being addressed, specifically what the program hopes to achieve, and an operating plan and budget, a description of the key leadership, and plans for evaluating the program's effectiveness. If the foundation is interested in considering the proposed program, additional information will be requested.

---

[1] This includes $76,551 in scholarships for children of employees, $264,075 to match employees' contributions to educational institutions, $113,100 paid as part of the Company's Architecture Program, $465,095 in commitments to United Way organizations, and $58,107 in miscellaneous contributions less than $1,500.

[2] This excludes three unusually large grants to well-established institutions totaling $1,015,993.

Cummins Engine Foundation

It should be noted that Cummins and its subsidiaries have manufacturing plants in Columbus, Seymour, Madison, and Plymouth, Indiana; Charleston, South Carolina; Jamestown, New York; Fostoria, Ohio; Cookeville and Memphis, Tennessee; Lake Mills, Iowa; and Sante Fe Springs, California. Proposals from plant communities outside southern Indiana should be submitted first to the local plant manager.

Grant Limitations
The foundation does not support political causes or candidates, or sectarian religious activities. Grants are not made to individuals.

Meeting Times
The board of directors of the Cummins Engine Foundation meets quarterly, in February, July, September, and December. The basic framework of the company's annual philanthropy plan and budget are set at the board meeting at the beginning of each year.

Publications
The foundation publishes an annual report.

Dayton Hudson Foundation
777 Nicollet Mall
Minneapolis, Minnesota 55402
(612) 370-6553

Contact Persons
Cynthia Mayeda, Managing Director
Vivian Stuck, Administrative Officer

Purpose
The Dayton Hudson Foundation is the major vehicle through which the Dayton Hudson Corporation contributes to nonprofit, tax-exempt organizations. The foundation policy emphasizes a strong obligation to those communities in which the corporation has operating company headquarters. The foundation's direction, therefore, is principally local, with activities concentrated in Minneapolis-St. Paul. The foundation gives a limited number national grants for programs that complement the local involvement of the operating companies, promote philanthropy, or that research and analyze preselected public-policy issues in the foundation's priority areas. On a more limited basis, the foundation makes grants in other communities where there are Dayton Hudson Corporation stores, including Target, Mervyn's, and Lechmere. (See Application Procedures below.)

Areas of Interest
The foundation concentrates its efforts in two focus areas: social action and the arts. Forty percent of the foundation's grants are made to programs and projects that result in economic and social progress for individuals and/or the development of community and neighborhood strategies that respond effectively to community social and economic concerns. Another forty percent goes to programs that result in artistic excellence and stronger artistic leadership in communities and/or in increased access to and use of the arts as a means of community expression. The remainder of the funds is contributed to programs and projects outside those two categories that either address special community needs and opportunities or represent innovative partnerships with other community leaders to solve problems.

In 1986 the foundation launched a special three-year initiative on school-dropout prevention. The effort, which is strongly results-oriented,

Dayton Hudson Foundation

provides increased funding beyond the small start-up grants in direct proportion to the results generated by the program: the more successful a program, the larger are subsequent grants. Other related issues include childcare, substance abuse prevention, and youth employment.

Financial Data (year ended 1/31/86)

Total grants paid:[1]	$	10,132,325
Number of grants paid:		899
Highest grant:[2]	$	86,000
Lowest grant:	$	400
Median grant size:	$	7,400

Application Procedures

The first step in applying for a grant is to identify the Dayton Hudson Company operating in your community. (A list appears at the end of this entry.) Areas of special interest, priorities and applications procedures may differ. If you apply to more than one Dayton-Hudson facility, you should indicate so in your formal request.

Generally the initial approach preferred is to send a one-page preliminary application letter that states the following: applicant's name, address, telephone number, and IRS tax-exempt status; the specific amount requested; and how the funds would be used. No additional information is needed at this stage. The foundation specifically requests that preliminary inquiries not be made by telephone or personal visit. Preliminary applications have no deadlines. The foundation or company usually responds to these inquiries within one month either by declining support or by asking for a formal application.

If a formal application is requested, it should be made in a letter of not more than two typewritten pages (four handwritten pages) that includes but is not limited to the following: (1) a request for a specific amount of money, with an explanation of how the funds will be used; (2) a description of the organization, including its purposes and objec-

---

[1] This grants analysis excludes all grants to local United Ways.
[2] This excludes 24 grants over $100,000 to major cultural and educational institutions.

Dayton Hudson Foundation

tives; and (3) the name(s) and qualifications of the person(s) who will administer the grant. If the request is to support a capital drive or specific project, the letter should include information about the need to be addressed, the geographical area and population to be served, and a timetable for the project.

Attached to each letter should be the following: (1) a copy of the organization's most recent tax-exempt ruling; (2) a list of the organization's officers and directors; (3) a financial report for the most recently completed year of operation; (4) an organizational budget for the current operating year showing anticipated expenses and income by sources; and (5) a donor's list, either complete or representative, showing private, corporate, and foundation contributors to the organization during the previous twelve months. Applications without the basic information and attachments listed above will not be considered until all such material is provided.

Grant Limitations
The foundation makes grants for general operations, specific projects, and capital purposes. The foundation rarely supports endowment programs. Grants are not made to individuals or to religious organizations for religious purposes, and are rarely made to national programs, health organizations, educational institutions, or advocacy or research groups. It should be noted that the foundation does not fund organizations during their first year of operation.

Meeting Times
The board of directors of the Dayton Hudson Foundation meets four times a year, in February, June, October, and December.

Publications
The foundation publishes an annual report and will make available upon request an information sheet, *Information for Applicants,* and a list of Dayton Hudson facilities.

Dayton Hudson Foundation

Operating Companies
Requests from Minnesota organizations should be addressed to the foundation. All other requests should be sent to the appropriate Dayton Hudson company listed below:

Michigan
Hudson's
Susan L. Kelly, Director
Region I Public Affairs
Dayton Hudson Department Store Company
21500 Northwestern Highway
Southfield, Michigan 48075
(313) 443-6220

Massachusetts
Lechmere
Elaine Ricci, Director
External Relations
275 Wildwood Street
Woburn, Massachusetts 01801
(617) 935-8320

Northern California, Nevada, Oregon, Utah, Washington
Mervyn's
Judy Belk, Manager
Public Affairs
25001 Industrial Boulevard
Hayward, California 94545
(415) 786-4778

Southern California, Arizona, Colorado
Mervyn's
Kathy Blackburn, Manager
Community Relations

Dayton Hudson Foundation

25001 Industrial Boulevard
Hayward, California 94545
(415) 786-7723

Georgia, Louisiana, Michigan, New Mexico, Oklahoma, Texas
Mervyn's
Valerie Carattini-Cook, Manager
Public Affairs
25001 Industrial Boulevard
Hayward, California 94545
(415) 786-7429

Target Stores
Store Manager at your local Target store.

Deer Creek Foundation
818 Olive Street
St. Louis, Missouri 63101
(314) 241-3228

Contact Person
Mary Stake Hawker, Administrator

Purpose
The Deer Creek Foundation's purpose is primarily, in its own words, "to advance and preserve governance of society by rule of the majority, with protection of basic rights as provided by the Constitution and the Bill of Rights, and in educational efforts related to this goal."

Areas of Interest
The foundation's priority is assisting individuals and groups working on action programs to advance government accountability, civil liberties, and civil rights that promise to have significant regional or national impact. Among the fields of interest are communications and free speech, equal rights, public policy, citizenship, education, film and media, civil and criminal justice, litigation and legal services, minority and ethnic groups and reproductive rights.

Financial Data (year ended 12/31/86)

Assets:	$	4,904,037
Total grants paid:	$	234,260
Number of grants paid:		33
Highest grant:	$	25,000
Lowest grant:	$	500
Median grant size:	$	5,000

Application Procedures
No specific application form is required. Applicants should submit a letter stating briefly the objectives of the project and program design, the qualifications of the organization and individuals concerned, the mechanism for evaluating the results, and a budget with amounts and sources of anticipated support. Proof of tax-exempt status from the IRS and the latest annual report, IRS Form 990, or audited financial statement should also be included, together with a list of officers and board members, a

Deer Creek Foundation

description of the organization's background and current activities, the current year operating budget, and sources of organizational support.

Grant Limitations
Grants are made only to organizations with Section 501(c)(3) tax-exempt status. The foundation does not normally support endowments, construction, equipment purchases, or general operating expenses.

Meeting Times
The board of directors of the Deer Creek Foundation meets in March, June, September, and December.

Publications
The foundation publishes a brochure containing grant application guidelines and application procedures. A list of past grantees is available upon request.

Design Industries Foundation for AIDS
Post Office Box 5176
FDR Station
New York, New York 10150
(212) 580-3311
(212) 502-0130

Contact Persons
George W. Slowik, Jr., Chairman of the Board
R. A. Radley, Executive Director

Purpose
The Design Industries Foundation for AIDS[1], DIFFA, was established in 1984 by concerned members and friends of the design, architecture, and furnishings professions. Its prime goal is to make grants to organizations providing direct services to people with AIDS, legal and financial assistance, education, housing, and those conducting research into the cure and treatment of the disease. DIFFA also supports public education and advocacy activities.

Through its national office, DIFFA coordinates a network of local fundraising and grantmaking advisory committees. As of January 1988 committees were active in northern California; southern Florida; Atlanta, Georgia; Chicago, Illinois; Boston, Massachusetts; Minnesota; Dallas and Houston, Texas; New York City; and Washington, D.C. Funds raised from the general public through local committees and at one-time-only fundraising events are awarded for work in the geographic areas from which they were collected and on the recommendation of the local DIFFA committee. Additional grants are made from national funds to groups operating both in other localities and nationally.

Areas of Interest
DIFFA seeks proposals that reflect its broad aims and purposes from qualified organizations and persons aimed at discovering the causes and methods of treatment of AIDS and AIDS-related diseases; hospitals, medical schools, and laboratories investigating the cause, methods for diagnosis and alternative treatments of AIDS; organizations providing health care and other forms of care, support, and similar services to persons

---

[1]Formerly called the Design and Interior Furnishings Foundation for AIDS.

Design Industries Foundation for AIDS

with AIDS and those affected by their illness; and other groups working to help people with AIDS and to educate the general public about the nature of the disease.

Financial Data (year ended 12/31/87)

Support and revenue:	$	1,149,722
Total grants paid:	$	226,582
Number of grants paid:		47
Highest grant:	$	15,000
Lowest grant:	$	586
Median grant size:	$	4,500

Application Procedures

There are no application deadlines. Proposals are reviewed throughout the year, and grants are awarded quarterly. Application forms are available upon request. Applicants are asked to include with their application form a cover letter describing how the proposed activity relates to DIFFA's goals and demonstrating that the applicant has the fiscal, management, and planning capacity to meet its stated objectives. The cover letter should be signed either by the organization's director, or the chair of its governing body.

Grant Limitations

There are no subject-matter limitations on the proposals DIFFA will consider, except that the proposed activity must be related to some aspect of the AIDS crisis. Grants are made to organizations engaged in charitable or educational activities that are either tax exempt or that are working with a tax-exempt fiscal agent.

Meeting Times

The board of trustees of the Design Industries Foundation for AIDS meets monthly and reviews grant applications quarterly.

Design Industries Foundation for AIDS

Publications
DIFFA publishes a brochure and fact sheet and will distribute grant application guidelines and forms upon request.

Geraldine R. Dodge Foundation, Inc.
95 Madison Avenue
Post Office Box 1239
Morristown, New Jersey 07960
(201) 540-8442

Contact Person
Scott McVay, Executive Director

Areas of Interest
The Geraldine R. Dodge Foundation concentrates its grantmaking activities in New Jersey, with a specific interest in the local Morristown/Madison area. The areas of emphasis include animal welfare, secondary education, the arts, and public interest and critical issues. The foundation's public interest/critical issues program supports projects working in fields such as teen pregnancy and sexuality, the environment, reduction of hazardous waste, energy, and public policy.

Financial Data (year ended 12/31/86)
Assets:	$ 127,108,281
Total grants paid:	$ 6,253,753
Number of grants paid:	196
Highest grant:	$ 200,000
Lowest grant:[1]	$ 5,500
Median grant size:[1]	$ 24,125

Application Procedures
Each program-interest area has a different deadline, and each is considered only once during the year. The deadlines for proposals are: January 1 for animal welfare and local projects in the Morristown/Madison area only; April 1 for secondary education; July 1 for the arts; and October 1 for public issues.

A preliminary inquiry is advisable before the submission of a detailed proposal. Grant requests should be initiated by a letter describing the proposed project, its expected impact, the qualifications of staff, a timetable, and other expected sources of funding. A copy of certified financial statements and proof of Section 501(c)(3) tax-exempt status should be

---

[1] This excludes 66 grants of $5,000 or less totaling $33,000.

Geraldine R. Dodge Foundation, Inc.

included. Interviews will be arranged only after the foundation has received a completed grant request. It is customary for an organization, whether or not it receives funding, to wait one year before submitting a subsequent proposal.

Grant Limitations
The foundation does not consider requests for support of higher education, health, or religion. Its focus on animal welfare is directed toward projects with national implications, and local humane activities are not considered for support. The foundation's focus on secondary education includes projects in New Jersey, at independent schools in the Northeast and Middle Atlantic states, and programs with national audiences.

The foundation ordinarily will not consider proposals for capital purposes, endowment funds, or deficit operations. It does not support scholarship funds or make direct awards to individuals, nor does it administer programs that it supports. The foundation typically does not consider requests for grants to conduit organizations that pass on funds to other organizations.

Meeting Times
The board of trustees of the Geraldine R. Dodge Foundation meets quarterly, in March, June, September, and December.

Publications
The foundation distributes an annual report that includes a description of its grants and application guidelines.

The William H. Donner Foundation, Inc.
500 Fifth Avenue
New York, New York 10111
(212) 719-9290

Contact Person
Donald S. Rickerd, President

Areas of Interest
The William H. Donner Foundation has national interests in two program areas. Its program in U.S.-Canadian relations supports policy studies and academic projects at the graduate level that offer promising opportunities for bilateral dialogue and problem-solving. Better management of the U.S. coastal marine zone and the nation's inland water resources is the primary objective of the ocean and inland water resources program. The foundation also makes some grants to cultural and arts institutions.

Preference is given to projects that are national in scope, although regional and local endeavors that may potentially have wider impact also receive consideration. Experimental endeavors for which seed money is not always readily available, and innovative policy research, especially policy studies of national issues, are of particular interest.

Financial Data (year ended 10/31/85)
Assets:	$ 42,337,185
Total grants paid:	$ 1,771,907
Number of grants paid:	50
Highest grant:	$ 152,000
Lowest grant:	$ 4,200
Median grant size:	$ 27,055

Application Procedures
After reviewing the complete description of the foundation's programs contained in its annual report, applicants should send a letter briefly describing the organization and the project. If the proposed project is of interest to the foundation, the applicant will be invited to submit a formal proposal for consideration. The foundation's policy is to review and respond to all inquiries.

The William H. Donner Foundation, Inc.

Grant Limitations
The foundation supports only tax-exempt organizations. The foundation does not fund construction or renovation of buildings, capital campaigns, annual charitable drives, research and travel, operating deficits, or loans. Individuals unaffiliated with nonprofit organizations are not eligible to apply for support for study, research, travel, or similar activities.

Meeting Times
The board of trustees of The William H. Donner Foundation, Inc., meets three times a year, usually in February, June, and October.

Publications
The foundation publishes an annual report.

Lucius and Eva Eastman Fund, Inc.
24120 Summit Woods Drive
Los Gatos, California 95030
(408) 353–2666

Contact Person
Lucius R. Eastman, Jr.

Areas of Interest
The Lucius and Eva Eastman Fund is committed to social change and supports a variety of grassroots organizations throughout the country. Some interests of the fund include women, community arts, litigation and civil rights, media and film, and peace/disarmament issues.

Financial Data (year ended 12/31/87)

Assets:	$	1,050,000
Total grants paid:	$	55,650
Number of grants paid:		44
Highest grant:	$	2,000
Lowest grant:	$	500
Median grant size:	$	1,000

Application Procedures
Requests for grants are accepted throughout the year. Each proposal should describe the project for which funding is sought, including a budget both for the project and the sponsoring organization. Information about the tax-exempt status of the organization, or about a tax-exempt fiscal agent, if applicable, must also accompany each proposal.

Grant Limitations
The fund states that only those requests for specific, well-focused projects are considered. Projects that have received substantial funding from other sources will not receive consideration.

Meeting Times
The board of directors of the Lucius and Eva Eastman Fund meets three times a year, in February, June, and October.

Lucius and Eva Eastman Fund, Inc.

Publications
The fund does not publish an annual report. Upon inquiry, a list of recent grantees and a brief description of application procedures will be provided.

The O. P. and W. E. Edwards Foundation
Hearthstone Village
South Londonderry, Vermont 05155
(802) 824-3770

Contact Person
David E. Gamper, President

Purpose
The O. P. and W. E. Edwards Foundation is a small, unstaffed foundation particularly interested in young people. Although most of its grants were specified in the donor's bequest, there is a discretionary grantmaking fund. With these moneys, the foundation supports groups with strong neighborhood ties that are able to intervene effectively at those critical times in a youth's life when he or she most needs help and support.

Its interests also include programs to help socially and economically deprived children get the start they need so that they may take advantage of opportunities to better their futures. It tends to favor organizations that take a comprehensive approach to problems either within their own programs or as integral parts a network of services in their communities. Most grants are made to organizations in Vermont; however, several grants are made in other areas and there are no geographic restrictions.

Areas of Interest
In the area of direct services to at-risk youth, the foundation looks for small programs that can work with young people in as holistic a manner as feasible. Organizations should have strong leadership with a recognized presence in the community and be able to follow through effectively on their contacts with their target population. This population should include but need not be limited to economically and socially disadvantaged youth. The foundation is also interested in supporting projects in special-issue areas such as truancy, juvenile delinquency and juvenile justice, teenage parenting, youth employability, chemical dependency, and the responsiveness of institutions.

In the prevention area, the foundation supports small organizations targeting economically disadvantaged children (and perhaps their families) at risk of becoming especially needy of social services later in their lives. This can include: work with young children in day care or after school programs; family issues such as parenting skills, child abuse and

The O. P. and W. E. Edwards Foundation

neglect, and domestic violence; and youth empowerment in general through implementation of prevention curricula in schools, focused educational outreach and follow-up activities, and training of service providers in prevention.

Recently grants have generally been grouped in the following categories: start-up funds for new, untested programs where a successful demonstration is likely to attract other longer-term support; grants for new projects of established organizations that are either likely to be institutionalized or have only a limited duration; and interim general support for organizations which, although undergoing a transition, seem likely to stabilize in the near future.

Financial Data (year ended 8/31/87)

Assets:	$	2,694,113
Total grants paid:[1]	$	134,837
Number of grants paid:		25
Highest grant:[2]	$	10,000
Lowest grant:	$	500
Median grant size:	$	3,000

Application Procedures

The foundation does not use application forms and has no established deadlines, although it notes that most of the estimated available funds have usually been allocated by August and February for the following six months. As an initial contact, applicants are advised to send a brief letter that describes the proposed project or program and the sponsoring organization, including an estimated budget and the amount requested. If the request falls within the foundation's guidelines and has a reasonable likelihood of receiving funding, a more detailed proposal will be requested and guidelines will be provided.

---

[1]This analysis is based only on discretionary grant awards. It excludes 16 grants totaling $175,200 paid to organizations specified by the donor.

[2]This excludes one unusually large grant of $50,000.

The O. P. and W. E. Edwards Foundation

Grant Limitations

The foundation does not make new grants to organizations whose annual operating budgets exceed $200,000 (although a tax-exempt fiscal sponsor's budget may be higher). Grants are made only to tax-exempt organizations and projects working with tax-exempt sponsors. The foundation does not make grants to individuals and only rarely contributes to capital campaigns. It is unlikely to fund research studies, films or publications.

Further, the fund prefers to support organizations in geographical locations that make site visits by one or more trustees possible, although occasionally grants are made based on references.

Meeting Times

The board of trustees of the O. P. & W. E. Edwards Foundation meets twice a year, in the summer and winter, to make grant decisions.

Publications

The fund distributes a description of its program interests and application procedures on request.

The Ford Foundation
320 East 43rd Street
New York, New York 10017
(212) 573-5000

Contact Persons[1]

Franklin A. Thomas, President
Robert Curvin, Urban Poverty
Norman R. Collins, Rural Poverty and Resources
Shepard L. Forman, Human Rights and Governance
Peter W. Stanley, Education and Culture
Enid C. B. Schoettle, International Affairs
Thomas F. Miller, Program-Related Investments
Barron M. Tenny, Vice President, Secretary and General Counsel

Purpose

The Ford Foundation is a private philanthropic institution chartered to serve the public welfare. The foundation works mainly by granting and lending funds for educational, developmental, research, and experimental efforts designed to produce significant advances on problems of worldwide importance.

Areas of Interest

There are two program divisions at the foundation: U.S. and international affairs programs and developing country programs. Cutting across these divisions are program interests that roughly coincide with the following broad categories: urban poverty, rural poverty and resources, human rights and social justice, governance and public policy, education and culture, international affairs, and population. In addition, the foundation uses a portion of its capital to make program-related investments (PRIs); in 1988–89, $100 million of the corpus of the endowment was earmarked for PRIs.

A review of grants made by the foundation in recent years reveals that while much of the support is directed toward established organizations, within each program interest a number of small grassroots community-based initiatives also received support. A brief description of each program interest follows.

---

[1]Grant requests should be addressed to the secretary of the foundation.

The Ford Foundation

Urban Poverty.   The largest single part of the foundation's 1988–89, program budget, over one-fifth, will be applied to problems of urban poverty. The foundation has organized its urban-poverty work into three broad categories. They are the physical, economic and social revitalization of low-income communities; services to children, youth, and families, including a new initiative in early childhood education and care; and cross-disciplinary research aimed at increasing knowledge about poverty in its many dimensions, ways to cope with it, and its relation to the larger economy.

Rural Poverty and Resources.   To help alleviate rural poverty, the foundation supports efforts to develop effective rural policies, to enhance agricultural productivity, to encourage more efficient and equitable management of land and water resources, to increase employment opportunities (particularly for women), and to strengthen rural community organizations. In the U.S. activities are funded that help develop more coherent rural policies, improve natural-resource management, and create income and employment opportunities for the rural poor. In its work overseas, the foundation emphasizes activities that promote agricultural and rural development.

Human Rights and Social Justice.   The principal aims of this program are promoting civil and political rights and broadening access to social and economic opportunities for minorities, women, refugees, migrants, and other disadvantaged groups. Substantial support goes to strengthen nongovernmental organizations monitoring and disseminating information about human rights violations and seeking remedies for victims, for groups promoting the free flow of ideas, for those working to protect the rights of minorities and women, for efforts to maintain strong and effective legal services for the poor, and for clarifying the rights of undocumented aliens and asylum-seekers and helping them obtain the protections of the law. The foundation continues to support efforts to advance the rights and opportunities of Blacks, Hispanics, and other minorities.

The Ford Foundation

In December 1987 the board of trustees of the foundation approved a two-year budget of $4.5 million for an AIDS initiative, approximately $3.0 million of which has been allocated for activities in the U.S.and $1.5 million of which has been allocated for work overseas. This initiative, housed within the Human Rights and Governance Program[2] has three parts:

1. Supporting a small number of national and intermediary organizations to synthesize, analyze, and disseminate current data on the demographic, social, and economic consequences of AIDS; to develop and evaluate policy options and strategies for state and local officials responsible for dealing with the disease; and to examine the ethical and legal implications of the AIDS crisis with due regard for the rights of HIV positive individuals and national requirements for public health and safety.
2. Establishing a national AIDS fund and six local consortia comprised of representatives of community foundations, state and local officials, other funders, and constituent groups to help develop local responses, and to support and learn from innovative preventive education and care giving programs.
3. Providing information and logistical support in developing countries for public health ministries and nongovernmental organizations concerned with developing fair and effective policies and preventive measures to contain the disease, and to share successful strategies.

Governance and Public Policy. Foundation activities in

[2]This funding is being administered by two organizations: the National AIDS Network and the National Community AIDS Partnership. For more information contact: Mr. Paul Kawata, Executive Director, National AIDS Network, 2033 M Street, N.W., Suite 800, Washington, D.C. 20036 (202) 293-2437; or Mr. Paul Van Ness, Executive Director, National Community AIDS Partnership, 2033 M Street, N.W., Suite 800, Washington, D.C. 20036 (202) 293-2437.

The Ford Foundation

the field of governance are aimed at strengthening democratic processes and institutions, promoting civic participation, improving the performance and service delivery of state and local governments, and enhancing the vitality of the nonprofit sector. In the area of public policy, grants are made for efforts to increase minority participation in the policy-making process, for studies to inform policy-making on various important social and economic issues, and for research on U.S. immigration and naturalization policies.

Education and Culture. In the U.S. the foundation's work in education has three principal objectives: broadening access to learning and improving the effectiveness of programs that serve disadvantaged groups; engagement of faculty in their teaching; and strengthening curricula and curricular resources in selected fields. The foundation has integrated its formerly separate programs for schools and higher education and broadened its grantmaking to include rural as well as urban schools. In developing countries the foundation seeks to encourage free inquiry and scholarship in key national colleges and universities and to strengthen research and training in the social sciences, including women's studies.

Support for the arts in the U.S. has two major goals: to assist the development of new work and innovative forms of expression in the performing arts and to enhance pluralism and diversity in the arts. Overseas the foundation assists programs to preserve and interpret traditional cultures and to enhance their contribution to contemporary society.

International Affairs. The premise of this program is that there is a continuing need for specialists in independent institutions who can provide authoritative analyses of important international issues for both policy makers and the public at large. To help meet this need, grants are made in the U.S. and abroad for research, training, the development of networks of analysts, and public information on seven topics: international

The Ford Foundation

economics and development; peace, security and arms control; international refugees and migration; U.S. foreign policy; international relations (particularly in developing countries); international organizations and law; and neglected fields of foreign-area studies.

Population. The foundation works in both the U.S. and the developing world to improve women's lives and the survival and healthy development of their children by supporting programs to strengthen reproductive health, the quality of family planning care, contraceptive safety, and the management of gynecological infections and sexually transmitted diseases. A second focus is research that informs policymakers and the public on the consequences of population change.

The foundation also makes PRIs in enterprises that advance its philanthropic purposes. PRIs are made in such fields as community development, low income housing, job development, education, and the arts. PRIs approved or paid in 1986 were predominantly in the area of urban poverty, with some support also for programs in rural poverty and resources, human rights and governance, and international development. Generally PRIs are made in projects for which commercial financing is not economically feasible.

Financial Data (year ended 9/30/87)

As of September 30, 1987, the assets of the foundation were $5.5 million. In FY 1987 the foundation approved grants and program-related investments totaling $204.3 million and $15.2 million, respectively.

Because complete 1987 grants data were not available for analysis when this entry was prepared, the following analysis is based on the foundation's grantmaking activities in FY 1986. In that year grants approved totaled $180 million and PRIs totaled $14.6 million. In conformity with the foundation's annual report, each program area combines grants made for programs in both the U.S. and developing countries. Note that in the case of multiyear commitments, these data represent only the part

215

The Ford Foundation

of the commitment actually paid in FY 1986. This analysis includes grants administered by the foundation as well as delegated-authority projects.

Application Procedures

Before a detailed formal application is made, applicants are urged to consult the foundation's most recent annual report and statement of current interests. A brief letter of inquiry is advisable in order to determine whether the foundation's interests and funds permit consideration of a proposal. If a proposal is submitted, it should be noted that there are no application forms. Proposals should set forth: (1) objectives; (2) the proposed program for pursuing objectives; (3) qualifications of persons engaged in the work; (4) a detailed budget; (5) present means of support and status of applications to other funding sources; and (6) tax-exempt status of the applicant.

Applications are considered throughout the year. Normally applicants may expect to receive an initial indication of whether the proposed request falls within the foundation's interests and budgetary limitations within one month after submitting an inquiry. Domestic applications should be sent to The Secretary, Ford Foundation, at the address in New York City. Applicants in foreign areas where the foundation has an office should direct proposals to the nearest foundation office.

The Ford Foundation
Analysis of 1985-86 Grantmaking Activity

	Total Grants Paid	Number of Grants	Highest Grant	Lowest Grant	Median Grant Size
Urban Poverty	$44,046,455	312	$6,200,000	$2,500	$50,000
Rural Poverty/Resources	$23,948,772	339	$1,425,686	$1,215	$34,000
Human Rights/Social Justice	$26,183,275	266	$1,585,000	$1,782	$47,850
Governance/Public Policy	$20,491,740	128	$2,500,000	$2,200	$50,000
Education/Culture	$27,319,174	271	$5,790,050	$1,457	$75,000
International Affairs	$20,346,434	206	$2,585,000	$2,635	$45,000
Population	$2,036,650	27	$281,365	$2,500	$50,000
Special Program Actions	$1,554,871	23	$500,000	$2,500	$25,000
Program-related Investments	$13,186,512	19	$1,500,000	$44,952	$500,000

The Ford Foundation

Grant Limitations

Most of the foundation's grant funds are given to organizations. While the foundation also makes grants to individuals, such grants are: (1) few in number relative to the demand; (2) limited to research, training, and other activities related to the foundation's program interests; and (3) subject to IRS limitations and requirements. The foundation does not award undergraduate scholarships, nor are grants awarded for purely local or personal needs. Most support for graduate fellowships is funneled through grants to universities and other organizations, which are responsible for the selection of recipients.

Grants are not made for medical projects (except as they affect population problems), programs for which substantial government support is readily available, religious activities as such, routine operating costs of institutions, or, except in rare cases, for the construction or maintenance of buildings.

Meeting Times

The board of trustees of The Ford Foundation meets quarterly.

Publications

Of particular relevance to potential grantees are the following Ford Foundation publications: the annual report, which contains a complete review of grants and financing, and the booklet titled *Current Interests,* which includes grant application procedures. *The Ford Foundation Letter* is a bimonthly publication that highlights issues of concern to the foundation and reports on grants. Periodically the foundation publishes reports describing particular programs or activities it has supported, and several films are available for purchase or rental. A list of publications and films may be obtained from The Ford Foundation, Office of Reports.

The Forum Institute
1616 P Street, N.W., Suite 100
Washington, D.C. 20036
(202) 328-5109

Contact Person
Terri K. Shuck, Executive Director

Purpose
The Forum Institute provides financial support to nonpartisan voter registration and education programs designed to increase citizen participation in the United States.

Areas of Interest
The Forum Institute makes grants to local tax-exempt organizations throughout the country that work on a grass roots level in their own communities to register and educate those voters who traditionally have had the lowest rates of political participation and representation, i.e., primarily low-income and minority. In addition, the Forum Institute supports organizations that conduct nonpartisan issue education in order to make people aware of their stake in the political process and create a more informed electorate.

Financial Data (year ended 12/31/87)

Support and revenue:	$	1,827,593
Total grants paid:	$	935,217
Number of grants paid:		20
Highest grant:[1]	$	50,417
Lowest grant:	$	2,000
Median grant size:	$	25,000

Application Procedures
The Forum Institute advises applicants to write or telephone and briefly describe their voter-participation project. If the project fits within the scope of the institute's program, a more detailed proposal will be invited. As much as possible, the Forum Institute's staff conducts site visits before making a funding recommendation to the board of directors.

---

[1]This excludes two unusually large grants totaling $549,589.

The Forum Institute

Grant Limitations
The Forum Institute does not consider requests for projects that do not involve voter registration, education, or participation activities, and it does not make grants to support partisan activities.

Meeting Times
The board of directors of The Forum Institute meets as needed to make grant awards, approximately four to six times a year.

Publications
None.

The Funding Exchange/National Community Funds
666 Broadway, 5th Floor
New York, New York 10012
(212) 260-8500

Contact Person
June Makela, Executive Director

Purpose
The Funding Exchange is a national network of community-based funds that support social-change efforts around a growing number of critical social and economic issues in their local communities. Its members are: Appalachian Community Fund (Knoxville), Bread and Roses Community Fund (Philadelphia), Baltimore Common Wealth (Baltimore), Chinook Fund (Colorado), Crossroads Fund (Chicago), Fund for Southern Communities (Georgia, North Carolina, and South Carolina), Haymarket People's Fund (New England), Headwaters Fund, (Minnesota), Liberty Hill Foundation (southern California), Live Oak Fund (Texas), McKenzie River Gathering Foundation (Oregon), North Star Fund (New York City), People's Resource of Southwest Ohio, Vanguard Public Foundation (San Francisco Bay area), and Wisconsin Community Fund (Wisconsin).[1]

The primary tasks of The Funding Exchange are to: (1) assist in the development of new community-based funds; (2) further the growth of existing funds; (3) expand the network of individual donors committed to social change philanthropy; (4) provide a variety of technical, fiscal, and advisory services to donors; (5) make donor-advised grants through its project, National Community Funds (NCF).

NCF was created in order to enable The Funding Exchange to respond to national as well as grass roots organizations outside the regions of its member funds. NCF assists individual funders by evaluating and disseminating information about important progressive trends and prospective grantees, administering grants, and maintaining information on legal and investment matters related to philanthropy. NCF staff research potential projects, look for common areas of interest among donors, and

---

[1]For further information about the activities of The Funding Exchange members, see their individual entries under Regional and Local Grantmakers. Each member fund has its own specific guidelines, individual funding priorities, and separate application procedures. In addition, most publish annual reports and regular newsletters. These materials are available upon request from their respective offices.

The Funding Exchange/National Community Funds

maintain a proposal clearinghouse. In addition, NCF has developed a network of resource people in its funding priority areas. NCF communicates with potential grantees and endeavors to keep grantees informed of any donor interest in their work.

Areas of Interest

NCF supports groups and projects primarily: (1) organizing in communities and workplaces around basic economic and social issues or providing resources for such organizing; (2) working for a more equitable distribution of power and wealth in society; or (3) working for a society without discrimination on the basis of race, sex, sexual orientation, economic status, or age. Groups must operate in a democratic manner and be responsive to the needs of the constituencies that they serve. In addition, groups and projects must have little or no access to traditional funding sources.

NCF's priorities include but are not limited to: (1) antiracist efforts as they relate to Black, Latin American, Native American, and Asian American communities; (2) community organizing around housing, health care, public services, welfare rights, rural issues; (3) energy and the environment, including organizations addressing issues such as nuclear power, safe energy alternatives, hazardous disposal of chemical wastes, pesticide abuse, land and water rights; (4) international issues, education and cultural activities around concerns such as Central and Latin America, Africa, Asia, and the Middle East; (5) lesbian and gay rights, including efforts to counter "new right" initiatives and parental rights; (6) women's movement activities, including women and work, reproductive rights, violence against women; and (7) workers' rights, including union democracy, occupational health and safety, farm workers' rights, and organizing the unorganized.

The Funding Exchange also has two special funds. The general fund extends to a national level the spirit of community-based control by relying on a committee of social-change activists to evaluate proposals and make funding decisions with a particular emphasis on organizing work in Third World communities. In 1987 The Funding Exchange launched the Paul Robeson Fund for Film and Video to provide an in-

The Funding Exchange/National Community Funds

stitutional source of funding for social- change-oriented media projects. Believing that films enhance organizing and inspire people to become involved, this fund complements the organizing focus of other Funding Exchange grantmaking on the national and local level. The Robeson Fund particularly emphasizes distribution, looking for applicants who have developed sound plans for getting their projects to communities that will be touched by the subject matter.

Financial Data (year ended 6/30/87)

At fiscal year end, June 30, 1987, The Funding Exchange listed total support and revenue for its national office as $5,423,029. Grants made by National Community Funds for the year totaled $2,822,307. The table below analyzes grants made by National Community Funds and the local Funding Exchange members combined by area of interest.

Application Procedures

Questions about the general fund and the Paul Robeson Fund, should be directed to the office, and interested applicants will be provided with application materials and deadline information.

The Funding Exchange/National Community Funds
Analysis of 1986-87 Grantmaking Activity

	Total Grants Paid	Number of Grants	Highest Grant	Lowest Grant	Median Grant Size
Community/Economic Issues	$726,806	238	$48,750	$50	$1,750
Environment/Safe Energy	$269,370	84	$31,000	$100	$1,500
Film and Video	$188,680	42	$17,500	$475	$3,500
Gay and Lesbian Rights	$120,754	54	$13,439	$25	$1,500
Government Accountability	$315,770	65	$78,250	$100	$1,500
Human Rights	$341,805	120	$26,978	$100	$2,000
International Issues	$1,086,732	287	$50,000	$100	$1,750
Peace/Disarmament	$472,666	108	$100,000	$20	$1,600
Resources for Organizing	$512,018	168	$27,000	$25	$1,500
Women's Rights	$508,875	168	$48,166	$100	$2,000
Worker's Rights	$194,181	65	$12,232	$150	$2,500

The Funding Exchange/National Community Funds

Otherwise, NCF does not require application forms or hard-and-fast procedures. Proposals should be brief (four to five pages), demonstrating that the project promotes social change, stating the problem the group or project is trying to solve, explaining how the project will operate, and providing information on the budget. In addition, the proposal package should include a brief cover letter describing the project, a copy of IRS notification of 501(c)(3) tax-exempt status for the project or its fiscal sponsor, and additional information such as the history of the organization, the past year's activities, a work plan for the next year, and a description of the group's organizational and decision-making structures. It should also include an explanation of the organization's funding sources, grass roots fundraising projects, and other groups with which the project has worked. Literature or other material produced about the group may be included, but applicants are asked not to send film, tapes, or videotapes.

Meeting Times
Grants are made from the general fund twice a year. Other grants are made throughout the year.

Publications
An annual report is published combining The Funding Exchange and National Community Funds.

Gannett Foundation
1101 Wilson Boulevard
Arlington, Virginia 22209
(703) 528–0800

Contact Persons
Chief Executive Officers of local Gannett Co., Inc., media properties[1]

Purpose
The Gannett Foundation makes grants available to the communities in which Gannett Co., Inc., newspapers, broadcasting stations, and outdoor advertising subsidiaries are located. These community-based grants are available in two ways: first, through a local grant program that provides extra support to help local organizations to continue to work effectively, to respond to new needs, or to take new approaches to old problems. Second, through its Community Priorities Program (CPP), the foundation has set up a means for communities to analyze their chief problems and needs, propose major projects to address them, and compete for substantial grants to get them started. CPP priorities are driven by the ascertainment process in each community, which typically involves the Gannett chief executive officer and a team of staff and community representatives. Issues addressed in each community reflect the work and research of that team.

Areas of Interest
Because Gannett's local grant program is decentralized, there is a great diversity among the grants. Taken together, they cover the full range of issues facing the country, including unemployment, poverty, housing, homelessness, crime, child care, health care, the elderly, urban decay, education, and racial tension. As of December 31, 1987, the foundation had awarded grants totaling about $308,000 for AIDS-related public education and services. The foundation requires that at least one-third of

---

[1]A full list appears in the foundation's annual report.

Gannett Foundation

each area's local grants address key community problems identified through the CPP ascertainment process.

Issues addressed by both CPP and the local grants program include teen pregnancy and teen mothers, homelessness, economic development, literacy, job training, and community efforts to cope with deteriorating central cities and loss of manufacturing jobs. Grants are also made to professional organizations of journalists and schools of journalism or mass communication for journalism education and strengthening the profession. Special areas of interest are freedom of the press, opportunities for minorities and women, continuing education, professionalism and ethics, and journalism research.

In addition, in September 1986, in cooperation with *USA Today* the foundation announced the Literacy Challenge, a two-year competitive grant program to bolster adult literacy efforts. Under the program, grants ranging from $40,000 to $100,000 are available to increase services addressing this problem through state-level coalitions and cooperative programs.

Financial Data (year ended 12/31/86)

Assets:	$ 577,757,400
Total grants awarded:	$ 19,051,296
Number of grants awarded:[3]	259
Highest grant:[4]	$ 250,000
Lowest grant:	$ 1,000
Median grant size:	$ 11,800

---

[3]These tabulations do not include grants totaling $801,222 awarded under the employee-matching gifts program; two programs for jouralists operated by the foundation, the Gannett Center for Media Studies (at Columbia University) and the Paul Miller Washington Reporting Fellowships (in Washington, D.C.); scholarship funds for children of employees and journalists; or 2,167 local grants under $5,000 each, which total $9,576,156.

[4]This figure omits one unusually large grant of $1 million awarded to set up a journalism center at Rochester Institute of Technology.

Gannett Foundation

Application Procedures

All recommendations for funding local programs originate with the local CEOs of the Gannett Co., Inc., properties. Application letters to the foundation will be returned for resubmission to the local CEO. The initial letter should include the project's purpose and cost; the amount of support requested; the completion date or timetable; other sources of revenue, actual or anticipated, and budgeted expenditures. In addition, the letter should include background on the organization and staff responsible for the project and documentation of IRS tax-exempt status.

Proposals are accepted throughout the year. Applicants should plan on 90 to 120 days for processing and decision on their proposal.

Applications dealing with journalism and mass communications and strengthening professionalism should be submitted directly to the Gannett Foundation in Rochester and addressed to The Vice-President/Education. Application for journalism grants must be made by the school or organization rather than the individual.

Grant Limitations

The foundation does not, as a general rule, make grants to local organizations not in Gannett-served communities or national or regional organizations unrelated to journalism; organizations serving religious purposes; elementary or secondary schools except for innovative special programs that serve disadvantaged or gifted students, enhance teaching skills or add a desirable education dimension not provided by regular school operating or capital budgets; political or legislative advocacy groups; endowments, loan programs, or annual contributions other than United Ways; multiple-year pledge campaigns; medical or other research unrelated to journalism; organizations in nations other than the U.S. and Canada; fraternal groups, athletic teams, veterans organizations, volunteer firemen, and similar organizations; programs that would financially benefit Gannett Co., Inc., properties.

Meeting Times

The full board of trustees of the Gannett Foundation meets quarterly, and its executive committee approves grants monthly.

Gannett Foundation

Publications

The foundation publishes an annual report, a brochure detailing guidelines for grant applications, and *Media Resource Guide,* a how-to manual
on press relations for community groups, along with numerous monographs and publications in the field of journalism.

Gannett Company Media Properties

As of February 1, 1988, the Gannett Company owned media properties
in the following locations:

Arizona	Minnesota
Arkansas	Mississippi
California	Missouri
Canada	Nebraska
Colorado	Nevada
Connecticut	New Jersey
Delaware	New Mexico
District of Columbia	New York
Florida	North Carolina
Georgia	Ohio
Guam	Oklahoma
Hawaii	Oregon
Idaho	Pennsylvnia
Illinois	South Dakota
Indiana	Tennessee
Iowa	Texas
Kansas	Vermont
Kentucky	Virgin Islands
Louisiana	Washington
Massachusetts	West Virginia
Michigan	Wisconsin

General Mills Foundation
Post Office Box 1113
Minneapolis, Minnesota 55440
(612) 540-3337

Contact Person
Reatha Clark King, Executive Director

Purpose
The General Mills Foundation serves as a channel through which General Mills, Inc., contributes to a variety of organizations and enterprises. There is an attempt to balance support between vital, established organizations and small, developing programs that promise to make important contributions in the future.

Areas of Interest
The foundation makes grants in the four general areas of education: social service, health, culture, and civic affairs. It has a particular interest in programs that encourage local initiatives in addressing community problems or opportunities, especially where the community has major plant facilities and a significant number of employees. (See list at the end of this entry.) In 1986 the vast majority of grants were awarded in the Minneapolis/St. Paul area, where General Mills has its corporate headquarters.

Financial Data (year ended 5/31/86)

Assets:	$ 16,530,422
Total grants paid:	$ 5,584,212
Number of grants paid:[1]	457
Highest grant:	$ 80,000
Lowest grant:	$ 1,000
Median grant size:	$ 5,000

Application Procedures
The foundation strongly requests that all initial inquiries be made by mail, not by telephone or personal visit. The foundation does not require

---

[1]This grants analysis does not include scholarships awarded to children of employees. Nor does it include the foundation's employee-matching gift contributions totaling $541,131.

General Mills Foundation

application forms. A brief letter with supporting documentation is an acceptable application. There are no application deadlines; proposals are accepted at any time.

The letter should include: a description of the purpose for which the grant is sought; specific details on how this purpose will be achieved by the grant; description of the constituency that will benefit from the project; evidence that the persons proposing the project are able to carry it to completion; a planned method of evaluation; a specific budget for the project as well as the operating budget for the organization's current fiscal year, showing anticipated sources of revenue as well as expenses; a brief description of the organization requesting support, with a list of officers and board members; an audited financial statement and the most recent IRS Form 990 (including Schedule A); a major donor list for the most recent and the current fiscal years listing the amount of support from each and sources of assured or anticipated support for the proposed project; and proof of Section 501(c)(3) tax-exempt status.

It is the practice of the foundation to seek additional relevant information on pending proposals from agencies and donors in the community that are likely to be well informed concerning a particular program or organization.

Grant Limitations

The foundation will not make grants to individuals; religious organizations for religious purposes; political campaigns; organizations without their own Sections 501(c)(3) and 509(a) rulings from the IRS; organizations designed primarily for lobbying; support travel by groups or individuals; national or local campaigns to eliminate or control specific diseases; basic or applied research, including but not limited to science, medicine, engineering, or energy; and recreation.

In general the foundation does not favor grants to subsidize publications, whether in print, on film, or for television; support conferences, seminars, workshops, or symposia; endowment campaigns or to capital funds for educational institutions; and fundraising campaigns.

General Mills Foundation

Meeting Times
The board of trustees of the General Mills Foundation meets periodically throughout the year.

Publications
The General Mills Foundation publishes an annual report containing application guidelines.

General Mills Subsidiaries
As of December 1987, General Mills had plant facilities in Buffalo, New York; Cedar Rapids, Iowa; Chicago and Saint Charles, Illinois; Los Angeles, Lodi, and Vallejo, California; Toledo, Ohio; Minneapolis, Minnesota; Great Falls, Montana; Johnson City, Tennessee; and Kansas City, Missouri.

General Service Foundation
Post Office Box 4659
1445 Pearl Street, Suite 201
Boulder, Colorado 80306
(303) 447-9541

Contact Person
Marcie J. Musser, Vice President and Treasurer

Purpose
The General Service Foundation, a private foundation, has determined that its most significant contribution can be made by addressing three basic long-term national and international problems: international peace, population, and resources. In general the foundation prefers to support experimental, demonstration, research projects and programs.

Areas of Interest
Within each area of activity, the foundation has established broad guidelines. For example, in the international peace program, the foundation is particularly interested in research and education on U.S. international relations that will contribute to international peace; international working groups concerned with increasing understanding and cooperation; program and policy analysis leading to the development of alternatives to war; and research and education on the relationships between economic, environmental, and political development and international peace. It will not support work addressing the military aspects of this issue.

The foundation's primary interest in the population area is in making contributions to organizations that are tax exempt under U.S. law and that conduct population work overseas, preferably in Latin America. Grants have been made to support programs that introduce and distribute family planning information and services including abortion and voluntary sterilization; programs that improve maternal and child health, family planning, and agricultural and economic development; and programs relating to reproductive health care and reproductive rights. Population interests in the United States include programs for adolescent pregnancy prevention and family life education and contraceptive development as well as programs relating to reproductive health and reproductive rights.

In the resources program, preference is given to programs that improve the use, management, and quality of water in the United States

General Service Foundation

(particularly west of the Mississippi River) and to programs that develop food, water, fuel, forage, forests, and fertilizer on a sustainable basis in developing countries and which are particularly tied into family planning education and services. Within these broad guidelines the foundation looks for initiatives at any level of the educational system that promise to develop integrative thinking and an international perspective.

Financial Data (year ended 12/31/86)

Assets:	$ 15,824,387
Total grants paid:[1]	$ 1,135,500
Number of grants paid:	45
Highest grant:	$ 61,500
Lowest grant:	$ 5,000
Median grant size:	$ 23,500

Application Procedures

There are no application deadlines; proposals are accepted throughout the year. Applicants who are uncertain as to whether their proposed project falls within the foundation's guidelines are urged to submit a letter of inquiry describing the project before preparing a formal proposal.

There are no application forms, but the foundation requests that formal proposals include the following: (1) name and address of the tax-exempt organization that will be responsible for the grant with proof that the applicant is currently tax exempt and not a private foundation; (2) brief statements of the purpose for which funds are sought, evidence supporting the need for the project, the project objectives, the amount requested, the person responsible for administration, qualifications of the organization and individuals responsible for carrying out the project, and what will be accomplished; (3) a one- or two-page summary of the proposed project or program, focusing on the solution to the problem;

---

[1]This excludes 15 discretionary grants made to arts organizations totaling $26,000. The foundation does not fund the arts through unsolicited project proposals. Rather, grants are made from a small discretionary fund and are distributed only at the personal request of a director.

General Service Foundation

(4) a budget for the project or program;(5) a statement regarding other funding obtained or requested and the plan for long-term funding; and (6) a copy of the applicant organization's last annual report (if available), or information including the organization's programs, its annual budget and financial statements, and a list of directors and officers.

Grant Limitations

In general, the foundation does not make contributions to operating budgets or to annual campaigns of established organizations. The foundation does not ordinarily contribute to capital (physical plant, equipment, endowment), to individuals or to relief programs.

Meeting Times

The board of directors of the General Service Foundation meets twice a year, in the spring and fall.

Publications

The foundation publishes an annual report.

HKH Foundation
33 Irving Place, 10th Floor
New York, New York 10003[1]
(518) 352-7391

Contact Person
Harriet S. Barlow, Adviser

Areas of Interest
The general program interests of the HKH Foundation are reversing the arms race, promoting environmental protection, and civil liberties.

Financial Data (year ended 12/31/87)
According to the foundation, while its assets at the end of 1987 were approximately $24 million, less than 10 percent of its grantmaking goes to the three areas identified above. In 1987 the foundation said there were approximately 20 grants made in these areas combined, averaging $5,000 to $20,000, for a total of $300,000. The following analysis is based on calendar year 1986.

Assets:	$	28,458,581
Total grants paid:	$	1,196,500
Number of grants paid:		23
Highest grant:[2]	$	30,000
Lowest grant:	$	5,000
Median grant size:	$	15,000

Application Procedures
The foundation does not review proposals on a competitive basis, i.e., choosing several among proposals submitted for a particular docket. Rather, the foundation focuses on its program areas, consults with activists and researchers, and formulates strategic plans. The foundation reports that sometimes this process results in support for current grantees, sometimes it produces support for new grantees, and occasionally it works to foster cooperative planning and action among organizations.

Thus, while the foundation welcomes the opportunity to learn about

---

[1] While the address of the foundation is in New York City, the contact person works in Blue Mountain, New York.
[2] This excludes one unusually large grant of $900,000.

HKH Foundation

the activities of organizations working in its fields of interest by receiving mailings, newsletters, and other information, it does not review or respond to solicitations or proposals for funding.

Foundation staff are willing to discuss the foundation's strategic planning and the perspectives of different organizations to help improve the effectiveness of the foundation, but these discussions are held only with the understanding that they are not about any one organization's specific funding needs.

Grant Limitations
The foundation does not make grants to individuals.

Meeting Times
The board of trustees of the HKH Foundation meets twice a year.

Publications
The foundation distributes a form letter stating its grantmaking policies and procedures as outlined above.

Harder Foundation
18301 East Eight Mile Road, Suite 213
East Detroit, Michigan 48021
(313) 772-4433

Post Office Box 7407
Tacoma, Washington 98407-7407

Contact Persons
Nathan B. Driggers, President (Michigan)
Del Langbauer, Vice-President (Washington)

Purpose
The Harder Foundation makes grants only for work on environmental issues. The foundation subscribes to the view that many individuals utilize common resources in such a way as to maximize his or her own gain at little personal short-term cost, the result being to exhaust the resource and being serious hardship to all who are dependent upon it. When restoration of the resource is possible, it is often at great cost and it must be borne by all citizens.

Areas of Interest
Particular interests include preservation of wilderness areas; preservation of biological species in their natural habitat; preservation of clean air, clear water, and clean soil and removal of chemical and other man-made pollutants; conservation of natural resources; and controlling population growth. Generally the foundation seeks to support activities that will provide the greatest possible improvement in environmental quality for the least possible cost. It also wants some reasonable assurance that measurable environmental benefits will occur during the time frame of the grant.

The foundation makes grants to national and local groups for environmental projects of national, regional, or local significance. Each year the foundation also makes a portion of its grants budget available for general support, particularly for small organizations that need basic operating expenses. Often such general-support grants are made to organizations that have recently completed successful project grants with the foundation. Occasionally they are made to new organizations to resolve an especially important environmental problem. In the latter case, the background and qualifications of officers and staff are especially important.

Harder Foundation

In addition, starting in 1985 the foundation made a limited number of grants to provide endowment funds for organizations working on environmental issues.

Financial Data (year ended 6/30/87)

Assets:	$	8,974,026
Total grants paid:	$	528,788
Number of grants paid:		36
Highest grant:	$	220,000
Lowest grant:	$	1,000
Median grant size:	$	7,000

Application Procedures

There are different application procedures depending on where an applicant is located. Projects west of the Mississippi River should direct their submissions to the western office in Washington state during the period from February 15 to July 25 each year. All others should be directed to the Michigan office. All proposals received after September 30 of any year are deemed to be proposals to be considered the next calendar year.

A request for project support should include the following items: (1) the name of the organization and the name, address, and telephone number of the contact person; (2) a full discussion of the problem to be addressed, the techniques to be used in the solution, and a clear statement of final objectives or "expected accomplishments" for the project (including specific information about what will be done and by whom); (3) a budget showing full costs for the project, committed and anticipated funding sources for the project, and the amount specifically requested from the Harder Foundation (no more than $15,000); (4) a timetable for the project; (5) a discussion of the qualifications of key individuals involved in the project; (6) concrete details concerning how the effectiveness of the project will be measured at its completion; (7) background information about the organization, including its record of past environmental accomplishments and disappointments; (8) a general budget for the organization; (9) the names, occupations and education of the or-

Harder Foundation

ganization's directors, officers and staff; and (10) a copy of the organization's letter from the IRS identifying it as tax exempt under Section 501(c)(3).

Groups applying for general operating support should submit: (1) the name, address, and telephone number of the organization and contact person; (2) the organization's most recent statement of assets and liabilities and operating financial statement; (3) the names, occupations, and education of its directors, officers, and staff; (4) its anticipated budget for the next year; (5) a discussion of its past environmental accomplishments and disappointments; (6) a statement of the environmental problems with which it is contending and their proposed solutions; (7) a description of how the effectiveness of its past, present, and prospective efforts may be measured, i.e., what it has and will accomplish for the environment; and (8) a copy of the organization's letter from the IRS identifying it as tax exempt under Section 501(c)(3). After a general support grant has been made, the final evaluation will include consideration of the organization's success during the period of the grant in increasing its membership (if appropriate) and in achieving its stated environmental goals.

Grant Limitations
The foundation makes grants to tax-exempt organizations only. Support is not available for environmental education, capital construction projects, individuals, and organizations sponsored by friends or acquaintances of foundation trustees. Research proposals will be considered only when they are in direct support of a developed plan for specific action to alleviate a pressing environmental problem. The foundation will not support projects normally funded by public tax funds.

Meeting Times
The board of trustees of the Harder Foundation meets once a year, in February.

Publications
The foundation publishes an annual report and distributes a program policy statement and detailed application guidelines.

The Edward W. Hazen Foundation
505 Eighth Avenue, 23rd Floor
New York, New York 10018
(212) 967-5920

Contact Person
Sharon King, Executive Director

Purpose
The Hazen Foundation is concerned primarily with young people and their value systems. The focus is on junior- and senior-high-school-age youth. Included are investigating new ways of obtaining accurate information on the realities of urban living for young people, furthering the interaction between schools and community organizations, and creating better understanding between cultural groups both domestic and international. This focus extends to an interest in the competence of teachers and the design and testing of teaching and learning models (particularly in the arts and humanities) and other programs working directly with young people.

Areas of Interest
The current priority is secondary school educational programs that include action and research in the following areas: (1) parental involvement in public education; (2) curricular ventures designed to improve the quality of teaching and learning; (3) equity for Black, Hispanic, and Asian refugee children as well as disadvantaged white adolescents in Appalachia and other areas of the country; (4) programs that increase the competence of adults, including seniors, in their work with young people; and (5) use of the arts as a vehicle for learning. The foundation also has added a new field of interest, juvenile justice, and continues to support media projects, particularly those aimed at youth, and a small number of projects addressing youth unemployment.

The foundation also supports efforts to advance volunteerism as a means of promoting youth development and values. Throughout its fields of interest, programs that have the potential for a national impact receive priority.

The Edward W. Hazen Foundation

Financial Data (year ended 12/31/86)

Assets:	$	8,783,770
Total grants paid:[1]	$	451,974
Number of grants paid:		61
Highest grant:	$	27,000
Lowest grant:	$	100
Median grant size:	$	5,000

Application Procedures

The foundation has no application forms but proposals must be submitted no later than January 15 or July 15 if they are to receive attention at the next semiannual meeting of the board of trustees. The foundation prefers an informal inquiry prior to the filing of a formal application. Proposals should be typewritten, single-spaced, and should address nine specific questions that are set forth in the foundation's guidelines brochure.

Grant Limitations

Generally the following are considered outside the foundation's primary field of operation: contributions to endowment or building funds, accumulated deficits, and ordinary operating budgets; and support for propaganda, efforts to influence legislation, conferences, institutes, and occasional seminars. Also, with rare exception, the foundation does not provide support for programs in medicine and the health sciences, law, engineering, and public and business administration. Individuals are not eligible for direct grants; awards are not offered for scholarships and fellowships. It usually does not support projects that are well established and have already been substantially funded by larger foundations or the government.

---

[1]This analysis includes program and discretionary grants made by the foundation; it does not include dues and memberships, miscellaneous small program grants, generally in amounts of $1,500 and under, or memorial grants.

The Edward W. Hazen Foundation

Meeting Times
The board of trustees of The Hazen Foundation has semiannual meetings, usually held in April and October. Additional meetings are called as necessary.

Publications
The foundation publishes a biennial report and a brochure, *General Information and Reports*. The list of grantees and financial statements are provided upon specific request.

The William and Flora Hewlett Foundation
525 Middlefield Road
Menlo Park, California 94025
(415) 329-1070

Contact Person
Roger W. Heyns, President

Purpose
The William and Flora Hewlett Foundation is a private foundation with broad charitable interests. It is wholly independent of the Hewlett-Packard Company and the Hewlett-Packard Company Foundation.

Areas of Interest
The foundation's resources are concentrated on the performing arts; education, particularly at the college and university level; population issues; environmental issues; and conflict resolution. Most grants are made to well-established national organizations, but smaller local groups receive support through a regional grants program that focuses on projects in the San Francisco Bay Area. The four priorities of the regional program are community development, youth employment, minority leadership development, and selected human services. The foundation will consider general, program, or project- support grants, and welcomes opportunities to fund programs with other grantmakers.

Performing Arts. Grants for the performing arts support classical music ensembles, professional theater and opera companies, and ballet and modern dance organizations for artistic, managerial, and institutional development. The foundation also makes some grants to groups providing services to Bay Area nonprofit film and video organizations.

Education. Institutional support is provided to colleges, universities, research libraries, and university presses. The foundation also supports teaching and research programs of academic institutions focusing on relations between the United States and Mexico.

Population. The foundation is particularly interested in the training of population experts; policy-related research; and family planning and other fertility-reducing programs.

The William and Flora Hewlett Foundation

Environment. This program has as its overall objective improving of decision-making on environmental issues, encouraging more intelligent and rewarding uses of the natural environment for education, conservation, and development.

Conflict Resolution. The foundation looks to alternatives to litigation and legislation in the process by which disputes are resolved. Grants, whose overall purpose is to support the development of the field of a whole, are made in three specific categories: theory development, support for mediators and other practitioners of third-party intervention techniques, and institutional support for organizations that train or educate potential users about conflict resolution.

Financial Data

The assets of the foundation were $565,201,000 on December 31, 1987. The foundation supplied the following two analyses of grants paid during 1987.

Special Projects

Total grants paid:	$ 5,694,133
Number of grants paid:	44
Highest grant:	$ 682,180
Lowest grant:	$ 5,616
Median grant size:	$ 75,000

Regional Grants Program

Total grants paid:	$ 3,536,525
Number of grants paid:	58
Highest grant:	$ 329,000
Lowest grant:	$ 9,550
Median grant size:	$ 50,000

Application Procedures

The foundation requests that, to facilitate its planning and evaluation process for arts grants, applicants adhere to the following deadlines: music

The William and Flora Hewlett Foundation

(January 1); theater (April 1); dance, and film and video (both July 1). Otherwise there are no application deadlines.

Initial contact with the foundation should be made by a brief letter of inquiry. The letter should contain a statement of the applicant's need for funds and enough factual information to enable staff to determine whether the application falls within the foundation's program or perhaps warrants consideration as a special project.

All inquiries are reviewed by the president and by a relevant program officer. The program officer will either (1) in consultation with the president, decline requests that seem unlikely to result in a project the foundation can support; (2) request further information if needed for a decision; or (3) present the request to the rest of the staff for discussion. Applicants who receive a favorable response to their initial inquiry will be invited to submit a formal proposal. All inquiries and proposals are reported to the board, including those declined at the staff level.

Grant Limitations

Normally the foundation will not make grants or loans to individuals; grants for basic research; capital construction fund contributions; grants in the medical or health-related fields; general fundraising drives; or grants intended directly or indirectly either to support candidates for political office or to influence legislation.

In addition, there are limitations within each program area. In the performing arts the foundation does not consider requests in the visual or literary arts; the humanities; elementary and secondary school programs; college or university proposals; community art classes; ethnic arts, including crafts, folk arts, popular music, and ethnic dance; recreational, therapeutic, and social service arts programs; individuals; one-time events such as seminars, conferences, festivals, or cultural foreign exchange programs; or touring costs. In education the foundation does not support proposals to fund student aid; construction; equipment purchases, including computers; education research; basic scientific research; health research; or health education programs. In the area of population the foundation will not consider support for biomedical research on repro-

The William and Flora Hewlett Foundation

duction, nor will it fund population education programs directed toward the general public.

Regional program grants are not made in support of the following: physical or mental health, law and related fields, criminal justice or juvenile delinquency, drug and alcohol addiction, or the problems of the elderly and the handicapped.

Meeting Times

The board of directors of The William and Flora Hewlett Foundation meets quarterly, in January, April, July, and October, to consider grant applications.

Publications

The foundation publishes an annual report that contains specific guidelines for applicants.

The Hitachi Foundation
1509 22nd Street, N.W.
Washington, DC 20037
(202) 457-0588

Contact Persons
Delwin A. Roy, President
Felicia B. Lynch, Vice-President/Program
Julie A. Banzhaf, Associate Program Officer

Purpose
The Hitachi Foundation was created in 1985 to help address the issues of the increasingly complex and technological world, increasingly international in scope. The foundation is committed to supporting programs that enable individuals to lead more productive lives and to participate with more awareness as citizens within this environment. The foundation is endowed by Hitachi, Ltd., of Tokyo.

Areas of Interest
The foundation makes grants in four general program areas: community and economic development, the arts, education, and technology and human resource development.

Community and Economic Development. The foundation places special emphasis on projects that offer innovative, creative, and practical approaches to concerns common to a number of communities; that stimulate the participation of community volunteers and the development of leadership capabilities; and that encourage the collaboration of a variety of local leaders. In this area the foundation will also consider projects that foster alliances between the business community and other sectors of society to address issues of global interdependency.

Arts. The foundation supports both visual and performing arts projects, particularly those that enhance the understanding of American and Japanese cultures. Special preference is giving to multidisciplinary projects, to projects that expand access to the arts for all segments of society, and to those that use the arts to improve education and learning.

Education. In this area the foundation emphasizes proj-

The Hitachi Foundation

ects that improve the quality of teaching and learning at all levels and show promise of enabling individuals fuller participation in our society and economy.

Technology and Human Resource Development. The foundation encourages projects that address the questions of technology transfer across institutions and countries, of access for all segments of society to technology, social and economic effects of upgrading technology, and of dysfunctional aspects of technology and how they affect social and economic systems.

Financial Data (year ended 3/31/87)

Assets:	$ 14,958,518
Total grants awarded:	$ 1,288,628
Number of grants awarded:[1]	40
Highest grant:	$ 200,000
Lowest grant:	$ 1,000
Median grant size:	$ 15,000

Application Procedures

The initial stage of a funding request should be a letter of no more than three pages. The letter should include a statement of need for the project and description of whom it will serve; a summary of proposed project activities, its specific purpose and how it is an improvement upon present practice; the amount of the grant being requested and other sources of funds to be committed to the project; a brief description of the applicant organization, its objectives, activities, and scope; and verification of tax-exempt status.

Preliminary requests received by the first of February, June, or October will be reviewed within four weeks. Otherwise, such requests will automatically be carried over to the next review period.

If the proposed project is of interest to the foundation, a detailed proposal will be requested. This proposal must include: a detailed explanation of the purpose and objectives of the proposed project or ac-

---

[1] This total includes one program-related investment of $15,000.

The Hitachi Foundation

tivity; a detailed narrative of the activities involved in achieving project goals; a description of the personnel or other organizations involved; a description of activities to disseminate the project to a broader audience and a description of how it will continue after funding (if appropriate); an itemized budget for the project; a current itemized budget for the organization, including sources of revenue and expenses and other sources of support committed or pending for the project; a schedule for completion of the project; an evaluation plan for the project; a brief history of the organization, a list of the governing board members, and a detailed statement of purpose and description of whom it serves; and a copy of the organization's 501(c)(3) tax-exempt letter from the Internal Revenue Service.

Grant Limitations
The foundation will not consider requests related to medical research or health-related activities; organizations whose activities or policies include specific political purposes; capital improvement projects or building funds; projects whose primary purpose is publications, conferences, seminars, or research; sectarian or denominational religious activities; endowments, fundraising campaigns, recruitment, or advertising; or funds for individuals including fellowships, scholarships, and stipends.

Meeting Times
The board of directors of The Hitachi Foundation meets three times a year, in February, June, and October.

Publications
The foundation publishes an annual report, a brochure describing its programs and procedures, and a newsletter, *Focus,* describing its grants and issues.

The Huber Foundation
Post Office Box 277
Rumson, New Jersey 07760
(201) 842-3733

Contact Persons
Hans A. Huber, President
Lorraine Barnhart, Program Director

Areas of Interest
The Huber Foundation focuses its grantmaking on the issues of reproductive freedom, population stabilization, and family planning. Only organizations that make a substantial commitment of time and resources to these issues will be considered for funding.

Financial Data (year ended 12/31/86)

Assets:	$ 15,270,178
Total grants paid:	$ 920,800
Number of grants paid:	40
Highest grant:	$ 125,000
Lowest grant:	$ 2,000
Median grant size:	$ 15,000

Application Procedures
There are no fixed deadlines for receipt of proposals, and the foundation has no formal application procedure. Organizations interested in applying for a grant should submit a letter describing the project together with a budget for the project and proof of the applicant's tax-exempt status. The foundation will request additional information if needed.

Grant Limitations
The foundation will not consider grants to individuals, to organizations located outside the U.S., or for capital campaigns, scholarships, endowment funds, research, or international projects.

Meeting Times
The board of trustees of The Huber Foundation holds four meetings at various times throughout the year.

The Huber Foundation

Publications

The Huber Foundation publishes an annual list of grantees that includes a general policy statement and financial information.

Ittleson Foundation, Inc.
645 Madison Avenue
New York, New York 10022
(212) 838-5010

Contact Person
David M. Nee, Executive Director

Areas of Interest
The Ittleson Foundation's grantmaking program is concentrated in the fields of health, welfare, and education for health and welfare with special emphasis on mental health, psychiatric, and behavioral science research.

Among the topics addressed by the foundation's grantees in fiscal 1985 were adolescent suicide, support services for Alzheimer's patients, the effects of federal-funding cuts on mental health services, support services for families in Family Court, arts broadcasts, and volunteer programs in jails and prisons. In 1986 and 1987 grants were also made for AIDS-related services and public education. In general, the foundation's grants supported a broad span of activities including publications, strengthening management, conferences and symposia, program and resource development, film, and general operations.

Financial Data (year ended 12/31/87)

Assets:[1]	$	15,668,006
Total grants paid:	$	917,784
Number of grants paid:		33
Highest grant:	$	130,000
Lowest grant:	$	3,633
Median grant size:	$	25,000

Application Procedures
The foundation has no application forms or deadlines. The foundation recommends that applicants write a brief letter to the executive director describing the work for which the funds are being sought, along with a budget. If the activity falls within the current scope of the foundation's interests, applicants will be asked to supply additional information as it may be required.

---

[1]As of December 31, 1986.

Ittleson Foundation, Inc.

Grant Limitations

As a matter of policy, the foundation does not usually contribute to the humanities or cultural projects, to general education, or to social agencies offering direct services to individuals. Furthermore, the foundation does not offer fellowships or scholarships of any kind, travel grants, or grants-in-aid to individuals.

Publications

The Ittleson Foundation does not publish an annual report. It will make a statement of policy available on request.

Jewish Fund for Justice
920 Broadway, Suite 605
New York, New York 10010
(212) 677-7080

Contact Person
Marlene Provizer, Executive Director

Purpose
The Jewish Fund for Justice is a national grantmaking organization through which the American Jewish community supports efforts to combat poverty and to nurture social and economic justice in the United States. Its resources are directed toward activities dealing with causes more than consequences of poverty and injustice, and most of its grants are made to local community organizing efforts that help dependent people achieve self-sufficiency.

Areas of Interest
The fund makes grants on a nondenominational basis to projects combatting poverty and the systemic disenfranchisement of low-income people in the United States. It is receptive to requests for general support as well as to special projects from nonprofit organizations addressing the causes of urban or rural poverty. Although from time to time the fund works to stimulate proposals addressing neglected issues, as a general rule it responds to initiatives from grant seekers.

In evaluating a proposed project, the fund inquires: Does it benefit and involve the poor either directly or through its strategic impact? Does it enable poor people to change the conditions that limit their lives? Does it improve the lives of the poor by addressing the systems, societal values, institutions, law, or policies that keep people poor? Does it operate at the community level or have strong community roots?

The fund is also interested in projects which, while meeting the above criteria, also encourage greater Jewish involvement in efforts to combat the causes of domestic poverty (financially, as activists or volunteers, and through involvement of other Jewish organizations); that provide the opportunities for its grants to leverage other financial support; and that take an approach or address an issue which is not yet attracting substantial financial support from the Jewish community.

Jewish Fund for Justice

Financial Data (year ended 12/31/87)

Support and revenue:[1]	$	497,281
Total grants paid:	$	123,374
Number of grants paid:		29
Highest grant:	$	5,000
Lowest grant:	$	1,940
Median grant size:	$	5,000

Application Procedures

Information about proposal deadlines is available on request, and there are no required application forms. The fund asks, however, that an applicant start the proposal with a one-paragraph description of its organization and the project or purpose for which funds are sought. The overall length of proposals (exclusive of supporting materials) is four double-spaced pages. In those four pages the fund asks that applicants tell the fund who they are, the problem to be addressed, the project's objectives, the proposed strategy for achieving them, how the project will be evaluated, and the applicant's qualifications.

As supporting materials, the fund requests a list of the members of the applicant's governing body; a complete financial statement for the most recent fiscal year (audited, if available); a project budget including a breakdown of projected expenditures and income; the most recently published materials of the applicant, such as a brochure, annual report, or newsletter; a list of major contributors; and proof of tax-exempt status.

Grant Limitations

The fund supports only those organizations that are tax exempt or working with a tax-exempt fiscal agent.

Meeting Times

The board of directors of the Jewish Fund for Justice reviews grant applications twice a year, in June and December.

---

[1]This figure is unaudited.

Jewish Fund for Justice

Publications
The fund publishes a brochure and a newsletter.

The Robert Wood Johnson Foundation
Post Office Box 2316
Princeton, New Jersey 08543-2316
(609) 452-8701

Contact Persons
Steven A. Schroeder, M.D., President
Edward H. Robbins, Proposal Manager

Purpose
The Robert Wood Johnson Foundation is a private philanthropy interested
in improving health in the United States. Its resources are concentrated
on improving access to personal health care for the most underserved
population groups; making health care arrangements more effective and
care more affordable; and helping people maintain or regain maximum
attainable function in their everyday lives.

Areas of Interest
The foundation defines its role as one that assists: development and testing
of new and previously untried approaches to health care problems; demonstrations to assess objectively the operational effectiveness and value
of selected new health care arrangements and approaches that have proven
effective in more limited settings; and projects designed to promote the
broader diffusion of programs that have been objectively shown to improve health status or to make health care more affordable.

　　By way of illustration, in 1984 the foundation, in cooperation with
the Pew Charitable Trusts and the U.S. Conference of Mayors, awarded
$25 million to coalitions in eighteen major cities to develop community-
based efforts to deliver hands-on health and health-related services to
homeless people. The foundation has also made grants aimed at bringing
health services to people who lack health insurance and cannot afford
care, and supported in-school adolescent health care clinics to address
the broad array of adolescent prevention and treatment needs. As of
February 1, 1988, the foundation had committed in excess of $20 million
to combat AIDS, making the foundation the largest private-sector funding
resource in this area.

　　While almost all of the foundation's grantmaking is directed toward
major well-established institutions, grants of $50,000 and less are made
by the president in consultation with the program staff. Referred to as

The Robert Wood Johnson Foundation

"president's grants" in the foundation's annual report, these grants do not require approval of the foundation's board of trustees and several support smaller public education, advocacy, service, and research programs working on innovative approaches within the foundation's areas of interest. Priority is given to programs and projects that address regional or national problems, but the foundation also awards a small number of grants to organizations in New Brunswick, New Jersey, where the foundation originated.

Financial Data (year ended 12/31/86)

At the end of 1986 the assets of the foundation were $804,599,529. Following is an analysis of the foundation's grantmaking activity, separating the general grants program from foundation fellowships and grants made from the president's fund.

Application Procedures

Grant applications are accepted throughout the year, and there are no formal application forms. Applicants should prepare a letter that briefly and concisely states the proposed project as well as its objectives and significance; the qualifications of the organization and the individuals involved; the mechanisms for evaluating results; and a budget. This letter should be accompanied by a copy of the applicant's proof of tax-exempt status under the Internal Revenue Code. Proposal letters should be addressed to the proposal manager. Applicants should keep in mind that it

The Robert Wood Johnson Foundation
Analysis of 1986 Grantmaking Activity

	Grants Program	Fellowships	President's Grants
Total Grants Paid	$93,183,882	$651,637	$770,014
Number of Grants	210	18	27
Highest Grant	$5,000,000	$52,120	$50,000
Lowest Grant	$10,000	$14,808	$5,998
Median Grant Size	$241,978	$46,475	$26,000

The Robert Wood Johnson Foundation

usually takes from six months to one year after an initial proposal letter is received for a grant award to be made.

Grant Limitations

Ordinarily preference will be given to organizations that have qualified for exemption under Section 501(c)(3) of the Internal Revenue Code and that are not private foundations as defined in Section 509(a). Public instrumentalities and government agencies are eligible for support.

The foundation's guidelines normally preclude support for the following types of activities: (1) ongoing general operating expenses; (2) endowment, construction, or equipment; (3) basic biomedical research; (4) international activities or programs and institutions outside the United States; and (5) direct support to individuals. In addition, the foundation does not support programs concerned solely with a specific disease or with broad public health problems except as they might relate to the foundation's three areas of interest.

Meeting Times

The board of trustees of The Robert Wood Johnson Foundation meets five times a year in February, May, July, October, and December.

Publications

The foundation publishes an annual report and application guidelines.

Joint Foundation Support, Inc.
40 West 20 Street, 10th Floor
New York, New York 10011
(212) 627-7710

Contact Persons

Nanette Falkenberg, Executive Director
Jim Metzinger, Program Officer

Purpose

Joint Foundation Support (JFS) was formed to provide the support services of a professional staff to several family foundations and individual donors. Although the specific interests of JFS members are quite different, all members share a general interest in social-change-oriented programs that fall within their common areas of interest. Grants are made to national organizations as well as to local grassroots programs in underserved areas of the country such as the South and Appalachia. It should be noted that grants made on the recommendation of JFS often represent only a portion of each individual member's total charitable contributions.

Areas of Interest

Among the specific interests of JFS members are programs to insure civil rights and civil liberties, to assist women and minority groups, to encourage self-help, to promote equality of opportunity and economic justice, to preserve the environment, and to foster disarmament and peace.

In 1986 about $1.2 million in grants made on JFS's recommendation was allocated for projects with a national focus and approximately $836,000 was allocated to local community-based projects. Of the grant total allocated for local efforts, 15 percent was divided between projects based in the South and the Midwest. Other centers of JFS grantmaking were New York City, Boston, Appalachia, the Southwest, California, and the Pacific Northwest.

Joint Foundation Support, Inc.

Financial Data (year ended 12/31/86)

Total grants awarded:[1]	$	2,010,777
Number of grants awarded:		189
Highest grant:[2]	$	60,000
Lowest grant:	$	500
Median grant size:	$	10,000

Application Procedures

Requests for grants should be submitted in a brief letter outlining the project for which funds are sought. Additional information should include a budget, evidence of tax-exempt status, and a list of other sources of support. If it is determined that a project falls within the funding priorities of any of the JFS members, a staff member will contact the project to request further materials or to set up an appointment. Meetings will not be scheduled before JFS receives a written submission.

Grant Limitations

JFS members prefer to apply their resources to projects for which other funds are not widely available and where a small grant can have a substantial impact. Grants are made only to tax-exempt organizations and not to individuals. Grants are generally not made to educational institutions or for research, scholarships, conferences, publications, or capital purposes.

Meeting Times

The boards of directors of the various members of Joint Foundation Support meet on a staggered basis several times throughout the year.

---

[1] In 1986 grants were paid by 10 foundations and individual donors. The JFS annual report specifically identifies each grant and the member grantmaker.

[2] This figure omits one unusually large grant made as part of a three-year commitment to an established cultural institution.

Joint Foundation Support, Inc.

Publications
JFS publishes an annual report that includes information on its past grant-making activities and the interests of each of the JFS members.

The W. Alton Jones Foundation, Inc.
232 East High Street
Charlottesville, Virginia 22901
(804) 295–2134

Contact Person
J. Pete Myers, Director

Purpose
The W. Alton Jones Foundation, Inc., focuses its support on two basic themes: "building a sustainable society" and "building a secure society."

Areas of Interest
The Sustainable Society Program seeks to promote the long-term sustainability of life by preserving our most precious natural resources: the diversity of the world's plant and animal species and the quality of land, air, and water. The program has two parts, conservation of biological diversity worldwide and protection of land, air, and water from pollution and toxic contamination. Throughout this program the foundation strives to support the education of the public and government; monitoring of government; development of parks and preserves and acquisition of environmentally significant lands; basic and applied research; policy development; litigation and mediation; training of resource specialists and development of indigenous conservation organizations, especially in the tropics and other species-rich areas.

The Secure Society Program has as its goal encouraging the development of a world that is secure from the peril of nuclear war without jeopardy to freedom and democracy. Only projects that bear directly on the risk of nuclear war will be considered. In recent years the foundation has funded projects falling into the following categories: public education through such means as election debates, high school curriculum development, television, lectures, books, films, and museum displays; journalist education through round tables, seminars, expert referral services, journalism schools, newsletters, and bulletins; policy development to help government with practical proposals on long-term strategic policy, technological change, strategic defense, crisis communications, and nuclear proliferation and terrorism; expanding the information base through research on the world's nuclear forces, the biological effects of a nuclear exchange, risks and costs of the Strategic Defense Initiative, as well as

The W. Alton Jones Foundation, Inc.

means of inhibiting nuclear proliferation; educating decision makers through such means as round tables and seminars; and improving U.S.-Soviet relations through private exchanges and collaborative efforts.

The foundation also has a small regional grants program that supports organizations in its immediate vicinity and supports a few organizations of traditional interest to the donor. In 1986 the foundation launched two-year pilot programs in three new areas: the arts, education, and urban issues. Currently these programs are entirely proactive; applications are neither sought nor accepted.

Financial Data (year ended 12/31/87)

Assets:[1]	$ 159,232,806
Total grants awarded:	$ 11,272,738
Number of grants awarded:	164
Highest grant:[2]	$ 300,000
Lowest grant:	$ 2,000
Median grant size:	$ 50,000

Application Procedures

Proposals must be received by the foundation on or before January 15, April 15, July 15, and October 15 to allow enough time for review. The foundation does not use application forms. Grant requests should be initiated by a succinct written proposal containing the following: a clear statement of objectives; a description of the organization, the project, and the staff; time frames for funding and completion of the project; what is original or unique about the project or, if general support is sought, about the organization; the organization's most recent financial statement; a detailed budget for the project showing its relation to the organization's overall financial situation; a copy of the organization's tax-exempt ruling under Section 501(c)(3) of the Internal Revenue Code. One copy of the

---

[1]These figures were supplied, without documentation, by the foundation.
[2]This figure omits a payment of $2.5 million, the sixth year of a seven-year $17.5-million commitment to the W. Alton Jones Cell Science Center in Lake Placid, New York.

The W. Alton Jones Foundation, Inc.

proposal is sufficient. Any supplementary materials that would help in evaluating the proposal may be attached.

Informal inquiries to determine whether a proposed project falls within funding guidelines may be made by phone or by letter. At this early stage, personal visits to the foundation are discouraged. Applicants, whether funded or not, are asked to wait one year after a grant is approved or declined before submitting another application.

Grants for projects and programs in Charlottesville and Albemarle County, Virginia, are administered under separate guidelines, which are available on request.

Grant Limitations
The foundation does not make grants to individuals or to conduit organizations that pass funds on to others. It does not make grants for building construction or renovation, scholarships, or endowments.

Meeting Times
The board of trustees of The W. Alton Jones Foundation, Inc., meets quarterly to review grant applications.

Publications
The foundation publishes an annual report and distributes guidelines for its regional grant program upon request.

The Henry J. Kaiser Family Foundation
2400 Sand Hill Road
Menlo Park, California 94025
(415) 854-9400

Contact Persons
Alvin R. Tarlov, M.D., President
Barbara H. Kehrer, Ph.D., Vice President

Purpose
The Henry J. Kaiser Family Foundation has as its broadly defined mission enhancing the quality of individuals lives and health. The foundation places at the core of all its grantmaking the promotion of health.

Areas of Interest
The foundation focuses all of its grants on health issues, broadly defined. Rather than funding medical research, the foundation supports programs and projects designed to improve two other determinants of health: individual behavior and socioeconomic and other major contributing factors to the gap between the quality of health care available and the quality of health of the people. In 1986 the foundation made several grants in support of AIDS-related programs of public education and services.

Grantmaking activity is divided into five program categories:

Health Promotion. This program focuses on programs to enhance health and prevent unnecessary illness, injury, and untimely death by encouraging changes in personal behavior and societal practices. The program aims to effect improvements by reducing risk behavior such as tobacco use, poor nutrition, poor physical fitness, alcohol or drug misuse, auto accidents, unintentional injuries, homicides, suicides and adolescent sexual activity leading to pregnancy.

Improving Health Care Outcomes. The goal of this pro-

The Henry J. Kaiser Family Foundation

gram is to seek, develop, and disseminate modifications in health care delivery that promise to improve outcomes as measured by patient functioning. Grants in this category have supported activities in research, development, applications, evaluation, and dissemination.

Health Professions Education Program. The foundation supports development of new approaches to medical education, research, and scholarship that recognize broadened concepts of medicine, health promotion, and functional health assessment, and that increase the opportunities for minorities in the health professions.

Health Care Financing. This has been a major interest of the foundation for twenty-five years. Previously the focus was principally development of prepaid group practices. Today the foundation no longer gives grants for the development of health maintenance organizations (HMOs), but it continues its commitment to projects of unusual potential related to alternative health care systems.

Health-related Programs in San Francisco. These grants support creative approaches to health service delivery in Alameda, Contra Costa, San Francisco, San Mateo, and Santa Clara counties. Grant recipients are community-based organizations, especially those whose major commitment is to the poor and disadvantaged. A principal focus of this program is serving the health needs of the elderly or disabled, with particular emphasis on the frail elderly. This program has made grants to support direct services for persons with AIDS. Its special focus with regard to AIDS is prevention activities in minority communities. An additional focus for Bay Area grants is projects dealing with youth. Within this program the foundation is particularly interested in model programs and in projects where a small grant can have an important impact. Most grants are made for one year only, and are in the range of $5,000 to $20,000.

The Henry J. Kaiser Family Foundation

Financial Data (year ended 12/31/86)

Assets:	$ 359,265,215
Total grants paid:	$ 8,440,345
Number of grants paid:[1]	107
Highest grant:	$ 750,000
Lowest grant:	$ 1,000
Median grant size:	$ 25,000

Application Procedures

Grant applications are reviewed throughout the year. The foundation requires no application forms. Each prospective applicant is requested to submit a preliminary letter that briefly describes the proposed project. This letter should include (1) a descriptive title of the project (up to ten words); (2) the primary contact person and that person's address and telephone number; (3) an outline of the plan and objectives of the project for which support is sought and why it is important to undertake; (4) an estimated budget; (5) information about the sponsoring organization and the individuals to be involved in the project; and (6) a copy of the institution's tax-exemption letter from the IRS.

Once foundation staff have reviewed the initial letter, a detailed proposal may be requested. In some cases a meeting with staff for further discussion or a site visit will also be scheduled.

Grant Limitations

As a general rule, the foundation does not support ongoing general operating expenses, capital campaigns or other fundraising events, construction of the purchase of equipment, or basic biomedical research. Grants are made only to organizations qualifying for tax exemption under Section 501(c)(3) of the Internal Revenue Code. The foundation may

---

[1]For purposes of this analysis, grants identified in the foundation's annual report as special projects fund grants but not itemized are not part of the tabulations. Similarly, matching gifts have been omitted. These two grants categories total $299,675 and $74,335, respectively.

The Henry J. Kaiser Family Foundation

not award grants to individuals or for legislation or support activities that seek to influence the legislative process.

Meeting Times
The board of trustees of The Henry J. Kaiser Family Foundation meets as needed to review grant applications.

Publications
The Henry J. Kaiser Family Foundation publishes an annual report and a brochure, "Information for Grant Applicants," which outlines the topics that should be addressed in a full proposal.

The Henry P. Kendall Foundation
One Boston Place
Boston, Massachusetts 02108
(617) 723-8727

Contact Person
Robert L. Allen, Vice-President

Purpose
The Henry P. Kendall Foundation was established for general purposes with special interests in arms control and environmental matters. The foundation's arms control and environmental programs have no geographic limitations; the remaining grant recipients in other categories are located primarily in Massachusetts.

Areas of Interest
The foundation's funding pattern is as follows: approximately forty percent of the foundation's grant dollar is allocated to arms control and environmental groups across the country. Educational and ecological programs are each allocated approximately twenty-five percent of the available budget. Social welfare organizations and projects receive less than ten percent of the foundation's available funds. A significant number of the foundation's grants reflect the long-standing interests of the family and the foundation's trustees.

Financial Data (year ended 12/31/85)
Assets:	$ 53,994,039
Total grants paid:	$ 2,207,110
Number of grants paid:	102
Highest grant:[1]	$ 80,000
Lowest grant:	$ 500
Median grant size:	$ 10,000

Application Procedures
The foundation prefers that interested applicants initiate contact by sending a complete proposal. The foundation reviews proposals throughout

---

[1]This excludes three unusually large payments of $450,490, $200,000, and $151,300 to, respectively, the Kendall Whaling Museum, Amherst College, and the Youth Project.

The Henry P. Kendall Foundation

the year and does not require completion of any specific application forms.

Meeting Times
The board of directors of The Henry P. Kendall Foundation meets as required.

Publications
The foundation does not publish an annual report.

**The Kresge Foundation
Post Office Box 3151
3215 West Big Beaver Road
Troy, Michigan 48007-3151
(313) 643-9630**

Contact Person
Alfred H. Taylor, Jr., Chairman

Purpose
The Kresge Foundation is an independent private foundation not affiliated
with any other corporation or organization. All funds are awarded on a
challenge basis, i.e., as partial support, and grants are made only for
construction or renovation of facilities, the purchase of major capital
equipment or an integrated system at a cost of at least $75,000, and real
estate purchases.

Areas of Interest
Grants are made to organizations operating in the fields of higher education, health and long-term care, social services, science and the environment, and public affairs. While most grants are made to well-established
traditional institutions, on several occasions funds have been awarded to
advocacy organizations that meet the foundation's criteria.

The foundation does not grant initial funds or total project costs.
Grants are for a portion of the costs remaining at the time of grant
approval. Recent deficits, declining use statistics, or less than two years
of operation are not viewed favorably by the foundation in its review of
applications.

Financial Data (year ended 12/31/86)
As of December 31, 1986, the assets of the foundation were $1.047 billion,
and during the year the foundation approved 151 grants totaling $45.1
million, the largest of which was a grant for $2.25 million to a nationally
recognized hospital. However, in keeping with the other entries in this
book, the following analysis is based on grant payments made in
1986.

The Kresge Foundation

Total grants paid:	$ 42,480,000
Number of grants paid:	153
Highest grant:	$ 1,500,000
Lowest grant:	$ 30,000
Median grant size:	$ 200,000

Application Procedures

There are no application deadlines; proposals are accepted throughout the year. However, organizations can make only one application in any twelve-month period.

The foundation's application forms and an outline of information required in proposals are available from the foundation. Applications are acknowledged when received, and a specific timetable for review is then provided. Grant decisions are usually reached within five months of application receipt. Written and telephone inquiries are encouraged prior to the submission of a full proposal.

Typical grantees will have raised some funds before applying to the foundation and will have outlined a fundraising strategy incorporating the use of a Kresge challenge grant for securing the balance of funds needed to complete the project. Any long-term financing (five years or more), regulatory approval (e.g., certificates of need, zoning) or purchase agreements (real estate) required for completion of the project must be formally committed or imminent (within one to two months of submission) prior to applying.

Grant Limitations

Requests specifically toward debt retirement, furnishings, church building projects, or projects that are complete at the time of application are not eligible for foundation support.

Meeting Times

The board of trustees of The Kresge Foundation meets regularly. Grant decisions are announced monthly from February through June and September through December.

The Kresge Foundation

Publications

The foundation publishes an annual report and distributes a brochure describing its policies and application procedures.

Levi Strauss Foundation
Levi's Plaza
1155 Battery Street
San Francisco, California 94111
(415) 544-6579

Mailing Address
Post Office Box 7215
San Francisco, California 94120-6906

Contact Person
Martha Montag Brown, Director of Contributions

Purpose
The Levi Strauss Foundation is the principal means by which Levi Strauss & Co. fulfills its social responsibility. Grants are made in Levi Strauss plant communities to local nonprofit organizations through two principal giving programs: community involvement team (CIT) grants and special emphasis grants. A list of communities in which Levi Strauss had operations as of 1988 follows at the end of this entry. While most support is directed exclusively to communities in which Levi Strauss has plants or distribution facilities, some grants are made to national and regional organizations for general support.

Areas of Interest
In 1988 the foundation's national and regional grantmaking was focused on community economic development. A 1988 immigration funding initiative supported education and counseling services to applicants for legalization in Levi Strauss communities. Grants were also made to support AIDS-related services and public education. Additionally the foundation awards grants to U.S.-based tax-exempt organizations that work in communities around the world where Levi Strauss has facilities.

Financial Data (year ended 12/31/87)
Assets:[1] $ 19,834,894

---

[1] The figures in this analysis were supplied by the foundation, without supporting documentation. They are, however, consistent with figures documented for previous years.

Levi Strauss Foundation

Total grants paid:[2]	$	2,248,463
Number of grants paid:		209
Highest grant:	$	100,000
Lowest grant:	$	500
Median grant size:	$	7,500

Application Procedures
The two major giving programs, CIT and the special emphasis grants program, each operate under their own application procedures.

Community Involvement Team. Organizations with clearly defined volunteer or modest financial needs should direct a letter of one or two pages to the local Levi Strauss facility. The letter should outline the organization's purpose, objectives, budget, and how CIT assistance would be used. The request will be reviewed by local CIT members. Once the CIT endorsed the need for funding, the regional manager of contributions may work with the organization on development of a grant application. Final review of the proposal will take approximately 90 days.

Special Emphasis Grants. Initial applications should be made by sending a one- to two-page letter that includes a brief statement of the organization's history and goals; purpose of the project and grant request; how the program fits the foundation's guidelines; target population to be served; and amount requested, project budget, and other sources of funds anticipated or committed. If the foundation determines that the project falls within the guidelines, a full proposal will be requested and an application outline provided. The application and review process usually takes 60 to 90 days, and all applicants are notified of the disposition of their requests.

---

[2]These tabulations include foundation grants only. Excluded are 1,007 employee social benefits grants (matching gifts, board service grants, and volunteerism grants) totaling $324,511.

Levi Strauss Foundation

Grant Limitations
Requests for projects for political or sectarian religious purposes; tickets for dinners or other special events; and sponsorship of advertising, research, conferences, travel, films, videos, and publications or (with the exception of United Way campaigns) ongoing general operating funds are not normally considered by the foundation. The foundation makes no grants to individuals.

Meeting Times
The application review committee of The Levi Strauss Foundation meets quarterly, in March, June, September, and December.

Publications
The foundation publishes an annual report and will make available a statement of program policy and guidelines, a list of approved grants, and a list of communities where the company has facilities.

Plant Facilities
As of 1987 the contact persons in communities with Levi Strauss facilities are as follows:

Location	Contact Person
Fayetteville, Harrison, Little Rock, Morrilton, Arkansas; Centerville, Tennessee; Warsaw, Virginia	Herman Davenport Manager of Contributions Levi Strauss Foundation 1500 Panatela Parkway Little Rock, Arkansas 72206
San Francisco, California	Myra Chow Manager of Contributions Levi Strauss Foundation 1155 Battery Street, LS/7 San Francisco, California 94111

Levi Strauss Foundation

Florence, Kentucky; Knoxville, Maryville, Mountain City, and Powell, Tennessee	Mary Ellen McLoughlin Manager of Contributions Levi Strauss Foundation One Regency Square, Suite 430 Knoxville, Tennessee 37901
Henderson, Nevada; El Paso and San Angelo, Texas	Mario Griffin Manager of Contributions Levi Strauss Foundation 1440 Goodyear El Paso, Texas 79936
Elizabethton and Johnson City, Tennessee	Julie White Manager of Contributions Levi Strauss Foundation 80 Allstate Parkway Markham, Ontario Canada L3R 8X6
Amarillo, Brownsville, Harlingen, Richardson, McAllen, San Antonio, and San Benito, Texas	Eduardo Gutierrez Manager of Contributions Levi Strauss Foundation 5800 Old Highway 90 San Antonio, Texas 78227

The Max and Anna Levinson Foundation
430 West San Francisco Street
Santa Fe, New Mexico 87501
(505) 989-8254
(505) 989-8255

Contact Person
Jutta von Gontard, Executive Director

Purpose
The Max and Anna Levinson Foundation is a small national foundation concerned with the "development of a more humane and rewarding society, in which people have greater ability and opportunity to determine directions for the present and future."

Areas of Interest
The foundation funds organizations and projects of national and international impact in the fields of peace and arms control, civil liberties and human rights, environment and energy, and the Jewish community.

In all its grants the foundation looks for projects that are concerned with promoting social change and social justice either by developing and testing alternatives or by responsibly modifying existing systems, institutions, conditions, and attitudes that block promising innovation. It seeks people and organizations that combine dedication and genuine concern with rigorous analysis and strategic plans and administrative and technical competence. Projects should be well timed and soundly conceived, and while admittedly risky should have reasonable prospects of effective impact. The foundation favors proposals that have some demonstrable product or effect within a year or two or shortly after the project grant period, although the primary and general goal may lie further in the future.

Financial Data (year ended 9/30/87)
Assets:[1]	$	4,946,000
Total grants paid:	$	333,672
Number of grants:		33
Highest grant:	$	22,500
Lowest grant:	$	1,000
Median grant size:	$	10,000

[1]As of September 30, 1986.

278

The Max and Anna Levinson Foundation

Application Procedures

Proposals may be submitted at any time but no later than December 15 for consideration at the next board meeting. There is no required format for applications. Proposals should be brief, two to six pages, and should address the following questions: (1) the "problem" or "opportunity" seeking to be addressed, including the scope, significance, and impact; (2) relevant to the above, the specific changes you are seeking to bring about; (3) activities to be carried out for which funds are sought; (4) a statement identifying why you believe your organization's efforts will be successful; and (5) the criteria that will be used to evaluate the extent to which the project's goals have been achieved. In addition, applicants should supply a budget, including expenditures and income from current and anticipated sources, relevant background about the organization and key individuals, and information on the organization's federal tax status.

Grant Limitations

Preference is given to tax-exempt organizations; however, in special circumstances, organizations that are not tax exempt will be considered for support. The foundation does not generally consider proposals for support to expand services currently offered; grants to individuals for travel, study, or similar purposes; tuition or fellowship programs; capital development programs; or projects of primarily local community significance. In addition, the foundation favors projects that cannot obtain traditional funding and that will benefit from small short-term start-up and matching grants.

Meeting Times

The board of directors of The Max and Anna Levinson Foundation meets twice a year, in January and September.

Publications

The foundation does not publish an annual report. However, a statement of general policies and a list of recent grant recipients are available upon request.

J. Roderick MacArthur Foundation
9333 Milwaukee Avenue
Niles, Illinois 60648
(708) 966–0143

Contact Person
Lance E. Lindblom, President

Purpose
The J. Roderick MacArthur Foundation supports organizations working to help those who are inequitably or unjustly treated by established institutions of society. The foundation seeks to foster discussion about and needed changes in these institutions by protecting and encouraging freedom of expression, human rights, civil liberties, and social justice, and by eliminating political, economic, social, religious, and cultural oppression.

Areas of Interest
The foundation supports efforts and projects, including litigation, throughout the world to (1) eliminate censorship and protect freedom of expression, including the freedom to hold and express opinions in all media of communications, both within and among nations; (2) foster human rights, including political, social, economic, and cultural rights; and (3) protect and foster civil liberties in the United States (including all constitutional rights) and encourage their eventual observance around the world. It should be noted that in 1987 the foundation made three grants to organizations working to halt discrimination against individuals with AIDS and AIDS-related conditions.

Financial Data (year ended 1/31/88)

Assets:[1]	$	26,000,000
Total grants paid:	$	2,000,000
Number of grants paid:		105
Highest grant:[2]	$	20,000
Lowest grant:[3]	$	2,200
Median grant size:	$	20,000

---

[1] Approximate.
[2] This excludes one unusually large grant of $200,000.
[3] This excludes two payments of membership support totaling $5,875 from special out-of-program funds for which no applications are accepted.

J. Roderick MacArthur Foundation

Application Procedures
Rather than first submitting a formal application with supporting materials, the foundation suggests that applicants send a preliminary letter of inquiry to determine foundation interest. This letter should describe succinctly the background, programs, personnel, and purposes of the organization and should briefly but thoroughly outline the proposal and its cost. If the foundation is interested, a formal application will be requested. It is important to specify the objectives of the proposed project, pointing out unique aspects and differentiating it from other similar projects. The duration of the project and other potential funding sources should be identified, and plans to evaluate the results of the project articulated.

Grant Limitations
Only nonprofit tax-exempt organization as defined in Section 501(c)(3) of the Internal Revenue Code are eligible for funding. The foundation cannot review a proposal unless it is submitted by a tax-exempt organization that takes full legal, fiscal, and administrative responsibility for the request. Capital projects, endowments, land or building acquisitions, ordinary social services of an ongoing nature, programs that are the routine responsibility of the government, university or other educational programs, economic development and training programs, organizations already supported by tax revenues, and religious church-based activities ordinarily will not be considered.

The foundation will not consider the purchase of blocks of tickets, support for benefits, solicitations from regular development campaigns, or annual contribution drives. Also excluded are requests for conference and seminar expenses; projects to erect statues, memorials, or the like; scholarships, internships, and fellowships; and loans.

The foundation does not make "pass-through grants" or grants to individuals. The foundation does not support grassroots organizing or demonstrations, and has no emergency discretionary funds.

Meeting Times
The board of directors of the J. Roderick MacArthur Foundation meets approximately six to eight times a year.

J. Roderick MacArthur Foundation

Publications

The foundation publishes brochures that describe its purposes, programs, and guidelines and that list previous grantees.

The John D. and Catherine T. MacArthur Foundation
140 South Dearborn Street
Chicago, Illinois 60603
(312) 726-8000

Contact Persons
Adele Smith Simmons, President
James M. Furman, Executive Vice-President
Ruth Adams, Director, Peace and International Cooperation Program
William Bevan, Director, Health Program
Peter H. Gerber, Director, Education Program
Kenneth W. Hope, Director, Fellows Program
Dan M. Martin, Director, World Environment and Resources Program
Rebecca R. Riley, Director, Special Grants Program

Purpose
The John D. and Catherine T. MacArthur Foundation was created for charitable and public service purposes. It has developed grantmaking programs within which it acts as a catalyst for useful change in American society, the world community, and within the Chicago area.

Areas of Interest
The foundation defines six areas of sustained emphasis: (1) health program, (2) MacArthur fellows program, (3) world environment and resources program, (4) peace and international cooperation program, (5) education program, and (6) special grants program. In these efforts the foundation has attempted to be an active rather than a reactive force, developing much of its program through board initiatives rather than in response to grant requests. The foundation also makes program-related investments.

>*Health Program.* This program is devoted primarily to research on mental health and on the biology of parasitic disease. Only programs generated and developed by foundation staff and advisers are funded under this program; it does not support discrete research projects proposed by individual investigators.
>*The MacArthur Fellows Program.* Perhaps the best publicized of the foundation's programs, the MacArthur fellowships

The John D. and Catherine T. MacArthur Foundation

are awarded to exceptionally creative individuals chosen through a confidential and anonymous screening process.

Peace and International Cooperation Program. Through this program the foundation seeks to expand and strengthen the field of international security studies and to increase public understanding of complex security issues.

World Environment and Resources Program. This program consists principally of the development and initial sustaining support of the World Resources Institute in Washington, D.C.

Education Program. This program focuses on literacy, with particular emphasis on programs for children aged four to fourteen years.

The Special Grants Program. This program fosters cultural and community activities in the Chicago area, with particular emphasis on community-based organizations that encourage resident participation, self-sufficiency, and self-determination, cooperative use of resources, and an enhanced community role in neighborhood revitalization.

Financial Data (year ended 12/31/86)

On December 31, 1986, the foundation's total assets were $2.271 billion, and during that year it authorized a grand total of $120,931,635 in grants and awards in all of its programs. Of that total, $8,111,000 was paid under the MacArthur fellows program, and $1,575,000 was paid by the foundation in support of the Palm Beach County Community Foundation.

Following is an analysis of grants made in 1986 grouped according to the priority categories identified in the foundation's 1986 annual report. While the names of these programs have since changed slightly, the data are still indicative of the extent of the foundation's involvement in these areas.

The John D. and Catherine T. MacArthur Foundation

Application procedures
The foundation does not accept unsolicited proposals in its health program, for the new initiatives in education and population, or for the MacArthur fellows program. In the other areas, application procedures vary.

The John D. and Catherine T. MacArthur Foundation
Analysis of 1986 Grantmaking Activity

	Total Grants Paid	Number of Grants	Highest Grant	Lowest Grant	Median Grant Size
PRIORITY INTERESTS					
Health	$12,351,143	41	$4,053,000	$2,500	$120,750
International Peace & Security	$13,799,541	103	$750,000	$3,500	$50,000
World Environment & Resources	$27,345,925	26	$12,516,000	$25,000	$205,000
SPECIAL GRANTS PROGRAM					
Fund for Neighborhood Initiatives	$1,692,000	54	$108,000	$6,000	$20,000
Technical Assistance Grants	$43,442	11	$14,000	$999	$3,000
Chicago Community Grants	$912,900	19	$150,000	$5,000	$40,000
Chicago Cultural & Special Initiatives	$6,793,500	103	$1,000,000	$2,500	$40,000
Program-related Investments	$5,070,000	6	$2,000,000	$500,000	$1,500,000
Other Grants	$690,650	6	$654,650	$3,500	$6,250
GENERAL GRANTS PROGRAM					
Mass Communications	$7,493,600	40	$2,500,000	$10,000	$30,000
Institutional Support	$9,865,000	3	$5,000,000	$1,865,000	$3,000,000
Program-related Investments	$4,000,000	3	$2,000,000	$500,000	$1,500,000
Other Grants	$7,495,211	34	$1,625,000	$5,000	$25,000
NEW PROGRAM INITIATIVES					
Education	$7,025,566	27	$1,000,000	$1,000	$100,000
Population	$5,770,000	9	$1,265,000	$100,000	$600,000

The John D. and Catherine T. MacArthur Foundation

Peace and International Cooperation Program. A limited number of grants has been made to disseminate new knowledge and enhance public awareness and discussion of these issues. Letters of inquiry of no more than two pages should be addressed to Ruth Adams, director of the program.

Special Grants Program. Chicago community grants are awarded primarily to neighborhood self-help groups to improve social and economic opportunities through revitalization of some of Chicago's poorest neighborhoods. Chicago cultural grants are awarded directly by the foundation for applications with budgets over $50,000 and through the City Arts I Program of Chicago's Department of Cultural Affairs for budgets under this amount. Applicants in this latter category should apply directly to the City Arts I Program. Additional information about the special grants program may be obtained by writing Rebecca Riley, director of the program.

Grant Limitations

Grants are not made available for the following programs or activities: programs or services that are among the routine or accepted responsibility of government; political activities or campaigns, attempts to influence legislation or development or dissemination of propaganda; capital campaigns, construction, equipment purchases, endowments, debt retirement, or already completed projects; general support of foundations or institutions, development campaigns, fundraising benefits; publications, conferences, or media production; religious programs; awards to individuals.

Meeting Times

The board of directors of The John D. and Catherine T. MacArthur Foundation meets regularly, and letters of inquiry are invited throughout the year.

Publications

The foundation publishes an annual report and individual program descriptions as well as a general programs and policies brochure.

A. L. Mailman Family Foundation
707 Westchester Avenue
White Plains, New York 10604
(914) 681-4448

Contact Person
Luba H. Lynch, Executive Director

Purpose
The A. L. Mailman Family Foundation is committed to strengthening the family. It supports projects that enhance the abilities of families to promote the intellectual, emotional, and ethical development of their members and serve as advocates for their children.

Areas of Interest
The foundation has a special interest in children and youth who are disadvantaged by reason of their race, socioeconomic status, life circumstances, or emotional or physical disabilities. It looks for creative and innovative projects that provide opportunities for all children to have a fair chance to grow and flourish. It is particularly interested in preventive projects that affect the welfare of vulnerable and at-risk children and families.

The foundation supports both projects and applied research. Projects must present innovative approaches to long-standing problems, current issues, or emerging needs; include a vehicle for broad replication and dissemination; be associated with a stable nonprofit institution; be operated by an institution and project staff with a good track record; and include a long-term plan that is not dependent on continued support.

Proposals for applied research will be considered when the implementation of the research program is in itself beneficial to the participants; there is a built-in plan for dissemination of the results; the investigators have a demonstrated ability to sustain the application of their research; and the research project is a collaborative undertaking involving the investigators, study participants, and practitioners.

In addition to its regular grants program, the foundation has established a small fund from which grants up to $5,000 are made to projects working to protect and promote reproductive rights and the health care of American families. Proposals are given special consideration when a small contribution can generate larger funding.

A. L. Mailman Family Foundation

Financial Data (year ended 12/31/86)

Assets:	$	14,097,547
Total grants paid:*	$	556,096
Number of grants paid:		20
Highest grant:	$	35,500
Lowest grant:	$	4,000
Median grant size:	$	19,498

Reproductive Rights Fund Grants

Total grants paid:	$	25,000
Number of grants paid:		5
Highest grant:	$	5,000
Lowest grant:	$	5,000
Median grant size:	$	5,000

Application Procedures

The deadlines for submitting proposals are October 1 and March 1. The first step in initiating a proposal is a letter of inquiry briefly describing the proposed project, the amount requested, the budget, and other funding sources. Also send a copy of the applicant's proof of tax-exempt status from the IRS. If the foundation is interested in a proposal, applicants will be invited to submit one.

A full grant application should include a two-page summary of the proposal; a description of the problem or issue that the proposed project will address; a statement on how the project relates to the foundation's interests; a review of similar efforts in the field and a rationale for the specific approach of the project; a fully developed project description and plans for implementation; staff qualifications and biographies; an assessment of the project's future implications and special contributions to the field; a plan for monitoring and evaluation; dissemination or replication plans; a detailed budget listing committed funds and potential funders with whom proposals are pending; and a projection of future

---

*This excludes grants totaling $200,000, representing historical and special commitments to well-established institutions, and small contributions totaling approximately $50,000.

A. L. Mailman Family Foundation

funding needs with proposed strategies to meet those budgetary needs without the foundation's continued support. Attached to the application should be a list of the members of the applicant's governing body and/ or advisory committee members and a letter from the governing body of the organization approving the project.

Grant Limitations
The foundation does not provide support for individuals, ongoing direct services, general operating expenses, capital expenditures, and endowment campaigns. Grant commitments of $50,000 or more must receive authorization at two consecutive meetings of the board.

Meeting Times
The board of directors of The A. L. Mailman Family Foundation meets twice a year, in January and June, to review grant proposals.

Publications
The foundation publishes an annual report.

The John and Mary R. Markle Foundation
75 Rockefeller Plaza, Suite 1800
New York, New York 10019-6908
(212) 489-6655

Contact Persons
Lloyd N. Morrisett, President
Dolores E. Miller, Secretary and Grants Manager

Purpose
The John and Mary R. Markle Foundation was established, in the words of the foundation, "to promote the advancement and diffusion of knowledge. . . and the general good of mankind." The foundation's current program concentrates on the improvement of all media, including services growing out of new technologies for the processing and transfer of information. The foundation is particularly interested in supporting promising ideas and innovative projects, and in working with grant recipients to achieve their objectives.

Areas of Interest
The foundation's grantmaking aims particularly at understanding the media's influence in society and realizing their potential for public benefit. Within this broad framework, the foundation supports programs in the following areas: (1) the potential of communications and information technologies to enhance political participation; (2) the benefits of communications and information technologies for an aging population; (3) developments in electronic publishing; (4) the educational and entertainment use and value of computer software in the home; and (5) analysis of issues of public policy and public interest in the communications field. Grants throughout these areas are made for research and demonstration projects. The foundation states that it has a general interest in all aspects of the media and related services and supports a wide range of efforts to improve them.

Financial Data (18 months ended 12/31/86)
Assets:	$ 72,548,034
Total grants paid:	$ 4,536,137
Number of grants:	52
Highest grant:	$ 500,000
Lowest grant:	$ 1,280
Median grant size:	$ 17,500

The John and Mary R. Markle Foundation

Application Procedures
The foundation does not have an application form for submitting a proposal; instead, it requests an informal letter outlining the project. This letter should include the project's objective, resources needed, personnel involved, and the methods to be used.

Grant Limitations
The foundation rarely awards funds for production of films, radio, or television programs. Support is not provided for endowments, building, or for individual scholarships.

Meeting Times
The board of directors of The John and Mary R. Markle Foundation awards grants three times a year, at its meetings in November, March, and June.

Publications
The foundation publishes an annual report.

The McIntosh Foundation
215 Fifth Street, Suite 100
West Palm Beach, Florida 33401
(305) 832-8845

Contact Person
Michael A. McIntosh, President

Areas of Interest
The McIntosh Foundation operates under broad general purposes. Its grants are limited primarily to the support of environmental litigation, conservation generally, and higher education.

Financial Data (year ended 12/31/86)
Assets:	$	21,024,662
Total grants paid:	$	634,800
Number of grants paid:		47
Highest grant:	$	55,000
Lowest grant:	$	1,000
Median grant size:	$	5,000

Application Procedures
The McIntosh Foundation has no formal application forms or specific proposal deadlines. Initial inquiries and requests for information should be made in writing. Proposals should include information about the nature of the project, the principals who will be involved in carrying it out, a budget, and some material covering the past history of the applicant organization. Proposals received by the foundation are acknowledged by mail, and, as a general rule, the foundation does not grant interviews to applicants.

Grant Limitations
The McIntosh Foundation makes no grants to individuals and does not consider requests for endowments or building funds.

Meeting Times
The board of directors of The McIntosh Foundation meets bimonthly.

The McIntosh Foundation

Publications

Upon written request, the foundation will provide a statement of program policy and guidelines for submitting grant applications. However, the foundation does not publish an annual report or a list of previous grantees.

Joyce Mertz-Gilmore Foundation
218 East 18 Street
New York, New York 10003
(212) 475-1137

Contact Persons
Larry E. Condon, President
Robert Crane, Vice-President, Program

Purpose
The Joyce Mertz-Gilmore Foundation is a private foundation with long-standing interests in promoting civil and human rights and democratic values as essential elements of a free society.

Areas of Interest
The foundation makes grants in four primary program areas:

> *Human Rights and Democratic Values.* The foundation's broadly defined concern in this area is to promote and secure human rights through support for programs addressing economic and social entitlements as well as civic and political safeguards. Of particular interest are projects that (1) foster democratic development at the community level in emerging democratic nations, (2) monitor and expose human-rights violations worldwide and promote the free flow of information within and between nations, and (3) protect and extend human rights under attack in the United States. In addition, the foundation has made at least one grant to protect individuals with AIDS from discrimination.
>
> *The Environment.* While the foundation considers support for programs addressing a range of serious environmental issues, it has targeted the problem of global warming as an area of special concern. It supports efforts to (1) mobilize the major environmental organizations to include global warming on their agendas, (2) inform the public and promote citizen action, particularly among the constituencies whose vocations or avocations would be drastically affected, and (3) attract the attention of legislators and government officials to the problem through national and international public policy research and analysis.
>
> The foundation also supports projects that address environmental issues directly affecting the New York metropolitan area.

Joyce Mertz-Gilmore Foundation

Alternative Defense and Common Security. Generally the foundation is interested in programs that increase participation in and expand the scope of the national security dialogue, and later the context of the confrontation between the United States and the Soviet Union. Of particular interest are programs that (1) offer alternative ways to conceptualize defense and security issues so as to improve the possibility for nuclear disarmament and to lessen the possibility of war, (2) explore bilateral and multilateral interactions that might increase the prospects for security among nations, and (3) broaden public participation in the defense and security dialogue in the United States to move it beyond its military focus.

New York City Programs. As part of its long-standing commitment to improving the quality of life for New York City residents, the foundation supports, with modest grants, community stabilization and development projects, advocacy programs, conservation efforts, performing arts groups, and cultural institutions. It also provides small planning and organizational development grants to community-based organizations with proven records.

The foundation occasionally funds projects in areas not listed above. However, these grants are made only if they are of special interest to the board of directors and only if requested by the foundation.

Financial Data (1/1/87 through 11/15/87)

Assets:[1]	$	28,410,268
Total grants paid:	$	3,130,341
Number of grants paid:[2]		184
Highest grant:	$	90,000
Lowest grant:	$	1,000
Median grant size:	$	10,000

---

[1]As of December 31, 1986.
[2]This figure and the tabulations below do not include 36 discretionary grants made at the initiative of the foundation and ranging from $366 to $350,000 and totaling $1,214,841.

Joyce Mertz-Gilmore Foundation

Application Procedures

There are no application deadlines. The foundation notes that, to the degree possible, proposals received from August through January will be considered by the board of directors at the spring meeting, and those received from February though July will be considered at the fall meeting.

Organizations seeking funds from the foundation must submit an application form which is available upon request. All inquiries and applications will be acknowledged, and the foundation will request additional information as needed. Applicants are advised that the foundation's staff is small and cannot give close attention to unsolicited full proposals. Furthermore, applicants are requested not to telephone the foundation regarding the status of their application, but to inquire by letter instead.

Grant Limitations

Foundation grants are made only to nonprofit charitable organizations with proof of tax-exempt status. The foundation does not provide funds for endowments, building construction or maintenance, primary operational support, political purposes such as lobbying or propaganda, programs consisting solely or primarily of conferences, sectarian religious concerns per se, individual scholarships, fellowships, loans, or travel, film or television production, publications, or annual fund appeals. It does not make grants to other private foundations. Within the New York City programs, funds are not provided for direct social services.

Meeting Times

The board of directors of The Joyce Mertz-Gilmore Foundation meets quarterly to review grant applications.

Publications

The foundation distributes a grants list, an application form, a brochure, and other information describing its programs and priorities.

The Charles Stewart Mott Foundation
1200 Mott Foundation Building
Flint, Michigan 48502-1851
(313) 238-5651

Contact Persons[1]
Judy Y. Samelson, Director of Communications
Fran Bell, Administrative Assistant

Purpose
The Charles Stewart Mott Foundation has long been interested and involved in community self-improvement—from within neighborhoods to within city hall—through education, social welfare, economic development, and environmental management. Since its founding in 1926, it has funded programs aimed at improving the quality of life for individuals and their communities.

The foundation's approach to grantmaking is guided by a series of principles and mission statements detailed in its annual report and management/philosophy statement, *Programs, Policies and Procedures.* The four principles into which grants are classified are opportunity for the individual, partnership with the community, effective functioning of community systems, and leadership as the mobilizer. It should be noted that most of the foundation's grantees are well-established programs and institutions, but within each principle there are several small grants to community-based or grassroots efforts. Special attention is directed to the grantmaking activities related to effective functioning of community systems.

The foundation is primarily interested in making grants that support action-oriented demonstration programs. It also seeks to fund unique

---

[1]General questions concerning the foundation's program and grantmaking procedures should be addressed to Judy Y. Samelson. Grant proposals should be clearly marked on the outside of the envelope and addressed as follows: Office of Proposal Entry, Mott Foundation, 1200 Mott Foundation Building, Flint, Michigan 48502-1851.

Contact persons in each of the foundation's program interests are: Jon Blyth, Job Training, Youth Employment, and Environment; Pat Edwards, Education and Leadership Development; Suzanne Feurt, Minority Higher Education, Community Foundations; Ruth Goins, Economic Development and Community-Based Organizations; Jack Litzenberg, Economic Development and Community-Based Organizations; Maureen Smyth, Environment; and Marilyn Steele, Community Identity and Stability.

The Charles Stewart Mott Foundation

approaches to solving community problems that if successful can be disseminated to or applied in other communities. Wherever possible, grants for seed money are preferred over those for general support.

Areas of Interest

In addition to its guiding principles, the foundation has identified seven missions, or current program areas: communities and neighborhoods, education, the environment, the Flint area, individuals and families, philanthropy, and exploratory and special projects.

Communities and Neighborhoods. The foundation seeks to improve communities and the quality of life of their residents through the support of a broad range of innovative institutions and programs, including efforts to improve community safety; expand economic opportunities through community-based entrepreneurship and job creation and by advancing the development of national policies to increase national competitiveness and strengthen the national economy; provide livable housing for low-income families through policy and research studies and support of a limited number of demonstration projects; and increase the effectiveness of community self-help groups seeking to revitalize neighborhoods.

Education. This area encompasses both efforts to develop community education as a means of making local educational institutions more relevant to the needs of their residents and support for the nation's historically and predominantly black colleges.

Environment. The foundation is committed to promoting a sustainable environment. It emphasizes preserving the natural order, conserving nonrenewable resources and wisely managing renewable resources in its support of model efforts to conserve energy and manage resources at the community level; efforts to preserve the land and water resources of the Great Lakes region; ways to reduce the threat from toxic substances; and

The Charles Stewart Mott Foundation

special initiatives offering unusual opportunities to contribute to the state of the art on global and national environmental problems.

Flint Area. In this area the foundation acknowledges its special obligation to Flint and Genesee County by supporting arts and recreation projects, economic revitalization efforts, and efforts to increase the capacity of the community and its local institutions to address economic and social problems.

Individuals and Families. Grants in this area are made to develop and disseminate long-term solutions to the problems of young people at risk; assist employment training and counseling programs for unemployed and underemployed adults; improve family services and family education programs; increase access for handicapped adults; enable seniors to remain independent; and prevent teenage pregnancy and expand the life options available to teenage parents and their children.

Philanthropy. In this area the foundation supports efforts to strengthen the philanthropy by providing technical assistance to community foundations and encouraging them to support low-income neighborhood groups in their local areas; encourage accountability by foundations and other charitable institutions; and promote volunteerism and the effective use and management of volunteers.

Special Projects. The foundation occasionally makes grants outside its regular programs where such support is likely to have a substantial effect or may lead to a continuing grantmaking interest. For example, the foundation has been supporting efforts to strengthen nonwhite community organizations and to train nonwhite community leaders in South Africa.

Further, the foundation engages in some international grantmaking employing two strategies: (1) supporting activities that are natural extensions of its current programs which will advance the goals and objectives of those programs; and (2) responding to new and special opportunities not included in current programs areas but which enable

The Charles Stewart Mott Foundation

the foundation to make a genuine contribution and enrich its overall programming.

In addition to making grants, the foundation also considers requests of a nongrant nature. It may make funds available for program-related investments, provide direct technical or fundraising assistance, or sponsor research and the dissemination of findings.

Financial Data (year ended 12/31/86)

Assets:	$ 736,873,249
Total grants paid:	$ 21,663,260
Number of grants paid:[2]	222
Highest grant:	$ 1,000,000
Lowest grant:	$ 15,000
Median grant size:	$ 40,000

Application Procedures

Applicants are strongly urged to read carefully the foundation's annual report and to examine their program objectives in light of the foundation's statement of program philosophy.

Grant applications to the Mott Foundation may be handled in one of two ways. The prospective grantee may either submit a brief letter outlining the details of the project or may send a full proposal. Both are processed as if they are requests for support. Projects are generally funded for a single year, but multiyear budgets may be submitted. In any event, the following basic information is needed: (1) a description of the project and what will be accomplished; (2) a statement of why the project is needed; (3) a statement concerning the population to be served; (4) a brief line-term budget including distribution of funds if a multiyear grant; (5) information on the organization seeking the funds and its accomplishments to date; and (6) the starting and ending dates and plans for postgrant funding and project evaluation.

Visits to the foundation's office are discouraged, except by invitation. The foundation advises that communication with individual trustees is

---

[2]This figure and the tabulations that follow do not include grants under $15,000.

The Charles Stewart Mott Foundation

highly discouraged. Applicants should allow about four months to process proposals.

Meeting Times
The board of trustees of The Charles Stewart Mott Foundation meets quarterly.

Publications
The foundation publishes an annual report that details each program interest and lists each grantee. Other foundation publications particularly helpful for grantseekers are *Programs, Policies and Procedures,* a booklet setting forth the foundation's program philosophies, and *Facts on Grants,* which contains a thorough summary of grant awards.

Ruth Mott Fund
1726 Genesee Towers
Flint, Michigan 48502
(313) 232-3180

1000 Wisconsin Avenue, N.W.
Washington, D.C. 20007
(202) 342-0519

Contact Person
Deborah Tuck, Executive Director

Purpose
The activities of the Ruth Mott Fund emphasize the importance of individuals taking personal responsibility for their world, and the view that while corrective action may in some instances be required, prevention is preferable to cure, whether for personal or social problems.

Areas of Interest
The fund's general guidelines state that programs should focus on topics of emerging significance, exemplify originality, offer the potential for application on a broader scale, and include an evaluation procedure based in part on specific objectives and identification of potential impact. The fund has identified four specific program priorities: the environment, health promotion, national and international security, and arts and special interests in Genesee County and Flint, Michigan. At the time this entry was being prepared, the foundation was reassessing its focus. This description is based on its program as administered in 1986.

During 1986 the foundation did not review unsolicited proposals in the area of the environment. Rather, requests for proposals were issued in the areas of global deforestation; alternative, sustainable agriculture; and toxic substances. Projects were funded solely at the fund's initiative. The goal of this process was to develop a grantmaking program in one or more of these three areas.

In the area of health promotion, the foundation supports efforts that foster general awareness, and understanding of preventive factors that alter attitudes and life-styles affecting health. Projects must focus on health issues affecting low-income sectors of the population, and emphasize one or more of the following preventive components: improved nutrition, stress control, exercise and fitness, smoking cessation, and reduced al-

Ruth Mott Fund

cohol and drug use. Proposals from new and modest-size organizations (with total budgets of less than $150,000 annually) are encouraged.

In the area of national and international security the fund supports projects and organizations working to foster public review and discussion of the factors that contribute to national security and science and technology related to the use of nuclear or space weapons by design or by accident.

The fund's arts program is the only area in which there is a geographic limitation. In this program grants are made only to activities in Genesee County, Michigan, and to beautification efforts, through landscaping and planting, in Flint.

Financial Data (year ended 12/31/85)

During calendar year 1985, the latest year for which figures were available, the fund's support and revenue totaled $2,840,130. The following grants analysis, however, is based on the 11-month period from December 1986 through October 1987.

Total grants paid:	$	1,446,278
Number of grants paid:		116
Highest grant:[1]	$	50,000
Lowest grant:	$	50
Median grant size:	$	10,000

Application Procedures

Applications should be sent to the fund's office in Michigan. There are no application deadlines, and no particular form is required. Applicants who would like an acknowledgment of proposal receipt are asked to include with their materials a self-addressed post card.

Proposals should not exceed twelve typewritten pages; brevity is appreciated. The foundation pays particular attention to the following points: What issues are being addressed and why are they important? What is the program plan and what are its measurable objectives? What

[1]This excludes one unusually large grant of $90,000.

Ruth Mott Fund

difference will the program make and how will it be evaluated? What are the plans for continued funding (if appropriate)? How might the program benefit people beyond those whom it immediately serves? What is the program budget? To whom have proposals been submitted and from whom has support already been received?

Appropriate supporting materials may be included. Minimally these should include: a summary of organizational history and activities, background of key personnel, a list of the members of the organization's governing body, a financial statement for the most recently completed fiscal year, and a copy of the organization's IRS tax-exemption letter.

Applicants are also asked to provide a one page summary including the name, address, and telephone number of the organization; the date submitted; the contact person and title; the total project budget; the amount requested; the period of time (with dates) for which funding is sought; and the organization's name as it appears on the IRS ruling of tax-exempt status. On the balance of the page applicants should summarize the purposes for which funds are sought, focusing on the issues and problems and how they will be addressed.

Grant Limitations
Generally the fund states that the following are low priorities: capital projects, major equipment purchases, land purchases, endowments, and renovations.

Meeting Times
The board of directors of the Ruth Mott Fund meets three times a year.

Publications
The fund publishes periodic multiyear reports.

Stewart R. Mott and Associates
Stewart R. Mott Charitable Trust
122 Maryland Avenue, N.E.
Washington, D.C. 20002
(202) 546-3732

1133 Fifth Avenue
New York, New York 10128
(212) 289-0006

Contact Persons
Anne B. Zill and Conrad Martin, Washington, D.C. office
Debbie Landau and Ronald Hanft, New York office

Background
Together, Stewart R. Mott and Associates and the Stewart R. Mott Charitable Trust[1] carry out the administrative responsibilities for Mr. Mott's personal philanthropy. Mr. Mott's assets derive from his inheritance. His father, C. S. Mott, was one of the largest stockholders of General Motors Corporation.

Stewart Mott received his education from M.I.T. and Columbia (B.A., 1961) and worked briefly as an English teacher before serving as an executive trainee in several of the companies controlled by his father. He established a Planned Parenthood clinic in Flint, Michigan, and volunteered for the national organization, giving speeches and soliciting funds. By 1968, eighty percent of his total personal charitable contributions, or $1.24 million, went to various population-control groups. In 1965 he discussed with his father a broadening of the family foundation's interests to include population control, arms limitation, and other new programs. When it was decided that such a broadening was not consistent with the foundation's goals, Stewart Mott embarked on his own program of philanthropy.

Areas of Interest
Mr. Mott's primary interests are: (1) peace, arms control, and foreign policy; (2) family planning and population issues; and (3) government reform and political education. His preference is to support activist proj-

---

[1]Grants are also by Mr. Mott under the name Spectemur Agendo.

Stewart R. Mott and Associates

ects rather than research-oriented activities, and projects that are national in scope, not local or regional grassroots efforts.

Financial Data

Mr. Mott is preparing a twenty-five year report on his charitable programs which is expected to be published by 1990. His Washington office estimates that each year a total somewhere between $500,000 and $1 million is distributed in small grants averaging $1,000. The figures below provide an indication of the level of direct grant support. However, they understate Mr. Mott's total charitable activities as they do not include the significant level of hands-on, in-kind support including conference

Stewart R. Mott and Associates
Five Year Summary of Grantmaking Activity
1982-1986

	1982	1983	1984	1985	1986	Total	Program as Percent of Total
Civil Rights & Liberties/ Women[2]	$29,575	$40,825	$54,300	$10,750	$11,300	$146,750	5.2%
Cultural	$70,667	$142,120	$49,600	$34,550	$27,800	$324,737	11.5%
Government Reform	$43,500	$216,550	$131,200	$81,663	$75,563	$548,476	19.4%
Peace	$209,081	$275,950	$161,200	$194,288	$94,603	$935,122	33.1%
Population	$169,268	$143,425	$133,500	$249,995	$116,809	$812,997	28.8%
Women[2]				$48,750	$4,500	$53,250	1.9%
Total	**$522,091**	**$818,870**	**$529,800**	**$619,996**	**$330,575**	**$2,821,332**	**100.0%**
Annual Funding as Percent of Total	18.5%	29.0%	18.8%	22.0%	11.7%	100.0%	

[2]Beginning in 1985, funding for women's programs is shown separate and apart from civil rights and civil liberties grants.

Stewart R. Mott and Associates

and seminar sponsorship, receptions, and the like provided on a regular basis by the Mott offices.

According to a now somewhat dated feature article in the May–August 1978 *Grantsmanship Center News*: "Mott's giving can be divided into four categories. He makes many small contributions, often in the form of benefit tickets. He gives 25 or 30 gifts exceeding $1,000 to organizations that he has a little more interest in. He makes perhaps a dozen grants of between $5,000 and $15,000 ... [a]nd finally, he makes a few very large contributions to organizations with which he is very involved." Rarely, the article reports, does Mr. Mott support more than a few new projects a year to any considerable extent.

Application Procedures
There is no formal application procedure. Brief letters are preferred over lengthy formal proposals. Requests should set forth: the project goals, the personalities involved, the tactics to be employed, how the group is structured, the planning process, the budgetary and tax status, and the amount requested. Proposals are reviewed in New York and Washington with Mr. Mott on a regular basis.

Publications
Upon request, a biography will be supplied.

Ms. Foundation for Women, Inc.
141 Fifth Avenue, Suite 6S
New York, New York 10010
(212) 353-8580

Contact Persons

Marie Wilson, Executive Director
Idelisse Malaze, Deputy Director
Sasha Hohri, Field Director

Purpose

The Ms. Foundation for Women, Inc., is a national multi-issue women's fund. It is committed to providing money and technical assistance to community-based activist women's organizations that have minimal or no access to conventional funding sources. The foundation hopes that its grants will enable groups to pursue larger grants from other sources and eventually become self-sustaining.

Areas of Interest

The foundation's focus is on survival issues: protection from violence and sexual assault in and outside the home; equal access to employment, job training, job safety, housing, credit, pensions, and health care; fair treatment within the criminal justice system; community and family sharing of responsibility for child care; education for both boys and girls that is nonsexist and multiracial; and the protection and furtherance of reproductive freedom.

Special consideration is given to groups that: support newly-emerging feminist issues as women organizing define them; have limited access to funding sources; encourage cooperation across race and class lines; are of special benefit to women of color and women isolated by geography or class; may be replicated by other groups or in other parts of the country; are run by women affected by the problem being addressed; and will empower women and girls to make their own decisions in the future.

In 1986 the foundation launched an economic development/technical assistance project offering women's organizations the opportunity to learn about the field of community-based economic development and receive technical assistance with special projects. The project's activities are aimed at grassroots women's organizations that are: starting small businesses to provide decent employment opportunities to their low-income constituents or to generate income; assisting low-income women and women of color to become self-employed or start small businesses; or affecting the economic development process in their communities

Ms. Foundation for Women, Inc.

through organizing and policy-making activities. Among other activities, the project offers an internship program through which an organization beginning an economic development project can have the opportunity to experience on-site training with another organization that is further along in the development of a similar project or activity.

Financial Data (year ended 12/31/86)

Support and revenue:	$	1,947,458
Total grants paid:	$	345,400
Number of grants paid:		47
Highest grant:	$	15,500
Lowest grant:	$	700
Median grant size:	$	8,000

Application Procedures

There are no proposal deadlines; however, applications should be received no later than six months prior to meetings of the foundation's board of directors. Applicants may write or telephone for application forms, but the forms are not required. In any event, the foundation asks that applicants, in five pages or less: (1) describe the organization and its purpose, history, constituency or membership (including race and class composition), decision-making structure, programs and accomplishments, and relationships to other organizations; (2) if applying for a specific project, outline the need, purpose, goals and methods, staff capabilities and responsibilities, time frame, and evaluation plans; and (3) describe the community in which the organization works and the need for the organization.

Applicants are also asked to attach to their submission: (1) the project budget, and if the project is only one part of the applicant's general work, an organizational budget; (2) a list of past and current funding sources and amounts and a list of potential funding sources and requests that are outstanding; (3) the names of other individuals or organizations (with telephone numbers) who are not part of the organization but are familiar with its work; and (4) proof of tax-exempt status. Other supporting materials such as brochures or newspaper clippings may be included.

Ms. Foundation for Women, Inc.

Grant Limitations
The foundation makes no grants to individuals, research, media and arts, litigation projects, or annual conferences. Generally, projects must be tax-exempt under Section 501(c)(3) of the Internal Revenue Code.

Meeting Times
The board of directors of the Ms. Foundation meets twice a year, in the spring and fall.

Publications
The foundation distributes an annual report, a list of grant awards, and guidelines for prospective applicants.

A. J. Muste Memorial Institute
339 Lafayette Street
New York, New York 10012
(212) 533-4335

Contact Person
Murray Rosenblith, Executive Director

Purpose
The A. J. Muste Memorial Institute has, as one of its programs, the funding and fiscal sponsorship of innovative and experimental projects which promote the principles and practice of nonviolent social change within its areas of interest. Grants are made to local, national, and international projects.

Areas of Interest
The institute looks to fund projects concerned with the issues to which A. J. Muste dedicated his life: peace and disarmament, social and economic justice, racial and sexual equality, and the labor movement.

Financial Data (year ended 12/31/87)

Assets:[1]	$	213,313
Total grants paid:[2]	$	41,800
Number of grants paid:		36
Highest grant:	$	2,500
Lowest grant:	$	500
Median grant size:	$	1,000

Application Procedures
Proposals must be no longer than five pages and must include: a description of the project, including its relevance, targeted community, and evidence of the group's ability to carry it out; a contact name, with day and evening telephone numbers; detailed project budget, annual organizational budget, and funding sources; list of advisers to the project or organization; amount requested (preferably a line item from the project budget); or, if applying for a sponsorship, the ceiling amount for transfer

---

[1]As of December 31, 1986.
[2]These tabulations reflect only grants made from discretionary funds and do not include 10 directed fiscal sponsorships totaling $129,473.

311

A. J. Muste Memorial Institute

between the time sponsorship is granted and the end of the calendar year.

Supporting material such as printed matter or press clippings may be attached. Applicants must submit two copies of the complete proposal and attachments and twenty-five copies of a one-page summary of the project. The institute makes between twenty-five and thirty-five grants per year in four cycles. Because deadlines vary from year to year, applicants are urged to contact the institute directly before submitting a proposal.

Grant Limitations
The institute does not fund organizations or projects that can secure funding from traditional sources and generally does not support projects that are budgeted at over $50,000, or organizations whose annual budget exceeds $500,000. Grants are not made to academic projects or individuals. The institute will not accept a new request from a previously funded group for two years after a grant.

Meeting Times
The board of directors of the A. J. Muste Institute meets approximately six times a year, and grant requests are considered at four of these meetings.

Publications
The institute publishes an annual report and grant application guidelines.

The Needmor Fund
1730 15th Street
Boulder, Colorado 80302
(303) 449-5801

Contact Persons
Virginia Stranahan, Coordinator
Lynn Gisi, Program Officer
Donna Sunn, Administrative Assistant

Purpose
The primary goal of The Needmor Fund is assisting groups of people working together to overcome problems, i.e., those forces and events that have an adverse and profound effect on their lives as individuals, families, and members of a community. It looks for grassroots, membership-controlled organizations, capable of setting out and implementing realistic strategies and goals within their communities. Preference is given to organizations whose membership represents traditionally disenfranchised populations.

Funds are allocated from the Broad Common Pool, which accepts proposals from throughout the United States; and from the Toledo Common Pool, a fund dedicated to organizations in Toledo, Ohio. In addition, Needmor makes a number of donor-directed grants reflecting the specialized interests and civic commitments of individual family members.

Areas of Interest
The fund's guidelines are process-oriented and do not identify specific funding priorities. A review of grants made in 1986 and 1987 illustrates a broad range of interest areas including, but not limited to, human rights, rural economic development, civil rights and civil liberties, labor issues and workers' education, economic rights, hunger, and natural resources.

In order to receive Needmor funding, an organization must demonstrate that is has the active involvement of its constituents in choosing its leadership, making policy, defining the problem, and planning and evaluating the program; and that it offers personal support and opportunities for learning in the context of collective work and action.

As each proposal is reviewed, the fund considers: Is this a project that empowers its constituents? Does it help people take control over their lives? Does the project serve to make the traditional power structure

The Needmor Fund

more responsive to community members? Is the organization made up of people at the local level? Does the proposed strategy seem realistic and sound? Does the leadership have the skills to direct the project successfully?

Needmor has also established a technical assistance grant program to enable the fund's current grantees to deal with internal management problems. Each organization is eligible to apply for one technical assistance grant, not to exceed $3,000, in a twelve-month period. The grant is to be used exclusively to improve the grantee's management and planning capabilities through the contracting of appropriate outside technical services.

Financial Data (year ended 12/31/86)

As of December 31, 1986, the assets of The Needmor Fund were approximately $5.4 million. Following is an analysis of all Needmor grants, excluding donor-directed contributions, based on the fund's fall 1986 and spring 1987 funding cycles.

Application Procedures

Deadlines for submitting proposals in 1988 were July 15 and January 15. However, the fund advises these deadlines vary slightly each year and specifically suggests that applicants telephone and recheck deadlines.

The first contact with the fund should be a telephone call or short

The Needmor Fund
Analysis of 1986-87 Grantmaking Activity

	The Broad Common Fund	The Toledo Fund	Technical Assistance Grants
Total Grants Paid	$899,800	$158,750	$23,924
Number of Grants Paid	50	11	9
Highest Grant	$35,000	$25,000	$3,000
Lowest Grant	$5,000	$3,000	$1,075
Median Grant Size	$20,000	$20,000	$3,000

The Needmor Fund

letter that states the history and goals of the organization, the nature of the project for which funding is sought, and the amount that will be requested from the fund. If the staff determine that a project falls within the fund's grantmaking criteria, a full written proposal will be requested, and specific guidelines and application forms will be provided. Before the staff submit a proposal to the fund's advisory committee for a final decision, every attempt is made to visit the applicant.

Grant Limitations
The Broad Common Pool does not consider proposals for funding in the following areas: scholarships/fellowships or other individual development projects; operating support for traditional community services; replacement of lost government funding; capital renovation, or purchase of land, buildings, or equipment; reduction or elimination of deficits; computer projects; film, television, or radio productions; books or publications; projects outside the United States. Grants to national organizations are rare.

Meeting Times
The fund has two grantmaking cycles each year. Funding decisions are usually made by the advisory committee of The Needmor Fund in May and November.

Publications
The fund distributes a program description, application guidelines and a list of grantees upon request.

The New World Foundation
100 East 85 Street
New York, New York 10028
(212) 249-1023

Contact Person
Colin Greer, President

Purpose
The New World Foundation is dedicated to the pursuit of equality and justice for the least privileged in society through support for programs with creative and innovative individuals working within them.

Areas of Interest
The foundation's grantmaking is directed toward minority and low-income people. Its major concerns are the broad areas of equal rights and opportunities, and encouraging economic and social equity through citizen participation in public policy at the local, regional, and national levels. The foundation is interested in the full participation of minorities, women, youth, and low-income people through organizing, public education, technical assistance, and policy development for economic, education, and health improvement.

The inextricable link between peace and justice is a key concern of the foundation, which is committed to the role of citizens through issue and group constituencies in helping to achieve the de-escalation of the nuclear arms race and the demilitarization of the economy.

The foundation will provide start-up money to initiate programs as well as funds for new projects created by established organizations.

Financial Data (year ended 9/30/86)

Assets:	$ 26,246,075
Total grants paid:	$ 1,575,000
Number of grants paid:	142
Highest grant:	$ 65,000
Lowest grant:	$ 500
Median grant size:	$ 10,000

The New World Foundation

Application Procedures

The foundation has no application forms or deadlines. Staff are generally unable to arrange appointments with prospective grantees prior to receipt and review of a written proposal.

A concise proposal, addressed to the president, should include: (1) a cover letter summarizing the proposal and stating the amount requested; (2) a project description, including objectives, with a timetable and strategies for achieving them; (3) a brief description of the sponsoring organization; (4) the organization's budget for the fiscal year for which funds are being sought and a budget for the specific project being proposed; (5) if possible, an audited report for the previous fiscal year or, otherwise, a financial statement; (6) a list of current sources of support and amount of income, and sources from which additional funds are being solicited; and (7) a copy of the IRS determination of federal tax-exempt status.

Grant Limitations

The foundation does not make contributions for general charitable purposes such as community fund drives, schools and hospitals, building and endowment funds, or other capital funding. It does not make grants to individuals, nor does it support scholarships, academic research, films, publications, media and arts projects, or direct social service delivery programs. It does not make general support grants to organizations that enjoy broad popular support, nor does it provide support for programs operating outside the U.S.

Meeting Times

The board of directors of The New World Foundation, Inc., meets quarterly, in September, December, February, and June.

Publications

The foundation publishes an annual report.

The New York Times Company Foundation, Inc.
229 West 43 Street
New York, New York 10036
(212) 556-1091

Contact Person
Arthur Gelb, President

Purpose
The New York Times Company Foundation, Inc., provides funding to strengthen community institutions and services in New York City and, to a growing extent, in the other communities from Maine to California served by New York Times affiliated companies. (See the complete list at the end of this entry.) A common theme in the foundation's 1986 grantmaking was the inseparable link between a free society and the need for greater equity and opportunity for all to participate in society's benefits.

Areas of Interest
Grants made in 1986 divide into five major categories: cultural affairs, education, community services, journalism, and environmental concerns. In the arts, grants were made to museums and libraries and major cultural institutions as well as to smaller performing arts groups. A special, continuing concern of the foundation in education and journalism areas is improving opportunities for minorities. The environment (including New York City's parks), community services, urban and national and international issues were additional areas supported by the foundation's grants.

Financial Data (year ended 12/31/86)

Assets:	$	1,696,762
Total grants paid:	$	4,300,494
Total number of grants:[1]		573
Highest grant:[2]	$	7,500
Lowest grant:	$	500
Median grant size:	$	4,000

---

[1] This number and the calculations below do not include grants to educational institutions made under the employee matching grant program.

[2] This excludes three unusually large grants of $100,000 and more made to well-established institutions.

The New York Times Company Foundation, Inc.

Application Procedures

Grants should be requested in a letter describing the purpose for which funds are sought and providing information concerning the costs of the specific venture and details of other potential sources of support. Proof of tax-exempt status under the Internal Revenue Code must accompany the letter.

Meetings with applicants are arranged at the discretion of the foundation only when such a meeting is essential to the determination of a response.

Grant Limitations

The foundation does not make grants to individuals, to sectarian religious institutions and causes, or for health-related purposes. In the urban affairs area, grants are generally not made on the neighborhood level. Some national and international activities receive contributions, but the majority of grants is concentrated in the greater New York area and in localities served by affiliates of The New York Times Company.

Meeting Times

The board of directors of The New York Times Company Foundation, Inc., meets at least twice annually, in the first and third quarter of each calendar year, to review the president's recommendations and approve grants.

Publications

The New York Times Company Foundation, Inc., publishes an annual report.

New York Times Company Locations

Alabama

Florence
Gadsden

Huntsville
Tuscaloosa

The New York Times Company Foundation, Inc.

New York Times Company Locations (cont.)

Arkansas
Fort Smith

California
Santa Barbara
Santa Rosa

Connecticut
Trumbull

Florida
Avon Park
Fernandina Beach
Gainesville
Lake City
Lakeland
Leesburg
Marco Island
Ocala
Palatka
Sarasota
Sebring

Georgia
Atlanta

Illinois
Moline

Kentucky
Harlan
Madisonville
Middlesboro

Louisiana
Houma
Opelousas
Thibodaux

Maine
Kennebunk
Madison

Mississippi
Booneville
Corinth

New Jersey
Cherry Hill

New York
New York

North Carolina
Hendersonville
Lenoir
Lexington
Wilmington

Pennsylvania
Avoca

Rhode Island
Newport

South Carolina
Spartansburg

The New York Times Company Foundation, Inc.

New York Times Company Locations (cont.)

Tennessee
Dyersburg
Memphis
New Tazewell

England
London

France
Neuilly-sur-Seine

Canada
Kapuskasing, Quebec

The New-Land Foundation, Inc.
1345 Avenue of the Americas, 45th Floor
New York, New York 10105
(212) 841–6000

Contact Person
Renee Schwartz, Secretary/Treasurer

Areas of Interest
The New-Land Foundation provides seed money, general operating support and support for special projects to organizations working in a variety of areas including education, health, welfare, the environment, law and civil rights, public policy, refugee issues, and arms control. It makes single and multiple year grant awards.

Financial Data (year ended 12/31/86)

Assets:	$ 17,717,464
Total grants paid:	$ 1,502,062
Number of grants paid:	121
Highest grant:[1]	$ 60,000
Lowest grant:	$ 1,000
Median grant size:	$ 7,000

Application Procedures
The foundation discourages telephone inquiries. Written contact with the foundation should be made by submitting a complete proposal, including a one-page summary that describes the project, the time period, the amount requested, and evaluation or follow-up plans. Applicants should also submit proof of tax-exempt status; an organizational and, if appropriate, project budget; a list of board members; and qualifications of key personnel. A copy of arms control and environmental proposals should be sent to Mr. Hal Harvey, Post Office Box 1266, Aspen, Colorado 81612.

Suggested dates for submitting grant requests are February 1 and August 1. Receipt of proposals is not acknowledged, and the foundation does not favor interviews. Grantseekers whose proposals are not approved generally are not advised.

---

[1]This omits one unusually large grant of over $250,000.

The New-Land Foundation, Inc.

Grant Limitations
The foundation makes grant awards only to tax-exempt organizations as defined in Section 501(c)(3) of the Internal Revenue Code. It makes no grants to individuals.

Meeting Times
The board of directors of The New-Land Foundation usually meets twice a year, in the spring and fall.

Publications
None.

Norman Foundation, Inc.
147 East 48 Street
New York, New York 10017
(212) 759-7185

Contact Person
Jody Weisbrod, Director

Purpose
The Norman Foundation supports projects that encourage a just, open, and democratic political system; a fair distribution of resources; and equality of opportunity. The foundation seeks to improve institutional arrangements and to identify public policy alternatives to achieve better, fairer results at all levels of modern American society.

Areas of Interest
The foundation supports projects addressing issues of national security and economic security. It also continues its long-standing commitment to making grants on behalf of civil rights and civil liberties issues that have a disproportionate impact on minorities, women, and poor people. In particular, the foundation seeks programs that aim to improve the effectiveness of community organizations and institutions through the use of skills training and broad-based mobilization.

The foundation provides seed money to initiate programs as well as funds for new projects created by established organizations. It seeks to provide a bridge between the initial needs of innovative programs and their achievement of greater support from the public, larger foundations, or government agencies.

Financial Data (year ended 12/31/87)[1]

Assets:	$ 20,733,984
Total grants paid:	$ 663,450
Number of grants paid:	52
Highest grant:	$ 25,000
Lowest grant:	$ 2,000
Median grant size:	$ 10,000

---

[1]These figures were supplied by the foundation in lieu of a grants list.

Norman Foundation, Inc.

Application Procedures

The foundation has no standard application form or procedures. A concise proposal, addressed to the program director, should contain the following information: (1) a cover letter briefly summarizing the proposal and stating the amount requested from the foundation; (2) a description of the specific project; (3) a statement of the objectives, a projected time-table for their achievement, and the strategies and methods to be used to attain them; (4) a brief description of the sponsoring organization; (5) the projected budget of the organization for the fiscal year during which funds are being sought, and a detailed budget for the specific project being proposed; and (6) the current sources of support and a list of sources from which additional funds are being solicited.

Each proposal will be assessed by its ability to fulfill the following criteria: talented personnel, including innovative, creative, and sound managerial and personal skills among the program's leadership; clearly articulated objectives and goals; active, ongoing equal-opportunity leadership development; and a substantial plan to acquire adequate support to complete the proposed project or to achieve self-sufficiency.

The foundation acknowledges receipt of proposals. Projects to be considered for a grant by the board of directors generally are notified six weeks after the acknowledgment, and at that time an interview or site visit will be arranged. The program director is generally unable to arrange appointments with prospective grantees prior to receipt and review of written proposals.

Grant Requirements

As a condition of each grant made, the foundation requires that a self-evaluation form provided by the foundation be completed by the grantee at the end of the grant year. Grantees will be asked to evaluate their progress—both successes and disappointments—against the goals and objectives stated in the proposal.

Grant Limitations

The foundation ordinarily makes grants only to tax-exempt organizations or to projects that have a tax-exempt sponsor. Further, the foundation

Norman Foundation, Inc.

does not usually support programs that deal with only local issues or involve only local constituencies.

The foundation does not make grants for general charitable purposes such as community-fund drives, building and endowment funds (or other capital funding), schools, or hospitals. It does not make grants to individuals, nor does it support scholarships, conferences, research, films, publications, media and arts projects, or direct social service delivery programs. It does not make grants to organizations that enjoy broad popular support or to programs operating outside the United States.

Meeting Times
The board of trustees of the Norman Foundation meets quarterly.

Publications
The foundation publishes triennial reports. Guidelines for grant applications and a list of grantees are available upon request.

Jessie Smith Noyes Foundation, Inc.
16 East 34 Street
New York, New York 10016
(212) 684-6577

Contact Persons
Stephen Viederman, President
Jael Silliman, Program Officer
Rachel Pohl, Program Officer

Purpose
The Jessie Smith Noyes Foundation is committed to two broad goals: first, preventing irreversible damage to the natural resources on which life depends, and, second, strengthening individuals whose leadership is crucial to the effective operation of institutions working to sustain natural systems.

Areas of Interest
The foundation has five specific programs, each with a specific geographic focus. They are: tropical ecology (Western Hemisphere); sustainable agriculture (United States, Canada, and third world); water resources (United States); population (third world); and integration/exploration. Throughout all program areas grants are made to support education and the development of leadership, interdisciplinary and international approaches to knowledge integration, networks and support groups (especially in the third world), experimental methods and techniques for population and resource management problems, dissemination of findings, and public-policy analysis.

As part of its population program, the foundation also supports some evaluation and demonstration projects in the New York City area designed to reduce adolescent pregnancy. Priority is given to improved public understanding and to developing new methods of communicating with teenagers.

Finally, in keeping with its long-term interest in improving the public schools, the foundation makes a limited number of grants to projects that offer unusual potential for stimulating new and adaptable approaches nationwide.

Jessie Smith Noyes Foundation, Inc.

Financial Data (year ended 12/31/86)

Assets:	$ 60,963,723
Total grants paid:[1]	$ 3,773,946
Number of grants paid:	101
Highest grant:	$ 100,000
Lowest grant:	$ 6,000
Median grant size:	$ 34,000

Application Procedures

The deadlines for submitting applications are December 15 (for consideration at the May meeting) and June 1 (for the November meeting).

Applications should be made in the form of a preliminary letter not longer than two pages. The following information should be included: (1) a brief statement of the project's objectives, process, outcomes, and their implications; (2) the amount requested, the total budget, and other potential and committed sources of support; and (3) the intended starting date and duration of the project. The foundation advises that supporting documents should not be submitted until specifically requested. Interviews are rarely scheduled before a written application has been received. Applicants should submit three copies of this initial letter. Letters should be directed to the executive director; thereafter, questions about the status of inquiries or proposals should be directed to a program officer.

If the proposed project falls within the guidelines, an applicant will be requested to submit additional information. Proposal deadlines are established at the time when a proposal is requested, generally within a month of the request.

Grant Limitations

Grants are made only to tax-exempt organizations. Programs limited to a narrow geographical area (with the exception of Greater New York) do not qualify for foundation support unless the problems addressed and the solutions proposed hold promise of general applicability. Normally

---

[1] This analysis excludes discretionary grants initiated by the directors and annual payments to charities specifically named by the founder.

Jessie Smith Noyes Foundation, Inc.

the foundation does not consider requests for endowment grants, capital construction funds, or general fundraising drives. Grants are not made to individuals or for individual scholarships or fellowships. Note that the foundation does not support demographic research or social science research related to population issues.

Meeting Times
The board of directors of the Jessie Smith Noyes Foundation meets twice a year, in May and November.

Publications
The foundation publishes an annual report and a brochure outlining its program guidelines and procedures.

Ottinger Foundation
1601 Connecticut Avenue, N.W., Suite 803
Washington, D.C. 20009
(202) 232-7333

Contact Person
Betsy Taylor, Executive Director

Areas of Interest
The Ottinger Foundation supports projects that promote democracy, economic justice, environmental preservation, and global peace. The foundation encourages submission of innovative proposals that seek to address causes rather than symptoms of problems. Most projects supported by the foundation include a strong component of citizen activism.

Financial Data (year ended 12/31/86)

Assets:	$	3,057,670
Total grants paid:	$	221,000
Number of grants paid:		43
Highest grant:	$	11,000
Lowest grant:	$	200
Median grant size:	$	5,000

Application Procedures
There are no application deadlines. Proposals should be written concisely and not exceed ten pages. Preference is given to proposals that include detailed and pragmatic discussions of strategy and project implementation rather than those that focus primarily on the need for support.

All applications should include the following information: (1)a clear statement of the need for support, the project's goals, an action plan for achieving those goals, and suggested methods for evaluating the project's success; (2) project and organizational line item budgets; (3) staff and organizational qualifications for carrying out the program; (4) lists of other sources of financial support already committed and sources to whom proposals have been sent; (5) proof of tax-exempt status; and (6) a list of other organizations involved in similar programs and a discussion of how the proposed project differs from them.

Ottinger Foundation

Grant Limitations
The foundation makes grants only to tax-exempt organizations in the United States. It does not make grants to organizations that traditionally enjoy popular support such as universities, museums, or hospitals. It does not support academic research, film or video projects, construction or restoration projects, profit-making businesses, or local programs without national significance.

Meeting Times
The board of directors of the Ottinger Foundation meets three times per year to review grant proposals.

Publications
None.

Peace Development Fund
44 North Prospect Street
Post Office Box 270
Amherst, Massachusetts 01004
(413) 256-8306

Pacific Peace Fund
5516 Roosevelt Way, N.E.
Seattle, Washington 98105
(206) 525-0025

Contact Persons
Meg Gage, Executive Director, Peace Development Fund
Dan Petegorsky, Executive Director, Pacific Peace Fund

Purpose
The Peace Development Fund and the Pacific Peace Fund make grants to organizations and projects working at the local level to promote global demilitarization, world peace, and nonviolent conflict resolution. The boards of directors especially seek groups of proven effectiveness. The funds also wish to encourage promising new peace groups and creative projects, particularly those involving constituencies new to the peace movement. The funds also operate a training program, the Exchange Project, which strengthens promising groups working for peace and social justice by teaching them grassroots fundraising, strategic planning, and other organizational development skills.

The Pacific Peace Fund supports groups working west of the Mississippi River. The Peace Development Fund supports groups east of the Mississippi.

Areas of Interest
The funds support the following specific areas: (1) halting and reversing the arms race; (2) relating the arms race to economic and social issues; (3) shifting the economy from military to nonmilitary production; (4) creating new strategies and materials for local use that can serve as models; and (5) finding new ways of overcoming despair about the possibility of a nuclear war, and fostering hope, cooperation, and action in peacemaking.

They especially seek to fund projects that: (1) focus on local com-

Peace Development Fund
Pacific Peace Fund

munities; (2) reach out to people not usually involved in the peace movement; (3) develop new approaches for educating the public about peace; (4) foster better coordination among peace groups; (5) show the potential to secure independent sources of funding; and (6) distribute usable materials for peace education and outreach.

At the time of publication the funds are initiating a new national grantmaking program, "Teaching Peace." This program supports peace education for young people in public and private programs, kindergarten through twelfth grade. It will offer competitive grants for creative, replicable programs in local schools and communities in the U.S.; research and evaluation of existing local programs in peace education; programs promoting new resources and successful models; programs that strengthen national networks; and training programs for peace educators.

Financial Data

During the year that ended May 31, 1987, the Peace Development Fund and the Pacific Peace Fund received $1,162,605 in contributions and revenue and made grant awards totaling $707,235. The following analysis of grants made was provided by the funds. It does not include donor-advised grants, designated grants, lobbying grants, and special projects.

Peace Development Fund

Total grants paid:	$	239,570
Number of grants paid:		62
Highest grant:	$	5,000
Lowest grant:	$	1,000
Median grant size:	$	3,300

Pacific Peace Fund

Total grants paid:	$	149,472
Number of grants paid:		44
Highest grant:	$	5,000
Lowest grant:	$	1,386
Median grant size:	$	3,500

Peace Development Fund
Pacific Peace Fund

Application Procedures

Application deadlines are January 2, April 20, and September 1. Proposals must be received at the funds' offices by these dates in order to be considered at the following board meeting. Organizations east of the Mississippi River should contact the Peace Development Fund. Applicants west of the Mississippi should contact the Pacific Peace Fund. There is an application form that must be completed and submitted with a formal proposal and supporting documentation. Applicants should contact the funds to request complete guidelines.

There are two funding cycles, in the spring and fall, for the Teaching Peace program. Applicants are advised to contact the Peace Development Fund for guidelines and deadlines.

Grant Limitations

Grants are made only to people and organizations working by peaceful, nonviolent means. Proposals are considered only for projects within the United States. In general, grants do not exceed $5,000, and often matching grants are required.

Meeting Times

The boards of directors of the Peace Development Fund and the Pacific Peace Fund award grants three times a year, in February, June, and October.

Publications

The funds publish a newsletter, *Peace Developments*, a statement of philosophy, and application guidelines. A list of grantees is contained in the newsletter, and audited financial statements are available upon request. The Exchange Project, a training program, also publishes a quarterly newsletter which is sent to participants.

The Pillsbury Company Foundation
Community Relations, M.S.3775
The Pillsbury Company
Pillsbury Center
Minneapolis, MN 55402-1464
(612) 330-4629

Contact Persons
John M. Stafford, President
Carol B. Truesdell, Vice President, Community Relations

Areas of Interest
The Pillsbury Company Foundation is the grantmaking vehicle of the Pillsbury Company's community relations division, through which the company strives to meet its commitment to be an outstanding corporate citizen.

The foundation's giving program is divided into two levels: first, the funding of programs in four categories—health and welfare, education, arts and culture, and civic and community. Second, the foundation directs major resources toward urgent needs of special interest to Pillsbury—youth and hunger. In addition to cash contributions, emphasis is placed on contributions of "noncash" resources such as products, company expertise and facilities, employee volunteers, and creative problem-solving assistance.

Priority is given to special one-time projects that will operate in Pillsbury headquarters, subsidiary, and plant communities and that uniquely address and seek solutions to the foundation's major areas of concern. The foundation states that it will, in the future, expand its participation to include national efforts in its focus area issues.

Financial Data (year ended 5/31/87)
In fiscal 1987 Pillsbury's charitable giving totaled $6,906,164. The grants analysis is by program area (see the table on the next page).

Application Procedures
There are no application deadlines; proposals are reviewed throughout the year. All proposals should be typewritten and should include the following information: (1) a request for a specific amount of money, date by which the funds are needed, and project timeline; (2) a project de-

The Pillsbury Company Foundation

scription, including explanation of community need, specific goals and objectives of the project, specific activities or methods for reaching the goals, and an evaluation plan; (3) an itemized project budget and sources of financial support, both committed and pending; (4) names and qualifications of the persons who will administer the grant; and (5) a brief description of the requesting organization's history and a statement of its purpose and objectives.

In addition, the proposal package should include a copy of the IRS ruling as to the organization's tax-exempt status under Section 501(c)(3); the most recent audited financial statements; a detailed organization budget for the current operating year; a list showing corporate and foundation support during the past twelve months; a list of the board of directors, officers, and their affiliations; and a copy of the organization's most recently filed IRS Form 990.

The foundation attempts to acknowledge proposals within thirty days of receipt. In order to permit careful investigation and assessment of proposals, notification of final action may take up to 120 days.

The Pillsbury Company Foundation
Analysis of 1986-87 Grantmaking Activity[1]

	Health and Welfare	Education	Arts and Culture	Civic and Community
Total Grants Paid	$1,310,508	$818,747	$692,937	$447,350
Number of Grants Paid	171	81	42	82
Highest Grant	$77,250	$106,669	$255,787	$60,000
Lowest Grant	$1,000	$1,000	$1,000	$1,000
Median Grant Size	$3,000	$3,500	$3,450	$2,625

[1]This grants analysis does not include grants under $1,000 totaling $79,466, which are not itemized in the foundation's annual report. Nor does it include the following categories: grants for scholarship programs ($248,875); employees matching gifts ($397,137); Burger King Education Programs ($1,069,839); Steak & Ale Charity Club ($30,298) or Law Enforcement Assistance Program ($126,000); gifts inkind ($5,457,214); United Way ($888,740); and other direct giving ($796,267).

The Pillsbury Company Foundation

Grant Limitations

The foundation does not fund appeals for product donations, except through the Second Harvest Food Bank Network; projects of religious denominations; efforts to influence legislation; fundraising events or advertising associated with such events; and capital and endowment campaigns. In addition, it does not make grants to individuals, to support travel for individuals or groups, or to grants operating for profit.

Meeting Times

The Charitable Contributions Committee of The Pillsbury Company Foundation considers grant requests throughout the year.

Publications

The Pillsbury Company Foundation publishes an annual report and a brochure on contributions policies and priorities.

Playboy Foundation
680 North Lake Shore Drive
Chicago, Illinois 60611
(312) 751–8000

Contact Person
Cleo Wilson, Executive Director

Purpose
The Playboy Foundation, part of the public affairs division of the company, is the primary vehicle by which Playboy Enterprises supports significant social and political causes and important charitable activities. Its goal, like that of the other programs within the division (government relations and community relations) is to support efforts reflecting the company's commitment to a safer, happier society that respects and protects individual rights and liberties as outlined in the Bill of Rights.

Areas of Interest
Grants awards typically support lobbying and litigation efforts of national significance and scope. Past grantees include organizations and projects concerned with First Amendment freedoms, gay and lesbian rights, government misconduct, reproductive freedom and the improved legal status of women, the abolition of capital punishment, and research on sexually transmitted diseases.

In addition to its grants program, the foundation operates a loan program (only for organizations that have had some previous association with the foundation or the company) and offers in-kind printing and postage. Guidelines for these programs are different from the grants program and should be requested separately.

Financial Data (year ended 6/30/88)
After many years of operating an active grants and in-kind contributions program, both activities were severely cut back in 1986 and 1987 due to a downturn in the company's revenues. It is expected, however, that the worst is over. For the fiscal year ending in 1988, the foundation expects to make contributions (cash and in-kind) totaling $100,000. Grants will range from $2,000 to $5,000.

Playboy Foundation

Application Procedures

Applications for grants are accepted on an ongoing basis, and no printed application form is used. Each proposal must, however, include the following: (1) a cover letter and brief summary of the background and purposes of the organization; (2) a description of the problem to be addressed, an explanation of how the project will address the problem and a rationale for the strategy; (3) a history of the organization and the individuals working on the project; (4) a copy of the IRS tax-exempt ruling for the organization; (5) a list of all major donors to the project and any other foundations where proposals may have been sent; (6) the name, address, and telephone number of a contact person who can provide additional information.

Since most Playboy Foundation grants are under $10,000, the proposal should highlight a special project that would benefit from a grant of this size. Grants are generally made for these kinds of special projects or individual cases rather than for general operating support.

In evaluating grant applications, the foundation takes into consideration the extent to which organizations provide equality of opportunity with respect to employment and promotion of staff, selection of board members, and service to clients.

Grant Limitations

No grants are made for scholarships, capital campaigns, endowments, or for religious purposes. The foundation does not make grants for the reduction of an operating deficit or to liquidate a debt.

Meeting Times

The board of directors of the Playboy Foundation meets several times a year to consider grant proposals.

Publications

The foundation publishes a brief brochure describing its priorities and grant-application procedures. The foundation does not publish an annual report.

339

Ploughshares Fund
Fort Mason Center, B-330
San Francisco, California 94123
(415) 775-2244

Contact Persons
Sally Lilienthal, President
Karen Harris, Program Director

Purpose
The Ploughshares Fund is a public foundation established in 1981 for the sole purpose of supporting organizations that will improve world security and prevent nuclear war. It specifically funds organizations and individuals whose work is focused on arms control that will lead to arms reduction and eventual disarmament. Encouraging a foreign policy founded on global collaboration, the fund emphasizes U.S.-Soviet cooperation as the cornerstone of world security.

Areas of Interest
In order to carry out its goal of encouraging arms control and improving U.S.-Soviet relations, the fund makes grants in the following categories: U.S.-Soviet dialogue, public education, and U.S. arms control and security policy. The fund also supports efforts to develop American political leadership and public constituencies for ending the arms race.

Over the last several years the fund has been increasing its support for efforts in regions of the country beyond the Northeast and Far West, where it feels the bulk of public education has historically been concentrated. In addition, the fund is particularly interested in groups and individuals who are reaching out to blue-collar workers, farmers, ranchers, students, veterans, women, and to minority and religious communities.

As a public foundation, Ploughshares also supports individuals directly and spends a portion of its resources on grassroots and national political lobbying. Ploughshares also initiates and executes its own programs when it perceives a particular opportunity to play a unique role, or when it finds a need that is not otherwise being met by any other organization.

Ploughshares Fund

Financial Data
On June 30, 1987, the assets of the Ploughshares Fund were valued at $1,803,183. Following are analyses of the grants made during the 12 months ended October 31, 1987 to organizations and to individuals:

Grants to Organizations
Total grants paid:	$	996,793
Number of grants paid:		108
Highest grant:	$	34,800
Lowest grant:	$	1,000
Median grant size:	$	10,000

Grants to Individuals
Total grants paid:	$	93,150
Number of grants paid:		13
Highest grant:	$	15,000
Lowest grant:	$	150
Median grant size:	$	5,000

Application Procedures
The initial request should be a letter briefly describing the project and indicating the financial needs. It should give the qualifications of the personnel involved and a concise description of the methods by which the project goals will be carried out. It should also identify other sources of existing support as well as those pending or contemplated. Proof of tax-exempt status and a list of the board of directors for sponsoring organizations should be enclosed. If it is determined that the project falls within the priorities and interests of the fund, a full proposal will be requested for further consideration. There are no application deadlines.

Grant Limitations
The fund does not support the production of films nor, as of this time, projects related to issues or activities in Central America or in the fields of human rights and nuclear energy.

341

Ploughshares Fund

Meeting Times
The board of directors of the Ploughshares Fund meets eight times a year to make decisions on grant applications.

Publications
The fund publishes an annual report that includes a complete list of grants and a statement of the fund's policies, programs, and guidelines.

The Prudential Foundation
751 Broad Street
15 Prudential Plaza
Newark, New Jersey 07102–3777
(201) 802–7354

Contact Person
Elisa D. Puzzuoli, Secretary

Purpose
The grantmaking activities of The Prudential Foundation reflect the company's belief that leadership on the part of business is essential to solving problems in local communities and nationwide and to keeping democratic processes and institutions vibrant and responsive to all citizens. As reductions have occurred in federal government funding of human service delivery programs, the needs of disadvantaged populations have increased, and the company has adopted the position that considerable private sector resources must be directed toward meeting their needs and for advocacy and research on their behalf.

Accordingly, the foundation has initiated and funded programs aimed at assisting disadvantaged populations and helped to implement projects conceived by disadvantaged persons. It also operates a social investment program that helps to finance socially desirable projects where the investment opportunities would not otherwise meet its risk-return requirements and provides substantial in-kind contributions of goods, services, and property to nonprofit organizations.

The foundation's preference is to support innovative and carefully considered approaches that address recognized problem areas or that anticipate major potential problems and opportunities before they arise. It also places high priority on catalytic grants that will stimulate others in the private or public sector to pursue opportunities to solve problems or to fund programs.

Areas of Interest
In December 1986 the foundation's trustees restructured the grantmaking guidelines. Generally, in priority order, the foundation's interests are health and human services, education, urban and community development, business and civic affairs, and culture and the arts.

The foundation has established specific standards and priorities within each area, which are listed in the foundation's annual report. However,

The Prudential Foundation

of particular note are the foundation's interest in increasing the access of disadvantaged parents to reduced-cost health services; community-based efforts that provide needed human services; efforts to enhance public awareness of economic relationships; innovative programs designed to improve basic-skills education in public school systems, especially in disadvantaged urban communities; efforts to foster the movement of disadvantaged persons into the mainstream of economic life and to provide jobs for single mothers and minority youth; efforts to support the efficiency and accountability of government; and improved management of water resources, toxic waste disposal, and ecologically sound land use.

Priority is given to national organizations and programs with potential impact in program areas consistent with the foundation's interests. The foundation also gives priority to organizations and programs located in and serving those metropolitan areas where The Prudential has a major economic interest, particularly New Jersey and the company's home city of Newark.

Financial Data (year ended 12/31/87)

The foundation reports that on December 31, 1987, its assets at market value were approximately $111.5 million, and that during the year it made 817 grants totaling approximately $7.8 million, excluding $1.7 million in grants made to match employee contributions and $2.1 million in grants to United Way agencies. The foundation was not, however, able to make a 1987 list of grants available. Hence the following analysis is based on grants paid in 1986.

Assets:	$ 117,410,000
Total grants paid:[1]	$ 5,125,830
Number of grants paid:[2]	148
Highest grant:	$ 277,000
Lowest grant:	$ 10,000
Median grant size:	$ 20,000

[1] This excludes $1,887,305 in grants made to match employee contributions and contributions totaling $1,967,706 to United Way agencies.
[2] This grants analysis excludes a total of $1,512,735 in grants of less than $10,000.

The Prudential Foundation

Application Procedures

Proposals are accepted and reviewed throughout the year, and based on scope or amount may be held over from one board meeting to the next. Initial contact with the foundation should consist of a letter or brief abstract of the proposed project. Applicants should, however, be prepared to supplement this letter with specific information as outlined in the foundation's annual report and to provide proof of tax-exempt status.

The foundation advises that every letter will receive a response, and that it is not generally helpful to request a telephone or in-person interview during the six-week period following submission of an initial letter. Thereafter, however, an organization may telephone or write the foundation to clarify the status of a request.

Grant Limitations

Generally the foundation does not make grants to: organizations which are not tax exempt or qualified to receive tax-deductible contributions; veterans', labor, religious, political, fraternal or external athletic groups, except in special cases where the project provides needed benefits or services to the community at large; individuals; single-disease health organizations seeking general operating funds; organizations that will redistribute the foundation's contribution to separate, independent tax-exempt organizations; and goodwill advertising.

Meeting Times

The board of trustees of The Prudential Foundation meets three times a year, in April, August, and December.

Publications

The foundation publishes an annual report.

Public Welfare Foundation
2600 Virginia Avenue, N.W.
Washington, D.C. 20037
(202) 965-1800

Contact Person
C. Glenn Ihrig, Executive Director

Purpose
The scope and purposes of the Public Welfare Foundation are broad. The foundation aims to promote general human welfare worldwide in instances where the need is both genuine and urgent and to help people help themselves within the limits of their resources in a manner that destroys neither their dignity nor their initiative. The foundation supports programs that enable people to utilize available resources and help themselves when circumstances beyond their control have deprived them of the chance to grow and develop.

Areas of Interest
The foundation has identified five funding priority areas: disadvantaged youth, population, the elderly, the environment, and criminal justice. In addition, the foundation has a long-standing involvement in arms control and peace issues.

The scope of the foundation's grantmaking also includes: AIDS-related services, education, and advocacy to combat discrimination; the arts, mainly projects that involve the disadvantaged and provide access to those who would not otherwise be able to participate; projects to improve the quality of education in the U.S.; projects supporting free speech and a free press where those freedoms are under attack; media projects, including local and national public radio and television where they involve causes of importance to the disadvantaged; disaster relief; and the needs of homeless children. Potential applicants working within the broad areas targeted by the foundation are encouraged to contact the office for a discussion with the appropriate program officer.

Financial Data
As of October 31, 1986, the assets of the foundation were $198,808,000, with total grants of $7,427,500 paid during the year. The following grants

Public Welfare Foundation

analysis distinguishes between the foundation's domestic and international grants programs.

Domestic Grants

Total grants paid:	$	6,177,300
Number of grants paid:		213
Highest grant:	$	250,000
Lowest grant:	$	2,000
Median grant size:	$	22,500

International Grants

Total grants paid:	$	1,250,200
Number of grants paid:		40
Highest grant:	$	78,000
Lowest grant:	$	2,500
Median grant size:	$	25,500

Application Procedures

The foundation requests that applicants not submit letters of inquiry or request preliminary meetings; rather, complete applications in writing should be submitted. Applications should include a complete description of the organization; a description of the project, including needs and problem statement, goals and objectives, plan of action, evaluation method, and long-term plans; the organization's most recent financial statement, audited, if possible; a line budget (including income and expenses) for the program for which funds are requested; proof of tax exemption; and a listing of officers, directors, and staff and their levels of compensation. The foundation prefers concise, informative proposals no longer than ten pages and will request additional supporting material when needed. To guide prospective applicants, the foundation offers a suggested outline for a complete proposal package in its annual report.

Requests may be submitted at any time and are reviewed daily by the foundation's screening committee. If a proposal is deferred for further consideration, it is assigned to a staff person, who will contact the applicant, and may request additional information, a meeting, or a site visit.

Public Welfare Foundation

It generally takes three months to investigate proposals once they are deferred.

Grant Limitations
Proposals in the following categories have been funded in rare instances and will be considered only when the application is consistent with the foundation's philosophy and offers direct assistance to the poor, disadvantaged, or handicapped: building construction, conferences, capital expenditures, efforts with a religious emphasis, foreign study, graduate work, individuals, publications, research projects, scholarships, seminars, and workshops.

Meeting Times
The board of directors of the Public Welfare Foundation meets regularly throughout the year.

Publications
The foundation publishes an annual report.

The Reed Foundation
30 Rockefeller Plaza, Suite 4528
New York, New York 10112–0119
(212) 977-5294

Contact Person
Reed Rubin, President

Areas of Interest
The Reed Foundation supports organizations working on the national and international level on a broad range of social issues with a strong emphasis on social justice. Its 1985 grants can generally be grouped in the following categories: civil rights/civil liberties, environment/conservation, education, foreign policy, peace, international cooperation, hunger and food policies, nuclear policy, women's rights; rural issues, and arts/culture. While most grants in this period were made to national organizations, a number of grants also went to community-based organizations serving disadvantaged populations in New York City.

Financial Data (year ended 12/31/85)

Assets:	$ 11,620,332
Total grants paid:	$ 2,107,400
Number of grants paid:	83
Highest grant:	$ 500,000
Lowest grant:	$ 1,000
Median grant size:	$ 5,000

Application Procedures
The foundation prefers that an applicant's initial contact be made with the submission of a full proposal (one copy). The foundation does not acknowledge receipt of applications. However, on some occasions after a proposal has been submitted, the foundation may request an interview.

Grant Limitations
The foundation makes no grants to individuals or for capital or building funds.

The Reed Foundation

Meeting Times
The board of directors of The Reed Foundation meets quarterly.

Publications
The foundation distributes a program policy statement.

Charles H. Revson Foundation
444 Madison Avenue
New York, New York 10022
(212) 935-3340

Contact Persons
Eli N. Evans, President
Lisa Goldberg, Vice-President

Purpose
The general purpose of The Charles H. Revson Foundation is the betterment of the human condition and the advancement of public welfare. Underlying the foundation's grantmaking program are the following themes: the forces shaping the future of New York City, the changing role of women, the impact of modern communications on education and other areas of life, and the need in a democratic society to keep government accountable to citizens. In some cases, these themes help to define a program; in others, they cut across grantmaking program lines.

Areas of Interest
The foundation's grantmaking activities are concentrated in the following program areas: urban affairs and public policy with special emphasis on New York City problems; education; biomedical research policy; and Jewish philanthropy and education. Most of the foundation's support goes to well-established organizations with a proven track record.

In addressing the problems and future of New York City, the foundation focuses on education, low-income housing, immigration, food and hunger, and legal services, funding primarily research and model programs with the potential for impact on public decision-making. One grant was made in 1986 to support a public education campaign on AIDS directed specifically to young people. The foundation does not support community-based or direct service delivery organizations.

Grants relating to the changing role of women emphasize the participation of women in politics and the political process. In addition to a series of foundation-sponsored fellowship programs designed to provide younger women with firsthand experience in policy-making at the city, state, and local levels, the foundation has supported research and training activities. Throughout its program the foundation desires to support organizations committed to increasing the participation of women and minority group members.

351

Charles H. Revson Foundation

The foundation supports a wide variety of organizations that address the problem of a lack of access to information about government activities and strengthen the voices of citizens in policy debate including projects in the area of U.S. international human rights policy and research that educates the public.

Financial Data (year ended 12/31/86)

Assets:[1]	$ 78,501,928
Total grants paid:	$ 13,549,000
Number of grants paid:	58
Highest grant:[2]	$ 500,000
Lowest grant:	$ 5,000
Median grant size:	$ 62,000

Application Procedures

The first step in initiating a formal grant request is to send a letter briefly outlining the proposed project to the foundation's president. The letter should include a description of the proposed project, expected results, plans for evaluation and future funding, other sources of support (if any), amount sought, the purpose and duration of the requested amount, and the background and purpose of the sponsoring organization. Attachments should consist of: the organization's latest audited financial statements, a copy of the IRS letter confirming tax-exempt status, a current and projected budget, and a list of the board of directors and their organizational affiliations.

Grant Limitations

The foundation generally does not approve grants in the following categories: individuals; community-based organizations; book projects; local arts groups; endowments; building, renovation, or construction; local or national health appeals; charity events; travel expenses; and general institutional support.

---

[1] At December 31, 1985.
[2] This excludes four unusually large grants totaling $7,250,000.

Charles H. Revson Foundation

Meeting Times
The board of directors of the Charles H. Revson Foundation meets quarterly.

Publications
The foundation publishes a report once every two years.

Rockefeller Brothers Fund, Inc.
1290 Avenue of the Americas
New York, New York 10104
(212) 373-4200

Contact Person
Benjamin R. Shute, Jr., Secretary

Purpose
The major objective of the Rockefeller Brothers Fund is to improve the well-being of all people through support of efforts in the U.S. and abroad that contribute ideas, develop leaders, and encourage institutions in the transition to global interdependence. It seeks to counter world trends of resource depletion, militarization, protectionism, and isolation that threaten cooperation, trade and economic growth, arms control, and conservation.

Four "touchstones" relating to the fund's approach to its substantive concerns (as opposed to specific areas of interest in and of themselves) are key to the fund's consideration of grant proposals: education of key individuals, special target groups, and the general public; leadership, i.e., the identification and encouragement of a new generation of leaders around the fund's specific program interests; leverage, i.e., using combinations of trustees and staff as well as related organizations to work toward common goals; and synergy, i.e., developing related projects so as to have an impact beyond the sum of the parts.

Areas of Interest
The fund makes grants in four general areas. The first, "one world," is made up of two components: sustainable resource use and world security (arms control and international relations), as well as the connections between global resource management and global security. This area is allocated the greatest share of the fund's grantmaking budget. The other three areas are New York City, the nonprofit sector, and special concerns.

The goal of the program in sustainable resource use is to encourage more efficient and renewable use of natural, human, and man-made resources using approaches that blend social, economic, and ecological concerns. Strategies supported by the fund include: defining and advocating the philosophy on a global basis through action-research and other projects that employ comprehensive approaches to resources manage-

Rockefeller Brothers Fund, Inc.

ment; and implementing the philosophy in areas such as forestry, agriculture, fisheries, and bioenergy in ways that create renewable resources that are less destructive to land, forest, air, water, and human resources.

The world security component has as its overriding objectives strengthening arms control, improving international relations, and encouraging development, trade, and finance. In the arms-control area the fund supports interdisciplinary analysis of specific nuclear and conventional arms issues, focusing particularly on collaborative efforts between the U.S. and Soviet groups; efforts to determine the effects of nuclear weapons use; and efforts to halt the spread of nuclear weapons capability to other countries and groups. In the area of international relations, the fund supports public information and education activities, including exchanges, internships, and joint work involving the industrialized nations, the Soviet Union, Eastern Europe, and East Asia.

In its New York City program, the fund stresses collaboration between the public sector and various private sector groups, particularly in relation to economic development policies and practices. In 1986 the fund initiated a special series of grants focusing on effective action on public health services, public policy development, and related issues involved with the AIDS crisis in New York City.

To promote the health and vitality of the nonprofit sector nationally and internationally, the fund supports basic research and public education with respect to nonprofits, efforts to develop new sources of income for and improved management of nonprofits, and greater international grantmaking.

The special concerns program allows the fund the flexibility to support emergency situations and compelling new opportunities. For example, the fund has supported a wide variety of efforts to promote human rights in South Africa.

Rockefeller Brothers Fund, Inc.

Financial Data (year ended 12/31/86)

Assets:	$ 220,733,767
Total grants paid:	$ 6,820,024
Number of grants paid:	130
Highest grant:[1]	$ 200,000
Lowest grant:	$ 2,000
Median grant size:	$ 30,000

Application Procedures

There are no application deadlines. Initially the fund recommends that applicants send a two- or three-page letter of inquiry to the fund's secretary, including a succinct description of the project or organization for which support is sought and its relationship to the fund's program, information about the principal staff involved, a synopsis of the budget, and an indication of the amount requested from the fund. All such inquiry letters are reviewed by one or more staff members who try to be prompt in notifying applicants when their projects do not fit program guidelines or exceed budgetary restraints. If a project is taken up for grant consideration, staff members will ask for additional information, including a detailed proposal and almost certainly a meeting with the project's principal organizers.

Grant Limitations

To qualify for a grant from the fund, applicants must be either a tax-exempt organization or an organization seeking support for a project that would qualify as tax exempt. The fund does not make grants to individuals, nor as a general rule does it support research, graduate study, or the writing of books or dissertations by individuals.

Meeting Times

The board of trustees of the Rockefeller Brothers Fund meets three times per year, in April, June, and November.

---

[1] This excludes three unusually large grants totaling $1,007,068.

Rockefeller Brothers Fund, Inc.

Publications

The fund publishes an annual report and a description of its program priorities.

Rockefeller Family Fund
1290 Avenue of the Americas
New York, New York 10104
(212) 373-4252

Contact Persons
Donald K. Ross, Director
Corinne Rafferty, Program Officer

Purpose
The purposes of the Rockefeller Family Fund are broad. The fund concentrates on developing solid, effective programs that will have impact beyond the scope of a single project. Identification of important issues and support of strong leaders and innovative ideas are keys to the fund's activities.

Areas of Interest
The fund concentrates on five general program areas: arms control, economic justice for women, the environment, institutional responsiveness, and citizen education and participation.

The arms control program supports efforts to reduce the risk of nuclear war and the economic and social consequences of the arms race. The fund's program area for women supports projects designed to promote economic justice and, in particular, those that seek to provide women with equitable employment opportunities and improve their work lives. In its program on the environment, the fund emphasizes conservation of natural resources and protection of health as affected by the environment. The institutional responsiveness program is the fund's most open-ended program interest. Its purpose is to help provide individuals and organizations with the means to influence the policies and actions of public and private institutions. The citizen education and participation program was initiated in 1986 to promote greater citizen involvement in political decision-making. In its first year, grants focused on qualified nonpartisan voter-education projects.

Financial Data (year ended 12/31/86)
Assets:	$ 27,749,266
Total grants paid:	$ 1,623,000
Number of grants paid:	82
Highest grant:	$ 55,000
Lowest grant:	$ 2,500
Median grant size:	$ 20,000

Rockefeller Family Fund

Application Procedures

There are no application deadlines and no special application form is required. The fund suggests that applicants submit the following materials: (1) a concisely written proposal describing the needs for the program, the objectives, a plan of action, staff and organizational qualifications, other organizations involved in similar programs and how the proposed project is similar or different, the amount requested, a line-item budget for the project, and the method of evaluation; (2) the organization's budget, including projected income sources, and if the organization has members, the average annual contribution per member; (3) the organization's most recent financial statement; and (4) the organization's certificate of tax-exempt status.

When the fund receives a proposal, an acknowledgment is sent within five days, unless the request is outside the fund's program areas, in which case the proposal is declined immediately. All proposals accepted for review are assigned to a program officer, who may request additional material, make a site visit, or meet with the applicant.

Grant Limitations

The fund does not make grants to support individuals, profit-making businesses, construction or restoration projects, lobbying activities, international programs, domestic programs dealing with international issues (other than arms control), or efforts to reduce an organization's debt.

Meeting Times

The full board of trustees of the Rockefeller Family Fund meets twice a year, usually in April and December. The executive committee, however, which reviews grant requests that have been investigated by the staff, generally meets every six weeks.

Publications

The fund publishes an annual report.

Samuel Rubin Foundation
777 United Nations Plaza
New York, New York 10017
(212) 697-8945

Contact Person
Cora Weiss, President

Purpose
The general purpose of the Samuel Rubin Foundation is to carry on the vision of its founder, whose life was dedicated to the pursuit of peace and justice and the search for an equitable reallocation of the world's resources. The foundation believes that these objectives can be achieved only through the fullest implementation of social, economic, political, civil, and cultural rights for all the world's people.

Areas of Interest
The foundation's emphasis is on national and international organizations. Its 1987 grant awards can generally be grouped into the following categories: civil and constitutional rights, environment, peace and disarmament, education, public policy, and arts and culture.

Financial Data (year ended 6/30/87)

Assets:	$ 11,640,900
Total grants paid:	$ 854,541
Highest grant paid:[1]	$ 30,000
Lowest grant paid:	$ 800
Median grant size:	$ 3,000

Application Procedures
The foundation prefers that an applicant's initial contact be made with the submission of a full proposal (one copy). The foundation does not acknowledge receipt of applications; however, after the proposal has been submitted, the foundation may request an interview.

---

[1]This excludes two unusually large grants of $235,000 and $80,000 made to, respectively, the Institute for Policy Studies and the Center for Constitutional Rights.

Samuel Rubin Foundation

Grant Limitations
The foundation makes no grants to individuals or for capital or building funds.

Meeting Times
The board of directors of the Samuel Rubin Foundation meets quarterly.

Publications
The foundation will distribute a program policy statement upon request.

The Scherman Foundation, Inc.
315 West 57 Street, Suite 2D
New York, New York 10019
(212) 489-7143

Contact Person
David F. Freeman, Executive Director

Areas of Interest
The main areas of interest of The Scherman Foundation, Inc., are conservation, disarmament and peace, family planning, human rights and
liberties, the arts, and social welfare. In the last two areas particularly,
priority is given to organizations in New York City. In the social welfare
field, grants are made to organizations concerned with social justice,
public affairs, and community self-help. For example, in 1987 a grant was
made to support a high school newspaper's AIDS education program.

Financial Data (year ended 12/31/86)

Assets:	$	36,391,869
Total grants paid:	$	2,497,200
Number of grants paid:		153
Highest grant:[1]	$	50,000
Lowest grant:	$	2,500
Median grant size:	$	12,500

Application Procedures
There are no application forms. Requests for grants should be made in
a brief letter outlining the purpose for which funds are sought. Helpful
information includes: a budget, names of the board of directors of the
organization, listing of key personnel, a recent financial statement listing
present sources of support, and evidence of tax-exempt status. If additional information is needed, the foundation will make a request. Note
that approximately one-third of the grants made by the foundation covered a two-year period.

---

[1]This excludes two unusually large grant awards totaling $225,000 to well-established
organizations.

The Scherman Foundation, Inc.

Grant Limitations

Grants are made only to tax-exempt organizations and to projects that fall within the scope of the foundation's interests. The foundation generally excludes from consideration all applications requesting grants for colleges, universities, and professional schools. No grants are made to individuals for any purpose.

Meeting Times

The board of directors of The Scherman Foundation, Inc., meets four times a year. Dates of meetings are not fixed.

Publications

The foundation publishes an annual report.

The Florence and John Schumann Foundation
33 Park Street
Montclair, New Jersey 07042
(201) 783-6660

Contact Person
William B. Mullins, President

Purpose
The Florence and John Schumann Foundation places special emphasis on organizations and projects that indicate a high level of community support (as evidenced by contributions of time or money from the group served), that hold the strong promise of becoming largely self-sufficient, and that offer the hope of permanent and positive change in the way society deals with particular problems.

Areas of Interest
In 1986 approximately one-half of the foundation's grant dollars went to organizations working on national issues. National priorities were international relations, population and the environment, early childhood development, and effective governance. In this area only projects having national significance are considered.

Approximately one-third of the foundation's support was allocated to New Jersey organizations, with high priority given to applications from Essex County and to projects with a statewide impact. The foundation is particularly interested in creative, innovative, and experimental programs and projects that involve community residents themselves in efforts to solve or alleviate problems.

The remaining fifteen percent of grant dollars was used to support institutions of special interest to the foundation's donors and trustees. These grants were all initiated by the foundation.

Financial Data (year ended 12/31/86)

Assets:	$ 51,652,873
Total grants paid:	$ 3,157,685
Number of grants paid:	115
Highest grant:[1]	$ 98,670
Lowest grant:	$ 1,000
Median grant size:	$ 10,000

---

[1]This excludes three unusually large grants totaling $425,000.

The Florence and John Schumann Foundation

Application Procedures

Proposal deadlines are January 15, April 15, August 15, and October 15, i.e., six weeks before meetings of the foundation's board of trustees. While action on a proposal may be reserved for a later quarter, the foundation replies promptly as to the status of all requests.

There is no standard application form. Rather, the foundation requests written proposals. The proposal should include a description of the organization's objectives, activities, and leadership; some detail of the purpose for which assistance is being requested; and the plan for accomplishing project goals. This proposal should be accompanied by: (1) the organization's latest financial statement; (2) an expense budget specifically identifying all sources of income; (3) the time frame and future funding plans; and (4) proof of the applicant's status as a tax-exempt public charity.

Grant Limitations

The foundation does not encourage proposals for capital campaigns, annual giving, endowment, or direct support of individuals.

Meeting Times

The board of trustees of The Florence and John Schumann Foundation meets four times a year, in March, June, September, and December.

Publications

The foundation publishes an annual report and application guidelines.

Seventh Generation Fund for Indian Development
Star Route
Lee, Nevada 89829
(702) 744-4231

Contact Person
Dagmar Thorpe, Executive Director

Purpose
The Seventh Generation Fund for Indian Development was created in 1977 by Daniel Bomberry and other Indian community activists to provide funding and technical assistance directly to Indian communities. It was founded on the premise that Indians need to move beyond the rhetoric of sovereignty toward concrete efforts to rebuild the economic and political infrastructures of Native communities. The fund has nurtured efforts by grassroots Indian communities to prevent exploitation of tribal natural resources, protect tribal and treaty-guaranteed rights to land, life, and water, and to strengthen Indian communities through rebuilding tribal economies and traditional ways of life. The fund also places special emphasis on projects organized by Native women to address the pressing needs of their families and communities.

Areas of Interest
The fund provides financial, technical, and management support directly to projects initiated and controlled by Native Americans which address those elements essential to revitalizing Native American communities. It is particularly interested in funding newly emerging issues that require immediate support to be addressed effectively and that lack access to other funding resources. Efforts supported by the fund use a variety of methods to accomplish the objective of continuing Native life including community education, action research, networking, coalition building, litigation, and public education.

Specifically, the fund is interested in projects addressing self-reliant economies, indigenous ways of life, land and natural resources, and Native women.

The interest in self-reliant economies includes efforts that demonstrate the economic viability of small-scale community development, use local renewable resources and human skills to provide basic goods and services, and are appropriate to Indian culture. Also of interest are re-

Seventh Generation Fund for Indian Development

development of self-reliant economies through food production, appropriate technology, and alternative energy use.

Indigenous ways of life covers efforts that restore indigenous forms
of political organization, modify existing governments along traditional
lines, or restore indigenous community systems and apply traditional
thought to contemporary issues.

In the area of land and natural resources, the fund supports efforts
to reclaim and live on aboriginal lands, and to protect tribal lands, resources, environment, and sovereignty. The special interest in Native
women encompasses efforts initiated by Indian women to promote the
spiritual, cultural, and physical well-being of the Native family in ways
consistent with Indian community/nation values and ethics.

Financial Data (year ended 6/30/87)

Support and revenue:	$	837,296
Total grants paid:[1]	$	109,590
Number of grants paid:		44
Highest grant:	$	7,500
Lowest grant:	$	75
Median grant size:	$	2,000

Application Procedures

Applications are accepted throughout the year; there are no application
deadlines. Applicants are urged to contact the fund to discuss the ap-
propriateness of their request. If the project meets the fund's initial
funding criteria, organizations may be invited to submit a proposal. However, a request for a proposal, the fund cautions, does not insure that a
grant award will follow.

A brief grant proposal of three pages should include the following:
a narrative that explains the problem that the project addresses, the goal
of the project, how the project intends to resolve or respond to that
problem, why that strategy will be effective; and a detailed budget in-

---

[1]This grants analysis is based on discretionary support only. It excludes $211,828 raised
by the fund on behalf of its projects in 41 separate grant awards from other funders.

Seventh Generation Fund for Indian Development

dicating both the funds the project will require to accomplish its goal and the status of its fundraising efforts.

Grant Limitations
In order to receive support from the fund, projects must be Indian-initiated and controlled and consistent with the fund's stated purpose and interests.

Meeting Times
The all-Indian board of directors of the Seventh Generation Fund meets three times a year, usually in October, February, and June.

Publications
The fund publishes an annual report, a magazine, and several newsletters.

The L. J. Skaggs and Mary C. Skaggs Foundation
1221 Broadway, 21st Floor
Oakland, California 94612-1837
(415) 451-3300

Contact Persons
Philip M. Jelley, Secretary and Foundation Manager
David Knight, Program Analyst

Purpose
The L. J. Skaggs and Mary C. Skaggs Foundation supports organizations made up of committed, enthusiastic individuals working on programs involved with the alleviation of social problems and concerns. It is also concerned with the enrichment and preservation of cultural and historic heritages, both in the United States and abroad. It seeks applications that propose unusual and untried solutions or innovative processes that may ultimately illuminate new solutions for the complex cultural and social concerns of society.

Areas of Interest
The foundation makes grants under six program categories: performing arts, social concerns, projects of historic interest, folklore/folklife, international grants, and special projects. Except for theater companies, performing arts applications may be submitted only by invitation of the foundation. In the performing arts, social concerns, and special projects categories, the vast majority of grants awarded in 1987 were made to northern California organizations.

In the area of social concerns, grants are made in three areas: women's and children's rights, the effect of mass media on human behavior and decision-making, and community organizing toward self and neighborhood empowerment.

Groups seeking international grants where funds are to be expended abroad must have a United States agency as sponsor or be registered and regulated by their government as a recognized charity. The foundation is particularly interested in supporting international women's organizations. With few exceptions, international grants will be made to organizations located on or around the Pacific Rim.

In addition to its regular grantmaking program, the foundation has established the Program Officer's Discretionary Grant Fund from which

The L. J. Skaggs and Mary C. Skaggs Foundation

small grants within the foundation's priority interests can be made without waiting for the annual board meeting. In 1986, 101 grants were made from this fund, in amounts up to $5,000 and totaling $296,025.

Financial Data (year ended 12/31/87)

Assets:[1]	$	14,247,504
Total grants paid:	$	2,504,600
Number of grants paid:[2]		198
Highest grant:	$	50,000
Lowest grant:	$	1,000
Median grant size:	$	7,500

Application Procedures

Telephone inquiries regarding program eligibility and direct communication with the foundation's directors are strongly discouraged. Requests should be initiated by a brief letter of intent to apply for funding during the following calendar year. Such letters are accepted from January 15 to June 1. They should describe the applying organization and the purpose for which the funds are sought. Information concerning the organization's income and expenses and materials outlining the expertise of key personnel should also be included.

If the foundation's staff determines that the proposed project is appropriate to the guidelines, a full proposal will be invited. All formal proposals and supporting documentation must be received by the foundation no later than September 1. Mass-mailed, photocopied, or printed funding requests are not given serious consideration. If a proposal or letter of intent does not fall within current guidelines, applicants are notified promptly.

All applicants are urged to read carefully the foundation's annual

---

[1] As of December 31, 1986.

[2] This total and the figures below omit three unusually large grants of $100,000 to $250,000 made to the San Francisco Opera Association, the American Folklore Society, and the University of Santa Clara.

The L. J. Skaggs and Mary C. Skaggs Foundation

report, grant policies and procedures information, and the foundation's most recent list of grantees before submitting a letter of intent.

Grant Limitations
Grants are made only to qualified tax-exempt charitable organizations. No grants are made to individuals, or for capital fund or annual fund drives, sectarian religious purposes, or to cover budget deficits. The foundation will not make grants to film production or distribution projects except in cases where the film relates to a major interest of the foundation. Grants are not made to residence-home programs or halfway houses.

Meeting Times
The board of directors of The L. J. Skaggs and Mary C. Skaggs Foundation meets annually in November to award grants.

Publications
The foundation publishes an annual report, a grants list, and a statement of grant policies and procedures.

The South Branch Foundation
c/o Gillen and Johnson
Post Office Box 477
Somerville, New Jersey 08876
(201) 722-6400

Contact Person
Peter S. Johnson, Administrator

Purpose
The South Branch Foundation operates a general grants program with particular emphasis on conservation, civil rights, cultural affairs, education, and animal welfare.

Areas of Interest
The foundation makes grants for national as well as local programs in such areas as: world population and family planning; protection of and advocacy for the environment; education programs, including minority scholarships; civil rights litigation; world peace; and community social services.

The foundation has no stated geographic restrictions. Its 1985 grants were awarded to organizations in Florida, New York, Pennsylvania, Maine, Massachusetts, New Jersey, Connecticut, and Washington, D.C.

Financial Data (year ended 12/31/87)

Assets:[1]	$	8,045,058
Total grants paid:	$	548,000
Number of grants:		28
Highest grant:	$	100,000
Lowest grant:	$	1,000
Median grant size:	$	10,000

Application Procedures
The foundation requires no application forms and has no fixed deadlines. Applications should take the form of a brief, concise report identifying the purposes for which funds are intended. The foundation does not grant interviews with applicants.

---

[1]As of December 31, 1986.

The South Branch Foundation

Grant Limitations
The foundation does not make grants to individuals or to building funds.

Meeting Times
The board of directors of The South Branch Foundation meets once a year, usually in January, at which time the budget for the year is set.

Publications
None.

The Philip M. Stern Family Fund
1601 Connecticut Avenue, N.W., Suite 803
Washington, D.C. 20009
(202) 232-7333

Contact Person
Betsy Taylor, Executive Director

Purpose
The Philip M. Stern Family Fund supports organizations working to empower the powerless, remedy inequities, secure social change, increase government accountability, and strengthen the workings of American democracy.

Areas of Interest
The fund's primary interests are: campaign finance reform; voter registration reform; investigative journalism; government accountability and whistleblower efforts; and technical assistance projects to strengthen progressive nonprofit groups, especially new groups lacking access to other sources of support.

Financial Data (year ended 1987)[1]

Total grants paid:	$	623,715
Highest grant:	$	25,000
Lowest grant:	$	250
Average grant size:	$	7,500

Application Procedures
The fund has no standard application forms, procedures or deadlines. A proposal accompanied by a short cover letter should be submitted to the executive director. Proposals are acknowledged, and the fund's staff will contact applicants if further information is needed. Generally the executive director is unable to arrange appointments with prospective grantees prior to receipt and review of written proposals.

Every proposal should include: (1) a statement of the problems to be addressed by the project; (2) a description of the organization or project proposed, including specific objectives, a projected timetable for

---

[1] The foundation does not distribute financial information, or a list of grants. The information provided is as summarized by the foundation for 1986–87.

The Philip M. Stern Family Fund

their achievement, and the strategies and methods that will be used to attain these objectives; (3) the projected budget of the organization for the fiscal year for which funds are being sought, and, if applicable, a detailed budget for the specific project proposed; (4) a list of current sources of support and sources from whom additional funds are being solicited; and (5) staff résumés or profiles. Preference is given to proposals that do not exceed ten pages.

Grant Limitations
The fund seldom supports capital or endowment campaigns.

Meeting Times
The board of directors of The Philip M. Stern Family Fund meets six times per year.

Publications
None.

The Streisand Foundation
Post Office Box 53369
Washington, D.C. 20009
(202) 331-8776

Contact Persons
Margery Tabankin, Executive Director
Cooki Collinet, Administrative Director

Purpose
The Streisand Foundation was started in 1986, and its spirit is embodied in the following statement made by Barbra Streisand at a live performance at her home in September of that year:

> I could never imagine myself wanting to sing in public again, but then, I could never imagine with all our advanced technology the starvation of bodies and minds and the possibility of nuclear winters in our lives—I could no longer remain silent, by my silence I was giving consent to the madness of nations spending billions of dollars on weapons that can never be used— and all at the expense of our schools, our farms, medical research, and research into safe sources of energy. Sometimes we forget the importance of one voice, of each of our voices, and the enormous difference it can make in all our lives—in history.

Areas of Interest
In 1987 most of the foundation's grants were made to organizations working on peace and the prevention of nuclear war. Remaining funds supported activities related to safe energy, preservation of the environment, and the protection of civil liberties.

Financial Data (1987)[1]
Total grants paid:	$	465,000
Number of grants paid:		30
Highest grant:	$	50,000
Lowest grant:	$	5,000
Median grant size:	$	10,000

---

[1]The foundation does not distribute a financial statement. Hence, its total assets are unknown. The grants analysis is based on total grants made in 1987.

The Streisand Foundation

Application Procedures
In order to be considered, the following items should be submitted to the foundation: (1) a short summary, one to three pages long, of the project proposed; (2) a complete proposal stating the problem, project goals, and strategies for achieving these goals, proposed solutions, and the value or impact on society; (3) budgets for both the organization and the specific project proposed; (4) a statement of current and projected income; and (5) a list of members of the organization's governing board.

In addition, applicants should submit an up-to-date copy of the their 501(c)(3) determination letter from the IRS. If an applicant is not a tax-exempt organization, but instead is working with a fiscal sponsor, a letter from the sponsoring organization agreeing to serve in that capacity along with a current copy of the sponsor's tax exemption determination letter must be provided.

Meeting Times
The board of directors of The Streisand Foundation does not have fixed meeting dates. Grants are made at least once per year.

Publications
The foundation distributes a brief description of its program interests and list of past grantees.

Sunflower Foundation
305 Madison Avenue, Suite 1166
New York, New York 10165
(212) 682-0889

Contact Persons
Kit Tremaine, President
Richard Parker, Executive Director

Purpose
The purpose of the Sunflower Foundation is to provide support for progressive groups involved in educating and organizing for change by addressing the root causes of problems in society rather than those treating the surface symptoms of the problems.

Areas of Interest
The broad interests of the foundation include community organizing, third world or women's organizing, legal and health care organizing, and related social and political activities. Occasionally the fund provides support for international groups interested in these activities.

Recent funding decisions covered a wide range of activities. Among the funded projects were groups working on the immediate shelter needs of the homeless, alternative farming and energy techniques designed to meet the environmental and economic needs of the future, legal assistance for Haitian immigrants, the mobilization of workers toward improvement of working conditions, conservation of threatened forest and mountain regions, and educational projects working to promote public awareness of the various cultures and species in society.

The foundation is exploring new ways of thinking about the future and specifically invites proposals from groups integrating holistic approaches to the problems confronting the planet Earth and its species.

Financial Data
As of December 31, 1984, the assets of the foundation were $13–15,000,000, including estimated values for oil and gas royalties. Although additional information was requested, the foundation declined to elaborate.

The foundation states that it makes no more than 100 grants per year totaling approximately $500,000 with the average grant size between

Sunflower Foundation

$3,000 and $5,000. Although a current grants list was not available for analysis, following is an analysis of the grants paid during the year ended December 31, 1984:

Total grants paid:	$	1,200,000
Number of grants paid:		85
Highest grant:	$	25,000
Lowest grant:	$	1,000
Median grant size:	$	7,500

Application Procedures

Applications to the foundation should include the following descriptions: the project (or that portion of a larger project) for which funding is sought and the amount requested; plans to achieve financial self-sufficiency; and the applicant's members, key staff, board members (if any), and goals. In addition, applicants should provide proof of tax-exempt status (or that of a sponsor) and the names of other foundations or donors from whom support is received, to whom proposals have been sent, and to whom it is contemplated proposals will be sent.

The foundation does not have a formal schedule; however, it suggests that proposals should be submitted six weeks before board meetings. Timely submission does not guarantee when a proposal will be considered. On occasion the foundation makes decisions at a preliminary meeting; other times proposals are held over to subsequent meetings.

Grant Limitations

The foundation does not support direct services provision, individuals, films, or books.

Meeting Times

The board of directors of the Sunflower Foundation meets three times per year, in July, November, and March.

Sunflower Foundation

Publications

The foundation does not publish an annual report. It will make guidelines available upon request.

Sunnen Foundation
7910 Manchester Avenue
St. Louis, Missouri 63143
(314) 781-2100

Contact Person
Samuel G. Landfather, Chairman, Grants Committee

Purpose
The Sunnen Foundation is a private foundation that makes grants to protect individual freedom of association and the First Amendment right to freedom of choice in religious beliefs.

Areas of Interest
Grants are made for specific goal-oriented activities, education, and litigation, the purpose of which is to protect individual freedom, particularly concerning contraception and abortion, separation of church and state, freedom from censorship (especially textbooks), and freedom of association. Projects with national scope and impact are given preference. Some grants are made for community support and for programs serving the handicapped and disadvantaged in St. Louis.

It should be noted that at the time this entry was prepared, the foundation was in a critical financial condition. Accordingly, its grants budget had been scaled down considerably, and the foundation had announced that no new grants would be made before 1989 at the earliest.

Financial Data (year ended 12/31/87)

Assets·	$ 13,941,313
Total grants paid:	$ 1,276,000
Number of grants paid:	45
Highest grant:	$ 150,000
Lowest grant:	$ 100
Median grant size:	$ 10,000

Application Procedures
Contact with the foundation should be by letter of application. The application should contain a definition of the problem, an outline of its solution, a project description and method of evaluation, the organization's qualifications to conduct the project, a total budget, and a specific

Sunnen Foundation

amount requested. Applications are accepted throughout the year. There are no deadlines.

Grant Limitations
With the exception of specific projects related to its primary areas of concern, grants are not made to general fundraising drives, religious bodies, educational institutions, environmental organizations, hospitals or medical charities, the arts, to name a few areas. In general the foundation does not support charities with broad-based public appeal or those involved with society's pervasive problems with which society as a whole can deal. No grants are made to individuals, and no support is available for scholarship, research, or travel.

Meeting Times
The board of directors of the Sunnen Foundation meets as necessary and continuously reviews grant applications.

Publications
None.

Threshold Foundation
873 Sutter Street
San Francisco, California 94109
(415) 771-4308

Contact Person
Drummond Pike, Foundation Manager

Purpose
Threshold Foundation is a cooperative and collaborative philanthropic endeavor based on donations from individuals. Its aim is to support initiatives that will produce "a planetary culture where there is a common respect for all life on earth and for the earth itself."

Areas of Interest
Threshold's grantmaking interests fall into five categories, each of which is directed by a committee of the foundation's donors. The committees are: planet, peace, person, social justice, and arts and media.

The Planet Committee seeks to reawaken a practical sense of ecological consciousness by supporting work related to issues such as toxic waste, tropical rain forests, and long-term alternative strategies of stewardship.

The Peace Committee's interests include peace education, innovative exchange projects between East and West, grassroots activities with national application, and exceptional efforts that address the imbalance between military needs and the needs of the American people.

The Person Committee supports projects that empower human beings and bring joy into their lives. Activities receiving support have included model projects representing new ideas in response to dysfunctional institutions and projects that promote traditional healing techniques.

The Social Justice Committee supports initiatives that address the poorest and most vulnerable in society. Areas of interest include: advocacy-oriented projects for groups with limited access to resources; creative strategies to deal with hunger and homelessness; and projects that explore and combat prejudice in society in all its forms.

The Arts and Media Committee identifies and promotes projects that enhance public awareness of exceptional individuals, ideas, and works-in-progress; inform and educate the public about issues of high priority;

Threshold Foundation

and touch audiences deeply, inspiring and empowering them to frame their lives with creativity and purpose.

Financial Data (year ended 12/31/86)

Support and revenue:	$	1,168,239
Total grants paid:	$	720,329
Number of grants paid:		54
Highest grant:	$	30,000
Lowest grant:	$	1,500
Median grant size:	$	12,000

Application Procedures

Threshold donors can sponsor one project annually, and an important part of Threshold's policy is the personal involvement of donors with sponsored projects. Donors serve as liaisons to the project, help with networking and implementation, provide follow-up advice and assistance in obtaining additional funds, and take primary responsibility for project evaluation. Whereas in 1984 the foundation did not accept unsolicited proposals, in 1986 unsolicited proposals were considered by the staff for possible sponsorship and presentation to the committees.

Grant Limitations

Only tax-exempt organizations or projects of tax-exempt sponsors are eligible to receive support.

Meeting Times

The grantmaking committees of the Threshold Foundation meet once a year to distribute foundation support.

Publications

The foundation publishes an annual report.

The Tides Foundation
1388 Sutter Street, 10th Floor
San Francisco, California 94109
(415) 771–4308

Contact Persons
Drummond Pike, Executive Director
Ellen Friedman, Associate Director

Purpose
The Tides Foundation is a public charity established in 1976 to promote innovative nonprofit and philanthropic activity. Its overall purpose is defined in the following statement made by its board of directors in 1981:

> The nonprofit sector is uniquely placed in American society to contribute substantively and imaginatively to the interacting forces seeking social justice, creative new approaches to economic enterprise, and an enlightened stewardship of our natural environment. The Tides Foundation desires an active role in this process. Expansion of the basic opportunity for everyone to participate in all aspects of social, political, and economic life based upon the best possible information is the essential stratagem from which the foundation's program is being developed.

The fund conducts its own programs, sponsors new initiatives, makes awards to outstanding individuals, and operates a general grantmaking program as well as several donor-advised funds.

Areas of Interest
The foundation has declared five general-issue areas for its work: land use, preservation, and stewardship; enterprise development and economic public policy; the environment and natural resources; peace education and international affairs; and community affairs and civil liberties.

The Tides Foundation

Financial Data (year ended 4/30/87)

Support and revenue:	$	8,708,400
Total grants paid:[1]	$	2,175,200
Number of grants paid:		170
Highest grant:[2]	$	56,000
Lowest grant:	$	2,000
Median grant size:	$	4,003

Application Procedures

The foundation requests that applicants first submit a two-page letter explaining the issue to be addressed, the organization's approach to the issue, the audience for the project, and the budget requirements and funding received. Following consideration of the initial inquiry letter, a full proposal and budget may be requested, and, on occasion, staff will make a site visit to the applicant organization. Applications are accepted throughout the year. There are no deadlines.

Grant Limitations

Grants are made only to tax-exempt organizations and to other organizations exclusively for charitable or educational purposes.

Meeting Times

The board of directors of The Tides Foundation meets three times a year.

Publications

The foundation publishes an annual report.

---

[1] This figure and the numbers that follow exclude 85 grants each under 2,000 totaling $68,610.

[2] This excludes two unusually large grants totaling $1,076,205.

Topsfield Foundation, Inc.
Route 169, Post Office Box 203
Pomfret, Connecticut 06258
(203) 928-2616

Contact Person
Paul J. Aicher, President

Areas of Interest
The Topsfield Foundation was founded in 1982 to focus on hunger, population, and peace. Until 1987 it focused its efforts on promoting citizen education and public involvement in the policy debates concerning international security.

As this entry was being prepared, the foundation had undertaken a major program assessment and was considering new fields of interest. It is most likely that the foundation will continue its traditional interest in the development of public policy, and it is expected that one new area of focus will be housing. New guidelines should be available by the end of 1988. In the meantime, while the foundation continues to meet its prior commitments, new grants are not being made and the foundation is no longer reviewing applications related to international security.

Financial Data (year ended 12/31/86)

Support and revenue:	$	211,991
Total grants paid:	$	159,850
Number of grants paid:		18
Highest grant:[1]	$	10,000
Lowest grant:	$	850
Median grant size:	$	4,500

Applications Procedures
While new guidelines are being formulated, the foundation requests that interested organizations send a one-page letter briefly describing their organization, the project for which funding is sought, the budget needs, and their tax-exempt status. All letters will be acknowledged, and if additional information is needed, it will be requested.

---

[1]This excludes two unusually large grants over $40,000 totaling $91,000.

Topsfield Foundation, Inc.

Grant Limitations

The foundation makes grants only to organizations that are classified as tax-exempt or that are considered projects of tax exempt organizations.

Meeting Times

The board of directors of the Topsfield Foundation, Inc., meets at least twice a year.

Publications

The foundation publishes an annual report and will distribute new application guidelines once its new program areas have been identified.

Town Creek Foundation
Post Office Box 159
Oxford, Maryland 21654[1]

Contact Person
Edmund A. Stanley, Jr., President

Purpose
The Town Creek Foundation is an unstaffed funding resource that was created in 1981 with the goal of playing a role in the achievement of a livable and sustainable environment and the search for a just society and a peaceful world.

Areas of Interest
Grants are made in the following program areas: (1) preservation and enhancement of the environment in the United States and monitoring federal, state, and local officials and bodies that are responsible for enforcement of legislation enacted to protect the environment; (2) dissemination, via public radio and television throughout the United States, of news and commentary significant to people concerned about the world around them and the future in order to provide them with a basis to examine what is happening and to act to improve many aspects of society and government; (3) the search for arms control and nuclear disarmament; and (4) improvement of the quality of life and opportunities for advancement for the people of Talbot County, Maryland, and its communities, where such opportunities have been adversely affected by economic and social conditions.

Financial Data (year ended 12/31/86)

Assets:	$ 16,710,000
Total grants paid:[2]	$ 1,165,500
Number of grants paid:	61
Highest grant:[3]	$ 10,000
Lowest grant:	$ 1,000
Median grant size:	$ 10,000

---

[1]As an unstaffed entity, the foundation does not have an telephone number where someone can be reached if further information is needed. All inquiries must be in writing.
[2]This grants analysis is based on the period January 1, 1986 through June 1, 1987.
[3]This excludes five unusually large grants of $100,000 and more totaling $600,000.

Town Creek Foundation

Application Procedures

The foundation welcomes inquiries and will consider proposals submitted between March 1 and November 1. Applicants should write a letter containing a concise statement of the program or project, the amount of funding requested, and a brief description of the organization making the application.

If, after studying this request, the trustees decide that there is a possibility of support, additional information will be requested, including the organization's ruling from the IRS identifying it as a 501(c)(3) tax-exempt organization, a copy of the organization's most recent financial statement, and a letter on the organization's letterhead signed by its chief executive officer on behalf of the governing body.

Grant Limitations

The foundation does not make grants to individuals, organizations classified as "private foundations," primary and secondary schools, hospitals, religious organizations, or capital- and building-fund campaigns. It does not make grants to colleges or universities except when some aspect of their work is an integral part of a program supported by the foundation.

Meeting Times

The board of directors of the Town Creek Foundation meets as a whole to review grant requests two or three times a year, at least, in the spring and fall.

Publications

The foundation publishes a brochure describing its program interests and application procedures.

Veatch Program
North Shore Unitarian Universalist Society
Plandome Road
Plandome, New York 11030
(516) 627-6576

Contact Persons
Barbara Dudley, Executive Director
Daniel Cantor, Program Officer
Marjorie Bowens-Wheatley, Program Officer

Purpose
The Veatch Program is a subdivision of the North Shore Unitarian Universalist Society, which was created by a personal bequest. The program is the vehicle used by the Society to further the ideals of Unitarian Universalism through support for organizations and institutions working to strengthen the democratic process and promote justice, equity, and compassion in human relations.

The program makes denominational grants to support regional, continental, and worldwide Unitarian Universalist projects. The program also makes nondenominational grants and loans in support of programs designed to address broad social, economic, and political problems in the United States. The material in this entry concentrates on the latter.

Areas of Interest
In its nondenominational grantmaking, Veatch supports organizations engaged in efforts to secure progressive changes in policies affecting the welfare of the general public, particularly the poor and disenfranchised. Grants are made to support projects working to alleviate inequity, injustice, and discrimination in the broader society, in addition to those which encourage the formulation and implementation of national policies that promote world peace. Particular attention is given to projects that increase citizen participation in the formulation of public policy, produce changes in the provision and distribution of services in ways that benefit the disadvantaged as well as those who seek to preserve civil rights and liberties.

The Veatch Program's 1987 annual report groups nondenominational grants under these categories: civil and constitutional rights, criminal-justice reform, economic justice, environmental protection, peace and

391

Veatch Program

disarmament, and general funding (which included grants for a variety of social-justice projects in the New York metropolitan area).

Financial Data (year ended 6/30/87)

In 1986–87 the Veatch program made denominational grants totaling $2,282,986. The data below analyze the nondenominational grants for the year.

Total grants paid:	$	4,517,014
Number of grants:		164
Highest grant:	$	310,000
Lowest grant:	$	1,000
Median grant size:	$	25,000

Application Procedures

The Veatch program has no application forms and no deadlines. Applications are considered throughout the year in the order in which they are received.

Applications should be concise and brief, preferably no more than ten to fifteen typewritten pages. They should include the following: (1) a one-page cover sheet including the name, address, and telephone number of the applicant; the contact person; amount being requested; the time period for which funding is being solicited; and a one-paragraph description of the proposed project; (2) an organizational profile, i.e., a description of the organization, including history, purpose and objectives, accomplishments, decision-making structure, sources of financial support, and staff composition; (3) Background of the problem(s) that the project seeks to address and an explanation of why the applicant is particularly well-qualified to undertake the proposed activities; (4) an outline of the specific activities to be undertaken during the course of the project with particular attention paid to what will be done; the methodology to be employed; the proposed timetable; and the impact and/or results anticipated; (5) an itemized budget detailing all proposed project costs in addition to a copy of the general operating budget of the organization;

Veatch Program

and a list of other sources and corresponding amounts of project support, committed and solicited.

Applicants should also submit copies of their operating budgets for the two preceding years showing income and expenditures, audited financial statements (if available), annual reports, and recent copies of IRS determination letters indicating their tax-exempt status under Sections 501(c)(3) and 509(a) of the Internal Revenue Code.

Receipt of applications is acknowledged by postcard. Once an application is deemed complete, every effort is made to provide a definitive response regarding support within ninety days.

Grant Limitations

The Veatch Program's nondenominational grantmaking is limited to U.S.-based organizations with a locus of activity in the U.S. Support is generally provided only to nonprofit tax-exempt organizations as defined under section 501(c)(3) of the Internal Revenue Code. The program does not make grants to individuals or government institutions, nor in the following categories: capital projects, endowments, scholarship funds, annual contribution drives, and historic preservation. Except in rare instances when the proposed activity is an integral part of efforts aimed at broader institutional change, the program does not make grants for: direct services, scientific or academic research, media programs, publications, conferences or seminars, and cultural programs.

Meeting Times

The board of governors of the North Shore Unitarian Universalist Veatch Program meets regularly throughout the year.

Publications

The Veatch Program publishes an annual report and a brochure.

The Villers Foundation
1334 G Street, N.W.
Washington, D.C. 20005
(202) 628-3030

25 West Street
Boston, Massachusetts 02111
(617) 338-6035

Contact Persons
Ronald F. Pollack, Executive Director
Susan K. Kinoy, Chief Grants Officer
Katherine S. Villers, Massachusetts Director

Purpose
The Villers Foundation was established in 1982 with a broad mandate to foster fundamental changes in institutions and attitudes affecting the elderly. The foundation places particular emphasis on the aged poor and near poor and seeks to nurture a movement of empowerment among the elderly.

Areas of Interest
The primary focus of the foundation's funding is assistance to facilitate organizing and advocacy among local and statewide groups engaged in aging empowerment with a lower-income orientation. The foundation also supports networking and coalition building by various national organizations around priority issues. Moreover, the foundation supports applied public policy research and special projects, along with the dissemination of the resulting information or materials to the public. Key issue areas and priorities for the foundation include health care, income security, and elders' contribution to society.

The Washington office focuses on efforts in different regions and localities throughout the country. Through the Massachusetts office, the foundation supports a special program of local grantmaking and technical assistance directed toward efforts within the state.

In particular the foundation looks for organizations with a good record and/or strong potential to affect major issues, a sense of long-range strategy, potential and interest for growth beyond present priority issues, strong leadership and excellent paid or volunteer staff, and strat-

The Villers Foundation

egies for increasing self-sufficiency. Minority groups and organizations of and for low-income people receive special attention.

In addition to its grantmaking activities, the foundation provides training and technical assistance for grassroots senior organizations, publishes materials, engages in research, and conducts conferences. The foundation also makes awards to recognize outstanding contributions by organizations and individuals to advocacy and empowerment, public policy analysis, and media coverage of issues affecting elders. As a result, in 1987 the IRS reclassified the foundation as an operating foundation.

Financial Data (year ended 12/31/87)

Assets:[1]	$ 16,807,708
Total grants paid:	$ 2,422,888
Number of grants paid:	176
Highest grant:	$ 100,000
Lowest grant:	$ 250
Median grant size:	$ 10,000

Application Procedures

Organizations working in Massachusetts should direct inquiries to the office in Boston; others should contact the Washington, D.C., office.

A request for support should be submitted as a concise (no more than five pages) description of the organization and the proposed project. This narrative should include: (1) a project description including what will be accomplished in terms of organization, program, and fundraising; (2) the background and track record of the organization and collaborating groups, i.e., why the organization is well-suited to carry out the project; (3) the significance of the project and its relationship to the mission and funding guidelines of the foundation; (4) a project timetable; (5) the name and résumé of the staff person or volunteer responsible for the project; (6) organization and project budgets for the current and previous years, including a description of other sources of support for the project

---

[1]This figure is an unaudited estimate of the market value of the Foundation's assets at year end.

The Villers Foundation

(committed and potential); and (7) a list of members of the organization's governing body with the affiliation of each member. The only attachment to this narrative should be proof of the tax-exempt status of the organization.

Grant Limitations
The foundation does not usually support social service models, the provision of services, facility construction, or biomedical research.

Meeting Times
The board of directors of the Villers Foundation meets quarterly to consider grant proposals.

Publications
The foundation has published a report for the period 1983–1985, and expects to publish an annual report. In addition, the foundation periodically prepares and disseminates other materials for use by community-based groups. It has also published a book entitled, *On the Other Side of Easy Street: Myths and Facts About the Economics of Old Age* and a book on long-term care is forthcoming in spring 1988.

The Windom Fund
2000 P Street, N.W., Suite 410
Washington, D.C. 20036
(202) 887-1957

Contact Person
Ellen Malcolm

Purpose
The Windom Fund, a private funding resource, makes tax-deductible grants to organizations that promote equality of opportunity for the disadvantaged in society: women, minorities, gays and lesbians, the poor, and the elderly. Often the projects receiving support are designed to affect public policy and to help citizens be more effective in the political process as voters, organizers, or public officials.

Areas of Interest
The fund is particularly interested in helping organizations that are new, higher-risk efforts with little access to traditional funding sources; those that are developing sound financial and administrative support systems; and those projects organized by and for women.

Financial Data (year ended 12/31/87)

Support and revenue:[1]	$	340,000
Total grants paid:[2]	$	260,500
Number of grants paid:		43
Highest grant:	$	10,000
Lowest grant:	$	500
Median grant size:	$	5,000

Application Procedures
On January 31, 1988, The Windom Fund's donor announced that the fund would cut back substantially on its grantmaking program and concentrate its support on those activities for which hard money is needed. Accordingly, in spring 1988 it was not accepting unsolicited proposals.

---

[1] This reflects support and revenue received by The Windom Fund during the eight-month period May 1 through December 31, 1987.

[2] The grantmaking budget for 1988 is expected to be about $50,000.

The Windom Fund

Grant Limitations
The fund does not give grants to individuals, nor does it provide support to programs in the following areas: social service delivery, the arts, film, research, or international affairs. Local projects are funded only if there is clear evidence of significant public policy impact.

Publications
The Windom Fund distributes a list of grantees.

The Winston Foundation for World Peace
401 Commonwealth Avenue
Boston, Massachusetts 02215
(617) 266-1014

Contact Persons
John Tirman, Executive Director
Nancy Stockford, Program Manager

Purpose
The Winston Foundation first started making grants in 1986. Its purpose is to contribute to world peace, primarily through the permanent prevention of nuclear war. Its primary focus is on public policy, reflecting a belief that in the postwar decades the political process, in the main, has failed to produce prudent decisions regarding the nuclear dilemma. A democracy needs an alert and active citizenry with access to accurate and sufficient information; it also needs governmental processes that are responsive to reasoned scientific and political analysis, that are effectively under civilian control and leadership, and that serve to build structures and relationships of world order and peace.

Areas of Interest
There are two general categories in which the foundation makes grants. The first encompasses conceptually inventive projects that have the promise to attack the problem of the nuclear arms race with freshness and daring. Examples of activities that have received support include projects devoted to citizen diplomacy, the creation of new constituencies for peace, and independent means of arms control and disarmament. The second category relates to building the "infrastructure" of the peace community, for example by improving skills, expertise, and public education.

Overall, the foundation is particularly interested in supporting innovative, "risk-taking" ventures and activist approaches to public policy. Although most of the foundation's grants assist national organizations, the foundation recognizes the fundamental contribution that local grassroots groups make to the peace process and attempts to leverage national grants in ways that will assist local communities.

The Winston Foundation for World Peace

Financial Data (year ended 12/31/87)

Assets:	$	2,683,278
Total grants paid:[1]	$	745,636
Number of grants paid:		54
Highest grant:	$	50,000
Lowest grant:	$	2,000
Median grant size:	$	12,500

Application Procedures

Deadlines for submitting proposals to the foundation are February 15, May 15, August 15, and November 15. The foundation does not use application forms. Applicants should submit a proposal that includes a concise statement of the organization's mission, resources, and approach to the problem being addressed. Why the applicant organization is uniquely well-suited to carry out the proposed project should be articulated. Easily transmitted examples of past work are welcome. The expected results of the project should be described, including outcomes that are less than desirable. The foundation stresses that background information such as project and organization budgets, and short biographies of key personnel, are essential.

The foundation staff tries to meet with applicants whenever possible, and is usually available for meetings in its Boston office. Application materials can be returned upon request, but otherwise are kept on file at the foundation's office.

The foundation advises that evaluation of funded projects is earnest, but informal. A brief written progress report is expected after six months, and a more full staff assessment is conducted after twelve months. Grants are generally considered to be for one year.

Meeting Times

The board of directors of The Winston Foundation for World Peace meets quarterly to review grant applications.

---

[1]This grants analysis is based on the 15 month period ended December 31, 1987.

The Winston Foundation for World Peace

Publications
The foundation publishes an annual report.

The Youth Project (Partnership for Democracy)
National Office
2335 18th Street, N.W.
Washington, D.C. 20009
(202) 483–0030

Contact Persons
Lorie Rubenstein, Executive Director
Kevin Reynolds, Administrative Assistant

Purpose
The Youth Project is a public charity that identifies and supports citizen organizations committed to social and economic justice and peace. It seeks to enable traditionally excluded constituencies—including Blacks, Hispanics, Native Americans, the rural white, women, and youth—to influence decision-making around issues having the greatest impact on their lives by providing the financial and technical assistance necessary for these groups to accomplish their goals. Originally focused on young people as activists, The Youth Project has broadened its mandate to support activists of all ages.

Foundation Structure The Youth Project has six field representatives and a national program representative. (See names, addresses, and telephone numbers listed at the end of this entry.) Field staff evaluate projects, help groups raise and manage funds, provide small discretionary grants, and assist groups in sharing resources. The national office manages all funds, provides assistance to nationally focused organizations, and coordinates the activities of all the field staff.

Areas of Interest
The Youth Project supports the process of citizen participation and seeks to enable grassroots citizen organizations to involve people in a myriad of issues affecting their lives, their regions, and the country at large. While The Youth Project does not specify funding categories, it generally supports efforts that encourage citizen participation in governance, the economy, foreign policy, and protection of the environment and natural resources.

The Youth Project provides local organizations with financial assistance in several ways. Initially, The Youth Project will provide seed funds

The Youth Project

to allow an organization to get firmly established. Once selected as a Youth Project grantee, an organization may be eligible for additional external funding. At this stage The Youth Project will help its grantees establish an entree to other foundations and to nonfoundation funding sources such as churches, corporations, individual donors, and the federal government. In addition, to insure long-term survival for its grantees, The Youth Project staff stresses that organizations must develop alternative, internal fundraising mechanisms, and assist organizations in achieving this goal.

In addition to funding and fundraising, The Youth Project offers local projects a wide array of other support services. The field staff offer advice and assistance with legal and management problems and help new organizations develop realistic goals, formulate feasible strategies, and choose appropriate tactics.

The Youth Project also operates a donor-advised fund program. Under special arrangements, The Youth Project acts as an advocate for local organizations and simultaneously provides individual donors with a vehicle for social change funding. Grants made from donor-advised funds are included in the following financial data.

Financial Data (year ended 6/30/87)

Support and revenue:	$	4,748,997
Total grants paid:	$	3,973,028
Number of grants paid:		204
Highest grant:	$	50,000
Lowest grant:	$	200
Median grant size:	$	5,000

Application Procedures

Organizations interested in applying for Youth Project support should contact the appropriate field staff person either by telephone or brief letter. Before an organization is funded, this staff will make an on-site visit, meet with the applicant's staff, leadership, and others who are active in the local community. A pre-funding memo is then written outlining

The Youth Project

the community and the issues involved, the organization's background, current status, and future plans, and the strengths and weaknesses of both the organization and its key leaders and staff. This memo is reviewed by the national office staff prior to funding. Once a project is approved, its staff is required to file monthly reports outlining the organization's development.

Publications
The Youth Project publishes an annual report. It also distributes *The Grass Roots Fundraising Book: How to Raise Money in Your Community* (2d ed., 1982) by Joan Flanagan and *Grassroots Fundraising Videotapes* with trainer Kim Klein. Both are available from the national office.

Field Staff
The Youth Project has several field offices. Following is a list of field staff and office addresses as of January 1, 1989.

Western Office

Jeff Anderson
The Willamette Building
534 SW 3rd Street, #510
Portland, Oregon 97204
(503) 228-1052

Territory

Oregon
Washington (state)
Idaho
California (San Francisco and
  north)
Nevada
Utah
Wyoming
Hawaii
Alaska

The Youth Project

Southwest Office

Frank Sanchez
Post Office Box 2501
Roswell, New Mexico 88201
(505) 623-1894

New Mexico
Oklahoma
Texas
Arizona
Colorado
California (south of San
   Francisco)

Midwest Office

Becky Glass
212 Third Avenue, North
Room 300 A
Minneapolis, Minnesota 55401
(612) 338-7572

Minnesota
Michigan (Upper Peninsula)
North Dakota
South Dakota
Nebraska
Iowa
Wisconsin
Kansas
Missouri

Chicago Office

Wilma Green
7725 North Paulina
Chicago, Illinois 60626
(312) 262-3065

Illinois
Indiana
Ohio
Michigan
Pennsylvania
New Jersey
New York

The Youth Project

Appalachian Office

Chuck Shuford	Tennessee
174 Idlewilde Drive	Arkansas
Winston-Salem, North Carolina	Louisiana
27106	Kentucky
(919) 773-1997	West Virginia
	North Carolina
	Virginia

Southern Office

Office Temporarily Vacant	Georgia
Contact National Office	South Carolina
	Alabama
	Florida
	Mississippi

National Office

National Program Representative	District of Columbia
2335 18th Street, N.W.	Maryland
Washington, D.C. 20009	Delaware
(202) 483-0030	National Projects

Financial Technical Assistance Program

Terry Miller
Post Office Box 40485
Portland, Oregon 97240
(503) 228-1052

11

Chapter Eleven
Regional and Local Grantmakers

Overview

The grantmakers described in this chapter have—like their national grant-maker counterparts in Chapter 10—demonstrated by their guidelines and recent grants a sensitivity to social- and economic-justice projects. They differ from those previously described in that they have specifically identified geographic limitations. As a result, they appear to fall more on one end or the other of what might be characterized as a continuum of social-justice funders. For example, while some of the community foundations listed in this chapter are highly cautious in their approach to risk-taking (conventional wisdom might suggest out of fear of offending wealthy donors in a local community), others welcome controversy and specifically invite proposals from those organizations working for unpopular causes. The overall impression they leave, when taken as a whole, is a greater willingness than many of the national funders described in Chapter 10 to take a chance that an investment in a new idea, or an unproven grantee, will pay off handsomely by producing substantial benefits in their own local communities.

In some instances, grantmakers' priorities are focused on a region made up of several states (not always contiguous); in others the focus might be several counties or a city. One of the few complaints received about the *The Grantseekers Guide*—dating back to the first edition published in 1981—has been that it segregates national from regional and local funders when there are several funders who fall somewhere in between. The reason they are differentiated is to respect those grant-makers who say they have specific geographic limits on their giving even if they do (occasionally or often) break their own rules. While grantseekers may not always like this book's organization, grantmakers favor it and have remarked that as a result they have received far fewer inappropriate inquiries and proposals than they had initially feared as a result of being included.

The lesson from the organization of *The Grantseekers Guide* is that these descriptions should be the first step in thoroughly researching funders, not the last. Be alert to cues. If the analysis of a grantmaker's giving patterns suggests flexibility in its geographic limitations, it is usually mentioned in the description. If further investigation of up-to-date materials corroborates the description, then a proposal from a national organization, or another group outside the funder's region of interest may be appropriate. Keep in mind, however, that flexibility is almost always directly related to reasonableness. While a local corporation or private foundation tied to the donor's hometown may occasionally support a national public interest law firm, a community foundation is not likely to venture far from home even in response to the most inviting of proposals.

While a grantmaker's size (measured either by assets, revenue, or grantmaking budget) is irrelevant when it comes down to determining how well a "foreigner's" proposal might be received, the tables that follow should be of more than passing interest. For example, they demonstrate that both the biggest funders and the smallest listed in this chapter are for the most part community foundations. Similarly, there are big corporate giving programs and small corporate giving programs.

All told, this chapter describes 107 grantmakers. There are 14 community foundations, characterized as such because they rely on gifts and bequests from individual members of the local community that, when pooled, yield income which is distributed back into the community. In addition there are 24 public charities, including a number of what are called by some "alternative community foundations," e.g., members of the Funding Exchange, created in recent years to respond specifically to local social- and economic-justice funding needs. Also described are 61 private foundations with local interests, and eight corporate-giving programs.

In the tables that follow, the grantmakers in this chapter are arranged by assets (if endowed), or support and revenue (if not endowed), as well as by size of grantmaking budget. While admittedly such information is less helpful in this chapter than in the preceding chapter, it is interesting nonetheless. For example, a quick review of the fifteen funders who reported assets of at least $100 million in 1986 or 1987 reveals that while more than one-half are on the East Coast, there are substantially more in the Midwest than in California.

Before getting carried away with the data, however, two disclaimers are in order: (1) the figures presented for assets (or support and revenue, as the case may be) are not from the same years, rather, they are merely the data most recently available when the chapter went to press; and (2) as far as the grantmaking budgets are concerned, while most represent grants paid, some are based on grants approved. Moreover, the grants data have been adjusted to reflect money available for discretionary grantmaking. While most grants data are based on a twelve month period, some others are for shorter or longer periods. Consult the individual entries, and particularly the footnotes to the financial data, for the qualifications and limitations.

Grantmakers Arranged by Assets

NAME	LOCATION	ASSETS	YEAR
McKnight Foundation, The	Minneapolis, MN	$711,287,990	1986
New York Community Trust/	New York, NY	527,356,153	1986
Knight Foundation	Akron, OH	460,555,993	1986
Irvine Foundation, The	Newport Beach, CA	423,008,466	1986
Joyce Foundation, The	Chicago, IL	269,180,079	1986
Chicago Community Trust, The	Chicago, IL	207,287,321	1987
Northwest Area Foundation	St. Paul, MN	198,850,966	1987
Boston Foundation	Boston, MA	190,451,103	1987
San Francisco Foundation, The	San Francisco, CA	178,641,014	1987
Penn Foundation, The	Philadelphia, PA	174,489,869	1987
Reynolds Foundation	Winston-Salem, NC	146,949,656	1987
Diamond Foundation, The	New York, NY	132,830,831	1986
Dodge Foundation, Inc.	Morristown, NJ	127,108,281	1986
Lyndhurst Foundation	Chattanooga, TN	112,402,318	1987
Cary Charitable Trust	New York, NY	101,103,243	1986
Calder Foundation, The	New York, NY	91,997,818	1986
Kaplan Fund, Inc., The	New York, NY	74,000,000	1987
Victoria Foundation, Inc.	Montclair, NJ	72,302,000	1987
California Community Foundation	Los Angeles, CA	71,299,000	1987
Atlanta Community Foundation	Atlanta, GA	68,019,271	1987
Bremer Foundation, The	St. Paul, MN	62,299,231	1986
Babcock Foundation	Winston-Salem, NC	57,261,523	1987
Gund Foundation, The	Cleveland, OH	56,241,398	1986
Minneapolis Foundation, The	Minneapolis, MN	56,089,430	1987
Philadelphia Foundation, The	Philadelphia, PA	48,808,973	1986
Graham Fund	Washington, DC	48,113,844	1986
Meyer Foundation	Washington, DC	45,094,233	1987
Rockefeller Foundation	Little Rock, AR	43,417,863	1987
Rubinstein Foundation	New York, NY	42,419,292	1987
Hyams Foundation, The	Boston, MA	41,692,009	1985
Clark Foundation	New York, NY	41,039,574	1986
New York Foundation	New York, NY	40,808,000	1987
Kroc Foundation	San Diego, CA	36,575,786	1986
Foundation for the Carolinas	Charlotte, NC	35,753,108	1986
Goldseker Foundation of Maryland, Inc.	Baltimore, MD	35,299,537	1986
Ameritech Foundation, The	Chicago, IL	33,919,772	1986
Zellerbach Family Fund, The	San Francisco, CA	31,456,925	1986
Gerbode Foundation, The	San Francisco, CA	31,376,387	1986
Columbia Foundation, The	San Francisco, CA	31,000,000	1987
New Hampshire Charitable Fund, The	Concord, NH	30,456,472	1986

Regional and Local Grantmakers

Grantseekers Arranged by Assets *(cont.)*

NAME	LOCATION	GRANTS PAID OR APPROVED	YEAR
Astor Foundation, The	New York, NY	30,115,555	1986
Woods Charitable Fund, Inc.	Chicago, IL	28,559,698	1986
Rosenberg Foundation	San Francisco, CA	28,000,000	1987
Fels Fund	Philadelphia, PA	26,910,310	1986
Field Foundation of Illinois, Inc.	Chicago, IL	24,625,433	1986
Fund for New Jersey	East Orange, NJ	20,191,159	1986
Memphis-Plough Community Foundation, The	Memphis, TN	18,388,489	1987
Virginia Environmental Endowment	Richmond, VA	18,166,087	1987
Cudahy Fund	Milwaukee, WI	17,835,873	1985
Haas, Jr. Fund	San Francisco, CA	17,377,406	1986
Blandin Foundation	Grand Rapids, MN	16,645,523	1987
Sapelo Island Research Foundation, The	Washington, DC	14,344,031	1987
Wieboldt Foundation	Chicago, IL	13,110,315	1987
Morgan Guaranty Trust Company	New York, NY	12,901,491	1986
Taconic Foundation, Inc.	New York, NY	12,662,647	1985
Southern Education Foundation, Inc.	Atlanta, GA	10,963,931	1987
Shaw Foundation	Boston, MA	9,674,650	1987
Peninsula Community Foundation	Burlingame, CA	8,637,032	1985
Hawaiian Foundation/Hawaii Community Foundation	Honolulu, HI	6,440,294	1986
New Prospect Foundation	Wilmette, IL	6,091,491	1986
Fel-Pro/Mecklenburger Foundation	Skokie, IL	5,094,799	1986
Minnesota Women's Fund, The	Minneapolis, MN	4,900,000	1986
Goldman Fund	San Francisco, Ca	4,643,000	1987
Irwin-Sweeney-Miller Foundation	Columbus, IN	3,186,000	1986
Boston Globe Foundation, The	Boston, MA	2,737,707	1986
Meyer Foundation, Inc.	Winter Park, FL	2,396,320	1986
Gerson Family Foundation, The	Beachwood, OH	2,286,000	1988
Bowsher-Booher Foundation	South Bend, IN	1,476,904	1986
Shalan Foundation, The	San Francisco, CA	1,452,448	1987
EMSA Fund, Inc.	Atlanta, GA	1,430,860	1986
Abelard Foundation	San Francisco, CA	1,100,000	1987
Pioneer Fund, The	Inverness, CA	900,000	1987
Ben & Jerry's Foundation	Ithaca, NY	654,944	1986
Bread and Roses Community Fund	Philadelphia, PA	297,775	1987
Bridgebuilders Foundation	Pittsburgh, PA	251,781	1986
A Territory Resource	Seattle, WA	132,288	1986

Grantmakers Arranged by Support and Revenue

NAME	LOCATION	SUPPORT AND REVENUE	YEAR
Community Foundation of New Jersey	Morristown, NJ	$1,609,605	1987
Piton Foundation, The	Denver, CO	1,567,801	1986
Fund for the City of New York	New York, NY	1,527,135	1987
North Star Fund	New York, NY	844,989	1987
Haymarket People's Fund	Boston, MA	831,560	1986
Women's Foundation, The	San Francisco, CA	566,058	1987
Vanguard Public Foundation	San Francisco, CA	506,563	1986
Liberty Hill Foundation	Santa Monica, CA	451,506	1987
Chicago Foundation for Women, The	Chicago, IL	387,588	1987
Discount Foundation, The	Washington, DC	329,142	1986
Hunt Alternatives Fund, The	New York, NY	315,982	1986
Fund for Southern Communities	Atlanta, GA	245,125	1987
Crossroads Fund, The	Chicago, IL	242,381	1986
Sophia Fund, The	Chicago, IL	229,513	1986
Live Oak Fund for Change, The	Austin, TX	201,377	1987
Nevada Women's Fund	Reno, NV	148,066	1987
Asian Foundation for Community Development	Oakland, CA	138,941	1986
Headwaters Fund	Minneapolis, MN	131,924	1986
Boston Women's Fund	Boston, MA	125,000	1986
Wisconsin Community Fund	Madison, WI	123,884	1987
McKenzie River Gathering Foundation	Eugene, OR	119,134	1987
Alaska Conservation Foundation	Anchorage, AK	104,921	1987
Chinook Fund	Denver, CO	90,000	1988
Sanford Foundation, The	Santa Rosa, CA	70,073	1986
Los Angeles Women's Foundation	Los Angeles, CA	61,047	1987
Astraea Foundation, The	New York, NY	35,000	1987
Appalachian Community Fund, The	Knoxville, TN	27,500	1987
Baltimore Common Wealth	Baltimore, MD	26,892	1987

Grantseekers Arranged by Grants Paid or Grants Approved

NAME	LOCATION	GRANTS PAID OR APPROVED	YEAR
New York Community Trust	New York, NY	$42,006,463	1986
Chicago Community Trust, The	Chicago, IL	32,000,000	1987
McKnight Foundation, The	Minneapolis, MN	31,648,302	1986
Penn Foundation, The	Philadelphia, PA	21,120,498	1987
Irvine Foundation, The	Newport Beach, CA	17,302,736	1986
San Francisco Foundation, The	San Francisco, CA	12,848,875	1987
Joyce Foundation, The	Chicago, IL	11,524,811	1987
Lyndhurst Foundation	Chattanooga, TN	11,032,643	1987
Diamond Foundation, The	New York, NY	8,907,978	1987
Kroc Foundation	San Diego, CA	8,623,974	1986
Gund Foundation, The	Cleveland, OH	8,097,537	1986
Boston Foundation	Boston, MA	7,909,704	1987
Knight Foundation	Akron, OH	7,906,587	1986
Northwest Area Foundation	St. Paul, MN	6,872,789	1987
Astor Foundation, The	New York, NY	6,568,355	1986
Dodge Foundation, Inc.	Morristown, NJ	6,253,753	1986
Cary Charitable Trust	New York, NY	6,225,807	1986
Kaplan Fund, Inc., The	New York, NY	5,827,000	1987
Reynolds Foundation	Winston-Salem, NC	5,811,145	1987
Morgan Guaranty Trust Company	New York, NY	5,571,718	1986
Blandin Foundation	Grand Rapids, MN	5,467,099	1987
California Community Foundation	Los Angeles, CA	4,730,642	1987
Rubinstein Foundation	New York, NY	4,304,786	1987
Calder Foundation, The	New York, NY	4,179,000	1986
Foundation for the Carolinas	Charlotte, NC	4,104,342	1986
Philadelphia Foundation, The	Philadelphia, PA	3,816,720	1987
Victoria Foundation, Inc.	Montclair, NJ	3,681,782	1986
Bremer Foundation, The	St. Paul, MN	3,492,314	1986
Babcock Foundation	Winston-Salem, NC	3,220,672	1987
Boston Globe Foundation, The	Boston, MA	3,014,371	1986
Hyams Foundation, The	Boston, MA	2,655,805	1985
Woods Charitable Fund, Inc.	Chicago, IL	2,435,380	1987
Borg-Warner Foundation	Chicago, IL	2,242,038	1986
New York Foundation	New York, NY	2,095,583	1987
Goldseker Foundation of Maryland, Inc.	Baltimore, MD	1,904,748	1986
Clark Foundation	New York, NY	1,776,728	1986
Graham Fund	Washington, DC	1,750,300	1986
Gerbode Foundation, The	San Francisco, CA	1,647,245	1986
New Hampshire Charitable Fund, The	Concord, NH	1,640,447	1986
Ameritech Foundation, The	Chicago, IL	1,625,817	1986
Rockefeller Foundation	Little Rock, AR	1,610,155	1987

Grantseekers Arranged by Grants Paid or Grants Approved *(cont.)*

NAME	LOCATION	GRANTS PAID OR APPROVED	YEAR
Field Foundation of Illinois, Inc.	Chicago, IL	1,574,822	1986
Meyer Foundation	Washington, DC	1,526,383	1987
Columbia Foundation, The	San Francisco, CA	1,412,749	1987
Piton Foundation, The	Denver, CO	1,367,840	1986
Zellerbach Family Fund, The	San Francisco, CA	1,347,869	1986
Rosenberg Foundation	San Francisco, CA	1,334,642	1987
Minneapolis Foundation, The	Minneapolis, MN	1,299,494	1987
Fund for New Jersey	East Orange, NJ	1,086,956	1986
Cudahy Fund	Milwaukee, WI	1,049,705	1986
Haas, Jr. Fund	San Francisco, CA	1,015,245	1986
Fel-Pro/Mecklenburger Foundation	Skokie, IL	993,172	1986
Virginia Environmental Endowment	Richmond, VA	916,217	1987
Taconic Foundation, Inc.	New York, NY	819,004	1985
April Trust, The	Washington, DC	796,540	1987
Fels Fund	Philadelphia, PA	763,183	1986
Irwin-Sweeney-Miller Foundation	Columbus, IN	651,242	1986
Wieboldt Foundation	Chicago, IL	490,525	1987
Sapelo Island Research Foundation, The	Washington, DC	468,738	1987
Goldman Fund	San Francisco, CA	414,583	1987
New Prospect Foundation	Wilmette, IL	393,700	1986
Peninsula Community Foundation	Burlingame, CA	383,619	1985
Haymarket People's Fund	Boston, MA	353,234	1986
Community Foundation of New Jersey	Morristown, NJ	350,027	1987
Shaw Foundation	Boston, MA	345,923	1987
Atlanta Community Foundation	Altanta, GA	326,785	1987
Bread and Roses Community Fund	Philadelphia, PA	293,315	1987
Shalan Foundation, The	San Francisco, CA	290,000	1987
Vanguard Public Foundation	San Francisco, CA	277,030	1986
Fund for the City of New York	New York, NY	271,217	1987
Minnesota Women's Fund, The	Minneapolis, MN	257,300	1986
Hunt Alternatives Fund, The	New York, NY	245,140	1986
Discount Foundation, The	Washington, DC	245,000	1987
Sophia Fund, The	Chicago, IL	208,000	1987
Southern Education Foundation, Inc.	Atlanta, GA	203,938	1987
Ben & Jerry's Foundation	Ithaca, NY	202,653	1986
Abelard Foundation	San Francisco, CA	176,000	1987
Women's Foundation, The	San Francisco, CA	170,000	1987
North Star Fund	New York, NY	169,790	1987

Regional and Local Grantmakers

A Territory Resource
221 Lloyd Building
603 Stewart Street
Seattle, Washington 98101
(206) 624-4081

Contact Person
Nora Hallett, Co-director

Purpose
A Territory Resource (ATR) is a public foundation organized in 1978 to increase the funds available for social-change activities in the Northwest and Northern Rockies. ATR's goal is to be a resource for organizations attempting to establish a society that is politically and economically democratic, equitable, and environmentally sound.

Areas of Interest
ATR funds projects that impact people in the states of Idaho, Oregon, Montana, Washington, and Wyoming.

It is interested in groups that are organizing people to work on social-justice activities; reaching effectively their constituencies and building lasting organizations that will be responsive to those constituencies; attempting activities with a realistic chance of success; and developing short- and long-range strategies. Other organizational strengths valued by ATR include direction by skillful leadership or staff, a self-sustaining financial plan, outreach to persons not before involved, and cooperative working relationships with other organizations that include shared research and the development of joint strategies.

In 1986 grants were made in the following issue areas: economic justice, the environment, Native Americans, women, energy, peace and disarmament, coalition building, and cultural work/education.

Financial Data (year ended 12/31/87)
Assets:[1]	$	132,288
Total grants paid:	$	163,280
Number of grants paid:		24
Highest grant:	$	19,000
Lowest grant:	$	2,500
Median grant size:	$	6,000

[1]As of December 31, 1986.

A Territory Resource

In addition to the regular grants analyzed above, the director has a discretionary fund available for grants under $1,000 for technical assistance. In 1986 ATR awarded 22 such grants totaling $8,734. The average technical assistance grant was $400. ATR also has an annual small cultural arts grants program. In 1986 three cultural grants, averaging $700 each, were awarded.

Application Procedures

ATR uses proposal forms and requires that they be completed and returned no later than February 1 or September 1. Three to eight weeks prior to the deadline prospective applicants should submit a one- to two-page project summary, including a general introduction to the group, the specific goals of the project, methods that will be used to achieve these goals, and the amount of funds needed. The ATR staff will review this summary and, if the project falls within its guidelines, will send the applicant a proposal form to be returned by the deadline.

The ATR staff reviews the application and requests clarification if necessary. Within two to three weeks the proposal is screened by the grant-review committee, which determines whether proposals will go to the board of directors for final consideration. At this point applicants are notified if their proposal has not been recommended. If the proposal has been recommended for consideration, the applicant may be asked for additional information and a site visit may be arranged. Proposals are considered by the board eight to ten weeks after the application deadlines. Applicants are informed of the board's decision within a week of the board meeting.

Grant Limitations

To be eligible for funding, a project must address fundamental issues facing the Northwest-Northern Rockies region and its inhabitants; have a direct impact on the people of Idaho, Montana, Oregon, Washington, and/or Wyoming; be actively working to change social institutions to make them more just, equitable, and humane; operate in a democratic, nondiscriminatory, humane manner, responsive to the project's constit-

A Territory Resource

uency; and be sponsored by a nonprofit, tax-exempt 501(c)(3) organization.

ATR generally will not fund projects that can be funded by traditional sources; projects sponsored by an individual or government agency; service projects; alternative institutions; or publications, conferences, media events, or arts or theater productions unless they are an integral part of other social change activities.

Meeting Times

The board of directors of A Territory Resource meets twice a year, in April and November, to consider grant applications.

Publications

ATR distributes a brochure containing grant guidelines, application procedures, and a list of grantees. ATR also publishes a quarterly newsletter on regional issues and grantees' activities.

Abelard Foundation
222 Agriculture Building
The Embarcadero
San Francisco, California 94105
(415) 989-0450

Contact Person
Leah Brumer, Executive Director

Purpose
The Abelard Foundation supports social-change organizations working toward a more democratic, just, and equitable society. The board is committed to the expansion and protection of civil rights and civil liberties; increased opportunities for the poor, the disenfranchised, and people of color; and expanded community involvement in and control over economic and environmental decisions.

Areas of Interest
The foundation supports community-based organizations in the western U.S. engaged in direct organizing, policy development, advocacy, or education on the following issues: resource policy (water, energy development, and agriculture); women; economic justice; workers' rights; third world issues (tribal sovereignty, immigration, etc.); criminal justice; and antimilitarism. Most grants are made to organizations working with a constituent base and committed to strengthening the skills and abilities of their members.

The Abelard staff advise other donors through Common Counsel, a shared grantmaking organization. These donors have interests similar to Abelard's, and also fund more extensively in the areas of Central America and media. Common Counsel also provides small technical assistance grants through its Grantee Exchange Fund.

Financial Data (year ended 12/31/87)

Assets:	$	1,100,000
Total grants paid:[1]	$	176,000
Number of grants paid:		25
Highest grant:	$	8,000
Lowest grant:	$	6,000
Median grant size:	$	7,000

---

[1]This grants analysis includes only grants made directly by the foundation. In addition, grants totaling $96,000 were made through Joint Foundation Support (see entry under National Grantmakers).

Abelard Foundation

Application Procedures

Groups working in Hawaii, California, the Pacific Northwest states, the Rocky Mountain states, and the Southwest should follow the application procedures outlined here. Groups working on urban projects in New York City and rural-based efforts along the eastern seaboard and into the South should refer to the listing for Joint Foundation Support, which advises on Abelard funding in those regions. Joint Foundation Support has its own application procedures.

There are no application deadlines; proposals are reviewed throughout the year. However, the staff will review only 100 proposals during each of the four funding cycles per year. Additional proposals are deferred to the next cycle. Therefore, applicants are encouraged to submit materials at least three months before any board meeting to assure they fall within the "first 100" limit.

Interested organizations may contact the foundation either by writing a brief letter of inquiry or by submitting a full proposal. Proposals should include the following: a letter summarizing the background and purposes of the organization requesting funds and stating how the funds will be used; a description of the project explaining the problem or issue to be addressed, how the project will address the problem, and why the strategy will be effective; résumés of the people who will do the work; a project schedule; a detailed budget for the project and for the sponsoring organization if the project is part of a larger, ongoing effort; information on fund-raising strategies, including the status of current requests and past sources of funding; proof of tax-exempt status; and a list of board members and other references familiar with the organization's work.

Grant Limitations

The foundation does not support social service programs offering ongoing or direct delivery of services; medical, educational, or cultural institutions; capital expenditures, construction, or renovation programs; programs undertaken at government initiative; and scholarship funds or other aids to individuals. Projects whose purpose is primarily to inform in a general way, or to study or research an issue for purpose of public education, and with little or no emphasis on policy change or implementation do

Abelard Foundation

not fall within Abelard's funding guidelines. Conferences are supported only when they are closely related to the initiation of new programs or organizations.

Meeting Times
The board of directors of the Abelard Foundation meets four times a year, in February, May, August, and November.

Publications
The foundation distributes a brochure describing its interests and a list of grantees.

Alaska Conservation Foundation
430 West Seventh Avenue, Suite 215
Anchorage, Alaska 99501
(907) 276-1917

Contact Person
Denny Wilcher, President

Purpose
The Alaska Conservation Foundation is a community foundation established in 1980 for the purpose of providing financial and organizational support to the environmental community in Alaska.

Areas of Interest
The foundation's particular interests include community and grassroots organizing around environmental issues, energy conservation and generation, hazardous waste and toxic substances, clean streams, and wildlands and wildlife protection. Grants are made both for general operating support and for carrying out specifically designated projects.

Financial Data (six months ended 6/30/87)

Support and revenue:[1]	$	104,921
Total grants paid:[2]	$	125,250
Total grants paid:		34
Highest grant:	$	15,000
Lowest grant:	$	250
Median grant size:	$	2,000

Application Procedures
The foundation distributes application guidelines upon request. Briefly, it requires information about the organization, structure, and legal status of an applicant and concise information on the organization or proposed project and needs to be served. Lengthy submissions are discouraged.

---

[1] In 1987 the foundation changed its fiscal year to end on June 30. For comparison, note that in the twelve-month period ended December 31, 1986, its total support and revenue was $357,759.

[2] The analysis of grants made is based on the nine-month period ended September 30, 1987. During the twelve-month period ended December 31, 1986, the foundation made grants totaling $235,808.

Alaska Conservation Foundation

There are three application deadlines. While the dates vary annually, they are generally six weeks in advance of meetings of the foundation's board of directors.

Grant Limitations

The foundation makes grants only to Alaska-based organizations. No grants are made for endowments, basic research, or lands acquisition.

Meeting Times

The board of directors of the Alaska Conservation Foundation meets three times a year. While the dates are not fixed, meetings usually occur in early February, May, and October.

Publications

The foundation publishes an annual report, application guidelines, and the *Alaska Conservation Directory*.

The Ameritech Foundation
30 South Wacker Drive, 34th Floor
Chicago, Illinois 60606
(312) 750-5223

Contact Person
Michael E. Kuhlin, Director

Purpose
The Ameritech Foundation was established late in 1984 to plan, develop, and implement the contributions program of Ameritech, the parent of the Bell companies serving Illinois, Indiana, Michigan, Ohio, and Wisconsin and several other communications-related companies. Priority is assigned to national and regional organizations with potential impact in program areas consistent with Ameritech Foundation and corporate objectives, a program emphasis that differentiates the foundation from Ameritech's Bell companies, which administer their own giving programs based on local and state-oriented needs.

Areas of Interest
The foundation has identified three areas for its programming: first, research and programs designed to determine ways that communications can contribute to the long-term betterment of society and quality of life; second, programs and activities that stimulate and improve the economic vitality of the Great Lakes area, including grants to major educational and cultural organizations; and third, research and development aimed at reshaping policy into forms more relevant to the current and future nature of the communications industry.

The foundation limits its contributions to significant organizations that are regional or national in orientation or impact. The foundation places a premium on innovation and creativity in reviewing grant applications.

Financial Data (year ended 12/31/86)

Assets:	$ 33,919,772
Total grants paid:	$ 1,625,817
Number of grants paid:	75
Highest grant:	$ 300,000
Lowest grant:	$ 1,000
Median grant size:	$ 10,000

The Ameritech Foundation

Application Procedures

Grant applications are accepted throughout the year. Preliminary inquiries by telephone or personal visits are discouraged. Rather, initial inquiry should be made by letter before a formal proposal is submitted. This letter should include a description of the organization, its history, and its purpose; an overview of the proposed project; a summary of the program's budget and an indication of the level of support requested; a list of sources and amounts of other funding obtained, pledged, or requested for the project; the population and geographic area served by the organization and/or project; and proof of 501(c)(3) tax-exempt status.

If the initial review is favorable, a formal proposal will be requested. There is no deadline for submitting proposals. If not, the foundation will convey the reasons for declining the opportunity to provide funding. Organizations are asked not to submit a preliminary proposal more than once in any twelve-month period.

Grant Limitations

The foundation does not make grants to individuals, to individual community organizations, local chapters of national organizations, religious groups for religious purposes, political activities or organizations established to influence legislation, or to national or international organizations with limited relationships to local Ameritech operations.

Meeting Times

The board of directors of The Ameritech Foundation meets four times a year, in March, June, September, and December.

Publications

The Ameritech Foundation distributes an annual report that sets forth application guidelines and includes a list of grants awarded.

The Appalachian Community Fund, Inc.
517 Union Avenue, Suite 206
Knoxville, Tennessee 37902
(615) 523–5783

Contact Person
Wendy Johnson, Executive Director

Purpose
The Appalachian Community Fund was created in 1986 to support community organizations addressing economic, environmental, and social-justice issues in the central Appalachian states of Kentucky, Tennessee, Virginia, and West Virginia.

Its mission is to be a source of new social-justice money for projects in the region, to provide technical assistance in fund-raising and organizational development to grassroots organizations, and to leverage money into the region from others for organizations addressing the root causes of social problems. It supports social change nationally and internationally through its participation in the New York-based Funding Exchange.[1]

Areas of Interest
The fund supports groups that are (1) organizing low-income and working people, or providing resources for such organizing; (2) working for a more equal distribution of wealth, resources, and power; (3) operating in a democratic manner and responding to the needs of their constituencies; (4) struggling for the rights of workers; (5) promoting self-determination in low-income and disenfranchised communities; (6) protecting the environment and developing appropriate technologies; (7) creating alternative arts and media linked to the struggle for social change; and (8) promoting peace and responsible U.S. foreign policy.

---

[1]For more information about The Funding Exchange, its programs and other members, see the entry under National Grantmakers for "The Funding Exchange."

425

The Appalachian Community Fund

Financial Data (year ended 6/30/87)[2]

Support and revenue:	$	27,500
Total grants paid:	$	20,000
Number of grants paid:		19
Highest grant:	$	2,000
Lowest grant:	$	500
Median grant size:	$	1,000

Application Procedures

The deadline for submitting a completed application to the fund is March 15; materials must be in the fund's office on that date no later than 5:00 P.M. If the deadline falls on a weekend, the following Monday is the due date. Application materials, including forms and guidelines, are available from the fund's office. The executive director of the fund and members of the grantmaking committee of its board of directors are available to answer questions about their process and to help prepare proposals if necessary. Applicants are urged to telephone or write with questions and for assistance.

The fund's application cover sheet is an essential part of the proposal. It must be entirely completed, and information must strictly be limited to the space provided. The remainder of the application cannot exceed five pages, not including appendixes such as budgets and lists of board members. Complete instructions appear in the guidelines. While additional materials may be provided, the fund advises that more information does not necessarily give the proposal a better chance of being funded.

Grant Limitations

The fund makes grants only to organizations in Central Appalachia. This region encompasses all of West Virginia; eastern Kentucky (the western border includes the counties of Lewis, Fleming, Bath, Montgomery, Clark, Madison, Garrar, Lincoln, Casey, Taylor, Green, Adair, Cumberland, and

---

[2]During the 12 months ending December 1987, the foundation increased its support and revenue to $75,000, enabling it to award 30 grants totaling $35,000 that ranged from $500 to $5,000, the median of which was $2,500.

The Appalachian Community Fund

Monroe); eastern Tennessee (including these western counties: Macon, Smith, DeKalb, Cannon, Coffee, and Franklin); and southwestern Virginia (including these easternmost counties: Rockingham, Augusta, Rockbridge, Botetort, Roanoke, Floyd, and Carroll).

Grants are made only to projects that have limited access to other sources of funds. The fund supports direct services only when those services are tied to social change programs, or when they are likely to empower the communities served. By law it can provide support only to organizations that conduct tax-exempt activities or have tax-exempt status. It does not fund groups that are involved in electoral campaigns or contribute substantially to support lobbying at federal, state, or local levels. No grants are made to individuals.

Meeting Times
Decisions on grant requests are made once a year by the board of directors of the Appalachian Community Fund, usually in June.

Publications
The Appalachian Community Fund publishes an annual report and grant guidelines.

The April Trust
1607 New Hampshire Avenue, N.W.
Washington, D.C. 20009
(202) 462-1155

Contact Person
Judith Y. Downey, Director

Purpose
The April Trust is a private charitable funding resource that makes grants to nonprofit organizations in the Washington, D.C., area. Its goal is to strengthen the quality of the leadership, financial viability, and program of organizations seeking to meet the needs of the community in the arts, education, health care, and human-service areas. Special attention is given to promising new approaches to difficult community problems as well as to projects of an original and pioneering, though yet unrecognized, nature. For this reason it is the policy of The April Trust to give priority to applications that have not received attention from other funding resources and to endeavors for which seed money is not readily available.

Areas of Interest
The trust's grantmaking activity falls under three broad categories: health and human services, the arts, and education. In fiscal 1987 approximately fifty-three percent of the trust's grant dollars were directed toward the health and human-services category, to support programs affecting poor children and families, special-needs children, day care issues, refugee needs, community mental health, and domestic violence. Grants in the arts, which comprised one third of 1987 grantmaking, included support for well-established institutions and for small, emerging, and experimental groups and programs. The remaining grants (fifteen percent) went to support education projects to enhance the quality of education in the D.C. schools and for miscellaneous projects and groups, including several specializing in technical assistance and management support services to the nonprofit sector.

Financial Data (year ended 5/31/87)

Total grants paid:	$	796,540
Number of grants paid:		65
Highest grant:	$	50,000
Lowest grant:	$	4,000
Median grant size:	$	10,000

The April Trust

Application Procedures
To initiate a request to The April Trust, applicants should submit a brief description of their organization and the proposed project, including the amount of support needed. Additional information will be requested by the staff if necessary. Telephone inquiries are welcome.

Grant Limitations
The trust supports projects only in the Washington, D.C., metropolitan area that are tax exempt as defined in Section 501(c)(3) of the Internal Revenue Code or that are working under the auspices of a tax-exempt fiscal sponsor. Funds are not normally provided for endowments, capital costs, or individuals.

Meeting Times
The board of directors of The April Trust meets three times a year, generally in May, November, and February, to review grant requests.

Publications
Application guidelines and a list of past grantees are available upon request.

Asian Foundation for Community Development
310 Eighth Street, Suite 305B
Oakland, California 94607
(415) 444-2680

Contact Person
Nelson P. Hall, Executive Director

Purpose
The purpose of the Asian Foundation for Community Development is to provide financial and technical assistance to organizations serving the Asian-Pacific communities in the San Francisco Bay Area of California. It seeks to increase the total grant dollars available for Asian-American issues, not only by providing funding, but also through its own advocacy and education programs.

Areas of Interest
In 1987 the foundation was primarily interested in employment and economic development projects that would serve low-income refugee and immigrant populations. In 1988 an additional priority will be efforts to counter anti-Asian violence and to promote better relations between Asians and other population groups.

The foundation has also indicated an interest in reviewing proposals for special innovative projects that address youth at-risk, including drop-outs and juvenile delinquents; job training and placement programs for adults no longer eligible for government assistance; unemployed and underemployed women; the impact of legalization, employer sanctions, and other provisions of the Immigration and Refugee Control Act of 1986.

Financial Data (year ended 12/31/86)
Support and revenue:	$	138,941
Total grants paid:	$	57,504
Number of grants paid:		6
Highest grant:	$	18,667
Lowest grant:	$	1,375
Median grant size:	$	9,231

Application Procedures
In 1987 the foundation had one grantmaking cycle, and the deadline for submitting proposals was December 31. Thereafter, the foundation ex-

Asian Foundation for Community Development

pected to conduct two cycles per year, one in the winter and one in the summer. Deadlines will vary, and applicants are urged to inquire before submitting proposals. The foundation suggests that initial contact should be by telephone, although staff will also respond to written inquiries.

Upon request the foundation will place organizations and individuals on its mailing list for announcements of grantmaking priorities and requests for proposals (RFPs). Although the foundation issues RFPs, the staff advise that the guidelines are flexible and that a significant portion of the foundation's grantmaking is in response to unsolicited proposals.

Meeting Times
The board of directors of the Asian Foundation for Community Development makes decisions on grant requests twice a year, usually in February and June.

Publications
The foundation publishes a newsletter twice a year.

The Vincent Astor Foundation
405 Park Avenue
New York, New York 10022
(212) 758-4110

Contact Person
Linda L. Gillies, Director

Purpose
The Vincent Astor Foundation limits its grantmaking activities, almost
without exception, to New York City. Its purpose is to support established
institutions and neighborhood programs that improve the quality of life
in the city.

Areas of Interest
The foundation supports organizations that encourage literacy, sponsor
the production of permanent low- and middle-income housing, and advocate for the preservation of open space and the thoughtful development
of the urban environment. Grants are also made to a limited number of
landmark preservation programs and to certain cultural institutions.

In addition to its regular grants program, the foundation also makes
grants of $5,000 or less from a discretionary fund with the approval of
the committee on grants but without requiring consideration by the full
board. Grants made from this fund may fall outside the foundation's usual
guidelines; they must, however, have a relationship to New York City or
its residents.

Financial Data (year ended 12/31/86)
The foundation's total assets as of December 31, 1986, were valued at
$30,115,555. Following are separate grants analyses for the foundation's
regular and discretionary grantmaking programs.

Regular grants
Total grants paid:	$	6,456,005
Number of grants paid:[1]		33
Highest grant:	$	50,000
Lowest grant:	$	10,000
Median grant size:	$	25,000

[1]This figure and the computations below do not include nine grants ranging from
$60,000 to nearly $1.5 million made to major established institutions.

The Vincent Astor Foundation

Discretionary grants

Total grants paid:	$	112,350
Number of grants paid:		42
Highest grant:	$	5,000
Lowest grant:	$	1,000
Median grant size:	$	2,500

Application Procedures

The foundation has no application forms and no formal deadlines for submission of proposals. Requests for grants should be in the form of a brief letter addressed to the director, describing the purpose for which funds are sought and providing a succinct description of the project, the sponsoring agency, and the estimated budget. If the proposal falls within the foundation's guidelines and appears to have a reasonable chance for funding, a meeting will be arranged and a more detailed proposal requested. The formal proposal should include (1) a description of the purpose of the grant, the names and qualifications of project staff, and plans for evaluating and continuing the project after termination of Astor Foundation support and disseminating project results; (2) a budget showing project cost, the amount requested from the foundation, and other actual or potential sources of funds; and (3) materials on the applicant, including background information, a list of governing board members, a copy of the most recently audited financial statement, copies of the determinations by the IRS indicating that the applicant is a tax-exempt public charity under Section 501(c)(3) of the Internal Revenue Code, and a copy of the most recent Form 990 and attachments filed with the IRS.

The foundation requires grantees to submit concise reports about projects it supports as well as financial accountings of the expenditure of grant money.

Grant Limitations

The foundation does not support projects involving the performing arts, medicine, mental health, advocacy, or research. Nor does it make grants to individuals or loans for any purpose.

The Vincent Astor Foundation

Meeting Times
The board of trustees of The Vincent Astor Foundation meets three times a year, in May, October, and December.

Publications
The foundation publishes an annual report.

The Astraea Foundation
666 Broadway, Suite 610
New York, New York 10012
(212) 529-8021

Contact Person
Kathy Acey, Executive Director

Purpose
The purpose of The Astraea Foundation is to raise and distribute funds for projects designed by and for women that advance the social, political, and cultural development of women and that enable women to challenge the institutions that oppress them. In addition, recognizing the lack of visibility of certain groups, the foundation is committed to multiracial, multiethnic outreach that includes women of all ages and sexual preferences.

Areas of Interest
The foundation encourages projects that promote a feminist perspective and work actively against racism, economic exploitation, ageism, and antigay attitudes in both their approach to issues and their organizational structure. Priority is given to projects involving women who have little access to funding, including women of color, working-class and poor women, lesbians, older women, and differently-abled women.

Astraea has supported a wide range of projects, including community groups working in the areas of labor, housing, reproductive rights, welfare advocacy, and gay rights; education activities, including programs addressing racism, anti-Semitism, homophobia, and health; projects addressing the legal rights of women, lesbians, and older women; social services provided in a manner promoting women's empowerment, including services for victims of domestic and sexual violence, prisoner-support projects, adult education for workingclass women and Latin immigrants, and a women's health clinic; cultural and media projects that document diverse aspects of women's culture and history; and women's organizing efforts against militarism, sexual violence, and political oppression.

Astraea also awards the specially endowed Margot Karle Scholarship to women undergraduates involved in working for social change and attending college within the City University of New York system.

The Astraea Foundation

Grants are made only to groups in the following geographic areas: Massachusetts, Connecticut, Rhode Island, New York, New Jersey, Pennsylvania, Washington, D.C., Maryland, and Delaware.

Financial Data (year ended 6/30/87)[1]

Support and revenue:[2]	$	35,000
Total grants paid:[3]	$	21,500
Number of grants paid:		24
Highest grant:	$	1,500
Lowest grant:	$	500
Median grant size:	$	1,000

Application Procedures
Completed applications to the foundation must be postmarked no later than May 31 and November 30 to receive consideration at the next funding cycle, and all applications must be submitted on forms provided by the foundation. Interested organizations should contact the foundation by telephone or mail and request an application form.

Grant Limitations
The foundation does not provide support for organizations outside the geographic areas identified in the areas of interest. It does not fund projects of individuals, except for cultural and media projects that are designed to serve as organizing tools for social change.

Meeting Times
The board of directors of The Astraea Foundation meets twice a year, in summer and winter, to consider grant requests.

---

[1]Astraea expects that its grantmaking budget will double in 1988 and that the maximum grant award will increase to $5,000 and that the maximum scholarship will increase to $1,000.

[2]This figure is approximate, because the foundation's audit was not complete when the entry was prepared.

[3]This grants analysis includes two Margot Karle Scholarships of $500 each.

The Astraea Foundation

Publications
The foundation publishes a brochure outlining its program interests and application procedures and a semiannual newsletter describing its grantees.

Metropolitan Atlanta Community Foundation, Inc.
50 Hurt Plaza, Suite 449
Atlanta, Georgia 30303
(404) 688-5525

Contact Person
Alicia Philipp, Executive Director

Purpose
The Metropolitan Atlanta Community Foundation supports local community-based programs by making grants from its discretionary funds and advising individual donors. Priority interests of the foundation are projects that clearly provide innovative responses to recognized community needs, help build internal stability, and collaborate with two or more organizations.

Areas of Interest
Grants are generally classified as social services, education, health, arts, and culture, or civics. It should be noted, for example, that the foundation has made several grants for AIDS-related services and public education. The foundation is particularly interested in innovative programs and projects that can exert a leverage or a multiplier effect or that, through research, planning, or evaluation, contribute significantly to the solution of important community problems.

Financial Data (year ended 6/30/87)

Assets:	$ 68,019,271
Total grants paid:[1]	$ 326,785
Number of grants paid:	118
Highest grant:	$ 10,000
Lowest grant:	$ 500
Median grant size:	$ 2,500

Application Procedures
Interested organizations seeking support should first telephone the foundation and discuss the proposed project with the staff in general terms.

---

[1]This grants analysis is based only on discretionary and field-of-interest funds housed at the foundation. Grants made from designated funds and donor-advised funds are not included.

Metropolitan Atlanta Community Foundation, Inc.

Qualified organizations will be sent specific grant application guidelines outlining the information and supplementary material that must be included in the formal grant proposal. Formal requests for support are due December 1, March 1, June 1, and September 1 for consideration at the next board of directors meeting. All grant proposals must include a copy of the organization's most current tax-exemption letter from the Internal Revenue Service.

Grant Limitations

Priority is given to organizations located in the following counties: Barrow, Butts, Cherokee, Clayton, Cobb, Coweta, DeKalb, Douglas, Fayette, Forsyth, Fulton, Gwinnett, Hall, Henry, Newton, Paulding, Rockdale, Spaulding, and Walton. Generally the foundation does not provide support for annual fund campaigns, operating support (other than start-up), religious organizations for sectarian purposes, research that is not of a community nature or does not have near-term results, conferences, films, endowments, lobbying, computer/word processing equipment, scholarships, requests for repeat funding for a project previously funded, and individuals.

Meeting Times

The board of directors of the Metropolitan Atlanta Community Foundation meets in January, April, July, and October.

Publications

The foundation publishes an annual report and grant application guidelines.

Mary Reynolds Babcock Foundation
102 Reynolda Village
Winston-Salem, North Carolina 27106
(919) 748-9222

Contact Person
William L. Bondurant, Executive Director

Areas of Interest
The Mary Reynolds Babcock Foundation provides grants and program-related investments (PRIs) or loans to tax-exempt organizations for programs to support active citizen participation in the following areas: environmental protection, development of public policy, education, well-being of children and adolescents, philanthropy, the arts, grassroots organizing, rural issues, and women's concerns. The majority (seventy-five percent) of grants is made to organizations working in North Carolina and the Southeast.

PRIs are made selectively by the foundation as a way to provide needed funds for philanthropic purposes while preserving the capital funds of the foundation. PRIs are chosen following much the same guidelines used for regular grants and are repaid after an agreed-upon period of time.

The foundation also makes interim grants between board meetings for projects needing emergency support. Interim grants do not exceed $7,000.

Financial Data (year ended 8/31/87)[1]

Assets:	$ 57,261,523
Total grants paid:	$ 3,220,672
Number of grants paid:	168
Highest grant:	$ 100,000
Lowest grant:	$ 550
Median grant size:	$ 20,000

---

[1]These figures were supplied by the foundation in lieu of a list of grants.

Mary Reynolds Babcock Foundation

Program-Related Investments

Total PRIs:	$	897,225
Number of PRIs:		11
Highest PRI:	$	100,000
Lowest PRI:	$	17,658
Median PRI size:	$	100,000

Interim Grants

Total interim grants paid:	$	108,901
Number of interim grants paid:		48
Highest interim grant:	$	5,000
Lowest interim grant:	$	550
Median interim grant size:	$	2,000

Application Procedures

Completed applications must be received by March 1 to be considered at the May board meeting, and by September 1 for the November meeting. If the deadline falls on a weekend or holiday, then the next business day serves as the official deadline. An application form, including an abstract page, will be provided by the foundation upon request. This form must be completed and signed by the applicant's chief executive officer or board chairman and returned with a full proposal.

The proposal should be no longer than five pages and should include descriptions of the following: the need for the proposed program, the program objectives and purposes, how the need will be met and the objectives accomplished, the location and duration of the program, a description of the applying organization, the qualifications of those involved in the program, and how the program will be evaluated.

Appended to the proposal should be a one-page, line-item budget identifying the projected expenses and income of the program. If the total budget for the organization is different from the program budget, a one-page summary of the organization's budget listing expenses and revenues should be included. The package should also include a list of the organization's governing board members with identification of their major organizational affiliation or occupation, and a certificate of tax-

Mary Reynolds Babcock Foundation

exempt status. Additional materials may be submitted to supplement the application if appropriate.

Grant Limitations
The foundation ordinarily does not provide funds to programs that benefit only one city or county. Exceptions to this policy are made when a program obviously has potential to transcend its community's geographic boundaries. Further, the foundation does not provide grants to individuals, for construction or restoration projects, international programs, film or video production, or activities of tax-supported educational institutions outside North Carolina. All of the above, the foundation notes, may be subject to an exception.

Meeting Times
The board of directors of the Mary Reynolds Babcock Foundation considers grant applications at its May and November meetings.

Publications
The foundation publishes an annual report.

Ben & Jerry's Foundation
Clinton Hall
108 North Cayuga Street
Ithaca, New York 14850
(607) 272-1813

Contact Person
Betsy Rice, Administrator

Purpose
Ben & Jerry's Foundation is funded by Ben & Jerry's Homemade, Inc., the ice cream manufacturer in Vermont, and most of its grants are made to projects in upstate New York, Vermont, and New Hampshire. Grants and loans are made for projects that are models for social change, projects infused with the spirit of generosity and hopefulness, projects that enhance people's quality of life, projects that exhibit creative problem-solving, and projects that are involved with community celebrations.

Areas of Interest
The foundation looks for organizations with creative and innovative approaches to social problems and ideas out of the ordinary that are going to make a lasting difference. It is particularly concerned with promoting peace and the celebration of community spirit that shows that people can work and live together and have fun.

A review of the first year and one-half of the foundation's operation shows that of the 111 grants made, most went to projects addressing the needs of children, the problems of poverty, and to arts programs. In addition, grants were made in the following areas: adults (the homeless, battered women, the elderly, and disabled); advocacy activities; community celebrations, mediation, labor, and business; the environment; peace; and health.

Financial Data (year ended 12/31/86)
Assets:	$	654,944
Total grants paid:[1]	$	202,653
Number of grants paid:		60
Highest grant:	$	10,000
Lowest grant:	$	300
Median grant size:	$	3,000

[1]Based on the list of grants paid during the 12 months ended March 31, 1987.

443

Ben & Jerry's Foundation

Application Procedures

The foundation's application deadlines are March 31, June 30, September 30, and December 31, and applications must be postmarked by these dates in order to be considered at the next meeting of the foundation's board. The foundation uses application forms which are available upon request.

In addition to the application forms, all applicants must submit a proposal no more than five pages long. Applicants should also provide an outline of the project budget, proof of tax-exempt status, a copy of their most recently completed tax return, and an abstract, or brief description, of the proposed project no more than one-half page in length.

Grant Limitations

Although the foundation will review all requests received, it tends not to make awards to state agencies and organizations with annual budgets of $500,000 or more. The foundation discourages applications for individual scholarships and will not fund projects outside of the continental United States.

Meeting Times

The board of directors of Ben and Jerry's Foundation meets quarterly to review grant applications.

Publications

The foundation will distribute on request a list of past grantees. It expects to publish an annual report beginning in 1988.

Blandin Foundation
100 Pokegama Avenue North
Grand Rapids, Minnesota 55744
(218) 326–0523

Contact Persons
Paul M. Olson, President
Kathryn L. Jensen, Vice-President Program
Charles P. Driscoll, Senior Program Officer
James Krile, Director of Blandin Community Leadership Program

Purpose
The Charles K. Blandin Foundation seeks to be a leading foundation serving Grand Rapids/Itasca County and the rural areas of Minnesota. The mission of the foundation is to help advance the quality of life in significant ways that have a long-term beneficial impact on the Grand Rapids/Itasca area. Throughout rural Minnesota, the foundation addresses the causes of problems that effect the viability of rural communities and the well-being of individuals.

Areas of Interest
The foundation divides its grantmaking program into five areas: education, leadership, economic development, health and human services, and arts and humanities.

More specifically, the foundation works to increase access and exposure to educational programs among rural Minnesota residents; develops and administers leadership programs to strengthen rural Minnesota communities; supports economic-development efforts that expand and diversify the rural economy to provide more jobs and lessen the reliance on large industries such as mining, forest products, and agriculture; helps rural communities meet the health and human service needs of their citizens; and supports projects that provide cultural opportunities and a richer, more creative life for Minnesota's rural communities.

In general, the foundation prefers projects that have a significant and long-lasting impact with clear plans for implementation that will be able to sustain themselves at the conclusion of the foundation's support. Each year the foundation sets specific objectives, and applicants are encouraged to telephone or write the foundation to determine which specific programs and services will be emphasized.

Charles K. Blandin Foundation

Financial Data (year ended 12/31/87)

Assets:	$ 16,645,523
Total grants paid:	$ 5,467,099
Number of grants paid:	157
Highest grant:	$ 800,000
Lowest grant:	$ 600
Median grant size:	$ 21,000

Application Procedures

The deadlines for submitting completed applications to the foundation are February 1 for review in May; May 1 for review in August; August 1 for review in November; and November 1 for review in February. Before making an application, the foundation requests that a preliminary inquiry be made concerning the nature of the project for which support is sought. This preliminary inquiry may be made in a short letter, a telephone call, or an appointment to meet with a member of the staff.

The foundation does not have grant application forms and needs only one copy of a full application. The full application must include: (1) a description of the applicant's organization; (2) a one-page summary of the proposed project; (3) a five- to ten-page detailed project description, including a budget; (4) a list of the members of the organization's governing body and staff; (5) the organization's most recent audited financial statement; (6) proof of the organization's tax-exempt status, and (7) a résumé of the person or persons who will be responsible for carrying out the project.

Grant Limitations

The foundation restricts its grants to the state of Minnesota. Applicant organizations must have nonprofit status as defined in Section 501(c)(3) of the Internal Revenue Code. Governmental units are also eligible for support provided the purpose of the request goes beyond the limits of expected government services.

The foundation does not support the following: capital campaigns; religious activities; medical research; publications, films, or video, except

Charles K. Blandin Foundation

for those reflecting unique subjects of special interest to the region or state; travel grants for individuals or groups; camping programs; ordinary governmental services; and grants to individuals.

Meeting Times

The board of trustees of the Charles K. Blandin Foundation meets quarterly to review grant applications.

Publications

The foundation publishes an annual report.

Borg-Warner Foundation
200 South Michigan Avenue
Chicago, Illinois 60604
(312) 322-8659

Contact Person
Ellen J. Benjamin, Director, Corporate Contributions

Purpose
Borg-Warner Corporation is a diversified manufacturing company involved in transportation, construction, consumer products, machinery, agribusiness, energy, and protective services. A large portion of Borg-Warner Foundation funds are given to organizations whose activities contribute significantly to the development of the company's home community, Chicago.

The contributions reflect Borg-Warner's concern that its grants, even small ones, make a difference, and every effort is made to respond not only to the needs of established institutions, but to new and innovative programs as well. In addition to the grantmaking activity of the foundation, each of the Borg-Warner operating divisions maintains budgets for making contributions in its own communities. It is noteworthy that the foundation has made at least one grant for AIDS-related public education.

Areas of Interest
In general, contributions are made to organizations seeking to sustain Chicago's major institutions and working to resolve urban problems in the inner city. Priorities include: civic affairs, which includes those working to insure effective and efficient government, provide legal services to the poor, improve the legal system, and promote individual freedom and dignity; culture, including the performing arts, galleries, libraries, museums, films, and public broadcasting; educational institutions and organizations; health care, with special consideration given to programs for the elderly and underserved or high-risk populations; neighborhood revitalization and economic development; and social welfare. Seed funds, capital support, endowment funds, matching gifts, general support, and support for special projects are available.

Borg-Warner Foundation

Financial Data (year ended 12/31/86)

Total contributions:[1]	$	2,242,038
Number of grants:		242
Highest grant:	$	206,000
Lowest grant:	$	1000
Median grant size:	$	5000

Application Procedures

All requests for funding should be accompanied by a letter summarizing the reason for the request, the amount of money sought, and the daytime phone number and relationship to the organization of a contact person regarding the request.

The proposal, of no more than ten pages, should state the purpose and history of the organization, objectives for the coming year and activities to carry them out, who is served, membership of the governing board, the current year's budget and audited financial statement from the previous year, size and source of corporate and foundation grants, proof of tax-exempt status, and a statement of needs to be met and of the agency's qualifications for meeting them.

Grant Limitations

Foundation activities are concentrated in the Chicago metropolitan area. Contributions are made only to nonprofit, tax-exempt organizations meeting the foundation's criteria. The Borg-Warner Foundation prefers to make unrestricted contributions directly to grantees and does not sponsor advertising in conjunction with philanthropy or purchase tickets to fundraising events. Grants are not available for medical or academic research or for individuals.

Meeting Times

The contributions committee of the Borg-Warner Foundation meets every other month to consider requests for contributions.

---

[1] These tabulations exclude grants made under Borg-Warner's employee-matching gifts program.

Borg-Warner Foundation

Publications

The Borg-Warner Foundation distributes an information packet that includes program guidelines and a list of contributions.

Boston Foundation
One Boston Place
Boston, Massachusetts 02108
(617) 723-7415

Contact Persons

Anna Faith Jones, Director
Wendy D. Puriefoy, Assistant Director
John F. Ramsey, Assistant Director
Robert R. Wadsworth, Assistant Director

Purpose

The Boston Foundation is a community foundation, a philanthropic organization to which any donor may make a gift or bequest of any size for the good of the people of greater Boston. Contributions are combined to create a permanent endowment for charitable purposes. The income from this endowment is distributed each year in ways that meet the changing needs of the community.

Areas of Interest

The foundation considers proposals to support programs that seek to meet in a significant way the health, human-service, housing, educational, recreational, environmental, and cultural needs of the greater Boston area. It favors programs that will serve a broad sector of the community and assist those who are not being adequately served by existing community resources; demonstration projects that propose practical approaches to specific community problems; programs that will help coordinate community services; programs that will provide leverage for generating additional funds and community support; and building, renovation, and energy-conservation projects that will improve the delivery of basic services.

The foundation typically makes grants for one year only. When the circumstances warrant it, however, a commitment may be made to a project for two or three years.

Financial Data (year ended 6/30/87)

Assets: $ 190,451,103
Total grants paid:[1] $ 7,909,704

---

[1]Total payments by the foundation in 1987, from all funds, totaled $12,846,816. These tabulations include only grants paid from general funds and discretionary, field-of-interest funds housed at the foundation.

Boston Foundation

Number of grants paid:		247
Highest grant:	$	250,000
Lowest grant:[2]	$	2,000
Median grant size:	$	25,000

Application Procedures

Proposals should be submitted a minimum of ten weeks before each scheduled foundation meeting. After submission of a proposal, a conference with the staff is normally necessary before a request can be considered. A longer advance period may be necessary in the case of proposals requiring an unusual amount of preliminary investigation.

Each proposal should include a cover letter signed by the organization's president and executive director summarizing the request and the amount requested; a report on the expenditure of any previous grant; the organization's most recent Section 501(c)(3) ruling from the IRS; a description of the organization's background, history, purpose, programs, and whom it serves; a list of board, officers, and staff; financial statements from the last three years, including current budget and most recent audit; project description including an estimate of the number of people to be served and specific plans for evaluating it; project budget; the amount requested from the foundation and other anticipated sources of funding; and the contact person and phone number.

Grant Limitations

Grants are made only to tax-exempt organizations as defined by Section 501(c)(3) of the Internal Revenue Code. The foundation does not consider more than one proposal from the same organization within a twelve-month period. In general, grants are not made from undesignated funds for general operating expenses; medical, scientific, or academic research; scholarships, fellowships, or loans; the writing, publication, or distribution of books or articles; conferences or symposiums; travel; the production or distribution of films, radio, or television programs; audio and/or video

---

[2]This figure excludes eight small grants of less than $2,000 each, totaling $7,497.

Boston Foundation

equipment; or capital campaigns of institutions that have nationwide support.

Furthermore, grants are not made from undesignated funds to individuals, small arts groups, religious programs or institutions, public or private schools, municipalities, organizations outside the greater Boston area, and national or international organizations.

Meeting Times
The Boston Foundation meets four times a year to consider grant requests, normally in March, June, September, and December.

Publications
The foundation publishes an annual report, a quarterly newsletter, and a brochure that includes program guidelines and application procedures.

The Boston Globe Foundation
Boston, Massachusetts 02107
(617) 929-2895

Contact Persons
George M. Collins, Jr., Executive Director
Suzanne T. Watkin, Associate Director

Purpose
The Boston Globe Foundation was formed in 1982 for the general purpose of strengthening the nonprofit voluntary sector by improving the operating efficiency of nonprofits, promoting and expanding voluntarism, promoting self-sufficiency and stability of income sources to nonprofits, and leveraging other financial and community resources to address community problems. Grants are made to local, national, and international nonprofit agencies and institutions throughout New England, but the major focus of grantmaking is the greater Boston area.

Areas of Interest
The foundation focuses its grantmaking in the broad areas of community services, culture and the arts, education, hospitals and health care, media business, and science and the environment.

> *Community Services, Arts, and Education.* In the community services area, support is given to such specific areas as counseling, corrections, accessibility and transportation for the handicapped, day care, job training, food assistance, housing, intercultural and race relations, leadership development, public safety, recreation and fitness, and shelter for the battered and homeless. Grants in the arts go to established institutions as well as small community-based programs, and include the visual and performing arts as well as historic preservation and restoration, libraries, museums, and public media. Grants in education are made for adult education, elementary and secondary education, community education on public issues, special education and training, and higher education.
> *Health, Media, and the Environment.* The foundation's program in hospitals and health care supports programs in community health care, family planning, hospice and home care,

The Boston Globe Foundation

mental health and mental retardation, and substance abuse as well as hospitals and medical research. Media business program grants are made to organizations working either to protect and promote freedom of the press or to advance the field of journalism. Finally, the science and the environment program supports such issues as animal welfare, conservation of natural resources, and environmental education.

The foundation also has extensive matching gift programs for cultural organizations and for higher education and it maintains giving programs for scholarships and summer camps.

Financial Data (year ended 11/30/86)

Assets:	$	2,737,707
Total grants paid:	$	3,014,371
Number of grants:[1]		480
Highest grant:	$	100,000
Lowest grant:	$	25
Median grant size:	$	5,000

Application Procedures

Requests for grants are accepted throughout the year. Applicants should expect the processing of proposals to require three to four months. The foundation asks that all complete proposals be submitted on special Boston Globe Foundation forms, which are provided upon request. Further, information is to be provided in outline form with additional narrative material appended if appropriate. Proposals will not be reviewed unless they include a copy of the IRS letter identifying the applicant as tax exempt pursuant to Section 501(c)(3).

The proposal itself should include information on the proposed project, its budget, goals, and anticipated results; the organization's overall program and operations; the population served; location; and manage-

---

[1]This figure and those below do not include matching gifts made to the United Way and to cultural and educational institutions of $290,000 and $24,365, respectively.

The Boston Globe Foundation

ment. The foundation's annual report presents in detail the specific questions to be addressed. In addition, the foundation asks its grant applicants to fill out an accessibility questionnaire as part of an effort to determine how best to address the problem of barriers to people with disabilities.

Grant Limitations
The foundation makes most of its grant awards to organizations in the greater Boston area. The foundation does not make grants to individuals, does not purchase tables or tickets at dinners or other functions, does not make contributions in the form of purchasing advertising, and does not usually make more than one grant per fiscal year to any one organization.

Meeting Times
The board of directors of the Boston Globe Foundation considers grant requests throughout the year.

Publications
The Boston Globe Foundation publishes an annual report and grant application forms.

Boston Women's Fund
31 St. James Avenue, Suite 902
Boston, Massachusetts 02116
(617) 542-5955

Contact Persons
Stephanie Borns, Executive Director
Elena Rivas de Zilles, Office and Outreach Coordinator

Purpose
The Boston Women's Fund was created in 1983 to help women address the growing inequities confronting women and children. The fund's broad goal is to improve women's lives by supporting grassroots women's groups that are working for social and economic justice. Grants of up to $2,500 are awarded to projects that are organized and operated by women and that have limited access to more traditional sources of support. Technical assistance is also provided.

Areas of Interest
The fund focuses on projects that work for social change by organizing women on their own behalf to address economic, sexual, racial, and social inequities. Special emphasis is given to (1) projects that strive to transcend barriers of race, age, and social class and encourage women of diverse backgrounds to work together; and (2) community-organizing projects and direct-service projects that empower women who are the most vulnerable and have the least access to resources (e.g., low-income women, women of color, single mothers, girls, lesbians, disabled women).

Financial Data (year ended 12/31/86)

Support and revenue:	$	125,000
Total grants awarded:	$	34,510
Number of grants awarded:		18
Highest grant:	$	2,500
Lowest grant:	$	500
Median grant size:	$	2,255

Application Procedures
Application deadlines are March 30 and October 30. Interested organizations should telephone the fund for guidelines and application forms.

Boston Women's Fund

In addition to requiring information about the organization making the request, the purpose of the grant, goals and objectives, and timetables, the proposal should demonstrate the following: (1) the group must be controlled by women; (2) it is committed to working toward a more just, human society free from all forms of inequality; and (3) its policy-making body reflects the population it serves in terms of race, class, age, and sexual orientation. Priority is given to projects with budgets under $60,000.

The application also requires information about income and expenses for the preceding year as well as anticipated income and expenses for the following year. Evidence of tax-exempt status under Section 501(c)(3) must be provided.

Grant Limitations
The fund makes grants only to organizations in the greater Boston area with proof of tax-exempt status or to projects working with a tax-exempt sponsor. It provides funds to an organization, project, or group only once during any given funding year. It does not support groups with substantial ongoing support or groups linked to large established institutions, alternative businesses (such as food co-ops and work collectives), nonprint media, conferences, cultural projects, and research and special events not integrally linked to organizing. Grants are not made to individuals.

Meeting Times
The allocations committee of the Boston Women's Fund meets twice a year, in the spring and fall, to consider grant applications.

Publications
The fund publishes a brochure, application guidelines, and a newsletter.

Bowsher-Booher Foundation
c/o First Interstate Bank
112 West Jefferson Boulevard
South Bend, Indiana 46601
(219) 237-3313

Contact Person
Robert R. Cleppe, Senior Vice-President and Trust Officer

Purpose and Areas of Interest
The Bowsher-Booher Foundation is an unstaffed family foundation incorporated for charitable, scientific, literary, and educational purposes primarily benefiting the general public of South Bend and St. Joseph County, Indiana. Its areas of interest include leadership development, citizenship, neighborhood revitalization, and families and children.

Financial Data (year ended 12/31/86)

Assets:	$	1,476,904
Total grants awarded:	$	107,572
Number of grants awarded:		13
Highest grant:	$	18,340
Lowest grant:	$	2,295
Median grant size:	$	6,000

Application Procedures
Potential applicants are asked to write a brief letter describing their organization, the purpose for which funds are sought, the amount requested, and other sources of funding. In order to receive consideration at the following board meeting, letters must be submitted by April 1 or October 1.

Grant Limitations
Grants are made only to support activities of tax-exempt organizations benefiting the residents of South Bend and St. Joseph County, Indiana.

Meeting Times
The board of directors of the Bowsher-Booher Foundation meets twice a year, in May and November, to review grant applications.

Publications
None.

Bread and Roses Community Fund
924 Cherry Street
Philadelphia, Pennsylvania 19107
(215) 928-1880

Contact Persons
Judy Claude
Rhonda Jordan

Purpose
The Bread and Roses Community Fund supports organizations within the five-county greater Philadelphia area and in Camden County, New Jersey, which are working for a more equitable distribution of resources, wealth, and power in society. The Community Fund supports progressive social change nationally and internationally through its participation in the New York-based Funding Exchange.[1]

Areas of Interest
Bread and Roses gives priority to groups that do not have access to traditional funding sources, especially those organizing in poor, working-class, or minority communities. Grants are also given to groups that provide support services to organizing efforts. The fund's grantmaking stresses organizations that challenge the root causes of social problems rather than those that treat symptoms.

Applications are evaluated using the following criteria: (1) organizations must express a commitment to working toward a society free from all forms of racial, sexual, and economic discrimination and inequality; (2) the activities of the organization must lead to systematic changes that will create a more humane and just society; (3) organizations must challenge existing institutions to become more responsive to the people they serve; (4) organizations must be democratically organized and responsible to the constituencies they serve; and (5) organizations must carry out their work in a nondiscriminatory manner.

---

[1]For more information about The Funding Exchange, its programs, and other members, see the entry under National Grantmakers for "The Funding Exchange."

Bread and Roses Community Fund

Financial Data (year ended 7/31/87)

Assets:	$	297,775
Total grants paid:	$	293,515
Number of grants paid:[2]		51
Highest grant:	$	5,000
Lowest grant:	$	500
Median grant size:	$	1,828

Application Procedures

Groups interested in applying for a grant from Bread and Roses should telephone the office for application forms. Applicants are required to complete written application forms and submit current literature and background materials. Grants are distributed twice a year, in February and July.

Once Bread and Roses has ascertained that an application falls within the funding guidelines and is complete, the application is distributed to members of the foundation's eighteen-person community funding board which may choose to interview the group or arrange an on-site visit. Following careful review and discussion, the funding board recommends approval or rejection and determines the grant size. Rejected groups may submit a written appeal requesting reconsideration. Final approval of funding recommendations is made by the Bread and Roses board of directors.

Grant Limitations

Bread and Roses funds organizations only within the five-county greater Philadelphia area and in Camden County, New Jersey. To be eligible for a grant from Bread and Roses, organizations must have IRS tax exemption or be carrying out tax-exempt work. Groups can apply either for general operating expenses or for specific projects. However, groups with annual budgets over $50,000 cannot submit a general support request; they must

---

[2]This grants analysis includes only grants made from discretionary funds. Omitted are 26 small emergency grants totaling $6,015 and 75 restricted or donor-advised grants totaling $194,250.

Bread and Roses Community Fund

apply for a special project grant. Human and social services such as health clinics and day-care services and groups linked to larger institutions generally are not funded.

Meeting Times
The board of directors of the Bread and Roses Community Fund meets six times a year. The community funding board meets from October through June to review grant applications.

Publications
The community fund publishes reports for donors, a newsletter entitled *Keeping in Touch,* and distributes application forms and guidelines upon request.

**The Otto Bremer Foundation
55 East Fifth Street, Suite 700
St. Paul, Minnesota 55101
(612) 227-8036**

Contact Person
John Kostishack, Executive Director

Purpose
The Otto Bremer Foundation is committed to encouraging the social and economic health of the communities served by Bremer-affiliated banks in Minnesota, North Dakota, and Wisconsin. Its major thrusts are a commitment to addressing rural poverty, the changing rural economy, early childhood education, and youth service opportunities. The foundation also makes a small number of regional grants and grants to relieve poverty in the city of St. Paul.

Areas of Interest
The programs of the foundation are organized into five areas of interest: community affairs, education, health, human services, and religion. Within all these areas the foundation has a special interest in projects that address the needs of women, Asian Americans, blacks, Chicanos, Native Americans, and other minority groups.

The community affairs program focuses on activities that address the needs of the general community and increase citizen participation.

The education program is directed primarily toward expanded community service opportunities for minority students and post-secondary educational institutions in Minnesota. The health program supports efforts to promote individual and community health, environmental quality, and health education.

The human-services program supports programs that address the needs of children, single-parent families, battered women, the elderly, the disabled, and the poor.

The foundation also provides support for programs of religious organizations, especially ecumenical programs that address critical community needs.

463

The Otto Bremer Foundation

Financial Data (year ended 12/31/86)

Assets:	$ 62,299,231
Total grants paid:[1]	$ 3,492,314
Number of grants:	350
Highest grant:	$ 144,859
Lowest grant:	$ 270
Median grant size:	$ 5,000

Application Procedures

Proposals are accepted throughout the year, and there are no deadlines. Applicants should plan to submit proposals for staff review three months prior to the date a funding decision is desired. The foundation encourages initial telephone or written inquiries concerning its interest in a particular project. Applicants are also encouraged to contact the foundation staff for assistance in developing a proposal.

Generally proposals should include: legal name, address, and brief description of the organization; name and telephone number of the contact person; documentation of the organization's nonprofit and tax-exempt status, including a copy of the ruling from the IRS; evidence that the request is endorsed by the board of directors of the organization, with a list of those members; a clear description of the project for which funds are being sought, what it is designed to achieve and how this will be accomplished; the names and qualifications of individuals responsible for implementing the project; a complete project budget, including an indication of the time period in which funds are to be spent; an audited financial statement, if available, for the organization's previous fiscal year, a current operating budget, and a copy of the most recently filed IRS Form 990: an indication of other funding sources to be approached and a description of future funding plans; and a description of the procedures for reporting expenditures and the progress of the project.

---

[1]This total and the tabulations below include $31,000 in program-related investments but do not include scholarships for employees' dependents totaling $27,500. Nor do they include matching gifts totaling $95,746 made to Federated Giving Campaigns.

The Otto Bremer Foundation

Grant Limitations

Grants are restricted to nonprofit tax-exempt organizations and are not made to individuals. They are made only to programs having a direct impact on the service areas of the twenty-five Bremer Banks in Minnesota, North Dakota, and Wisconsin and in the city of St. Paul. (See the list that appears at the end of this entry.) Grants are rarely made to organizations in other communities unless they significantly affect the geographic areas of interest to the foundation.

Meeting Times

The board of trustees of The Otto Bremer Foundation meets monthly.

Publications

The foundation publishes an annual report.

Affiliates

Following is a list of locations in Minnesota, North Dakota, and Wisconsin where there are Bremer-affiliated banks and agencies. A complete list, including specific corporate names, is included in the foundation's annual report.

Minnesota

Alexandria
Baxter
Brainerd
Brandon
Breckenridge
Crookston
Detroit Lakes
Fisher
International Falls
Inver Grove Heights
Marshall
Milroy
Redwood Falls
Rice
St. Cloud
Shelly
South St. Paul
Warren
Watertown
Willmar

The Otto Bremer Foundation

North Dakota
Berthold
Carrington
Casselton
Fordville
Forest River
Glenfield
Grafton
Hoople
Kensal
Lansford

Larimore
Leonard
Lisbon
Max
Minnewaukan
Minot
Richardton
Rugby
St. Thomas
Woodworth

Wisconsin
Amery
Bayfield
Colfax
Danbury

Deer Park
Frederic
La Pointe
Siren
Washburn

Bridgebuilders Foundation
1310 Commonwealth Building
Pittsburgh, Pennsylvania 15222
(412) 471-7502

Post Office Box 247
Sun Valley, Idaho 83353
(208) 726-8400

Contact Persons
Katie Klingelhofer, Trustee
Molly Dolan, Administrative Assistant

Purpose
The main objective of the Bridgebuilders Foundation[1] is to provide support for community groups that tend to form bridges between various racial, social, and ethnic groups, particularly those that are not able to find funding through conventional channels. The foundation limits its contributions to western Pennsylvania and the Northern Rockies, although each year a few contributions are made outside those geographic areas.

Areas of Interest
The foundation's primary interests are community projects of all types, including, in particular, self-help organizations, organizations promoting social and economic justice through positive social change, third world groups, organizations working to promote peace, and environmental groups.

Financial Data (year ended 12/31/87)
Assets:[2]	$	251,781
Total grants approved:	$	35,350
Number of grants approved:		27
Highest grant:	$	5,000
Lowest grant:	$	350
Median grant size:	$	1,000

---

[1]Formerly the Pittsburgh Bridge & Iron Works Charitable Trust
[2]At December 31, 1986

467

Bridgebuilders Foundation

Applications Procedures

All requests should be received by May 1 or November 1 for consideration at the next board meeting. The foundation has no rigid requirements for proposals. All applications should include the organization's latest annual report, a partial list of previous grants received, and any materials that describe the program, such as brochures, public announcements, and so forth. A copy of the IRS letter of determination of tax-exempt status must also be included.

Grant Limitations

In addition to its stated geographic preferences, the foundation does not make grants to individuals, to United Way campaigns, to traditional health care facilities, or to capital fund drives.

Meeting Times

The board of trustees of the Bridgebuilders Foundation meets to consider grants twice a year, in June and December.

Publications

The foundation publishes an annual report.

The Louis Calder Foundation
230 Park Avenue, Room 1530
New York, New York 10169
(212) 687-1680

Contact Persons
Paul R. Brenner, Trustee
Peter D. Calder, Trustee

Purpose
The grantmaking program of The Louis Calder Foundation is directed toward promoting the health, education, and welfare of the people of the New York Metropolitan area.

Areas of Interest
The foundation's current funding priorities are health and welfare programs, education and cultural projects, and medical research. While many of the foundation's grantees are well-established institutions, a number are community and neighborhood efforts addressing such issues as youth employment, teen parenting, housing, homelessness, and education for disadvantaged youth. The foundation has also made a number of grants for AIDS-related basic medical research. Applicants are encouraged to submit proposals on a challenge, matching-grant basis, particularly in the case of proposed funding in excess of $50,000.

Financial Data (year ended 10/31/86)
Assets:	$ 91,997,818
Total grants paid:	$ 4,179,000
Number of grants:	165
Highest grant:	$ 250,000
Lowest grant:	$ 3,500
Median grant size:	$ 15,000

Application Procedures
Applications should be sent to the foundation office between November 1 and March 31 in order to be considered during the same fiscal year. The foundation has no formal application form. A letter from one to three pages will ordinarily suffice; it should include a concise statement of the purpose of the grant and the amount of the funding requested. Accom-

The Louis Calder Foundation

panying the letter should be a copy of the IRS letter of determination confirming the applicant's status as a tax-exempt public charity; a brief description of the nature, history, and activities of the applicant (in pamphlet form, if available); a current list of directors or officers; a copy of the latest audited financial report or a summary, if included in an official publication of the organization; a detailed budget for the project, program, or organization, as applicable; and a statement of other foundations that currently contribute to the applicant or the project and the amounts of their commitments.

Grant Limitations
The foundation does not make grants to individuals, private foundations, governmental organizations, or publicly operated educational and medical institutions. Grants for endowments, building funds, or capital development and grants payable over a period of years are made only rarely.

Meeting Times
The trustees of The Louis Calder Foundation have no set schedule of meetings.

Publications
The foundation publishes an annual report.

California Community Foundation
3580 Wilshire Boulevard, Suite 1660
Los Angeles, California 90010
(213) 413-4042

4050 Metropolitan Drive, Suite 300
Orange, California 92668
(714) 937-9077

Contact Persons
Jack Shakely, Executive Director
Paul J. Vandeventer, Vice-President/Orange County
Gloria De Necochea, Senior Program Officer

Purpose
The California Community Foundation is a nonprofit organization established to administer philanthropic gifts and distribute grants to improve the human condition through nonprofit agencies in southern California. Grant requests will be considered only from organizations located in or offering services to the citizens of greater Los Angeles, including Los Angeles, Orange, Riverside, San Bernardino, and Ventura counties.

Areas of Interest
The foundation has established several broad categories in which grants are made: the arts and humanities, education, environment, health and disability, human services, public affairs and community development, and animal welfare. The foundation emphasizes grants for model programs and/or projects that strengthen management and fund-raising skills for nonprofits.

Financial Data (year ended 6/30/87)
The assets of the California Community Foundation were $71,299,000 at year end, and all grants paid by the foundation (including those specifically directed by the donor) totaled $4,730,642. The following analysis is based only on the unrestricted grants of the foundation and those grants made when donors have specified a particular field of interest but not a specific recipient. Also excluded from the tabulations is one unusually large grant of $200,000 made to the Los Angeles Zoo.

471

California Community Foundation

Total grants paid:	$	1,744,802
Number of grants paid:		210
Highest grant:	$	65,578
Lowest grant:	$	25
Median grant size:	$	2,674

Application Procedures
There are no deadlines, and proposals may be submitted at any time. Applicants should submit one copy of their proposal with a cover letter typed on the organization's letterhead that is signed by a board officer authorized to sign for the corporation. Attached to the proposal should be one copy of (1) the list of the organization's governing body, including professional, business, or community affiliations and indicating any paid staff members serving on the board; (2) the complete financial statement for the most recent fiscal year (audited if available) and the organization's most recent IRS Form 990; (3) budgets for the current and immediately preceding year; (4) the current annual report or statement of program activities; and (5) an IRS letter confirming the applicant's tax-exempt status.

Grant Limitations
In addition to the geographic limitations set forth above, unless otherwise designated specifically by a donor to the foundation, grants will not be made for endowments; annual campaigns, dinners, or special events; building campaigns; sectarian purposes; individuals; routine operating support; existing obligations; or films (unless they focus on the foundation's service area).

Meeting Times
Grantmaking decisions are made by the California Community Foundation's distribution committee, which meets four times a year.

Publications
The foundation publishes an annual report, which encompasses detailed listings of grants and instructions for preparing a proposal. Through its

California Community Foundation

Funding Information Center, the foundation has produced and makes available a comprehensive guide to researching and approaching foundations, *The Funding Information Center Handbook*. The handbook is available free to nonprofit organizations.

Mary Flagler Cary Charitable Trust
350 Fifth Avenue, Room 6622
New York, New York 10118
(212) 563-6860

Contact Person
Edward A. Ames, Trustee

Purpose
The Mary Flagler Cary Charitable Trust conducts its grantmaking activities in two areas: music and conservation of natural resources. The trust makes grants both for general operating support and for specific projects or objectives. The music grants program is restricted to New York City; environmental grants are limited to the eastern coastal states.

Areas of Interest
In the program area of music, the trust's primary interests are the development of young orchestral musicians and the enrichment of musical performance in New York City, including the support of new and experimental music. Whenever possible, the trust seeks to give help to the disadvantaged, minority group members, and women in the pursuit of their music studies and careers. Music grants are made in the areas of performance, generally for orchestral concert seasons rather than individual events or festivals; for ensembles and presenting organizations that provide opportunities for the performance of new and experimental music, and for organizations that commission new music or provide direct services to composers; for institutional support for the advanced training of instrumentalists seeking orchestral careers; and for community music schools and other institutions that offer basic music training for young people who would otherwise not have such an opportunity.

In its conservation program, the trust's purpose is to preserve coastal barrier islands and beaches in their natural state, to discourage public subsidy of private development in critical coastal areas, and to further an ecosystem approach to the management of resources in the coast zone. Grants are made to support land acquisition programs, with a current emphasis on Virginia, North Carolina, and Florida; for legal protection of barrier islands and in coastal wetlands; and for ecosystem management, particularly for programs with a strong scientific component.

The trust also makes grants under its urban environment grant pro-

Mary Flagler Cary Charitable Trust

gram, which has as its purpose the support of community initiatives and development of local leadership to work on environmental problems within low-income neighborhoods of New York City.

Financial Data (year ended 6/30/86)

Assets:	$ 101,103,243
Total grants paid:	$ 6,225,807
Number of grants:[1]	63
Highest grant:[2]	$ 100,000
Lowest grant:	$ 3,700
Median grant size:	$ 12,000

Application Procedures

The trust does not use a grant application form. Instead, as a first step, a letter should be sent to the trust containing a concise statement of the program or project, the amount of funding requested and how it fits within the overall budget of the applicant, a brief description of the nature and activities of the applicant, its legal name, and a current list of officers and directors or trustees.

If, after studying a written grant request, the trustees decide that there is a possibility of support, additional information will be requested, including (1) complete tax information, with rulings on tax exemption status under Internal Revenue Code Section 501(c)(3) and tax classification determination that the applicant is "not a private foundation" under Section 509(a); (2) a copy of the applicant's most recent audited financial statement; and (3) an official letter or request on the organization's letterhead, signed by its chief executive officer on behalf of its governing body.

---

[1]This figure includes one program-related loan of $50,000. Not included are moneys paid in support of the Mary Cary Flagler Arboretum ($3 million) and for maintenance and support of the family collections ($540,000 total).

[2]This figure omits two unusually large grants to The Nature Conservancy and the National Orchestra Association of $1 million and $600,000, respectively.

Mary Flagler Cary Charitable Trust

Grant Limitations

The trust does not make grants to individuals, to organizations outside of the U.S., for endowments or building fund campaigns, or to colleges or universities except when some aspect of their work is an integral part of an established program of the trust. Grant renewals are not automatic and cannot be guaranteed from year to year. Music grants are not made to individual composers or performers.

Meetings

The trustees of the Mary Flagler Cary Charitable Trust meet at least once every month.

Publications

The Mary Flagler Cary Charitable Trust publishes a brochure, *Program Guidelines and General Information,* and will make a grants list and financial information available on request.

The Chicago Community Trust
222 North LaSalle Street, Suite 1400
Chicago, Illinois 60601
(312) 372-3356

Contact Persons
Bruce L. Newman, Executive Director
Trinita Logue, Assistant Director

Purpose
The Chicago Community Trust was created in 1915 to serve the needs of Chicago. The trust has continued since that time as a positive force for the Chicago area, a community foundation endowed by the community for the community. The trust manages over 250 different funds, many with specific restrictions. It provides funding support for a vast array of organizations and institutions.

Areas of Interest
The trust makes grants in five broadly defined areas: (1) hospitals, and health and medical programs; (2) social services; (3) arts and humanities; (4) education; and (5) civic affairs. The trust supports nonprofit organizations whose services improve the quality of life in the greater Chicago community. Taken together, they cover every aspect of life in the area, from health and mental health, youth, aging, civil rights and liberties, homelessness and hunger, to the arts. In 1986–87 the trust made at least one grant for AIDS-related services and public education.

The trust also makes technical assistance grants available to nonprofits. It has set up the Joint Foundation Energy Conservation and Facilities Improvement Fund in cooperation with five other area foundations in order to assist groups in financing improvements that will increase energy efficiency and allow recipient organizations to use savings from these improvements for the delivery of services.

Financial Data (year ended 9/30/87)
The assets of The Chicago Community Trust total $207,287,321. Grant awards made during the year from discretionary funds, donor-designated, and donor-advised funds totaled over $32 million. The analysis that follows is based only on discretionary funds.

The Chicago Community Trust

The Chicago Community Trust
Analysis of 1986-87 Grantmaking Activity[1]

	Total Grants Paid	Number of Grants	Highest Grant	Lowest Grant	Median Grant Size
Health and Medical	$176,290	7	$30,000	$2,290	$18,250
Social Services	$2,168,034	69	$500,000	$1,000	$15,000
Arts and Humanities	$2,100,395	49	$240,000	$7,000	$30,000
CityArts II	$450,000	49	$12,000	$5,350	$10,200
Education	$1,686,010	15	$1,000,000	$7,500	$50,000
Civic Affairs	$2,615,900	48	$400,000	$3,000	$32,500

[1]Excluded from this analysis of discretionary grants are: fellowships, scholarships, and student loans totaling $1,881,055; grants and loans from the Joint Foundation Energy Conservation and Facilities Improvement Fund totaling $315,200; loans made by a joint project of the trust and the Illinois Department of Children and Family Services, totaling $431,137; and in the arts category, major unrestricted and matching grants to 13 cultural arts institutions, totaling $6.84 million.

Application Procedures

The trust does not use a printed application form or a required format for applications. However, all applications must include a cover letter and brief summary of the background and purposes of the request for funds; approval in writing for the submission of the request from the chief executive officer or other authorized individual; a copy of the organization's 501(c)(3) tax-exemption letter from the IRS; a list of members of the agency's governing board; a copy of the most recent audited financial statement, if available, and the current financial statement and operating budget for the agency. All proposals should be on 8½ × 11 paper. Two copies should be sent to the attention of the assistant director.

The trust publishes a question and answer brochure, *Information for Prospective Grantees,* which outlines in greater detail additional information that should be included in each proposal, as appropriate, in the general categories of background information, purpose and objectives, evaluation, and budget and financial information. It is recommended that each applicant request the brochure and review it thoroughly before preparing application materials.

The Chicago Community Trust

Grant requests may be submitted at any time. Upon receiving a request, the trust will confirm receipt and indicate the staff member to whom it has been assigned for evaluation. Within two to three weeks that staff member will contact the applicant to request necessary additional information and/or to indicate a time period within which a decision will likely be made by the executive committee. As a general rule, decisions are made within ninety days of receipt of a request.

Technical assistance grants of up to $2,000 are made from a special fund. These grants are made to help agencies obtain consultant services for board development, program development, management improvements, bookkeeping, and training in proposal development and fundraising. The trust will provide a special form and brochure on this program upon request. Technical assistance grants are made at the discretion of the executive director with concurrence from the chairman of the executive committee, and are considered apart from regular grant requests. In general, highest priority is given to organizations with annual budgets of $350,000 or less.

Grant Limitations

The trust will not fund outside of Cook County. It will not, as a matter of general policy, make grants for scholarships, individuals, religious purposes, endowments, or for operating support of government agencies. Nor will the trust make grants for the general operating support, the construction, or reconstruction of physical facilities or the purchase of equipment for agencies or institutions that are principally engaged in program activities undertaken by a large number of similar agencies or institutions; for the purchase of computer hardware or for the acquisition of electronic data processing capabilities in the absence of a feasibility study documenting the need for such a system, the benefits, and its costs; for writing, publishing, producing, or distributing audio, visual, or printed materials; for conferences, festivals, exhibitions, or meetings; or for deficit reduction or debt liquidation.

Meeting Times

The executive committee of The Chicago Community Trust meets four times a year to review grant applications.

The Chicago Community Trust

Publications

The Chicago Community Trust distributes a variety of materials for donors and potential grantees, including an annual report; *The Community Trust Review,* which includes background on the trust and each of its funds; a pamphlet describing the Technical Assistance Grant Program; another on guidelines, policies, and procedures for applicants; a description of the cultural arts program; and *The Trust Quarterly,* a newsletter that lists grant awards, profiles agencies, and announces news of trust activities and initiatives.

The Chicago Foundation for Women
332 South Michigan Avenue, Suite 1419
Chicago, Illinois 60604
(312) 922-8762

Contact Persons
Pam Anderson, Executive Director
Kris Torkelson, Program Officer

Purpose
The goal of The Chicago Foundation for Women is to fund organizations
and projects that address the needs of women of all economic, ethnic,
and racial backgrounds. In order to benefit the whole society, the foundation works to remove obstacles that prevent women from achieving
their full potential in all aspects of their lives. Grants are made only to
organizations and projects in the Chicago metropolitan area.

Areas of Interest
The foundation will provide funding for both new projects and for
strengthening the contributions and self-sufficiency of ongoing programs.
Proposals should address one or more of the foundation's major goals:
(1) to encourage changes in policies and systems to provide full participation by women; (2) to foster prevention of problems, early intervention, support, and enrichment programs for young girls, adolescents, or
older women; (3) to create leadership opportunities for women; and (4)
to respond with new or unique approaches to the current and emerging
needs and interests of girls and women that promote independence,
cultural opportunities, and economic and social advancement.

Financial Data (year ended 6/30/87)

Support and revenue:	$	387,588
Total grants paid:[1]	$	156,000
Number of grants paid:		63
Highest grant:	$	5,000
Lowest grant:	$	1,000
Median grant size:	$	2,500

[1]The grants analysis is based on grants approved in the fall 1986 and spring 1987
funding cycles.

The Chicago Foundation for Women

Application Procedures

Proposals should be no more than five pages long and must include: (1) a cover sheet with a one-paragraph summary of the purpose of the request, the amount requested, the population to be served, the size of the budget, and a contact person and telephone number; (2) a narrative describing the purpose of the grant, the plan for achieving project or organizational goals, and how the achievements will be evaluated; (3) a brief history of the organization; (4) the rationale or criteria by which the organization or project meets the foundation's priorities and interests; and (5) the total amount requested and a breakdown of how the funds would be used.

In addition, the following materials must accompany proposals: a copy of the organization's 501(c)(3) determination letter from the IRS or the letter of agreement from a fiscal agent and a copy of the sponsoring organization's proof of tax-exempt status; a list of personnel and members of the organization's governing body; a list of other funders being approached and a list of past supporters; and complete budgets for the current year as well as for the previous and following years. If the proposal is for a specific project, both project and organizational budgets should be provided.

Grant Limitations

Grants are made only to organizations and projects in the Chicago metropolitan area, and all applicants must have obtained or be eligible for 501(c)(3) status from the Internal Revenue Service, or have the support of a tax-exempt fiscal agent.

The foundation does not support religious organizations for religious purposes, individual efforts, capital drives, endowments, or campaigns to elect candidates to public office.

Meeting Times

The board of directors of The Chicago Foundation for Women meets in the spring and fall to review grant proposals.

Publications

The foundation publishes a brochure, application guidelines, and a newsletter.

Chinook Fund
1245 East Colfax Avenue, Suite 216
Denver, Colorado 80218
(303) 830-2070

Contact Person
Chris Takagi, Executive Director

Purpose
The Chinook Fund supports grassroots Colorado organizations working for social change. The fund supports progressive social change nationally and internationally through its participation in the New York-based Funding Exchange.[1]

Areas of Interest
The fund is interested in organizations and projects that work for a society free of discrimination based on race, sex, age, religion, economic status, sexual orientation, and ethnic background; promote international peace and an end to corporate building of weapons; defend political and human rights and promote a just U.S. foreign policy; promote self-determination in low-income, agricultural, and disenfranchised communities; defend the rights of workers; create arts and media dealing with the struggle for social justice; oppose the destruction of the natural environment; and defend the rights of persons with disabilities.

Financial Data
The fund operates on a calendar year, and 1988 will be its first complete year of operations. For the twelve months ending December 31, 1988, the fund projects that its support and revenue will be $90,000 and that its expenses, including grants, will be $85,000. The grantmaking budget for the fund's spring 1988 funding cycle is $25,000; the budget for the fall 1988 cycle is $35,000. It is expected that grants will range from $1,000 to $2,500.

Application Procedures
The deadline for submitting completed applications for the fund's spring funding cycle is February 21; the deadline for the fall cycle is August 21.

---

[1] For more information about The Funding Exchange, its programs and other members, see the entry under National Grantmakers for "The Funding Exchange."

Chinook Fund

Applications must either be delivered to the fund's office by 5:00 P.M., or postmarked no later than the deadline. The fund uses application forms which are available upon request, and telephone calls from applicants with questions are accepted.

Among the items of information requested on the application forms are the number of women and minorities on the governing body of the applicant organization, a description of the organizational structure and decision-making process of the applicant; and identification of the constituency served by the applicant and the issues or problems addressed by the organization. The fund also requests that applicants submit a budget and timeline for the specific project for which funding is sought.

Grant Limitations
The fund generally will not support organizations with access to traditional funding, i.e., those groups with annual budgets in excess of $100,000; organizations whose sole purpose is to provide services; and individuals or groups not operating under the fiscal sponsorship of an organization tax-exempt under Section 501(c)(3).

Meeting Times
Decisions on grant applications are made by a twelve-person grantmaking committee composed of Colorado activists and submitted to the board of directors of the Chinook Fund for ratification. Grant awards are announced twice a year, in June and December.

Publications
The fund distributes a brochure describing its program interests and anticipates distributing a list of grant awards.

Robert Sterling Clark Foundation
112 East 64 Street
New York, New York 10021
(212) 308-0411

Contact Person
Margaret C. Ayers, Executive Director

Areas of Interest
The Robert Sterling Clark Foundation conducts grants programs in three major areas: (1) improving the performance of public institutions in New York City and State, including concentration on human-services delivery, housing and economic development, environmental management, and the budgetary process; (2) strengthening the management of cultural institutions; and (3) insuring access to family planning services.

In the first field, the foundation supports efforts designed to monitor human-services-delivery programs to insure that funds are not wasted and that recipients of service are well served; to insure the preservation and protection of the environment in accordance with federal and state mandates; to encourage linkages between the public and private sectors to promote the development of New York's economic base; and to improve the effectiveness and accountability of city and state agencies.

In its program to strengthen the management of cultural institutions, the foundation's grantmaking takes two forms: (1) management-support grants to cultural institutions and arts-service organizations for one-time projects designed to generate new sources of earned and/or contributed income, reduce operating costs through resource sharing, and improve internal management; and (2) foundation-initiated grants made to a limited number of small cultural institutions for general support. Eligibility is limited to institutions in New York City and the greater metropolitan area.

In its final program priority the foundation seeks proposals from organizations whose work is aimed at protecting reproductive freedom and insuring access to family planning services. The foundation funds projects at the national level making use of litigation, public policy analysis, public education, and research to achieve these objectives.

Financial Data (year ended 10/31/86)
As of October 31, 1986, the assets of the foundation were $41,039,574,

Robert Sterling Clark Foundation

and during that year the foundation paid 92 grants totaling $1,776,728, the highest of which was $60,000 and the lowest of which was $1,500. The foundation advises that grants averaged between $25,000 and $30,000. However, the 1986 grants list was not provided, hence the following analysis—which would appear comparable—is based on grants paid in 1985.

Total grants paid:	$ 1,762,093
Number of grants paid:	83
Highest grant:	$ 75,000
Lowest grant:	$ 1,000
Median grant size:	$ 17,500

Application Procedures

The foundation prefers that contact be initiated when a prospective applicant submits a full proposal. The foundation does not use pre-prepared application forms. Proposals are accepted throughout the year and should not exceed ten pages. If the applicant is requesting support for a particular project, the proposal should include the following: (1) description of the project; (2) project budget; (3) expected results; (4) detailed workplan; (5) plans for evaluation; (6) plans for future support; (7) other contributors; and (8) the names of other organizations to which the proposal has been submitted.

In addition, the foundation requires that the following information accompany all proposals: (1) a one-page proposal summary; (2) the organization's budget for the past year, the current year, and a projected budget; (3) the organization's most recent audited financial statement; (4) proof of tax-exempt status; (5) the names and occupations of the board of directors; (6) major sources of current financial support; (7) résumés of key staff; and (8) examples of past accomplishments.

Grant Limitations

The foundation makes no grants to individuals or for building or endowment funds.

Robert Sterling Clark Foundation

Meeting Times
The board of directors of the Robert Sterling Clark Foundation meets quarterly, in January, April, July, and October. The board considers proposals throughout the year.

Publications
The foundation publishes an annual report, and will make available upon request an information sheet titled *Program Guidelines and Grant Application Procedures.*

The Columbia Foundation
1090 Sansome Street
San Francisco, California 94111
(415) 986-5179

Contact Person
Susan Clark Silk, Executive Director

Purpose
The Columbia Foundation makes grant awards to projects that address critical social issues, support the rights of the disadvantaged, enrich the cultural life of the community, and improve international understanding. For the most part, grants are made to organizations operating in the San Francisco Bay Area.

Areas of Interest
The program priorities of the foundation in 1987 were: preservation of the natural environment; enhancement of urban community life and culture; international and cross-cultural understanding; reversal of the arms race worldwide; and protection of basic human rights. The foundation prefers to award grants to projects that offer promise of significant positive impact. The foundation states that it will not assume obligation for permanent support; however, it will consider grants for more than one year when the goals of a project require support over a period of time.

Financial Data (year ended 5/31/87)

Assets:	$ 31,000,000
Total grants paid:	$ 1,412,749
Number of grants paid:	198
Highest grant:	$ 125,000
Lowest grant:	$ 100
Median grant size:	$ 7,150

Application Procedures
Grant applications are accepted on an ongoing basis, and review can take two to three months. The foundation prefers that interested applicants submit a preliminary inquiry letter to the executive director before completing a formal proposal. If the project is to be considered by the foundation's board of directors, a proposal and proposal summary sheet will

The Columbia Foundation

be requested. Grant applications are accepted throughout the year. Generally applications must be received at least three months prior to board meetings in order to be considered.

Full proposals should contain the following information: (1) a description of the need for the project or activity, statement of objectives and strategies for attaining them, time frame for the project, and description of the project evaluation procedure; (2) information on the organization, including a statement of goals, qualifications of key staff, a description of the organization's decision-making structure, and its history of accomplishments; (3) financial information, including the specific project budget, the total organizational budget for the current fiscal year, income and expense statements for the previous fiscal year, sources of prior funding, and a list of pending or proposed applications for funds.

All proposals must be accompanied by a list of the organization's board of directors and evidence that the governing body has authorized a request to the foundation. In addition, copies of federal and state determinations that the organization is a public charity must be included.

Grant Limitations

The foundation limits its grantmaking for all local and regional programs to the San Francisco Bay Area. The foundation prefers not to consider projects in the fields of health, specialized scientific research, or religion. The foundation generally does not provide support for endowments, building campaigns, ordinary operating budgets of established organizations, individual fellowships or scholarships, or for agencies that are wholly supported by federated campaigns or heavily subsidized by government funds. Ordinarily the foundation will consider grants only to organizations certified by the IRS as public charities.

Meeting Times

The board of directors of The Columbia Foundation meets four times a year.

Publications

The foundation publishes an annual report, and will make available upon request a foundation profile, grants list, and proposal summary sheet.

Community Foundation of New Jersey
Knox Hill Road
Post Office Box 317
Morristown, New Jersey 07960
(201) 267-5533

Contact Persons
Sheila C. Williamson, Executive Director
Barbara A. Gille, Program Officer

Purpose
The Community Foundation of New Jersey was established to accept philanthropic gifts from individuals, corporations, and organizations and make grants to improve the quality of life for residents of the state of New Jersey. While much of its resources are restricted to the particular interests of its donors, the foundation operates a modest unrestricted grantmaking program.

In its unrestricted grantmaking, the foundation seeks out innovative programs having a multiplier effect or contributing to the solution or easing of important community problems. It is particularly interested in preventive projects and projects that enable nonprofit organizations to reduce their costs, increase efficiency, and become more self-sufficient. It stresses that ideas should be significant, feasible, have impact, and involve people capable of carrying them through successfully.

The foundation looks favorably on projects leading to coalition building and encourages challenge grants. It provides support for special projects and makes modest loans and program-related investments.

Areas of Interest
The foundation makes grants in the following areas: community development, to encourage economic and leadership development and neighborhood revitalization; cultural affairs, to facilitate access to well-established institutions and foster awareness of new and emerging groups; education, to prepare students more effectively for employment, motivate teachers, lower dropout rates, and address the high rate of urban illiteracy; environment and conservation, to preserve natural resources and plan for orderly future development; health, to promote health, prevent institutionalization, and facilitate access to health care delivery systems; social

490

Community Foundation of New Jersey

services and welfare, to respond to changing community needs and encourage efforts to address significant social problems; and religion.

On the horizon, the foundation identifies the following interests: the problem of homelessness; sensitizing state residents to needs emerging as a result of reduced government spending; and working to lower school dropout rates and insure that effort and good grades will result in job opportunities for young people when they graduate from high school.

Financial Data (year ended 6/30/87)

Support and revenue:[1]	$	1,609,605
Total grants paid:	$	350,027
Number of grants paid:		66
Highest grant:	$	92,892
Lowest grant:	$	25
Median grant size:	$	2,000

Application Procedures

There are no application deadlines; proposed projects are reviewed throughout the year. Potential applicants are urged to review the foundation's program priorities as they appear in its annual report and then contact the program officer to discuss the concepts and potential of their program. Applicants may, alteratively, send a one-page letter explaining the scope of the project for which funds are sought. If the project addresses an area of interest to the community and a strong need is demonstrated, additional materials may be requested and a meeting set up.

Grant Limitations

The foundation makes grants only for charitable or educational activities serving the residents of the state. Grants from its unrestricted fund are not made for operating budgets, capital needs, or sectarian, religious programs and grants are not made to individuals.

---

[1]This figure and the analysis below combine the foundation's operating fund and restricted funds. While the foundation's annual report distinguishes each fund's revenue, its list of grants does not separate unrestricted from restricted payments.

Community Foundation of New Jersey

Meeting Times
The board of trustees of the Community Foundation of New Jersey meets six times a year to consider grant proposals.

Publications
The foundation publishes an annual report.

The Crossroads Fund
343 South Dearborn, Suite 604
Chicago, Illinois 60604
(312) 987-0941

Contact Persons
Jacqueline Schad, Executive Director
Judy Hatcher, Associate Director

Purpose
The Crossroads Fund is a publicly supported foundation that provides grants and technical assistance to grassroots organizations working for progressive social change in the Chicago area. Crossroads supports social change nationally and internationally through its participation in the New York-based Funding Exchange.[1]

Areas of Interest
Crossroads invites applications from organizations that are: (1) working for a society free of discrimination based on race, sex, age, religion, economic status, sexual preference, ethnic background, or physical and mental disabilities; (2) struggling for the rights of workers; (3) promoting self-determination in low-income and disenfranchised communities; (4) creating alternative arts and media linked to the struggle for social change; (5) promoting international peace and a just U.S. foreign policy; and/or (6) defending political and human rights.

Priority is given to those groups that operate in the Chicago metropolitan area, that are based in minority and other oppressed communities, that operate in a democratic manner and are responsive to the constituencies they serve, that provide direct services only when tied to social-change programs or when they are likely to empower the communities served, and that may have difficulty securing funding from larger private and public funding sources.

---

[1]For more information about The Funding Exchange, its programs, and other members, see the entry under National Grantmakers for "The Funding Exchange."

The Crossroads Fund

Financial Data (year ended 12/31/86)

Support and revenue:	$	242,381
Total grants paid:	$	124,181
Number of grants paid:		72
Highest grant:	$	5,450
Lowest grant:	$	50
Median grant size:	$	2,000

Application Procedures

Organizations interested in applying should telephone or write the fund to request an application packet. Deadlines for submitting applications change each year, so applicants should contact Crossroads for specific information.

The grantmaking committee of the fund screens proposals and selects the strongest applications for interviews by members of the Crossroads board. Any group not funded on its initial application may reapply at the next deadline. Organizations receiving a grant must wait one year before reapplying.

Grant Limitations

The Crossroads Fund cannot support groups that do not have tax-exempt status or do not conduct charitable activities. In addition, The Crossroads Fund does not generally support groups whose sole purpose is to provide direct services, groups with access to traditional funding sources, and individuals.

Meeting Times

The board of directors of The Crossroads Fund meets bimonthly, and funding decisions are made twice a year.

Publications

The Crossroads Fund publishes an annual report, funding guidelines, application materials, and grants lists.

Patrick and Anna M. Cudahy Fund
Post Office Box 11978
Milwaukee, Wisconsin 53211
(414) 271–6020

Contact Person
Judith Borchers, OSB, Executive Director

Purpose
The Patrick and Anna M. Cudahy Fund is a general purpose, family foundation that directs most of its support to local organizations in Chicago and Milwaukee. However, on rare occasions grants are made to national groups.

Areas of Interest
The fund's interests are broad. A review of its 1985 and 1986 grants lists suggests four program areas: identification with the dispossessed (including international relief, international self-development projects, advocacy organizations working for systemic change, domestic relief organizations, and domestic self-development projects working for local community change); persistent national issues (including education, arms control, environment, farm policies, race relations, and economics); institutional support (including higher education, youth-serving agencies, inner-city education, elderly, medical, disabled, pregnancy prevention, and religion); and arts and culture.

It should be noted that when this material was being prepared, the fund was undergoing an assessment of its program interests that are likely to change.

Financial Data (year ended 12/31/86)

Assets:[1]	$	17,835,873
Total grants paid:	$	1,049,705
Number of grants paid:		103
Highest grant:[2]	$	50,000
Lowest grant:	$	400
Median grant size:	$	8,000

---

[1]At December 31, 1985
[2]This excludes one unusually large grant of $69,200.

Patrick and Anna M. Cudahy Fund

Application Procedures

There are no application deadlines. However, in order to receive prompt consideration, grant proposals must be submitted at least one month prior to the quarterly meetings of the fund's board of directors.

Proposals should include a brief description of the organization, an outline of the proposed project, a financial summary of both the organization and the project, and a copy of the organization's ruling from the IRS classifying it as taxexempt under Section 501(c)(3). Completed proposals will be acknowledged by the fund's staff. Where appropriate, site visits and interviews may be conducted. Groups are informed of the decision of the directors usually within a week of the meeting.

Grant Limitations

The fund does not make grants to individuals, loans, or provide support for endowment funds.

Meeting Times

The board of directors of the Patrick and Anna M. Cudahy Fund meets quarterly, generally in March, June, September, and December.

Publications

The fund distributes application guidelines and a list of recent grantees.

The Aaron Diamond Foundation
1270 Avenue of the Americas, Suite 2624
New York, New York 10020
(212) 757-7680

Contact Persons
Vincent McGee, Executive Director
Kate Chieco, Program Officer
Marsha Bonner, Program Officer
Ann Gael, Grant Administrator

Areas of Interest
The Aaron Diamond Foundation is a private foundation that concentrates
its support on programs and initiatives benefiting the people of New York
City in three program areas: medical research, education, and culture. A
review of its 1987 grants list reveals that within these areas the foundation
has made several grants for AIDS-related medical research. It also supported advocacy efforts by and on behalf of young people (particularly
minorities and new immigrants) related to education and adolescent
pregnancy prevention; international human rights organizations, and arms
control education projects; and groups working to protect civil rights
and civil liberties, especially freedom of speech.

Financial Data (year ended 12/31/87)

Assets:[1]	$ 132,830,831
Total grants paid:	$ 8,907,978
Number of grants paid:	189
Highest grant:[2]	$ 341,500
Lowest grant:	$ 500
Median grant size:	$ 25,000

Application Procedures
There are no deadlines for submitting proposals. Initial contact with the
foundation should be a letter of request addressed to the executive
director. A short proposal should be enclosed. The proposal should provide a history of the project, an outline of the goals to be achieved and
the methods by which they will be accomplished, a budget, and a schedule
for implementing the proposed activity. Applicants are requested to in-

[1]As of December 31, 1986
[2]This excludes a one-time out-of-program grant of $500,000.

497

The Aaron Diamond Foundation

clude their most recent annual financial statement, a list of board members and financial supporters, and a copy of the letter from the IRS certifying that the applicant is a public charity, or its equivalent, under Section 501(c)(3) of the Internal Revenue Code. The foundation staff will respond to each applicant in writing and may request additional materials or a meeting.

Grant Limitations
The foundation accepts proposals only from organizations and projects in New York City. It does not support projects concerning the AIDS crisis that are not strictly biomedical research; capital projects such as buildings, renovations, land purchases, and endowments; any projects related to theater; or private schools. The foundation does not make grants to individuals, to fund specific artistic productions, films, or book projects, nor does it make loans.

Meeting Times
The board of directors of The Aaron Diamond Foundation meets four times a year on a flexible schedule.

Publications
The foundation publishes guidelines for applicants, and a grant report for 1986 and 1987 is forthcoming.

The Discount Foundation
37 Temple Place, Third Floor
Boston, Massachusetts 02111
(617) 426–7471

Contact Person
Susan Chin, Executive Director

Purpose
The Discount Foundation is a private foundation that supports charitable and educational activities designed to achieve progressive social change by means of citizen organizing in the northeastern quadrant of the United States.

Areas of Interest
In 1988 the foundation focused on organizations working on housing-policy reform and/or empowering low-income minority citizens. At the February 1988 board meeting, only applications related to housing were considered. Within this area, the foundation was looking for organizing activities directed toward systemic public policy remedies for the declining availability and affordability of decent housing for low-income people with a particular focus on the preservation of low-cost housing (including publicly assisted housing). At the 1989 meeting, the foundation will consider proposals specifically from organizations in poor minority communities as well as organizations seeking housing policy reform.

Because the current program areas are new and the guidelines may change, interested applicants are urged to contact the foundation and request current program and application information before preparing a proposal.

Financial Data (year ended 9/30/87)
Support and revenue:[1]	$	329,142
Total grants paid:	$	245,000
Number of grants paid:		37
Highest grant:	$	15,000
Lowest grant:	$	2,000
Median grant size:	$	7,500

[1]For the 12 months ended June 30, 1986.

The Discount Foundation

Application Procedures

Applications are considered once a year. In 1987 the filing deadline was November 30. Applicants should contact the foundation for current deadline information.

The foundation requires that specific documents be assembled and submitted as part of an application. The format is clearly described in the foundation's statement of application requirements. In addition to the submission of a comprehensive proposal, an organizational and (if appropriate) project budget, and proof of Section 501(c)(3) tax-exempt status, the foundation requires that a three-page summary of the proposed activities be prepared. Among other things, the summary must include: (1) a detailed narrative statement of the applicant's purpose, objectives, and their social importance, with specific reference to the foundation's substantive and geographic interests; (2) past accomplishments; and (3) references.

Grant Limitations

The foundation supports activities only in the northeast United States, i.e., Connecticut, Delaware, Illinois, Indiana, Kentucky, Maine, Maryland, Massachusetts, Michigan, New Hampshire, New Jersey, New York, Ohio, Pennsylvania, Rhode Island, Vermont, Virginia, Washington, D.C., West Virginia, and Wisconsin. Grants are made only to publicly supported charitable organizations whose Section 501(c)(3) status is confirmed by a current IRS determination or ruling letter. Applications intended to support projects or individuals may be submitted by a qualified sponsoring organization.

Meeting Times

The board of directors of The Discount Foundation meets twice a year, in the spring and fall.

Publications

The foundation does not publish an annual report. Application guidelines are distributed upon request.

EMSA Fund, Inc.
20 Westminster Drive
Atlanta, Georgia 30309
(404) 874-8877

Contact Person
Alice Franklin, President

Areas of Interest
The EMSA Fund, Inc., is a small, unstaffed family foundation. Its grant-making is focused on progressive grassroots organizations that promote self-determination in low-income and traditionally disenfranchised communities, protect the environment, create alternative visual and performing arts, and address responsible foreign policy and peace.

It prefers advocacy organizations rather than direct service providers and rarely funds activities with broad public appeal and support. Most of its grants are directed toward local organizations in Georgia and Colorado, although awards are occasionally made to national organizations headquartered in these two states.

Financial Data (year ended 12/31/86)

Assets:[1]	$	1,430,860
Total grants paid:[2]	$	63,450
Number of grants paid:		56
Highest grant:[3]	$	5,000
Lowest grant:	$	25
Median grant size:	$	200

Application Procedures
The fund does not use application forms and has no deadlines. All inquiries should be in writing. As an initial contact, the fund prefers to receive a brief (two pages maximum) letter explaining the organization seeking funds and the proposed project, the need to be met, past accomplishments and disappointments, and expected results. Budget information, including

---

[1]This figure is an approximation of the foundation's assets.
[2]The fund made several major commitments to well-established institutions for the three years 1986 through 1988. Thereafter it is expected that the total grants budget will increase, as will the number of grants to progressive organizations.
[3]This excludes one unusually large grant of $30,250.

EMSA Fund, Inc.

the specific amount requested from the fund, should be provided, as well as proof of tax-exempt status (or proof of the tax-exempt status of a solid fiscal sponsor). Supporting materials such as brochures or newspaper clippings may be submitted. If additional information is needed, the fund will contact the applicant.

Grant Limitations
The fund does not make grants to individuals, for disease research, or to organizations with broad public appeal.

Meeting Times
Decisions on grant requests are made by the EMSA Fund, Inc., at least quarterly.

Publications
None.

Fel-Pro/Mecklenburger Foundation
7450 North McCormick Boulevard
P.O. Box 1103
Skokie, Illinois 60076-8103
(312) 761-4500
(312) 674-7700
(312) 674-7701, ext. 411 (direct dial)

Contact Person
Celene Peurye, Director, Corporate Contributions Program

Purpose
Fel-Pro is a privately held, family-owned company that manufactures and markets automotive and industrial gaskets, sealing products, and specialized lubricants. The activities of the foundation focus specifically on the communities and neighborhoods where the company operates and where its employees live in the six-county Chicago metropolitan area.

The foundation supports both special projects and general operating needs of organizations whose programs meet one or more of the following criteria: serving significant numbers of Fel-Pro employees; serving disadvantaged community areas or advocating for the disadvantaged; and serving the community's general population, particularly as it reflects the diverse multiethnic and racial composition of the Fel-Pro workforce.

Areas of Interest
The foundation has four programs for supporting eligible organizations: a grants program, in-kind contributions, the Fel-Pro Matching Gifts Program, and the employee administered Fel-Pro Better Neighborhood Fund. The grants program and neighborhood fund are described below. Information about in-kind and matching contributions is available by writing to the director of the corporate contributions program.

The grants program has three components: general program grants made in response to unsolicited proposals, foundation-initiated programs grants made in response to a specific request for proposals (RFP) issued by the foundation, and employee-initiated program grants, which include the Fel-Pro Better Neighborhood Fund.

General program grants are made in five areas: advocacy, corporate social responsibility, environment, human services, and vocational training. Each is briefly described below.

Fel-Pro/Mecklenburger Foundation

Advocacy. The foundation supports organizations working for causes such as affirmative action, civil rights, legal aid, and consumer information. It also supports efforts to address the underlying societal conditions that contribute to the needs served by the foundation in the areas of human services and vocational training described below.

Corporate Social Responsibility. Support is offered to promote, study, or implement programs incorporating social responsibility and ethics in business, especially in the automotive industry and related fields.

Environment. The foundation's interest in the environment provides the basis for supporting organizations which advocate for the environmental needs and interests of employees and which serve to protect or enhance natural resources, land, parks, and recreation areas in and adjacent to the urban areas in which Fel-Pro employees live.

Human Services. In this program area, contributions are made primarily to programs serving key neighborhoods where Fel-Pro employees reside or that address special problems of concern to Fel-Pro employees. Priority is given to programs or organizations that provide direct services relevant to the Fel-Pro workforce; serve basic human needs; are accessible by location, service philosophy, and delivery to the general population, particularly minorities, women, and other disadvantaged groups; and are community-based.

Vocational Training. Contributions in this interest area are made primarily to organizations whose programs address employment needs of minorities and women. Priority is given to community-based programs that provide training for jobs in the automotive industry, industries projected to have significant growth, or in nontraditional occupations. Particular consideration may be given to programs that take a comprehensive approach to the needs of trainees by, for example, providing supportive services that enable a trainee to participate in the program.

Fel-Pro/Mecklenburger Foundation

Foundation-initiated program grants are made in areas of special interest to the foundation. In 1986 a number of grants were made in a specific neighborhood. In addition, there was particular interest in two areas, human needs and culture, with the latter limited to a select number of museums, zoos, and public radio and television stations. A number of special grants were also made to organizations working against apartheid in South Africa. Proposals from eligible organizations are accepted only when they are received in response to a foundation-initiated RFP. For information to determine whether your organization qualifies for a foundation-initiated program grant, contact the director of the corporate contributions program in writing.

The Fel-Pro Better Neighborhood Fund is administered by an employee committee. Support is available to community-based organizations in all program categories, with special attention given to social welfare, youth, economic development, and community revitalization. Educational agencies such as day care programs and public and private schools may also be eligible. Applications must be endorsed by a Fel-Pro employee and must include evidence of participation by that employee or by a member of his or her immediate family. Organizations seeking support from this program should first ascertain whether a Fel-Pro employee is involved in their activities. A special application form is available only to the employee through the Fel-Pro personnel department.

Financial Data (year ended 12/31/86)
Assets: $ 5,094,799

General and Foundation-Initiated Grants
Total grants paid:[1]	$	878,519
Numbers of grants paid:		131
Highest grant:	$	160,000
Lowest grant:	$	100
Median grant size:	$	2,000

[1] These tabulations do not include 147 matching gifts, totaling $21,544, made by the foundation.

Fel-Pro/Mecklenburger Foundation

Better Neighborhood Fund

Total grants paid:	$	114,653
Numbers of grants paid:		148
Highest grant:	$	1,500
Lowest grant:	$	74
Median grant size:	$	750

Application Procedures

As noted above, unsolicited proposals are not accepted for foundation-initiated program grants or for the Fel-Pro Better Neighborhood Fund. These programs require a RFP and special application form, respectively.

For organizations seeking a general program grant, there are no formal application deadlines, and the foundation does not require the completion of specific forms. Rather, applicants must submit a concise statement of the following: the organization's history, purpose, and achievements; how the program serves Fel-Pro communities, employees, and other foundation priorities; whether the request is for support of a special project or for general operating purposes. Also included should be a current budget for the whole organization and, if appropriate, a special project, as well as budgets for the previous year; audited financial statements for the last complete fiscal year, a letter of auditability, or other evidence of sound fiscal management; proof of tax-exempt status; a list of officers and board members showing their affiliations; a list of current corporate, foundation, or major individual donors; and a list of accrediting agencies, if appropriate.

All eligible requests to the foundation are acknowledged. A site visit or interview may be scheduled at the foundation's initiative with representatives of the applicant's staff or board.

Grant Limitations

Grants are generally restricted to the six-county Chicago metropolitan area and primarily focused in Cook County. Within these boundaries, priority in reviewing requests is given to programs serving key neighborhoods where Fel-Pro employees reside and communities adjacent to the company's plant and headquarters.

Fel-Pro/Mecklenburger Foundation

The foundation generally declines to support organizations not meeting its guidelines and those that are not classified as tax exempt under Section 501(c)(3) of the Internal Revenue Code; hospitals, research associations, and health-related organizations; conferences, institutes, and special events; religious or political organizations, including lobbying groups; organizations receiving support through federated campaigns supported by the foundation; individuals; organizations that have received a contribution from the foundation during the previous twelve-month period; organizations whose solicitations are simply direct mail appeals; capital campaigns or endowment funds; and ad books or goodwill advertising, tickets, raffles, benefits, and other events.

Meeting Times
General program grants are reviewed bimonthly by the board of directors of the Fel-Pro/Mecklenburger Foundation. Foundation-initiated program grants are reviewed annually, and employee-initiated program grants are reviewed monthly.

Publications
The foundation publishes guidelines on its programs.

Samuel S. Fels Fund
2214 Land Title Building
100 South Broad Street
Philadelphia, Pennsylvania 19110
(215) 567-2808

Contact Person
Kathryn Smith Pyle, Executive Director

Purpose
The Samuel S. Fels Fund is a local foundation with interests in human services, education, the arts, and scientific research. Within these broad categories, the fund seeks to support projects that help to demonstrate and evaluate ways to prevent, lessen, or resolve contemporary social problems, or that seek to provide permanent improvement in the provision of services. The fund's interest in scientific research is largely limited to support for scientific institutions established by Mr. Fels during his lifetime.

Areas of Interest
The fund's priorities are organizations and projects located within the city of Philadelphia and directed toward making permanent improvements in community services, specifically in the areas of education, science and health, the arts, and community programs. The fund prefers to make grants on a modest scale that will have maximum impact upon institutions and service patterns in Philadelphia. Priority is given to innovative projects with strong evaluation components. The fund seeks programs that monitor public responsibilities, strengthen neighborhood life, improve public education, and provide forums for public issues. The fund also promotes increased stability for arts organizations.

Financial Data (year ended 12/31/86)

Assets:	$ 26,910,310
Total grants paid:	$ 763,183
Number of grants paid:	131
Highest grant:[1]	$ 60,000
Lowest grant:	$ 500
Median grant size:	$ 4,568

---

[1] This figure omits three major grants of $125,000 and over for research, university chair endowment, and professional education and training.

Samuel S. Fels Fund

Application Procedures

Grant proposals are considered throughout the year, except for arts applications, which are reviewed only twice annually, in January and June. In general, the fund accepts only one proposal from an organization per year. The fund provides applicants with a proposal outline on request. Preliminary inquiries concerning possible applications may be made by telephone. The fund specifically discourages preliminary letters or abbreviated proposals, since only full proposals are accepted for board consideration.

The full proposal should include a cover sheet (provided by the fund). The body of the proposal should include, in no more than five pages, the following information: (1) a summary of the proposal; (2) background on the organization, including its history and the history of the problem to be addressed, its purpose and goals, a summary of activities and accomplishments (with highlights of the past year, including people involved and specific events), the constituency or membership, and a description of interaction with other organizations; (3) the funding request and plans for the coming year, including a description of the organization (or project) program objectives and events and activities planned, number of people involved, number of staff involved, and a timetable; and (4) a description of how the program will be evaluated.

Attachments should include résumés of top staff; a board of directors list including addresses and occupation (indicating any minority, low-income, consumer and/or neighborhood representatives); an annual operating budget for the organization and a project budget (if appropriate); a list of funding sources including past major contributors and amounts, recent applications with results, and anticipated future funding sources; a recent financial statement (audited if available); an annual report (if available); relevant newspaper or magazine articles about the organization's program; and a copy of the most recent IRS letter certifying the applicant's tax-exempt status (and a copy of the IRS letter formally approving a change of name, if appropriate).

Notification of approval or nonapproval of a grant is usually provided within two weeks after a decision by the board of directors. Progress reports from approved grantees stating what has been accomplished and

Samuel S. Fels Fund

providing appropriate financial reports are required by the fund at least annually.

Grant Limitations

The fund generally excludes from its grantmaking program contributions to building and development funds, scholarships, fellowships, and grants-in-aid to individuals for travel. Ordinarily the fund also avoids making grants for continuing major programs of large institutions and contributions to endowment funds and to national organizations.

Meeting Times

The board of directors of the Samuel S. Fels Fund meets monthly to consider grant applications.

Publications

The fund publishes an annual report and will make available upon request a fact sheet about its grantmaking program.

Field Foundation of Illinois, Inc.
135 South LaSalle Street
Chicago, Illinois 60603
(312) 263-3211

Contact Person
Handy L. Lindsey, Jr., Executive Director

Purpose
The Field Foundation of Illinois, Inc., states that its sole objective is to play a constructive and responsible role in meeting the diverse and ever-changing needs of the greater Chicago area. The foundation makes an effort to achieve a balance between supporting young, struggling, grass-roots, community-based programs and older, established institutions.

Areas of Interest
The foundation considers only applications in the fields of health, welfare, education, cultural activities, and civic affairs from institutions and agencies primarily serving the people of the Chicago metropolitan area.

The distribution of grants paid during the 1985–1986 fiscal period was as follows: 19 percent of the grants budget went for cultural programs, including conservation; 21 percent of the year's grants went to community welfare programs; another 21 percent was awarded to education programs; 24 percent went for health; and 15 percent of the grant moneys went toward addressing the urban crisis.

In considering applications, the board of directors attempts to ascertain the social need for the specific program or project, and the applicant organization's ability to meet this need effectively, including proper control of expenses and the use of volunteers.

Financial Data (year ended 4/30/86)

Assets:	$	24,625,433
Total grants paid:	$	1,574,822
Number of grants paid:		68
Highest grant:	$	70,000
Lowest grant:	$	4,881
Median grant size:	$	17,317

Field Foundation of Illinois, Inc.

Application Procedures

The foundation has no application forms. Letters of request should briefly describe the project, the proposed budget, and the history and background of the organization. All applications must include copies of letters from the IRS indicating the applicant's tax-exempt status under Sections 501(c)(3) and 509(a) of the Internal Revenue Code.

Applications from hospitals have additional criteria that are not repeated here, but which are fully enumerated in the foundation's annual report.

Grant Limitations

The foundation supports only projects primarily serving the people of the Chicago metropolitan area. Operating support of a program will normally be of a short duration, generally one to three years. Requests for continuing operating support will not be considered.

No grants for regular operating support are made to member agencies of the United Way of Metropolitan Chicago, or to member agencies of other community chests in the metropolitan area. The foundation does not support scholarships, fellowships, or other requests from individuals; medical research or national health agency appeals; organizations or committees whose efforts are aimed at influencing legislation; private schools; conferences, seminars, or meetings; the costs of printed materials; organizations working to achieve religious purposes; general operating budgets of neighborhood health centers or clinics, day care centers for children, or small cultural groups.

Meeting Times

The board of directors of the Field Foundation of Illinois, Inc., meets quarterly.

Publications

The foundation publishes an annual report.

Foundation for the Carolinas
301 South Brevard Street
Charlotte, North Carolina 28202
(704) 376-9541

Contact Person
William L. Spencer, President and Chief Professional Officer

Areas of Interest
The Foundation for the Carolinas is a community foundation serving North and South Carolina, with a particular long-standing interest in the Charlotte-Mecklenburg area. Its grantmaking is divided into the following categories: programs for senior adults, human services, education, religion, arts, youth programs, health, public and civic leadership, and environment and historic preservation. In partnership with the Charles Stewart Mott Foundation, a neighborhood grants program was initiated in 1985 to improve low-income communities and strengthen neighborhood leadership.

In distributing its unrestricted grant funds, the foundation gives priority to seed grants to initiate promising new projects, to innovative and efficient approaches for meeting community needs and opportunities, to challenge gifts that require other donors to make matching gifts, to organizations working cooperatively with other programs in their community, and to applicants that demonstrate a plan for funding and likely support from other sources. Most grants are $5,000 and less.

Financial Data (year ended 12/31/86)

Assets:	$	35,753,108
Total grants paid:[1]	$	4,104,342
Number of grants paid:[2]		270
Highest grant:	$	400,000
Lowest grant:	$	2,000
Median grant size:	$	5,000

---

[1] The foundation's annual report does not distinguish between unrestricted grants and grants made at the direction of individual donors. Hence this analysis includes both restricted and unrestricted grants. As a measure of the foundation's growth, it should be noted that during the eleven-month period ended November 30, 1987, the foundation had distributed $6,753,990 in grants.
[2] This grants analysis excludes 537 grants of $2,000 and less totaling $280,678.

513

Foundation for the Carolinas

Application Procedures

The deadlines for submitting complete formal proposals to the foundation are February 1, May 1, August 1, and November 1. The foundation requests that prior to submitting an application form, applicants send the foundation a brief letter of intent, outlining the purpose of the request, how much will be requested, the anticipated date of application, and the current tax status of the organization. Application forms, which must be completed, will then be provided.

Applicants should provide fifteen copies of their proposal and one copy of their most recent audit to the foundation by the required deadline. Attachments to the application form should include a cover letter (not more than two pages) addressing concisely the objectives and background of the project, a demonstrated need for the project, specific plans and timetables, current and long-term funding plans of the organization, and the qualifications of the applicant organization and the personnel who will be responsible for the project. Applicants should also provide an overall budget for the organization as well as a budget for the specific project (showing income and expenditures), a list of members of the applicant organization's governing body, and a copy of the applicant's official notice of tax-exempt status from the Internal Revenue Service.

Grant Limitations

The foundation limits its discretionary funding to organizations recognized by the IRS as tax exempt under Section 501(c)(3) of the Internal Revenue Code and serving the communities from which the foundation derives its support. Generally, the foundation does not support capital campaigns, general operating budgets of existing organizations, publication of books, or conferences.

Meeting Times

The board of directors of the Foundation for the Carolinas meets quarterly to review grant proposals.

Publications

The foundation publishes an annual report.

The Fund for New Jersey
57 Washington Street
East Orange, New Jersey 07017
(201) 676-5905

Contact Person
Mark M. Murphy, Executive Director

Purpose
The purpose of The Fund for New Jersey is to help New Jersey citizens and organizations become both informed on the critical issues facing the state, and effective, responsible participants in efforts to address these issues.

Areas of Interest
The fund's interests span the broad spectrum of serious public policy issues in New Jersey. The fund states explicitly that the parameters of its interests are open-ended, with particular emphasis on public-policy research, oversight of government activities, citizen-action efforts, and collaborative problem-solving programs.

The fund lists its recent grantees in these five broad categories: (1) general information and research efforts (focusing on New Jersey-oriented public issues); (2) public education issues; (3) urban revitalization; (4) environment and land use; and (5) problems of the poor and underrepresented. In addition to its regular grants, the fund made a number of small between-meeting grants of $5,000 or less, available at the discretion of the executive director. The fund will also consider program-related investments within its guidelines.

Financial Data (year ended 12/31/86)
Assets:	$	20,191,159
Total grants awarded:	$	1,086,956
Number of grants awarded:		77
Highest grant:	$	75,000
Lowest grant:	$	326
Median grant size:	$	5,000

Application Procedures
The fund has no application forms. Application should be made in letter or proposal form and should be accompanied by a detailed budget and

515

The Fund for New Jersey

a copy of the organization's determination letter from the IRS indicating tax-exempt status.

The fund has established several specific criteria for reviewing and evaluating the proposals that it receives. The fund does not rely on any mechanical process or quantitative measure of proposed projects. Instead, the following questions are raised:

> 1. How closely does the proposal match the grantmaking priorities of the fund? Does the group seek to effect public policy or does the group provide a service? (Note: eighty-five percent of the fund grants go to activities that encompass effecting public policy and only fifteen percent is reserved for organizations that directly provide services.)
>
> 2. What is the organization's capacity to carry out the proposed project? Is there a rough balance between the organizational objectives and the available administrative, intellectual, and budgetary resources? (The fund examines the organization's recent project record, checks with individuals familiar with the organization and its efforts, reviews publications, reports, and other products of the organization.)
>
> 3. Assuming the group is capable of doing what it proposes, how effective will the program be? Does the organization propose to work on a problem that can reasonably be expected to be modified, corrected, or changed, or is the organization attempting to accomplish the impossible?
>
> 4. What is the financial need of the applicant? What are the other sources of revenue for the project? Are grants available from public agencies for the project and would acceptance of such funds be appropriate for the projects? (Ordinarily the fund will give preference to organizations that cannot or should not accept public funds.)
>
> 5. What is the geographic scope of the organization's activities? Municipal? Regional? Countywide? Statewide? (In general, the fund gives higher priority to projects that seek

The Fund for New Jersey

to affect policy on a statewide basis rather than one that is local.)

6. Are there other organizations that are working on the same problem or in the same field? Is there something special or unique about the applicant organization that should be preserved or strengthened, or if the organization ceased to operate, would its place easily be filled by some other existing group?

Grant Limitations

Grants are made only to organizations that have applied for or received federal tax-exempt status under Section 501(c)(3). In a limited number of cases, the fund will provide new organizations with legal counsel to assist with the incorporation and application for tax exemption.

In addition to the fund's geographical restrictions, applications are not accepted for support of individuals, capital projects (including acquisition, mortgage retirement, renovation, or equipment), and, as a general rule, for day care centers, drug treatment programs, health-care delivery, scholarships, or curricular changes in educational institutions. Only rarely does the fund approve grants to tax-supported agencies.

Meeting Times

The board of trustees of The Fund for New Jersey considers proposals four times per year.

Publications

The fund publishes an annual report and a list of publications produced with its support.

Fund for Southern Communities
552 Hill Street, S.E.
Atlanta, Georgia 30312
(404) 577-3178

Contact Persons
Nan Orrock, Executive Director
Edris Branch, Grants Officer

Purpose
The Fund for Southern Communities supports organizations challenging social, political, and economic injustice in North Carolina, South Carolina, and Georgia. The fund also supports progressive social change nationally and internationally through its participation in the New York-based Funding Exchange.[1]

Areas of Interest
The fund invites applications from organizations: (1) working against discrimination based on race, sex, age, religion, economic status, sexual preference, ethnic background, or physical and mental disabilities; (2) struggling for the rights of workers; (3) promoting self-determination in low income and disenfranchised communities; (4) protecting the environment and developing appropriate technologies; (5) creating alternative arts and media; (6) promoting peace and responsible U.S. foreign policy; and (7) working for an equitable distribution of economic and political power.

A variety of issues are included under the fund's guidelines, which include, but are not limited to, health care, housing, community organizing, women's rights, third world concerns, civil rights, antiracist organizing, workers' rights, lesbian and gay rights, safe energy and appropriate technology, economic development, criminal justice, law reform, alternative culture and media, militarism and peace, international issues, civil liberties, and Native American rights and cultures.

---

[1]For more information about The Funding Exchange, its programs, and other members, see the entry under National Grantmakers for "The Funding Exchange."

Fund for Southern Communities

Financial Data (year ended 6/30/87)[2]

Support and revenue:	$	245,125
Total grants paid:	$	82,760
Number of grants paid:		52
Highest grant:	$	2,600
Lowest grant:	$	560
Median grant size:	$	1,500

Application Procedures

The fund accepts applications throughout the year, and makes grants three times a year, in the spring, summer, and fall. To obtain an application, telephone or write to the fund. Staff is available to answer questions about eligibility before an application is completed. All applicants are required to submit an eight-page request consisting of a four-page application form plus a four-page narrative. Complete instructions come with the application package.

After an initial review of the applications, the board selects the strongest proposals and requests interviews. At this time applicants no longer under consideration are notified. Following a second evaluation by the board, final decisions are made. The whole process takes about three months.

Grant Limitations

Although requests must be submitted from projects or programs operating in North Carolina, South Carolina, or Georgia, a project may operate in one or more of these states. The fund awards seed grants to new projects, and general support and project grants to small organizations. Applicants with an annual budget of $20,000 or more must request support for a specified purpose; grants to these organizations are not made for general support. Direct-service applicants are discouraged from applying, unless the services are tied to social-change programs or are likely to empower the community to be served.

---

[2]This analysis includes only unrestricted funds and grants from those funds.

519

Fund for Southern Communities

Meeting Times
The board of directors of the Fund for Southern Communities meets three times a year to make grant awards.

Publications
The fund publishes an annual report, grants listings, a quarterly newsletter, brochures, and application forms.

Fund for the City of New York
121 Sixth Avenue, 6th Floor
New York, New York 10013
(212) 925–6675

Contact Person
Anita Nager, Grants Administrator

Purpose
The Fund for the City of New York is a public operating foundation, established by the Ford Foundation in 1968, to be alert to opportunities to improve the quality of life in the city and the management of the public business. The fund both initiates programs and responds to requests from others.

Areas of Interest
In its grantmaking and in its operating programs, the fund concentrates on children and youth, housing, and recently the AIDS epidemic. At the same time, the fund takes the full range of government and nonprofit activities in New York City as its field of endeavor, and is prepared to consider contributions to any promising and significant opportunity to improve things. The fund looks for promising new ideas, projects, leaders, and for opportunities where private help will make public resources go further. It selects projects based upon the importance of the problems they address, the ability and track record of the people who are proposing them or would carry them out, and the degree to which the fund has anything special to offer.

Four kinds of grants are made by the fund: (1) grants to advocacy organizations—watchdog grants—to help strengthen government accountability; (2) general support grants to outstanding service delivery agencies to help identify best practice and to encourage the survival and growth of excellent programs; (3) short-term consultancy grants to allow the managers of government and nonprofit agencies to engage expert assistance to turn good ideas into workable propositions and to get through other sticking points in developing and improving programs; (4) incubator grants to provide a temporary home, organizational support, and cash assistance to important new institutions and programs.

In addition to its grantmaking, the fund operates several projects. Of significant importance is the Cash Flow Loan Program. Established in

Fund for the City of New York

1976, the fund makes bridge loans of $10,000 or less to small nonprofit New York City organizations against government grants and contracts that have been delayed in bureaucratic processing. The fund also operates a special loan program in cooperation with the New York City Department of Housing Preservation and Development for housing administrators. Cash flow loans range from $2,000 to $10,000. Another program inaugurated in 1986 is the Nonprofit Computer Exchange, designed to meet the need for computer-related research and support services for groups seeking to computerize.

Financial Data (year ended 9/30/87)

Support and revenue:	$	1,527,135
Total grants paid:	$	271,217
Number of grants paid:		32
Highest grant:	$	50,000
Lowest grant:	$	700
Median grant size:	$	7,500

Application Procedures

Organizations interested in applying to the fund for an outright grant should submit a brief letter describing the project. Once the fund determines that the proposed project is appropriate to its guidelines, specific application instructions will be forwarded to the applicant.

Applications to the Cash Flow Loan Program, on the other hand, are usually initiated during a telephone conversation between the fund and the potential borrower. During that conversation, the fund ascertains whether the group has a government contract, whether the delay in payments has caused severe cash flow problems, and other realistic sources of assistance. The group is then asked to submit a letter containing: (1) a brief program description; (2) details on the government contract, its purpose, amount, and status within the bureaucracy; (3) the reasons that a loan is required, how much is needed, and exactly how the funds would be used; (4) a definite repayment schedule based on when moneys are expected from the funding source; and (5) the name and phone number

Fund for the City of New York

of an official who can verify the information provided. Applicants must also submit copies of their tax-exempt status and most recent financial report. Loans may be denied if a group has too many outstanding loans, the organization is unstable, or its cash flow problems are caused by poor management. The average time between request and loan delivery is three to five working days.

The fund assumes the administrative costs of the loan program, but the cost of the fund's borrowing is passed on to the loan recipients via a two percent service charge that is deducted from the loans when they are made. If the fund is repaid in full within two months or less, one-half of the service charge is refunded.

Grant Limitations
The fund makes grants in New York City only. The fund does not provide grants to cover deficits of ongoing programs, simple expansion, or projects that are part of the normal expenses of government. The fund does not assume long-term funding responsibilities for any group or project, nor does it fund academic studies.

Meeting Times
The board of directors of the Fund for the City of New York meets five times a year.

Publications
The fund publishes a report every three years, and will make available information about its loan program and computer exchange upon request.

The Wallace Alexander Gerbode Foundation
470 Columbus Avenue, Suite 201
San Francisco, California 94133
(415) 391-0911

Contact Person
Thomas C. Layton, Executive Director

Purpose
The Wallace Alexander Gerbode Foundation is primarily interested in innovative positive programs directly impacting residents of the five Bay Area counties (Alameda, Contra Costa, Marin, San Francisco, and San Mateo) and the state of Hawaii. The foundation will, on occasion and as a second priority, award grants to efforts that it finds exceptionally compelling in other northern California communities.

Areas of Interest
The foundation's interests generally fall into the following categories: arts, education, environment, health, and urban affairs.

Financial Data (year ended 12/31/86)
As of December 31, 1986, the assets of the foundation were $31,376,387. The foundation makes both grants and program-related investments. These are analyzed separately below.

Grant Awards
Total grants approved:	$	1,647,245
Number of grants approved:		114
Highest grant:[1]	$	75,000
Lowest grant:	$	500
Median grant size:	$	6,500

Program-related Investments
Total PRIs approved:	$	800,000
Number of PRIs approved:		5
Highest PRI:	$	250,000
Lowest PRI:	$	100,000
Median PRI size:	$	100,000

[1]This excludes one unusually large grant of $225,000 payable over three years to the National Hispanic University.

The Wallace Alexander Gerbode Foundation

Application Procedures
There is no standard format for application to the foundation, and proposals are accepted throughout the year. The foundation prefers that initial contact be made in a letter of inquiry, including a short description of the project and the proposed budget.

Grant Limitations
The foundation generally does not support direct services, deficit budgets, general operating funds, building and equipment funds, endowments, general fund-raising campaigns, religious purposes, publications, scholarships, and grants to individuals.

Meeting Times
The board of directors of The Wallace Alexander Gerbode Foundation meets six times per year.

Publications
The foundation publishes an annual report. A statement of program policy and grant application guidelines is available upon request.

The Benjamin S. Gerson Family Foundation
5 Sherwood Court
Beachwood, Ohio 44122
(216) 464-0621

Contact Person
Eleanor Gerson, Chairperson

Purpose
The Benjamin S. Gerson Family Foundation is a small, unstaffed grant-maker. It was established in 1973 to support organizations working to effect progressive social change, remedy inequities, increase access of opportunity, and promote self-help, as well as those organizations working for preservation of existing freedoms and values.

Areas of Interest
Grants are made in a number of areas, including programs for women, civil rights and civil liberties, and local community organizations. Grants for operational programs are almost always confined to the greater Cleveland area. However, grants may be made to national organizations working on issues of concern to the foundation.

Financial Data (year ended 12/31/87)

Assets:[1]	$	2,286,000
Total grants paid:	$	95,000
Number of grants paid:		19
Highest grant:	$	5,000
Lowest grant:	$	1,000
Median grant size:	$	4,000

Application Procedures
The deadline for submitting applications is October 31. Interested applicants are encouraged to telephone the foundation to discuss a request prior to submitting a formal proposal. There are different requirements depending on the amount requested, and brief, concise proposals are appreciated.

Requests for over $1,000 require the submission of a cover letter

---

[1]Approximate market value as of January 31, 1988

The Benjamin S. Gerson Family Foundation

summarizing the request and a formal proposal. The letter, no more than two typewritten pages, must state the need to be addressed, the objectives of the program, how the funds will be used, the expected outcomes, and the anticipated length of the project. The formal proposal should include a short history of the organization and its current activities; a statement of the need or problem to be addressed (with reference to specific objectives, plans for implementation, and staff qualifications); and the project's budget, other sources of funding, and plans for future funding if the project is to be ongoing. Copies of the organization's proof of tax-exempt status, current budget, annual report, and audited financial statements should also be provided. The contact person's name, title, and telephone number should also be clearly identified. Additional supporting materials may also be included. Two copies must be provided.

For requests of $1,000 or less, information should include a summary of the organization's history and purpose, a description of the objectives of the request, the need to be met, the amount requested for the project, and the total cost of the project. An indication of the organization's viability, current budget, and annual report, along with a description of board and staff and evidence of tax-exempt status are required. Two copies should be provided.

Grant Limitations
The foundation does not provide support for individuals, religious purposes, or to meet budget deficits. Requests for capital campaigns, endowments, conferences, and research are funded only infrequently.

Meeting Times
The board of directors of The Benjamin S. Gerson Family Foundation meets once a year, in January, to consider grant requests.

Publications
The foundation distributes guidelines upon request.

Richard and Rhoda Goldman Fund
1090 Sansome Street, 3rd Floor
San Francisco, California 94111
(415) 788-1090

Contact Person
Duane Silverstein, Executive Director

Purpose
The purpose of the Richard and Rhoda Goldman Fund is broadly defined to support programs that will enhance the quality of life of residents of the San Francisco Bay Area, and grants are restricted to projects in this geographic region.

Areas of Interest
The fund directs the majority of its grants toward organizations and projects addressing problems related to the elderly, the environment, and civic affairs. Education, health, and social services are also areas of interest, and work on issues of peace and disarmament receives modest support.

Financial Data (year ended 10/31/87)

Assets:	$ 4,643,000
Total grants paid:	$ 414,583
Number of grants paid:	51
Highest grant:	$ 50,000
Lowest grant:[1]	$ 1,250
Median grant size:	$ 7,500

Application Procedures
To initiate a grant request to the fund, write a brief letter of inquiry, including a description of the project and budget information. The fund responds to all personal letters of inquiry but does not acknowledge mass mailings and form letters. If the fund is interested in potentially supporting a project, additional information will be requested of the applicant. There are no application deadlines.

---

[1]These computations do not include eight grants of $1,000 and less which were made completely at the discretion of the board of trustees and not in response to grant applications.

Richard and Rhoda Goldman Fund

Grant Limitations

The fund does not support projects outside the San Francisco Bay Area. It generally does not support deficit budgets, endowments, general fund-raising campaigns, conferences, building funds, general operating budgets of established organizations, grants or scholarships to individuals, or basic research. It will consider applications only from organizations certified by the IRS as public charities.

Meeting Times

Decisions on grant applications are made quarterly by the board of directors of the Richard and Rhoda Goldman Fund.

Publications

The fund will distribute an annual report upon request.

Morris Goldseker Foundation of Maryland, Inc.
5 East Read Street
Baltimore, Maryland 21202
(301) 837-5100

Contact Person
Timothy D. Armbruster, President

Purpose
The purposes of the Morris Goldseker Foundation of Maryland, Inc., are
to improve broadly the quality of life in metropolitan Baltimore with a
special emphasis on programs that serve the disadvantaged. Of particular
interest are programs that increase access and opportunity, promote
independence and personal achievement, strengthen institutions and systems of delivery, attract other resources, improve efficiency of operations,
address long-term solutions to community problems, strengthen neighborhoods, and strengthen the private, nonprofit sector.

Areas of Interest
The foundation has identified five program interests: community affairs,
education, housing, human services, and medicine and public health. It
has elected, however, not to set specific priorities within these areas,
preferring to maintain the greatest possible flexibility to initiate projects
and respond to changing community needs.

Applicants are encouraged to demonstrate how ongoing programs,
once initiated, will be sustained, as usually the foundation does not award
grants for longer than one year and does not consider itself a long-term
source of funds. Priority is given to projects not normally financed with
public funds.

Financial Data (two-years ended 12/31/86)
Assets:	$ 35,299,537
Total grants awarded:	$ 1,904,748
Number of grants:	47
Highest grant:	$ 160,000
Lowest grant:	$ 500
Median grant size:	$ 25,500

Morris Goldseker Foundation of Maryland, Inc.

Application Procedures

To apply for support, a brief preliminary letter describing the project should be submitted to the foundation. The letter should include background information about the applicant, a statement of need and objectives, methods for accomplishing objectives, a proposed program budget, and the amount sought from the foundation. Evidence of Section 501(c)(3) and 509(a) tax-exempt status should also be provided. The foundation staff will review the materials and promptly notify applicants if a more fully developed proposal is appropriate. If so, a Proposal Development Form and appropriate guidelines will be supplied, and the staff will answer questions and provide such other assistance as may be necessary.

Preliminary letters and grant proposals are welcomed throughout the year; however, there are specific deadlines for submitting fully developed proposals. These deadlines are December 1, April 1, and August 1. Applicants are advised to submit preliminary letters as early as possible before the deadlines, because the proposal development process may be time-consuming.

Grant Limitations

The foundation does not consider advocacy and/or political action groups as prime interests for grantmaking. It does not have a program in cultural affairs, and does not award grants in support of endowments, individuals, building campaigns, deficit financing, annual giving, publications, and religious purposes. Usually the foundation does not award grants in support of operating budgets, and grants are not typically made to organizations formed for the purpose of raising or allocating funds. Grant activities are restricted to the Baltimore metropolitan area, and principally Baltimore City.

Meeting Times

The selection committee and trustees of the Morris Goldseker Foundation of Maryland, Inc., consider grant requests three times annually, in March, June, and October.

Morris Goldseker Foundation of Maryland, Inc.

Publications

The foundation publishes an annual report and a brochure outlining program guidelines.

Philip L. Graham Fund
1150 15th Street, N.W.
Washington, D.C. 20071
(202) 334-6640

Contact Person
Mary Bellor, Secretary

Purpose
The Philip L. Graham Fund has as its purpose the awarding of grants for charitable, scientific, literary, and educational concerns, including raising the standards of excellence in professional journalism and helping to enhance and improve the quality of life in communities where The Washington Post Company has business interests.[1]

Areas of Interest
The fund conducts its grantmaking activity in two broadly defined categories, journalism and community assistance. Journalism grants are directed to academic programs, chairs, and professorships at the post-graduate level; minority journalist training and scholarship; legal and First Amendment concerns; and programs whose goal is to improve the practice of professional journalism.

Community assistance grants are made in the areas of arts and humanities, civic and community projects, education, and health and human services to support special needs or projects of organizations formed in and operating for the benefit of communities in which The Washington Post Company has a significant business presence. Of particular interest are programs that address a specific need, promote self-sufficiency or produce lasting benefit. Among the issues addressed by the fund's 1986 grantees were hunger, homelessness, infant care, battered women, and educational enrichment programs. Grants from the fund went to support such programs and activities as direct services, building funds, capital campaigns, and litigation.

---

[1] As of December 1987, The Washington Post Company had business interests in the District of Columbia; Detroit, Michigan; Jacksonville, Florida; and Hartford, Connecticut.

Philip L. Graham Fund

Financial Data (year ended 12/31/86)

Assets:	$ 48,113,844
Total grants paid:	$ 1,750,300
Number of grants:	91
Highest grant paid:	$ 100,000
Lowest grant paid:	$ 3,000
Median grant size:	$ 10,000

Application Procedures

Deadlines for receipt of proposals are April 1, August 1, and November 1. The fund has no application forms. The preferred format is a brief letter containing the following information: (1) a general statement describing the organization, its purposes, and its goals; (2) a description of the project for which funding is sought and its anticipated benefits; (3) a project budget; (4) the specific amount requested from the fund and a list of other funding sources from which the organization is seeking assistance, if any; (5) a copy of the organization's most recent financial statement; (6) a copy of the IRS determination of tax-exempt status; and (7) if the program is expected to be a continuing one, information on how it will be funded in the future.

Grant Limitations

The fund makes grants only to organizations that are tax-exempt public charities as defined in Section 501(c)(3) of the Internal Revenue Code. The fund makes grants primarily in the Washington, D.C., metropolitan area. No grants are made to individuals, or for research, conferences, workshops, seminars, or travel expense; production of films or publications; tickets for benefits or support for fund-raisers; courtesy advertising; annual campaigns; or sectarian religious purposes. Grants usually are not made for general support or for national purposes or concerns.

Meeting Times

The board of trustees of the Philip L. Graham Fund meets three times a year.

Philip L. Graham Fund

Publications
The Philip L. Graham Fund publishes an annual summary of grants and application guidelines.

The George Gund Foundation
One Erieview Plaza
Cleveland, Ohio 44114-1773
(216) 241-3114

Contact Persons
David Bergholz, Executive Director
Daniel E. Berry, Program Officer
Judith G. Simpson, Program Officer

Purpose
The programs of The George Gund Foundation are directed toward enhancing the ability of individuals to understand the social, cultural, economic, and physical environments in which they live and increasing the ability of individuals to cope with changes that are constantly taking place.

Preference is given to pilot projects, innovative programs, and studies that hold the promise of significant benefits with broad applicability. Most of the foundation's grants are awarded to organizations in northern Ohio. Grantees are encouraged, however, to disseminate their work broadly, since the foundation knows that problems in this region are often relevant to other parts of the country and the world.

Areas of Interest
The foundation has established six program areas: education, economic and community revitalization, human services, the arts, environmental quality, and civic affairs. In addition, in 1986 the foundation began a funding program to support research on the cause, treatment, and prevention of hereditary degenerative diseases of the retina. Grants in the first three areas listed above have the highest priority and were allocated approximately sixty-nine percent of the grants committed in 1986.

In the education program the objective is to foster individual skills in living in, improving, and preserving society and the environment by providing better education at all levels from preschool through adult programs. Particular emphasis is placed on new concepts and methods of teaching and learning and on encouraging equal educational opportunity. Also stressed are programs of research, policy formulation, and balanced public education on issues of arms control, disarmament, and preventing nuclear proliferation.

The George Gund Foundation

The economic and community revitalization program area is mostly concerned with ameliorating the effect of change brought by the decline of the industrial sector. Priority is given to programs to nurture entrepreneurship, develop new technologies, retrain workers, and preserve the strong residential character of the city's neighborhoods. Of particular interest are programs that create jobs, particularly for those who have been left out of the economic mainstream.

Through the human services program, the foundation gives priority to projects that will assist abused children and battered women, improve management and service delivery capacity of human service systems, and preserve reproductive choice.

The arts program seeks to strengthen cultural institutions and improve arts education and outreach programs.

The environmental quality program focuses on education, improved land use, conservation of natural resources, health protection initiatives, and for historic preservation. The grants program for 1986 gave special attention to acid rain, preserving the Great Lakes ecosystem, and improved hazardous waste disposal.

The civic affairs program supports education and research related to strengthening the effectiveness of governmental organization and functions.

Financial Data (year ended 12/31/86)

Assets:	$ 56,241,398
Total grants awarded:	$ 8,097,537
Total number of grants:	299
Highest grant:	$ 178,755
Lowest grant:	$ 750
Median grant size:	$ 16,595

Application Procedures

Proposals submission deadlines are January 15, April 15, August 15, and October 15. While no special forms are required, applications should normally be a letter or formal statement that includes a one-page abstract

The George Gund Foundation

of the proposal summarizing the program, a current board list, current organizational budget, a copy of the IRS classification letter, the most recent audited financial statement, an outline of sources of income for the current fiscal year, and a list of other funding sources approached for support of the proposal.

The abstract should include background on the organization's history and mission, its activities or research conducted as antecedents to the proposed project, and documentation of the need for the project. The project description should clearly state the project's goals and objectives, activities planned to meet the objectives, a project schedule, qualifications of key personnel, and evaluation methods. A detailed budget indicating all anticipated income sources and expenditures for the project should be included.

All proposals are screened and evaluated by the staff before presentation at trustee meetings. Organizations submitting proposals outside of the foundation's interests and priorities will be notified promptly.

Grant Limitations

The foundation does not make direct awards to individuals nor does it administer programs that it supports. Grants are limited to purposes and activities in the United States, and the great majority of grants are limited to Cuyahoga County and northeast Ohio. With the exception of the foundation's special initiative program on retinal degenerative disease research, the foundation does not make grants in the health or medical fields. Grants for general operating support will be considered only if the need is for a limited duration and will substantially strengthen the work and improve the future position of the organization. Rarely does the foundation consider building or endowment grants.

All grantees must have satisfied IRS requirements as nonprofit, tax-exempt agencies having public charity status, or be approved as qualified government-related agencies or religious institutions.

Meeting Times

The board of trustees of The George Gund Foundation meets quarterly, in March, June, October, and December.

The George Gund Foundation

Publications
The foundation publishes an annual report.

Evelyn and Walter Haas, Jr. Fund
1160 Battery Street, Suite 400
San Francisco, California 94111
(415) 544–6575

Contact Persons
Melissa Bannett, Executive Director
Lois Kapteina, Administrative Assistant

Purpose
The Evelyn and Walter Haas, Jr., Fund was organized to support cultural, educational, and human welfare projects that enrich the lives of residents of the San Francisco Bay Area by promoting various strategies that will lead to increased self-sufficiency.

Areas of Interest
The fund has a particular interest in programs that maintain older adults in the community, assist the hungry and homeless, focus on selected community development programs in San Francisco's Mission District, and encourage corporate social responsibility efforts within the business community.

Financial Data (year ended 12/31/86)
Assets:	$ 17,377,406
Total grants paid:	$ 1,015,245
Number of grants paid:[1]	75
Highest grant:[2]	$ 55,000
Lowest grant:	$ 1,200
Median grant size:	$ 5,000

Application Procedures
Before a formal application to the fund is made, it is suggested that applicants submit a brief one- or two-page letter outlining the purpose of and need for the project, background of the sponsoring organization,

---

[1]This figure does not include grants of $1,000 or less made by the foundation across all its program areas.

[2]This omits two unusually large grants of $200,000 and $84,800 made to the Jewish Community Federation and the Regents of the University of California, respectively.

Evelyn and Walter Haas, Jr. Fund

project budget, the amount requested, and potential and actual sources of funding.

If the fund requests a formal proposal, the proposal should include: (1) a full description of the objectives, scope, and anticipated outcome of the project; (2) the plan for continuing the project after completion of the fund support; (3) a budget for the project, a current financial report, and a statement of actual income (including sources) and disbursements for the last fiscal year; (4) the names and qualifications of key personnel; (5) a list of the members of the organization's governing body; and (6) an IRS letter of determination indicating that the applicant is a public charity.

All applications, including those that are clearly outside the fund's declared interests, are reviewed by the trustees. The fund will acknowledge all requests upon receipt and applicants will be notified of the final disposition of their request within ninety days.

Grant Limitations
The fund does not normally provide support to individuals. While the trustees occasionally initiate grants to organizations outside the Bay Area, financial support is generally restricted to programs in San Francisco and Alameda counties. The foundation does not make grants to other private foundations, general fund-raising campaigns, or for deficit budgets, religious purposes, conferences, publications, or research projects.

Meeting Times
The board of trustees of the Evelyn and Walter Haas, Jr. Fund meets periodically, at least four times per year.

Publications
The fund publishes an annual report.

The Hawaiian Foundation
The Hawaii Community Foundation
Hawaiian Trust Company, Limited
Post Office Box 3170
Honolulu, Hawaii 96802
(808) 525-8548

Contact Person[1]
Mark O'Donnell, Acting Secretary

Purpose
The Hawaiian Foundation is a community foundation created to respond to community problems, explore solutions, and serve as a catalyst for constructive community change within its priority fields of interest.

Areas of Interest
The Hawaiian Foundation Distribution Committee has identified six general areas of emphasis for its grantmaking activities. These are, in order of priority: problems of youth, families in crisis, rural communities in Hawaii, preservation of irreplaceable artifacts or records of Hawaii and the transmitting of knowledge of cultural or historical value, environmental concerns, and community-based economic development. Grants are made in support of educational, scientific, recreational, or social welfare programs in the state of Hawaii.

Financial Data (year ended 12/31/86)
Assets:	$	6,440,294
Total grants paid:[2]	$	50,600
Number of grants paid:		16
Highest grant:	$	6,500
Lowest grant:	$	2,000
Median grant size:	$	3,000

---

[1]For application information, write to the Charitable Trust Department.
[2]This analysis includes only grants made from unrestricted general funds. It should be noted that the foundation made grants totaling $335,696 from restricted donor-advised funds in 1986.

The Hawaiian Foundation

Application Procedures

Proposals are due December 1 and June 1. The foundation publishes an information sheet, *Grant Application Procedures,* that outlines in detail the information which must be included in proposals. It is recommended that grant applicants secure a copy and follow the instructions carefully. Ten copies of the proposal and attachments should be submitted. Telephone inquiries concerning the submission of funding requests are welcome.

Grant Limitations

The Committee of the Hawaiian Foundation will consider programs and projects carried out by Hawaii organizations only. The organizations must be tax-exempt public charities as defined in Section 501(c)(3) of the Internal Revenue Code.

Meeting Times

The Hawaiian Foundation Committee meets four times a year, but considers grant applications only in January and July.

Publications

The foundation publishes an annual report and an information sheet on application procedures.

Haymarket People's Fund
42 Seaverns Avenue
Boston, Massachusetts 02130
(617) 426–1909

Contact Persons
Tommie Harris
Hillary Smith
Robert Chu
Louise Profumo
Pam Rogers

Purpose
Haymarket supports projects working only within the six New England states. Its goals are to help people understand the sources of social and economic injustice and how to change them; to support people trying to take control of their lives by challenging established power, learning to use leadership, and developing self-respect; and to work toward a society that is non-oppressive and life-supporting. Haymarket supports progressive social change nationally and internationally through its participation in the New York-based Funding Exchange.[1]

Areas of Interest
Haymarket funds groups organizing around issues of community empowerment, racial discrimination, peace, rights of people with disabilities, women, gay/lesbian rights, energy/environment, older people's rights, and workplace democracy. In addition, the fund supports groups doing public education and organizing on international issues.

Financial Data (year ended 12/31/86)
Support and revenue:[2]	$	831,560
Total grants paid:	$	353,234
Number of grants paid:		200
Highest grant:	$	28,748
Lowest grant:	$	50
Median grant size:	$	1,000

---

[1]For more information about The Funding Exchange, its programs, and other members, see the entry under National Grantmakers for "The Funding Exchange."
[2]This figure includes $664,388 in unrestricted support and revenue and $167,172 in restricted funds.

Haymarket People's Fund

Application Procedures

Haymarket's grantmaking is carried out by nine regional boards through-out New England: New Hampshire, Maine, Vermont, Hartford, New Haven, greater Boston, western Massachusetts, Rhode Island, and southeastern Massachusetts. Each is comprised of four to twelve people who are activists in their region.

Deadlines for proposals in the greater Boston area are February 15, May 1, August 15, and November 1. Projects working in more than two Haymarket funding regions should submit proposals no later than March 1 or September 1. All other proposals must be submitted no later than January 15, May 15, and September 15. Interested organizations should contact Haymarket to receive application forms. All applicant groups proposing activities within the fund's guidelines are interviewed before grant decisions are made.

Grant Limitations

Haymarket funds only within New England. Priority is given to groups and projects that involve working class and/or third world people and women, conduct community or workplace organizing, and support organizing.

Funding is not usually provided to beginning projects, organizations having access to significant government or corporate support, or groups linked to large, established organizations. Haymarket does not fund activities not clearly linked to organizing, human service organizations, alternative businesses or institutions, groups with budgets of more than $100,000, or groups with no fundraising plans other than Haymarket.

Meeting Times

Decisions on grant requests are made quarterly by the Boston Regional Board of the Haymarket People's Fund. Decisions on regional grants are made semi-annually; all other grant awards are made three times a year.

Publications

The Haymarket People's Fund publishes an annual report. Complete information on application procedures and guidelines as well as an audited financial statement are available upon request.

Headwaters Fund
122 West Franklin Avenue, #110
Minneapolis, Minnesota 55404
(612) 879–0602

Contact Person
Steven Newcom, Executive Director

Purpose
The Headwaters Fund is a Twin Cities charitable fund established in 1984 to make grants to local social change organizations whose projects address the social, economic, and racial conditions of disadvantaged people and work to eliminate obstacles to full participation in society. The fund supports progressive social change nationally and internationally through its participation in the New York-based Funding Exchange.[1]

Areas of Interest
The fund does not specify distinct areas of interest. It will consider proposals from projects meeting the following criteria: located in the greater Twin Cities area; addressing root causes of social problems rather than symptoms; operating in a democratic manner and responsible to their constituency; empowering people to help themselves through community organizations; based in the community with constituent leadership; working in a cooperative manner with other groups in the community; limited in access to traditional grant sources; nondiscriminatory as to race, sex, sexual preference, and national origin; and tax-exempt or working through a tax-exempt fiscal sponsor.

Financial Data (year ended 6/30/86)

Support and revenue:	$	131,924
Total grants paid:[2]	$	100,210
Number of grants paid:		23
Highest grant:	$	5,000
Lowest grant:	$	750
Median grant size:	$	5,000

---

[1]For more information about The Funding Exchange, its programs, and other members, see the entry under National Grantmakers for "The Funding Exchange."
[2]This grants analysis is based upon the 1987 spring and fall funding cycles.

Headwaters Fund

Application Procedures
The grant application process should be initiated by a letter or telephone call requesting application guidelines and forms. The forms require the following types of information: a brief history of the organization; a description of the organizational structure, the constituency (or community the project will try to reach), project goals, purpose of the grant, and funding strategy for the entire project; an itemized budget for both the organization and the proposed project; a copy of the organization's affirmative action policy; and a list of other sources of support over the preceding three years. Evidence of tax-exempt status must also be supplied.

Grant Limitations
Headwaters cannot legally fund organizations whose activities primarily involve lobbying (work that seeks to influence a federal, state, or local legislative body), electoral campaigns, direct union organizing, and business or profit-making organizations. The fund will not consider requests for individual efforts, academic research, religious events, or large-budget projects.

Meeting Times
The board of directors of the Headwaters Fund makes decisions on grant applications twice a year, in the summer and winter.

Publications
The fund publishes an annual report and will distribute application guidelines and forms upon request.

The Hunt Alternatives Fund
1255 Fifth Avenue
New York, New York 10029
(212) 722–7606

500 East 8th Avenue, Suite #100
Denver, Colorado 80203
(303) 839–1933

Contact Persons
Alice Radosh, Executive Director (New York and Dallas Projects)
Lauren Casteel, Executive Director (Denver Projects)

Purpose
The Hunt Alternatives Fund was established to provide financial and technical assistance to projects in New York City, Denver, and Dallas. Its primary concern is to support programs that struggle against disenfranchisement, discrimination, physical and mental disabilities, violence, and poverty. The fund seeks to encourage new endeavors as constructive alternatives to traditional solutions by supporting projects that promote individual empowerment.

Areas of Interest
The fund accepts proposals for projects that serve the disadvantaged in ways that are noninstitutional and nontraditional and that demonstrate cooperative efforts and networking to maximize personnel, facilities, expertise, and planning resources. Starting in 1985 the fund focussed on one issue each year. For example, in 1985 it concentrated on women of color; in 1986, affordable housing; and in 1987, the needs of children. In addition, the fund has supported projects concerning: the homeless, community development, and services for the chronically mentally ill.

Financial Data (year ended 11/30/86)

Support and revenue:	$	315,982
Total grants paid:	$	245,140
Number of grants paid:		83
Highest grant:	$	13,000
Lowest grant:	$	500
Median grant size:	$	2,500

The Hunt Alternatives Fund

Application Procedures
Initial contact with the fund should be a two-page letter that outlines the project for which funds are sought, demonstrates proof of Section 501(c)(3) tax-exempt status by an attached copy of an IRS determination letter, and designates a person (with an address and telephone number) for follow-up contact. New York City and Dallas projects should address their correspondence to the New York City address, and Denver projects to the Denver office, as indicated above.

Grant Limitations
The fund supports only public charities recognized by the IRS and located in metropolitan New York, Denver, or Dallas. It does not support institutional or general program needs; federal, state, county, or municipal agencies; and arts, cultural, educational, or religious projects, except those concerned primarily with the stated interests of the fund.

Meeting Times
The board of directors of the Hunt Alternatives Fund meets periodically, as necessary.

Publications
The fund publishes an annual report and publication guidelines.

The Hyams Foundation
One Boston Place, 32nd Floor
Boston, Massachusetts 02108
(617) 720–2238

Contact Persons
Elizabeth B. Smith, Executive Director
Susan R. Perry, Administrative Assistant

Purpose
The Hyams Foundation[1] supports both new and continuing programs in human services and community development in metropolitan Boston with the income from three funds: The Godfrey M. Hyams Trust, the Sarah A. Hyams Fund, and the Isabel F. Hyams Fund.

Areas of Interest
The foundation centers its grantmaking activities in the following areas: community development and housing, crime prevention, cultural programs, education, environment, land conservation, medical research, and human services (including adult education, alcoholism and drug abuse, courts and corrections, counseling, elderly, emergency services, handicapped, health, job development and training, legal aid, technical assistance, temporary shelter and the homeless, and youth). Requests may be made for operating expenses, special programs, renovations, building projects, and program-related investments.

Beginning in 1984, the foundation's trustees decided to undertake initiatives in four priority areas: housing and economic development, refugee services, adolescent pregnancy, and women in prisons. In 1986 at least one grant was awarded for AIDS-related services and public education.

Financial Data (year ended 12/31/85)[2]

Godfrey M. Hyams Trust
Assets: $ 39,104,589

---

[1]The foundation was formerly known as the Godfrey M. Hyams Trust.
[2]In December, 1985, the Godfrey M. Hyams Trust, the Sarah A. Hyams Fund, and the Isabel F. Hyams Fund were combined to form The Hyams Foundation. The first two funds in the new foundation are grantmaking entities; the Isabel F. Hyams Fund uses all of its income for services in East Boston. The grantmaking entities have similar areas of interest and procedures. To comport with the foundation's annual report for 1984-85, grants made by the two funds are analyzed here separately.

The Hyams Foundation

Total grants paid:[3]	$	2,520,305
Number of grants paid:		176
Highest grant:	$	87,000
Lowest grant:	$	217
Median grant size:	$	10,000

Sarah A. Hyams Fund

Assets:	$	2,587,420
Total grants paid:	$	135,500
Number of grants paid:		26
Highest grant:	$	20,000
Lowest grant:	$	1,200
Median grant size:	$	4,250

Application Procedures

A single application should be made to The Hyams Foundation, rather than individual or duplicate applications to the separate funds. There are no application deadlines and no required forms. The foundation does, however, strongly recommend that applicants follow the guidelines and suggested format published in its annual report and available on request.

The main body of the proposal should not exceed ten pages. Attachments should include copies of IRS determination letters establishing that the organization is a tax-exempt public charity and proof of incorporation in Massachusetts (with first-time proposals). Six copies of the completed proposal should be mailed to the foundation's executive director.[4]

---

[3]This total and the tabulations below do not include $401,330 in program-related investments made by the Godfrey M. Hyams Trust.

[4]General inquiries should be directed to the secretary to the directors rather than to the executive director.

The Hyams Foundation

Applicants should not request an appointment before submitting a written proposal. When the staff determines that a proposal meets the eligibility requirements and is complete, a meeting with the applicant organization's director will be requested. The review process takes from two to six months.

Grant recipients are expected to submit a financial statement (audited, if possible) as well as a full report on funded program. The report should include a statement of the progress made on the program, goals as set forth in the original proposal, the number of persons actually served by the program, income and expenses for the project, specifically, and the organization as a whole, the number of staff employed, and program achievements, as well as problems encountered.

Grant Limitations

Applicants must be Massachusetts charitable corporations and tax-exempt public charities as defined in Section 501(c)(3) of the Internal Revenue Code. Most grants are made to agencies serving the Boston metropolitan area.

The trustees will not consider applications from educational institutions for standard educational or capital programs. Consideration will be given only to experimental programs of educational institutions designed to meet the social welfare needs of the community. In addition, no grants are made for educational curriculum development, conferences, film production, or scholarships; to any municipal, state, or federal agency; to national or regional organizations; to religious organizations for religious purposes; to hospital capital campaigns; or to one organization for the programs of another which is not tax-exempt.

Meeting Times

The board of trustees of the Hyams Foundation meets approximately six times a year, from September through June.

The Hyams Foundation

Publications

The Hyams Foundation publishes an annual report which includes detailed information on guidelines and application procedures, financial information, and a full list of grants.

The James Irvine Foundation
450 Newport Center Drive, Suite 545
Newport Beach, California 92660
(714) 644-1362

One Market Plaza
Steuart Street Tower, Suite 2305
San Francisco, California 94105
(415) 777-2244

Contact Person
Dennis A. Collins, President

Purpose
The broadly defined goal of The James Irvine Foundation is to promote the general welfare of the people of California. The foundation is dedicated to enhancing the social, economic, and physical quality of life throughout the state, and to enriching the intellectual and cultural environment.

The more specific goals of its grantmaking are to enhance equal opportunity; to improve the economic and social well-being of the disadvantaged and their communities; to foster communication, understanding, and cooperation among diverse groups; to promote civic participation, social responsibility, public understanding of issues, and sound public policy development; and to enrich the quality and diversity of educational, cultural, health and human services programs statewide.

Areas of Interest
Grants are made for higher education, the arts, medicine and health care, community services and youth programs both to well-established institutions and to less mature organizations which exhibit the capacity to realize their potential. Of particular interest are projects that encourage and sustain leadership, seek solutions to new and long-standing problems, and strive to leverage results. The foundation supports demonstration projects and collaborative projects, as well as programs with a statewide focus or the potential for significant regional impact.

The foundation will consider requests for institutional and program development, policy studies and capital projects; it specifies, in the latter case, that it expects applicants to attract most of the funds from other sources and to demonstrate financial capacity to support continuing operational costs without further recourse to the foundation.

The James Irvine Foundation

Financial Data (year ended 12/31/86)

In 1986, grant authorizations by categories, were allocated as follows: higher education, $6.6 million (35 percent); cultural programs, $5.6 million (30 percent); community services, $2.4 million (13 percent); medicine and health care, $1.4 million (7 percent); youth, $1.2 million (6 percent); and special projects, $1.6 million (9 percent). The following analysis is based on grants paid in 1986:

Assets:	$ 423,008,466
Total grants paid:	$ 17,302,736
Number of grants paid:	209
Highest grant:	$ 2,000,000
Lowest grant:	$ 1,875
Media grant size:	$ 25,000

Application Procedures

Prospective applicants are requested to submit a preliminary letter briefly outlining the project or need for which support is sought. The letter and enclosures should provide general information about the applicant organization, including a financial statement identifying all income sources; project scope, budget, and timetable; and plans for funding the activity. Copies of federal and state tax exemption letters and evidence that the applicant is a public charity should accompany the letter. Preliminary letters are accepted throughout the year.

Foundation staff will suggest a meeting with applicants whose preliminary requests appear to be in keeping with the foundation's current interests and funding guidelines. Additional information and a site visit may be scheduled. Projects selected at this stage will then go on to one of the foundation's two distribution committees for further consideration and possible recommendation to the board.

For the purposes of processing inquiries and applications, the foundation has divided the state into northern and southern regions. Letters and applications from the northern regions, which extends to but does not include San Luis Obispo, Kern, and San Bernardino Counties, should

The James Irvine Foundation

be directed to the San Francisco office. Inquiries and applications from these three counties and southward should be sent to the Newport Beach office.

The board takes formal action on grant requests twice a year. Upon recommendation of staff, the distribution committees may take interim action on applications. Higher education proposals are acted upon by the full board once a year, in September.

Grant Limitations
By trust provisions, grants are limited to charitable uses in the state of California and for the benefit of charities which do not receive a substantial part of their support from taxation nor exist primarily to benefit tax-supported entities. Grants are generally not made to sectarian or religious organizations or private pre-collegiate schools for activities primarily benefitting their own members; for basic research; for films or publishing activities; or for festivals or conferences.

Meeting Times
The distribution committees of the James Irvine Foundation meet twice a year, generally in May and November, to consider applications. These meetings are followed by a meeting of the Board of Directors at which final action is taken.

Publications
The James Irvine Foundation publishes an annual report which includes a full list and description of grants and information for potential applicants.

Irwin-Sweeney-Miller Foundation
420 Third Street
Post Office Box 808
Columbus, Indiana 47202
(812) 372-0251

Contact Person
Susan Ingmire, Program Officer

Purpose
The primary focus of the Irwin-Sweeney-Miller Foundation is on creative programs in social justice (including those focusing on the economically disadvantaged), religion, community development, and the arts in the city of Columbus and Bartholomew County, Indiana.

Areas of Interest
The foundation provides support for operating budgets, start-up, and special projects when programs clearly can be seen to meet a present need and have high potential for immediate impact.

Financial Data (year ended 12/31/86)

Assets:	$ 3,186,000
Total grants paid:	$ 651,242
Number of grants paid:	55
Highest grant:[1]	$ 50,000
Lowest grant:	$ 59
Median grant size·	$ 1,500

Application Procedures
A brief letter of inquiry describing the proposed project is the preferred method of initial contact. If the project is of interest to the foundation, a formal proposal will be requested. The foundation acknowledges receipt of inquiries and proposals, and encourages personal meetings with applicants before proposals are reviewed by the foundation's board of directors.

---

[1]This excludes one unusually large grant of $254,385 made for general operating expenses of a community center in Columbus, Indiana.

Irwin-Sweeney-Miller Foundation

Grant Limitations
The foundation's support is primarily limited to the local area of Columbus, Indiana. Generally the foundation does not provide support for annual campaigns, deficit financing, capital and endowment funds, matching gifts, and scholarships or fellowships.

Meeting Times
The board of directors of the Irwin-Sweeney-Miller Foundation meets twice a year to review grant applications.

Publications
The foundation publishes a biennial report.

The Joyce Foundation
135 South LaSalle Street, Suite 4010
Chicago, Illinois 60603–4886
(312) 782–2464

Contact Persons
Craig Kennedy, President
Joel Getzendanner, Program Director

Areas of Interest

The Joyce Foundation awards grants primarily in the fields of conservation, culture, economic development, education, government, and health. The foundation has a long-standing commitment to efforts aimed at helping poor people enter the social and economic mainstream. This emphasis is especially important in the fields of economic development, education, government, and health.

Preference is given to organizations with a base or programs in Illinois, Indiana, Iowa, Michigan, Minnesota, Missouri, Ohio, and Wisconsin. A limited number of conservation grants are made in North and South Dakota, Kansas, and Nebraska. The foundation rarely moves beyond the Midwest, and then for projects of special interest or merit.

Conservation. The foundation supports projects related to groundwater protection, soil conservation, and the Great Lakes. In 1987 the foundation began inviting proposals in the area of biotechnology for developing environmentally sound regulations for the testing of new organisms. The foundation will also establish a program in air during 1988.

Culture. The foundation seeks to encourage artistic excellence and cultural diversity throughout the Midwest. Special attention is given to new and emerging arts organizations of exceptional promise. This interest centers on arts groups that have reached a critical juncture in their organizational development. This emphasis enables the foundation to support efforts aimed at improving organizational management and artistic development.

Economic Development. This program focuses on four specific strategies for improving long-term employment opportunities for low-income and minority individuals: job-training programs, projects aimed at stimulating job-creation activities

The Joyce Foundation

in low-income communities, job placement, and open housing efforts that make suburban job markets accessible to minority jobseekers. There is also a strong interest in economic development policy and in encouraging citizen participation in the creation and monitoring of local and state economic development programs.

Education. In higher education the foundation has two priorities: collaborations between collegiate and precollegiate institutions that address the foundation's precollegiate interests; and improving the recruitment and retention of low-income students. Public and private institutions are considered under the first priority; the second is limited to private colleges.

In precollegiate education the foundation's overarching priority is changing the structure of the public schools serving low-income youth. To this end, it is most interested in projects that spark change in teaching, school leadership, institutional arrangements, parent involvement, and counseling.

Government. The foundation seeks to encourage greater citizen participation in the electoral process as well as innovative efforts to strengthen the public's understanding of and participation in state and local budget-making processes through the Midwest. Projects focusing on the rights of citizens as they relate to the electoral process, those that reduce procedural barriers to voting, and direct voter registration programs are considered. Additionally the foundation supports independent analyses of state and local government budget-making processes that have strong citizen participation components.

Health. Primary prevention of adolescent pregnancies— preventing the first birth—continues to be the sole interest of the foundation's health program. The foundation is seeking model program initiatives that reach large numbers of youths and have the potential to be replicated throughout the Midwest. Another area of interest are projects that help create a positive environment for the development and implementation of primary prevention programs within the region. This includes advocacy,

The Joyce Foundation

research, policy, and education efforts directed toward the general public, state and local policy officials, or others that would foster community consensus on family planning issues for adolescents. The foundation is also strongly interested in efforts geared toward building a Midwest coalition around the issue of primary prevention.

Financial Data (year ended 12/31/87)

The foundation's assets as of December 31, 1986, were reported at $269,180,079. The grants analysis below is based on grants made in the year ending December 31, 1987, and totaling $11,524,811.

The Joyce Foundation
Analysis of 1987 Grantmaking Activity

	Total Grants Paid	Number of Grants	Highest Grant	Lowest Grant	Median Grant Size
Conservation	$2,843,528	73	$100,000	$5,000	$40,000
Culture	$1,322,663	66	$75,000	$3,000	$15,000
Economic Development	$2,283,649	62	$150,000	$1,500	$35,000
Education	$2,519,004	70	$132,844	$1,000	$30,000
Government	$1,255,180	40	$100,000	$1,785	$20,000
Health	$654,442	17	$100,000	$20,000	$30,000
Miscellaneous	$646,345	55	$150,000	$400	$5,000

Application Procedures

Preliminary inquiries should be made by submitting a brief program or project description. The foundation will respond in writing to all inquiries as quickly as possible. If the initial response is positive, the foundation will request a full proposal, to be reviewed at a joint meeting of the staff and the directors. (The foundation will provide format guidelines upon request.) Results of that meeting will be reported to the applicants in writing.

Proposal deadlines are as follows: economic development and education, January 15; conservation and health, May 15; and culture and

The Joyce Foundation

government, August 15. Applicants in the field of higher education should contact the foundation at least two months prior to the January 15 deadline to request a higher-education questionnaire.

The foundation makes a number of small grants of $5,000 or less between regularly scheduled meetings of the board. These grants are given for special projects and in response to immediate funding needs.

Grant Limitations

The Joyce Foundation concentrates its grantmaking activities in the Midwest, supporting organizations with a midwestern base or constituency.

Applicants must be prepared to document their tax-exempt status by providing copies of the ruling or determination letters of the IRS under Sections 501(c)(3) and 509(a) of the Internal Revenue Code. In addition, all organizations must be prepared to submit complete financial information and to have the results of a grant audited. Projects and programs needing support over a period of several years will be given closer consideration if they provide plans for financial support from others that would permit phasing out funding from The Joyce Foundation. The foundation does not make grants to individuals.

Meeting Times

The board of directors of The Joyce Foundation meets three times a year, in spring, summer, and fall, to consider grant requests.

Publications

The foundation publishes an annual report and distributes program and policy guidelines.

The J. M. Kaplan Fund, Inc.
330 Madison Avenue, 33rd Floor
New York, New York 10017
(212) 661-8485

Contact Person
Suzanne Davis, Executive Director

Purpose
The J. M. Kaplan Fund works to improve existing American institutions and to create new ones. The fund describes its role as" to reinforce New York's honorable tradition of progressive social policy, to strike whatever blow we can for fairness and justice, and to encourage talented people to make wonderful things happen." While the fund makes some national grants in its areas of interest, it favors local efforts and national organizations based in New York.

Areas of Interest
The fund's grantmaking activities are concentrated in three areas: (1) land use: conservation and enhancement of natural resources; parks, gardens, farmlands, and open space; architecture, historic preservation, and strong neighborhoods; and rational planning by government, including avoidance of nuclear explosion; (2) civil liberties and human needs: assistance to organizations involved in the struggle for a more just society, including First Amendment and other legal protections; basic public services; and worldwide human rights; (3) the arts: libraries, writers' organizations, special publications, and poetry; exhibitions and catalogues; and chamber, choral, and jazz groups of the highest order. Arts grants particularly emphasize New York.

Financial Data (year ended 11/30/87)
Assets:	$ 74,000,000
Total grants paid:	$ 5,827,000
Number of grants paid:[1]	177
Highest grant:[2]	$ 390,000
Lowest grant:	$ 1,000
Median grant size:	$ 18,500

---

[1]This figure excludes 20 matching grants, averaging under $7,000 each, initiated by individual trustees of the fund.

[2]This figure excludes two major grants of $390,000 for the J. M. Kaplan Center for N.Y.C. Affairs at the New School for Social Research, and $377,000 to the Association to Benefit Children.

The J. M. Kaplan Fund, Inc.

Application Procedures
Requests to The J. M. Kaplan Fund are considered between March 1 and October 15, and grant decisions are made on a rolling schedule. A clear, concise letter accompanied by budgets, sources of income, board and staff lists, an IRS tax-exemption letter, and Form 990 serves as the application. Other information will be requested if there is trustee interest in the proposal. The fund states that as much as possible they make grants quickly, flexibly, and without red tape. The fund primarily supports activities that take place in the New York area.

Grant Limitations
Generally the fund does not contribute to operating budgets of educational, medical, or cultural institutions; building programs; charitable organizations that solicit contributions from the general public; organizations whose main activities take place outside the New York area; films or video; scholarships, fellowships, research projects, prizes, study, travel, or personal ventures in the arts. The fund supports only tax-exempt, nonprofit organizations and makes no grants to individuals.

Meeting Times
The board of trustees of The J. M. Kaplan Fund meets as needed.

Publications
The fund publishes an annual report that sets forth its program interests, a list of the previous year's grantees, and a condensed financial statement.

Knight Foundation
One Cascade Plaza, 8th Floor
Akron, Ohio 44308
(216) 253-9301

Contact Person
Creed C. Black, President

Purpose
The Knight Foundation is a private, independent foundation that works to assess and respond to the changing needs of communities in which the Knight-Ridder company has newspaper and other business enterprises. (See complete listing at the end of this entry.) In its grantmaking, the foundation seeks to enhance the quality of life in those communities and encourage educational, cultural, economic, social, and civic betterment. The foundation also supports projects that offer special promise of advancing the quality and effectiveness of a free press in America and worldwide.

Areas of Interest
The foundation's grantmaking falls generally within the broad categories of education, culture, journalism, health, and welfare. In 1986 education represented 40.1 percent of grants paid by the foundation; cultural, 29.8 percent; welfare, 8.6 percent; health, 7.7 percent, and journalism, 7.6 percent. Support took the form of endowment, capital, program, matching, and general-support grants and fellowships.

Financial Data (year ended 12/31/86)

Assets:	$ 460,555,993
Total grants paid:	$ 7,906,587
Number of grants:	166
Highest grant:[1]	$ 333,000
Lowest grant:	$ 1,000
Median grant size:	$ 16,500

[1]This figure omits three unusually large grants of $1 million each to endow a chair or department at Cornell University, the University of Miami, and the University of Akron.

Knight Foundation

Application Procedures

Deadlines are January 15, April 15, July 15, and October 15. Proposals must be received at foundation offices by 5:00 P.M. on those dates; any requests arriving too late for one grant cycle will be carried over to the next. Only written applications can be considered. Telephone and personal interviews are explicitly discouraged unless initiated by the foundation.

The Knight Foundation does not use application forms. Organizations seeking grant support should submit a brief letter on the letterhead of the organization to the president of the foundation. That letter must include the following information: a brief description of the organization; the need for the project, what it will accomplish and a timetable for its duration; and the total cost of the project and the specific amount being requested from the foundation. If other foundations are being approached, they should be listed and any commitments noted.

In addition, the proposal should have the following attachments: a list of the governing board and officers showing their business, professional, and community affiliations; a copy of the most recent letter from the Internal Revenue Service determining the organization's current tax-exempt status; a copy of the organization's most recent audited financial statements; and a written endorsement by the organization's chief executive officer if the request comes from someone other than the CEO. If additional information is needed, it will be requested.

All applicants will be notified in writing of the foundation's final decision regarding their proposals, usually within two weeks after the meeting that concludes each grant cycle. The trustees prefer not to consider applications from any organization more frequently than once every twelve months, regardless of the result of the previous request.

Grant Limitations

All applicants must have a letter of determination from the IRS identifying them as public charities as defined in Section 501(c)(3) of the Internal Revenue Code. Unless the proposed project is in keeping with other program objectives of the foundation, applicant organizations must be located within one of the Knight Foundation eligible cities (see list be-

Knight Foundation

low). The foundation does not make grants to individuals, nor does it make grants for annual fund-raising campaigns, for ongoing general operating support, or for operating deficits.

Meeting Times
The board of trustees of the Knight Foundation meets quarterly, in March, June, September, and December, to consider grant requests.

Publications
The Knight Foundation publishes an annual report and makes a current list of eligible cities available on request.

Knight Foundation Eligible Cities[2]

Alabama
Mobile

Arizona
Tucson

California
Long Beach
Pasadena
San Jose

Colorado
Boulder

Florida
Boca Raton
Bradenton
Miami
Tallahassee

Georgia
Columbus
Macon
Milledgeville

Indiana
Fort Wayne
Gary

Kansas
Wichita

Kentucky
Lexington

Michigan
Detroit
Flint

---

[2]This list was current as of June 1, 1987.

Knight Foundation

Minnesota
Duluth
St. Paul

Mississippi
Biloxi

New York
Albany

North Carolina
Charlotte

North Dakota
Grand Forks

Ohio
Akron

Oklahoma
Oklahoma City

Pennsylvania
Philadelphia
State College

Rhode Island
Providence

South Carolina
Columbia
Myrtle Beach

South Dakota
Aberdeen

Tennessee
Nashville

Virginia
Norfolk

The Joan B. Kroc Foundation
8939 Villa La Jolla Drive, Suite 201
San Diego, California 92037
(619) 453-3737

Contact Person
Joan B. Kroc, President

Purpose
The Joan B. Kroc Foundation was established in 1984 to initiate and support programs and activities to help people accept and overcome conditions that may undermine their sense of individual worth and family love. All of the foundation's programs focus on human needs.

Areas of Interest
Most of the foundation's activities involve communication and education aimed at fostering understanding and encouraging people to take an active role in improving the quality of their lives. Most recently the foundation has focused on major research in psychoneuroimmunology, an in-patient hospice for San Diego, and programs designed to increase voter participation and to prevent nuclear war. In these last two areas, while a couple of grants have been made to national organizations, most of the foundation's support has gone to projects working in California, and specifically San Diego.

In 1986 the distribution of grants paid, by program area, was as follows: educational programs and services in chemical dependency, 60 percent; medical research and education, 11 percent; human services, 8 percent; education in nuclear arms and arms control, 16 percent; and voter education, 5 percent.

Financial Data (year ended 12/31/86)
Assets:	$ 36,575,786
Total grants paid:	$ 8,623,974
Number of grants paid:	39
Highest grant:[1]	$ 500,000
Lowest grant:	$ 500
Median grant size:	$ 25,000

---

[1]This excludes two unusually large grants totaling $4,918,415.

The Joan B. Kroc Foundation

Application Procedures
The foundation's 1986 annual report says that the foundation generates its programs internally. As of that time, it did not fund any unsolicited grant requests or proposals.

Grant Limitations
The foundation does not sponsor religious events or participate in the fund-raising activities of other organizations.

Publications
The Joan B. Kroc Foundation publishes an annual report.

Liberty Hill Foundation
1320 C Third Street Promenade
Santa Monica, California 90401
(213) 458–1450

Contact Person
Michele Prichard, Executive Director

Purpose
Liberty Hill Foundation provides support for progressive social change and grassroots community organizations. While the foundation limits its funding to the southern California area, it supports progressive social change nationally and internationally through its participation in the New York-based Funding Exchange[1] and through its donor-advised program.

Areas of Interest
Liberty Hill funds groups involved in educating the community about social and economic conditions and in organizing people to confront fundamental problems affecting their lives. Grantmaking in 1987 was reported in the foundation's annual report under the broad categories of women, Central America, militarism and peace, community organizing, and social and economic justice.

The foundation welcomes applications from organizations in Los Angeles and San Diego counties that are working against discrimination based on race, sex, age, religion, economic status, sexual preference, physical disability, or ethnic background. The foundation is also interested in projects to promote the rights of workers, encourage self-determination in low-income communities, protect the environment, and promote peace and responsible U.S. foreign policy. The foundation prefers to support projects unlikely to be funded by traditional sources.

Financial Data (year ended 6/30/87)

Support and revenue:	$	451,506
Total grants awarded:	$	148,691
Number of grants awarded:		70
Highest grant:[2]	$	7,435
Lowest grant:	$	100
Median grant size:	$	1,738

---

[1] For more information about The Funding Exchange, its programs, and other members, see the entry under National Grantmakers for "The Funding Exchange."

[2] This omits two donor-advised grants of $27,000 and $10,000. The foundation notes that the highest grant from discretionary funds rarely exceeds $4,000.

Liberty Hill Foundation

Application Procedures

Groups seeking funding should call the office for application guidelines and deadline information. The application form includes a cover sheet which should be filled out and attached to a detailed proposal. The proposal should contain a description of the group, together with information about its history, purposes, and budget.

A month after the proposal deadline, the Community Funding Board holds a screening meeting to review proposals and select groups for further discussion. Groups so selected will be asked to meet with two board members to review their proposal and to resolve any questions that were raised by the board at the screening meeting. At its decision meeting the following month, the board members report on each interview, present answers to questions raised previously, and decide, by majority vote, which groups are to be funded and for what amounts.

Meeting Times

Each year two the Liberty Hill Foundation holds funding cycles, entailing two Community Funding Board meetings each, are held in Los Angeles, and one funding cycle of two meetings is held in San Diego.

Publications

The foundation publishes an annual report, newsletter, brochure, and application guidelines.

Limantour Foundation
One Post Street, Suite 1925
San Francisco, California 94104–5223
(415) 399–0447

Contact Persons
Victor Honig
Lorraine Honig

Purpose
The Limantour Foundation is a small, unstaffed, and unendowed family foundation started in 1975 to support progressive social change activities and community organizing in the San Francisco Bay Area. It supports projects just getting started and provides seed grants and small grants to projects at critical stages in their development. The foundation is particularly interested in opportunities to leverage its contributions by cooperating with other grantmakers.

Areas of Interest
The foundation's directors support groups that are working, through organization and education, toward solutions to current economic and social problems. Priority is given to groups dealing with peace, poverty, discrimination, and environmental issues. The foundation also supports alternative cultural organizations, media projects, and alternative press-related activities; from time to time the foundation makes interest-free loans to tax-exempt organizations with temporary cash flow problems.

Financial Data (year ended 8/31/87)
Total grants paid:	$	54,857
Number of grants paid:		35
Highest grant:	$	3,000
Lowest grant:	$	500
Median grant size:	$	1,500

Application Procedures
The foundation does not have specific guidelines and does not use application forms. Interested applicants should telephone before submitting formal proposals. If a proposal is invited, included with the materials submitted should be a budget, recent financial statements (if available),

Limantour Foundation

and evidence of the applicant's federal tax-exempt status or the tax-exempt status of a fiscal sponsor.

Grant Limitations
The foundation does not support the preparation of books; research; conferences; or capital, plant, facilities, and equipment purchases. It makes grants only to tax-exempt organizations or projects with tax-exempt fiscal sponsors.

Meeting Times
The board of directors of the Limantour Foundation meets as necessary to consider grant requests.

Publications
The foundation publishes an annual report.

The Live Oak Fund for Change
Post Office Box 4601
Austin, Texas 78765
(512) 476-5714

Contact Persons
Timothy M. Fuller, Executive Director
Liliana Schaffer, Administrative Assistant

Purpose
The Live Oak Fund for Change supports grassroots organizations working to bring about fundamental social, political, and economic change. Its grantees are organizations committed to community involvement as the means of promoting equality, peace, and respect for the environment. The fund supports progressive social change nationally and internationally through its participation in the New York-based Funding Exchange.[1]

Areas of Interest
The program interests of the fund include: (1) grassroots groups struggling with injustice in the areas of housing, health, energy, environment, and minority, women's, and lesbian/gay rights (with priority given to low-income and working-class people); (2) workplace organizations striving to improve urban and rural working conditions, eliminate discrimination, and increase worker participation in the formulation of business policy; (3) advocacy groups working for institutional change in areas such as law enforcement, prison reform, consumer rights, economic democracy, social service programming, and international human rights; and (4) cultural and educational groups seeking to develop community awareness through media, art, and communications.

Factors that determine whether an organization will be funded include its level of community participation and the likelihood that the organization will carry out its proposed goals as projected from its membership, past achievements, and staff competencies.

In addition to its regular grants program, the fund makes discretionary interim emergency grants up to $500.

---

[1]For more information about The Funding Exchange, its programs, and other members, see the entry under National Grantmakers for "The Funding Exchange."

The Live Oak Fund for Change

Financial Data (year ended 6/30/87)

Support and revenue:	$	201,377
Total grants paid:[2]	$	42,694
Number of grants paid:		27
Highest grant:	$	5,000
Lowest grant:	$	250
Median grant size:	$	1,000

Application Procedures

The deadlines for submitting formal, completed applications to the fund are October 1 and March 1. However, initial contact with the fund should be a brief letter describing the organization or project for which funds are sought. If, after reviewing this submission, the staff determine the request meets the fund's guidelines, specific instructions will be provided for submitting a formal request.

Grant Limitations

Support is provided only to Texas-based tax-exempt organizations or charitable activities with tax-exempt sponsors. The fund does not support lobbying or electoral campaigns, direct union organizing, profit-making ventures, or activities that benefit private interests.

Meeting Times

The funding council of The Live Oak Fund for Change meets twice a year, in December and June.

Publications

The fund publishes an annual report and distributes two newsletters a year.

---

[2]This excludes 13 grants totaling $90,958 designated by specific donors. It includes three emergency grants of $500 or less totaling $1,194.

Los Angeles Women's Foundation
6030 Wilshire Boulevard, Suite 303
Los Angeles, California 90036
(213) 938-9828

Contact Person

Elizabeth L. Bremner, Executive Director

Purpose

The Los Angeles Women's Foundation is dedicated to reshaping the status of women and girls in southern California through purposeful philanthropy. The foundation administers a grants program and provides training in fund-raising and financial management for programs serving women and girls.

The foundation makes grants to organizations that both serve the needs of women and girls and encourage self-sufficiency and economic independence. Applicants must confirm their commitment to empowerment by showing the active involvement of program participants in program and organizational decisions and program development. The majority of the foundation's grants are awarded to groups focusing on the needs of low-income and underserved women and girls.

Areas of Interest

Applications are considered in two categories: (1) organizational development, addressing issues concerned with the development of long-term organizational stability; and (2) program development, expanding a service, increasing services, or providing a new service. Applications for program support must be based on documented needs and have the potential to provide or initiate long-term solutions.

Consideration is given to programs and projects serving the following areas: health and safety, programs dedicated to insuring basic needs such as housing, food, health care, and a safe environment are met; economic empowerment, activities geared toward enhancing the economic power and self-sufficiency of women and girls; education, both improving educational opportunities and improving access to education and training; social welfare, programs working to reverse social trends and conditions that have a negative effect on women and girls; and quality of life, programs that enhance the quality of life for women, girls, and the communities in which they live.

Los Angeles Women's Foundation

Financial Data (year ended 6/30/87)

Support and revenue:	$	61,047
Total grants paid:[1]	$	30,000
Number of grants paid:		10
Highest grant:	$	5,000
Lowest grant:	$	1,000
Median grant size:	$	3,000

Application Procedures

The deadlines for submitting completed application forms to the foundation are December 18 and June 17. Organizations interested in applying to the foundation for support should telephone or write the foundation for a copy of the funding guidelines and grant application forms. The forms clearly state that the maximum grant available from the foundation is $5,000. Five copies of the application form and of the required attachments must be submitted. Members of the foundation's grants review committee may make a site visit to an applicant organization.

Grant Limitations

At the time this entry was prepared, only organizations located in and serving Los Angeles County were eligible for support. The foundation does not consider requests for individuals, operating deficits, endowments, educational scholarships for individuals, capital campaigns, conferences and meetings, sectarian services, fund-raising event tickets, advertising in event programs, or salaries and administrative costs (except as they relate to proposed program development).

Meeting Times

The grants review committee makes recommendations to the board of directors of the Los Angeles Women's Foundation twice a year. Decisions are announced in April and October.

This analysis is based on the foundation's first funding cycle in spring 1987.

Los Angeles Women's Foundation

Publications
The foundation publishes an annual report, funding guidelines, and a list of past grantees.

Lyndhurst Foundation
701 Tallan Building
Chattanooga, Tennessee 37402
(615) 756-0767

Contact Person
Jack Murrah, Executive Director

Purpose
The goal of the Lyndhurst Foundation is to stimulate broad community support for projects and organizations whose goals and interests are consistent with the foundation's program areas which focus primarily on revitalization through education, the arts, and civic affairs. The foundation's support is concentrated in Chattanooga; however, grants are also made to state and regional projects.

Areas of Interest
The foundation's grantmaking is focused on community development, education, and the arts. Grants in the community-development area support broad-based development and revitalization projects, including the upgrading of low-income housing. The foundation's interest in education is usually directed at elementary and secondary schools. Arts organizations receive grants to help increase or diversify audiences, improve management, or strengthen earnings potential.

Financial Data (year ended 12/31/87)

Assets:[1]	$	112,402,318
Total grants paid:	$	11,032,643
Number of grants paid:[2]		67
Highest grant:[3]	$	100,000
Lowest grant:	$	755
Median grant size:	$	54,000

[1]This analysis was provided by the foundation in lieu of a grants list.
[2]This number does not include Lyndhurst Prizes or Teacher Awards, 35 of which were granted in 1987.
[3]This excludes eleven grants over $100,000 made to established educational and cultural institutions and one unusual grant of $5,634,946 for a major local urban revitalization effort.

Lyndhurst Foundation

Application Procedures

Deadlines for grant requests are generally January 25, March 25, June 25, August 25, and October 25. However, the foundation requests that applicants check directly with staff for specific dates or changes in schedule.

A grant request should be initiated by a letter of no more than three pages describing the project for which support is being sought. Attachments should include: (1) a description of the organization, a list of directors and staff, and a copy of the annual organizational budget; (2) proof of tax-exempt status from the IRS; and (3) an estimated project budget with tentative line items.

All grant requests are reviewed by the foundation's staff before presentation to the board of trustees. Applicants will be notified of the board's decision following regular meetings. Grant recipients are required to submit semiannual reports of activities and expenditures.

Grant Limitations

Most of the foundation's grantmaking activities are concentrated in Chattanooga. Grants will not be awarded to support endowment funds, capital projects, deficit operating budgets, or religious organizations. Grants to individuals are made only at the initiative of the foundation.

Meeting Times

The board of directors of the Lyndhurst Foundation meets five times a year.

Publications

The foundation publishes an annual report.

McKenzie River Gathering Foundation
454 Willamette
Eugene, Oregon 97401
(503) 485-2790

3558 S.E. Hawthorne
Portland, Oregon 97214
(503) 233-0271

Contact Persons
Linda Reymers, Program Director (Eugene)
Debra Ross, Development Director (Portland)

Purpose
The McKenzie River Gathering Foundation funds groups in Oregon working to challenge social and economic inequities and, through its participation in the New York-based Funding Exchange[1], supports progressive
social change nationally and internationally.

Areas of Interest
Generally the foundaton's grants can be grouped in the following categories: human rights, peace and solidarity, and environmental protection.
Recent grants have supported projects affecting people of color, women,
lesbians and gay men, Central America, South Africa, Middle East peace,
nuclear disarmament, progressive media, low-income organizing, pesticide reform, toxic wastes, and wilderness protection. Of particular interest are groups that practice affirmative action in their groups composition
and program outreach.

Financial Data (year ended 6/30/87)

Support and revenue:[2]	$	119,134
Total grants paid:	$	60,962
Number of grants paid:		49
Highest grant:	$	2,000
Lowest grant:	$	500
Median grant size:	$	1,400

---

[1] For more information about The Funding Exchange, its programs, and other members,
see the entry under National Grantmakers for "The Funding Exchange."

[2] This analysis includes only unrestricted funds and grants from those funds. It should be
noted that donor-advised and board-of-director grants for the year totaled $219,686.

McKenzie River Gathering Foundation

Application Procedures
The foundation has two funding cycles per year, one each in the spring and fall. Applicants are encouraged to contact the foundation's Eugene office to discuss the proposed project, obtain application forms (which are required), and ascertain application deadlines. The process itself includes a community oral presentation in an open meeting conducted by the grantmaking committee, where applicants are asked to make a presentation to the group on their project and to respond to questions from committee members and other applicants.

Grant Limitations
All groups must be located in Oregon and be unlikely to receive sufficient funding from other sources. The foundation generally does not fund food co-ops, health centers, alternative schools, or social services unless these projects are promoting social change beyond their basic function.

Meeting Times
The board of directors of the McKenzie River Gathering Foundation makes decisions on grant proposals twice a year, no later than December 31 and June 30.

Publications
The foundation publishes an annual report. Application forms and guidelines are available upon request.

The McKnight Foundation
410 Peavey Building
Minneapolis, Minnesota 55402
(612) 333-4220

Contact Person
Russell V. Ewald, Executive Vice-President

Purpose
The McKnight Foundation seeks to identify and respond to the needs of individuals in ways that will lead to their full potential as human beings, and through its grantmaking, to support and enhance the capacity of community resources to help address those needs. In so doing, the foundation also strives to enhance the ability and willingness of public and private institutions to respond efficiently and humanely to the changing needs of groups and individuals. The foundation supports organizations that demonstrate effective leadership and administration and appear likely to have a major favorable impact on their area of concern and on the community.

Grantmaking activity is concentrated in Minnesota, and proposals from organizations outside Minnesota ordinarily will not be considered. However, the directors occasionally may take the initiative to identify projects outside the state for support.

Areas of Interest
The foundation has a primary interest in human and social services that address basic needs and help alleviate or resolve problems faced by members of the community. The foundation supports new programs or expansion of existing ones that respond to economic, social, or physical problems. Among the areas funded in this program are the aged, emergency services, employment training and placement, housing, law and corrections, minorities, neighborhood services, urban and rural development, women, and youth and family.

The foundation also makes a limited number of grants in education, health, and the arts. Recent grants have focused, for example, on increasing access to education or to health care for disadvantaged or underserved populations. The foundation is interested in conservation, and supports some experimental energy programs and other conservation efforts. In the arts, housing, and neighborhoods, the foundation has developed major

The McKnight Foundation

programs which are the primary focus of grantmaking in these fields. Similarly a large-scale five-year program to address the priority needs of nonmetropolitan Minnesota responds to issues identified by special regional teams and administered by six regional organizations; the program will consider a limited number of proposals for nonmetropolitan programs.

Financial Data (year ended 12/31/86)

Assets:	$ 711,287,990
Total grants paid:[1]	$ 29,748,302
Number of grants paid:[2]	334
Highest grant:	$ 850,000
Lowest grant:	$ 710
Median grant size:	$ 41,000

Application Procedures

The foundation requires that organizations considering submission of a proposal write a brief letter describing the organization and summarizing the proposed project and amount of support to be requested. The foundation will then give an informal indication of the likelihood of support, which will help to focus the time and attention of both the foundation and the applicant on the most productive efforts.

Deadlines for the receipt of completed grant proposals are March 1, June 1, September 1, and December 1. Upon foundation discretion, exceptions may be made to this schedule if an unusual situation requires an immediate response. Grantees will be required to submit complete annual program and financial reports.

---

[1] It should be noted that in addition to these grants the foundation also made program-related investments totaling $1.9 million.

[2] Excluded from this figure and the analysis below are major grants to public media, scientific research grants and fellowships, human service awards, gifts to United Ways, and several major grants to educational institutions and the State of Florida made under the McKnight Programs in Higher Education in Florida. Taken together, these excluded categories of grants total $10,261,943.

The McKnight Foundation

Grant Limitations
The foundation will not approve grants to religious organizations for religious purposes; for biomedical research; to individuals or to other private foundations (with the exception of McKnight Awards in Plant Biology and in Human Service); or to national fund-raising campaigns, ticket sales, dinners, and similar activities. Eligible applicants must be classified by the IRS as tax-exempt public charities, and must maintain adequate accounting procedures.

Meeting Times
The board of directors of The McKnight Foundation meets quarterly, in May, August, November, and February.

Publications
The McKnight Foundation publishes an annual report that includes a list of grants and a description of programs and priorities; a quarterly grants list; and policies and procedures for grantmaking.

The Memphis-Plough Community Foundation
1755 Lynnfield Road, Suite 249
Memphis, Tennessee 79901
(901) 761-3806

Contact Person
Gid H. Smith, President

Areas of Interest
The Memphis-Plough Community Foundation is a general-purpose community foundation that focuses its giving on Memphis, Shelby County, western Tennessee, northern Mississippi and the surrounding vicinity. It administers donor-advised funds and operates an unrestricted grantmaking program.

Grants from the unrestricted fund are diverse and not limited to one or more fields of interest. Examples of projects funded in 1986 include aid to the homeless, seed money for an alcohol and drug abuse clearinghouse, and start-up funds for a program to help the children of ex-offenders. Support has also been provided to programs working on issues such as family planning, teenage pregnancy, and organ transplants, and to meet emergency needs of local charities. The foundation is interested in one-time projects that need seed money to get started and that would have a significant impact on the community.

Financial Data (year ended 4/30/87)
At the close of its fiscal year, the assets of the foundation were $18,388,489. Following is an analysis of grants made from the foundation's unrestricted grantmaking program as provided by the foundation in lieu of a grants list. It excludes grants made from designated funds where the donor recommends the specific grant recipient.

Total grants paid:[1]	$	42,631
Number of grants paid:		8
Highest grant:	$	6,000
Lowest grant:	$	471
Median grant size:	$	5,328

[1] This includes one grant of a computer with a fair market value of $6,460.

587

The Memphis-Plough Community Foundation

Application Procedures

The deadlines for submitting completed applications are May 15 and November 15. The foundation advises that applicants should inquire by letter or telephone initially to determine if their project fits within the foundation's guidelines. If the guidelines are met, grant application forms and guidelines will be mailed to the applicant. Attachments to the application forms should include a cover letter outlining the objectives of the project, proof of tax-exempt status, a detailed program budget, current financial statements, a list of officers and board members, and supplemental materials supporting the need for the proposed project.

Grant Limitations

The foundation considers only those proposals that will benefit the geographic areas it serves and are submitted by organizations that are tax-exempt under Section 501(c)(3) of the Internal Revenue Code. It prefers not to fund requests that are repetitive of past foundation grants or duplicate the efforts of other charitable organizations.

The foundation will not consider requests for endowment, building fund, or capital campaigns; operating expenses and budget deficits; annual giving campaigns at educational, religious, medical, and liberal arts institutions; or direct financial aid to individuals.

Meeting Times

The board of governors of The Memphis-Plough Community Foundation makes final decisions on grant requests twice a year, in June and December.

Publications

The foundation publishes an annual report and newsletters and distributes unrestricted fund grant guidelines.

Bert and Mary Meyer Foundation, Inc.
2913 Corinne Drive
Orlando, Florida 32803
(407) 645–4227

Contact Persons
Barbara C. Portee, President
Franklin D. Williams, Executive Director

Purpose
The Bert and Mary Meyer Foundation is a small family fund committed to supporting constituency controlled organizations striving for social change in the rural Southeast.

Areas of Interest
The foundation is particularly interested in farm-worker organizations and invites applications from self-governing groups whose objectives include analyzing their own reality, appreciating their cultural identity, creating and executing strategies to affect decisions that control their lives, and networking with like-minded groups with similar objectives. Because of the increasingly large numbers of farm workers who are from Central America, the foundation also places priority on grassroots organizing efforts aimed at educating and Activating communities in the Southeast on human rights and self-determination issues in Central America. The foundation makes a limited number of multiyear grants.

Financial Data (year ended 12/31/86)

Assets:	$	2,396,320
Total grants paid:	$	140,823
Number of grants paid:[1]		26
Highest grant:	$	40,000
Lowest grant:	$	400
Median grant size:	$	3,000

Application Procedures
Applicants are invited to call the foundation office before submitting a proposal to clarify the foundation's focus and to request a copy of the application form. The foundation has a spring and a fall grant cycle;

---

[1]This figure excludes various small travel grants totaling $5,923.

Bert and Mary Meyer Foundation, Inc.

however, an organization can receive funding only once within a twelve-month period. Applications must be received by March 31 for the spring cycle and September 30 for the fall cycle.

During the month following each deadline, all proposals are reviewed prior to the foundation's board meeting. This review usually includes a site visit, which is arranged by staff or board members at a mutually convenient time. Grant announcements are made in late May and late November, and grants are distributed in July and January. Grant recipients are required to submit a report on the use of the grant by the end of the grant period; this report must be made before a new application will be accepted.

Grant Limitations
Grant proposals are not accepted during April, May, June, October, November, and December.

Meeting Times
The board of directors of the Bert and Mary Meyer Foundation, Inc., meets twice a year to review grant proposals.

Publications
The foundation publishes an information sheet for grant applicants, an application form, and a list of grants and loans.

Eugene and Agnes E. Meyer Foundation
1400 16th Street, Northwest, Suite 360
Washington, D.C. 20036
(202) 483–8294

Contact Persons

Julie L. Rogers, President
Irene S. Lee, Program Officer

Purpose

The Eugene and Agnes E. Meyer Foundation supports projects and programs that respond to the changing needs of the greater Washington, D.C., metropolitan area. It has no rigid rules on the selection of projects. Its policy is to use its funds so as to promote community improvement, participation, and responsibility.

Areas of Interest

The foundation makes grants for a wide variety of projects, principally grouped into the following categories: community service, education, health and mental health, law and justice, and arts and humanities. In 1987 two areas of particular interest to the foundation were addressing unmet community needs and enabling disadvantaged groups such as the poor and homeless, recent immigrants, and young people at risk to become self-sufficient. Grants were also made in response to the growth of the Hispanic community; homelessness, hunger, and unemployment; the need for AIDS-related services and public education; and to strengthen community organizations.

Financial Data (year ended 12/31/87)[1]

Assets:	$ 45,094,233
Total grants paid:	$ 1,526,383
Number of grants paid:	111
Highest grant:	$ 40,000
Lowest grant:	$ 500
Median grant size:	$ 13,751

---

[1]The figures in this analysis were provided by the foundation in lieu of a grants list.

Eugene and Agnes E. Meyer Foundation

Application Procedures
The foundation suggests that initial inquiries should be made in a brief letter that includes a short narrative about the project and the funding sought. This letter should be received between one and two months prior to proposal deadlines to allow ample time for review and response. Formal proposals are due by 5:00 P.M. on the following dates: April 1 (for consideration at the June board meeting), August 1 (for October consideration), and December 1 (for the February meeting).

For the proposal itself, no specific application form is required; however, a proposal outline that must be followed is provided in the foundation's annual report. All applications are subject to staff review, possibly including an interview and/or site visit. Notification of the board's decision is made in writing by the end of the month in which the board meets. Applicants are asked not to telephone the foundation to ascertain whether a project was approved.

Grant Limitations
In view of its concern with local issues, the foundation does not contribute to programs that are national or international in scope. The foundation distributes its funds to tax-exempt organizations and makes no grants to individuals. As a general rule, the foundation does not support projects that are sectarian in character; nor does it support capital campaigns or endowment drives.

Meeting Times
The board of directors of the Eugene and Agnes E. Meyer Foundation meets in formal session five times per year. Three of these meetings are reserved for review of proposals.

Publications
The foundation publishes an annual report.

The Minneapolis Foundation
500 Foshay Tower
821 Marquette Avenue
Minneapolis, Minnesota 55402
(612) 339-7343

Contact Person
Marion G. Etzwiler, President

Purpose
The Minneapolis Foundation is a community foundation established to support the public well-being and improve the quality of life in the seven-county Minneapolis/St. Paul metropolitan area. The foundation administers a broad range of restricted and unrestricted funds and makes grants for a variety of purposes and projects.

This summary highlights the priorities and interests of three grantmaking programs: the Undesignated Funds Grantmaking Program, the McKnight Neighborhood Self-Help Initiatives Program, and the Minneapolis Emergency Fund. The Minnesota Nonprofits Assistance Fund, operated by the foundation, appears in Appendix V which describes cash flow loan funds generally. The Minnesota Women's Fund, administered by the foundation, is described as a separate entry.

Areas of Interest
Each of the three grantmaking programs has its own grantmaking priorities and interests, financial data, application procedures, proposal deadlines, and grant limitations; hence each is separately described below.

The Undesignated Funds Grantmaking Program The role of the Undesignated Funds Grantmaking Program is twofold: to assist both new and established organizations to be responsive to the changing needs of the community and to focus the community's attention on important issues and problems. Grants are allocated in six major categories: human services, community affairs, education, health (including AIDS), arts, and the environment.

The program's major concerns are programs that address the underlying causes of specific problems rather than those dealing only with the symptoms. These include, for example,

593

The Minneapolis Foundation

projects that work to bring about social change, that advocate for the rights of disadvantaged people, or that are preventive in nature; programs that work to combat racism, sexism, and other forms of discrimination; new, innovative programs that require start-up funds; community studies, original artistic works, and other projects to help citizens understand their problems and options, foster refinement of public policies and encourage interinstitutional coordination and cooperation; established organizations that are relevant to community needs; and educational programs that will benefit the work of local community service organizations.

Applicants to this program must provide evidence of tax-exempt status (and evidence the applicant is not a private foundation), show proof of registration with the Minnesota Department of Commerce under the Charitable Solicitation Law, comply with all nondiscrimination statutes and ordinances, and be incorporated as a nonprofit corporation in the State of Minnesota.

In addition, applicants must establish the following organizational characteristics: program staff capability, sound fiscal policies and responsible financial management, a plan for future funding (if applicable), the capacity for evaluation of the results of the project for which funding is sought, an elected board of directors with policy-making authority, a board of directors that reflects the organization's constituencies, the ability to describe the relationship between the proposed project and other similar programs, and the ability to show the proposal does not represent unnecessary duplication of services.

McKnight Neighborhood Self-Help Initiatives Program (MNSHIP) This program was established in 1981 to provide support for the initiatives of neighborhoods in the pursuit of neighborhood improvement, effective service delivery, social and economic opportunity, improved quality of life, and the need for self-determination and institutional change.

MNSHIP encourages applications from informal neighbor-

The Minneapolis Foundation

hood organizations with a track record of resident participation and emerging neighborhood groups with the potential to become ongoing organizations. It is especially interested in organizations with the following characteristics: neighborhood (not just geographic, but also the emotional, historical, ethnic, and other boundaries which residents use to define "where they live"); self-help (the extent to which the residents affected by issues are involved in and benefit from the project); local initiative (programs developed by and accountable to neighborhood citizens); cooperation and caring; self-sufficiency; self-sustaining; leverage; and performance.

MNSHIP is particularly interested in projects that represent efforts to overcome poverty-related problems. It provides operating support, capital and equipment needs in areas including but not limited to employment, advocacy, economic development, health, crime prevention, energy, housing, human services, technical assistance, and special projects.

Minneapolis Emergency Fund (MEF) The general purposes of this program are to provide emergency and/or interim funding to organizations when other sources of funding are not available; to provide short-term interim funding; and to provide emergency funding to individuals upon referral from nonprofit, tax-exempt social service agencies (but only when the funds can be channeled through the referring agency and no other sources of funding are available).

Financial Data (year ended 3/31/87)
On March 31, 1987, the total assets of the foundation were $56,089,430. Following is an analysis of each of the three grantmaking programs described above.

Application Procedures
The foundation's annual report clearly spells out the application procedures for each grantmaking program, and applicants are strongly advised

The Minneapolis Foundation

The Minneapolis Foundation
Analysis of 1986-87 Grantmaking Activity

	Undesignated Fund Program	MNSHIP Program Grants	MNSHIP Technical Assistance Grants	MEF Program Grants[1]
Total Grants Paid	$487,639	$657,683	$29,795	$124,377
Number of Grants Paid	47	31	18	38
Highest Grant	$38,000	$44,900	$2,500	$23,009
Lowest Grant	$300	$6,580	$300	$365
Median Grant Size	$10,000	$15,000	$2,000	$1,441

[1]This analysis is based on grants awarded during the year ended March 31, 1986.

to request a copy before contacting the foundation about potential support. Briefly, however, the high points are reviewed below.

The Undesignated Funds Grantmaking Program

The deadlines for submitting formal applications for support are March 1 and September 1. Applicants are encouraged to initiate the application process by writing a letter of inquiry to the foundation briefly describing the organization for which a grant is sought, the need the program is designed to meet, the plan of the program, a budget summary, the amount of funding sought, and a description of how the project fits within this program's guidelines. Following review, a more detailed application will be requested if staff determine that the project fits within the foundation's guidelines. An outline of the formal application, which must not exceed seven pages, appears in the foundation's annual report.

The Minneapolis Foundation

McKnight Neighborhood Self-Help Initiatives Program (MNSHIP)

The deadlines for applying for MNSHIP support are July 15 and January 15. Applicants are encouraged to telephone the foundation to explore potential support, or with questions about the guidelines and preparation of grant requests. Specific information, as outlined in the foundation's annual report, must be submitted. Applications failing to follow the format will not be considered.

Minneapolis Emergency Fund (MEF)

There are no application deadlines for MEF support. Applicants to this program are encouraged to contact the foundation by letter or telephone. The following information should accompany requests for emergency funding: a brief description of the applicant, an explanation of the nature of the emergency and why it occurred, a plan to prevent a recurrence of the emergency situation, the amount requested, the list of other sources of funds that have been contacted and the results, and an assessment of the impact on the applicant if the emergency cannot be resolved.

Grant Limitations
In the Undesignated Funds Grantmaking Program, the foundation gives low priority to capital or construction drives, endowments, scholarships, medical research, and recurrent requests from an organization for the same purpose for which a grant was made in the past. The foundation will not consider grants to the following types of organizations or for the following purposes: religious organizations for direct religious activities; annual contributions to ongoing operating budgets; deficit financing; multiyear support; dollar-for-dollar replacement of reduced or eliminated government funding; membership in civic organizations or trade associations; individuals; political organizations or campaigns; fraternal or-

The Minneapolis Foundation

ganizations, societies, or orders; courtesy advertising or benefit tickets; telephone solicitations; and national fund-raising efforts.

MNSHIP grants will not be made to the capital costs of constructing new housing stock, projects created and/or operated by public agencies or departments, and individuals.

Meeting Times

The Distribution Committee of The Minneapolis Foundation meets twice a year, in May and November, to act on Undesignated Funds grant requests. MNSHIP grant decisions are made by the committee in September and March.

Publications

The foundation publishes an annual report.

The Minnesota Women's Fund
500 Foshay Tower
821 Marquette Avenue
Minneapolis, Minnesota 55402
(612) 339-7343

Contact Person
Ellen O'Neill, Program Officer

Purpose
The Minnesota Women's Fund is a permanent endowed fund of The Minneapolis Foundation. Its purpose is to assist in removing barriers to the economic, educational, physical, emotional, social, artistic, and personal growth of women and girls and to encourage the advancement and full participation of women and girls in society.

Organizations applying for support must fall within one of more of the following broad areas of concern: advocating long-term change for women and girls; enabling women and/or girls, as a group, to achieve economic self-sufficiency; encouraging the development of positive self-images for young and adolescent girls through prevention, early intervention, and enrichment programs; increasing the range of choices and expanding opportunities available to women and girls; or working toward the elimination of prejudice based on race, gender, class, sexual or affectional preference, age, or physical ability.

The fund supports programs, projects, groups, and organizations within the State of Minnesota that address the root causes of problems rather than symptoms; are directed toward removing barriers for women and girls as a group within institutions and systems, or creating alternative systems or models; and promote fundamental social, political, or economic change so that women and girls as a group can move toward equity in society.

Areas of Interest
Special consideration is given to proposals that address the needs of low-income women and children, and/or issues of discrimination; or which have limited access to traditional funding sources. The fund specifically encourages emerging grassroots groups and informal groups of women who have come together for a specific project with a charitable purpose

The Minnesota Women's Fund

to apply for support. The fund provides funds for start-up expenses, new and special projects, programs, and general operating costs.

Financial Data (year ended 3/31/86)
Between the time fund-raising first started in 1984 and March 31, 1986, the fund had secured $4.9 million in gifts and pledges. Its goal is to establish a $10 million endowment. The following is based on the fund's first full year of grantmaking.

Total grants paid:	$	257,300
Number of grants paid:		28
Highest grant:	$	10,000
Lowest grant:	$	2,500
Median grant size:	$	10,000

Application Procedures
The deadlines for submitting formal proposals to the fund are May 15 and November 15. Applicants are encouraged to telephone or write the fund to explore potential eligibility for support, or with questions about the guidelines and preparation of grant requests. Application materials will be provided upon request.

The staff and the community advisory committee review each grant request. The advisory committee is chosen through a public application process and must be balanced by geography, race, and income. The advisory committee makes funding recommendations to the distribution committee of The Minneapolis Foundation. Staff make every effort to talk with each applicant during the review process to gain further information as needed.

Grant Limitations
The fund does not provide grants for individuals, capital fund drives, endowments, campaigns to elect candidates to public office, programs that promote religious activities, programs or projects out of the State

The Minnesota Women's Fund

of Minnesota, or programs inconsistent with nondiscrimination and equal employment opportunity statutes and ordinances.

Meeting Times
The distribution committee of The Minneapolis Foundation makes grants from The Minnesota Women's Fund twice a year, in January and July.

Publications
The fund publishes an annual report.

Morgan Guaranty Trust Company
Morgan Guaranty Charitable Trust
23 Wall Street
New York, New York 10015
(212) 483-2058

Contact Person

Roberta A. Ruocco, Assistant Vice-President, Community Relations and
Public Affairs

Areas of Interest

Morgan Guaranty Trust Company supports a broad range of programs in
New York City. Its program interests include education, urban affairs,
housing, health and related services, arts, the environment, and international affairs. In each area of giving, Morgan looks for long-term solutions to problems and supports programs and organizations that advocate
and press for the implementation of those solutions.

Examples of its interests particularly significant for this publication
include preserving and strengthening families and communities and improving the quality of life for those that are educationally, economically,
and social disadvantaged by making grants to support both direct-service
organizations as well as those advocating on hunger and housing issues;
enhancing the role of parents in improving the quality of education in
the New York City public school system; facilitating constructive responses to critical issues that affect the health of young and old alike and
improving access to essential services, particularly for low-income people;
and enabling cultural communities—including smaller, less established
programs—to flourish.

A review of Morgan's 1986 grants shows that its grant dollars, excluding employee-matching gift contributions, were distributed as follows: education received 26.8 percent; urban affairs, 19.7 percent; housing,
3.3 percent; health and related services, 17.9 percent; arts, 15.4 percent;
environment, 2.1 percent; and international affairs, 14.8 percent.

Financial Data (year ended 12/31/86)

Assets:	$ 12,901,491
Total grants paid:[1]	$ 5,571,718

---

[1]This excludes a $600,000 contribution to the Tri-State United Way and grants made to
match employee contributions.

Morgan Guaranty Trust Company

Number of grants paid:		398
Highest grant:[2]	$	150,000
Lowest grant:	$	1,500
Median grant size:	$	10,000

Application Procedures

Morgan accepts both proposals and proposal letters throughout the year. There are no deadlines. It uses an application form available upon request from the public affairs office.

Information submitted to Morgan must include the primary goals of the organization, including a statement on the segments of the population to which its efforts are primarily directed; the applicant's latest annual report (if available); a brief history of the organization; a list of the members of its governing body; a list of senior staff members and the number of persons on the full staff; the applicant's most recent audited financial statement, or if none are available, an indication of when an audit can be expected; a current operating budget, including sources of projected income for the year; a list of public and private sector supporters and amounts contributed for the most recently completed fiscal year, and for the current year-to-date; an outline of any plans for enlarging the organization's base of support; and a copy of the organization's most recently filed IRS Form 990.

Requests for specific projects must include the project's primary purpose, the names of the people who will direct it and their qualifications, how its results will be evaluated, its anticipated duration, its budget, and when funds are needed.

Requests for capital support must include a description of the program, the total amount of funds needed, the amount raised to-date, and the anticipated completion date of the campaign.

Proposals will not be considered until all requested information has been submitted, after which time a decision will be reached within three months. Morgan discontinues consideration of all proposals that remain incomplete for two months after they are initially acknowledged by the

---

[2]This excludes five unusually large grants of $100,000 and more totaling $612,470.

Morgan Guaranty Trust Company

public affairs office. Applicants whose proposals have been turned down are not encouraged to reapply for one year.

Grant Limitations

Morgan makes grants only to organizations that are tax exempt as described in Section 501(c)(3) of the Internal Revenue Code and that are not classified as private foundations. It rarely contributes to projects outside New York City, except in the field of education. Grants made outside New York are likely to be made to national organizations.

Morgan does not give to individuals or to churches and other religious organizations unless the programs for which funds are sought are entirely secular in nature. Further, in 1986, Morgan had a policy of not supporting drug-related programs, work with specific diseases and disabilities, scholarly research, and scholarships and fellowships.

Meeting Times

The contributions committee of Morgan Guaranty Trust Company meets frequently.

Publications

Morgan publishes an annual report and grant application guidelines.

Nevada Women's Fund
Post Office Box 50428
Reno, Nevada 89513
(702) 786-2335

Contact Person
Fritsi H. Ericson, Executive Director

Purpose
The Nevada Women's Fund is a community foundation created in 1982 to respond to inadequate funding of many women's and girls' programs and projects in the state. Through public support the fund helps women by making grants in recognition of and in response to the special needs of women.

Areas of Interest
The fund supports educational and charitable projects relevant to women and girls in Nevada, including training and counseling to become self-sufficient and self-supporting; scholarships, internships, and projects that promote career development for women and girls in nontraditional fields such as science, the arts, the professions, athletics, and business; counseling and training programs for displaced homemakers, single, minority, rural, disabled, and elderly women; children's services; and organizations helping women and families in emergency or crisis situations.

All grantees must be Nevada residents or organizations working on a project that will benefit women and girls in Nevada. Grants are awarded for specific projects to be accomplished within specified time frames, and preference is given to applicants who are not likely to receive funding from more traditional sources. All grantees are required to participate in an evaluation process during the grant period and to submit a final report on their work.

Financial Data (year ended 12/31/87)

Support and revenue:	$	148,068
Total grants paid:	$	40,050
Number of grants paid:		15
Highest grant:	$	5,000
Lowest grant:	$	500
Median grant size:	$	2,500

Nevada Women's Fund

Total scholarships paid:	$	21,525
Number of scholarships paid:		23
Highest scholarship:	$	1,525
Lowest scholarship:	$	500
Median scholarship size:	$	1,000

Application Procedures

Interested applicants should write or telephone the fund and request a copy of the grantmaking criteria and application guidelines. Deadlines for submitting applications vary, so applicants should be certain to ask about the timing of a request.

Among the items that must be included in a grant application to the fund are descriptions of the documented need for the program, measurable objectives, clear and concise program procedures, an evaluation scheme related to the identified objectives, the personnel involved in the program and their qualifications, a detailed budget, including other sources of funding and the specific proposed use of grant funds from the fund, a time schedule for meeting objectives, and a timetable for reporting to the fund on progress toward meeting the program objectives.

There are separate application procedures and guidelines for scholarships that can be used by Nevada residents for education outside the state. Among the factors the fund takes into consideration in making scholarship awards are need, goals, previous and current community involvement, plans after completing course of study, and the nontraditional field a candidate desires to enter.

Grant Limitations

The fund supports only projects in Nevada. Requests for endowments and building funds receive low priority.

Meeting Times

The board of directors of the Nevada Women's Fund meets monthly. In the fall the board considers grant applications. In the spring the board considers scholarship applications.

Publications

The fund publishes an annual report.

The New Hampshire Charitable Fund
One South Street
Post Office Box 1335
Concord, New Hampshire 03301
(603) 225-6641

Contact Person
Lewis M. Feldstein, President

Purpose
The New Hampshire Charitable Fund is New Hampshire's statewide community foundation. Established in 1962, the fund makes grants, loans, and scholarship awards to respond to community problems and needs across the state.

Areas of Interest
The fund's grantmaking focuses principally on the arts and humanities, education, the environment, health, social and community services, and the voluntary sector. The directors particularly seek opportunities where a moderate-size grant can effect a significant result in the state.

In addition, the fund has identified six specific issues for consideration: education, aimed principally at support for research and model programs to spark improvements in public schools statewide; long-term care for the elderly, with the emphasis upon affordable community alternatives to institutional care; public policy analysis, to sharpen and refine analysis and debate of issues important to New Hampshire, particularly through institutions of higher education; health promotion, through support for programs that emphasize prevention and life-style changes; mediation as a means of resolving environmental issues, in particular; and voluntary organizations, with the emphasis on pooled resources for liability and health insurance for nonprofits and their employees.

Financial Data (year ended 12/31/86)
At year end, The New Hampshire Charitable Fund reported assets of $30,456,472 and total grants paid of $1,640,447.[1]

---

[1] This total reflects the combined assets and grantmaking activity of The New Hampshire Charitable Fund and The New Hampshire Charitable Directed Fund, in compliance with the fund's annual report. The table incorporates the grantmaking of trusts affiliated with the fund within these common issue areas. The grants analysis does not include donor-directed grants made through the fund or The New Hampshire Charitable Directed Fund, nor does it include scholarship grants and loans totaling $691,510 made under the Student Aid Program.

The New Hampshire Charitable Fund

The New Hampshire Charitable Trust
Analysis of 1986 Grantmaking Activity

	Total Grants Paid	Number of Grants	Highest Grant	Lowest Grant	Median Grant Size
Arts and Humanities	$530,814	125	$189,069	$100	$1,200
Education	$237,275	86	$46,500	$100	$1,100
Environment	$238,329	49	$54,000	$100	$1,200
Health	$218,380	59	$35,000	$100	$2,000
Social/Community Services	$1,000,925	187	$100,000	$50	$1,200
Voluntary Sector	$90,250	19	$25,000	$100	$2,000

Application Procedures

Application deadlines are February 1, May 1, August 1, and November 1. Application letters should explain carefully the purpose of the project and describe how it will be accomplished. Each submission must include an itemized income and expense budget for the project, the organization's operating budget, and last available financial statement, along with a copy of the IRS tax-exemption letter.

Proposal guidelines are available from the fund on request. The fund notes that program staff are happy to discuss project ideas, either by telephone or personal interview, before a formal application is submitted.

Grant Limitations

Grant and loan eligibility is limited to tax-exempt organizations and public agencies in the state of New Hampshire. General operating support is usually not provided from discretionary funds for ongoing programs, and grants will not be made for endowments or to eliminate deficits. Generally grants are not made for capital projects such as acquisition of land, buildings, major equipment, or the construction or renovation of facilities. (Two of the affiliate trusts are an exception to this rule. The Smith Foundation will consider capital requests, and the Bean Foundation will consider capital requests for such projects in Amherst or Manchester.)

The New Hampshire Charitable Fund

Meeting Times
Grantmaking decisions are made quarterly by The New Hampshire Charitable Fund and affiliated trusts.

Publications
The New Hampshire Charitable Fund publishes an annual report and grant application guidelines.

New Prospect Foundation
1420 Sheridan Road, #9A
Wilmette, Illinois 60091
(708) 256–3886

Contact Person
Frances Lehman, President

Purpose
The New Prospect Foundation supports efforts directed toward the alleviation of pressing social problems in the Chicago metropolitan area. Priority is given to organizations that have strong local support and representation, clear objectives, and well-defined spheres of activity. Special consideration is given to those with modest budgets that have no constituency from which to draw financial support and that might have difficulty in qualifying for funding from traditional sources.

Areas of Interest
The foundation emphasizes its support for activities to enhance opportunities for employment, housing, health, and welfare. Programs focused on minorities and low-income groups are of particular interest. The foundation also supports organizations seeking to guarantee legal and civil rights and those whose activities are undertaken in the public interest.

Financial Data (year ended 12/31/86)
As of December 31, 1986, the assets of the foundation were valued at $6,091,491, and during that year the foundation made grants totaling $393,700. However, since this grants list was not provided for analysis, the following—which would appear comparable—is based on grants paid in 1985.

Total grants paid:	$	410,796
Number of grants paid:		102
Highest grant:[1]	$	12,500
Lowest grant:	$	500
Median grant size:	$	2,500

---

[1] This figure excludes two unusually large grants of $90,000 and $48,500 made to the Jewish Vocational Services and Businessmen and Professional People in the Public Interest, respectively.

New Prospect Foundation

Application Procedures

Although the foundation does not use application forms or have any specific guidelines, the following should be included in any proposal: a description of the problem to be addressed, a description of the proposed project or the methods that will be used to address the problem, evaluation procedures (if relevant), a project budget, and the amount needed from the foundation.

Other documents that should be submitted, as appropriate, are a list of the applicant's board members, an organizational budget, the applicant's most recent audit, documentation of tax-exempt status under Section 501(c)(3), a list of current funders, and other materials the applicant thinks will support the request.

Grant Limitations

The foundation does not ordinarily support programs related to the arts, basic research, or higher education. Mass-mailed proposals and other solicitations receive minimal consideration.

Meeting Times

The board of directors of the New Prospect Foundation meets quarterly.

Publications

None.

New York Community Trust
Community Funds, Inc.
415 Madison Avenue
New York, New York 10017
(212) 758-0100

Contact Persons
Lorie A. Slutsky, President
Richard A. Mittenthal, Vice-President, Program
Joyce Bove, Vice-President, Special Projects

Purpose
New York Community Trust and Community Funds, Inc., are comprised of many individual funds ranging in size from a few thousand dollars to several million dollars. Many of the grant awards are made to organizations at the suggestion of the donor. The discretionary awards are made by a distribution committee composed of prominent residents of the New York City area.

Areas of Interest
Combining the interests of individual donors with the general purpose of enhancing the quality of life in the New York City area has enabled the trust to build a flexible pattern of grant activity that is responsive to the changing needs of the New York constituency. Among the programmatic interests are arts and culture, arts in education, civic and government affairs, the environment, economic development, education and training, handicapped services, health (including AIDS), housing, human justice, mental health, social service, and welfare.

Financial Data (year ended 12/31/86)

Assets:[1]	$ 527,356,153
Total grants paid:[2]	$ 42,006,463
Number of grants paid:[3]	606
Highest grant:[4]	$ 748,000
Lowest grant:	$ 10,000
Median grant size:	$ 27,500

---

[1] The assets of New York Community Trust/Community Funds, Inc., and the Fairfield County Cooperative Foundation, Inc., are combined, in conformity with the trust's financial statements.

[2] This total represents all grants made in 1986, including those made from designated and donor-advised funds. It does not include $217,000 in loan guarantees.

[3] This figure and the computations below do not include $3,061,166 in grants under $10,000 each that are not itemized in the trust's annual report.

[4] This omits two unusually large grants of $5,501,250 and $1,100,000 to the Museum of Broadcasting and the YMCA of Long Island, Inc., respectively.

New York Community Trust

Application Procedures

Applicants are specifically requested not to telephone for appointments or to discuss a proposed project until a letter describing the project or a proposal has been submitted. Applicants should phone and ask the receptionist for the trust's general data sheet entitled *Information for Grant Applicants* and for any additional grantmaking guidelines in your specific program area.

It is suggested that an original copy of the proposal is not necessary, a photocopy is sufficient. An original cover letter on the applicant's letterhead should accompany the proposal and should include the applicant's telephone number, a one-page summary of the proposal, the results expected, and the amount requested. The cover letter should be signed by the chief executive officer on behalf of the applicant's governing body.

The trust does not use an application form, but it has established both general guidelines and specific guidelines for each program interest.[5] Briefly, the full proposal should include, in no more than ten pages, the following information: what need will be met and how it will be met, who specifically will be served, the applicant's qualifications and a discussion of similar programs, the budget for the project and what other sources of support may be forthcoming, a detailed description of the project evaluation, how the project will be supported after the grant expires, and a timetable. If the trust is not the only funding source being approached, the names of other sources contacted should also be included. Participation of other funders is encouraged.

Supporting materials should include a brief background of the organization, identification of the organization's board members, the organization's most recent audited financial statement, a copy of the organization's current operating budget, and evidence of tax-exempt status.

All proposals are acknowledged with a postcard, and the trust notes that sometimes applicants may not hear again from the staff for six to

---

[5]As of 1986 specific grantmaking guidelines were available for organizations seeking support for aging, arts and culture, arts in education, economic development, education, family and child welfare, girls and young women, handicapped, health, housing, human justice, mental health, neighborhood revitalization, social services and welfare, visual handicaps, youth, and youth employment.

New York Community Trust

eight weeks following acknowledgment. The trust may request a meeting to obtain additional information if it appears that a meeting would be productive.

Grant Limitations
The distribution committee concentrates primarily on organizations in the New York City area. Grants for programs outside this area generally result from donors' suggestions. There is a general policy against giving grants to individuals, and grants for endowments, building campaigns, deficit financing, films, general operating support, and religious purposes are rarely made.

Meeting Times
The distribution committee of the New York Community Trust/Community Funds, Inc., meets bimonthly, in February, April, June, July, October, and December.

Publications
An annual report and specific application guidelines are available upon request.

New York Foundation
350 Fifth Avenue, Room 2901
New York, New York 10118
(212) 594–8009

Contact Person
Madeline Lee, Executive Director

Areas of Interest
The New York Foundation makes grants in the metropolitan New York area to groups that are working on problems of pressing concern to disadvantaged, handicapped, or minority populations. In general, the foundation supports projects that have strong community roots and that seek to enable members of New York's neediest groups to make some difference in their own lives. Nearly one half of the foundation's grants are made to projects serving youth or the elderly. The foundation also considers support for public education and advocacy programs whose effect is to increase the participation of its target populations in public debate on issues of pressing concern. The foundation is particularly interested in reviewing proposals to coordinate and improve communication among programs working on similar issues.

Projects stand the best chance of receiving a grant if they: (1) involve New York City or a particular neighborhood of the city; (2) address a critical need of a disadvantaged population and involve those affected in seeking to meet that need; (3) are strongly identified with a particular community; (4) require an amount of funding to which a New York Foundation grant would make a substantial contribution; and (4) clearly identify a role for the foundation's funds.

Although the foundation supports a diversity of issues, all its grants fall into one of the following categories: start-up grants to new, untested programs, frequently involving a high element of risk; grants for new community projects of established institutions that offer a high probability of ongoing support in the future, or that anticipate only a limited life; general support to organizations meeting the foundation's guidelines, usually relatively new programs; and grants offering technical assistance, either by support of organizations providing technical assistance or by direct provision of services to grantees.

New York Foundation

Financial Data (year ended 12/31/87)

Assets:[1]	$ 40,808,000
Total grants paid:	$ 2,095,583
Number of grants paid:	93
Highest grant:	$ 50,000
Lowest grant:	$ 1,500
Median grant size:	$ 25,000

Application Procedures

The foundation's deadlines for proposals are November 1, March 1, and July 1. Compliance with these deadlines never guarantees consideration at the next board meeting, however. Considerable staff work must be completed before the board considers grant requests, and in some instances this process may take three months or longer. Therefore, it is generally unwise to count on the foundation in meeting emergency needs or in beginning a program within a very short period of time.

The foundation does not use application forms. A simple letter outlining the project, the budget need, and the amount requested will be sufficient for the foundation's initial review. Applicants will usually receive a response to this initial letter within ten days. If the foundation decides that a project fits within its guidelines, the applicant will receive proposal information and required financial forms. The foundation staff meets personally with applicants to evaluate proposed projects and will visit the program site before making recommendations to the board.

Grant Limitations

The foundation does not make grants to individuals and rarely supports capital campaigns. It is unlikely to fund research studies, films, conferences, or publications, unless initiated by the foundation itself. The foundation makes no grants outside the United States.

---

[1]Unaudited.

New York Foundation

Meeting Times
The board of directors of the New York Foundation meets three times a year, in February, June, and October.

Publications
The foundation publishes an annual report.

North Star Fund
666 Broadway, 5th Floor
New York, New York 10012
(212) 460-5511

Contact Persons
Marjorie Fine, Executive Director
Monona Yin, Associate Director
Betty Kapetanakis, Program Associate

Purpose
The North Star Fund makes grants to projects that bring New York City people together to work for social, economic, and political change. The fund limits its direct funding to projects in New York City, but supports progressive social change nationally and internationally through its participation in The Funding Exchange.[1]

North Star invites those groups that meet the following criteria to apply: (1) working actively in New York City communities and workplaces; (2) organizing low-income and working people or supporting such organizing; (3) working actively against racism, sexism, economic exploitation, ageism, and antigay attitudes in their approach to issues and in their organizational structure; and (4) operating in a manner that is democratic and responsive to the constituency being served.

Areas of Interest
The fund supports groups that educate the community on social and economic conditions and organize people to confront fundamental problems affecting their lives. In addition, some consideration is given to organizations doing education work within local communities on national and international issues of direct concern to those communities; films, videotapes, and slide shows specifically related to New York City community organizing efforts; cultural projects that are accessible to a broad range of people and raise the consciousness of their audience; and research of direct use to local organizing efforts.

Loans of up to $1,000 are also made from a revolving loan fund established by the fund. Loans are made only to ease immediate cash flow problems, i.e., when a grant has been approved and payment has

---

[1]For more information about The Funding Exchange, its programs, and other members, see the entry under National Grantmakers for "The Funding Exchange."

North Star Fund

not yet been received, front money for an event where success is relatively guaranteed, or for a fund-raising mailing.

Under exceptional circumstances North Star will make emergency grants of up to $300. Groups should submit a one-page letter explaining the emergency or telephone the office. North Star will reply within forty-eight hours. In 1986 twenty-two emergency grants were made totaling $6,800.

Financial Data (year ended 1/31/87)

Support and revenue:[2]	$	844,989
Total grants paid:	$	169,790
Number of grants paid:		112
Highest grant:	$	5,675
Lowest grant:	$	300
Median grant size:	$	1,750

Application Procedures

Application deadlines are in January, May, and October. Potential grantees should telephone or write the fund and request an application form. The form contains summary sheets and outlines the information necessary to complete the proposal. All funding decisions are made by a board of twelve people who are politically active in New York City and who represent a broad range of progressive perspectives. Members of the North Star Community Funding Board may request an interview. Any group not funded on its initial application may reapply in six months. Groups receiving a grant must wait one year before reapplying.

Grant Limitations

North Star can legally fund a wide variety of groups, including those that are not incorporated or tax-exempt. For further information, contact the fund. No grants are made to groups solely providing alternative services, groups with access to traditional funding sources, and individual efforts.

---

[2]This figure includes support and revenue figures for both general and restricted funds.

North Star Fund

Meeting Times

The North Star Fund Community Funding Board meets monthly and makes funding decisions three times a year.

Publications

North Star publishes an annual report and a newsletter. Grant guidelines and a grantee list are contained in the application forms.

Northwest Area Foundation
West 975 First National Bank Building
St. Paul, Minnesota 55101-1373
(612) 224-9635

Contact Persons
Terry Saario, President
Karl N. Stauber, Vice-President, Program
Barbara H. Henrie, Senior Program Officer
Cris Stainbrook, Senior Program Officer

Purpose
The Northwest Area Foundation, operating under new guidelines announced in the fall of 1985, targets its resources to achieve two major goals: to focus, deepen, and enhance public dialogue so that the region's citizenry may make more effective decisions concerning important regional issues; and to build individual and organizational capacity to address those issues after foundation support terminates. Its support is limited to organizations in Minnesota, Iowa, North Dakota, South Dakota, Montana, Idaho, Oregon, and Washington.

Areas of Interest
The foundation concentrates its funding on regional economic vitality, responsibly meeting basic human needs, enhancing and conserving natural resources, and promoting access to the arts. Each program is briefly described below.

> *Economic Development.* The largest number of grants awarded in 1986 was in this area. Public policy programs, leadership training and technical assistance programs, and development funds received grants. In rural areas these grants primarily assist communities struggling to recover from depression in mining and agricultural sectors and Indian reservations. In urban areas grants are targeted to disadvantaged populations and poor neighborhoods.
>
> *Basic Needs.* The thrust of this area is enhancing the potential of individuals. In both rural and urban settings the foundation promotes proactive, comprehensive, cost-effective models of supportive services. The foundation also stresses in-

621

Northwest Area Foundation

novative responses to housing needs and a variety of long-term strategies for food sufficiency.

Wise Use of Resources. Recognizing the region's historical dependence upon its natural resources, the foundation makes grants to projects dealing with issues such as water policy, sustainable farming, environmental quality, and habitat restoration.

Arts. The foundation supports a variety of artistic activities, stressing accessibility to the arts for a variety of communities. Grants are targeted both to strengthen the capacities of local arts organizations and to support touring and other outreach efforts in opera, dance, and drama.

In addition to traditional grants, the foundation also makes some moneys available for program-related investments. These may take the form of low-interest loans, equity, or other financing mechanisms, and are used to support projects for which other funding may not be available.

Financial Data (year ended 2/28/87)

Assets:	$ 198,850,966
Total grants paid:	$ 6,872,789
Number of grants paid:	201
Highest grant:[1]	$ 166,250
Lowest grant:	$ 475
Median grant size:	$ 21,000

Application Procedures

Applications are accepted throughout the year. The foundation asks that preliminary inquiries be made by letter rather than by phone. The first step in applying for support from the foundation is to request a copy of its *Guidelines for Grant Applicants,* which describes in detail the foundation's funding interests, policies, and procedures. It contains an appli-

[1]This figure excludes three unusually large grants of $250,000 and over awarded for housing development and for museum acquisitions.

Northwest Area Foundation

cation cover sheet, which must accompany the proposal, and an outline of the information required in the grant application. Application review and a final decision may require as long as three or four months to complete. Application and decision-making procedures for program-related investments are similar to those for traditional grant proposals. In general, the grant proposal must provide detailed information about the applicant organization, the proposed project, and the project's finances.

The foundation considers the following factors in its review of applications: the relevance of the proposed project to the foundation's funding priorities, the need addressed in the proposal and other past or ongoing attempts to meet it; the potential benefits of the project; the project's potential to serve as a model; the capability of the applicant organization and its staff to achieve the desired results, the adequacy of the projected activities, budget, and timetable to achieve the desired results; cooperation with other organizations working in the same field; the likelihood of future support from other sources; and the quality of the applicant's plan for evaluating and disseminating the results of the project.

Grant Limitations

The foundation accepts grant applications from nonprofit organizations in Minnesota, Iowa, North Dakota, South Dakota, Montana, Idaho, Oregon, and Washington. It has a policy limiting a single grant to a maximum of $300,000. It does not make grants for operating budgets, expansion or duplication of existing programs, scholarships, fellowships, travel, publications, films, or audiovisual materials, except in special circumstances. It will not provide grants for capital campaigns, physical plants, equipment, endowments, annual fund drives, propaganda, lobbying activities, or religious activities.

Meeting Times

The board of directors of the Northwest Area Foundation meets bimonthly to make decisions on proposal requests.

Northwest Area Foundation

Publications
The foundation publishes an annual report and a newsletter, *Northwest Report,* and distributes a brochure, *Guidelines for Grant Applicants.*

Nu Lamdba Trust
125 Princeton Road
Menlo Park, California 94205
(415) 326-3701

Contact Person
Nancy L. Kittle

Purpose and Areas of Interest
Nu Lambda Trust is an unstaffed funding resource that supports service and advocacy projects located in northern California and Wyoming that are seeking to produce progressive change in society and promote a more equitable distribution of resources in their local areas.

It is particularly interested in supporting projects that address issues of the environment and social and economic justice. The trust prefers to know that its support will not be necessary year after year and favors special projects over general operating support. Generally its funding is directed to projects that lack access to more traditional sources of support.

Financial Data (year ended 6/30/87)
Total grants paid:[1]	$	139,500
Number of grants paid:		39
Highest grant:	$	7,500
Lowest grant:[1]	$	1,000
Median grant size:	$	3,000

Application Procedures
The best way to initiate a grant request to the trust is to write a brief letter of inquiry describing the proposed project and the amount requested. Because the trust is unstaffed, it specifically prefers not to get telephone calls at this early stage. All letters of inquiry will receive a response, and if the proposed project is determined to fall within the trust's guidelines, a more complete proposal will be requested. Proposals should not exceed ten typewritten pages and should always include evidence of tax-exempt status of the applicant organization or its tax-exempt fiscal agent, as appropriate.

---

[1]This figure excludes several contributions of less than $1,000.

Nu Lambda Trust

Grant Limitations

Support is limited to projects in northern California and Wyoming. Requests for brick and mortar projects are usually not considered. All grantees must be tax-exempt organizations or projects working under the auspices of a tax-exempt fiscal sponsor.

Meeting Times

Decisions on grant requests are usually made twice a year, in December and June.

Publications

None.

Peninsula Community Foundation
1204 Burlingame Avenue
Post Office Box 627
Burlingame, California 94010-0627
(415) 342-2477

Contact Person
Bill Somerville, Executive Director

Purpose
The mission of the Peninsula Community Foundation is to provide funding for local charitable organizations so that they can meet changing needs in San Mateo County and the Palo Alto area. The general policy of the foundation is to make grants for innovative and creative projects and programs in the areas of health, social service, education, and cultural affairs.

Areas of Interest
While the foundation does not define specific priority areas, its annual report divides grants into the following categories: culture, social service, youth, seniors, education, health, environment, and emergency assistance. The foundation identifies itself as a "first funder," or a provider of seed funds, for new projects and ideas.

Financial Data (year ended 12/31/85)
Assets:	$	8,637,032
Total grants paid:[1]	$	383,619
Number of grants paid:		94
Highest grant:	$	65,976
Lowest grant:	$	125
Median grant size:	$	750

Application Procedures
There are no specific application deadlines, however applicants are urged to submit proposals at least two months in advance of the quarterly meetings of the foundation's distribution committee. Applicants may tele-

---

[1]This figure and the analysis below are based only on grants made from unrestricted and general field-of-interest funds.

Peninsula Community Foundation

phone or submit a letter of intent briefly describing their proposed project before submitting a formal proposal in order to find out if their ideas are potentially fundable.

The foundation distributes grant application guidelines that specify what should be included in a proposal. In brief, proposals should contain information about the specific purpose for which funds are sought, the community need for the project, the qualifications of key personnel, evaluation plans, and other grants received, and applications pending. In addition, applicants must submit their latest operating budget and statement of assets, a list of members of the governing body and the members' principal occupations, proof of federal tax exemption, and evidence that the proposal to the foundation has been approved by the applicant's governing body. If the application is accepted for consideration, a site visit will be arranged.

Grant Limitations
Organizations applying for funds should be serving the citizens of San Mateo County and the Palo Alto area.

Meeting Times
The distribution committee of the Peninsula Community Foundation meets four times a year, in February, May, August, and November, to review grant applications.

Publications
The foundation publishes an annual report and application guidelines. The guidelines are available in English, Spanish, Tagalog, Tongan, Samoan, Japanese, Vietnamese, Portuguese, and large type.

The William Penn Foundation
1630 Locust Street
Philadelphia, Pennsylvania 19103-6305
(215) 732-5114

Contact Person
Bernard C. Watson, President

Purpose
The William Penn Foundation is a private regional foundation that confines its grantmaking to the support of programs addressing local needs in the metropolitan Philadelphia area, including Bucks, Chester, Delaware, Montgomery, and Philadelphia counties in Pennsylvania and Camden County, New Jersey.

Areas of Interest
In 1987 the foundation began operating under new grantmaking guidelines developed in connection with its fortieth anniversary. The newly defined principal interests of the foundation are as follows.

Culture. The chief focus of the foundation's support for cultural programs is to promote high quality in performances and exhibits, to increase access to the arts, and to promote conservation of cultural artifacts.

Environment. Grants in this area are made with the goal of improving urban development patterns by preserving and creating urban open space, assisting land banking efforts, supporting community gardening, enhancing public parks, and supporting urban planning projects. Support in this one issue area only extends to the geographic area encompassing southeastern Pennsylvania and southern New Jersey and includes suburban and rural areas. The foundation is interested in the preservation of natural resources, including protection of agricultural areas, wetlands, stream valleys, shorelines, aquifers, and trails; fostering an "environmental ethic"; and promoting the monitoring of natural areas and their uses.

Human Development. The foundation allocates the largest percentage of its giving to support programs that address the educational, human services, and health care needs of in-

The William Penn Foundation

dividuals and families. The foundation's interest in children seeks especially to improve the health status of infants and toddlers at risk, to promote sound emotional development, to teach parenting skills and child care, and to enhance intellectual development. For adolescents, the program focuses on the capability of adolescents to become productive adults, youth employment, developing the personal skills necessary to achieve their highest potential, and expanding undergraduate education for minorities, particularly in math and science. For the elderly the foundation's priority is programs to help them live independently in a healthy, safe, and supportive environment.

Community Fabric. In this program area the foundation concentrates on relations between the people and the institutions upon which they rely to make society function. Of particular interest are projects that improve human relations among cultural, racial, ethnic, age, and other groups; increase and renovate low-income housing and provide permanent housing for the homeless; train law and justice system officials; improve the effectiveness of community institutions; increase access to community-based health care; and improve adult education and literacy.

In addition, the foundation initiates grants, in two program areas: national and policy grants and international peace/international development grants. The international program currently focuses on Africa and the Caribbean Basin. Unsolicited proposals in these two areas are not accepted.

The foundation prefers to make grants for projects that receive help from several sources and organizations that do not expect total support from the foundation. A demonstration of multiple support is interpreted as documentation of broad interest in the proposed program.

The William Penn Foundation

Financial Data (year ended 12/31/87)

Assets:	$ 174,489,869
Total grants paid:[1]	$ 21,120,498
Number of grants paid:	240
Highest grant:	$ 1,250,000
Lowest grant:	$ 1,000
Median grant size:	$ 50,000

Application Procedures

The foundation accepts and reviews written requests for support throughout the year. There are no formal deadlines. A single copy of a proposal is sufficient, and the foundation has no standard application form. The foundation states that there is no reason for proposals to be lengthy, elaborate, or expensively packaged. There are, however, a few rules to follow. Because the foundation reviews only written requests, potential applicants are advised not to telephone for an appointment with the staff. If additional information is required, applicants will be contacted.

A complete application should have the following elements: a one-page summary outline, information about the organization making the request, a complete description of the proposed project, and background financial data. Included with every request should also be proof of tax-exempt status from the IRS, a list of the officers and directors of the organization, the organization's most recent annual program report, and the most recent financial statement, preferably audited. Each of these elements is more completely described in the foundation's guidelines.

Grant Limitations

Foundation grants are limited to organizations in the five southeastern Pennsylvania counties and Camden County, New Jersey, which are defined as tax-exempt public charities under Section 501(c)(3) of the Internal Revenue Code. In the case of the environment program area, geographic eligibility encompasses a larger area—approximately a 100-

---

[1] These tabulations do not include matching gifts and various small grants totaling $672,959. All figures were provided by the foundation.

The William Penn Foundation

mile radius of Philadelphia. The organization does not fund grants to individuals or for scholarships, fellowships, or travel. Nor does it support religious activities, political lobbying or legislative activities, organizations wishing to distribute grants at their own discretion, tax-exempt organizations that pass funds on to nonexempt groups, profit-making enterprises, loans, programs concerned with a particular disease, addiction treatment programs, recreational programs, or films.

Meeting Times
The board of directors of The William Penn Foundation meets five times a year, in January, April, July, October, and December, to consider grant requests.

Publications
The foundation publishes an annual report that includes application guidelines. It also distributes a brochure entitled *New Directions and Guide to Applying for a Grant.*

James C. Penney Foundation
1633 Broadway, 39th Floor
New York, New York 10019
(212) 830-7490

Contact Persons
Anne Romasco, Managing Director
Joy Harvey, Administrative Assistant

Purpose
The James C. Penney Foundation is a small family foundation established by the late J. C. Penney and Caroline A. Penney. The foundation continues the philanthropic spirit of the founders by its giving to underfunded domestic sectors. Building on the premise that basic human rights must be guaranteed, the foundation is guided by several fundamental goals: empowering politically and economically disenfranchised people, fostering individual autonomy and progress toward self-reliance, influencing public opinion and policy to promote human dignity and social justice, and supporting innovative efforts to determine and address the underlying causes of problems.

Areas of Interest
In 1988 the foundation's program interests focused on community renewal (homelessness and hunger, low-income housing, and community economic development); the environment (toxic chemical issues including source reduction, control of chemical exposures, occupational health, and renewable energy); peace (alternative security, economic consequences of the military budget, new constituencies, and leadership development); and strengthening youth and family (domestic violence, high school dropout, youth employment, and teenage pregnancy).

Priority is given to activities that increase self-sufficiency, develop the potential of emerging leaders, or use volunteers creatively; serve as model programs with potential for replication; and involve specific projects. Support for grassroots groups is emphasized, but proposals from

James C. Penney Foundation

national organizations are considered when they work to strengthen local groups through networking, coalition building, or by providing resources and leadership development.

Financial Data (year ended 12/31/87)

Assets:	$	4,341,963
Total grants paid:[1]	$	385,991
Number of grants paid:		50
Highest grant:	$	10,000
Lowest grant:	$	500
Median grant size:	$	7,000

Application Procedures

There are no application deadlines. Proposals are accepted throughout the year. Initial contact should be in the form of a two- to three-page letter that briefly describes the organization, the project, and the funding requested. If the project falls within the foundation's priorities and interests, a full proposal will be invited, and the foundation will provide a form cover sheet and specific instructions. It should be recalled that an invitation to submit a proposal indicates only the foundation's interest in a project; it does not mean the proposal will be presented to the board of directors. Before any proposal is submitted to the board for approval, a site visit or personal meeting with the applicant will be arranged.

Grant Limitations

Funding is primarily limited to programs in the northeastern United States and parts of Appalachia as far south as North Carolina. While grants are made for a one-year period, the board may consider applications for renewals. The foundation does not make grants for capital improvements, media production, films, the arts, cultural events, academic research, scholarships, or individuals. Retroactive funding is not considered, and there are no discretionary funds available for emergency funding.

---

[1]This figure and the analysis below exclude two board-member-advised grants totaling $93,100 and one program-related investment of $100,000.

James C. Penney Foundation

Meeting Times
The board of directors of the James C. Penney Foundation meets three times a year to consider requests for funding. At each meeting the date of the following meeting is set.

Publications
The foundation will provide a copy of its guidelines and a list of grantees on request. It will also provide a copy of its seven-year report for the years 1980–1986.

The Philadelphia Foundation
Two Mellon Bank Center, Suite 2017
Philadelphia, Pennsylvania 19102
(215) 563-6417

Contact Person
Jacqueline A. Akins, Acting Director

Purpose
The Philadelphia Foundation is a community foundation serving the greater Philadelphia area, including Philadelphia, Delaware, Montgomery, Chester, and Bucks counties. It was established in 1918 and includes 121 funds created by individuals and families. The foundation is a broad-based, flexible organization engaged in activities that directly affect the quality of life in southeastern Pennsylvania.

Empowerment was established by the foundation's board as a specific funding criterion in 1983. Empowerment refers to the processes that increase the ability of individuals and groups to gain control over their lives and to participate effectively in collective and institutional efforts to solve common problems. The foundation, in adopting this policy, seeks to expand and enhance the day-to-day practice of society's democratic ideals. All organizations have some elements of empowerment; few agencies fully meet all the criteria.

An organization that empowers will have, to varying degrees, some or all of the following characteristics: (1) primarily serve or represent a disadvantaged sector(s) of society; (2) operate within an organizational structure that has the active involvement of the program's constituents/clients in defining the problem to be addressed, making policy and planning and evaluating the program; (3) promote collective action and mutual support in solving personal and social problems; (4) improve the individual's ability to assert control over his/her own life and to help others; (5) advance individual skills and understanding through group activities, cooperative work, and learning through action; and (6) address the causes of the problem affecting the constituent group.

Areas of Interest
The foundation has five specific priorities. The percentage of total funds distributed during 1985–86 fiscal year are indicated: community affairs,

636

The Philadelphia Foundation

33 percent; social services, 26 percent; education, 15 percent; health, 15 percent; and culture, 9 percent. Religion, 2 percent, is funded only when specifically directed by a donor.

The foundation utilizes a number of criteria for evaluating proposals, including: community need, administrative effectiveness, and empowerment (as described above). These criteria enable the foundation to concentrate its resources on small and developing organizations that are operated by and/or empower minority and low-income people.

Financial Data (year ended 4/30/87)

Assets:[1]	$ 48,808,973
Total grants paid:	$ 3,816,720
Number of grants paid:	348
Highest grant:[2]	$ 65,976
Lowest grant:	$ 276
Median grant size:	$ 8,000

Application Procedures

The deadlines for submitting formal applications are July 31 and January 15. Proposals are not accepted between August and October, or from February to April. Applicants are urged to submit proposals well in advance of the actual deadlines. The earlier a proposal is submitted, the earlier it is reviewed and the more time is available for the applicant to submit any supplementary material.

Application forms are required and, along with outlines for both project and general-support proposals, are available upon request. Applicants are strongly advised to review the foundation's grantmaking criteria before submitting a proposal.

Organizations can apply for funding for specific programs or projects,

---

[1] As of April 30, 1986. At the end of the foundation's 1987 fiscal year its assets at market value were approximately $60 million.

[2] This excludes two unusually large grants totaling $225,102. Grant awards usually fall in the range from $500 to $15,000. Grant awards that exceed this range are generally from funds in which the donor has designated specific agencies or areas to receive income.

The Philadelphia Foundation

or for general support. The foundation advises that agencies with total budgets greater than $400,000 should apply for specific projects and those with less than $400,000 should apply for general support. It is difficult for staff to meet with applicants before a written proposal has been submitted, and not every organization will receive a field visit.

Grant Limitations
The foundation has set a low priority on a number of areas and therefore rarely funds the following (except as directed by a donor in a trust instrument): capital campaigns, conferences, deficit financing, endowments, government agencies, individuals, large-budget agencies ($1 million and over), national organizations, private schools, publications, religion, research projects, scholarships, tours and trips, umbrella-funding organizations, and agencies outside Philadelphia, Delaware, Montgomery, Chester, and Bucks counties.

Meeting Times
The Distribution Committee of The Philadelphia Foundation meets twice a year to vote on grant applications, usually in early November and late April.

Publications
The foundation publishes an annual report and distributes information especially for applicants upon request.

The Pioneer Fund
Box 33
Inverness, California 94937
(415) 669-1122

Contact Person
Armin Rosencranz, Executive Director

Purpose
The Pioneer Fund has two primary interests: assisting emerging documentary filmmakers with particular film projects, and stimulating innovative projects intended to illuminate or ameliorate significant public-policy aspects of public school education. Grants in filmmaking are limited to Pacific Coast filmmakers. Grants in public education are limited to northern California.

Areas of Interest
The fund makes grants to tax-exempt organizations that support emerging (i.e., experienced but not well recognized) documentary filmmakers. In the area of education it makes grants to organizations that address significant public-policy aspects of public school education and that cannot secure funding from conventional sources. "Public policy" denotes structural, organizational, and financial issues such as budgeting, teacher seniority and tenure, collective bargaining, and parent and student empowerment.

Financial Data (year ended 6/30/87)

Assets:	$	900,000
Total grants paid:	$	71,210
Number of grants paid:		31
Highest grant:	$	5,000
Lowest grant:	$	500
Median grant size:	$	2,500

Application Procedures
Applications are reviewed throughout the year. The preferred form of initial contact with the fund is a letter or telephone call to the executive director that briefly describes the project and requests a proposal summary sheet.

The Pioneer Fund

Grant Limitations
The fund supports only organizations with evidence of public charity tax-exempt status. It does not provide support for endowments, building campaigns, accumulated deficits, and ordinary operating expenses, nor does it make grants to individuals. In the film area the fund ordinarily does not make either seed or distribution grants, and does not support instruction or performance documentaries or student film projects. In the education area the fund does not support school site or curriculum enrichment programs.

Meeting Times
The board of directors of The Pioneer Fund meets three times a year to consider grant applications.

Publications
The Pioneer Fund will provide a profile, a proposal summary sheet, and a grants list upon request.

The Piton Foundation
Kittredge Building
511 16th Street, Suite 700
Denver, Colorado 80202
(303) 825–6246

Contact Persons
Samuel Gary, Chairman
Mary Gittings, Executive Director

Purpose

The Piton Foundation is committed to fostering community processes and developing resources that enable citizens to come together to solve community problems. It also promotes strong cooperative arrangements between the public and private sectors with an emphasis on local involvement and self-determination. The foundation is particularly interested in: (1) improving conditions for those inadequately served by society; (2) increasing the ability of people to control the decisions that affect their own lives; and (3) strengthening the nonprofit voluntary sector.

Areas of Interest

The foundation primarily supports programs in Colorado and has five specific categories in which grants are made: (1) community self-help initiatives, which is designed to strengthen neighborhoods and build constituencies; (2) organizational capacity building and leadership training, which supports programs that provide skills and resources for personal achievement, leadership development, and organizational renewal; (3) economic development, which promotes a strong economic base in selected neighborhoods, job preparation, and training opportunities; (4) affordable housing, which includes housing production and financing mechanisms, counseling and support services, and planning and housing policy; and (5) improving conditions and opportunities for individuals and families, particularly women and children, which offers the opportunity for people to control their lives through educational advancement and support services that meet basic needs.

The foundation also has a general and discretionary grant program that allows allocation of funds to cultural, civic, conservation, and health programs that contribute to the quality of life in Denver. In addition, it makes loans and program-related investments and administers the Eight

The Piton Foundation

South Fifty-Four East, Inc., Fund and the Gary-Williams Oil Producers Employee Advised Fund.

In all program areas the foundation is interested in funding projects that fulfill one or more of the following criteria: (1) provide essential support to organizations operating within the foundation's areas of interest; (2) identify and address critical needs; (3) improve the operating efficiency of nonprofits; (4) leverage other financial and community resources to address community problems; (5) promote and expand volunteerism; (6) promote self-sufficiency or stability of income sources; (7) address root causes of community problems; (8) advocate policy and systemic changes when appropriate; (9) promote projects initiated by the people most directly affected; and (10) increase opportunities for personal achievement.

Financial Data (year ended 11/30/86)

Support and revenue:	$	1,567,801
Total grants paid:[1]	$	1,367,840
Number of grants paid:		65
Highest grant:	$	68,000
Lowest grant:	$	1,000
Median grant size:	$	20,000

Program-related Investments

Total PRIs paid:	$	789,702
Number of PRIs:		9
Highest PRI:	$	250,000
Lowest PRI:	$	3,000
Median PRI size:	$	35,410

Application Procedures

The foundation has no application deadlines and reviews inquiries and proposals throughout the year. Applicants should submit a brief letter

---

[1]This excludes $41,906 in nongrant contributions made in support of various civic and cultural organizations in the Denver metropolitan area and a total of $106,406 in awards made to various foundation grantees on a one-time basis for legal, accounting, and other expenses.

The Piton Foundation

(no more than three pages) describing the proposed project. It should include: (1) a brief history of the organization; (2) a concise description of the program, needs addressed, goals, opportunities presented to the foundation, and specific amount requested; and (3) an organizational budget with income and expenses. If the program described in the letter is consistent with the foundation's objectives and areas of interest, a staff member will contact the organization and ask for a more detailed application, and, if appropriate, arrange for a site visit. Application review and a final decision may take as long as four months to complete.

Grant Limitations
Ordinarily the foundation will not consider requests for support of basic research, long-term operations support or programs, building fund campaigns, debt reduction, or endowments.

Meeting Times
There are no regularly scheduled meetings of The Piton Foundation's board of directors. Meetings are called as the need arises.

Publications
The foundation publishes an annual report.

Z. Smith Reynolds Foundation
101 Reynolda Village
Winston-Salem, North Carolina 27106-5199
(919) 725-7541

Contact Persons
Thomas W. Lambeth, Executive Director
Joseph E. Kilpatrick, Assistant Director

Purpose
The Z. Smith Reynolds Foundation supports a wide variety of charitable activities in North Carolina only. In recent years the foundation has taken greater initiative to seek out new funding possibilities both for well-established institutions and leadership projects at the grassroots level.

Areas of Interest
The foundation's grants are generally grouped into the following six categories: criminal justice, women's issues, minority issues, economic/community development, environmental quality, and education.

Criminal Justice, Women, and Minorities. In criminal justice the foundation's goal is to help reduce North Carolina's reliance on incarceration by demonstrating the value of alternatives to imprisonment. In the area of women's issues, the focus is on putting economic independence for women at the top of the public policy agenda for the state. Grantmaking in the area of minority issues is spread generally among projects aimed at empowering Black people and opening the doors of opportunity.

Economic Development, Environment, and Education. In the area of economic/community development, the foundation is particularly interested in community projects that will help promote economic independence for women, minorities, and other disadvantaged groups. It should be noted that the foundation has made at least one grant to decrease the incidence of AIDS. Protecting North Carolina's environment and preserving ecologically sensitive areas are the goals of the foundation's grantmaking in the environmental quality area. And finally, in education, the foundation has made preschool, elementary, and

Z. Smith Reynolds Foundation

secondary education its priority, with special emphasis on projects that improve the quality of teaching and combat the problem of school dropouts.

In addition, the foundation has a catchall miscellaneous grantmaking program. Grants in this category have been made to projects working in such areas as grassroots organizing, the arts, intergenerational programs, and various social service programs for constituencies, including the elderly, the mentally ill, gays, and farmers.

Financial Data (year ended 12/31/87)[1]

Assets:[2]	$ 146,949,656
Total grants approved:	$ 5,811,145
Number of grants approved:	202
Highest grant:[3]	$ 375,000
Lowest grant:	$ 500
Median grant size:	$ 20,000

Application Procedures

The foundation requires that every applicant fill out and submit a three-page form in addition to a proposal. One copy of the complete application package must be postmarked or delivered to the office no later than February 1 or August 1 to be considered. The application form includes detailed instructions concerning deadlines, procedures, and proposal guidelines for submitting a complete application package. Applicants are also advised to review the guidelines contained in the foundation's annual report.

In brief, the application form asks for background information on both the organization and the project, including a breakdown of board

---

[1] The figures in this analysis were provided by the foundation in lieu of a grants list for 1987.

[2] This represents the combined assets of the Zachary Smith Reynolds trust and the W. N. Reynolds trust.

[3] This does not include a payment of $750,000 to Wake Forest University made as part of a continuing contractual commitment.

Z. Smith Reynolds Foundation

and staff membership by sex and minority representation, fiscal information, and the need for the project. The form must be signed by an authorized official of the organization. The proposal, which is not to exceed three single-spaced pages, must state the amount requested in the first paragraph. Attachments must include a one-page, line-item budget, including anticipated income and expenditures for the organization's current fiscal year and for the proposed project, a board of directors list with a description of how they are elected; and proof of tax-exempt status as a public charity from the IRS. Additional supporting materials for the proposal are optional.

Grant Limitations
The terms of the foundation's charter limit its grantmaking to charitable activities in the state of North Carolina. The policy is to make grants only to nonprofit, tax-exempt organizations falling under Section 501(c)(3) of the Internal Revenue Code or to governmental units. No grants are made to individuals for any purpose. Organizations that operate both within and outside the state may be eligible for consideration for programs operated exclusively in North Carolina. In general, the foundation gives very low priority to endowments and to brick-and-mortar projects.

Meeting Times
The board of trustees of the Z. Smith Reynolds Foundation meets twice annually to consider grant applications, the second Friday in May and the second Friday in November.

Publications
The foundation publishes an annual report and an application form.

Winthrop Rockefeller Foundation
308 East Eighth Street
Little Rock, Arkansas 72202
(501) 376-6854

Contact Person[1]
Mahlon Martin, President

Purpose
The Winthrop Rockefeller Foundation is committed to improvement of the quality of life in Arkansas. It implements this philosophy by encouraging broad-based leadership, entrepreneurial activities, and educational improvements. The foundation's emphasis is reflected in projects that eliminate existing barriers to a strong and diverse economy; encourage the prudent use of local and state resources; and build cooperative relationships among business, government, and education.

In addition to its grantmaking program, the foundation has initiated several programs including foundation-directed public policy projects, the Winthrop Rockefeller Fellows Program, and program-related investments. The foundation is also collaborating with the Shorebank Corporation and South Shore Bank to create a new corporation in Arkansas to increase human and capital resources for innovative rural economic development.

Areas of Interest
The foundation has selected education, civic affairs and economic development as its three primary areas for grantmaking. These programs are supplemented by grants made for leadership development and community empowerment and for public policy and advocacy. In addition the foundation makes small discretionary grants, usually not more than $2,000, for technical assistance and precollegiate education programs.

The foundation's interest in economic development encompasses

---

[1]Pre-proposal inquiries and letters should be directed to the staff person responsible for the program area in which support is sought. Economic development proposals should be addressed to the President, Thomas C. McRae; education proposals should go to Jacqueline Cox New, Senior Program Officer; leadership development and community empowerment proposals should be directed to Freeman McKindra, Senior Program Officer; public policy and advocacy proposals should go to Wendy Margolis, Director of Communications and Public Policy; and requests for mini-grants should be sent to the attention of Carolyn Hamm, Grants Manager.

Winthrop Rockefeller Foundation

two priorities: strengthening local economies and creating mechanisms that will provide the capital and human development needed to create employment opportunities in rural areas. The foundation is interested specifically in innovative programs that will help farmers stay on their land and in small business. In the education program five priority areas have been identified: education reform initiated at the building and district levels; a study of the impact of the state's educational reform efforts; innovative pre-service education for teachers and administrators; education for high risk youth; and the precollegiate mini-grant program.

The foundation's goals in the area of civic affairs include: (1) the development of effective leadership that enables poor, minority and disenfranchised citizens of Arkansas to better control their futures; and (2) strengthening human and other resources needed for community development and institutional effectiveness. Proposals for public policy projects must include plans for disseminating information and findings to the public.

In 1984 the foundation established the Community Incentive Program to offer basic assistance to agencies in Arkansas whose needs cannot be addressed through the regular grants program. These funds are used for projects that have the potential for significantly improving the quality of life in the communities in which they are located. Applicants must not be previous grantees of the foundation, and only those projects concerned with community development, education, or economic development will be considered. Applicants must represent minority concerns. Under this program the foundation will consider requests for general operating support, construction and equipment purchases if deemed critical to the agency's programmatic future. Consideration is not, however, limited strictly to these items. Grant awards in this program will not exceed $10,000.

Winthrop Rockefeller Foundation

Financial Data (year ended 12/31/87)

Assets:[2]	$	43,417,863
Total grants authorized:	$	1,610,155
Number of grants authorized:		104
Highest grant:[3]	$	60,000
Lowest grant:	$	400
Median grant size:	$	20,000

Technical Assistance Mini-grants

Total discretionary grants:	$	27,900
Number of discretionary grants:		30
Highest grant:	$	1,000
Lowest grant:	$	500
Median grant size:	$	1,000

Application Procedures

For the regular grants program, the foundation suggests that applicants first telephone, write a brief letter, or stop by the office. If it is determined that the project is likely to qualify for a grant, applicants may be asked to submit a formal proposal, no more than four pages long. Initial contact should not be made by sending a full proposal. The foundation has established a precise format and outline all proposals must follow if they are to receive consideration. These guidelines are spelled out in the annual report. Initial contact with the foundation must take place at least eight weeks prior to the quarterly meetings of the foundation's board of directors, if applicants expect prompt consideration. All applicants must provide proof of tax-exempt status.

Formal applications for training and technical assistance grants are not required. These grants are at the discretion of the foundation's president and may be made at any time. Applicants to the Community Incentive Program should follow the same guidelines as the regular grants program.

---

[2] Unaudited.
[3] This excludes one unusually large grant of $165,549.

Winthrop Rockefeller Foundation

Grant Limitations
The foundation does not make grants for annual or general fund drives, emergencies, most types of research, trips (unless they are part of a complete program's budget), scholarships or fellowships directly to individuals. With the exception of the Community Incentive Program (see above), the foundation does not support construction or equipment purchases.

Meeting Times
The board of the Winthrop Rockefeller Foundation meets quarterly, the first weekend of March, June, September, and December.

Publications
The foundation publishes an annual report that includes specific application guidelines.

Rosenberg Foundation
210 Post Street
San Francisco, California 94108
(415) 421-6105

Contact Person
Kirke Wilson, Executive Director

Purpose
The Rosenberg Foundation makes grants in the state of California for projects to benefit children and youth, with particular emphasis on minorities, low income families, and immigrants. Usually the foundation itself does not operate programs.

Areas of Interest
The foundation has two priority grantmaking categories. The first focuses on children in poverty and their families in rural and urban areas of California. In this area, the foundation is particularly interested in programs that reduce dependency, promote self-help, create access to the economic mainstream, or that address the causes of poverty among children and families. The second focus is the changing population of California. The emphasis of this program is on programs and activities that promote the full social, economic, and cultural integration of immigrants as well as minorities into a pluralistic society.

The foundation states that grants are made for projects that have the greatest feasibility and significance. Feasibility of a project includes the extent to which the leadership, setting, scale, and design are adequate to achieve its goals. Significance includes the importance of issues addressed and the potential of the project as a model, a source of permanent institutional reform, or a contribution to public social policy related to children and youth. The foundation also pays particular attention to projects sponsored by groups they are designed to serve.

Financial Data (year ended 12/31/87)
Assets:	$ 28,000,000
Total grants paid:	$ 1,334,642
Number of grants paid:	68
Highest grant:	$ 80,000
Lowest grant:	$ 500
Median grant size:	$ 19,779

Rosenberg Foundation

Application Procedures

The Rosenberg Foundation does not use standardized application forms, but prefers brief letters of inquiry that describe the proposed project, the applicant organization, and the estimated budget. If the project appears to fall within the foundation's program priorities, a complete application will be requested. That application must include a full narrative proposal, an itemized budget, and materials describing the applicant organization. The foundation publishes a full listing of the required contents of this application, which is available on request.

After an application has been accepted, the foundation staff usually arranges a visit to the project site. Because the foundation reviews a large number of applications, there is normally a two- or three-month waiting period before applications are considered by the board.

Grant Limitations

Except for a small number of grants in the field of philanthropy, the foundation does not make grants for programs outside California. Foundation policy also precludes grants to continue or expand projects started with funds from other sources or to match grants from other sources. Grants to purchase equipment, produce films, or publish materials are made only when such activities are a necessary part of a larger project supported by the foundation. No grants are made to individuals or for basic research, construction, scholarships, or operating expenses of ongoing programs.

Meeting Times

The board of directors of the Rosenberg Foundation meets monthly except during July and August.

Publications

The foundation publishes an annual report.

Helena Rubinstein Foundation
405 Lexington Avenue
New York, New York 10174
(212) 986-0806

Contact Person
Diane Moss, Executive Director

Areas of Interest
The Helena Rubinstein Foundation is primarily concerned with programs that benefit women and children in New York City. The foundation carries out its grantmaking activities within four broad program areas: education, community services, the arts, and health care and medical research. Within the education area, the foundation has shown particular interest in programs that make the visual and performing arts accessible to minority and disadvantaged public school children, and in fellowship and scholarship programs for women.

Community service grants in 1987 targeted programs for improving options and opening vistas for at-risk children and teenagers, including pregnancy prevention; parenting workshops; job training and placement; tutoring; counseling; and artistic, athletic, and recreational activities. A second focus area was support for programs designed to alleviate problems of the elderly, the disadvantaged, and the handicapped, including food distributions, camp vacations, senior centers, special education, and self-help groups.

In the arts, support was given to professional training and education and cultural institutions in performing and visual arts. Emphasis was placed upon programs for the disadvantaged and on programs for the schools.

In health care and medical research, the foundation made grants for ongoing support of treatment and research of eye diseases, cancer, birth defects, and children's blood diseases.

Financial Data (year ended 5/31/87)

Assets:	$	42,419,292
Total grants paid:	$	4,304,786
Number of grants:		242
Highest grant paid:	$	300,000
Lowest grant paid:[1]	$	2,000
Median grant size:	$	8,000

[1]This figure excludes miscellaneous small grants totaling $46,170.

Helena Rubinstein Foundation

Application Procedures

The foundation has no required application form, and it accepts proposals throughout the year. Organizations seeking funds are asked not to make telephone inquiries. The preferred means of contact is a brief letter outlining the project, its aims, budget, amount requested, other funding sources, and a short history of the organization.

Every proposal or inquiry is acknowledged in writing. If it is one the foundation is able to consider, more detailed information will be requested and, where feasible, a meeting or site visit will be arranged.

Grant Limitations

Grants are made only to federally tax-exempt, nonprofit organizations, generally for a one-year period. A grant may be considered for renewal on the basis of reports received, site visits, the foundation's priorities, and availability of funds. Grants are not made to individuals. Scholarship and fellowship grants are made directly to colleges and universities which, in turn, select recipients. Grants are not made for film or video projects, and the foundation does not make loans or provide emergency funds. Grants are rarely made to endowment funds and capital campaigns. Funding of new proposals is limited by ongoing and long-range commitments and fiscal constraints.

Meeting Times

The board of directors of the Helena Rubinstein Foundation holds semi-annual meetings, in May and November.

Publications

The Helena Rubinstein Foundation publishes an annual report.

The San Francisco Foundation
685 Market Street, 9th Floor
San Francisco, California 94105
(415) 543-0223

Contact Person
Robert M. Fisher, Director

Purpose
The San Francisco Foundation seeks out and encourages projects that add to the quality of life in the Bay Area by contributing to the aesthetic, physical, and social well-being of the community. Usually such projects fall into one or more of the following areas: (1) enhancing the enjoyment and appreciation of life through the arts, culture, and the humanities; (2) developing public policy; testing new methods of addressing problems; changing institutional behavior; and coordinating the activities of two or more established agencies.

The foundation's grantmaking is limited to the following counties in northern California: Alameda, Contra Costa, San Francisco, San Mateo, and Marin.

Areas of Interest
The foundation's activities can be grouped into the following broad general categories: the arts and humanities, community health, education, environment, and urban affairs.

Arts and Humanities. Grants are made according to the following priorities: performing arts, visual arts, literary arts, multidisciplinary arts, humanities, and related activities. Grantmaking in this area is designed to enhance the capacity of both individuals and communities to think creatively and critically about the aesthetic, ethical, and humanitarian issues of our times. There is an emphasis on projects that support organizational development, usually over a period of several years.

Community Health. These grants assist special populations in achieving and maintaining good physical, social, and mental health. Emphasis is placed on helping children, youth, and the elderly, with highest priority given to the needs of ethnic minorities and the disabled of all age groups. Program priorities

The San Francisco Foundation

are improving access to and delivery systems for direct services, health promotion, planning human-services systems to improve greater responsiveness to client needs, and organizational development to improve services. In 1986 and 1987 the foundation made a number of grants for AIDS-related services and public education.

Education. This program seeks to improve learning among elementary and secondary school children and to promote equal access to high quality education. Current program priorities include students with special needs and school and teacher improvement. A special interest is expressed in collaborative efforts.

Environment. The focus of this program is on the protection, rejuvenation, and public appreciation of the San Francisco Bay/Delta ecosystem through support for projects designed to instill an enlightened environmental ethic in government, business, the independent sector, and the general public. Specific program priorities include preservation of natural resources, public policy development, and environmental education. There is also a growing interest in programs that enhance the urban environment, with particular focus on low-income neighborhoods.

Urban Affairs. These grants are awarded to promote equal access and eliminate discrimination among disadvantaged populations, foster community and economic development, and to strengthen the capacity of individuals, institutions, and communities to address and solve problems. The priorities are projects concerned with housing, community development, community justice and civil rights, employment, economic development, civic participation, and communications.

In addition to the grants described above, the foundation provides short-term technical assistance grants to permit organizations to bring in expert assistance to strengthen management or otherwise improve the capacity to deliver services.

The San Francisco Foundation

Financial Data (year ended 6/30/87)

The foundation's assets, including unrestricted, restricted, and donor endowment funds totaled $178,641,014 as of June 30, 1987. During that year the annual report shows payments of $12,848,875 for grants, awards, and loans. The table below shows a breakdown of grants from unrestricted and field-of-interest funds by program category.

The San Francisco Foundation
Analysis of 1986-87 Grantmaking Activity

	Total Grants Paid	Number of Grants	Highest Grant	Lowest Grant	Median Grant Size
Education	$1,321,524	62	$170,000	$3,500	$25,000
Community Health	$1,886,919	163	$101,500	$3,000	$20,000
Urban Affairs	$1,826,302	132	$100,000	$5,000	$23,000
Arts and Humanities	$1,351,665	159	$50,000	$2,000	$10,000
Environment	$812,478	49	$88,400	$2,500	$15,000
Technical Assistance	$365,985	49	$19,000	$1,000	$4,000

Application Procedures

Interested applicants are encouraged to secure a copy of the foundation's annual priority statements and technical assistance guidelines, and to telephone the foundation both to arrange to attend one of the foundation's workshops, "How to Apply for a Grant" and to ascertain the foundation's current and forthcoming deadlines for proposal submission.

The first step in applying is to submit a letter of intent of no more than three pages. The letter should be addressed to the intake coordinator and should cover the following: (1) a project outline including goals, methods, project budget, and how much is requested from the foundation as well as from other potential sources of funding; (2) definition of the problem or issue to be addressed, expected results of project and how the project fits the foundation's goals; and (3) a description of the organization's purpose, programs, size of annual budget, and sources of current support.

Letters of intent are reviewed by staff, and applicants are notified

The San Francisco Foundation

within six weeks whether a full proposal is encouraged. If so, the foundation will send an application package with complete instructions on the requirements for the proposal. All proposals are reviewed by a program executive, and recommendations are prepared for the foundation's board of trustees. The process of review and recommendation for proposals normally takes three to five months.

Grant Limitations
The foundation makes grants only to tax-exempt nonprofit organizations with appropriate financial records and controls. Grants are not made for endowments, budget deficits, medical research, direct assistance to individuals, or for scholarships.

Meeting Times
Grantmaking decisions are made by the board of trustees of The San Francisco Foundation, which meets at approximately two-month intervals.

Publications
The foundation publishes an annual report and distributes information on guidelines, procedures, and deadlines for applications.

The Sanford Foundation
Post Office Box 14983
Santa Rosa, California 95402[1]

Contact Person
Patricia S. Turner, Executive Director

Purpose
The goal of The Sanford Foundation is to enhance the quality of life in specific communities by providing technical staff assistance and direct financial support to qualifying tax-exempt organizations that address social and cultural concerns facing society. The geographic interests of the foundation are Claremont and the Pomona Valley, Santa Rosa and Walnut Creek, California; Eugene, Oregon; and Mendham, New Jersey. Grants for projects outside these areas are not considered.

Areas of Interest
The foundation's priority interests are social, civic, youth, the elderly, and cultural programs. In the social program area the foundation supports programs that help people become self-reliant and projects dealing with the causes of domestic violence. The focus of grants made in the civic area is promoting productivity and foster the work ethic and grassroots community development programs. The youth category emphasizes programs that strive to develop the full potential of children by providing experiences that promote independent thinking, acceptance of responsibility, and physical and social skill development. In the elderly category the foundation supports projects that encourage seniors to lead independent and productive lives. Finally, in the cultural category the foundation seeks programs that foster understanding and appreciation of cultural heritages or the performing arts.

The foundation will consider requests for seed money for pilot programs that are innovative and can serve as models for action in other communities. Preference is given to projects that address the causes of problems rather than just treating the symptoms and to those with potential for independent funding. The foundation's intent is to provide funds that will act as a challenge or catalyst, thereby enabling grantees

---

[1]Just as this entry was being finalized, the foundation moved. While the post office box number is current as of March 1988, a telephone number was not available.

The Sanford Foundation

to secure additional funding. As a general rule, grants are made on a nonrecurring basis.

In addition, the foundation offers low-cost seminars and workshops to local nonprofit groups on subjects such as fund-raising, board development and management, budgeting, and volunteer management. For further information, contact the foundation.

Financial Data (year ended 8/31/86)

Support and revenue:	$	70,073
Total grants paid:	$	43,685
Number of grants paid:		62
Highest grant:	$	5,000
Lowest grant:	$	15
Median grant size:	$	100

Application Procedures

Interested applicants should submit one copy of a letter, no more than two pages, signed by both the president of the governing board and the director of the organization. Initial letters are due by February 1 for consideration in the spring and by August 1 for consideration in the fall.

The letter should include: (1) a general introduction to the organization; (2) a concise description of the project, including the specific goals and projected methods to achieve those goals; (3) a project budget; (4) the amount of money and/or type of technical assistance requested from the foundation; and (5) evidence of Section 501(c)(3) tax-exempt status. If it appears the request falls within the foundation's guidelines, an application form will be sent. When that is received, the applicant will be contacted to arrange a site visit and discuss the proposal more thoroughly.

Grant Limitations

The foundation will not consider proposals for direct grants, scholarships, or fellowships to individuals; endowments; operating budgets of United Way member agencies; projects of sectarian or religious organizations

The Sanford Foundation

whose principal benefit is for their own members or adherents; propagandizing or influencing elections or legislation; and government agencies or institutions primarily supported by tax revenues.

Meeting Times
The board of directors of The Sanford Foundation meets twice a year, in the spring and fall.

Publications
The foundation distributes a brochure describing its interests and application procedures.

The Sapelo Island Research Foundation
57 Forsythe Street, Suite 300
Atlanta, Georgia 30303
(404) 525–6444

Contact Person
Alan McGregor, Executive Director

Purpose
After many years as an operating foundation, The Sapelo Island Research Foundation became a grantmaking organization in the mid-1980s. Approximately half of its grantmaking budget goes to support research in marine biology at the University of Georgia Marine Institute on Sapelo Island and to other work on Sapelo Island itself. The other half goes to social-concern projects, first in the three counties surrounding Sapelo Island (McIntosh, Glynn, and Long), and second in the rest of the state of Georgia. On occasion, the foundation supports projects of regionwide significance.

Areas of Interest
The primary interests of the foundation are in the areas of environmental, biological, marine, and coastal sciences. However, in addition, the foundation makes grants to a variety of grassroots projects sharing a basic commitment to empowerment and providing leverage for people to help themselves. Among the issues addressed are the environment, employment, pay equity, civil liberties, peace, voter registration, hunger, and civil rights and race relations.

Financial Data (year ended 6/30/87)
Assets:	$	14,344,031
Total grants authorized:	$	468,738
Number of grants authorized:		31
Highest grant:[1]	$	20,000
Lowest grant:	$	2,500
Median grant size:	$	10,000

---

[1]This excludes one unusually large grant of $175,000.

The Sapelo Island Research Foundation

Application Procedures
Applicants are requested to make all preliminary inquiries by letter, which the foundation says it will respond to immediately. Before submitting a formal proposal, a brief two- or three-page summary of the project with a budget and proof of tax-exempt status should be sent to the foundation. It should include a clear identification of the problem, the project's goals and strategies for achieving these goals, the proposed solution, and the value that such a project has for society. If the idea of the project falls within the foundation's primary areas of interest, the applicant will be contacted and asked to submit a formal proposal.

Formal proposals requested by the foundation must include: (1) background information on the project, including past accomplishments; (2) objectives of the proposal, plan of development, strategies for implementation, and anticipated results; (3) method of evaluation, including what criteria will be used; (4) a complete organizational budget; (5) a calendar of project activity; and (6) information about other support received or being requested. The deadlines for submitting proposals once requested by the foundation are March 15 and September 15. Grants are awarded six to eight weeks later, and successful applicants will be notified promptly.

Grant Limitations
The activities of the foundation are limited primarily to coastal Georgia, with some support for projects in other parts of the state and projects with regionwide significance.

Meeting Times
The board of directors of The Sapelo Island Research Foundation meets twice a year, in June and December.

Publications
The foundation publishes a brochure identifying its program interests, application guidelines, and recent grant awards.

The Shalan Foundation
82 Second Street, #300
San Francisco, California 94105
(415) 543–4561

Contact Persons
Catherine Lerza, Executive Director
Diana Campoamor, Communications Director
Terri Lowe, Administration

Purpose
The Shalan Foundation supports organizations that explore, develop, and advocate policies that will result in structural changes in the economic system leading to greater social justice and environmental balance.

Areas of Interest
The foundation is interested in projects aimed at improving public policy in resource management, including agriculture and timber, and industrial policy, including policy issues related to employment and investment. The foundation also supports projects that attempt to improve citizens' ability to participate effectively in public-policy decision-making, including coalition building, campaign finance reform, and economic education. The foundation's primary focus is the western United States, particularly California; however, some grants are made to national organizations.

Financial Data (year ended 9/30/87)

Assets:[1]	$	1,452,448
Total grants authorized:	$	290,000
Number of grants paid:		24
Highest grant:	$	50,000
Lowest grant:	$	5,000
Median grant size:	$	10,000

Application Procedures
Funding requests are collected and reviewed after March 1 and July 15. The foundation prefers to receive a short summary proposal or a letter describing the project for which funds are sought. Foundation staff will

---

[1]Unaudited.

The Shalan Foundation

provide an acknowledgment of receipt, review this initial submission after the dates above, and then request more detailed information if there is serious interest in a specific proposal.

Grant Limitations

The foundation primarily supports activities in the western part of the United States, and particularly California. However, grants are made occasionally to national public-policy organizations. The foundation does not support social or direct service programs; medical, cultural, or educational institutions, including museums and clinics; construction or renovation programs; scholarships or other assistance to individuals, including university research fellowships; media, including periodicals, radio, or television programs, investigative journalism, films, or videotapes; international programs or programs dealing with international issues; voter registration projects; and groups where the highest paid staff member receives more than three times the salary of the lowest full-time staff person.

Meeting Times

The board of directors of The Shalan Foundation meets twice a year, in the spring and fall, to make funding decisions.

Publications

The foundation publishes grant guidelines and grantee lists, but does not publish financial data.

Gardiner Howland Shaw Foundation
45 School Street
Boston, Massachusetts 02108
(617) 451-9206

Contact Persons
Kenneth S. Safe, Trustee
Ellen DeBay, Assistant

Purpose
The Shaw Foundation was established for the study, prevention, correction, and alleviation of crime and delinquency, and the rehabilitation of adult and juvenile offenders. The foundation limits its grants to programs in Massachusetts.

Areas of Interest
The foundation concentrates its support on projects that explore new ideas and approaches to criminal-justice issues. One half of the foundation's support is awarded to programs working on specific problems in the courts. Within this area, priority is given to programs that: (1) offer alternative sentencing options through restitution, community work service, pretrial diversion, home confinement, specialized probation, or other means; (2) resolve disputes outside the criminal courts through mediation, arbitration, conciliation, and other pretrial settlement techniques; (3) encourage or expand the use of substitutes for confinement; or (4) strengthen the role of the community in the courts or improve the responsiveness of the courts to community needs.

The other half is divided between two emphases. Thirty percent of available grant funds goes to former grant recipients, mostly for programs serving minority or female offenders and helping committed juveniles or adults return to crime-free lives in the community. The remaining twenty percent goes to support new ideas or approaches to criminal justice problems.

Financial Data (year ended 4/30/87)

Assets:	$	9,674,650
Total grants paid:	$	345,923
Number of grants paid:[1]		32
Highest grant:	$	38,500
Lowest grant:	$	500
Median grant size:	$	8,150

---

[1]This figure and the computations below do not include $28,023 in miscellaneous grants for justice-related projects, technical assistance, and emergency assistance.

Gardiner Howland Shaw Foundation

Application Procedures

Deadlines for applications are January 2, May 1, and September 1 for consideration at the meeting the month after each deadline. Grant applicants are asked to submit brief proposals, three to five pages in length, explaining the problem to be addressed, clients to be served, program objectives and methods, evaluation plan, and the specific grant request. The following materials must be attached: (1) IRS proof of tax-exempt and public charity status; (2) brief profiles of staff and key volunteers; (3) names of board members (with affiliations); (4) budget for the proposed project and the organization; (5) an independent audit, IRS Form 990, or a Massachusetts Form PC; and (6) plans for future funding.

Grant Limitations

The trustees of the Shaw Foundation have made it a policy not to fund substance abuse or mental health counseling, the arts, endowments, capital requests, or proposals from individuals. The foundation does not consider requests for proportional support of programs that happen to serve offenders among a much larger, more diverse client group.

Meeting Times

The board of trustees of the Gardiner Howland Shaw Foundation meets to consider grant applications in February, June, and October.

Publications

The foundation publishes an annual list of grants.

The Sophia Fund
53 West Jackson Boulevard, Room 825
Chicago, Illinois 60604
(312) 663-1552

Contact Person
Sunny Fischer, Executive Director

Purpose
The founder of The Sophia Fund envisions this funding resource as a means to work in partnership with those active in addressing the concerns of women and to encourage others to increase the pool of resources directed specifically to women's issues. The fund attempts to respond to the economic, social, cultural, and political inequalities women experience. The fund's primary interest is in Chicago; however, several grants are made to national organizations.

Areas of Interest
The fund focuses on four different issues: economic justice, domestic violence, reproductive rights, and efforts to increase the amount of traditional philanthropic resources directed to women's issues. The rationale for its support of organizations working on economic justice is that barriers to achieving economic equity must be addressed before women will be able to take care of their own human needs and those of their children. Its support for projects working on domestic violence and reproductive rights is grounded in a belief that the right to determine what happens to one's body, one's health, and one's safety is fundamental to living a free and productive life. Preference is given to social change efforts rather than to social services.

Generally the fund seeks to be responsive to advocacy organizations that attempt to foster long-term change by empowering women to take control over their own lives. It supports groups working to increase public awareness and education about the effect on women of laws, public policy, and services. Most of the fund's support is concentrated in the Chicago area, but a small number of national organizations may be considered for grants.

The Sophia Fund contributes to general operating expenses and special projects. Grants are usually under $10,000 and most often in the form of marketable securities. Generally a six-month and annual report

The Sophia Fund

are necessary, and there may be other requirements that are part of the grant agreement. Renewed funding depends on a reapplication and evaluation process and on the current focus of the fund.

Financial Data (year ended 6/30/87)

Support and revenue:[1]	$	229,513
Total grants paid:	$	208,000
Number of grants paid:		60
Highest grant:	$	10,000
Lowest grant:	$	500
Median grant size:	$	3,500

Application Procedures

There are two application deadlines: March 1 and September 1. These deadlines will be extended to the first workday after these dates when the deadline falls on a weekend or a holiday.

To apply for a grant, applicants should prepare a proposal, not more than five pages long, which includes: (1) a description of the sponsoring organization and populations served; (2) the issue being addressed; (3) method of addressing the issue; (4) past accomplishments of the organization or a brief history of its work in the community; and (5) a plan to evaluate the work.

In addition, the following should be attached: an itemized budget for the project and sponsoring organization (with current and projected foundation and corporate support); a list of staff and board members and résumés of those responsible for the project or program; the organization's latest audited financial statement (if available); the organization's most recently completed IRS Form 990; and proof of tax-exempt status.

Grant Limitations

The fund does not support individuals, scholarships or fellowships, medical research, or religious organizations for religious purposes.

---

[1]For the year ended June 30, 1986

The Sophia Fund

Meeting Times
Grant decisions are made twice a year.

Publications
The fund publishes a brochure that includes its application guidelines and a list of recent grant awards.

Southern Education Foundation, Inc.
135 Auburn Avenue, 2nd Floor
Atlanta, Georgia 30303
(404) 523–0001

Contact Persons
Elridge W. McMillan, President
Jean Sinclair, Program Officer

Purpose

The Southern Education Foundation has as its principal purpose the advancement of equal and quality educational opportunity for Blacks in southern states. A major ingredient in many of the programs funded by the foundation is the evidence of innovative, people-oriented approaches to finding solutions to educational inequities.

Areas of Interest

The foundation's grantmaking program addresses a continuum of educational concerns, from preschool to postgraduate and professional development. In elementary and secondary education the foundation stresses the resolution of issues as opposed to the delivery of services. In higher education it is concerned primarily with the needs of Black colleges. The foundation also emphasizes networking and bringing new players with innovative solutions to problems of race and class into education. Generally the foundation prefers to fund specific programs or projects rather than to make grants for general operating support.

The foundation also operates a program of its own in education and public policy. Some preference is given to activities that complement or supplement this program. In lieu of a grant, the foundation sometimes issues contracts to qualified agencies or individuals to perform services.

A small portion of the foundation's resources is allocated to local activities that are somewhat outside the specifically defined interest in education.

Financial Data (year ended 3/31/87)

Assets:	$ 10,963,931
Total grants paid:	$ 203,938
Number of grants paid:	32
Highest grant:	$ 30,000
Lowest grant:	$ 1,330
Median grant size:	$ 4,045

Southern Education Foundation, Inc.

Application Procedures

The foundation accepts proposals throughout the year. However, the deadline for proposals to be considered at the spring meeting of the board is February 1; for the fall meeting it is September 1. Interested organizations should send a letter of inquiry to the foundation describing generally the problem to be met and its proposed solution. Staff will respond to such inquiries and provide advice about whether a formal proposal should be prepared.

Proposals should include the following information: (1) organization name and address; (2) purpose of project; (3) background of need; (4) plan of operation; (5) length of proposed activity; (6) anticipated results; (7) method of project evaluation; (8) itemized budget for the total project and amount requested from the foundation; (9) demonstration of additional financial support; (10) qualifications of project director or person responsible for operating the project; and (11) proof of the organization's tax-exempt status.

Grant Limitations

The foundation will not award more than $30,000 to any organization during one year. The foundation does not award grants for individual research, fellowships, scholarships, or loans. Grants are not made for building construction, annual fund-raising campaigns, or travel. By charter, the foundation is restricted to grantmaking that benefits residents of the South.

Meeting Times

The board of trustees of the Southern Education Foundation meets twice a year, in the spring and fall.

Publications

The foundation publishes an annual report, quarterly newsletter, giving guidelines, and research and conference reports.

Taconic Foundation, Inc.
745 Fifth Avenue
New York, New York 10151
(212) 758-8673

Contact Person
Jane Lee J. Eddy, Executive Director

Purpose
The Taconic Foundation directs most of its grants to programs in the New York City area that are aimed at furthering equality of opportunity in various aspects of national life, including those related to economic well-being.

Areas of Interest
The foundation places special emphasis on youth employment, housing, and related aspects of land use policy. Some support is also available for projects related to broader civil rights issues, voting rights, voter registration and education, and to other programs serving children and youth.

Financial Data (year ended 12/31/85)
Assets:	$ 12,662,647
Total grants paid:	$ 819,004
Number of grants paid:	37
Highest grant:[1]	$ 30,800
Lowest grant:	$ 500
Median grant size:	$ 10,000

Application Procedures
The foundation does not require a special application form and reviews proposals throughout the year. The foundation specifically requests proposals that have well-defined goals, specific plans for achieving them and for financing the project, and that take into consideration other related work. In order to be eligible for grants from the Taconic Foundation, applicants must provide proof of tax-exempt status.

---

[1]This figure omits two unusually large grants of over $200,000 made to the Potomac Institute and the Smokey House Project.

Taconic Foundation, Inc.

Grant Limitations

The foundation does not make grants to local community programs outside New York City except in special instances directly related to the foundation's program priorities. Regional projects are occasionally supported, and national programs only rarely. Nor does the foundation make grants for the following purposes: buildings or endowments, higher education, scholarships and fellowships, the elderly, arts and cultural programs, mass media, crime and justice, health, medicine, mental health, the environment, and international programs.

Meeting Times

The board of directors of the Taconic Foundation meets four to six times per year.

Publications

The foundation publishes a biennial report and distributes, on request, a yearly listing of grants.

Van Ameringen Foundation, Inc.
509 Madison Avenue
New York, New York 10022
(212) 758-6221

Contact Persons
Patricia Kind, President and Treasurer
Eleanor Sypher, Assistant to the President

Purpose
The Van Ameringen Foundation is primarily devoted to furthering the field of mental health and related social issues. The foundation provides support for programs that respond to changing conditions and is receptive to exploring emerging needs. The underlying philosophy is that mental illness and mental health affect many aspects of human behavior and daily life. The focus is on projects in the New York metropolitan area, with occasional grants made to projects in the Boston to Washington, D.C., corridor. Rarely does the foundation make grants on a regional or national basis.

Areas of Interest
Within its program interest, the broad field of mental health, the foundation's present concern is with access to and delivery of appropriate and effective therapeutic care. The foundation is particularly interested in preventive and early intervention strategies, especially those that work in tandem with education programs; programs that demonstrate the relative merits of various therapies; programs that feature the creative mixing of public and private efforts on behalf of mental health clients; programs that increase the accessibility of mental health services to the poor and needy; and programs incorporating self-help models. Several grants have been made for AIDS-related services, including the problems of turnover, stress, and burnout among health care professionals and volunteers working with AIDS victims.

In rare instances the foundation will make highly selective grants to cultural, environmental, and recreational projects within its geographic scope.

Van Ameringen Foundation, Inc.

Financial Data (year ended 12/31/86)

Assets:	$ 15,759,227
Total grants paid:	$ 1,104,674
Number of grants paid:	36
Highest grant:	$ 100,000
Lowest grant:	$ 1,250
Median grant size:	$ 25,000

Application Procedures

The foundation does not use application forms and does not have established deadlines. It is suggested that contact with the foundation be initiated by letter and proposal eight weeks prior to the month of a board meeting. The letter should provide a concise statement of the aims and significance of the proposed work and state clearly the duration and amount of requested support. The proposal, which should not exceed five typewritten pages, should state: (1) the project design; (2) the qualifications of the organization and individuals involved; (3) evaluation mechanisms; and (4) a budget noting all planned expenditures and anticipated sources of income. Proof of tax-exempt status must be attached and recent financial statements should be included.

Grant Limitations

Applications outside the geographic focus of the foundation are not encouraged, and regional or national grants are made only occasionally. Foundation policy excludes consideration of applications for endowment purposes, capital projects, annual fund-raising drives, and support of international activities and institutions in foreign countries. Grants are made to tax-exempt organizations; under no circumstances are grants made in direct support of individuals.

Meeting Times

The board of directors of the Van Ameringen Foundation, Inc., considers grant proposals three times annually, generally in March, June, and November.

Van Ameringen Foundation, Inc.

Publications

The foundation has two publications, an annual report and a booklet, *The Foundation and Its Program,* which includes application procedures.

Vanguard Public Foundation
14 Precita Avenue
San Francisco, California 94110
(415) 285-2005

Contact Person
Beth Rosales, Executive Director

Purpose
The Vanguard Public Foundation supports groups organizing to confront fundamental problems affecting their lives and working toward a redistribution of wealth and power. Although the foundation concentrates its direct funding on projects located within the nine San Francisco Bay Area counties, through its participation in the New York-based Funding Exchange,[1] the foundation supports progressive social change nationally and internationally.

Areas of Interest
Vanguard functions on the premise that the value of the foundation lies in its ability to respond effectively to the priorities that community leadership, in turn, derives from its constituencies. Vanguard, therefore, encourages applications for support from and for these communities: (1) low-income and working-class groups promoting self-determination for traditionally disenfranchised communities; (2) groups working to end racism, sexism, homophobia, and economic exploitation, with priority given to those working for the rights of women, third world people, Native Americans, lesbians, gay men, the disabled, youth, and the elderly; and (3) groups addressing the underlying systemic causes of poverty and injustice with programs to alter those systems. Priority is also given to organizations promoting peace and a responsible foreign policy.

Financial Data (year ended 6/30/86)
It should be noted that contributions to the Vanguard Public Foundation are divided equally between the community and donor boards, which make funding decisions at separate meetings. The maximum grant each

---

[1]For more information about The Funding Exchange, its programs, and other members, see the entry under National Grantmakers for "The Funding Exchange."

Vanguard Public Foundation

board can make is $5,000, so that a project can receive as much as $10,000. Grantmaking activity of both boards is combined below.

Support and revenue:	$	506,563
Total grants paid:	$	277,030
Number of grants paid:		103
Highest grant:	$	5,000
Lowest grant:	$	500
Median grant size:	$	2,500

Application Procedures

A statement of Vanguard's funding guidelines and an application form can be obtained by telephoning the foundation. Proposal deadlines are July 1, October 1, January 1, and April 1.

In addition to the application, a written proposal of no more than five pages must be submitted. The proposals should include: (1) a brief history of the organization and description of its structure and decision-making process; (2) a description of the membership, including advisory committee and/or board of directors and of the constituency served in terms of race, sex, sexual preference, disability, age, geographic region, etc.; (3) a statement of the organization's purpose, goals, and methods for achieving them; (4) a description of the project for which support is sought, if applicable; (5) budget and other financial information; (6) a description of relations with other groups working on the same or similar issues; (7) a self-evaluation including strengths and weaknesses as an organization; (8) proof of tax-exempt status, or, if applicable, that of the project's fiscal sponsor; and (9) the names of three individuals or groups, with phone numbers, who are familiar with the applicant's work.

Preliminary screening by the advisory funding boards will determine whether the project is to be rejected at this point or the applicant to be scheduled for an interview. After the interview the final funding decision will be made at the next board meeting. Applicants should expect the whole process to last approximately five months. Past grantees may apply for additional funding on a schedule described in the foundation's application package.

Vanguard Public Foundation

Meeting Times

The community and donor boards of the Vanguard Foundation each meet quarterly.

Publications

The Vanguard Foundation publishes an annual report and a newsletter, and distributes program guidelines and application forms upon request.

Victoria Foundation, Inc.
40 South Fullerton Avenue
Montclair, New Jersey 07042
(201) 783-4450

Contact Person
Catherine M. McFarland, Executive Officer

Areas of Interest
The Victoria Foundation primarily supports projects in Newark, New Jersey. Its principal areas of interest are education, environment, ethnic and geographic communities, and youth and families.

Education grants support a variety of core and enrichment programs in the public and private schools, promote greater readiness for and access to college education for disadvantaged students, and support other educational programs such as career guidance and adult literacy. In the environment area, grants are made to groups that are addressing urgent environmental problems within New Jersey, including toxics, preservation of pinelands, wildlife, and shoreline, and resource recovery.

Through its ethnic and geographic communities grants, the foundation supports self-help programs within minority and disadvantaged communities dealing with issues including housing, job training, health services, and education. Youth and family grants provide support for programs dealing with such issues as adolescent pregnancy and parenting, mental health and counseling, wellness promotion, tutoring and training, and families in crisis.

In addition to these areas, the foundation makes grants for a miscellany of issues including drug and alcohol abuse, support services for small businesses, and services to prisoners. A particular focus of 1986 grantmaking was employment training.

Financial Data (year ended 12/31/87)

Assets:	$	72,302,000
Total grants paid:	$	3,681,782
Number of grants paid:[1]		134
Highest grant:	$	100,000
Lowest grant:	$	6,000
Median grant size:	$	20,000

[1] This figure omits 32 miscellaneous small grants totaling $68,500.

Victoria Foundation, Inc.

Application Procedures

Prospective grantees may submit either a brief letter outlining the details of the project or a full proposal. The foundation prefers a concise two-page summary of the project. Deadlines for receiving proposals are March 15 for spring consideration and September 15 for fall. The following basic information should be included: proof of the applicant's tax exempt status from the IRS; names and affiliations of the board of directors; description of the project indicating what it is expected to accomplish; explanation of need for project; constituency to be served; a budget showing projected sources of income and anticipated expenditures; information about the organization and its accomplishments to date; starting and ending dates together with any plans for postgrant funding and evaluation; and indication of persons who will implement and bear ultimate responsibility for the program.

Grant Limitations

Organizations outside the state of New Jersey are requested not to apply for grants. Rare out-of-state grant awards are made at the initiation of the foundation and not in response to applications. The foundation makes no grants to individuals or for programs dealing with specific diseases, afflictions, geriatric needs, or day care.

Meeting Times

The board of trustees of the Victoria Foundation meets semiannually, in May and December.

Publications

The foundation publishes an annual report.

Virginia Environmental Endowment
1051 East Cary Street
Post Office Box 790
Richmond, Virginia 23206-0790
(804) 644-5000

Contact Person
Gerald P. McCarthy, Executive Director

Purpose
The purpose of the Virginia Environmental Endowment is to improve the quality of the environment in Virginia. It funds projects related to water quality and the effects of water pollution on human health and the environment in the Ohio River and Kanawha River valleys, particularly those that actively involve people in developing solutions to environmental needs. The endowment prefers constructive, results-oriented projects carried out by existing organizations. Activities that bring business, government, and environmental groups together to address environmental opportunities are encouraged.

Areas of Interest
The endowment makes grants within two major program areas: the Virginia Program and the Water Quality Program. The Virginia Program focuses specifically on improving the quality of the environment, locally and statewide, for the benefit of the citizens of the Commonwealth of Virginia. Within this area the priorities are: the Chesapeake Bay; land use; waste management; toxic substances and their effects on human health, water quality, and the environment; local environmental improvement; environmental mediation; and environmental law and public policy. Proposals submitted to the Water Quality Program must specifically address water quality and the effects of water pollution on public health and the environment in the Ohio River and Kanawha River valleys. Eligible activities include research, education, and action-oriented projects that promote regional cooperation and citizen participation.

Financial Data (year ended 3/31/87)

Assets:	$	18,166,087
Total grants authorized:	$	916,217
Number of grants authorized:		38
Highest grant:	$	55,000
Lowest grant:	$	1,220
Median grant size:	$	21,432

Virginia Environmental Endowment

Application Procedures

Proposals must be received by the endowment by 5:00 P.M. Eastern time, on January 15, May 15, and September 15. When these dates fall on a weekend, the following Monday is the deadline.

The endowment does not use application forms, nor does it review preliminary proposals. Applicants should submit four copies of their full proposal signed by the chief executive officer or board chairman.

Proposals should include: (1) a project description (about five pages) stating the need for the project, its objectives and purposes, and its significance in relation to other work being done in the field; (2) information about the organization, qualifications of key personnel, a list of the board members, and proof of tax-exempt status; (3) a line-item budget showing all sources and amounts of matching funds, all anticipated income and expenses, and plans for future support; (4) a project schedule; (5) plans for continuing project activities and raising financial support beyond the grant period; and (6) a detailed plan for evaluation stating method and criteria.

Grants are normally made for up to one year. Matching funds are usually required, and challenge grants may be offered to provide leverage in fund-raising efforts. Approved grants are paid in installments on a reimbursement basis. Grantees are required to submit periodic reports of progress and expenditures as well as a final evaluation report at the end of the grant period.

Grant Limitations

Ordinarily funds are not provided for overhead, indirect costs, building funds, endowments, or lawsuits.

Meeting Times

The board of directors of the Virginia Environmental Endowment usually meets in March, July, and November.

Publications

The endowment publishes an annual report.

Wieboldt Foundation
53 West Jackson Boulevard, Suite 930
Chicago, Illinois 60604
(312) 786-9377

Contact Person
Anne C. Hallett, Executive Director

Purpose
The Wieboldt Foundation is a private foundation incorporated in Illinois, primarily interested in Chicago. The foundation looks for organizations that have been created by community residents and that are controlled by and accountable to them. It seeks to support organizations that serve as vehicles through which neighborhood people themselves can define issues and develop their own strategies for dealing with these issues. Typical grantee organizations of the foundation are governed by neighborhood residents and pursue a multi-issue agenda.

Areas of Interest
Approximately sixty percent of the foundation's grants are made to neighborhood-based organizations that give local residents a structure for decision-making and action on issues of concern. A high priority is enabling citizens in the city's poorest neighborhoods to shape their own future and to oversee and implement investment of resources in their neighborhoods. Most of the remaining budget is devoted to groups that support the work of community organizations through policy development, advocacy, technical assistance and expertise, and by pushing the frontiers of thinking and action.

Financial Data (year ended 12/31/86)[1]

Assets:	$	10,114,961
Total grants paid:	$	395,000
Number of grants paid:		54
Highest grant:	$	22,000
Lowest grant:	$	1,000
Median grant size:	$	6,000

---

[1]Although complete data were not available for analysis, it should be noted that on December 31, 1987, the assets of the foundation were valued at $13,110,315 and that during that calendar year the foundation made 54 grants totaling $490,525.

Wieboldt Foundation

Application Procedures

The foundation does not use standard application forms, and it reviews proposals throughout the year. Applications received by the first of the month are usually placed on that month's grantmaking agenda.

Applications should include a summary page with a one- or two-sentence description of the organization or program for which funding is sought; the total budget of the organization, the total amount of the project, if appropriate, and the amount requested from the foundation; and a summary of the request.

The main body of the proposal (excluding financial information) should not exceed ten pages, and the foundation requests that applicants not bind their proposals or reproduce them on both sides of the page. Proposals should include: (1) information about the history, program, and activities of the applicant organization, including its structure, membership, and staff; (2) information about how the organization increases the skills and competence of leaders and staff members; (3) a listing of officers and members of the organization's governing body, including their work and/or community affiliations; and (4) financial information about the organization.

The financial information should include: the organization's total budget of expenses and potential income for the year for which support is sought, including a list of anticipated and committed income from foundations and corporations; the total budget of expenses and anticipated income of the project for which support is requested (if different); a financial report showing actual expenses and income from the most recently completed budget year, including a list of sources of income from foundations and corporations; a copy of the organization's most recent audit; and information establishing the tax-exempt status of the applicant.

Meeting Times

The board of directors of the Wieboldt Foundation meets ten times a year, every month except August and December.

Publications

The foundation publishes an annual report.

Wisconsin Community Fund
222 South Hamilton Street, Suite 4
Madison, Wisconsin 53703
(608) 251-6834

Contact Persons
Elizabeth Lawrence
Steven Starkey

Purpose
The Wisconsin Community Fund is a progressive foundation established to support positive social change for the people of Wisconsin. It supports organizations and activities working to create a more just and harmonious world by making small grants of seed money and ongoing support on a project basis and for general operating expenses. The fund supports progressive social change nationally and internationally through its participation in the New York-based Funding Exchange.[1]

Areas of Interest
The fund supports organizations based in Wisconsin that reach out to and involve their constituencies, work toward the empowerment of individual citizens, challenge societal institutions and attitudes, organize low-income and minority peoples, operate in a cooperative manner, and demonstrate limited access to more traditional sources of funding.

Financial Data (year ended 6/30/87)

Support and revenue:	$	123,884
Total grants paid:	$	57,000
Number of grants paid:		23
Highest grant:	$	7,000
Lowest grant:	$	1,000
Median grant size:	$	2,500

Application Procedures
Groups interested in applying for a grant should contact the fund by telephone or in writing to determine the precise dates of the spring and fall funding cycles. Next, no more than two weeks after a cycle has begun,

---

[1]For more information about The Funding Exchange, its programs, and other members, see the entry under National Grantmakers for "The Funding Exchange."

Wisconsin Community Fund

a one-page letter should be sent to the fund; it should describe the organization (or project, if applicable) and have a sentence about the amount of funding requested. Organizations fulfilling the fund's guidelines will then receive application packages to be completed and returned to the fund (in 15 copies) within one month.

Grant Limitations
The fund supports only groups working in Wisconsin and having federal tax-exempt status or a tax-exempt fiscal sponsor. Groups may apply for general operating expenses or specific project support; however, in order to qualify for operating support, an organization's annual administrative budget may not exceed $30,000. The fund does not support the projects of individuals, national projects, social service agencies, academic research, religious projects, and cultural or media projects that are not part of a larger educational or organizing effort.

Meeting Times
The community funding board of the Wisconsin Community Fund meets in the spring and fall to consider grant requests.

Publications
The fund publishes an annual newsletter that includes information on the timetables for each funding cycle. The fund also distributes a brochure describing its guidelines.

The Women's Foundation
3543 Eighteenth Street, #9
San Francisco, California 94110
(415) 431-1290

Contact Persons
Roma Guy, Executive Director
Paula Ross, Allocations Coordinator

Purpose
The Women's Foundation is a community foundation that provides grants
to women's and girls' projects and educates women about financial management and philanthropy in northern California. The foundation's grantmaking is for the purpose of improving the economic, social, cultural,
and political status of women and girls.

Areas of Interest
Grants are made for resource development that strengthens the self-
sufficiency and income base of organizations. The target populations of
the foundation are low-income women and girls in the following categories: disabled women and girls, women and girls of color, women under
age 40, lesbians, women over age 60, and single mothers. Preference is
given to organizations in which one or more of the members of the target
populations are involved in the organization's planning and decision-
making. Organizations from rural areas are particularly encouraged to
apply.

Financial Data (year ended 12/31/87)

Support and revenue:[1]	$	566,058
Total grants paid:	$	170,000
Number of grants paid:		38
Highest grant:	$	10,000
Lowest grant:	$	2,500
Median grant size:	$	5,000

---

[1]These figures were supplied by the foundation in lieu of a grants list.

The Women's Foundation

Application Procedures

Applicants should write or telephone the foundation and request guidelines and application forms. If the foundation determines that the proposed project meets its guidelines, an application will be invited and a site visit will be scheduled. Request of a site visit should be interpreted as sincere interest in the organization's objectives but not as a guarantee that the organization will receive a grant.

The foundation awards grants in two funding cycles annually, with deadlines that vary from year to year. Applicants should check with the foundation regarding forthcoming deadlines and should expect the entire process, from deadline to final decision, to take from four to six months.

Grant Limitations

Grants are made only to organizations in northern California, from San Luis Obispo, Kern, and Inyo counties north to the Oregon state line. Grants are not usually made for support of general operating costs (direct services and administrative overhead), individuals, scholarships, capital improvements, endowments, loans, research, literary publications, films, videotapes (unless they are an instrument for resource development), and government agencies, (unless the organizational leadership originates in the community).

Meeting Times

The allocations committee of The Women's Foundation holds a series of meetings twice a year, in the spring and fall.

Publications

The foundation publishes an annual report and a quarterly newsletter, and provides funding guidelines and application forms upon request.

Woods Charitable Fund, Inc.
Three First National Plaza, Suite 2010
Chicago, Illinois 60602
(312) 782-2698

Post Office Box 81309
Lincoln, Nebraska 68501
(402) 474-0707

Contact Persons
Jean Rudd, Executive Director
Pam Baker, Director, Lincoln Office

Purpose
The Woods Charitable Fund is a private foundation that limits its grant-making to organizations located in and directly serving the residents of Illinois and Nebraska, and more particularly the metropolitan communities of Chicago and Lincoln.

Areas of Interest
In Chicago, while the fund's activities include education and the arts, its support is primarily directed toward community-organizing activities that stress citizen involvement and development of neighborhood leaders. Grants are made for exploratory planning projects; general operating support; specific projects to support new initiatives or one-time needs; research or consulting assistance for training board members, volunteers, and staff, and education in public policy; collaborative projects; evaluations to improve management or programs; and matching grants to encourage support from other sources.

In addition, the fund has identified several special interests in Chicago, specifically public school reform, government accountability, public policies affecting families, and comprehensive and collaborative approaches to problem-solving joining nontraditional partners from the academic, community, government, business, public service, and religious sectors.

In Lincoln, the fund actively solicits proposals both for new initiatives and to improve or evaluate the effectiveness of existing programs. In 1986 priority interests were arts and humanities; the development of community strengths through promotion of community improvement, participation, and responsibility; historic preservation; and local leader-

Woods Charitable Fund, Inc.

ship development and economic issues affecting the future of the city and the state.

Financial Data (year ended 12/31/87)

In 1987, 79 percent of the grants made were paid to organizations in Chicago and 21 percent were paid to organizations in Lincoln.[1] The grantmaking activities of these two geographic areas are analyzed separately below:

Chicago Grants Program

Total grants paid:	$	1,926,376
Number of grants paid:		154
Highest grant:	$	75,000
Lowest grant:	$	300
Median grant size:	$	10,000

Lincoln Grants Program

Total grants paid:	$	509,004
Number of grants paid:		40
Highest grant:[2]	$	40,000
Lowest grant:	$	200
Median grant size:	$	9,000

Application Procedures

The fund has different application procedures for each program. While both are briefly described below, applicants are advised to request a copy of the fund's annual report, which includes program priorities, funding limitations, and procedures, before inquiring about support.

Chicago

Applicants should initially telephone the fund staff or submit a brief two-page summary request. If a proposal is requested, the outline provided in the fund's annual report should be used by the applicant as a guide

---

[1] On December 31, 1986, the assets of the fund at market value were $28,559,698.

[2] This excludes one unusually large grant of $100,000.

Woods Charitable Fund, Inc.

and checklist. In Chicago no proposals are considered at the March board meeting, which is used for planning evaluation. Thus, the timetable for submitting proposals is as follows:

Submission Dates	Board Meeting
March 1 – April 15	June[3]
June 1–July 15	September
September 1–October 15	December

Lincoln

In Lincoln applicants should initially telephone the fund staff or submit a brief two-page summary request. If it appears worthwhile to prepare a proposal, directions are clearly spelled out in the annual report, and the following timetable will apply.

Submission Dates	Board Meeting
December 1 –February 1	March
March 1–May 1	June
June 1–August 1	September
September 1–November 1	December

In both Chicago and Lincoln, proposals that arrive well before the deadline have a better chance for careful review. Proposals neither clearly within the fund's priority areas, nor clearly ineligible, are screened by the fund's local board members. If at least one board member seeks board meeting discussion of the proposal, it can be considered for funding.

Grant Limitations

Limitations on the fund's grants also vary by geographic area.

Chicago

The fund will not consider fund-raising benefits or program advertising; individual needs; endowments; scholarships or fellowships; residential

---

[3]The foundation's once-a-year review of arts proposals occurs at this meeting.

Woods Charitable Fund, Inc.

care, treatment programs, clinics, or recreation programs; social services, except special projects with a clear public policy strategy or projects expressly planned for wide duplication; health care institutions; medical and scientific research; national health, welfare, educational, or cultural organizations or their state or local affiliates; and religious programs.

Lincoln
While the fund makes grants in diverse fields, the following areas are not eligible for grant review: individual needs; endowments; scholarships and fellowships; national health, welfare, educational, or cultural organizations, or their state or local affiliates; medical or scientific research; fundraising benefits or program advertising; religious activities; capital projects in health care institutions; government agencies or projects; and college or university proposals that do not involve students and/or faculty in projects to benefit the metropolitan region.

Meeting Times
The board of trustees of the Woods Charitable Fund meets quarterly, in March, June, September, and December.

Publications
The fund publishes an annual report and application guidelines.

The Zellerbach Family Fund
120 Montgomery Street, Suite 2125
San Francisco, California 94104
(415) 421–2629

Contact Person
Edward A. Nathan, Executive Director

Purpose
The Zellerbach Family Fund uses its resources to support innovative programs that are unlikely to gain the immediate support of individual donors and which, through a modest investment, can bring significant services to many persons. Grants are directed primarily but not exclusively to programs and projects within the San Francisco Bay Area.

The fund emphasizes that with the exception of its community arts program, which works from grant requests, most projects supported by the fund are developed by advisory groups and staff. Furthermore, with the exception of community arts, the fund advises it is committed to projects under way and does not expect to make grants to new programs in the next few years.

Areas of Interest
The fund's grantmaking is primarily in two general areas: first, projects that address critical human needs in mental health, education, and social services; and second, programs in community arts.

In the fund's human needs program, priority is given to projects emphasizing early intervention to promote family stability as well as efforts to improve private sector collaboration and integration within public services. Grants also assist language and reading development and increased understanding of diverse cultures through curriculum development. Grants made in this program are generally divided into the following categories: children and families, education, programs for people with special needs, and refugees. The fund aids in project development, evaluation, and dissemination. While the fund notes that few new programs are currently under consideration for support, the fund has an interest in reviewing new ideas concerned with primary prevention in mental health, foster care, child welfare, and minority youth.

Support for community-based performing arts groups is channeled through the Community Arts Distribution Committee. In 1975 the fund's

The Zellerbach Family Fund

board of directors established the committee to permit community artists to participate directly in the grantmaking process. The committee reviews and develops grant proposals and makes specific dollar recommendations. Community arts grants are divided into the following categories: community organizations (ongoing support); dance; theater; festivals, arts events, exhibits, murals; films, video, publications, poetry; and music.

Financial Data (year ended 12/31/87)

As of December 31, 1987, the assets of the fund were approximately $30,331,891. And during the calendar year, the fund paid grants totaling $1,312,865, of which $250,000 was distributed through the Community Arts Distribution Committee. Unfortunately, at the time this entry was prepared complete data were not available to analyze the fund's 1987 grantmaking activities. Hence, the following analysis is based on the $1,347,869 in grants paid in 1986.

Human Needs

Total grants paid:	$	1,105,126
Number of grants paid:		62
Highest grant:	$	98,464
Lowest grant:	$	930
Median grant size:	$	11,519

Community Arts

Total grants paid:	$	233,743
Number of grants paid:		134
Highest grant:	$	5,000
Lowest grant:	$	375
Median grant size:	$	1,500

Application Procedures

Grant applications are accepted by the fund throughout the year and should be addressed to the executive director. Human-need-related programs should include the following information: (1) a half-page summary of the purpose of the proposed project (a more detailed presentation

The Zellerbach Family Fund

may accompany the summary); (2) an itemized budget with clear indication of the source of income, indicating specifically support from federations, foundations, community fund-raising efforts, and public sources;
(3) a list of the persons and foundations to whom the project request
has been directed, and a statement of anticipated sources of current and
future income; (4) a statement indicating the community support and
identifying the project's leadership, including evidence of the competence and the preparation of the leadership to direct the proposed project;
and (5) evidence that the applicant is a tax-exempt organization.

Community arts groups should provide: (1) a brief statement of the
purpose of the program, its goals, number of persons participating, the
audience or persons toward whom the efforts are directed; (2) information about the leadership of the organization; (3) press clippings and
a few statements from community groups or experts who appreciate the
value of the program; (4) the most recent income and expense statement
for the organization; (5) detailed projected income and expense statement for the project, identifying the most essential budgetary items; (6)
a list of all contributions and grants from others, as well as other groups
that have received or will receive an application; and (7) information
about tax-exempt status. Eight copies of the request must be provided.

Grant Limitations
The fund does not make grants to individuals or for endowment funds.

Meeting Times
The board of directors of The Zellerbach Family Fund meets quarterly.
The Community Arts Distribution Committee generally meets every seven
weeks.

Publications
The fund publishes an annual report that contains program policy statements and grant application guidelines.

I

Appendix I
The Funding Search Revisited
By Michael S. Seltzer*

Since the first edition of The *Grant Seekers Guide* appeared in 1980, nonprofit organizations have been buffeted by dramatic cutbacks in government funding and increased competition for foundation and corporate grants. With characteristic dedication and hard work, nonprofit leaders have continued their efforts in spite of these obstacles. Increasingly, these organizations—traditional nonprofit institutions and progressive social-change groups alike—have sought ways to diversify their funding base. No longer can any one kind of funding source, such as foundations or government, be viewed as sufficient to meet financial needs. A broad base of support is a requisite for a strong and independent organization.

In the exploration for new sources of support and revenue "The Funding Search" checklist is offered once more (in a revised form) as a tool for staff, board members, and volunteers. Not all sources are necessarily appropriate to all organizations, nor are they all capable of providing the same level of support. Each source, or approach in the case of individuals, should be reviewed with a critical eye. Ask questions such as: Have we ever explored this possibility? Do we share mutual interests? Do we have contacts or leads? Once answers to such questions have been assessed, you can then plan systematically how best to approach new prospects.

Other steps that can be helpful in planning your funding search include: (1) checking the reference materials listed in the bibliography and located at the Foundation Center Libraries and Cooperating Collections (see Appendix VII); (2) speaking with local community leaders, checking with other nonprofits in your area, and looking into other programs similar to your own in other parts of the country; and (3) contacting appropriate national organizations or coalitions and drawing on current or prospective funders and management support organizations for advice (see Appendix VI).

This kind of information-gathering and "prospecting" for new ways to generate support for nonprofits is critical to any successful fund-raising.

---

*Michael S. Seltzer is a nonprofit and foundation consultant in New York City. He is the author of *Securing Your Organization's Future: A Complete Guide to Fundraising Strategies.* (See bibliography for description and ordering information.)

Appendix I. The Funding Search Revisited

Individuals
☐ Face-to-face solicitation
☐ Direct mail
☐ Special events
☐ Planned giving
☐ Earned or venture income projects

Foundations
☐ Family foundations
☐ Community foundations
☐ Local foundations
☐ Local public charities
☐ National foundations

Businesses and Corporations
☐ Neighborhood stores
☐ Banks, utility companies, department stores, etc.
☐ Corporations with headquarters or facilities in your community
☐ Large national corporations
☐ Trade associations

Government (grants and contracts)
☐ Local government units
☐ State government units
☐ Federal government units

Religious Institutions
☐ Individual churches, synagogues, and other faith communities
☐ Metropolitan and regional religious bodies
☐ Metropolitan and regional ecumenical bodies
☐ Religious federated organizations
☐ National religious bodies

Federated Fund-raising Organizations
☐ United Way
☐ Other community chests
☐ Alternative funds

Appendix I. The Funding Search Revisited

Associations of Individuals
- ☐ Neighborhood or community-based associations
- ☐ Labor unions
- ☐ Citywide associations
- ☐ National associations

List of sources reprinted with permission in substantially the same form from Michael S. Seltzer, *Securing Your Organization's Future: A Complete Guide to Fundraising Strategies,* (New York: 1987), pp. 407–8, by permission of The Foundation Center.

II

Appendix II
Sources of Religious Support

Following is a list of religious resources for social-justice organizations alphabetically arranged and grouped by religious tradition. First a few words on how the list was put together and what it contains. Then a word of caution.

The list that follows is by no means complete. Furthermore, inclusion does not guarantee that grant moneys or other resources are available from the program listed. Part of the reason for this disclaimer is the somewhat unscientific "snowball" method by which the list was compiled. First a list of religious grantmakers known to publish guidelines was put together. Other organizations identified by various social-justice grantseekers and grantmakers alike were added. Then the list was circulated. Some groups were added, others deleted. The result is a hodgepodge of national and regional programs. The only ones specifically excluded are congregationally based programs, of which there are too many to list in this limited space. But as with every rule, there are one or two exceptions.

Now the caution. The advisory committee for this book debated at length how to balance the needs of grantseekers for information with the desires of religious grantmakers for anonymity. There was no easy solution. What follows is a compromise. Three grantmakers with well-known national programs are not only listed here but also are described in detail in the chapter on national grantmakers: The Campaign for Human Development, the Jewish Fund for Justice, and the Veatch Program. These grantmakers are identified in the list that follows with a cross-hatch symbol (#). Before contacting one of them, please consult the complete entry. Other grantmakers that will distribute program information on request are identified with an asterisk (*). For those that issue guidelines, by all means write and request a copy before submitting a proposal. Then go ahead and submit a proposal if and only if you qualify. For all the others, before you write, try to find someone in your community who may know something about the program—another organization that may have received support, a pastor known to be an active supporter of previous social-justice activities, or a local congregant who may be a part of your own organization or circle of friends. Learn on your own first. Then, if that fails, write a brief letter.

Most of all, respect the religious grantmaker, the process, and the complexities as you would anyone else who supports your work. In so doing, you will make it easier to include more information on church funding sources in the next publication. Now, if you have read Chapter 6 by Doug Lawson from start to finish, you're ready to begin your search for resources from church-related funding sources.

NOTE: Those organizations with their own entries in *The Grant-seekers Guide* are marked with a cross-hatch symbol (#). Organizations that are known to issue program guidelines and make grants are marked with an asterisk (*). All others may or may not have funding programs or other resources. Research thoroughly before contacting them.

American Baptist Churches
Board of National Ministries
Valley Forge, PA 19481
Matthew Guiffrida
(215) 768-2000

Office of Issue Development
Valley Forge, PA 19481
Thelma Mitchell
(215) 768-2000

**The Christian Church
(Disciples of Christ)**
General Reconciliation
    Committee*
Post Office Box 1986
Indianapolis, IN 46206
Rev. Ernest J. Newborn
(317) 353-1491

Episcopal Church
Coalition for Human Needs*
Episcopal Church Center
815 Second Avenue
New York, NY 10017
Father Earl A. Neil
(212) 867-8400 ext. 249

Parish of Trinity Church*
74 Trinity Place
New York, NY 10006
Rev. James Callaway
(212) 285-0812

Presiding Bishop's Fund*
for World Relief
Episcopal Church Center
815 Second Avenue
New York, NY 10017
Nancy L. Marvel
(212) 867-8400

Women of the Episcopal Church*
United Thank Offering Committee
Episcopal Church Center
815 Second Avenue
New York, NY 10017
Willeen Smith
(212) 867-8400

**Evangelical Lutheran Church
in America**
Commission for Church and
    Society*
8765 West Higgins Road
Chicago, IL 60631
Fran Burnford
(312) 380-2561

Division for Social Ministry
 Organizations*
8765 West Higgins Road
Chicago, IL 60631
Rev. Charles Miller
(312) 380-2561

Jewish
Jewish Community Council of
 Metropolitan Detroit
Urban Affairs Fund
163 Madison Avenue, Suite 225
Detroit, MI 48226
Miriam Schay
(313) 962-1800

Jewish Fund for Justice#
1334 G Street, N.W.
Washington, D.C. 20005
Lois Roisman
(202) 638-0550

Urban Affairs Foundation
Community Relations Committee
234 McKee Place
Pittsburgh, PA 15213
Lou Borman
(412) 681-8000

Local Tzedakab Collectives
Brandeis Hillel Tzedakah
 Collective
415 South Street
Waltham, MA 02254

Chevrat Tzedakah of Fobrangen
7319 Cedar Avenue
Takoma Park, MD 20912

Highland Park Minyan
Tzedakah Collective
17 Harrison Avenue
Edison, NJ 08817

Ma Tov Tzedakah Collective
Temple Shalon
1015 South Hillside Avenue
Saccasunna, NJ 07876

The Sudbury (Massachusetts)
 Tzedakah Collective
19 Pine Needle Road
Wayland, MA 10778

Ziv Tzedakah Fund
263 Congregational Lane, #708
Rockville, MD 20852

Lutheran Church - Missouri Synod
Board for Social Ministry
 Services*
1333 South Kirkwood Road
St. Louis, MO 63122
Dr. Al M. Senske
(314) 965-9000

Mennonite Bodies
Mennonite Central Committee
21 South 12th Street
Akron, Pa 17501

Mennonite Mutual Aid
 Association*
Fraternal Grant Fund
110 North Main Street
P.O. Box 483
Goshen, IN 46526
Mr. John Liechty, Fraternal
 Activities Manager
(800) 348-7468

Appendix II. Sources of Religious Support

Presbyterian Church (USA)
Presbyterian Hunger Program*
100 Witherspoon Street
Louisville, KY 40202
Coleen Shannon
(502) 580-1900

Self-Development of People Fund*
100 Witherspoon Street
Louisville, Ky 40202
Fred Walls
(502) 580-1900

Thank Offering*
100 Witherspoon Street
Louisville, KY 40202
(502) 580-1900

Reformed Church in America
National Office
475 Riverside Drive
New York, NY 10115
Rev. Eugene Heideman
(212) 870-2841

The Religious Society of Friends (Quakers)
Friends Committee on National
  Legislation
245 Second Street, N.E.
Washington, D.C. 20002
(202) 547-6000

American Friends Service
  Committee
National Office
1501 Cherry Street
Philadelphia, PA 19102
Asia Bennett
(215) 241-7000

Regional Offices
980 North Fair Oaks Avenue
Pasadena, CA 91103

2160 Lake Street
San Francisco, CA 94121

92 Piedmont Avenue, N.E.
Atlanta, GA 30303

407 South Dearborn Street
Chicago, IL 60605

4211 Grand Avenue
Des Moines, IA 50312

317 East 25th Street
Baltimore, MD 21218

2161 Massachusetts Avenue
Cambridge, MA 02140

15 Rutherford Place
New York, NY 10003

915 Salem Avenue
Dayton, OH 45406

814 N.E. 40th Street
Seattle, WA 98105

The Roman Catholic Church
United States Catholic Conference
Campaign For Human
  Development#
1312 Massachusetts Avenue, N.W.
Washington, D.C. 20005
Douglas M. Lawson
(202) 659-6650

Orders of Catholic Priests and Nuns

Claretian Priests and Brothers
Claretian Social Concerns
  Committee
San Gabriel Mission
537 West Mission Drive
San Gabriel, CA 91776
Fr. Gary Smith
(818) 282-5191

Claretian Priests and Brothers
Claretian Social Development
  Fund*
400 North Euclid Avenue
Oak Park, IL 60302
Rev. Tom Joyce
(312) 427-4351

Dominican Fathers and Brothers
Dominican Social Action Fund
1727 West 33rd Avenue
Denver, CO 80211
Fr. Jerry Stookey
(303) 296-9225

The Franciscans*
Chicago, St. Louis Province of the
  Sacred Heart
St. Anthony Fund for the Poor
3140 Mermec Street
St. Louis, MO 63118
Bro. Bill Schultz
(314) 353-3132

Franciscan Friars of Santa Barbara
  Province*
The Poverello Fund
133 Golden Gate Avenue
San Francisco, CA 94102
Jose Medina
(415) 431-7522

Franciscan Sisters of Perpetual
  Adoration
Human Development Fund
Saint Rose Convent
912 Market Street
LaCrosse, WI 54601
Sr. Cecilia Corcoran
(608) 782-5610

Franciscan Sisters of the Poor
Charity Fund
191 Joralemon Street
Brooklyn, NY 11201
(718) 625-4530

Foundation Mothers of the
  Nativity
225 Carol Avenue
Putnam, NY 10803

Humility of Mary
Grants for the Poor
Villa Maria, PA 16155

Jesuit Quest for Justice Fund
Jesuit Society Ministries
222 N.W. Hoyt
Portland, OR 97210
Fr. Terrence Shea
(206) 329-9791 (Seattle)

Jesuit Quest for Justice Fund
Jesuit Social Ministries
Loyola Marymount University
P.O. Box 45041
Los Angeles, CA 90045
Fr. Mike Mandala
(213) 642-3170

Marianist Sharing Fund
Central Province
267 East 8th Street
St. Paul, MN 55101
Fr. Robert Moosbrugger
(612) 292-8622

Marianist Sharing Fund*
New York Province
4301 Roland Avenue
Baltimore, MD 21210
Richard E. Ullrich
(301) 366-1324

Missionaries of La Salette*
Office of the Provincial
P.O. Box 6127
Hartford, CT 06106

National Committee for Justice
Passover Fund
2111 East Madison Avenue
El Cajon, CA 92021

Our Lady of Mt. Carmel
Route 2
Carroll, Iowa 54101

Our Lady of Victory Missionary
  Sisters*
Resource Sharing Fund
Victory Knoll, Box 109
Huntington, IN 46750
Sr. Virginia Schmitt
(219) 356-0628

Pallottine Brothers*
Immaculate Conception Province
Center for Apostolic Causes
Post Office Box 573
Pennsauken, NY 08110
Msgr. Ralph F. Firneno
(215) 649-3577

Provincial Education
Social Development Fund
303 West Barry Avenue
Chicago, IL 60657

St. Mary's Bertand Hall
Wasatch Fund Project
Notre Dame, IN 46556

School Sisters of St. Francis
International Office
1501 South Layton Boulevard
Milwaukee, WI 53215
Sr. Bernadette
(414) 384-4105

The Sisters of St. Francis of
  Philadelphia*
Our Lady of Angels Convent -
  Glen Riddle
Aston, PA 19014
Sr. Miriam Eileen Murray
(215) 459-4125

Sisters of St. Joseph
Team for Apostolic Ministry
Mount Marie
Holyoke, MA 01040
Sr. Lorrie Villemaere
(413) 536-0853

Sisters of St. Joseph of Peace*
Congregational Sharing Fund
Ascension House
302 West 106 Street
New York, NY 10025
Sr. Mary Anne Vincent
(212) 663-8123

Sisters of St. Joseph of
  Carondelet*
Aid to the Needy Fund
St. Joseph's Provincial House
Latham, NY 12110
Sr. Jean Whalen
(518) 785-7050

Sisters of Loretto*
Special Needs Fund
3001 S. Federal Boulevard
Box 1113
Denver, CO 80236
Sr. Nancy Finneran
(301) 922-8215

Sisters of Mercy Health
  Corporation*
Program Development Fund
28550 Eleven Mile Road
Farmington Hills, MI 48018
Susie George
(313) 478-9900

Sisters of Mercy*
Mercy Action, Inc.
Mercy Center
1320 Fenwick Lane, Suite 610
Silver Spring, MD 20910
Sr. Mariann Horning
(301) 587-6310

Sisters of Mercy
Mercy Fund
3333 Fifth Avenue
Pittsburgh, PA 15213
Sr. Judith Stojhovic
(412) 578-6188

Sisters of Mercy
Tithing Fund
1437 Blossom Road
Rochester, NY 14610
Sr. Celeste
(716) 288-2710

Sisters of Notre Dame De
  Namier*
Ohio Province
On the Side of the Poor Fund
701 East Columbia Avenue
Cincinnati, OH 45215
Sr. Mary Elaine Tarpy
(513) 821-7448

Sisters of Providence
9 East Ninth Avenue
Spokane, WA 99202
(509) 455-4884

Sisters of Providence
Poverty and Justice Fund
St. Mary of the Woods
Saint Gabriel Province
931-B Woodlawn Avenue
Indianapolis, IN 46203
Sr. Marshal Speth
(317) 635-7171

Social Justice Committee of the
  Xaverian Brothers*
Old Mission
Santa Barbara, California 93105
Bro. Thomas Moore Page
(805) 682-4713

Southern Baptist Convention
Home Mission Board
2715 Peachtree Road, N.E.
Atlanta, GA 30305
Harold Wilcox
(404) 873-4041

Unitarian Universalist Association
Unitarian Universalist Service
  Committee, Inc.
International Program
78 Beacon Street
Boston, MA 02108
Mary Lania
(617) 742-2120

North Shore Unitarian Universalist
  Association
Veatch Program#
Plandome Road
Plandome, NY 11030
Joshua Reichert
(516) 627-6560

Unitarian Universalist Social
  Concerns Panel Fund*
First Unitarian Society
900 Mount Curve
Minneapolis, MN 55403
Rev. Koran Aresian
(612) 377-6608

The United Church of Christ
Board for World Ministries
14 Beacon Street
Boston, MA 02108

Board for World Ministries
Post Office Box 179
115 North Jefferson Street
St. Louis, MO 63166

Commission for Racial Justice
105 Madison Avenue
New York, NY 10016
(212) 683-5656

Commission for Racial Justice
5113 Georgia Avenue, N.W.
Washington, D.C. 20001

Council for Indian Ministry
122 West Franklin Avenue,
  Room 300
Minneapolis, MN 55404

Office for Church in Society
110 Maryland Avenue, N.E.
Washington, D.C. 20002

United Church Board for
  Homeland Ministries*
Division of American Missionary
  Association
132 West 31 Street
New York, NY 10001
Faith A. Johnson
(212) 239-8700

United Church Board for
  Homeland Ministries*
The American Missionary
  Association
Office of Family Life and Women's
  Issues
132 West 31 Street
New York, NY 10001
Rev. Theodore Erickson
(212) 239-8700

United Church Board for World
  Ministries*
World Hunger Action
475 Riverside Drive, 16th Floor
New York, NY 10115
Rev. Neill Richards
(212) 870-2951

United Methodist Church
Board of Church and Society
110 Maryland Avenue, N.E.
Washington, D.C. 20002
(202) 488-5600

Board of Church and Society
Department of Peace and World
  Order
777 United Nations Plaza
New York, NY 10017

Board of Discipleship
National Youth Ministry
  Organization
Youth Services Fund
Post Office Box 840
Nashville, TN 37202

Board of Global Ministries*
National Division
Office of Urban Ministries
475 Riverside Drive, Room 332
New York, NY 10115
Rev. Kinmoth Jefferson
(212) 870-3832

Board of Global Ministries*
National Division
Town and Country
475 Riverside Drive, 3rd Floor
New York, NY 10115
Gladis Campbell
(212) 870-3835

Board of Global Ministries*
National Division
Women in Crisis
475 Riverside Drive, 3rd Floor
New York, NY 10115
Peggy Halsey
(212) 870-3835

Board of Global Ministries
Office of Health & Welfare
Kendall Funds
475 Riverside Drive, Room 350
New York, NY 10115
(212) 870-3910

Board of Global Ministries*
Women's Division
Call to Prayer/Self-Denial Offering
  Funds
475 Riverside Drive, Room 1503
New York, NY 10115
Sandra Wilder
(212) 870-3735

Board of Global Ministries*
Women's Division
Community Action Fund
475 Riverside Drive, Room 1502
New York, NY 10115
Chiquita G. Smith
(212) 870-3766

Board of Global Ministries
National Division
Food, Land and Justice
475 Riverside Drive, 3rd Floor
New York, NY 10115
(212) 870-3835

Commission on the Status and
  Role of Women
1200 Davis Street
Evanston, IL 60201

General Commission on Religion
  and Race*
Minority Group Self-
  Determination Fund
110 Maryland Avenue, N.E.
Washington, D.C. 20002
Kenneth Deere
(202) 547-4270

Appendix II. Sources of Religious Support

Ecumenical Organizations

Appalachian Development
  Projects Committee
Commission on Religion in
  Appalachia
864 Weisgarber Road, N.W.
Knoxville, TN 37919

Church Women United in the
  U.S.A.*
475 Riverside Drive, Room 572
New York, NY 10115
Pat Williams
(212) 870-2355

Church Women United in the
  U.S.A.*
Intercontinental Grants Program
475 Riverside Drive, Room 572
New York, NY 10115
Joyce Yu
(212) 870-2355

Colorado Council of Churches
1370 Pennsylvania, Suite 100
Denver, CO 80203
Gilbert Horn
(303) 861-1884

Joint Strategy Action Committee
475 Riverside Drive, Room 903
New York, NY 10115
John DeBoer
(212) 870-3105

Lutheran Resources Commission
733 15th Street, N.W., Suite 900
Washington, D.C. 20005
Lloyd Foerster
(202) 639-8280

National Council of Churches
Division of Church and Society
475 Riverside Drive
New York, NY 10115

Project Reach Out
2025 East Fulton Street
Grand Rapids, MI 49503

Wheat Ridge Foundation*
104 S. Michigan Avenue
Chicago, IL 60603
Robert J.L. Zimmer
(312) 263-1182

World Council of Churches
Program to Combat Racism
150 Route de Ferney
1211 Geneva 20
Switzerland
Dr. Anwar Barkat

III

Appendix III
Alternative Federated Funding Programs

If you've heard the line "I gave at the office" one too many times in your efforts to raise funds from individuals, perhaps it is time for you to explore workplace fund-raising. Chapter 8 by Bob Bothwell at the beginning of this book is an excellent introduction. Before you take it to the bank, however, consult the lists that follow.

If you are considering starting a local federation of charities to solicit payroll deductions, before you march into a corporate headquarters or state government office and demand participation in their payroll deduction program, you should consult the first list. This is a list of seasoned resource people—grouped by subject matter—who can provide good advice so that you can benefit from the experiences of the others who have gone before you, learn from their mistakes, and maximize their successes. Some are organizers who have been where you are; others coordinate what is in essence a trade association.

National federations are listed next. This list indicates the people that should be contacted by national organizations that want to join an existing federation.

The last list contains the names and contact persons at existing and developing local alternative funds as of January 1988 around the country. It should be consulted by local organizations seeking to join an existing federation engaged in payroll deduction solicitation. Since almost all these funds limit membership geographically to either the immediate vicinity of the city in which they are located or statewide, they are grouped by subject and then listed alphabetically by state. Those funds still in their developmental stages are identified with an asterisk (*).

Resource People for Starting New Local Federations

Arts Funds
Milton Rhodes
President
American Council for the Arts
570 Seventh Avenue
New York, NY 10018
(212) 245-4510

Black United Funds
Bill Merritt
President
National Black United Fund
Room 821
2090 Adam Clayton Powell
  Boulevard
New York, NY 10027
(212) 866-5400

Appendix III. Alternative Federated Funding Programs

Health Funds
John Sellman
President
Combined Health Appeal of
   America
1101 King Street, Suite 501
Alexandria, VA 22314
(703) 838-5508

Social Action, Environmental, and Women's Funds
Steve Paprocki
Director of Field Operations
c/o National Committee for
   Responsive
Philanthropy
2001 S Street, N.W., Suite 620
Washington, D.C. 20009
(202) 387-9177
(612) 690-2520

Robert Bothwell
Executive Director
National Committee for
   Responsive
Philanthropy
2001 S Street, N.W., Suite 620
Washington, D.C. 20009
(202) 387-9177

Nan Langen Steketee
Alliance for Choice in Giving
c/o Center for Responsible
   Funding
924 Cherry Street, Suite 508
Philadelphia, PA 19107
(215) 925-6140

Dyan Oldenburg
Alliance for Choice in Giving
c/o Women's Funding Alliance
119 South Main Street, Suite 330
Seattle, WA 98104
(206) 467-6733

Federations of National Organizations

Don Sodo
Executive Director
National Service Agencies
10686 Crestwood Drive
Manassas, VA 22110
(703) 368-1365

Jim Barr
Executive Director
National Voluntary Health
   Agencies
1137 North Highland Avenue
Arlington, VA 22201
(703) 467-5913

Richard Leary
Executive Director
International Service Agencies
4733 Bethesda Avenue, #805
Bethesda, MD 20814
(301) 652-4494

Operating and Developing Alternative Funds

Arts Funds

Cozie Simon
Ft. Wayne Fine Art Foundation
114 East Superior Street
Ft. Wayne, IN 46802
(219) 424-0647

Allan Cowen
President
Greater Louisville Fund for the
    Arts
609 West Main Street
Louisville, KY 40202
(502) 582-1821

Anne Baker
United Arts Council
429 Landmark Center
St. Paul, MN 55102
(612) 292-3222

Mel Lowenstein
Executive Director
St. Louis Arts-Education Council
40 North Kings Highway
St. Louis, MO 63108
(314) 367-6330

Marvin Miller
Executive Director
Arts & Sciences Council
121 West Seventh Street
Charlotte, NC 28202
(704) 372-9667

Joseph Walls
Executive Director
The Arts Council, Inc.
311 West Fourth Street
Winston-Salem, NC 27101-2802
(919) 723-1960

Mary McCullough-Hudson
Fine Arts Fund
2649 Erie Avenue
Cincinnati, OH 45208
(513) 871-2787

Richard C. McCauley
President
Performing Arts Fund
Post Office Box 1312
Dayton, OH 45401
(513) 222-2787

Zee Harris
Executive Director
Allied Arts Foundation
One Santa Fe Plaza
Oklahoma City, OK 73102
(405) 278-8900

Molly Teague
The Allied Arts of Greater
    Chattanooga
20 Bluff View
Chattanooga, TN 37403
(615) 756-2787

Evelyn Vitek
United Performing Arts Fund
929 North Water Street
Milwaukee, WI 53202
(414) 273-7121

Black United Funds

Pam Brooks
Brotherhood Crusade
200 East Slauson Avenue
Los Angeles, CA 90011
(213) 231-2171

Toni Cook
Bay Area BUF
1440 Broadway, Suite 403
Oakland, CA 94612
(415) 763-7270

Henry English
Illinois BUF
2336 East 71st Street
Chicago, IL 60649
(312) 933-7535

Bob Cheeks
Baltimore BUF
600 North Arlington Avenue
Baltimore, MD 21217
(301) 467-7460

Brenda Rayford
BUF of Michigan
2187 West Grand Boulevard
Detroit, MI 48208
(313) 894-2200

Lloyd Oxford
New Jersey BUF
24 Commerce Street, #417-18
Newark, NJ 07102
(201) 624-0909

Kermit Eady
New York City BUF
144 West 125 Street
New York, NY 10027
(212) 663-7600

Amina Anderson
BUF of Oregon
Post Office Box 12406
Portland, OR 97212
(503) 282-7973

Linda Richardson
Pennsylvania BUF
4601 Market Street, Second Floor
Philadelphia, PA 19139
(215) 748-0150
(800) 232-5191

Cleo Glenn-Johnson
Executive Director
Houston BUF*
c/o Ingrando House
5151 Martin Luther King
   Boulevard
Houston, Texas 77021
(713) 644-1561

Environmental Funds

Kalman Stein
Michelle Miller
Environmental Federation of
   California
916 New Montgomery, Suite 231
San Francisco, CA 94104
(415) 882-9330

Jim Abernathy
Jim Eychaner
Environmental Fund of
   Washington*
Post Office Box 12322
Seattle, WA 98101
(206) 464-7320 (Abernathy)
(206) 625-1367 (Eychaner)

Health Funds[1]

Michelle Cassano, Chairman
National Voluntary Health
Agencies of AK*
c/o American Diabetes
  Association
201 East Third Avenue, Suite 301
Anchorage, AK 99501
(907) 276-3607

Margaret Jean Daniel
Executive Director
CHA of Alabama
National Voluntary Agencies of AL
16 Office Park Circle, Suite 14
Birmingham, AL 35223
(205) 879-1326

Tanya Goosev
Executive Director
CHA of Fresno
1350 O Street, Suite 205
Fresno, CA 93721
(209) 268-5000

Gloria DeRobles
Executive Director
CHA of California
1631 Executive Court
Sacramento, CA 95864
(916) 481-2908

Maxine Coover
Executive Director
Combined Health Agencies Drive
Post Office Box 232301
4699 Murphy Canyon Road
San Diego, CA 92123-0007
(619) 492-2017

Executive Director
CHA of Santa Barbara County
1235 B Veronica Springs Road
Santa Barbara, CA 93105
(805) 687-7070

Edward J. Hendricks, CAE
Executive Director
CHA of Colorado*
14291 East Fourth Avenue, #205
Aurora, CO 80011
(303) 366-1505

Peter J. Flierl
Executive Director
Greenwich Health Association*
189 Mason Street
Greenwich, CT 06830
(203) 869-0200

Robert O. Holt
Executive Director
CHA of South Central
  Connecticut
1125 Dixwell Avenue
Hamden, CT 06514
(203) 785-9328

Warren P. Dunbar
President
CHA for Business & Industry
99 Woodland Street
Hartford, CT 06105
(203) 549-0700

Blake Smith
President
CHA of Broward County*
1398 SW 19th Street
Boca Raton, FL 33432
(305) 771-6700

---

[1]Combined Health Appeal is abbreviated "CHA."

Merle Evanchyk
Chairman
CHA of Central Florida*
c/o Epilepsy Association
Post Office Box 531059
Orlando, FL 32853
(305) 422-1439

Alex Mitchell
CHA of Hillsborough County*
c/o National Society to
Prevent Blindness
4511 North Hines Avenue,
  Suite 140
Tampa, FL 33614
(813) 874-2020

Rosemary Stevens
CHA of West Palm Beach*
c/o Leukemia Society of America
324 Datura Street, Suite 312
West Palm Beach, FL 33401
(305) 882-2445

Maureen Fraser
Chairman
CHA of Georgia*
c/o Cystic Fibrosis Foundation
1655 Tullie Circle, Suite 111
Atlanta, GA 30329
(404) 325-6973

Donald R. Ford
CHA of Hawaii*
c/o American Lung Association of
  Hawaii
245 North Kukui Street
Honolulu, HI 96717
(808) 537-5966

Richard Pokora
President
Quad-City Council of Voluntary
Health Agencies
c/o Redeemer Lutheran Church
1107 Tanglefoot Lane
Bettendorf, IA 52722
(319) 355-5405

B.J. Hall
Executive Director
CHA of Iowa
1111 Office Park Road
West Des Moines, IA 50265
(515) 224-1451

Jerry Woolley
CHA of Illinois
c/o American Diabetes
  Association
Six North Michigan Avenue, Suite
  1202
Chicago, IL 60602
(312) 346-1805

Joyce Horan
CHA of Kentucky*
c/o Leukemia Society, Inc.
710 West Main Street, Suite 100
Louisville, KY 40202
(502) 584-8490

Tricia Medrano
Chairman
CHA of Louisiana*
c/o Leukemia Society of America
3101 West Napoleon Avenue,
  Suite 134
Metairie, LA 70001
(504) 525-2338

Michael Petit
Executive Director
CHA of Maine
c/o National Health Agencies of
  Maine
197 Lancaster
Portland, ME 04101
(207) 774-9280

Robert C. Whitney
Executive Director
Combined Health Agencies
1521 Edgewood Street, Suite C
Baltimore, MD 21227-2028
(301) 644-4483

Suzanne T. Shaffer
Executive Director
CHA of the National Capital Area
(Washington, D.C.)
4853 Cordell Avenue
Bethesda, MD 20814
(301) 656-9111

Mark W. Mulligan
CHA of Northeast Massachusetts*
c/o American Lung Association
Middlesex County
Post Office Box 265
Five Mountain Road
Burlington, MA 01803
(617) 272-2866

Clair M. Carvalho
CHA of Southeast MA
c/o Easter Seal Society
1145 Purchase Street
New Bedford, MA 02740
(617) 997-1553

Kirk N. Joslin
CHA of Central Massachusetts*
c/o Massachusetts Easter Seal
  Society
484 Main Street, Sixth Floor
Worcester, MA 01608
(617) 757-2756

Robert G. Smith
Chairman
CHA of Michigan
c/o American Lung Association
403 Seymour Avenue
Lansing, MI 48914-9989
(517) 484-4541

Roman Lucky
Acting Executive Director
CHA of Minnesota*
c/o P.M.I.
416 East Hennepin Avenue
Minneapolis, MN 55414
(612) 379-5351

Ken Lucy
CHA of Southeastern Missouri*
c/o Muscular Dystrophy
  Association
100 Broadway, Second Floor
Cape Girardeau, MO 63701
(314) 335-4400

Stanlee Dull
CHA of Montana*
c/o American Diabetes
  Association
Post Office Box 2411
Great Falls, MT 59403
(406) 761-0908

Curt Gordon
Executive Director
Combined Health Agencies Drive
of Nebraska
2728 South 114 Street
Omaha, NE 68144
(402) 334-1814

Sharon Murray
CHA of New Hampshire
c/o National Easter Seal Society of
New Hampshire and Vermont
555 Auburn Street
Manchester, NH 03103
(603) 623-8863

Pat Johnson
New Jersey CHA*
c/o Lupus Foundation of New
  Jersey
Post Office Box 320
Elmwood Park, NJ 07407
(201) 791-7868

Sheila Small
Executive Secretary
CHA of the Capital District
212 Point of Woods
Albany, NY 12203
(518) 869-5230

Shannon Maloy Roscini
Executive Director
CHA of Syracuse and Onondaga
  County
7145 Henry Clay Boulevard
Liverpool, NY 13088
(315) 457-7395

Carol Demoulin
Greater Rochester CHA*
c/o Leukemia Society of America
233 Alexander Street
Rochester, NY 14607
(716) 263-2440

William Carnes
CHA of Central Ohio*
c/o Muscular Dystrophy
  Association, Inc.
1110 Morse Road, Suite 216
Columbus, OH 43229
(614) 888-5142

Robyn Boswell
Acting Chairperson
CHA of Oklahoma*
c/o Muscular Dystrophy
  Association
5601 Northwest 72 Street, Suite
  218
Oklahoma City, OK 73132
(405) 722-8001

Ester Beatty
CHA of Central Pennsylvania*
c/o Leukemia Society of America
6000 B. Linglestown Road
Harrisburg, PA 17112
(717) 652-6520

Betsy McKelvey
CHA of Middle Tennessee
NHACFC State Coordinator
Post Office Box 121361
Nashville, TN 37212
(615) 297-0351

Pam Mueller
CHA of Dallas*
c/o Leukemia Society of America
2522 McKinney, Suite 200
Dallas, TX 75201
(214) 871-1600

Sharon Archer
CHA of Greater Houston
c/o Leukemia Society of America
8705 Katy Freeway, Suite 405
Houston, TX 77024
(713) 973-2222

Roger Weis
Co-Chairman
Peninsula CHA*
c/o Leukemia Society of America,
Inc.
Post Office Box 21
2101 Executive Drive
Hampton, VA 23666
(804) 838-9351

Diane Watson
Co-Chairman
Peninsula CHA*
c/o American Lung Association
11116 Jefferson Avenue
Newport News, VA 23601
(804) 595-1184

Jayna Eller
Chairman
CHA of Central Virginia*
c/o Cystic Fibrosis Foundation
Post Office Box 14776
3602 Floyd Avenue
Richmond, VA 23221
(804) 355-2464
(800) 572-3213 (VA only)

Brenda Daley
CHA of Roanoke Valley*
c/o Leukemia Society of America
2728 Colonial Avenue, Suite 103
Roanoke, VA 24015
(703) 343-7567

Tom Heine
Executive Director
Wisconsin CHA
2000 Engel Street, Suite 103
Madison, WI 53713
(608) 222-8825

Social Action Funds

Jim Stratton
Community Share/Alaska
Post Office Box 103800
Anchorage, AK 99501
(907) 276-1917

Bill Watanabe
Ron Kuramoto
Alan Woo
Los Angeles Asian Fund
c/o Little Tokyo Service Center
244 South San Pedro, #411
Los Angeles, CA 90012
(213) 680-3729 (Watanabe)
(213) 381-5068 (Kuramoto)
(213) 623-2313 (Woo)

Katrina B. Miesner
Johanna B. Brownell
The Progressive Way,
San Francisco-Oakland
477 15th Street, #200
Oakland, CA 94612
(415) 839-6768

Mike Russell
Peace Fund, Sonoma County, CA*
Post Office Box 946
Petaluma, CA 94952
(707) 762-1865

Christine Karim
Community Share/Colorado
c/o Community Resource Center
3005 West Gill Place
Denver, CO 80219
(303) 922-2325

Shawn de Loyola
Idaho Sponsoring Committee*
c/o C.A.P.A
Post Office Box 1956
Boise, ID 83701
(208) 345-1872

Larry Dansinger
The Maine Share*
Post Office Box 110
Stillwater, ME 04489
(207) 827-3107

Mike Mazepink
Community Share/Baltimore, MD
3028 Greenmont
Baltimore, MD 21218
(301) 889-0071

Lisa Doucett
Massachusetts Foundation for
  Children
18 Claremont Avenue
Arlington, MA 02174
(617) 648-6207

Ken Sinkler
Bob Cordt
Action for Boston Community
Development
178 Tremont Street
Boston, MA 02111
(617) 357-6000

Debra Furry
Community Works
25 West Street
Boston, MA 02111
(617) 423-9555

Peter Friedland
Fund for the Hungry and
  Homeless of
Greater Springfield, MA*
145 State Street
Springfield, MA 01103
(413) 785-1257

Jean Anderson
Cooperating Fund Drive
1619 Dayton Avenue, Suite 323
St. Paul, MN 55104
(612) 647-0440

Clifford Wilson
United Black Community Fund
Post Office Box 5382
St. Louis, MO 63115
(314) 531-3045

Mike Schechtman
Scott Crichton
Community Share/Montana*
25 South Ewing, #513
Post Office Box 1029
Helena, MT 59601
(406) 442-6615 (Schechtman)
(406) 449-8801 (Crichton)

Mary Fran Flood
Community Services Fund
2202 South 11 Street
Lincoln, NE 68502
(402) 475-3040

Ann Painter
Community Share/New Mexico*
Post Office Box 1701
Corrales, NM 87048
(505) 898-1858

Gloria Duus
Native American Family Fund*
Post Office Box 4186
Yahtahey, NM 87375
(505) 722-2144

Rebecca Reich
Big Apple Coalition for Housing*
c/o U.H.A.B.
40 Prince Street, 2d Floor
New York, NY 10012
(212) 226-4119

David Austin
North Carolina Sponsoring
   Committee*
1025 Lakewood Avenue
Durham, NC 27707
(919) 489-0296

Chip Bromley
Natalie Graham
Community Share/Cleveland
3130 Mayfield
Cleveland Heights, OH 44118
(216) 371-4285

Ann Doley
Mike Burke
Bread and Roses Community
   Fund
924 Cherry Street, 2d Floor
Philadelphia, PA 19107
(215) 928-1880

Joe Vanni
Fund for Community Progress/
Community Share of Rhode Island
533 Branch Avenue
Providence, RI 02904
(401) 331-3863

Peggy Matthews
Community Share/Knoxville, TN
517 Union Avenue, #203
Knoxville, TN 37902
(615) 522-1604

Barbara Toomer
Community Share/Utah*
347 South 400 East
Salt Lake City, UT 84111
(801) 364-7765

Mary Kay Wright
Pride Foundation*
Dean Witter Reynolds
3400 188th Street, SW, #101
Lynwood, WA 98037
(206) 464-4040

Paul Haas
Community Progress Alliance*
Post Office Box 31151
3601 Fremont Avenue North
Seattle, WA 98103
(206) 632-1285

Beatrice Kelleigh
Northwest AIDS Foundation*
818 East Pike
Post Office Box 3449
Seattle, WA 98122
(206) 322-0304

KC Spengler
Seattle Food Resource Network*
Post Office Box 31151
3601 Fremont Avenue North
Seattle, WA 98103
(206) 632-1285

Richard Berling
Access to Community Services
c/o M.A.R.C.
501 East Badger Road
Madison, Wisconsin 53713
(608) 237-3630

Nicolle Gotthelf
Denise Matyka
Community Share of Wisconsin[2]
14 West Mifflin Street, Suite 316A
Madison, Wisconsin 53703
(608) 256-1066 (Gotthelf)
(608) 256-8823 (Matyka)

Kevin Ronnie
Roger Quindell
A Choice, Milwaukee, WI
4417 West North Avenue
Milwaukee, WI 53208
(414) 444-6010

Women's Funds

Liz Bremner
Los Angeles Women's Fund*
6030 Wilshire Boulevard, #303
Los Angeles, CA 90036
(213) 939-9828

Rachel Johnson
Illinois Women's Fund
Sponsoring Committee*
c/o Illinois NOW LDEF
2220 Country Club Drive, #13
Woodbridge, IL 60517
(312) 929-0643

Maxine Brown
President
Fund for Women, Inc.*
239 South Fifth Street
Louisville, KY 40202
(502) 585-3434

Karen Zelemyer
Women's Funding Coalition
c/o Women in Need
410 West 40 Street
New York, NY 10018
(212) 695-7330

Lynn Yeakel
Tanya Thomas
Womens Way
125 South Ninth Street, #602
Philadelphia, PA 19107
(215) 592-7212

Dyan Oldenburg
Women's Funding Alliance
119 South Main Street, #330
Seattle, WA 98104
(206) 467-6733

---

[2]Community Share of Wisconsin is the result of a merger in 1988 between Madison
Sustaining Fund and Aid to Wisconsin Organizations.

IV

Appendix IV
IOLTA Programs (Interest on Lawyers' Trust Accounts):
A New Resource for Access to Justice Projects

IOLTA, the Interest on Lawyers' Trust Accounts program, is a relatively new concept for providing support for law-related charitable and educational products and providing legal services to low-income people. The program allows lawyers to place nominal or short-term client trust funds, which typically would be co-mingled in a regular checking account, in an interest-earning NOW account. The interest earned on these funds is periodically remitted by financial institutions to a designated administrative body. The administrative entities then disburse the funds for various law-related programs according to priorities and procedures that vary from state to state but generally operate much the same as foundation guidelines. First introduced in Florida in 1981, the program now operates in forty-five states and the District of Columbia. In eleven states lawyers are required to participate; in the remaining states, participation is voluntary.

There is no doubt that IOLTA programs make a significant difference in the quantity of funding available for law-related programs throughout the country. In the first six years, over $110 million was raised through IOLTA, and grants totaling over $74 million have been made. IOLTA's potential continues to increase as more states adopt the program and as states which currently make lawyers' participation voluntary increase their participation levels.

While almost all IOLTA programs limit their funding to organizations and projects operating within their respective states, their areas of interest vary significantly. Some states use their funds for law-related education programs and law school scholarships. Others use their funds to support social-justice organizations such as legal services back-up programs, organizations that advocate on behalf of welfare recipients, and tax-exempt public interest law firms that provide legal help to Central Americans seeking political asylum. Hence it is essential that grantseekers write their local IOLTA program and request grant proposal information.

The American Bar Association Commission on IOLTA operates an IOLTA clearinghouse in Chicago. The clearinghouse maintains files on every IOLTA program and works with the state IOLTA directors to network information across the nation. The list of IOLTA programs in operation as of August 1987 follows. For more information contact:

Debra S. Baxter, Director
ABA IOLTA Clearinghouse
750 North Lake Shore Drive
Chicago, IL 60611
(312) 988-5748

Alabama
Reginald Hamner
Post Office Box 671
415 Dexter Street
Montgomery, 36101
(205) 269-1515

Alaska
In the process of hiring a director. Interim correspondence through:

Debra O'Regan
Executive Director
Alaska Bar Association
Post Office Box 10029
Anchorage, AK 99510
(907) 272-7469

or

Mary Hughes, President
Alaska Bar Foundation
509 West Third Avenue
Anchorage, 99501
(907) 274-7522

Arizona
David A. Williams
IOLTA Program Coordinator
Arizona Bar Foundation
363 North First Avenue
Phoenix, 85004
(602) 252-4804

Arkansas
Susanne Roberts
Executive Director
Arkansas IOLTA Foundation
Suite 337
209 West Capitol Avenue
Little Rock, 77201
(501) 376-1801

California
LeRoy Cordova
Executive Director
Legal Services Trust Fund
State Bar of California
555 Franklin Street
San Francisco, 94102
(415) 561-8249

Colorado
Meredith McBurney
Executive Director
Colorado Lawyer Trust Account
Foundation (COLTAF)
1900 Grant Street, Suite 950
Denver, 80203-4309
(303) 863-7221

Connecticut
Susan Fair
Executive Director
Connecticut Bar Foundation
10 Grand Street
Hartford, 06106
(203) 525-1275

Delaware
Donald J. Wolfe, Jr., Esq.
Potter, Anderson & Corroon
350 Delaware Trust Building
Wilmington, 19801
(302) 658-6771

District of Columbia
Zona Hostetler
IOLTA Administrator

or

Constance Pena
Asst. IOLTA Administrator
District of Columbia Bar
Foundation IOLTA Program
Suite 503
918 Sixteenth Street, N.W.
Washington, D.C. 20006
(202) 466-3030

Florida
Jane E. Robertson
Executive Director
Florida Bar Foundation
Suite 102
880 North Orange Avenue
Orlando, 32801
(305) 843-0045

Georgia
Len Horton
IOLTA Director
State Bar of Georgia
11th Floor
84 Peachtree Street
Atlanta, 30303
(404) 527-8700

Hawaii
Carol Yamani
IOLTA Program Director
Hawaii Bar Foundation
Post Office Box 26
Honolulu, 96810
(808) 537-1868

Idaho
Barbara Anderson
IOLTA Program Director
Idaho Law Foundation
Boise, 83701
(208) 342-8958

Illinois
Ruth Ann Schmitt
Executive Director
Lawyers Trust Fund of Illinois
Suite 3416
55 East Monroe Street
Chicago, 60603
(312) 372-5906

Iowa
John Courtney, Director
Lawyer Trust Account
    Commission
Iowa Supreme Court
State Capitol, Room 23
Des Moines, 50319
(515) 281-3718

727

Appendix IV. IOLTA Programs

Kansas
Art Thompson
IOLTA Program Director
Kansas Bar Foundation
Post Office Box 1037
Topeka, 66601
(913) 234-5696

Kentucky
Gregory Fuchs, Administrator
Kentucky IOLTA Fund
West Main at Kentucky River
Frankfort, 40601
(502) 564-3795

Louisiana
Dixie G. Smith
Executive Director
Louisiana Bar Foundation
630 Camp Street
New Orleans, 70130
(504) 561-1046

Maine
Nancy Chandler
IOLTA Director
Maine Bar Foundation
Post Office Box 5430
Augusta, 04330
(207) 622-7523

Maryland
Robert Rhudy
Executive Director
Maryland Legal Services
  Corporation
34 Market Place, Suite 402
Baltimore, 21202
(301) 576-9494

Massachusetts
Lonnie Powers
Executive Director
Massachusetts Legal Assistance
  Corporation
20 West Street, Third Floor
Boston, 02111
(617) 574-9258

Michigan
Linda Rexer
Michigan State Bar Foundation
306 Townsend Street
Lansing, 48933-2083
(517) 372-9030

Minnesota
Judith Rehak, Director
Lawyer Trust Account Board
Minnesota Supreme Court
318A State Capitol
St. Paul, 55155
(612) 296-6822

Mississippi
Angie K. Cook
IOLTA Director
Mississippi State Bar
Post Office Box 2168
Jackson, 39205
(601) 948-4471

Missouri
Glenn Baker
Executive Director
Missouri Lawyer Trust Account
  Foundation
Post Office Box 63
Jefferson City, 65102
(314) 634-8117

Montana
Susan Peters
IOLTA Coordinator
State Bar of Montana
Post Office Box 4669
Helena, 59604
(406) 442-7660

Nebraska
Miden G. Ebert
Executive Director
Nebraska Lawyer Trust Account
  Foundation
Post Office Box 81809
Lincoln, 68501
(402) 475-7091

Nevada
Heather Elliott
Project Coordinator
IOLTA Project
Nevada Law Foundation
Post Office Box 2371
Sparks, 89432
(702) 359-2626

New Hampshire
Gail Kinney
Executive Director
New Hampshire Bar Foundation
18 Centre Street
Concord, 03301
(603) 224-6942

New Mexico
Sigrid Olson
Executive Director
New Mexico Bar Foundation
Post Office Box 27439
Albuquerque, 87125
(505) 265-1797

New York
Lorna Blake
Executive Director
IOLTA Fund of the State of New
  York
270 Broadway, Suite 1012
New York, 10007
(212) 587-4910

North Carolina
Martha W. Lowrance
Director
North Carolina State Bar Plan for
  IOLTA
Post Office Box 2687
Raleigh, 27602-2687
(919) 828-0477

North Dakota
Les Torgerson
Executive Director
North Dakota State
Bar Foundation
Post Office Box 2136
Bismarck, 58502
(701) 255-1404

Ohio
Randall M. Dana
IOLTA Program Director

or

Billy Kitts
IOLTA Coordinator
Ohio Public Defender
8 East Long Street
Columbus, 43215
(614) 466-5394

Oklahoma
Edward H. Palmer
Executive Director
Oklahoma Bar Foundation
Post Office Box 53036
Oklahoma City, 73152
(405) 524-2365

Oregon
Ann Bartsch
Executive Director
Oregon Law Foundation
Post Office Box 1689
Lake Oswego, 97034
(503) 620-0222

Rhode Island
Helen McDonald
Director
Rhode Island Bar Foundation
91 Friendship Street
Providence, 02903
(401) 421-5740

South Carolina
Sam M. Pierson III
Executive Director
South Carolina Bar Foundation
Post Office Box 11039
Columbia, 29211
(803) 799-6653

South Dakota
William K. Sahr
Executive Director
South Dakota Bar Foundation
222 East Capitol
Pierre, 57501
(605) 224-7554

Tennessee
Barri E. Bernstein
Executive Director
Tennessee Bar Foundation
3622 West End Avenue
Nashville, 37205
(615) 383-7421

Texas
Patricia Moran
Executive Director
Texas Equal Access to Justice
    Foundation
Post Office Box 12487
Capitol Station
Austin, 78711
(512) 463-1444

Utah
Michael Keller
Secretary/Treasurer
Utah Bar Foundation
425 East First South
Salt Lake City, 84111
(801) 532-3333

Vermont
Charles (Bud) Ochmanski
Executive Director
Vermont Bar Foundation
Post Office Box 100
Montpelier, 05602
(802) 223-2020

Virginia
Sharon Brooks
Staff Assistant
Virginia Law Foundation
Ross Building, Suite 1000
801 East Main Street
Richmond, 23219
(804) 786-2061

Washington
Barbara Clark
Executive Director
Legal Foundation of Washington
600 Central Building
810 Third Avenue
Seattle, 98104
(206) 624-2536

Wisconsin
M. Clark Johnson
Executive Director
Wisconsin Trust Account
    Foundation
Post Office Box 14197
Madison, 53714-0197
(608) 273-2595

V

Appendix V
Emergency Cash Flow Loan Funds

The guiding principle behind the emergency cash flow loan concept is that nonprofit organizations need special capital resources when government contracts, contract reimbursements, or other guaranteed funds are delayed in bureaucratic red tape. Nonprofit organizations typically have small cash reserves, and while a profit-making business can go to a bank and get a loan, banks are often reluctant to make loans to nonprofit agencies. Nonprofits, in the eyes of a bank, have no profit margin in their operations and most of the time, compounding the problem, government grants and contracts forbid the payment of interest with their funds.

The first emergency loan funds in the country date back to the early 1970s. They grew out of spontaneous needs to help nonprofit human-services agencies quickly through emergency situations. In the process of providing assistance, these emergency fund programs have developed a structure and become part of the established foundation community in the areas where they are located. Each of the cash flow loan programs is different because each is guided by the unique needs of its own community. In general, however, all provide short-term low-interest and no-interest loans to organizations that meet their lending criteria.

Some cash flow loan programs go further. The Donors Forum in Chicago advocates for long-term solutions of these cash flow problems. The cash flow loan program in Denver, for example, provides technical and managerial assistance to organizations that apply (whether or not the loan is granted) so that the organizations can avoid problems in the future or can be prepared to handle problems when they arise. Others, such as the Foundations-Corporations Emergency Fund Committee in San Francisco, work with government agencies to change procedures so that there are no disruptions in fund flows. The committee also supports and initiates legislation to change the manner in which government entities contract and reimburse nonprofit agencies.

Cash flow loan programs are not a first-time source of funds. They are designed to meet short-term crisis situations when guaranteed moneys have been delayed and all other remedies have been exhausted. The administration of each program is different. Application procedures, qualifying criteria, maximum loan size, loan period, interest rates, and repayment plans vary.

Following is a list of several cash flow loan programs in operation as of March 1988. Please note that each program has specific geographic limitations, usually the metropolitan area in which the program is located. For more information, contact these loan programs directly.

The Arts and Education Council
of Greater St. Louis
Revolving Loan Fund
40 North Kings Highway
St. Louis, Missouri 63108

Associated Grantmakers of
Massachusetts
Emergency Loan Fund
Suite 417
294 Washington Street
Boston, Massachusetts 02108

Edyth Bush Charitable
Foundation, Inc.
Emergency Loan Fund
650 Barnett National Bank
Building
Post Office Drawer F
Winter Park, Florida 32789

Community Cash Flow Fund
The Technical Assistance Center
Suite A504
1385 South Colorado Boulevard
Denver, Colorado 80222

The Community Foundation of
Santa Clara County
Emergency Grant/Loan Fund
42-D South First Street
San Jose, California 95113

Nonprofit Financial Assistance
Center
Emergency Loan Fund
Suite 500
166 West Washington Boulevard
Chicago, Illinois 60602

Fund for the City of New York
Cash Flow Loan Program
419 Park Avenue South
New York, New York 10016

The Minneapolis Foundation
Minnesota Emergency Fund
500 Foshay Tower
821 Marquette Avenue
Minneapolis, Minnesota 55402

Northern California Grantmakers
Arts Loan Fund
116 New Montgomery Street
San Francisco, California 94105

Northern California Grantmakers
Emergency Fund Committee
116 New Montgomery Street
San Francisco, California 94105

The Playboy Foundation
919 North Michigan Avenue,
5th Floor
Chicago, Illinois 60611

Peninsula Community Foundation
Emergency Grant/Loan Fund
1204 Burlingame Avenue
Post Office Box 627
Burlingame, California 94010-0627

California Community Foundation
Emergency Loan Fund
Suite 1660
3580 Wilshire Boulevard
Los Angeles, California 90010

United Way of Orange County
Emergency Loan Fund
13252 Garden Grove Boulevard
Garden Grove, California 92643

VI
Appendix VI
Management Support Organizations

Management support organizations (MSOs) are a relatively new institution in the nonprofit sector distinct in subtle ways from technical assistance providers. MSOs specialize in providing information and services that make the management of a nonprofit organization run more efficiently and perform more effectively to help the nonprofit realize its goals. Technical assistance providers, by contrast, typically concern themselves with imparting knowledge about nuts and bolts—for example, how to design energy efficient workspace, or what kind of telephone, computer, or word processing system will work best for your organization.

While each MSO is different, with its own specialty and way of working, a few general observations can be made. Typically MSOs are themselves small nonprofit organizations that rely on a core staff supplemented by other professionals and volunteers to serve clients that are usually other small to medium-size nonprofits in the local area. Their services are available for a fee that may vary from zero to the going commercial rates depending on the client's ability to pay, and the income the MSO derives from a combination of these fees and grants or contracts from third parties, such as foundations or government agencies. This last point is worthy of elaboration. In the last few years the number of funders willing to consider paying for management consulting services has grown. Sometimes this service is provided only on the funder's own initiative to current grantees; other times funders will accept proposals. On occasion, funders have been known to make support conditional on the grantee first securing the services of an MSO known to the grantmaker. If you find yourself in this position, remember to ask the funder for a list of several MSOs so that you have the opportunity to determine which one will work best for you.

This appendix contains a list of MSOs known to various members of the National Network of Grantmakers, the book advisory committee, and grantees as having experience working specifically with community-based organizations seeking to effect progressive social and economic justice. But before running out to hire one of these organizations, do some homework. For one thing, this list is far from exhaustive. Its focus is on organizations that provide primarily on-site consulting services. It therefore excludes a number of valuable resources such as regional associations of grantmakers (e.g., the Donor's Forum of Chicago, Associated Grantmakers of Massachusetts, the Minnesota Council on Foundations, the Southern California Association of Philanthropies) which often provide formal and informal management services and keep lists of local MSOs; grantmakers that also provide management assistance in the regular course of reviewing and administering grant proposals and awards (e.g., the Youth Project, Capp Street Foundation, the Campaign for Human Development); organizations that provide only organized training programs, seminars, or conferences; large for-profit consulting firms that may have pro bono departments to assist nonprofits; and individuals working without institutional affiliation. A good reference book to check is *The Nonprofit Management Association 1986 Directory of Members*, published every two years. There is probably a copy in your local Foundation Center Cooperating Collection (see Appendix VII), or it is available from the association (c/o Terry Barreiro, Post Office Box 2350, Minneapolis, Minnesota 55402, $25.00.) A second reason for doing some checking is that inclusion on this list is not an endorsement. What has been good practical management consulting for one organization—that is, advice that has been taken to heart and has worked—may not be good for another. Check the organization out for yourself. Ask about the types of services offered, the level of experience, and the fees, and be certain to tell them clearly what you want to get out of the arrangement. If it sounds like you have found a match, that is great. If not, try another one. Management support organizations work best when the match between their services and the clients' needs is a good one.

Center for Community Change
1000 Wisconsin Avenue, N.W.
Washington, D.C. 20007
(202) 342-0519

21 Sutter, 3rd Floor
San Francisco, California 94104
(415) 397-7322

1103 Santa Fe Drive
Denver, Colorado 80204
(303) 893-2149

Center for Management Assistance
One West Armour Boulevard
Kansas City, Missouri 64111
(816) 561-5505

Center for Organizational and Community Development[1]
225 Furcolo Hall
University of Massachusetts
Amherst, Massachusetts 01003
(413) 545-2038

---

[1]Formerly the Citizen Involvement Training Project

Community Resource Exchange
4th Floor
17 Murray Street
New York, New York 10007
(212) 349-6113

Independent Community Consultants
Planning and Training Office
Post Office Box 141
Hampton, Arkansas 71744
(501) 798-4510

Research and Evaluation Office
Post Office Box 1673
West Memphis, Arkansas 72301
(501) 735-8431
(501) 735-3040

Management Assistance Group, Inc.
Suite 305
1835 K Street, N.W.
Washington, D.C. 20036
(202) 659-1963

Western Regional Office
2685 Puesta del Sol Road
Santa Barbara, California 93105
(805) 569-0364

The Management Center
215 Leidesdorff Street, 4th Floor
San Francisco, California 94108
(415) 781-1953

Midwest Academy
225 West Ohio Street
Chicago, Illinois 60610
(312) 645-6010

Northern Rockies Action Group
9 Placer Street
Helena, Montana 59601
(406) 442-6615

Pacific Institute for Community Organizations
171 Santa Rosa Avenue
Oakland, California 94610
(415) 655-2801

The Philadelphia Clearinghouse
419 South 15th Street
Philadelphia, Pennsylvania 19146
(215) 546-2140

Public Interest Public Relations
A Division of M. Booth &
  Associates
225 West 34 Street
New York, New York 10122
(212) 736-5050

The Support Center
1410 Q Street, N.W.
Washington, D.C. 20009
(202) 462-2000

Suite H
3052 Clairmont Drive
San Diego, California 92117
(619) 275-0880

75 Lily
San Francisco, California 94102
(415) 552-7584

5th Floor
166 West Washington Street
Chicago, Illinois 60606
(312) 461-9300

Suite 408
14 Beacon Street
Boston, Massachusetts 02108
(617) 227-5514

Suite 1101
17 Academy Street
Newark, New Jersey 07102
(201) 643-5774

Suite 1208
36 West 44 Street
New York, New York 10036
(212) 302-6940

525 N.W. 13th Street
Oklahoma City, Oklahoma 73103
(405) 236-8133

15 East 5th Street
Tulsa, Oklahoma 74103
(918) 586-5112

Suite 504
57 Eddy Street
Providence, Rhode Island 02903
(401) 521-0710

Suite 244
1755 Lynnfield Road
Memphis, Tennessee 38119
(901) 685-2175

Suite 3800
1801 McKinney
Houston, Texas 77010
(713) 739-1211

The Technical Assistance Center
Suite A504
1385 South Colorado Boulevard
Denver, Colorado 80222
(303) 691-9610

Telecommunications Cooperative Network
Suite 1805
505 Eighth Avenue
New York, New York 10018
(212) 714-9780

VII

Appendix VII
The Foundation Center

The Foundation Center is an independent agency that researches, stores, and disseminates information on philanthropic programs. The center operates four reference libraries which offer a wide variety of materials, including books and periodicals, foundation annual reports, newsletters, press clippings, and center publications. The New York City and Washington, D.C., libraries also keep on file IRS tax returns for all currently operating private foundations in the U.S. The Cleveland and San Francisco collections house the tax returns for foundations in the midwestern and western states respectively. The center libraries are open to the public. Please telephone them for more information and their specific hours of operation.

In addition, the center has cooperating collections in most major cities in the U.S. Generally these collections are located within public institutions such as libraries; however, in some instances the cooperating collection may be housed and maintained by foundations or area associations of foundations. A list of these cooperating collections as of December 1987 follows the listing of Foundation Center–operated facilities. To check on new locations, telephone toll–free 1-800-424-9836.

Foundation Center Reference Libraries

The Foundation Center
79 Fifth Avenue
New York, New York 10003
(212) 620-4230

The Foundation Center
Kent H. Smith Library
1442 Hanna Building
1422 Euclid Avenue
Cleveland, Ohio 44115
(216) 861-1933

(Covers Illinois, Indiana,
  Kentucky, Michigan, Missouri,
  Ohio, Pennsylvania, and
  Wisconsin)

The Foundation Center
1001 Connecticut Avenue, N.W.
Washington, D.C. 20036
(202) 331-1400

The Foundation Center
312 Sutter Street
San Francisco, California 94108
(415) 397-0902

(Covers Alaska, Arizona,
  California, Colorado, Hawaii,
  Idaho, Montana, Nevada, New
  Mexico, Oregon, Utah,
  Washington, and Wyoming)

Collections Operated in Cooperation with the Foundation Center

Alabama

Birmingham Public Library
2100 Park Place
Birmingham, 35203
(205) 226-3600

Huntsville-Madison County
Public Library
108 Fountain Circle
Huntsville, 35804
(205) 536-0021

University of South Alabama
Library Building
Reference Department
Mobile, 36688
(205) 460-7025

Auburn University at
Montgomery Library
Montgomery, 36193-0401
(205) 271-9649

Alaska

University of Alaska
Anchorage Library
3211 Providence Drive
Anchorage, 99508
(907) 786-1848

Arizona

Phoenix Public Library
Business and Sciences
Department
12 East McDowell Road
Phoenix, 85004
(602) 262-4636

Tucson Public Library
Main Library
200 South Sixth Avenue
Tucson, 85701
(602) 791-4393

Arkansas

Westark Community College
  Library
Grand Avenue at Waldron Road
Fort Smith, 72913
(501) 785-7000

Little Rock Public Library
Reference Department
700 Louisiana Street
Little Rock, 72201
(501) 370-5950

California

Peninsula Community Foundation
1204 Burlingame Avenue
Burlingame, 94011-0627
(415) 342-2505

California Community Foundation
Funding Information Center
Suite 1660
3580 Wilshire Boulevard
Los Angeles, 90010
(213) 413-4042

Community Foundation for
Monterey County
420 Pacific Street
Monterey, 93940
(408) 375-9712

California Community Foundation
Suite 300
4050 Metropolitan Drive
Orange, 92668
(704) 937-9077

Riverside Public Library
3581 7th Street
Riverside, 92501
(714) 787-7201

California State Library
Reference Services, Room 309
914 Capitol Mall
Sacramento, 95814
(916) 322-4570

San Diego Community Foundation
Suite 410
525 "B" Street
San Diego, 92101
(619) 239-8815

The Foundation Center
312 Sutter Street
San Francisco, 94108
(415) 397-0902

Grantsmanship Resource Center
Junior League of San Jose
Community Foundation of
Santa Clara County
Suite 220
960 West Hedding
San Jose, 95126
(408) 244-5280

Orange County Community
Development Council
1440 East First Street, 4th floor
Santa Ana, 92701
(714) 547-6801

Santa Barbara Public Library
Reference Section
40 East Anapamu
Post Office Box 1019
Santa Barbara, 93102
(805) 962-7653

Santa Monica Public Library
1343 Sixth Street
Santa Monica, 90401-1603
(213) 458-8603

Tuolomne County Library
465 South Washington Street
Sonora, 95370
(209) 533-5707

Colorado
Pikes Peak Library District
20 North Cascade Avenue
Colorado Springs, 80901
(303) 473-2780

Denver Public Library
Sociology Division
1357 Broadway
Denver, 80203
(303) 571-2190

Connecticut
Danbury Public Library
170 Main Street
Danbury, 06810
(203) 797-4527

Hartford Public Library
Reference Department
500 Main Street
Hartford, 06103
(203) 525-9121

D.A.T.A.
30 Arbor Street
Hartford, 06106
(203) 232-6619

D.A.T.A.
Suite 502
25 Science Park
New Haven, 06513
(203) 786-5225

Delaware
Hugh Morris Library
University of Delaware
Newark, 19717-5267
(302) 451-2965

District of Columbia
The Foundation Center
1001 Connecticut Avenue, N.W.
Washington, D.C. 20036
(202) 331-1400

Florida
Volusia County Public Library
City Island
Daytona Beach, 32014
(904) 252-8374

Jacksonville Public Library
Business, Science & Industry
  Department
122 North Ocean Street
Jacksonville, 32202
(904) 633-3926

Miami-Dade Public Library
Humanities Department
101 West Flagler Street
Miami, 33132
(305) 375-2665

Orlando Public Library
101 East Central Boulevard
Orlando, 32801
(305) 425-4694

Selby Public Library
1001 Boulevard of the Arts
Sarasota, 33577
(813) 366-7303

Leon County Public Library
Community Funding
Resources Center
1940 North Monroe Street
Tallahassee, 32303
(904) 478-2665

Palm Beach County
Community Foundation
Suite 340
324 Datura Street
West Palm Beach, 33401
(305) 659-6800

Georgia
Atlanta-Fulton Public Library
Ivan Allen Department
1 Margaret Mitchell Square
Atlanta, 30303
(404) 688-4636

Hawaii
Thomas Hale Hamilton Library
General Reference
University of Hawaii
2550 The Mall
Honolulu, 96822
(808) 948-7214

The Hawaiian Foundation
Resource Room
130 Merchant Street
Bancorp Tower, Suite 901
Honolulu, 96813
(808) 538-4540

Idaho
Caldwell Public Library
1010 Dearborn Street
Caldwell, 83605
(208) 459-3242

Illinois
Belleville Public Library
121 East Washington Street
Belleville, 62220
(618) 234-0441

DuPage Township
300 Briarcliff Road
Bolingbrook, 60439
(312) 759-1317

Donors Forum of Chicago
Room 430
53 West Jackson Boulevard
Chicago, 60604
(312) 431-0265

Evanston Public Library
1703 Orrington Avenue
Evanston, 60201
(312) 866-0305

Sangamon State University Library
Shepherd Road
Springfield, 62708
(217) 786-6633

Indiana
Allen County Public Library
900 Webster Street
Fort Wayne, 46802
(219) 424-7241

Indiana University Northwest
Library
3400 Broadway
Gary, 46408
(219) 980-6580

Indianapolis-Marion County
Public Library
40 East St. Clair Street
Indianapolis, 46204
(317) 269-1733

Iowa
Public Library of Des Moines
100 Locust Street
Des Moines, 50308
(515) 283-4259

Kansas
Topeka Public Library
Adult Services Department
1515 West Tenth Street
Topeka, 66604
(913) 233-2040

Wichita Public Library
223 South Main
Wichita, 67202
(316) 262-0611

Kentucky
Western Kentucky University
Division of Library Services
Helm-Cravens Library
Bowling Green, 42101
(502) 745-3951

Louisville Free Public Library
Fourth and York Streets
Louisville, 40203
(502) 561-8600

Louisiana
East Baton Rouge Parish Library
Centroplex Library
120 St. Louis Street
Baton Rouge, 70821
(504) 389-4960

New Orleans Public Library
Business & Science Division
219 Loyola Avenue
New Orleans, 70140
(504) 596-2583

Shreve Memorial Library
424 Texas Street
Shreveport, 71101
(318) 226-5894

Maine
University of Southern Maine
Center for Research & Advanced
   Study
246 Deering Avenue
Portland, 04102
(207) 780-4411

Maryland
Enoch Pratt Free Library
Social Science & History Dept.
400 Cathedral Street
Baltimore, 21201
(301) 396-5320

Massachusetts
Associated Grantmakers
of Massachusetts
Suite 501
294 Washington Street
Boston, 02108
(617) 426-2608

Boston Public Library
Copley Square
Boston, 02117
(617) 536-5400

Western Massachusetts
Funding Resource Center
Campaign for Human
   Development
Chancery Annex
73 Chestnut Street
Springfield, 01103
(413) 732-3175 ext. 67

Walpole Public Library
Common Street
Walpole, 02081
(617) 668-5497 ext. 340

Grants Resource Center
Worcester Public Library
Salem Square
Worcester, 01608
(617) 799-1655

Michigan
Alpena County Library
211 North First Avenue
Alpena, 49707
(517) 356-6188

University of Michigan-Ann Arbor
Reference Department
209 Hatcher Graduate Library
Ann Arbor, 48109-1205
(313) 764-1149

Henry Ford Centennial Library
16301 Michigan Avenue
Dearborn, 48126
(313) 943-2337

Purdy Library
Wayne State University
Detroit, 48202
(313) 577-4040

Michigan State University
   Libraries
Reference Library
East Lansing, 48824
(517) 353-9184

Farmington Community Library
32737 West 12 Mile Road
Farmington Hills, 48018
(313) 553-0300

University of Michigan-Flint
Library
Reference Department
Flint, 48503
(313) 762-3408

Grand Rapids Public Library
Sociology & Education Dept.
Library Plaza
Grand Rapids, 49502
(616) 456-4411

Michigan Technological
University Library
Highway U.S. 41
Houghton, 49931
(906) 487-2507

Minnesota
Duluth Public Library
520 Superior Street
Duluth, 55802
(218) 723-3802

Southwest State
University Library
Marshall, 56258
(507) 537-7278

Minneapolis Public Library
Sociology Department
300 Nicollett Mall
Minneapolis, 55401
(612) 372-6555

Rochester Public Library
Broadway at First Street, S.E.
Rochester, 55901
(507) 285-8002

Saint Paul Public Library
90 West Fourth Street
St. Paul, 55102
(612) 292-6311

Mississippi
Jackson Metropolitan Library
301 North State Street
Jackson, 39201
(601) 944-1120

Missouri
Clearinghouse for
Midcontinent Foundations
University of Missouri-Kansas City
Law School, Suite 1-300
52nd Street & Oak
Kansas City, 64113
(816) 276-1176

Kansas City Public Library
311 East 12 Street
Kansas City, 64106
(816) 221-2685

Metropolitan Association for
Philanthropy, Inc.
Suite 150
5585 Pershing Avenue
St. Louis, 63112
(314) 361-3900

Springfield-Greene County Library
397 East Central Street
Springfield, 65801
(417) 866-4636

Montana
Eastern Montana College Library
Reference Department
1500 North 30th Street
Billings, 59101-0298
(406) 657-2262

Montana State Library
Reference Department
1515 East 6th Avenue
Helena, 59620
(406) 444-3004

Nebraska
University of Nebraska,
Lincoln
106 Love Library.
Lincoln, 68588-0401
(402) 472-2526

W. Dale Clark Library
Social Sciences Department
215 South 15th Street
Omaha, 68102
(402) 444-4826

Nevada
Las Vegas-Clark County
Library District
1401 East Flamingo Road
Las Vegas, 89119
(702) 733-7810

Washoe County Library
301 South Center Street
Reno, 89505
(702) 785-4190

New Hampshire
The New Hampshire Charitable
  Fund
One South Street
Concord, 03301
(603) 225-6641

Littleton Public Library
109 Main Street
Littleton, 03561
(603) 444-5741

New Jersey
Cumberland County Library
800 East Commerce Street
Bridgeton, 08302
(609) 455-0080

The Support Center
17 Academy Street, Suite 1101
Newark, 07102
(201) 643-5774

County College of Morris
Masten Learning Resource Center
Route 10 & Center Grove Road
Randolph, 07869
(201) 361-5000, ext. 470

New Jersey State Library
Governmental Reference
185 West State Street
Trenton, 08625
(609) 292-6220

New Mexico
Albuquerque Community
  Foundation
6400 Uptown Boulevard, N.E.
Suite 500-W
Albuquerque, 87110
(505) 883-6240

New Mexico State Library
325 Don Gaspar Street
Santa Fe, 87503
(505) 827-3824

New York
New York State Library
Cultural Education Center
Humanities Section
Empire State Plaza
Albany, 12230
(518) 474-7645

Suffolk Cooperative
Library System
627 North Sunrise Service Road
Bellport, 11713
(516) 286-1600

Bronx Reference Center
New York Public Library
2556 Bainbridge Avenue
Bronx, 10458
(212) 220-6575

Brooklyn in Touch
Room 1508
101 Willoughby Street
Brooklyn, 11201
(212) 237-9300

Buffalo & Erie County Public
  Library
Lafayette Square
Buffalo, 14203
(716) 856-7525

Huntington Public Library
338 Main Street
Huntington, 11743
(516) 427-5165

Levittown Public Library
Reference Department
One Bluegrass Lane
Levittown, 11756
(516) 731-5728

The Foundation Center
79 Fifth Avenue
New York, 10003
(212) 620-4230

SUNY/College at Old
Westbury Library
223 Store Hill Road
Old Westbury, 11568
(516) 876-3156

Plattsburgh Public Library
Reference Department
15 Oak Street
Plattsburgh, 12901
(518) 563-0921

Adriance Memorial Library
93 Market Street
Poughkeepsie, 12601
(914) 485-4790

Queens Borough Public Library
89-11 Merrick Boulevard
Jamaica, 11432
(718) 990-0700

Rochester Public Library
Business & Social Sciences
   Division
115 South Avenue
Rochester, 14604
(716) 428-7328

Staten Island Council on the Arts
Room 311
One Edgewater Plaza
Staten Island, 10305
(718) 447-4485

Onondaga County Public Library
335 Montgomery Street
Syracuse, 13202
(315) 473-4493

White Plains Public Library
100 Martine Avenue
White Plains, 10601
(914) 682-4488

North Carolina
The Duke Endowment
Suite 1100
200 South Tryon Street
Charlotte, 28202
(704) 376-0291

Durham County Library
300 North Roxboro Street
Durham, 27701
(919) 683-2626

North Carolina State Library
109 East Jones Street
Raleigh, 27611
(919) 733-3270

The Winston-Salem Foundation
229 First Union National Bank
   Building
Winston-Salem, 27101
(919) 725-2382

North Dakota
Western Dakota Grants
Resource Center
Bismarck Junior College Library
Bismarck, 58501
(701) 224-5450

North Dakota State University
The Library
Fargo, 58105
(701) 237-8876

Ohio
Stark County District Library
715 Market Avenue North
Canton, 44702
(216) 452-0665

Public Library of Cincinnati &
Hamilton County
Education Department
800 Vine Street
Cincinnati, 45202
(513) 369-6940

The Foundation Center
Kent H. Smith Library
1442 Hanna Building
1422 Euclid Avenue
Cleveland, 44115
(216) 861-1933

The Public Library of Columbus
   and Franklin County
Main Library
96 South Grant Avenue
Columbus, 43215
(614) 227-9500

Dayton and Montgomery County
Public Library
Grants Information Center
215 East Third Street
Dayton, 45402-2103
(513) 227-9500, ext. 211

Toledo-Lucas County Public
  Library
Social Service Department
325 Michigan Street
Toledo, 43624
(419) 255-7055 ext. 221

Ohio University-Zanesville
Community Education and
  Development
1425 Newark Road
Zanesville, 43701
(614) 453-0762

Oklahoma

Oklahoma City University Library
N.W. 23rd at North Blackwelder
Oklahoma City, 73106
(405) 521-5072

Tulsa City-County Library System
400 Civic Center
Tulsa, 74103
(918) 592-7944

Oregon

Library Association of Portland
Government Documents Room
801 S.W. Tenth Avenue
Portland, 97205
(503) 223-7201

Oregon State Library
State Library Building
Salem, 97310
(503) 378-4274

Pennsylvania

Northampton County Area
  Community College
Learning Resources Center
3835 Green Pond Road
Bethlehem, 18017
(215) 865-5358

Erie County Public Library
3 South Perry Square
Erie, 16501
(814) 452-2333 ext. 54

Dauphin County Library System
Central Library
101 Walnut Street
Harrisburg, 17101
(717) 234-4961

Lancaster County Public Library
125 North Duke Street
Lancaster, 17602
(717) 394-2651

The Free Library of Philadelphia
Logan Square
Philadelphia, 19103
(215) 686-5423

University of Pittsburgh
Hillman Library
Pittsburgh, 15260
(412) 624-4423

Economic Development Council
  of Northeastern Pennsylvania
1151 Oak Street
Pittston, 18640
(717) 655-5581

James V. Brown Library
12 East 4th Street
Williamsport, 17701
(717) 326-0536

751

Rhode Island
Providence Public Library
Reference Department
150 Empire Street
Providence, 02903
(401) 521-7722

South Carolina
Charleston County Public Library
404 King Street
Charleston, 29403
(803) 723-1645

South Carolina State Library
Reader Services Department
1500 Senate Street
Columbia, 29201
(803) 734-8666

South Dakota
South Dakota State Library
State Library Building
800 North Illinois Street
Pierre, 57501
(605) 773-3131

Sioux Falls Area Foundation
404 Boyce Greeley Building
321 South Phillips Avenue
Sioux Falls, 57102-0781
(605) 336-7055

Tennessee
Knoxville-Knox County Public
  Library
500 West Church Avenue
Knoxville, 37902
(615) 523-0781

Memphis-Shelby County Public
  Library
1850 Peabody Avenue
Memphis, 38104
(901) 725-8876

Public Library of Nashville and
  Davidson County
8th Avenue, North and Union
  Street
Nashville, 37203
(615) 244-4700

Texas
Amarillo Area Foundation
1000 Polk
Post Office Box 25569
Amarillo, 79105
(806) 376-4521

The University of Texas
The Hogg Foundation for Mental
  Health
Austin, 78712
(512) 471-5041

Corpus Christi State University
  Library
6300 Ocean Drive
Corpus Christi, 78412
(512) 991-6810

Dallas Public Library
Grants Information Service
1515 Young Street
Dallas, 75201
(214) 670-1487

Pan American University
Learning Resource Center
1201 West University Drive
Edinburg, 78539
(512) 381-3304

El Paso Community Foundation
El Paso National Bank Bldg.
Suite 1616
El Paso, 79901
(915) 533-4020

Funding Information Center
Texas Christian University Library
Ft. Worth, 76129
(817) 921-7664

Houston Public Library
Bibliographic & Information
  Center
500 McKinney Avenue
Houston, 77002
(713) 224-5441, ext. 265

Lubbock Area Foundation
502 Commerce Bank Building
Lubbock, 79401
(806) 762-8061

Funding Information Library
507 Brooklyn
San Antonio, 78215
(512) 227-4333

Utah
Salt Lake City Public Library
Business & Science Department
209 East Fifth Street
Salt Lake City, 84111
(801) 363-5733

Vermont
State of Vermont Department of
  Libraries
Reference Services Unit
111 State Street
Montpelier, 05602
(802) 828-3261

Virginia
Grants Resources Collection
Hampton Public Library
4207 Victoria Boulevard
Hampton, 23669
(804) 727-6234

Richmond Public Library
Business, Science & Technology
  Department
101 East Franklin Street
Richmond, 23219
(804) 780-8223

Washington
Seattle Public Library
1000 Fourth Avenue
Seattle, 98104
(206) 625-4881

Spokane Public Library
Funding Information Center
West 906 Main Avenue
Spokane, 99201
(509) 838-3364

West Virginia
Kanawha County Public Library
123 Capital Street
Charleston, 25301
(304) 343-4646

Wisconsin
Marquette University Memorial
  Library
1415 West Wisconsin Avenue
Milwaukee, 53233
(414) 224-1515

University of Wisconsin-Madison
Memorial Library
728 State Street
Madison, 53706
(608) 262-3647

Wyoming
Laramie County Community
College Library
1400 East College Drive
Cheyenne, 82007
(307) 838-3364

Collections Operated in Other Countries

Australia
Victorian Community Foundation
94 Queen Street
Melbourne Vic 3000
607-5922

Canada
Canadian Center for Philanthropy
Suite 4080
3080 Yonge Street
Toronto, Ontario M4N 3N1
(416) 484-4118

England
Charities Aid Foundation
14 Bloomsbury Square
London WC1A 2LP
01-430-1798

Mexico
Biblioteca Benjamin Franklin
Londres 16
Mexico City 6, D.F.
(525) 591-0244

Puerto Rico
Universidad Del Sagrado Corazon
M.M.T. Guevarra Library
Correo Calle Loiza
Santurce, 00914
(809) 728-1515 ext. 357

Virgin Islands
College of the Virgin Islands
   Library
Saint Thomas
U.S. Virgin Islands, 00801
(809) 774-9200 ext. 487

VIII

**Appendix VIII
State and Regional Grantmaking Directories**

One of the most valuable resources for community-based organizations is the local philanthropic community. This publication cannot provide data on all local foundations and corporate-giving programs. Therefore, following is a list of directories organized by state or region. State directories are listed first; regional directories follow. When the information is known, reference is made to availability and price. State and regional directories are almost always available in the Foundation Center libraries and the geographically appropriate cooperating collection (see Appendix VII); they need not be purchased.

Alabama

Birmingham Public Library. *Alabama Foundation Directory*. 1982–83. 56 pp. Contains listings of 193 foundations. Available from Reference Department, Birmingham Public Library, 2020 Park Place, Birmingham, Alabama 35203. $5.00 prepaid.

See *Foundation Profiles of the Southeast: Alabama, Arkansas, Louisiana, Mississippi*. Contains listing of 212 Alabama foundations.

Arizona

Junior League of Phoenix, Inc. *Arizona Foundation Directory*. 1986. 80 pp. Contains listings on 150 Arizona foundations, plus out-of-state foundations. Available from the Junior League of Phoenix, Inc., 1949 E. Camelback Road, Post Office Box 10377, Phoenix, Arizona 85064. $15.00 prepaid.

Arkansas

Jerry Cronin and Earl Anthes. *Guide to Arkansas Funding Sources*. Independent Community Consultants, Inc., 1986. 103 pp. Contains profiles of 218 foundations in Arkansas and neighboring states that make grants in Arkansas. Available from Independent Community Consultants, Inc., Box 1673, West Memphis, Arkansas 72301. $13.00, plus $1.50 postage and handling.

See *Foundation Profiles of the Southeast: Alabama, Arkansas, Louisiana, Mississippi*. Contains listings of 148 Arkansas foundations.

Appendix VIII. State and Regional Grantmaking Directories

California
Gould, Morgan, ed. *Guide to California Foundations*. 6th edition. San Francisco, 1985. 585 pp. Contains listings of 749 California foundations. Available from Northern California Grantmakers, 334 Kearny Street, San Francisco, California 94102. $17.00 plus $2.00 postage and handling.

Logos Associates. *The Directory of the Major California Foundations*. 1st edition. 1986. 94 pp. Contains listings on 97 + California foundations. Available from Logos Associates, 7 Park Street, Room 212, Attleboro, Massachusetts 02730. $19.95 plus $.63 shipping.

San Diego Community Foundation and the Junior League of San Diego, Inc. *The San Diego County Foundation Directory*. 1985. Contains listing of 123 grantmakers. Available from the San Diego Community Foundation, 625 Broadway, Suite 1015, San Diego, California 92101. $20.00 includes postage.

Sternberg, Sam. *National Directory of Corporate Charity: California Edition*. 1981. 450 + pp. Contains listing of 620 California corporations. Available from Regional Young Adult Project, 330 Ellis Street, Room 506, San Francisco, California 94102. $14.95 plus $2.00 shipping (plus sales tax for California residents).

Tobey, Patricia Blair and Irving R. Warner, eds. *Where the Money's At, How to Reach Over 500 California Grant-Making Foundations*. Los Angeles, ICPR Publications, 1978. 536 pp. Contains listing of 525 California foundations. Available from Irving R. Warner, 3235 Berry Drive, Studio City, California 91604. $17.00.

Colorado
Junior League of Denver, Inc., the Denver Foundation, the Attorney General of Colorado, co-sponsors. *Colorado Foundation Directory*. 5th edition. Based on 1983 and 1984 990-PF returns. Contains listing of approximately 250 Colorado foundations. Available from Colorado Foundation Directory, Junior League of Denver, Inc., 6300 East Yale Avenue, Denver, Colorado, 80222. $10.00. Checks payable to Colorado Foundation Directory.

Connecticut
Burns, Michael E., ed. *1985-1986 Connecticut Foundation Directory*. OUA/DATA, 1985. 350 pp. Contains listing of approximately 865 Connecticut foundations. Available from DATA, 880 Asylum Avenue, Hartford, Connecticut 06103. $25.00 prepaid.

Burns, Michael E., ed. *1986–1987 Guide to Corporate Giving in Connecticut.* 1986. 350 pp. Available from DATA, 880 Asylum Avenue, Hartford, Connecticut 06103. $26.50 plus $2.00 postage and handling.

Logos, Inc. *Directory of Major Connecticut Foundations.*
1982. 49 pp. Contains listing of 61 Connecticut foundations. Available from Logos, Inc., 7 Park Street, Room 212, Attleboro, Massachusetts 02703. $19.95.

Delaware
United Way of Delaware. *Delaware Foundations.* Wilmington, 1983. 120 pp. Contains listing of 154 Delaware foundations. Available from United Way of Delaware, Inc., 701 Shipley Street, Wilmington, Delaware 19801. $14.50.

District of Columbia
Community Foundation of Greater Washington, Inc. *Directory of Foundations of the Greater Washington Area.* Based on 1985 990-PF returns filed with the IRS. 142 pp. Contains listing of 400+ grantmaking foundations in the metropolitan Washington area. Available from Community Foundation of Greater Washington, 3221 M Street, N.W., Washington, D.C. 20007. $12.00 plus $1.50 postage and handling.

Florida
The Complete Guide to Florida Foundations. Miami, 1986. Available from the publisher, John L. Adams and Company, Inc., Post Office Box 561565, Miami, Florida 33156. $55.00.

Taylor, James H. and John L. Wilson. *Foundation Profiles of the Southeast: Florida.* 1983. 130+ pp. Contains listing of 780 Florida foundations. Available from James H. Taylor Associates, Inc., 804 Main Street, Williamsburg, Kentucky 40769. $39.95 prepaid.

Georgia
Taylor, James H. and John L. Wilson. *Foundation Profiles of the Southeast: Georgia.* 1983. 85 pp. Contains listing of 457 Georgia foundations. Available from James H. Taylor Associates, Inc., 804 Main Street, Williamsburg, Kentucky 40769. $39.95 prepaid.

Hawaii
Like, Alu. *A Guide to Charitable Trusts and Foundations in the State of Hawaii.* Honolulu, 1986. 302 pp. Contains listing of 143 foundations, 25

local service organizations, and 13 church funding sources. Available from Alu Like, Inc., 401 Kamakee Street, 3rd floor, Honolulu, Hawaii 96814. $30.00 for nonprofit organizations; $35.00 for profit-making organizations.

Idaho
Caldwell Public Library. *Directory of Idaho Foundations*. 1984. 23 pp. Contains listing of 89 Idaho foundations. Available from Caldwell Public Library, 1010 Dearborn Street, Caldwell, Idaho 83605. $3.00 prepaid.

Illinois
Capriotti, Beatrice J. and Frank J., III. *Illinois Foundation Directory*. 1985. 327+ pp. Contains entries on approximately 1900 foundations. Available from the Foundation Data Center, Kenmar Center, 401 Kenmar Circle, Minnetonka, Minnesota 55343. $275.00 (includes annual seminar). Update service by annual subscription, $210.00.

Dick, Ellen A., ed. *The 1986 Directory of Illinois Foundations*. Contains entries on 399 foundations. Available from Donors Forum of Chicago, 53 West Jackson Boulevard, Suite 430, Chicago, Illinois 60604. $35.00.

Levy, Susan M., ed. *The Chicago Corporate Connection: A Directory of Chicago Area Corporate Contributors, Including Downstate Illinois and Northern Indiana*. 2nd edition. 1983. 213 pp. Contains listing of approximately 200 area corporations. Available from Donors Forum of Chicago, 53 West Jackson Boulevard, Suite 430, Chicago, Illinois 60604. $18.50 plus $1.50 postage and handling, prepaid.

Levy, Susan M., ed. *Donors Forum Members Grants List of 1983*. 1984. 253 pp. Contains listing of approximately 103 grantmakers. Available from Donors Forum of Chicago, 53 West Jackson Boulevard, Suite 430, Chicago, Illinois 60604. $20.00 plus $1.50 postage and handling.

Indiana
Spear, Paula Reading, ed. *Indiana Foundations: A Directory*. 3rd edition. Indianapolis, 1981. 164 pp. Contains listing of 288 Indiana foundations. Available from Central Research Systems, 320 North Meridian, Suite 1011, Indianapolis, Indiana 46204. $24.75 prepaid.

Iowa
Holm, Daniel H. *Iowa Directory of Foundations*. Dubuque, 1984. 108 pp. Available from Trumpet Associates, Inc., Post Office Box 172, Dubuque, Iowa 52001. $19.75 plus $2.00 postage and handling.

Appendix VIII. State and Regional Grantmaking Directories

Kansas

Hart, Eloise B., ed. *Directory of Kansas Foundations*. compiled by the Junior League of Kansas City, 1986. 378 pp. Contains listings of approximately 300 foundations. Available from Topeka Public Library, 1515 West 10th Street, Topeka, Kansas 66604. $25.00. Checks payable to Topeka Public Library.

Talbot, Linda, ed. *Directory of Greater Kansas City Foundations*. 1st edition. 1986. Compiled by Jarie Midgett. 74 pp. Contains listings on 281 foundations. Available from Clearinghouse for Mid-Continent Foundations, Post Office Box 22680, Kansas City, Missouri 64113. $25.00 plus $3.00 postage and handling.

Townsley, Connie, ed. *Directory of Kansas Foundations*. Topeka, Association of Community Arts Agencies of Kansas, 1979. 128 pp. Contains listing of 255 Kansas foundations. Available from Association of Community Arts Agencies of Kansas, Post Office Box 62, Oberlin, Kansas 67749. $5.80.

Kentucky

Dougherty, Nancy C., ed. *A Guide to Kentucky Grantmakers*. 1982. 19 pp. Contains listing of 101 foundations. Available from The Louisville Foundation, Inc., 623 West Main Street, Louisville, Kentucky 40202. $6.00 prepaid.

Taylor, James H. and John L. Wilson, eds. *Foundation Profiles of the Southeast: Kentucky, Tennessee, Virginia*. 1981. 153 pp. Contains listing of 117 Kentucky foundations. Available from James H. Taylor Associates, Inc., 804 Main Street, Williamsburg, Kentucky 40769. $39.95 prepaid.

Louisiana

See *Foundation Profiles of the Southeast: Alabama, Arkansas, Louisiana, Mississippi*. Contains listing of 229 Louisiana foundations.

Maine

Burns, Michael E., ed. *Guide to Corporate Giving in Maine*. 1984. 74 + pp. Contains listings on 218 corporations. Available from OUA/DATA, 81 Saltonstall Avenue, New Haven, Connecticut 06513. $15.00.

Center for Research and Advanced Study. *Directory of Maine Foundations*. 7th edition. University of Southern Maine, 1986. 35 pp. Contains listing of 74 Maine foundations. Available from the Center for Research and Advanced Study, University of Southern Maine, 246 Deering Avenue, Portland, Maine 04102. $6.00.

Center for Research and Advanced Study. *Maine Corporate Funding Directory*. 1984. 100 pp. Contains listings on approximately 75 corporations. Available from the Center for Research and Advanced Study, University of Southern Maine, 246 Deering Avenue, Portland, Maine 04102. $5.50.

Maryland

Office of the Attorney General. *1984 Annual Index Foundation Reports*. Baltimore, Office of the Attorney General, 1985. Contains listing of 380 Maryland foundations. Available from the Office of the Attorney General, 7 North Calvert Street, Baltimore, Maryland 21202. $35.00 prepaid.

Massachusetts

Burns, Michael E., ed. *Guide to Corporate Giving in Massachusetts*. 1983. 97 pp. Contains listings on 737 foundations. Available from OUA/DATA, 81 Saltonstall Avenue, New Haven, Connecticut 06513. $30.00 plus $1.50 postage and handling.

Simmons, Gracelaw and Linda C. Coe, eds. *Massachusetts Grantmakers*. Boston, 1986. Contains listing of 385 foundations and corporations. Available from Associated Grantmakers of Massachusetts, Inc., 294 Washington Street, Suite 417, Boston, Massachusetts 02108. $25.00 plus $3.00 handling.

The Social Service Planning Corporation. *Private Sector Giving: Greater Worcester Area*. 1983. 184 pp. Contains listings on approximately 150 foundations. Available from the Social Service Planning Corporation, 340 Main Street, Suite 329, Worcester, Massachusetts 01608. $12.50 plus $2.25 postage and handling for photocopy (printed edition depleted).

Logos Associates. *Directory of the Major Greater Boston Foundations*. 1981. 48 pp. Contains listing of 56 Boston area foundations. Available from Logos Associates, 12 Gustin, Attleboro, Massachusetts 02703. $19.95 prepaid.

Michigan

Council of Michigan Foundations and Michigan League for Human Services. *The Michigan Foundation Directory*. 5th edition. 1986. 213 pp. Contains listing of 859 Michigan foundations. Available from the Michigan

League for Human Services, 300 North Washington Square, Suite 311, Lansing, Michigan 48893. $15.00 for members, $18.00 for nonmembers.

Minnesota

Capriotti, Beatrice J. and Frank J., III, eds. *Minnesota Foundation Directory*. 1987. 327+ pp. Contains listings of approximately 700 foundations. Available from the Foundation Data Center, Kenmar Center, 401 Kenmar Circle, Minnetonka, Minnesota 55343. $275.00 (includes annual seminar). Update service by annual subscription, $210.

Minnesota Council on Foundations. *Guide to Minnesota Foundations*. Minneapolis, 1983. 149 pp. Contains listing of 420+ Minnesota foundations. Available from University of Minnesota Press, 2037 University Avenue, S.E., Minneapolis, Minnesota 55414. $14.95 plus sales tax for state residents.

Mississippi

See *Foundation Profiles of the Southeast: Alabama, Arkansas, Louisiana, Mississippi*. Contains listing of 54 Mississippi foundations.

Missouri

Swift, Wilda H., ed. *The Directory of Missouri Foundations*. 1985. 126 pp. Contains listings on 788 foundations. Available from Swift Associates, Post Office Box 28033, St. Louis, Missouri 63119. $15.00 plus $2.10 shipping.

Montana

McRae, Kendall and Kim Pederson. *The Montana and Wyoming Foundations Directory*. 4th edition. 1986. Contains listing of 65+ Montana foundations. Available from Grant Assistance, Eastern Montana College Library, 1500 North 30th Street, Billings, Montana 59101. $6.00 prepaid.

Nebraska

Junior League of Omaha. *Nebraska Foundation Directory*. Omaha, 1985. 30 pp. Contains listing of approximately 200 foundations. Available from Junior League of Omaha, 808 South 74th Plaza, Omaha, Nebraska 68114. $6.00.

Nevada

Honsa, Vlasta and Annetta Yousef. *Nevada Foundation Directory*. 1985. 64 pp. Contains listing of 41 foundations. Available from Community

Relations Department, Las Vegas-Clark County Library District, 1401 East Flamingo Road, Las Vegas, Nevada 89109. $10.00 plus $2.00 postage.

New Hampshire

Burns, Michael E., ed. *Guide to Corporate Giving in New Hampshire.* 1984. 89 pp. Contains listings of 239 corporations. Available from OUA/ DATA, 81 Saltonstall Avenue, New Haven, Connecticut 06513. $15.00.

Office of the Attorney General. *Directory of Charitable Funds in New Hampshire.* 3rd edition. Concord, 1976. 107 pp. Contains listing of 400 New Hampshire foundations. Supplemented annually. Available from the Office of the Attorney General, State House Annex, Concord, New Hampshire 03301. $2.00. Annual supplement, $2.00.

New Jersey

Logos Associates. *The Directory of Major New Jersey Foundations.* 1983. 56 pp. Available from Logos Associates, 7 Park Street, Room 212, Attleboro, Massachusetts 02703. $19.95.

Mitchell, Janet A., ed. *The New Jersey Mitchell Guide: Foundations, Corporations, and Their Managers.* Princeton, 1985. 150+ pp. Contains listing of 116 foundations and 500 corporations in New Jersey. Available from The Mitchell Guide, 195 Nassau Street, Post Office Box 413, Princeton, New Jersey 08542. $65.00 prepaid.

New Mexico

Murrell, William G. and William M. Miller, eds. *New Mexico Private Foundations Directory.* Tijeras, New Moon Consultants, 1982. 77 pp. Contains listing of approximately 45 foundations. Available from New Moon Consultants, Post Office Box 532, Tijeras, New Mexico 87059. $10.00 plus $1.00 postage.

New York

Mitchell, Rowland C., Jr., ed. *The New York City Mitchell Guide: Foundations, Corporations, and Their Managers.* 2nd edition. Contains listing of 2,183 foundations and 537 corporations. Available from Rowland L. Mitchell, Jr., Box 172, Scarsdale, New York 10583. $150.00 prepaid.

Mitchell, Rowland L., ed. *The Mitchell Guide to Foundations, Corporations, and Their Managers: Long Island.* 1984. Contains listing of 149 foundations and 125 corporations. Available from The Mitchell Guide, Post Office Box 413, Princeton, New Jersey 08542. $30.00 prepaid.

Mitchell, Rowland L., ed. *The Mitchell Guide to Foundations, Corporations, and Their Managers: Upper Hudson Valley.* 1984. Contains listing of 61 foundations and 125 corporations.Available from The Mitchell Guide, Post Office Box 413, Princeton, New Jersey 08542. $25.00 prepaid.

Mitchell, Rowland L., ed. *The Mitchell Guide to Foundations, Corporations and Their Managers: Westchester.* 1984. Contains listings on 148 foundations and 58 corporations. Available from The Mitchell Guide, Post Office Box 413, Princeton, New Jersey 08542. $30.00 prepaid.

Mitchell, Rowland L., ed. *The Mitchell Guide to Foundations, Corporations and Their Managers: Western New York State.* 1984. Contains listings on 125 foundations and 132 corporations. Available from The Mitchell Guide, Post Office Box 413, Princeton, New Jersey 08542. $30.00 prepaid.

Mitchell, Rowland L., ed. *The Mitchell Guide to Foundations, Corporations and Their Managers: Central New York State.* 1984. Contains listings on 62 foundations and 125 corporations. Available from The Mitchell Guide, Post Office Box 413, Princeton, New Jersey 08542. $25.00 prepaid.

Monroe County Library System. *Guide to Grantmakers: Rochester Area.* 2nd edition. Rochester, 1983. 220 pp. Contains listing of 140 organizations. Available from the Urban Information Center, Monroe County Library System, 115 South Avenue, Rochester, New York 14604. $14.00 prepaid.

North Carolina
Shirley, Anita Gunn. *Grantseeking in North Carolina: A Guide to Foundation and Corporate Giving.* 1985. 637 pp. Contains listings of 589 foundations and 362 corporations. Available from North Carolina Center for Public Policy Research, Post Office Box 430, Raleigh, North Carolina 27602. $35.00 plus $2.50 postage and handling.

Taylor, James H. and John L. Wilson. *Foundation Profiles of the Southeast: North Carolina, South Carolina.* 1983. 100 + pp. Contains listing of 492 foundations. Available from James H. Taylor Associates, Inc., 804 Main Street, Williamsburg, Kentucky 70769. $39.95 prepaid.

Ohio
United Way of Summit County. *Guide to Charitable Foundations in the Greater Akron Area.* 1981. 48 pp. Contains listing of 38 Akron foundations.

Available from Grants Department, United Way of Summit County, Post Office Box 1260, 90 North Prospect Street, Akron, Ohio 44304. $7.50.

Ohio Attorney General's Office. *Charitable Foundations Directory of Ohio*. Columbus, 1984. 105 pp. Contains listing of 1,800 Ohio foundations. Available from Charitable Foundations Directory, Attorney General's Office, 30 East Broad Street, 15th Floor, Columbus, Ohio 43215. $6.00.

Richardson, Carol and Judy Tye. *Directory of Dayton Area Grantmakers*. 1983. 29 pp. Contains listing of 22 foundations. Available from Belinda Hogue, 449 Patterson Road, Apt. A, Dayton, Ohio 45419. $1.25 postage and handling.

Roy, Cynthia Hastings. *The Source: A Directory of Cincinnati Foundations*. The Junior League of Cincinnati, 1985. 120 pp. Contains listings of 259 foundations. Available from the Junior League of Cincinnati, Grantsmanship Committee, Regency Square, 2334 Dana Avenue, Cincinnati, Ohio 45208. $9.85 (Ohio residents, $10.32).

Oklahoma

Broce, Thomas E., ed. *Directory of Oklahoma Foundations*. Norman, Oklahoma, 1982. 284 pp. Contains listing of 150 Oklahoma foundations. Available from the University of Oklahoma Press, 1005 Asp Avenue, Norman, Oklahoma 73019. $22.50 plus $.86 postage.

Reid, Dee. *Oklahoma Foundations Directory*. 1986. Contains listings of approximately 200 foundations. Available from Foundation Research Project, Post Office Box 1146, Oklahoma City, Oklahoma 73101-1146. $20.00 plus $2.00 postage and handling.

Oregon

United Way of the Columbia-Willamette. *The Guide to Oregon Foundations*. 1984. 215 pp. Contains listing of 300 Oregon foundations. Available from United Way of the Columbia-Willamette, 718 W. Burnside, Portland, Oregon 97209. $15.00.

Pennsylvania

Kletzien, S. Damon. *Directory of Pennsylvania Foundations*. 3rd edition, 1981. 300 pp. Contains listing of 2,300 Pennsylvania foundations. Available from Directory of Pennsylvania Foundations, Post Office Box 336, Springfield, Pennsylvania 19064. $37.50 postpaid (plus Pennsylvania sales tax of $2.25 unless exempt). Check payable to "Directory of Pennsylvania Foundations. "

Rhode Island

Burns, Michael E., ed. *Guide to Corporate Giving in Rhode Island*. 1984. 58 pp. Contains listing of 188 corporations. Available from OUA/DATA, 81 Saltonstall Avenue, New Haven, Connecticut 06513. $15.00.

Council for Community Services. *Directory of Grant-Making Foundations in Rhode Island*. 1983. 47 pp. Contains listing of 91 foundations. Available from the Council for Community Services, 229 Waterman Street, Providence, Rhode Island 02906. $8.00 prepaid.

South Carolina

Middletown, Anne K., ed. *South Carolina Foundation Directory*. 2nd edition. Columbia, 1983. 51 pp. Contains listing of 203 South Carolina foundations. Available on inter-library loan from South Carolina State Library, Post Office Box 11469, Columbia, South Carolina, 29211.

Taylor, James H. and John L. Wilson. *Foundation Profiles of the Southeast: North Carolina, South Carolina*. 1983. 100 + pp. Contains listing of 49 South Carolina foundations. Available from James H. Taylor Associates, Inc., 804 Main Street, Williamsburg, Kentucky 40769. $39.95 prepaid.

Tennessee

City of Memphis. *Tennessee Directory of Foundations and Corporate Philanthropy*. 3rd edition. 1985. Contains listing of 58 foundations and 21 corporations. Available from Executive and Management Services, Room 508, City Hall, 125 North Mid-America Mall, Memphis, Tennessee 38103. $30.00 plus $2.50 postage and handling. Diskette available ($30.00).

Texas

Chumney, Cardes, ed. *The Hooper Directory of Texas Foundations*. 9th edition. 1986. 238 pp. Contains listing of approximately 1,400 Texas foundations. Available from Funding Information Center, 507 Brooklyn, San Antonio, Texas 78215.

Herfurth, Sharon, Karen Fogg, and Lynn Bussey. *Directory of Dallas County Foundations*. 1984. 310 pp. Contains list of 268 foundations. Available from Urban Information Center, Dallas Public Library, 1515 Young Street, Dallas, Texas 75201. $14.75 plus $2.35 postage and handling.

Rhodes, Catherine and the Junior League of Fort Worth. *Directory of Tarrant County Foundations*. 1983. Contains listing of 110 foundations. Available from Funding Information Center, Texas Christian University Library, Ft. Worth, Texas 76129. $3.00.

Utah
Gaber, Mary. *The Directory of Utah Foundations*. 1984. 200 pp. Contains listing of 200 foundations. Available from MG Enterprises, 839 East South Temple #107, Salt Lake City, Utah 84102. $35.00 plus $2.50 postage and handling.

Jacobsen, Lynn Madera. *A Directory of Foundations in Utah*. 1985. 265 pp. Contains listing of 163 foundations. Available from University of Utah Press, 101 University Services Building, Salt Lake City, Utah 84112. $50.00.

Vermont
Burns, Michael E., ed. *OUA/DATA's 1984-1985 Guide to Corporate and Foundation Giving in Vermont*. 1984. 28 pp. Contains listing of 132 corporations and 56 foundations. Available from OUA/DATA, 81 Saltonstall Avenue, New Haven, Connecticut 06513. $15.00.

McGovern, Denise M. *A Directory of Foundations in the State of Vermont*. Willimantic, Connecticut, Eastern Connecticut State College Foundation, Inc., 1975. 24 pp. Contains listing of 41 Vermont foundations. Available from Eastern Connecticut State College Foundation, Inc., Post Office Box 431, Willimantic, Connecticut 06226. $3.00.

Virginia
Grants Resource Library of Hampton, Virginia. *Virginia Foundations 1985*. 200 + pp. Contains listing of 500 foundations. Available from Grants Resources Library, Hampton City Hall, 9th Floor, 22 Lincoln Street, Hampton, Virginia 23669. $16.00 prepaid.

Washington
Office of the Attorney General. *Charitable Trust Directory*. 1985. 202 pp. Contains listing of 968 Washington organizations. Available from the Office of the Attorney General, Temple of Justice, Olympia, Washington 98504. $4.00.

West Virginia
Seeto, William, ed. *West Virginia Foundation Directory*. Terra Alta, 1979. 49 pp. Contains listing of 99 West Virginia foundations. Available from

West Virginia Foundation Directory, Box 96, Route 1, Terra Alta, West Virginia 26764. $7.95.

Wisconsin

Hopwood, Susan H., ed. *Foundations in Wisconsin: A Directory 1986.* 171 pp. Contains listing of 643 Wisconsin foundations. Available from The Foundation Collection, Marquette University Memorial Library, 1415 West Wisconsin Avenue, Milwaukee, Wisconsin 53233. $16.00 plus $2.00 shipping.

Wyoming

Darcy, Kathy. *1985 Wyoming Foundations Directory.* 3rd edition. 1986. 82 pp. Contains listing of 45 Wyoming foundations. Available from Laramie County Community County Library, 1400 East College Drive, Cheyenne, Wyoming 82007. $3.00.

McRae, Kendall and Kim Pederson, *The Montana and Wyoming Foundations Directory.* 4th edition. 1986. Contains listing of 65+ Montana foundations. Available from Grant Assistance, Eastern Montana College Library, 1500 North 30th Street, Billings, Montana 59101. $6.00 prepaid.

REGIONAL GRANTMAKING DIRECTORIES

Taylor, James H. and John L. Wilson. *Foundation Profiles of the Southeast: Alabama, Arkansas, Louisiana, Mississippi.* 1983. Available from James H. Taylor Associates, Inc., 804 Main Street, Williamsburg, Kentucky 40769. $39.95 prepaid.

Taylor, James H. and John L. Wilson. *Foundation Profiles of the Southeast: Kentucky, Tennessee, Virginia.* 1981. 153 pp. Available from James H. Taylor Associates, Inc., 804 Main Street, Williamsburg, Kentucky 40769. $39.95 prepaid.

Taylor, James H. and John L. Wilson. *Foundation Profiles of the Southeast: North Carolina, South Carolina.* 1983. 100+ pp. Available from James H. Taylor Associates, Inc., 804 Main Street, Williamsburg, Kentucky 40769. $39.95 prepaid.

Selected Bibliography

Listed here are some of the many periodicals and books related to fund-raising, management, and organizing. The list is by no means exhaustive. Rather, it is made up of selected publications recommended by various grantseekers and grantmakers alike over the years as particularly useful for community-based social- and economic-justice initiatives. Most of these materials are available at the Foundation Center libraries cooperating collections, or your local public library. For convenience, however, the most recently available information on the publisher's address and the price of the publication are included.

Reprints and Brochures

Foundation Center, The. 79 Fifth Avenue, New York, NY 10003. The Foundation Center prepares and distributes a number of brochures on using the center's facilities, researching grantmaking activities, and philanthropy. Many of these materials are free of charge. Specifically recommended are: *What Makes a Good Proposal?* and *What Will a Foundation Look for When You Submit a Grant Proposal?*

Grantsmanship Center, The. 1031 South Grand Avenue, Los Angeles, California 90015. The Grantsmanship Center publishes a number of reprints of articles that have appeared in the *Grantsmanship Center News*. Prices vary according to the length of the article, from $3.00 to $4.00 each, and quantity discounts are available. Among the articles that have stood the test of time are: "Program Planning and Proposal Writing" (expanded version), "Researching Foundations" (Parts I and II), "Community Foundations," "Exploring Corporate Giving," and "How Foundations Review Proposals and Make Grants."

Periodicals

Council on Foundations. *Foundation News*. To subscribe, write, Foundation News, 1828 L Street, N.W., Washington, D.C. 20036. Published bimonthly. $29.50/yr.

Foundation Center, The. *Foundation Grants Index Bimonthly*. This publication updates the *Foundation Grants Index Annual* (see below). To subscribe, write the publisher, 79 Fifth Avenue, New York, New York 10003. Published six times a year. $28/yr.

Grantsmanship Center, The. *Whole Nonprofit Catalog.* Quarterly. Available from the publisher, 1031 South Grand Avenue, Los Angeles, California 90015. Free.

————. *Grassroots Fundraising Journal.* Bimonthly. Each issue features a practical article on a specific fundraising method or issue, and includes ideas submitted by readers. Order from Grassroots Fundraising Journal, 517 Union Avenue, Suite 206, Knoxville, Tennessee 37902. $20.00 per year.

Independent Sector. *Update.* Monthly. Contains information about volunteers and fundraising for nonprofits. Available to members of Independent Sector, 1828 L Street, N.W., Washington, D.C. 20036.

Lutheran Resources Commission—Washington (An adjunct agency of the Lutheran Council in the U.S.A.)*Newsbriefs.* To subscribe, write the publishers at 733 15th Street, N.W., Suite 900, Washington, D.C. 20005. Published monthly. $60/yr.

National Committee for Responsive Philanthropy. *Responsive Philanthropy.* To subscribe, write the committee at 2001 S Street, N.W., Suite 620, Washington, D.C. 20009. Published quarterly. Subscription price is $25/yr. for individuals and $25-$200 for organizations (depending on the level of annual income).

Northern Rockies Action Group. *NRAG Papers.* To subscribe, write the publisher, 9 Place Street, Helena, Montana 59601. Published quarterly. $12/yr.

Books

Allen, Herb, ed. *The Bread Game, the Realities of Foundation Fundraising,* revised-expanded edition. San Francisco: 1981. This book, a joint venture of the Regional Young Adult Project, is written in an easy-to-read style. It is a short, fun book on the "nature and feeding habits of the beasts known as foundations."

Alvo, Stella and Kate Shackford. *Funding for Social Change Volume I: How to Become an Employer and Gain Tax-Exempt Status.* New York: 1977. This book is an excellent primer that includes information on incorporation, applying for tax exemption, and the responsibilities of being an employer.

American Association of Fund Raising Counsel, Inc. *Giving USA: Estimates of Philanthropic Giving in 1987 and the Trends They Show*. 1986. 103 pp. Available from the American Association of Fund Raising Counsel, Inc., 500 Fifth Avenue, New York, New York 10036. $60.00.

Bennett, Paul. *Up Your Accountability: How to Improve Your Service-ability and Funding Credibility by Upping Your Accounting Ability*. Washington, D.C.: Taft Products, Inc., 1973. This book, although some-what dated, provides a good introduction to nonprofit money management. It explains the principles and procedures of accounting for nonprofit organizations. Out of print.

Center for Third World Organizing. *Directory of Church Funding Sources*. Oakland, California: Center for Third World Organizing, 1986. Approximately 45 pp. This contains a list of religious funding sources, including both local and national levels, with contacts, deadlines, restrictions, and other useful information. Available from the Center for Third World Organizing, 3681 Martin Luther King, Jr. Way, Oakland, CA 94609. $5.95.

Conference Board, The. *Annual Survey of Corporate Contributions 1984 Edition*. 1984. This survey presents data on contributions ratios based on financial data and number of employees, and it tracks the distribution of contributions among different types of grantees. All data are derived from the Conference Board's own surveys and IRS documents. Available from The Conference Board, 845 Third Avenue, New York, NY 10022. $15.00.

Flanagan, Joan. *The Grass Roots Fundraising Book*. 2d rev. ed. 1982. This book provides a compilation of fundraising how-to information, including a detailed analysis on how to choose an event that will be the most profitable for your organization, a description of what steps should be taken to arrange the event, and who should do what. Available from the publisher, 180 North Michigan Avenue, Chicago, Illinois 60601, or from The Youth Project, National Office, 2335 18th Street, N.W., Washington, D.C. 20009. $8.95.

—————. *The Grass Roots Organization: Getting Started and Getting Results in Nonprofit, Charitable, Grass Roots, and Community Groups*. Chicago: Contemporary Books,1981. This book presents an excellent picture of how to make an organization function effectively. It includes chapters on such subjects as a strategy for self-sufficiency, how to make meetings fair and effective, boards of directors (their members and committees), and the publicity committees. Available from the publisher, 180 North Michigan Avenue, Chicago, Illinois 60601. $8.95 (paper).

Selected Bibliography

Fojtik, Kathleen M. *The Bucks Start Here: How to Fund Social Service Projects*. Ann Arbor: Domestic Violence Project, Inc., 1978. This is a practical guide to the rules and requirements of grantmaking agencies. It includes a number of handy appendixes and references. Available from the publisher, Post Office Box 7052, Ann Arbor, MI 48104. $5.00.

Ford Foundation, The. *Meeting the Challenge: Foundation Response to AIDS*. New York: The Ford Foundation, 1987. This report, prepared on the basis of interviews with foundation trustees and staff in mid-1987, assesses the role of foundations in responding to the AIDS crisis. It is available from the Foundation Center, 79 Fifth Avenue, New York, New York 10003. $6.50.

Forum Institute, The. *Search for Security: A Guide to Grantmaking in International Security and the Prevention of Nuclear War*. Washington D.C.: The Forum Institute, 1985. This book offers a roadmap to grantseeking and grantmaking in international security and the prevention of nuclear war. t provides information on approximately eighty foundations, including annotated lists of all 1984 international security grants, a grants analysis by type of activity and issue focus, assets, total grantmaking, and application procedures. Contact the publisher about availability at 1616 P Street, N.W., Suite 100, Washington D.C. 20036. $45.00.

Foundation Center, The. *The Comsearch Printouts*. These printouts arrange foundation information derived from the National Grants Index into subject categories and geographic areas. In the 1987 series, there were 66 subject printouts, 20 geographic printouts, 26 broad topic printouts, and three special-topic printouts. The materials are updated periodically. For a current list of *Comsearch Printouts*, contact The Foundation Center, 79 Fifth Avenue, New York, NY 10003. $18 each for the subject printouts on paper. $7 each for printouts on microfiche.

———. *The Foundation Directory*. 11th Edition. New York: Columbia University Press, 1987. This reference contains information on all American foundations whose assets exceed $1,000,000 or whose annual grants total $100,000 or more, over 5,000 foundations in all. The entries contain brief information on the foundation purpose, financial data, key officers, and grant application procedures. The directory also is indexed by foundation name, subject, geographic focus, names of donors, types of support, and by names of donors, trustees, and officers. Available from The Foundation Center at the address above, or from the publisher at, 136 South Hudson, Irvington-on-Hudson, NY 10533. $85.00.

————. *Source Book Profiles*. no.2. A looseleaf series providing in-depth profiles of the 1,000 largest U.S. foundations on a two-year cycle. Five hundred profiles issued annually plus updates. Profiles include an analysis of grants by subject, type of grant, type of recipients, geographic preference, sample grants, policies, guidelines, and application procedures. Available from The Foundation Center at the address above. Subscription price: $295 for 1988 annual subscription; $285 for complete set of 500 *Profiles* issued in 1987. Both years, ordered together, $520.

————. *The Foundation Grants Index*. 16th ed. New York: The Foundation Center, 1987. This volume describes 40,000 actual grants totaling $2.2 billion awarded by major foundations. It is indexed by subject areas, recipients, key words, and geographic focus. Available from the publisher at 79 Fifth Avenue, New York, NY 10003. $46.

————. *AIDS: A Status Report on Foundation Funding*. New York: The Foundation Center, 1987. This book provides an overview of the state of AIDS funding by foundations during the period 1983 through 1986. It includes basic contact information about the funders, lists of AIDS-related grants, and data on recipients and grant awards. Available from the publisher at the address above. $20.

Funding for Justice Project. *Church Funds for Social Justice*. 1984. 94 pp. Lists local, regional, and national church and church organizations that fund social change. Available from 122 West Franklin Avenue, Room 218, Minneapolis, Minnesota 55404. $8.00 plus postage.

Grambs, Marya, and Pam Miller. *Dollars and Sense: A Community Fundraising Manual for Women's Shelters and Other Non-Profit Organizations*. San Francisco: Western States Shelter Network, 1982. 135 pp. Explains a variety of fundraising methods, including a discussion of how to help organization members overcome barriers to asking for money. Contains anecdotes and exercises for practice. Available from Western States Shelter Network, 870 Market Street, Suite 1058, San Francisco, CA 94102. $22.00.

Gross, Malvern J., Jr., and William Warshauer, Jr. *Financial and Accounting Guide for Nonprofit Organizations*. 3d rev. ed. New York: John Wiley & Sons, 1983. This is basically a readable reference book that concentrates on different types of accounting systems and options for financial statements. It includes a useful section on setting up and keeping books for a small organization. Available from the publisher's warehouse, One Wiley Drive, Somerset, New Jersey 08875, Attn: Order Department. $59.95.

Selected Bibliography

Horgen, Gregory C. *Playing the Funding Game: Where It Is, How to Get It, Keep It, Increase It and Manage It for Your Special Project or Organization*. Sacramento: Human Services Development Center, 1981. This book clearly states some of the common sense principles of grant-seeking, starting with the initial steps of incorporation through post-grant evaluation. It identifies various types of prospective donors (from the usual corporate-giving programs to the less common unions and the unthinkable elements of philanthropy, adult-bookstore operators, the Mafia, and so on). Out of print.

Kahn, Si. *Organizing: A Guide for Grassroots Leaders*. New York: McGraw-Hill, 1982. This book is filled with the kind of sensible and astute advice only an experienced organizer can provide. It includes chapters on constituencies, leadership, strategy, tactics, and culture, all well illustrated by examples. Available from the publisher, 1221 Avenue of the Americas, New York, NY 10020. $7.95, paper. $12.95, cloth.

King, George V. *Deferred Gifts: How to Get Them*. Ambler, Pennsylvania: Fundraising Institute, 1981. This book emphasizes the marketing and management aspects of deferred giving, a fundraising program aimed at securing gifts that can be used by the recipient only after the donor's death, e.g., bequests, life insurance gifts, and trusts. It includes advice on identifying and approaching donors. Available from the publisher, Post Office Box 365, Ambler, PA 19002. $44.95.

Klein, Kim. *Fundraising for Social Change*. Washington, D.C.: CRG Press, 1985. Describes techniques for low-budget organizations to develop and maintain a fundraising program in their community, with particular emphasis on individual donors. Available from Kim Klein, 517 Union Avenue, Knoxville, TN 37902. $20.00.

Lee, Lawrence. *The Grants Game: How to Get Free Money*. San Francisco: Harbor Publishing, Inc., 1981. This book is a practical guide to the rules of the game and the pitfalls to avoid from the planning stages to the follow-through. Out of print.

Lydenberg, Steven. *Rating America's Corporate Conscience*. Reading, Massachusetts: Addison-Wesley, 1986. 499 pp. The major objective of this book, prepared for the Council on Economic Priorities, is to influence consumer-buying patterns. It matches consumer products to their Fortune 500 manufacturers, profiles each company, and rates each for factors such as representation of women and minorities on the board of directors and in top management, involvement in South Africa, conventional and nuclear weapons contracting, and corporate giving. It provides excellent insight into underlying factors that influence corporate grantmaking. $14.95.

Marshall, Sue, and Neil Mayer. *Neighborhood Organizations and Community Development*. Washington, D.C.: Urban Institute, 1985. 230 pp. Contains descriptions of projects by groups in HUD's Neighborhood Self-Help Development Program, and provides a wealth of ideas for community groups and funders. Available from University Press of America, 4720 Boston Way, Lanham, MD. 20706. $10.00.

Merrill Lynch. *How to Read a Financial Report*. 5th ed. 1984. This booklet is a good introduction on how to read corporate annual reports. It contains useful information pertinent to foundation annual reports as well. Available free of charge from your local Merrill Lynch office.

Moskowitz, Milton, Michael Katz, and Robert Levering, eds. *Everybody's Business, an Almanac: The Irreverent Guide to Corporate America*. New York: Harper & Row, 1980. While somewhat dated, the value of this book lies in the way it tells the corporate story, not in its statistical analysis. Through a combination of profiles, short essays, and background facts, the editors reveal the corporate personalities of about 317 large corporations. The entries, grouped by industry, include information on the corporation's founding and history, its reputation, and public image. Available from the publisher, 10 East 53 Street, New York, NY. 10022. $9.95.

National Directory of Corporate Public Affairs. Washington, D.C.: Columbia Books, Inc., 1988. Contains listings on approximately 1,500 corporations, including their political and grantmaking activities and officers responsible for corporate contributions activity. Available from the publisher, 1350 New York Avenue, N.W., Suite 207, Washington, DC 20005. $65.00.

Nielsen, Waldemar A. *The Golden Donors*. New York: E.P. Dutton, 1985. 468 pp. This book puts forth Nielsen's view of the role that the really big (assets over $250 million) foundations play in setting and meeting public policy demands at both the national and regional levels. $25.00.

Pifer, Alan. *Philanthropy in an Age of Transition*. New York: The Foundation Center, 1984. This book contains a series of essays by the former president of the Carnegie Corporation of New York that articulates his views on some of the major social issues of the last 20 years. It provides good insight into the way a well-respected member of the grantmaking community thinks and analyzes problems and issues. Available from the publisher, 79 Fifth Avenue, New York, NY 10003. $12.50.

Powell, Walter W. *The Nonprofit Sector: A Research Handbook*. New Haven: Yale University Press, 1987. 464 pp. A compilation of scholarly articles on the sociological, political, economic, and legal aspects of nonprofit organizations. Available from the publisher, 92A Yale Station, New Haven, CT 06520. $45.00.

Price, A. Rae, ed. *Increasing the Impact*. Battle Creek, Michigan: W. K. Kellogg Foundation, 1985. 234 pp. This collection of essays by experienced communications and public affairs officers at foundations and nonprofits explores communications in the high technology era, everything from television coverage for a town meeting to communicating by computer. It's filled with both practical tips and how-tos as well as a wealth of ideas adaptable to many organizations. Available from the foundation at 400 North Avenue, Battle Creek, MI 49016. Free.

Public Media Center. *Index of Progressive Funders*. 1985. 466 pp. Lists foundations that fund public interest and progressive organizations, including information on the kinds of projects receiving funding and lists of recent grantees with the amount received. Available from Public Media Center, 466 Green Street, San Francisco, CA, 94113. $40.00.

Read, Patricia. *Foundation Fundamentals: A Resource Guide for Grantseekers*. 3d ed. New York: The Foundation Center, 1986. This book is a comprehensive guide to the reference tools available at The Foundation Center that includes insights into how foundations operate and how best to approach them. Topics covered include what are foundations, how foundations fit into the total funding picture, who gets foundation grants and how to present your ideas to a foundation. Available from the publisher, 79 Fifth Avenue, New York, NY 10003. $9.95.

Russell, John M. *Giving and Taking: Across the Foundation Desk*. New York: Teachers College, 1977. This book is a small philosophical treatise on foundation management written by the former president of the John and Mary R. Markle Foundation. It is not a how-to book, but it does contain valuable insights into the attitudes of foundation executives toward would-be grantees. Out of print.

Seltzer, Michael S. *Securing Your Organization's Future: A Complete Guide to Fundraising Strategies*. New York: The Foundation Center, 1987. This book is designed as a complete guide to fundraising, including an overview of funding sources for nonprofits and how to secure funding from individuals, foundations, businesses, corporations, and the government. It also discusses new, emerging funding opportunities and provides a blueprint for designing and implementing your own funding strategies. Available from the publisher, 79 Fifth Avenue, New York, NY 10003. $19.95.

Standard & Poor's Corporation. *Standard & Poor's Register of Corporations, Directors and Executives.* New York: McGraw-Hill, 1988. (Published every January.) This three-volume set is one of the best references on corporations, who runs them, what they do, and how much money they have. For ordering information, contact Standard & Poor's Corporation, 25 Broadway, Post Office Box 992, New York, NY 10275.

Sternberg, Sam. *The National Directory of Corporate Charity.* San Francisco: Regional Young Adult Project, 1984. 500 pp. This information is based on U.S. corporations with gross annual sales of $200 million or more. Each entry includes, minimally, the company name and address, subsidiaries, and the name of the public affairs officer. Data on corporate giving, whether or not there is an associated foundation, may also be provided. Out of print.

Taft Corporation. *Taft Corporate Giving Directory, 1988 Edition.* Washington, D.C.: Taft Corporation,1987. This directory profiles 564 major corporate giving programs and foundations. Each entry includes contact person, funding priorities, plant locations, recent grants, and more. Available from the publisher, 5130 MacArthur Boulevard, N.W., Washington, DC 20016. $297.

U.S. Internal Revenue Service. *Tax-Exempt Status for Your Organization.* IRS Publication 557. 44 pages. This pamphlet explains the requirements and rules necessary for an organization that seeks recognition by the Internal Revenue Service as a tax-exempt organization under Section 501(c) and classification as "not a private foundation" under Section 509(a). Available from your local IRS district office. Free.

Vecchito, Daniel W. *An Introduction to Planned Giving: Fund Raising Through Bequests, Charitable Remainder Trusts, Gift Annuities and Life Insurance.* Washington, D.C.: The Taft Group, 1984. 177 pp. Contains full description of planned giving programs, including how to avoid overpaying income, capital gains, and estates taxes. Available from The Taft Group, 5130 MacArthur Boulevard, N.W., Washington, DC 20016. $24.95.

Women's Action Alliance. *Struggling Through Tight Times.* New York: Women's Action Alliance, 1985. This resource handbook designed primarily for women's organizations can help organizations learn to diversify their funding base, improve their management, assess their potential for income-generating projects, and acquire new analytical skills. Out of print.

White, Virginia P. *Grants: How to Find Out About Them and What to Do Next.* New York: Plenum Press, 1979. This book provides a good overview of identifying potential funding sources and developing a fundraising strategy. Available from the publisher, 233 Spring Street, New York, NY 10013. $19.50.

Who's Who in America, 45th Edition 1988–1989. Chicago: Marquis Who's Who, Inc., 1988.

Index of Contact Persons

New names were included in the second printing of this third edition which are not included in this index.

Index of Contact Persons

Index of Contact Persons

Index of Grantmakers by Geographic Priorities

This index groups grantmakers with specific geographic interests and limitations by state, which can be misleading to one who does not read carefully. Many funders specify a city, county, or region within a state—for example, the five-county region know as the Bay Area of northern California. Others define their geographic limitations as a major metropolitan area which may encompass more than one state; greater Philadelphia, for example, may include Camden County, New Jersey, or the District of Columbia may include northern Virginia and parts of Maryland. There are also grantmakers who specify interests in terms of a region of the country whose boundaries may be open to interpretation; the *Southwest,* the *Pacific basin,* the *Southeast,* and *Appalachia* are all examples. Where the specific list of states for a funder is ambiguous, this list errs on the inclusive rather than the exclusive side.

Every effort has been made to identify the specific geographic interests of corporations that favor communities where they have facilities and other major business interests, but in the case of major companies with multiple subsidiaries, the reference may be incomplete.

Index of Grantmakers by Fields of Interest

This index represents the editors' judgment of the subject-matter interests of the funders whose program interests are described in Chapters 10 and 11. In response to requests by grantseekers and grantmakers alike for greater specificity, several of the general categories used in the last edition of *The Grantseekers Guide* have been subdivided. Whereas the last edition had 52 indexed categories and 25 cross-references, this edition uses 74 and 54, respectively.

The index remains, however, fraught with pitfalls. Many grantmakers describe their priorities in language that defies easy "key word" categorization. For example, one funder may use the word "education" to mean only educational programs in classrooms, another may use the word in the broader sense of "public information," and a third may mean both. While every attempt has been made to list funders according to the categories they use to describe their own programs, tempered with the reality of their grants lists, each category is subject to wide variation.

Moreover, while some funders have defined interests evidenced by their guidelines and grants lists that make them easily susceptible to categorization, others deliberately take a more open-ended approach to their grantmaking, making it next to impossible for any two people to use the same categories to describe their priorities.

In sum, while we have tried to err on the side of inclusion rather than exclusion the material that follows merely represents the interpretations of the editors. Moreover, it is based on information available in late 1987 through early 1988, and may not stand the test of time. Its greatest utility is as a place to start research. The ultimate authority on the interests of any grantmaker is always that funder's annual reports, grants lists, and other printed materials.

Asian Americans and Pacific Islanders (see also Minority and Ethnic Groups)

Community Development (see Economic and Community Development)

Community Organizations and Organizing

Comparable Worth (see Employment and Labor Issues)

Computers

Conflict Resolution

Conservation (see Environment and Natural Resources)

Consumer Rights

Criminal Justice

Economic Issues and Policy

Education

Elderly, (see Older Persons)

Emergency Funding

Employment and Labor Issues

Energy, (see Environment and Natural Resources)

Environment and Natural Resources

Equal Rights, (see also Civil Rights and Civil Liberties)

Live Oak Fund for Change, The, 575

Los Angeles Women's Foundation, 577

MacArthur Foundation, J. Roderick, 280

Minneapolis Foundation, The, 593

Muste Memorial Institute, A.J., 311

New World Foundation, The, 316

Norman Foundation, Inc., 324

Sophia Fund, The, 668

Stern Family Fund, The Philip M., 374

Threshold Foundation, 383

Windom Fund, The, 397

Ethics

CarEth Foundation, The, 173

Crowe Foundation, Pettus, 187

Fel-Pro/Mecklenburger Foundation, 503

Haas, Jr. Fund Evelyn and Walter, 540

Seventh Generation Fund for Indian Development, 366

Families

Bowsher-Booher Foundation, 459

Chicago Community Trust, The, 477

Clark Foundation, The Edna McConnell, 181

Edwards Foundation, The O.P. and W.E., 208

Ford Foundation, The, 211

Hawaiian Foundation, The, 542

Ittleson Foundation, Inc., 251

Kroc Foundation, TheJoan B., 569

Levi Strauss Foundation, 274

Mailman Family Foundation, A.L., 287

McKnight Foundation, The, 584

Morgan Guaranty Trust Company, 602

Mott Foundation, The Charles Stewart, 297

Nevada Women's Fund, 605

Piton Foundation, The, 642

Seventh Generation Fund for Indian Development, 366

Victoria Foundation, Inc., 681

Woods Charitable Fund, Inc., 691

Zellerbach Family Fund, The, 695

Family Planning, (see Reproductive Rights)

Farms and Farming, (see Agriculture and Rural Affairs)

Fellowships, (see Scholarships and Fellowships)

Film and Media

Benton Foundation, The, 153

Boehm Foundation, The, 159

Borg-Warner Foundation, 448

Campaign for Human Development, 169

Chinook Fund, 483

Deer Creek Foundation, 418

Eastman Fund, Inc., Lucius and Eva, 206

Ittleson Foundation, Inc., 251

Limantour Foundation, 573

Live Oak Fund for Change, The, 575

North Star Fund, 618

Hazardous Wastes (see Toxics)

Health Care, Physical and Mental

Hispanics (see also Minority and Ethnic Groups)

Historic Preservation

Homelessness

Housing

Hunger, (see Food, Hunger, and Nutrition)

Human Rights

Human Services (see Social and Human Welfare)

Humanities (see Arts and Culture)

Immigration (see Refugees and Immigration)

Interim Grants (see Emergency Funding)

**Nuclear Power, (see
Environment and Natural
Resources)**

**Nuclear War, (see Peace and
Disarmament)**

**Occupational Safety and
Health**

Older Persons

Organizing (see Community Organizations and Organizing)

Pay Equity

Peace and Disarmament

Index of Grantmakers by Fields of Interest

Rural Economic Development (see Economic and Community Development)

Rural Poverty

Scholarships and Fellowships

Workers Rights

Young People

Index of Grantmakers

About the Editors

Jill R. Shellow is a graduate of the Georgetown University Law Center and a law clerk at Caplin & Drysdale, Chartered. She is the editor of the first two editions of *The Grantseekers Guide* and has spent more than twelve years raising money from the private and public sectors for nonprofit organizations, in capacities ranging from professional to volunteer and board member. Prior to starting law school she was the director of issues development at People for the American Way, and, prior to that, she was the development officer and secretary of the Urban Institute.

Nancy C. Stella is a public relations consultant and writer in Washington, D.C., specializing in issues marketing, media relations, and in helping nonprofits to communicate their views and recommendations on issues of public policy. She is director of communications for The Center for Population Options and was, formerly, director of communications at People for the American Way. Prior to that, she was an account executive with Public Interest Public Relations, Inc.